# HISTORY OF ART

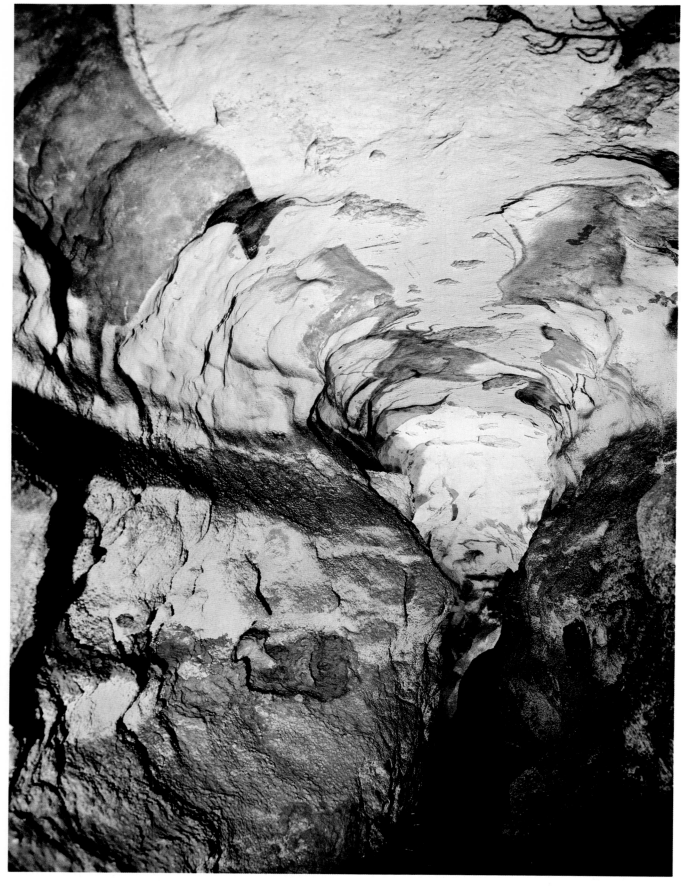

*AXIAL GALLERY, LASCAUX CAVES, FRANCE*
15,000–10,000 B.C. (figure 31)

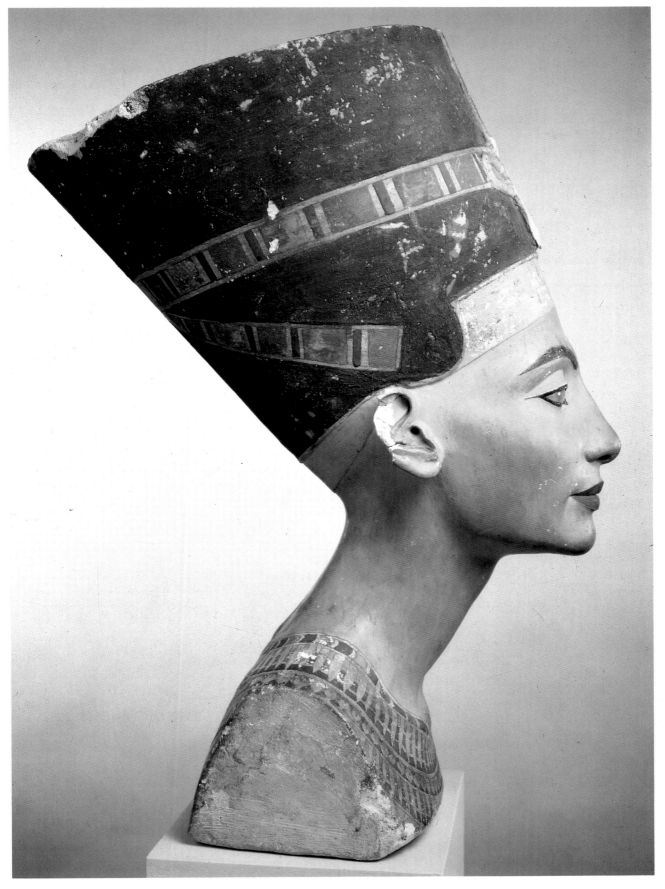

*QUEEN NOFRETETE, FROM EGYPT*
c. 1360 B.C. (figure 101)

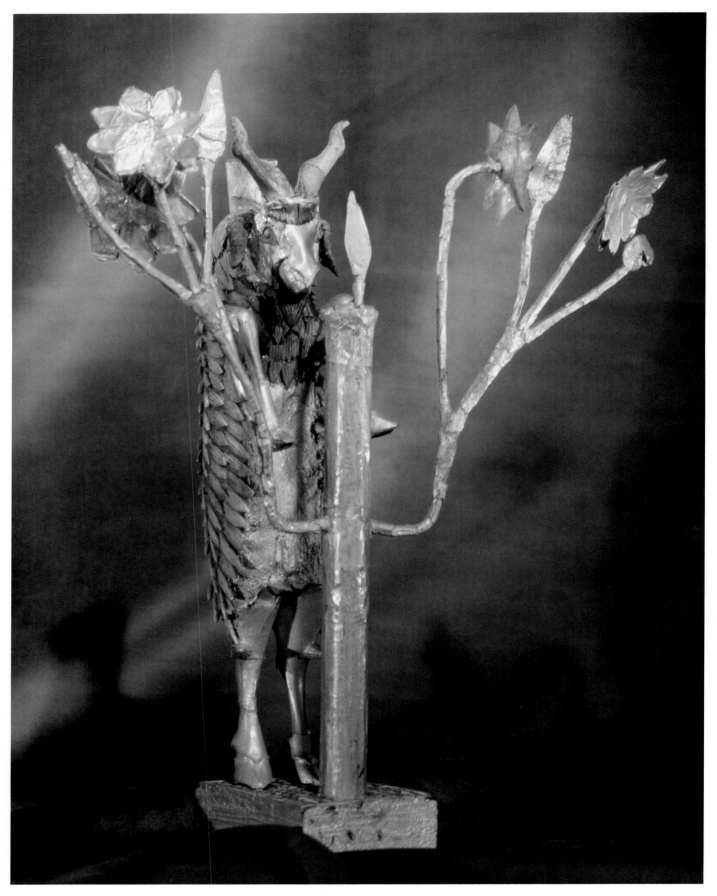

*RAM AND TREE, FROM UR IN SUMER*
c. 2600 B.C. (figure 112)

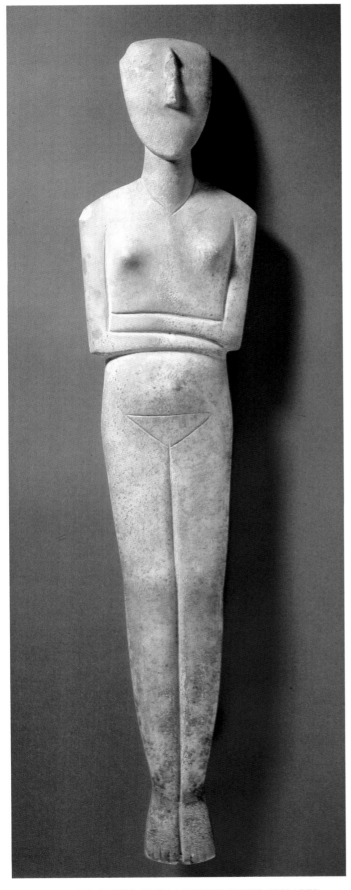

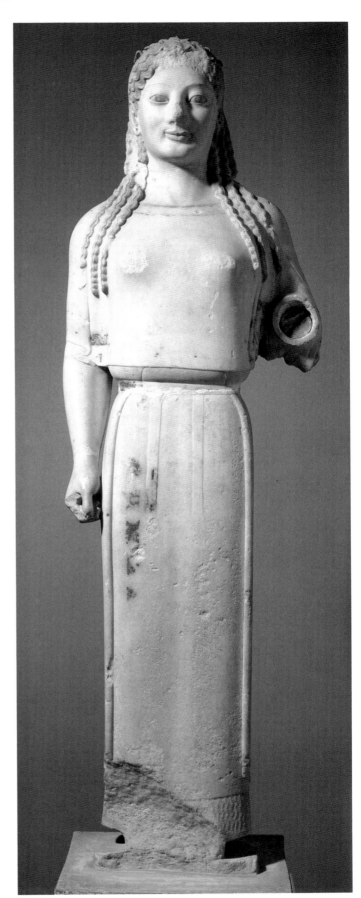

CYCLADIC STATUE, FROM AMORGOS IN THE CYCLADES
2500–1100 B.C. (figure 137)

ARCHAIC GREEK KORE
c. 530 B.C. (figure 171)

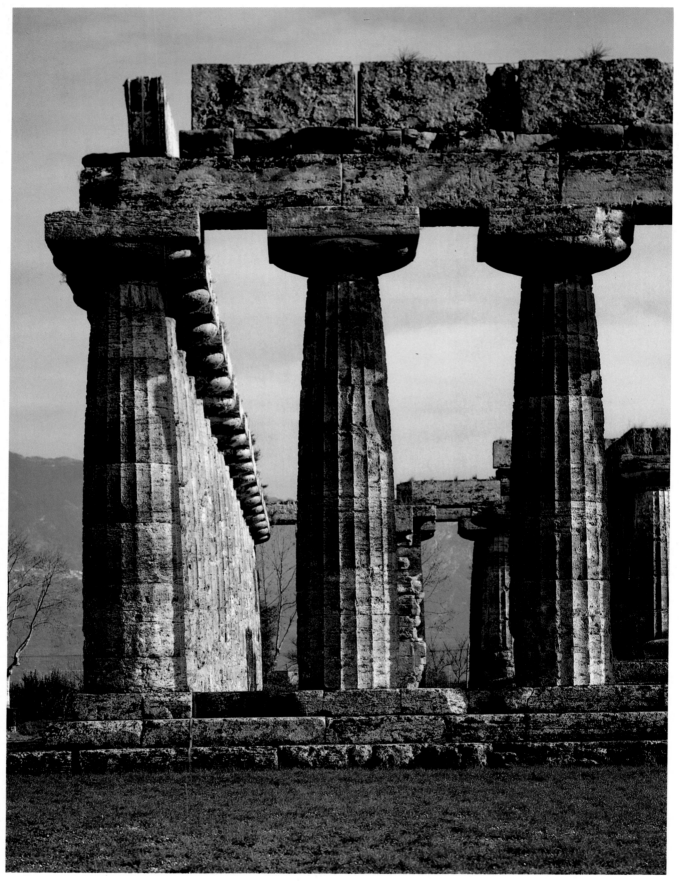

*THE "BASILICA," A DORIC GREEK TEMPLE IN PAESTUM, ITALY*
c. 550 B.C. (figure 184)

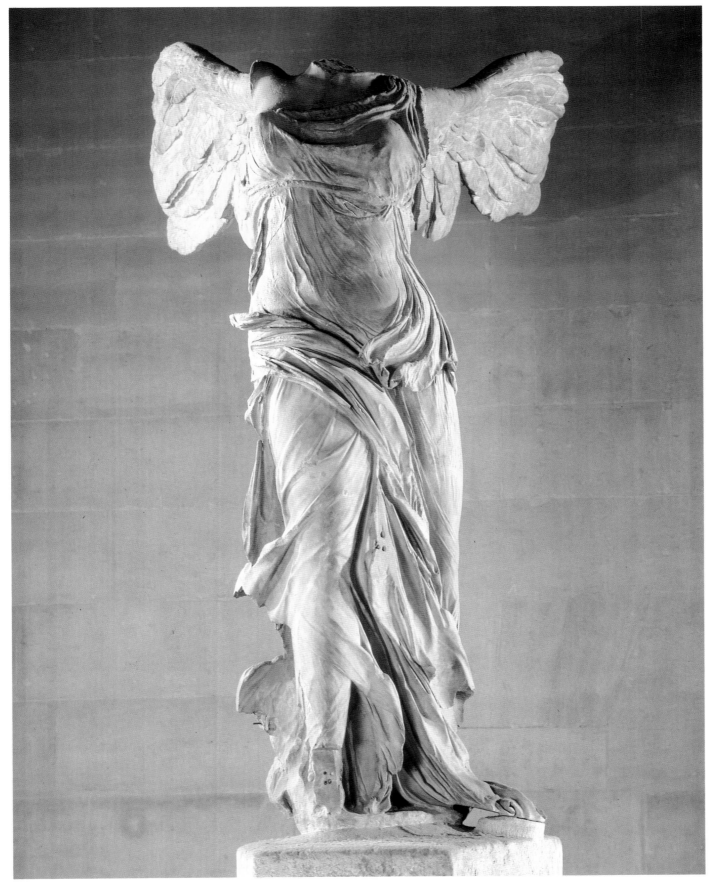

*NIKE OF SAMOTHRACE, A HELLENISTIC SCULPTURE*
c. 200–190 B.C. (figure 229)

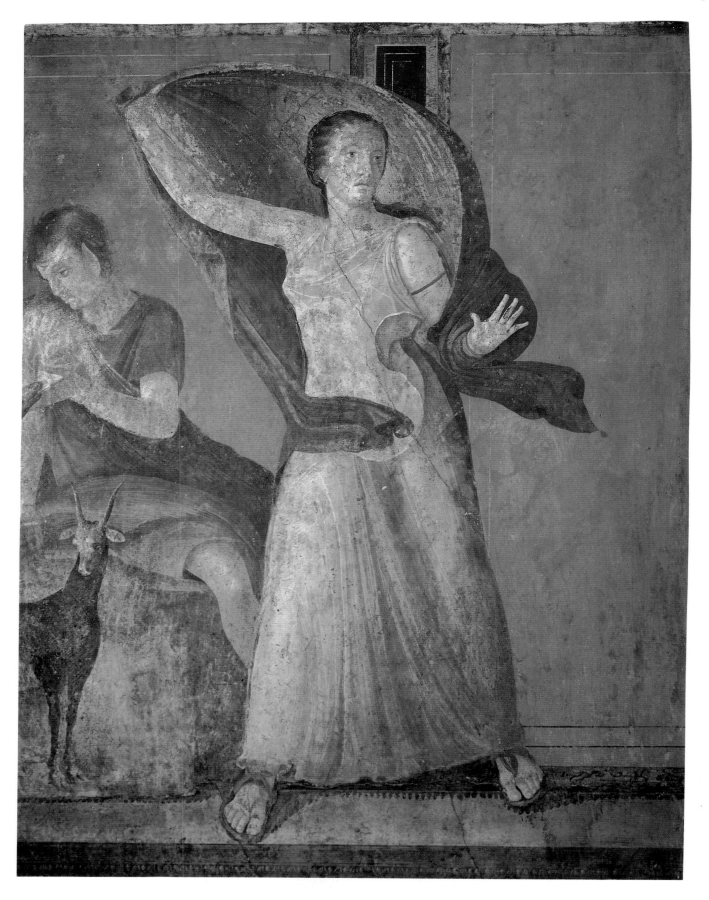

*WOMAN WITH A VEIL, FROM A ROMAN WALL PAINTING IN POMPEII, ITALY*
c. 50 B.C. (figure 311)

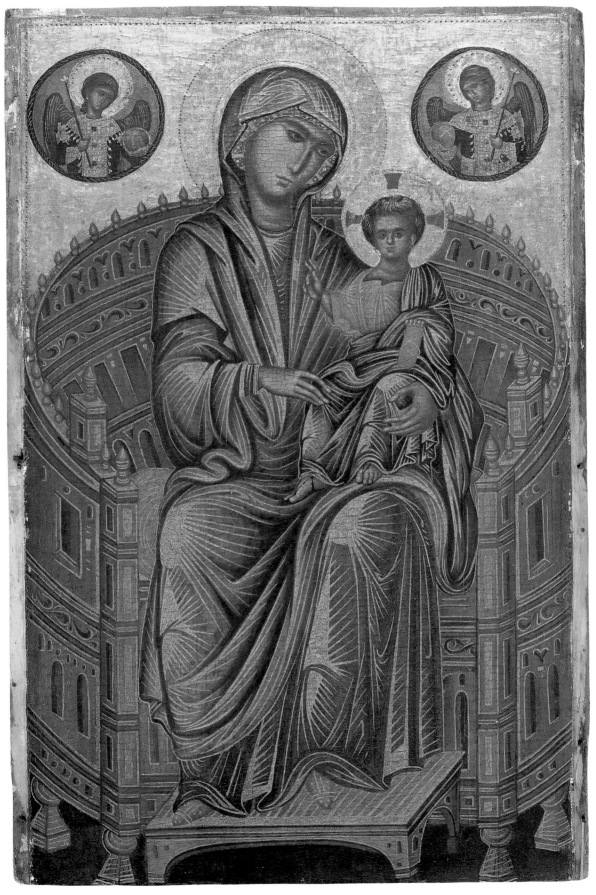

*MADONNA ENTHRONED, A BYZANTINE PANEL PAINTING*
Late 13th century (figure 358)

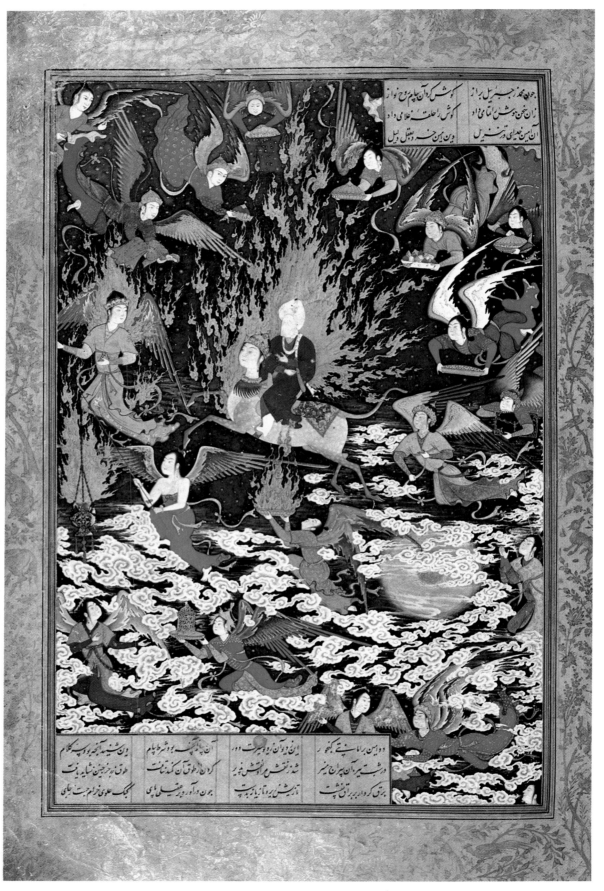

*THE ASCENSION OF MOHAMMED, FROM A PERSIAN MANUSCRIPT*
1539–43 (figure 383)

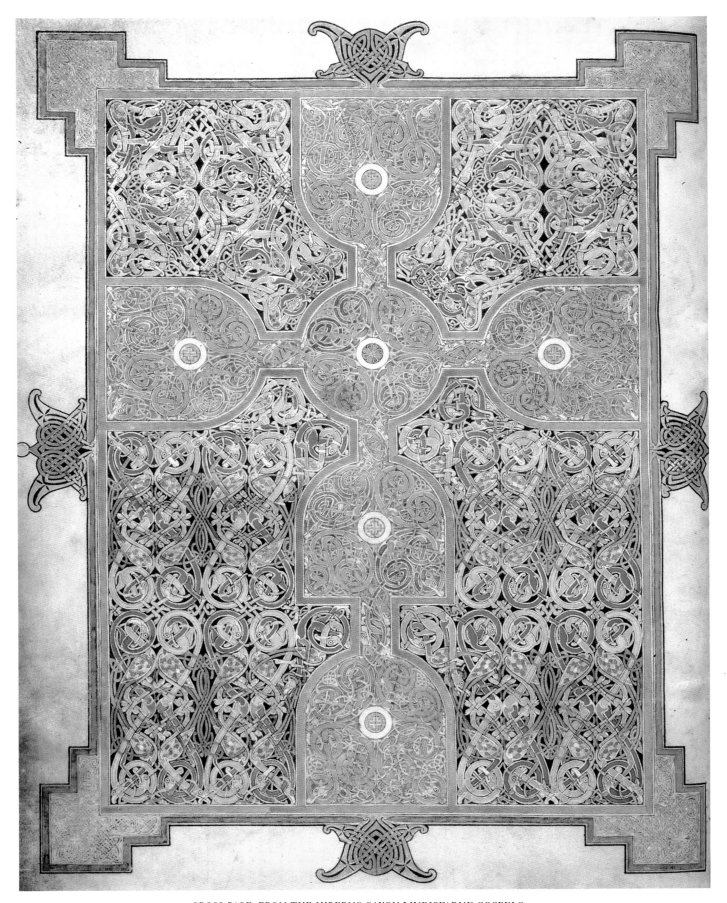

*CROSS PAGE, FROM THE HIBERNO-SAXON* LINDISFARNE GOSPELS
c. 700 (figure 387)

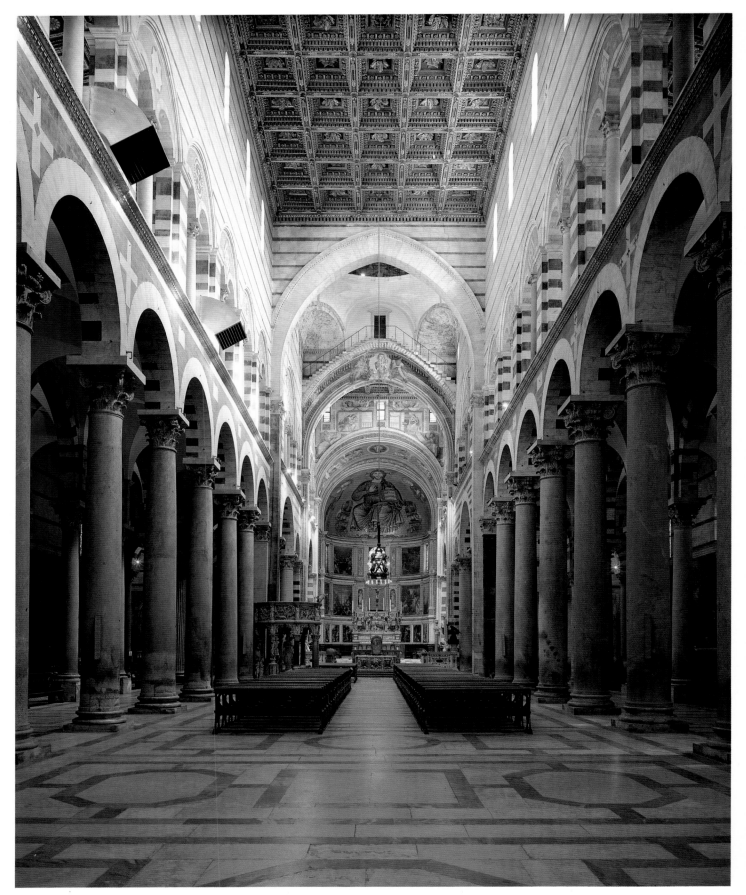

*PISA CATHEDRAL*
1053–1272 (figure 430)

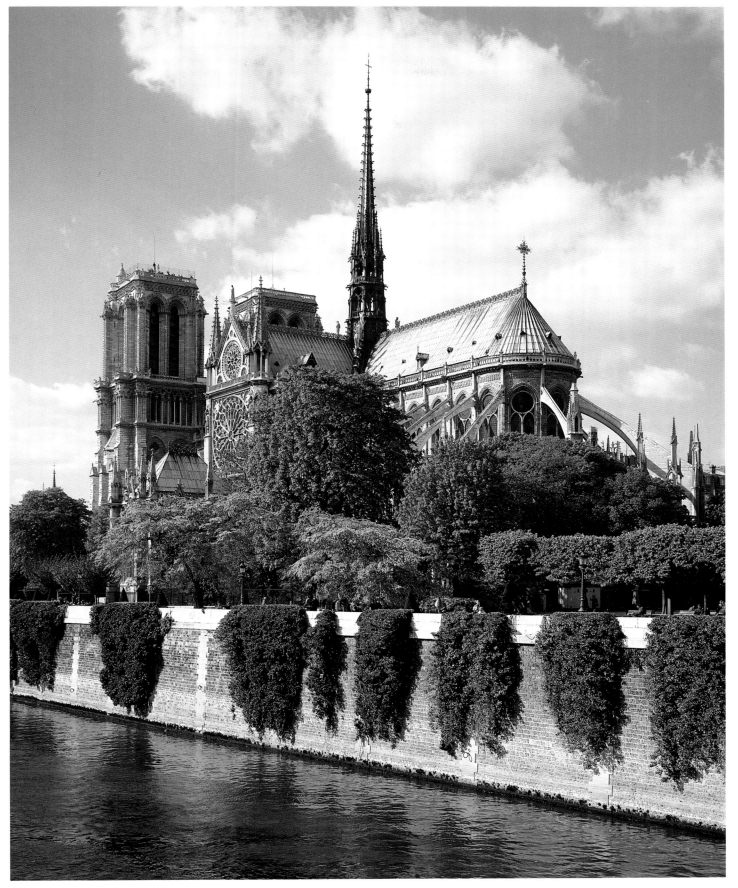

*NOTRE-DAME CATHEDRAL, PARIS*
1163–c. 1250 (figure 455)

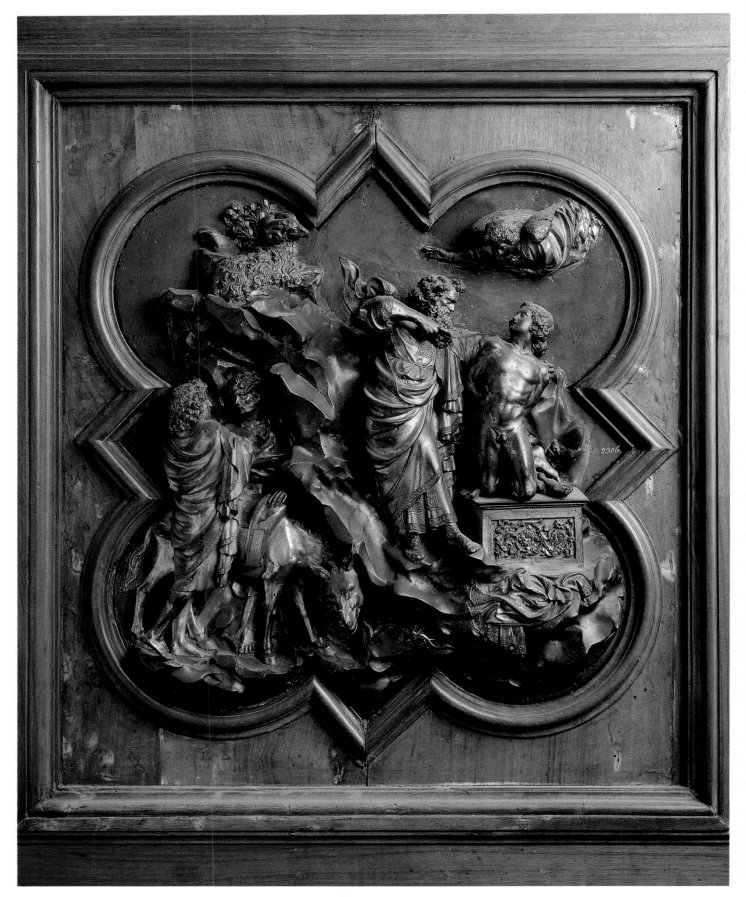

*LORENZO GHIBERTI. THE SACRIFICE OF ISAAC*
1401–02 (figure 516)

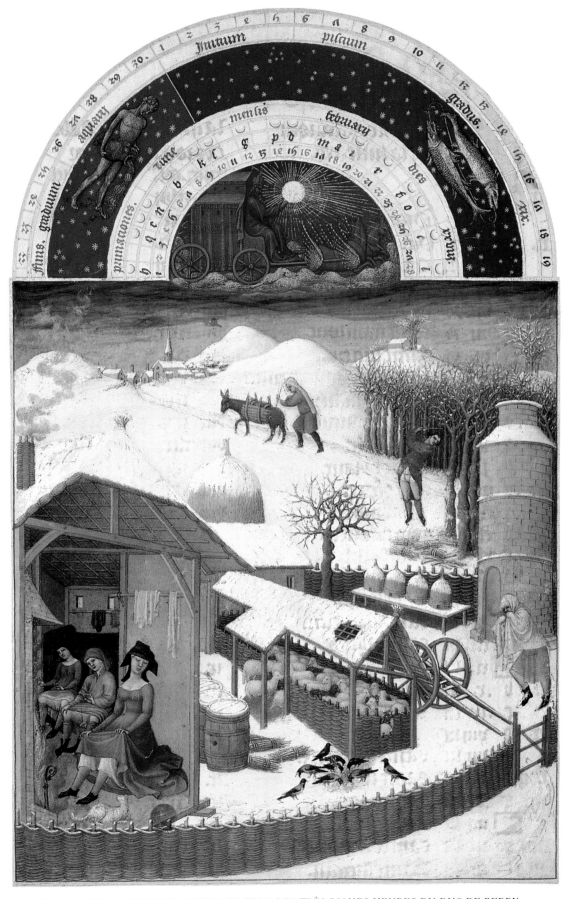

*THE LIMBOURG BROTHERS. FEBRUARY, FROM* LES TRÈS RICHES HEURES DU DUC DE BERRY
1413–16 (figure 542)

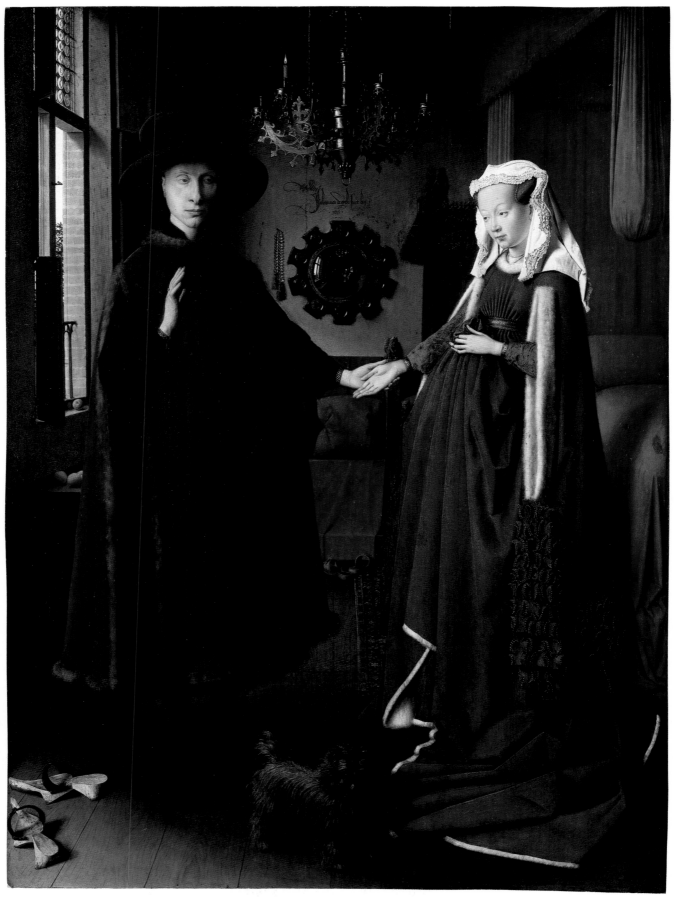

*JAN VAN EYCK. WEDDING PORTRAIT*
1434 (figure 553)

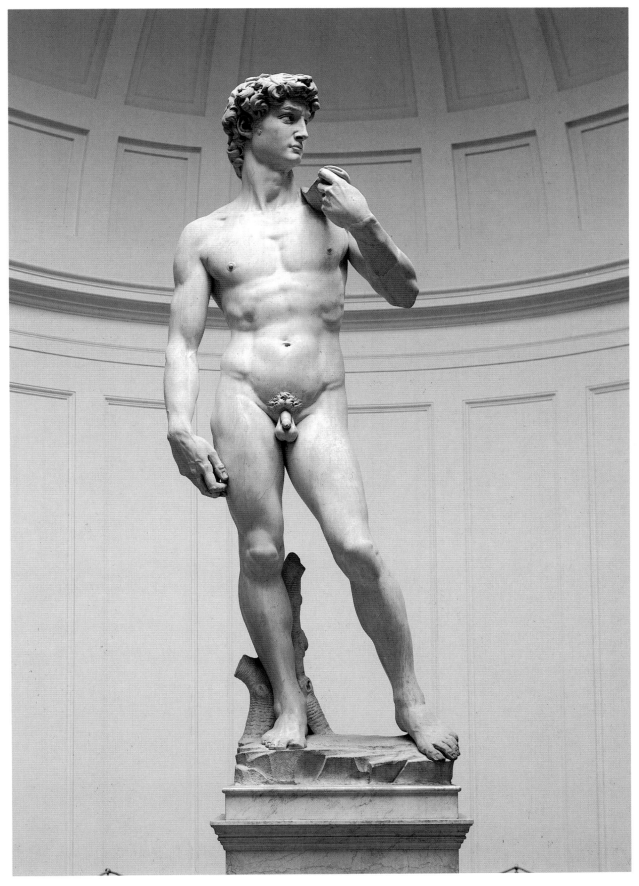

*MICHELANGELO. DAVID*
1501–04 (figure 652)

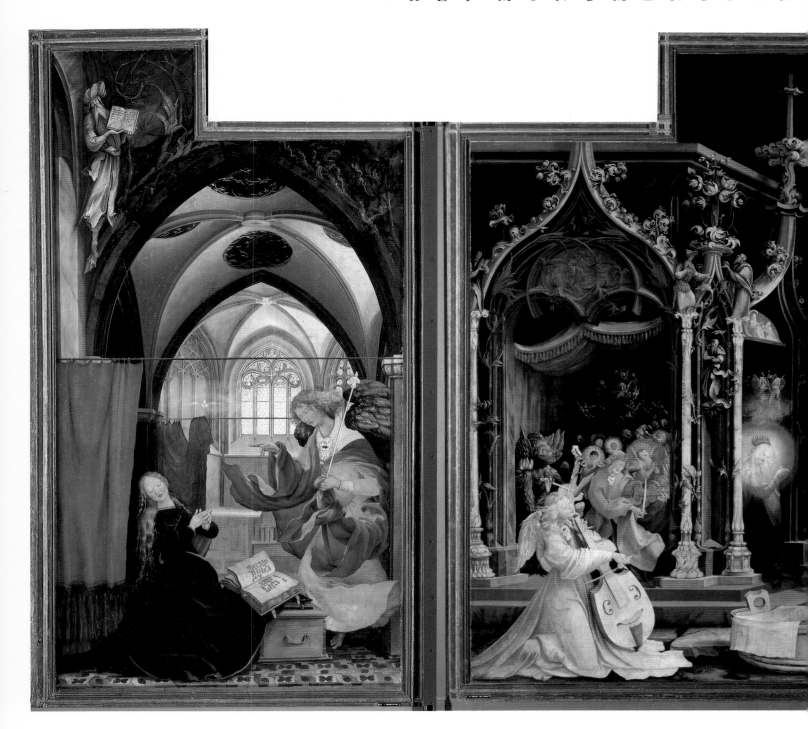

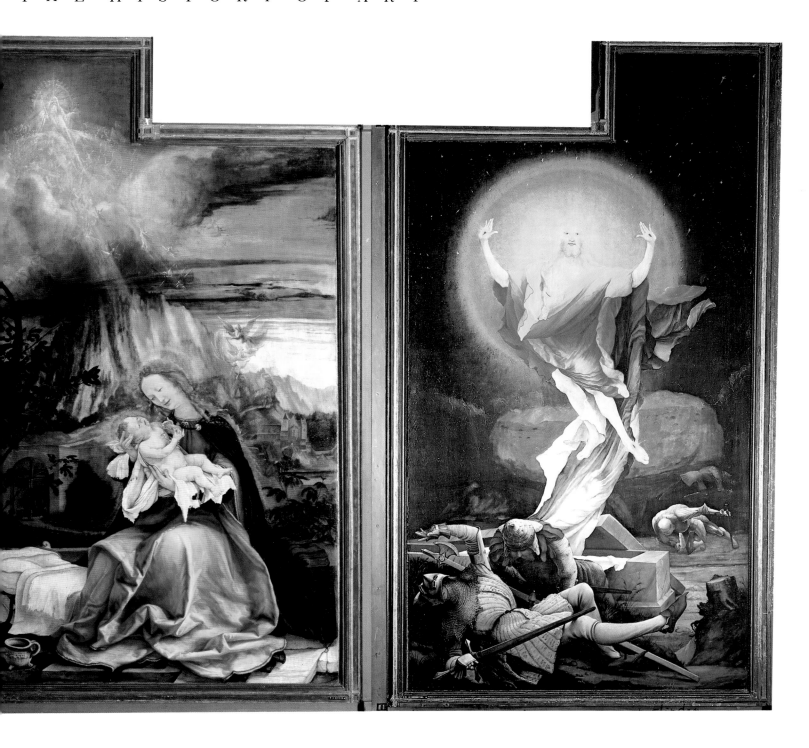

*MATTHIAS GRÜNEWALD. ISENHEIM ALTARPIECE, SECOND VIEW*
c. 1510–15 (figure 711)

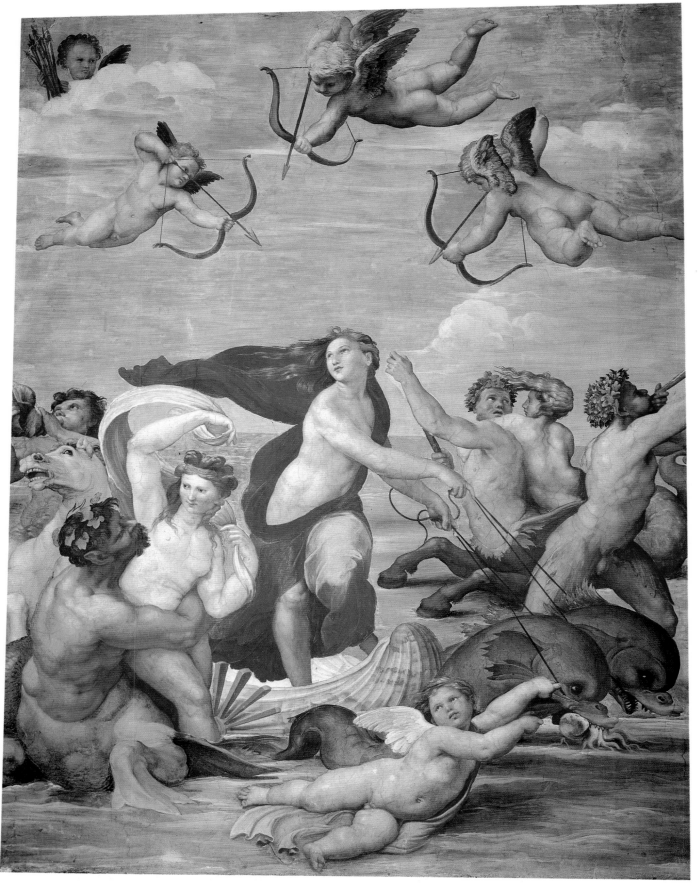

*RAPHAEL. GALATEA*
1513 (figure 673)

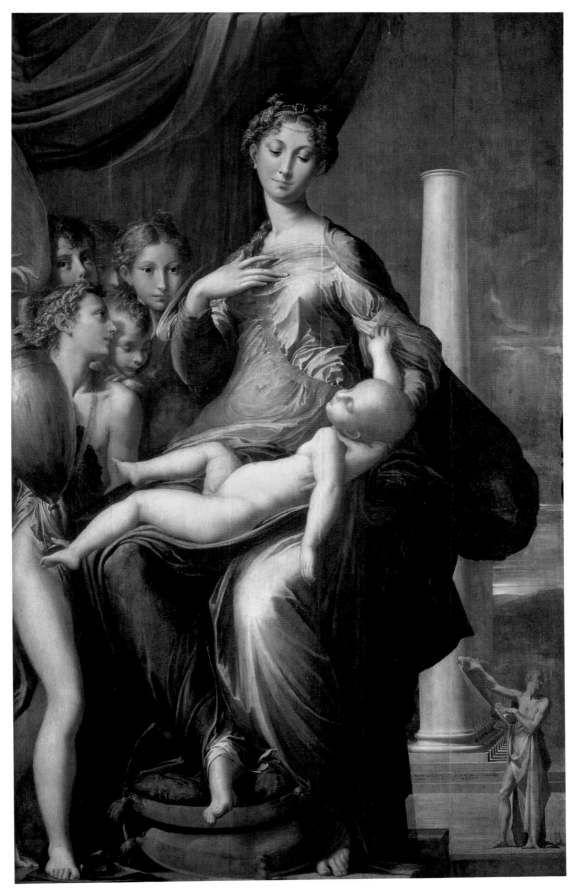

*PARMIGIANINO. THE MADONNA WITH THE LONG NECK*
c. 1535 (figure 684)

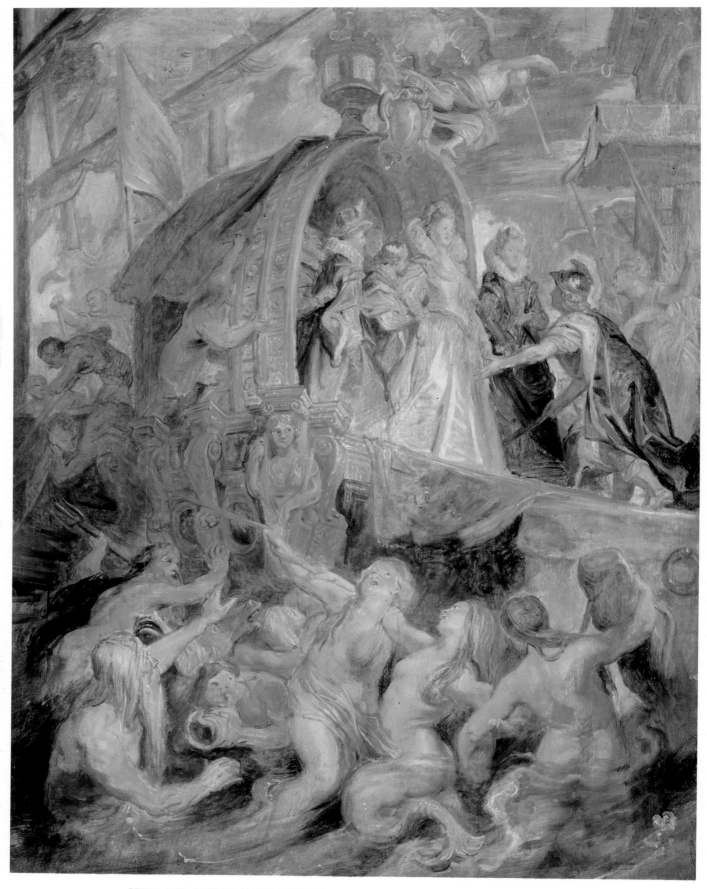

*PETER PAUL RUBENS. MARIE DE'MEDICI, QUEEN OF FRANCE, LANDING IN MARSEILLES*
1622–23 (figure 774)

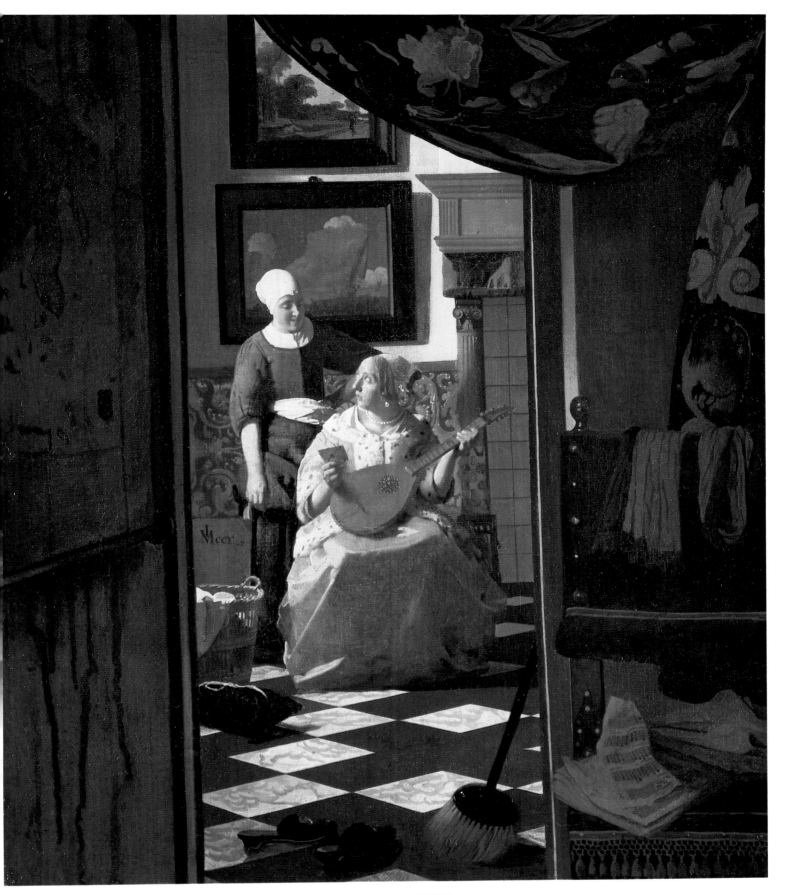

*JAN VERMEER. THE LETTER*
1666 (figure 794)

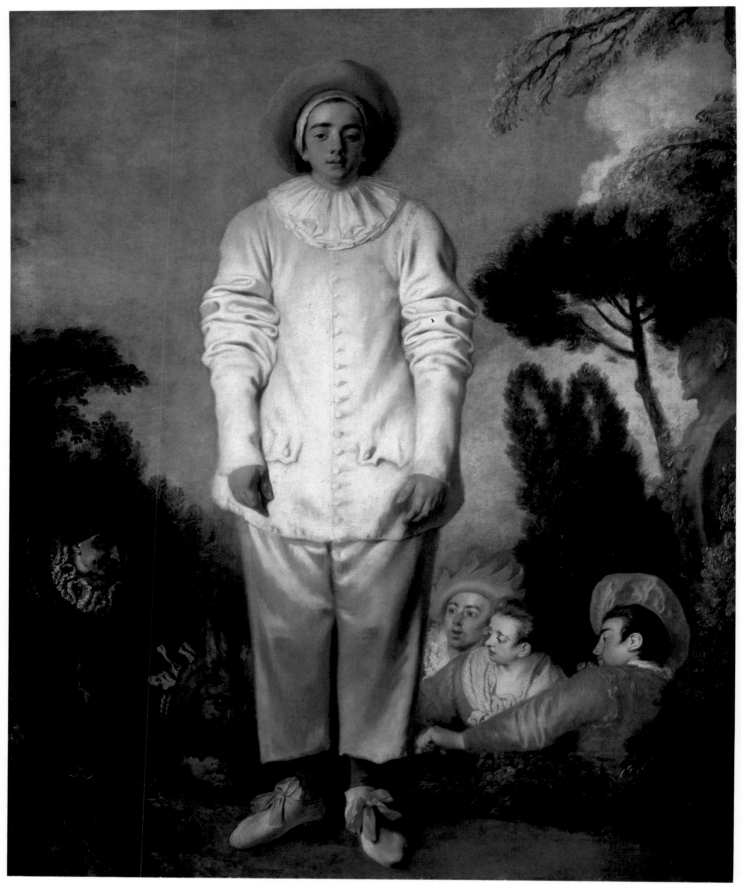

*JEAN-ANTOINE WATTEAU. GILLES AND FOUR OTHER CHARACTERS FROM THE COMMEDIA DELL'ARTE*
c. 1719 (figure 819)

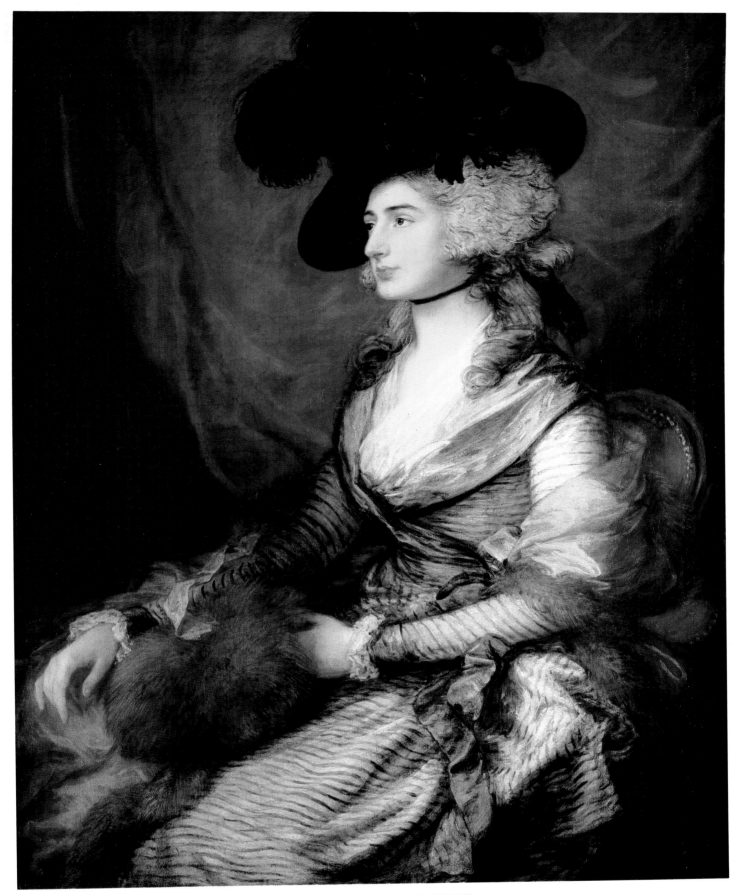

*THOMAS GAINSBOROUGH. MRS. SIDDONS*
1785 (figure 834)

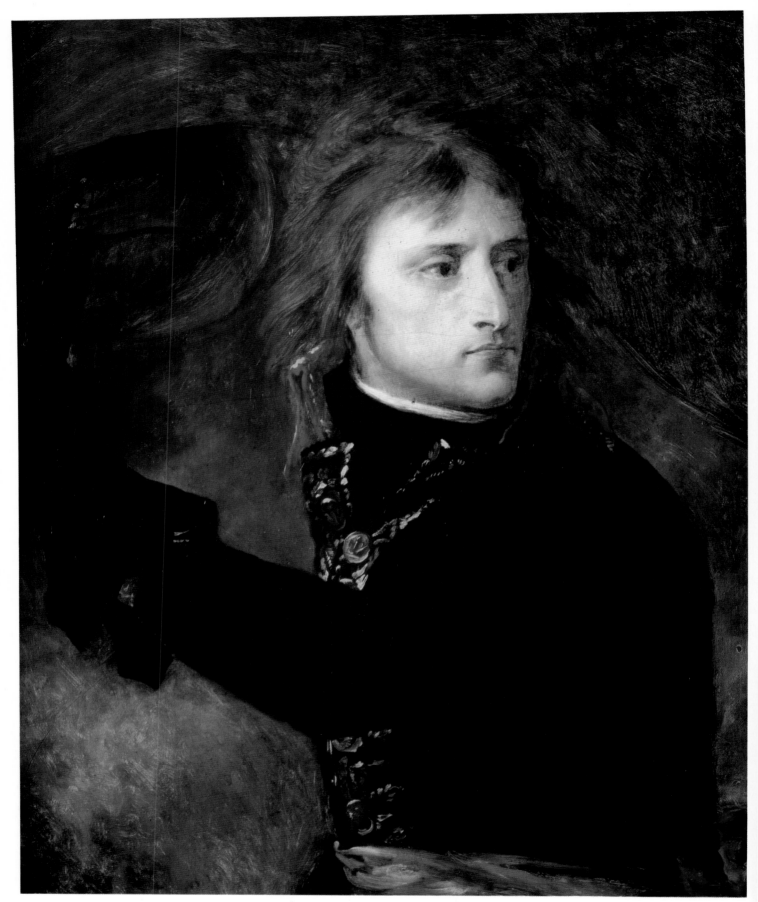

*ANTOINE-JEAN GROS. NAPOLEON AT ARCOLE*
1796 (figure 859)

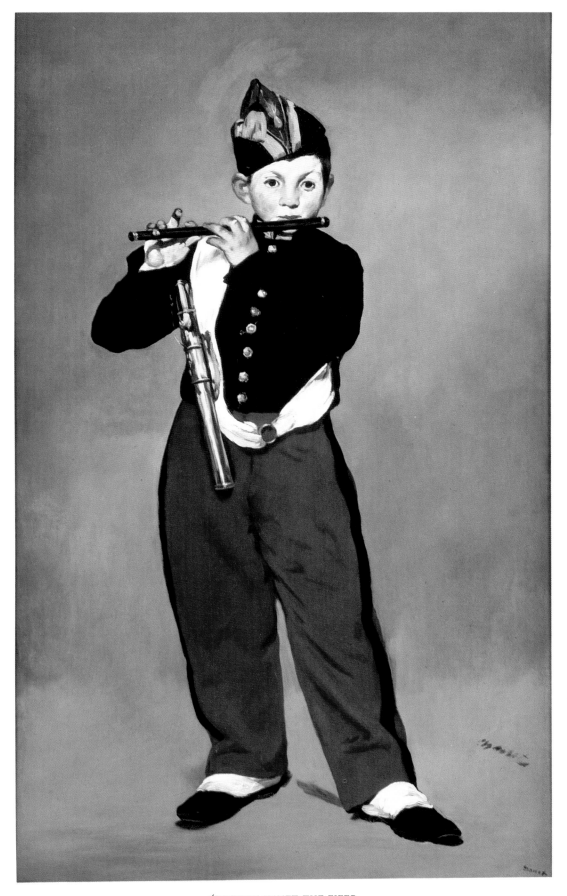

*ÉDOUARD MANET. THE FIFER*
1866 (figure 912)

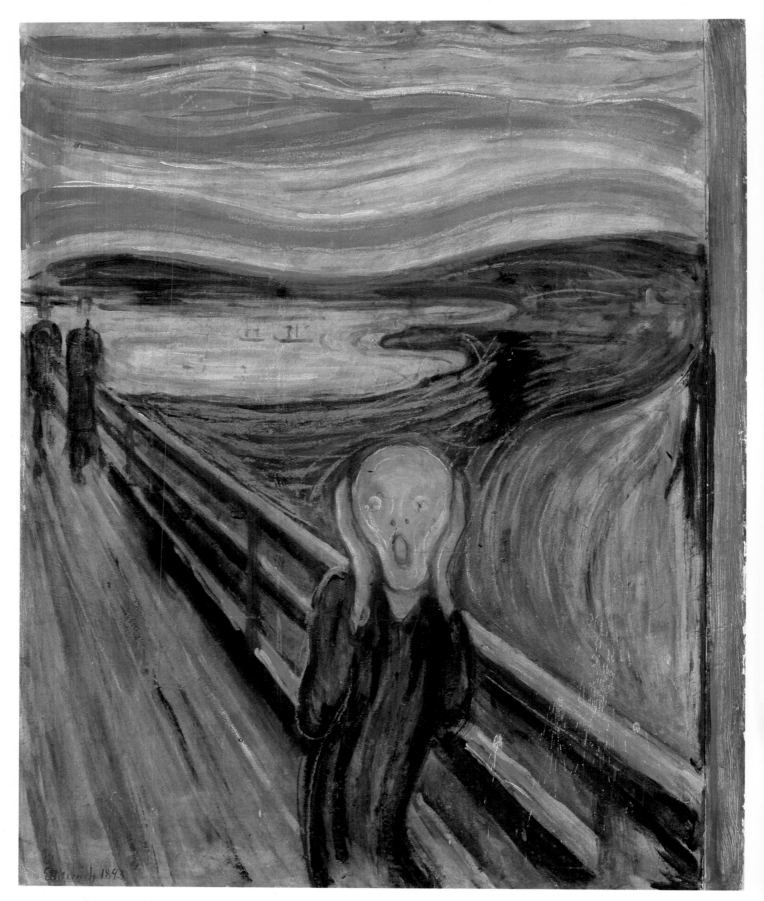

*EDVARD MUNCH. THE SCREAM*
1893 (figure 958)

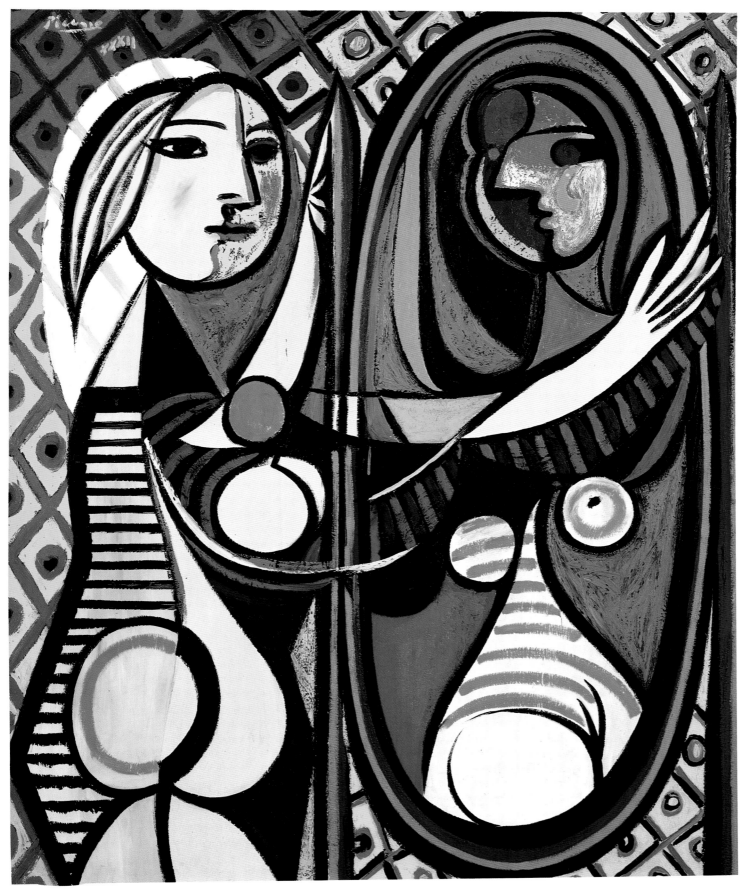

*PABLO PICASSO. GIRL BEFORE A MIRROR*
1932 (figure 12)

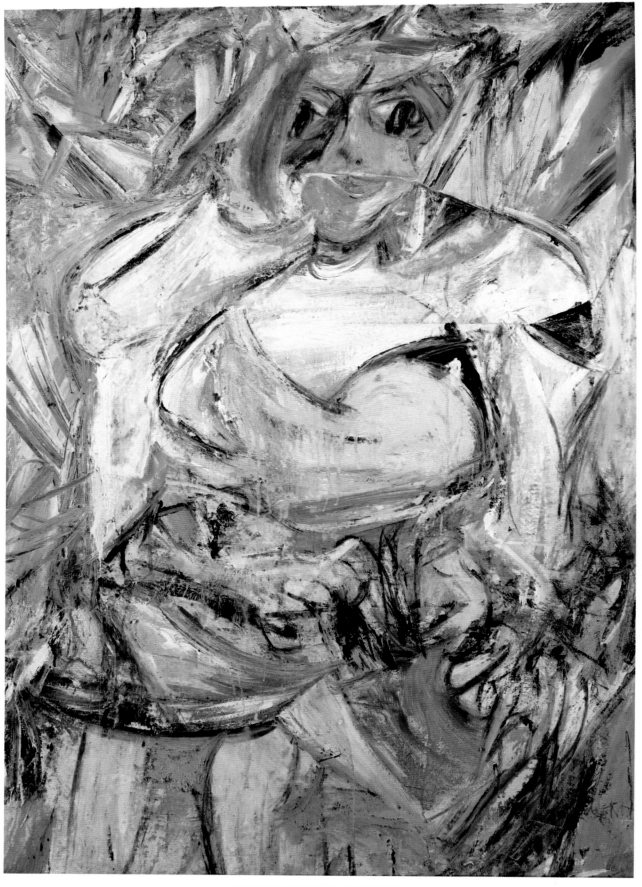

*WILLEM DE KOONING. WOMAN II*
1952 (figure 1037)

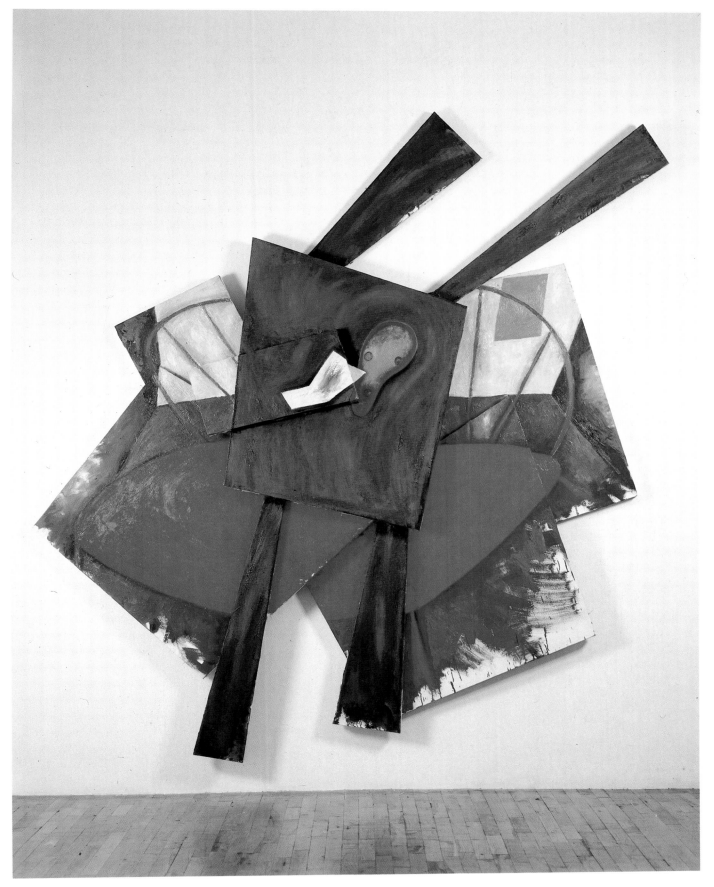

*ELIZABETH MURRAY. MORE THAN YOU KNOW*
1983 (figure 1063)

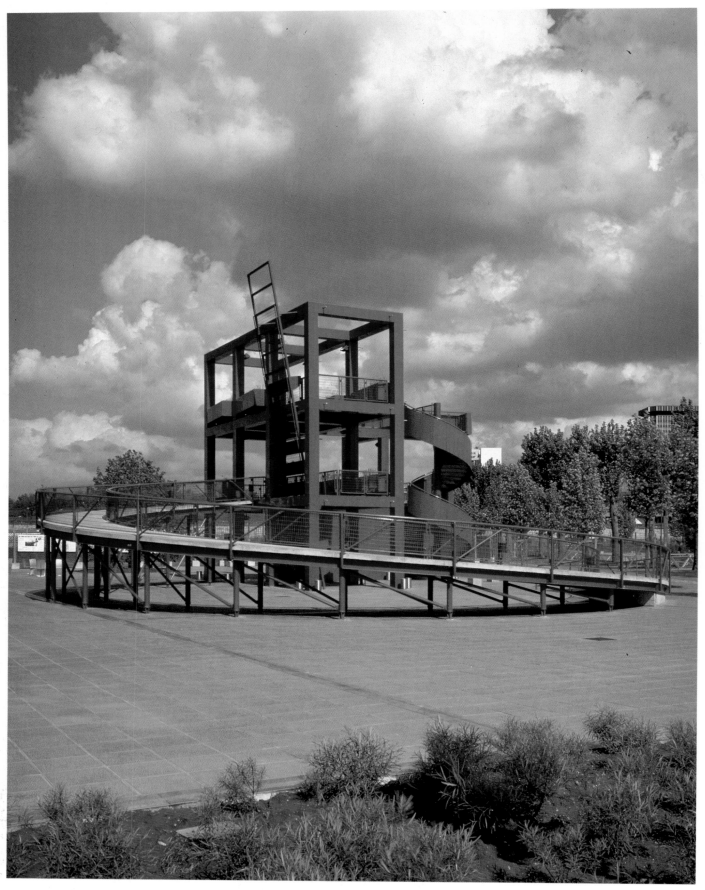

*BERNARD TSCHUMI ARCHITECTS. FOLIE P6, PARC DE LA VILLETTE, PARIS*
Designed 1983 (figure 1118)

# HISTORY OF ART

FOURTH EDITION

# H. W. JANSON

# HISTORY

HARRY N. ABRAMS, INC., NEW YORK

REVISED AND EXPANDED BY

# ANTHONY F. JANSON

# OF ART
VOLUME
ONE

PRENTICE HALL, INC., ENGLEWOOD CLIFFS, NEW JERSEY

Project Managers: Sheila Franklin Lieber, Julia Moore
Editor: Julia Moore
Designer: Bob McKee
Rights and Reproductions/
Picture Researcher: Jennifer Bright

On the front cover: *Poseidon (Zeus?)*. c. 460–450 B.C.
National Archeological Museum, Athens (fig. 206)
On the back cover: Pylon of Ramesses II, Temple of
Amun-Mut-Khonsu, Luxor. c. 1260 B.C. (fig. 96)

Library of Congress Cataloging-in-Publication Data
Janson, H. W. (Horst Woldemar), 1913–
History of art / by H. W. Janson.—4th ed. / revised and expanded
by Anthony F. Janson.
p.    cm.
Includes bibliographical references and index.
ISBN 0-13-388448-1 (Prentice-Hall : pbk. : v. 1). —ISBN
0-13-388455-4 (Prentice-Hall : pbk. : v. 2).
1. Art—History.   I. Janson, Anthony F.   II. Title.
N5300.J3   1991
709—dc20                                                    90-7405
                                                              CIP

*Note on the Picture Captions*
Each illustration is placed as close as possible to its first
discussion in the text. Measurements are given throughout,
except for objects that are inherently large: architecture, architectural
sculpture, interiors, and wall paintings. Height precedes width.
A probable measuring error of more than one percent is
indicated by "c." Titles of works are those designated by the museums
owning the works, where applicable, or by custom. Dates are
based on documentary evidence, unless preceded by "c."

First Edition 1962
Revised and Enlarged in 1969
Second Edition 1977
Third Edition 1986
Fourth Edition 1991

# CONTENTS

# PREFACE AND ACKNOWLEDGMENTS
## TO THE FIRST EDITION

The title of this book has a dual meaning: it refers both to the events that *make* the history of art, and to the scholarly discipline that deals with these events. Perhaps it is just as well that the record and its interpretation are thus designated by the same term. For the two cannot be separated, try as we may. There are no "plain facts" in the history of art—or in the history of anything else, for that matter; only degrees of plausibility. Every statement, no matter how fully documented, is subject to doubt, and remains a "fact" only so long as nobody questions it. To doubt what has been taken for granted, and to find a more plausible interpretation of the evidence, is every scholar's task. Nevertheless, there is always a large body of "facts" in any field of study; they are the sleeping dogs whose very inertness makes them landmarks on the scholarly terrain. Fortunately, only a minority of them can be aroused at the same time, otherwise we should lose our bearings; yet all are kept under surveillance to see which ones might be stirred into wakefulness and locomotion. It is these "facts" that fascinate the scholar. I believe they will also interest the general reader. In a survey such as this, the sleeping dogs are indispensable, but I have tried to emphasize that their condition is temporary, and to give the reader a fairly close look at some of the wakeful ones.

I am under no illusion that my account is adequate in every respect. The history of art is too vast a field for anyone to encompass all of it with equal competence. If the shortcomings of my book remain within tolerable limits, this is due to the many friends and colleagues who have permitted me to tax their kindness with inquiries, requests for favors, or discussions of doubtful points. I am particularly indebted to Bernard Bothmer, Richard Ettinghausen, M. S. İpşiroğlu, Richard Krautheimer, Max Loehr, Wolfgang Lotz, Alexander Marshack, and Meyer Schapiro, who reviewed various aspects of the book and generously helped in securing photographic material. I must also record my gratitude to the American Academy in Rome, which made it possible for me, as art historian in residence during the spring of 1960, to write the chapters on ancient art under ideal conditions.

H. W. J.
1962

# PREFACE AND ACKNOWLEDGMENTS
## TO THE FOURTH EDITION

This, the fourth edition of H. W. Janson's *History of Art,* preserves most of the text of the previous one. At the same time, it presents a number of major changes and additions. There are now more than 550 illustrations in color—three times the number of the previous edition—and all illustrations are integrated with the text. In addition, a special color section, Key Monuments in the History of Art, sets the stage for our survey by presenting thirty-one masterpieces of painting, sculpture, and architecture that eloquently show how great artists from the Old Stone Age to the present have responded to that most human of impulses, the urge to create art. New illustrations show works *in situ,* adding a new dimension of visual context to the narrative of art history. There are diagrams and architectural drawings that have never appeared in *History of Art,* as well as many improved diagrams and plans.

Less immediately apparent perhaps, but no less important, is the complete reorganization of Part Four, devoted to the modern world. The distinction between Neoclassicism and Romanticism is now drawn more clearly. Twentieth-century painting now has a more straightforward chronological organization. A separate chapter is devoted to sculpture since 1900, which has followed a rather different path from painting. Modern architecture begins with Frank Lloyd Wright, while its antecedents, including the Chicago School and Art Nouveau, have been placed in earlier chapters where they properly belong. I have also taken the opportunity throughout to make numerous adjustments in the text and headings; to bring the record of art history up-to-date; and to add a number of artists, including half again as many women as were in the previous edition. In this connection, it should be noted that the masculine gender is used in referring collectively to artists and some other groups of people only to avoid awkward circumlocutions and repetitive language.

The expanded Introduction now includes a brief discussion of line, color, light, composition, form, and space. This section is intended to help the beginner become more sensitive to visual components of art. The decision to incorporate basic elements of art appreciation—a subject that lies outside the traditional scope of art history—is based on the conviction that one must first learn how to look at art in order to understand it, since the works of art themselves remain the primary document. Most people who read this book do so to enhance their enjoyment of art, but often feel uneasy in looking at individual works of art. The new material address-es that obstacle by providing some general observations on viewing art, without resorting to formulaic guidelines that too often get in the way.

In making these revisions, I am mindful that changing anything in a book that has become an institution is not a task to be undertaken lightly. My primary aim has been to preserve the humanism that provided the foundation of this book and to integrate my own approach and writing style as seamlessly as possible into *History of Art* as it has evolved over almost thirty years. Further, I am quite aware that asserting the traditional value of the aesthetic experience runs counter to the "new art history," which sees art essentially as a conveyor of meaning determined by social context. The influence of the semiotic approach—an interest of mine that goes back more than a decade—can be detected in the Introduction's reference to language and meaning. Nevertheless, it is arguably more suited to the written word than to the visual arts, stemming as it does largely from French literary criticism and linguistics. Moreover, it can be seen as embodying a distinctly Post-Modernist sensibility (discussed toward the end of the book), in which the artist and his creation are relegated to secondary considerations. The book's traditional approach is based on my belief that ignoring the visual and expressive qualities of a work in order to make it conform to a theoretical construct risks depriving us of much of art's pleasure, purpose, and inherent worth by turning its study into a scholastic exercise.

I am greatly indebted to two former colleagues: Michael McDonough for his helpful suggestions on modern architecture and Joseph Jacobs for his stimulating ideas about contemporary art. At Harry N. Abrams, Inc., I have been fortunate to have the collaboration of Senior Editor Julia Moore, who was responsible for editing and for tracking the myriad revisions. Project Manager Sheila Franklin Lieber provided strong support and made consistently helpful suggestions early in the revision process. Bob McKee redesigned the entire book with intelligence and aplomb. Jennifer Bright worked miracles in the herculean task of securing hundreds of new photographs. In finding solutions to the complex problems of integrating color—without sacrificing the high quality production for which this book is known—Shun Yamamoto performed with the greatest professionalism. I am especially grateful to Paul Gottlieb for his unfailing support, sound advice, and good humor. Lastly, it is only fitting that this edition be dedicated to the memory of Fritz Landshoff, whose impact on me was so profound.

A. F. J.
1990

# INTRODUCTION

## ART AND THE ARTIST

"What is art?" Few questions provoke such heated debate and provide so few satisfactory answers. If we cannot come to any definitive conclusions, there is still a good deal we can say. Art is first of all a *word*—one that acknowledges both the idea and the fact of art. Without it, we might well ask whether art exists in the first place. The term, after all, is not found in every society. Yet art is *made* everywhere. Art, therefore, is also an object, but not just any kind of object. Art is an *aesthetic object*. It is meant to be looked at and appreciated for its intrinsic value. Its special qualities set art apart, so that it is often placed away from everyday life—in museums, churches, or caves. What do we mean by aesthetic? By definition, aesthetic is "that which concerns the beautiful."

Of course, not all art is beautiful to our eyes, but it is art nonetheless. And no matter how unsatisfactory, the term will have to do for lack of a better one. Aesthetics is, strictly speaking, a branch of philosophy which has occupied thinkers from Plato to the present day. Like all matters philosophical, it is inherently debatable. During the last hundred years, aesthetics has also become a field of psychology, a field which has come to equally little agreement. Why should this be so? On the one hand, people the world over make much the same fundamental judgments, since our brains and nervous systems are the same. On the other hand, taste is conditioned solely by culture, which is so varied that it is impossible to reduce art to any one set of precepts. It would seem, therefore, that absolute qualities in art must elude us, that we cannot escape viewing works of art in the context of time and circumstance, whether past or present. How indeed could it be otherwise, so long as art is still being created all around us, opening our eyes almost daily to new experiences and thus forcing us to readjust our understanding?

## Imagination

We all dream. That is imagination at work. To imagine means simply to make an image—a picture—in our minds. Human beings are not the only creatures who have imagination. Even animals dream. A cat's ears and tail may twitch as he sleeps, and a sleeping dog may whine and growl and paw the air, as if he were having a fight. Even when awake, animals "see" things. For no apparent reason a cat's fur may rise on his back as he peers into a dark closet, just as you or I may get goose bumps from phantoms we neither see nor hear. Clearly, however, there is a profound difference between human and animal imagination. Humans are the only creatures who can tell one another about imagination in stories or pictures. The urge to make art is unique to us. No other animal has ever been observed to draw a recognizable image spontaneously in the wild. In fact, their only images have been produced under carefully controlled laboratory conditions that tell us more about the experimenter than they do about art. There can be little doubt, on the other hand, that people possess an aesthetic faculty. By the age of five every normal child has drawn a moon pie-face. The ability to make art is one of our most distinctive features, for it separates us from all other creatures across an evolutionary gap that is unbridgeable.

Just as an embryo retraces much of the human evolutionary past, so the budding artist reinvents the first stages of art. Soon, however, he completes that process and begins to respond to the culture around him. Even children's art is subject to the taste and outlook of the society that shapes his or her personality. In fact, we tend to judge children's art according to the same criteria as adult art—only in appropriately simpler terms—and with good reason, for if we examine its successive stages, we find that the youngster must develop all the skills that go into adult art: coordination, intellect, personality, imagination, creativity, and aesthetic judgment. Seen this way, the making of a youthful artist is a process as fragile as growing up itself, and one that can be stunted at any step by the vicissitudes of life. No wonder that so few continue their creative aspirations into adulthood.

Given the many factors that feed into it, art must play a very special role in the artist's personality. Sigmund Freud, the founder of modern psychiatry, conceived of art primarily in terms of sublimation outside of consciousness. Such a view hardly does justice to artistic creativity, since art is not simply a negative force at the mercy of our neuroses but a positive expression that integrates diverse aspects of personality. Indeed, when we look at the art of the mentally ill, we may be struck by its vividness; but we instinctively sense that something is wrong, because the expression is incomplete.

Artists may sometimes be tortured by the burden of their genius, but they can never be truly creative under the thrall of psychosis. The imagination is one of our most mysterious facets. It can be regarded as the connector between the conscious and the subconscious, where most of our brain activity takes place. It is the very glue that holds our personality, intellect, and spirituality together. Because the imagination responds to all three, it acts in lawful, if unpredictable, ways

that are determined by the psyche and the mind. Thus, even the most private artistic statements can be understood on some level, even if only an intuitive one.

The imagination is important, as it allows us to conceive of all kinds of possibilities in the future and to understand the past in a way that has real survival value. It is a fundamental part of our makeup. The ability to make art, in contrast, must have been acquired relatively recently in the course of evolution. The record of the earliest art is lost to us. Human beings have been walking the earth for some two million years, but the oldest prehistoric art that we know of was made only about 35,000 years ago, though it was undoubtedly the culmination of a long development no longer traceable. Even the most "primitive" ethnographic art represents a late stage of development within a stable society.

Who were the first artists? In all likelihood, they were shamans. Like the legendary Orpheus, they were believed to have divine powers of inspiration and to be able to enter the underworld of the subconscious in a deathlike trance, but, unlike ordinary mortals, they were then able to return to the realm of the living. Just such a figure seems to be represented by our *Harpist* (fig. 1) from nearly five thousand years ago. A work of unprecedented complexity for its time, it was

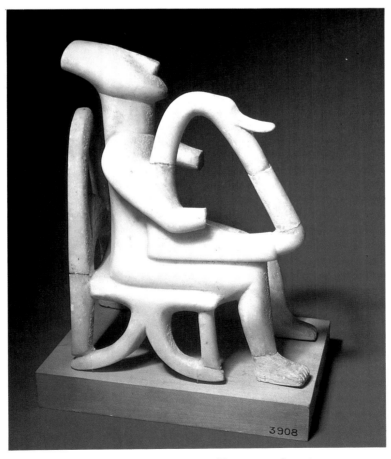

1. *HARPIST,* so-called Orpheus. Marble statuette from Amorgos
in the Cyclades. Latter part of the 3rd millennium B.C.
Height 8½″ (21.5 cm). National Archeological Museum, Athens

carved by a remarkably gifted artist who makes us feel the visionary rapture of a bard as he sings his legend. With this artist-shaman's unique ability to penetrate the unknown and his rare talent for expressing it through art, he gained control over the forces hidden in human beings and nature. Even today the artist remains a magician whose work can mystify and move us—an embarrassing fact to civilized people, who do not readily relinquish their veneer of rational control.

In a larger sense art, like science and religion, fulfills our innate urge to comprehend ourselves and the universe. This function makes art especially significant and, hence, worthy of our attention. Art has the power to penetrate to the core of our being, which recognizes itself in the creative act. For that reason, art represents its creator's deepest understanding and highest aspirations; at the same time, the artist often plays an important role as the articulator of our shared beliefs and values, which he expresses through an ongoing tradition to us, his audience. A masterpiece, then, is a work that contributes to our vision of life and leaves us profoundly moved. Moreover, it can bear the closest scrutiny and withstand the test of time.

## Creativity

What do we mean by making? If, in order to simplify our problem, we concentrate on the visual arts, we might say that a work of art must be a tangible thing shaped by human hands. This definition at least eliminates the confusion of treating as works of art such natural phenomena as flowers, seashells, or sunsets. It is a far from sufficient definition, to be sure, since human beings make many things other than works of art. Still, it will serve as a starting point. Now let us look at the striking *Bull's Head* by Picasso (fig. 2), which seems to consist of nothing but the seat and handlebars of an old bicycle. How meaningful is our formula here? Of course the materials used by Picasso are fabricated, but it would be absurd to insist that Picasso must share the credit with the manufacturer, since the seat and handlebars in themselves are not works of art.

While we feel a certain jolt when we first recognize the ingredients of this visual pun, we also sense that it was a stroke of genius to put them together in this unique way, and we cannot very well deny that it is a work of art. Yet the handiwork—the mounting of the seat on the handlebars—is ridiculously simple. What is far from simple is the leap of the imagination by which Picasso recognized a bull's head in these unlikely objects; that, we feel, only he could have done. Clearly, then, we must be careful not to confuse the making of a work of art with manual skill or craftsmanship. Some works of art may demand a great deal of technical discipline; others do not. And even the most painstaking piece of craft does not deserve to be called a work of art unless it involves a leap of the imagination.

But if this is true are we not forced to conclude that the real making of the *Bull's Head* took place in the artist's mind? No, that is not so, either. Suppose that, instead of actually putting the two pieces together and showing them to us, Picasso merely told us, "You know, today I saw a bicycle seat and handlebars that looked just like a bull's head to me." Then there would be no work of art and his remark would not even strike us as an interesting bit of conversation. Moreover, Picasso himself would not have felt the satisfaction of having created something on the basis of his leap of the imagination alone. Once he had conceived his visual pun, he could never be sure that it would really work unless he put it into effect.

Thus the artist's hands, however modest the task they may have to perform, play an essential part in the creative process. Our *Bull's Head* is, of course, an ideally simple case, involving only one leap of the imagination and a manual act in response to it—once the seat had been properly placed on the handlebars (and then cast in bronze), the job was done. The leap of the imagination is sometimes experienced as a flash of inspiration, but only rarely does a new idea emerge full-blown like Athena from the head of Zeus. Instead, it is usually preceded by a long gestation period in which all the hard work is done without finding the key to the solution to the problem. At the critical point, the imagination makes connections between seemingly unrelated parts and recombines them.

Ordinarily, artists do not work with ready-made parts but with materials that have little or no shape of their own; the creative process consists of a long series of leaps of the imagination and the artist's attempts to give them form by shaping the material accordingly. The hand tries to carry out the commands of the imagination and hopefully puts down a brushstroke, but the result may not be quite what had been expected, partly because all matter resists the human will, partly because the image in the artist's mind is constantly shifting and changing, so that the commands of the imagination cannot be very precise. In fact, the mental image begins to come into focus only as the artist "draws the line somewhere." That line then becomes part—the only fixed part—of the image; the rest of the image, as yet unborn, remains fluid. And each time the artist adds another line, a new leap of the imagination is needed to incorporate that line into his ever-growing mental image. If the line cannot be incorporated, he discards it and puts down a new one.

In this way, by a constant flow of impulses back and forth between his mind and the partly shaped material before him, he gradually defines more and more of the image, until at last all of it has been given visible form. Needless to say, artistic creation is too subtle and intimate an experience to permit an exact step-by-step description; only the artist himself can observe it fully, but he is so absorbed by it that he has great difficulty explaining it to us.

The metaphor of birth comes closer to the truth than would a description of the process in terms of a transfer or projection of the image from the artist's mind, for the making of a work of art is both joyous and painful, replete with surprises, and in no sense mechanical. We have, moreover, ample testimony that the artist himself tends to look upon his creation as a living thing. Perhaps that is why creativity was once a concept reserved for God, as only He could give material form to an idea. Indeed, the artist's labors are much like the Creation told in the Bible; but this divine ability was not realized until Michelangelo described the anguish and

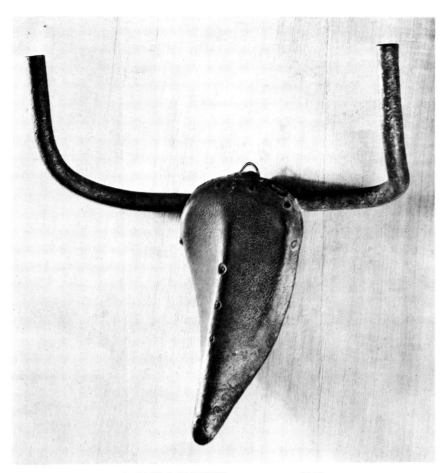

2. PABLO PICASSO. *BULL'S HEAD.* 1943.
Bronze cast bicycle parts, height 16⅛″ (41 cm).
Galerie Louise Leiris, Paris

glory of the creative experience when he spoke of "liberating the figure from the marble that imprisons it." We may translate this to mean that he started the process of carving a statue by trying to visualize a figure in the rough, rectilinear block as it came to him from the quarry. (At times he may even have done so while the marble was still part of the "living" rock; we know that he liked to go to the quarries and pick out his material on the spot.)

It seems fair to assume that at first Michelangelo did not see the figure any more clearly than one can see an unborn child inside the womb, but we may believe that he could see isolated "signs of life" within the marble—a knee or an elbow pressing against the surface. To get a firmer grip on this dimly felt, fluid image, he was in the habit of making numerous drawings, and sometimes small models in wax or clay, before he dared to assault the "marble prison" itself. For that, he knew, was the final contest between himself and his material. Once he started carving, every stroke of the chisel would commit him more and more to a specific conception of the figure hidden in the block, and the marble would permit him to free the figure whole only if his guess as to its shape was correct.

Sometimes he did not guess well enough—the stone refused to give up some essential part of its prisoner, and Michelangelo, defeated, left the work unfinished, as he did with *St. Matthew* (fig. 3), whose very gesture seems to record the vain struggle for liberation. Looking at the block, we may get some inkling of Michelangelo's difficulties here. But could he not have finished the statue in *some* fashion? Surely there is enough material left for that. Well, he probably could have, but perhaps not in the way he wanted, and in that case the defeat would have been even more stinging.

Clearly, then, the making of a work of art has little in common with what we ordinarily mean by "making." It is a strange and risky business in which the maker never quite knows what he is making until he has actually made it; or, to put it another way, it is a game of find-and-seek in which the seeker is not sure what he is looking for until he has found it. (In the case of the *Bull's Head* it is the bold "finding" that impresses us most; in the *St. Matthew*, the strenuous "seeking.") To the non-artist, it seems hard to believe that this uncertainty, this need-to-take-a-chance, should be the essence of the artist's work. We all tend to think of "making" in terms of the craftsman or manufacturer who knows exactly what

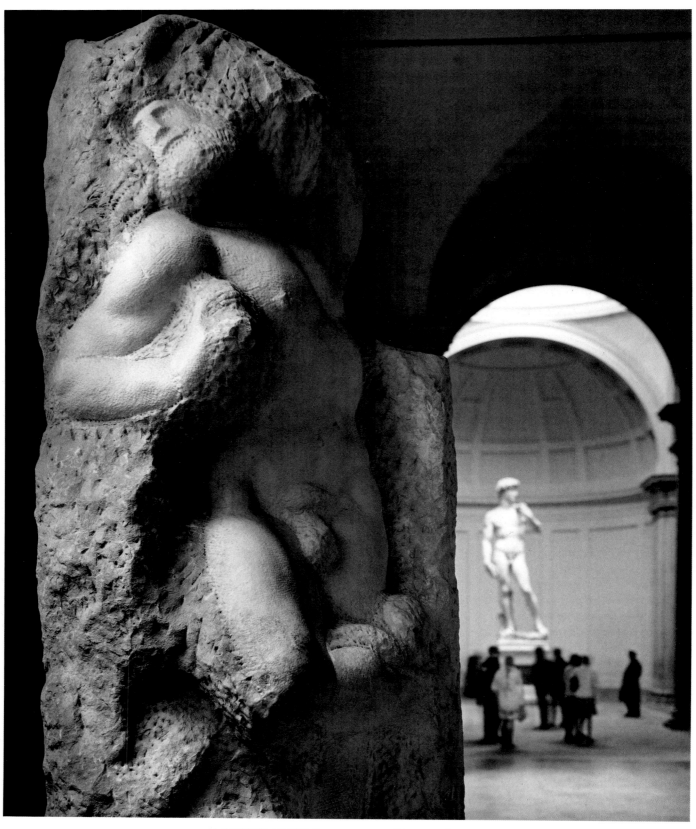

3. MICHELANGELO. *ST. MATTHEW* (foreground). 1506.
Marble, height 8'11" (2.7 m).
Galleria dell'Accademia, Florence

he wants to produce from the very outset, picks the tools best fitted to the task, and is sure of what he is doing at every step. Such "making" is a two-phase affair: first the craftsman makes a plan, then he acts on it. And because he—or his customer—has made all the important decisions in advance, he has to worry only about the means, rather than the ends, while he carries out his plan. There is thus comparatively little risk, but also little adventure, in his handiwork, which as a consequence tends to become routine. It may even be replaced by the mechanical labor of a machine.

No machine, on the other hand, can replace the artist, for with him conception and execution go hand in hand and are so completely interdependent that he cannot separate the one from the other. Whereas the craftsman attempts only what he knows to be possible, the artist is always driven to attempt the impossible—or at least the improbable or unimaginable. Who, after all, would have imagined that a bull's head was hidden in the seat and handlebars of a bicycle until Picasso discovered it for us; did he not, almost literally, "make a silk purse out of a sow's ear"? No wonder the artist's way of working is so resistant to any set rules, while the craftsman's encourages standardization and regularity. We acknowledge this difference when we speak of the artist as *creating* instead of merely *making* something, although the word has been done to death by overuse, and every child and fashion designer is labeled "creative."

Needless to say, there have always been many more craftsmen than artists among us, since our need for the familiar and expected far exceeds our capacity to absorb the original but often deeply unsettling experiences we get from works of art. The urge to penetrate unknown realms, to achieve something original, may be felt by every one of us now and then; to that extent, we can all fancy ourselves potential artists—mute inglorious Miltons. What sets the real artist apart is not so much the desire to *seek*, but that mysterious ability to *find*, which we call talent. We also speak of it as a "gift," implying that it is a sort of present from some higher power; or as "genius," a term which originally meant that a higher power—a kind of "good demon"—inhabits the artist's body and acts through him.

One thing we can say about talent is that it must not be confused with aptitude. Aptitude is what the craftsman needs; it means a better-than-average knack for doing something. An aptitude is fairly constant and specific; it can be measured with some success by means of tests that permit us to predict future performance. Creative talent, on the other hand, seems utterly unpredictable; we can spot it only on the basis of *past* performance. And even past performance is not enough to ensure that a given artist will continue to produce on the same level: some artists reach a creative peak quite early in their careers and then "go dry," while others, after a slow and unpromising start, may achieve astonishingly original work in middle age or even later.

## Originality

Originality, then, ultimately distinguishes art from craft. We may say, therefore, that it is the yardstick of artistic greatness or importance. Unfortunately, it is also very hard to define; the usual synonyms—uniqueness, novelty, freshness—do not help us very much, and the dictionaries tell us only that an original work must not be a copy. Thus, if we want to rate works of art on an "originality scale," our problem does not lie in deciding whether or not a given work is original (the obvious copies and reproductions are for the most part easy enough to eliminate) but in establishing exactly *how* original it is. To do that is not impossible. However, the difficulties besetting our task are so great that we cannot hope for more than tentative and incomplete answers. This does not mean that we should not try; quite the contrary. For whatever the outcome of our labors in any particular case, we shall certainly learn a great deal about works of art in the process.

A straightforward copy can usually be recognized as such on internal evidence alone. If the copyist is a conscientious craftsman rather than artist, he will produce a work of craft; the execution will strike us as pedestrian and thus out of tune with the conception of the work. There are also likely to be small slipups and mistakes that can be spotted in much the same way as misprints in a text. But what if one great artist copies another? In using another work as his model, the artist does not really copy it in the accepted sense of the word, since he does not try to achieve the effect of a duplicate. He does it purely for his own instruction, transcribing it accurately yet with his own inimitable rhythm. In other words, he is not the least constrained or intimidated by the fact that his model, in this instance, is another work of art. Once we understand this, it becomes clear to us that the artist *represents* (he does not *copy*) the other work, and that his artistic originality does not suffer thereby.

A relationship as close as this between two works of art is not as rare as one might think. Ordinarily, though, the link is not immediately obvious. Édouard Manet's famous painting *Luncheon on the Grass* (fig. 4) seemed so revolutionary a work when first exhibited more than a century ago that it caused a scandal, in part because the artist had dared to show an undressed young woman next to two men in fashionable contemporary dress. People assumed that Manet had intended to represent an actual event. Not until many years later did an art historian discover the source of these figures: a group of classical deities from an engraving after Raphael (fig. 5). The relationship, so striking once it has been pointed out to us, had escaped attention, for Manet did not *copy* or *represent* the Raphael composition—he merely *borrowed* its main outlines while translating the figures into modern terms.

Had his contemporaries known of this, the *Luncheon* would have seemed a rather less disreputable kind of outing to them, since now the hallowed shade of Raphael could be seen to hover nearby as a sort of chaperon. (Perhaps the artist meant to tease the conservative public, hoping that after the initial shock had passed, somebody would recognize the well-hidden quotation behind his "scandalous" group.) For us, the main effect of the comparison is to make the cool, formal quality of Manet's figures even more conspicuous. But does it decrease our respect for his originality? True, he is "indebted" to Raphael; yet his way of bringing the forgotten old composition back to life is in itself so original and creative that he may be said to have more than repaid his

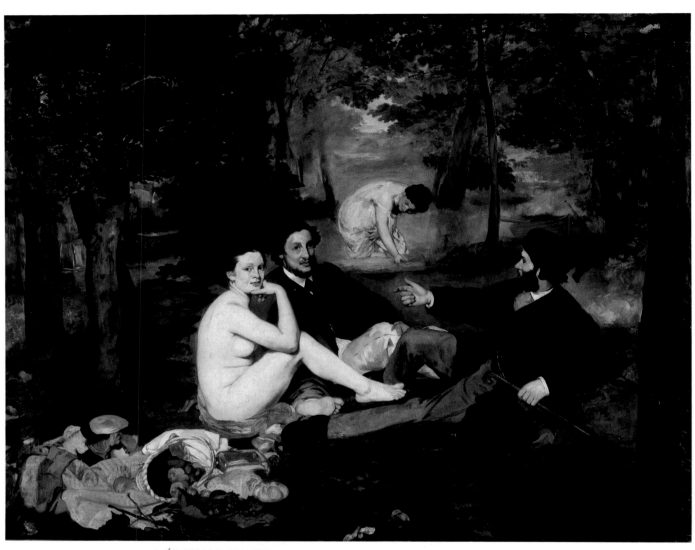

4. ÉDOUARD MANET. *LUNCHEON ON THE GRASS (LE DÉJEUNER SUR L'HERBE)*.
1863. Oil on canvas, 7′ × 8′10″ (2.1 × 2.6 m).
Musée d'Orsay, Paris

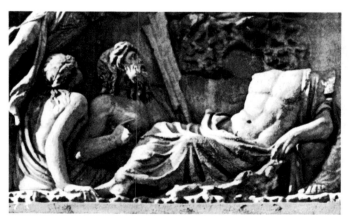

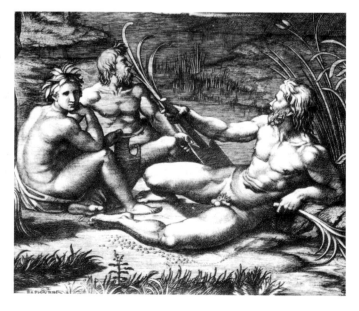

5. *(above)* MARCANTONIO RAIMONDI, after RAPHAEL
*THE JUDGMENT OF PARIS* (detail). c. 1520. Engraving

6. *(right)* RIVER GODS. Detail of Roman sarcophagus.
3rd century A.D. Villa Medici, Rome

debt. As a matter of fact, Raphael's figures are just as "derivative" as Manet's; they stem from still older sources which lead us back to ancient Roman art and beyond (compare the relief of *River Gods* (fig. 6).

Thus Manet, Raphael, and the Roman river gods form three links in a chain of relationships that arises somewhere out of the distant past and continues into the future—for the *Luncheon on the Grass* has in turn served as a source of more recent works of art. Nor is this an exceptional case. All works of art anywhere—yes, even such works as Picasso's *Bull's Head*—are part of similar chains that link them to their predecessors. If it is true that "no man is an island," the same can be said of works of art. The sum total of these chains makes a web in which every work of art occupies its own specific place; we call this *tradition*. Without tradition—the word means "that which has been handed down to us"—no originality would be possible; it provides, as it were, the firm platform from which the artist makes a leap of the imagination. The place where he lands will then become part of the web and serve as a point of departure for further leaps.

And for us, too, the web of tradition is equally essential. Whether we are aware of it or not, tradition is the framework within which we inevitably form our opinions of works of art and assess their degree of originality. Let us not forget, however, that such assessments must always remain incomplete and subject to revision. For in order to arrive at a definitive view, we should be able to survey the entire length of every chain. And that we can never hope to achieve.

If originality distinguishes art from craft, tradition serves as the common meeting ground of the two. Every budding artist starts out on the level of craft by imitating other works of art. In this way, he gradually absorbs the artistic tradition of his time and place until he has gained a firm footing in it. But only the truly gifted ever leave that stage of traditional competence and become creators in their own right. None of us, after all, can be taught how to create; we can only be taught how to go through the motions of creating. If the aspiring artist has talent, he will eventually achieve the real thing. What the apprentice or art student learns are skills and techniques—established ways of drawing, painting, carving, designing; established ways of *seeing*.

Nevertheless, one of the attributes that distinguishes great artists is their consummate technical command. This superior talent is recognized by other artists, who admire their work and seek to emulate it. This is not to say that facility alone is sufficient. Far from it! Ample warning against such a notion is provided by the academic painters and sculptors of the nineteenth century, who were as a group among the most proficient artists in history—as well as the dullest. Still, complete technical command is a requisite of masterpieces, which are distinguished by their superior execution.

If the would-be artist senses that his gifts are not large enough for him to succeed as a painter, sculptor, or architect, he may take up one of the countless special fields known collectively as "the applied arts." There he can be fruitfully active in less risky work—illustration, typographic design, industrial design, and interior design, for example.

All these pursuits stand somewhere between "pure" art and "traditional" craft. They provide some scope for originality to their more ambitious practitioners, but the flow of creative endeavor is cramped by such factors as the cost and availability of materials or manufacturing processes, accepted notions of what is useful, fitting, or desirable; for the applied arts are more deeply enmeshed in our everyday lives and thus cater to a far wider public than do painting and sculpture. Their purpose, as the name suggests, is to beautify the useful—an important and valued end, but limited in comparison to art pure-and-simple.

Nevertheless, we often find it difficult to maintain the distinction between fine and applied art. Medieval painting, for instance, is to a large extent "applied," in the sense that it embellishes surfaces which serve other, practical purposes as well—walls, book pages, windows, furniture. The same may be said of much ancient and medieval sculpture. Greek vases, as we shall see, although technically pottery, were sometimes decorated by artists of very impressive talent. And in architecture the distinction breaks down altogether, since the design of every building, from country cottage to cathedral, reflects external limitations imposed upon it by the site, by cost factors, materials, technology, and by the practical purpose of the structure. (The only "pure" architecture is imaginary, unbuilt architecture.) Thus architecture is, almost by definition, an applied art, but it is also a major art (as against the other applied arts, which are often called the "minor arts").

The graphic arts form a special case of their own. Drawings are original works of art; that is, they are entirely by the artist's own hand. With prints, however, the relationship between artist and image is more complex. Prints are not unique images but multiple reproductions made by mechanical means. Perhaps the distinction between original and copy is not so critical in printmaking after all. The printmaker must usually copy onto his plate a composition that was first worked out in a drawing, whether his own or someone else's. From the beginning, most prints have been made, at least in part, by craftsmen whose technical skill is necessary to ensure the outcome. Woodcuts and engraving in particular were traditionally dependent on craftsmanship, which may explain why so few creative geniuses have made them and have generally been content to let others produce prints from their designs. Although it does not require the artist's intervention at every step of the way, printmaking usually involves the artist's supervision and even active participation, so that we may think of the process as a collaborative effort.

## Meaning and Style

Why do we create art? Surely one reason is an irresistible urge to adorn ourselves and decorate the world around us. Both are part of a larger desire, not to remake the world in our image but to recast ourselves and our environment in *ideal* form. Art is, however, much more than decoration, for it is laden with meaning, even if that content is sometimes slender or obscure. Art enables us to communicate our understanding in ways that cannot be expressed otherwise. Truly a painting (or sculpture) is worth a thousand words, not only in its descriptive value but also in its symbolic significance. In art, as in language, we are above all inventors of symbols that convey complex thoughts in new ways. We must think of art not in terms of everyday prose but of poetry, which is free to rearrange conventional vocabulary and syntax in order to convey new, often multiple, meanings and moods. A work of art likewise suggests much more than it states. And like a poem, the value of art lies equally in what it says and how it says it: it communicates partly by implying meanings through pose, facial expression, allegory, and the like.

But what is the *meaning* of art—its iconography? What is it trying to say? Artists often provide no clear explanation, since the work is the statement itself. (If they could say what they mean in words, they would surely be writers instead.) Fortunately, certain visual symbols and responses occur so regularly over time and place that they can be regarded as virtually universal. Nevertheless, their exact meaning is specific to each particular culture, giving rise to art's incredible diversity.

The meaning, or content, of art is inseparable from its formal qualities, its *style*. The word *style* is derived from *stilus*, the writing instrument of the ancient Romans; originally, it referred to distinctive ways of writing—the shape of the letters as well as the choice of words. Nowadays, however, style is used loosely to mean the distinctive way a thing is done in any field of human endeavor. It is simply a term of praise in most cases: "to have style" means to have distinction, to stand out. But something else is implied, which comes to the fore if we ask ourselves what we mean when we say that something "has no style." Such a thing, we feel, is not only undistinguished but also undistinguishable; in other words, we do not know how to classify it, how to put it into its proper context, because it seems to point in several directions at once. Of a thing that *has style,* then, we expect that it not be inconsistent within itself—that it must have an inner coherence, or unity, that it possess a sense of wholeness, of being all of a piece. These are the qualities we admire in things that have style, for style has a way of impressing itself upon us even if we do not know what particular *kind* of style is involved.

In the visual arts, style means the particular way in which the forms that make up any given work of art are chosen and fitted together. To art historians the study of styles is of central importance; it not only enables them to find out, by means of careful analysis and comparison, when and where (and by whom) a given work was produced, but it also leads them to understand the artist's intention as expressed through the style of his work. This intention depends on both the artist's personality and the setting in which he lives and works. Accordingly, we speak of "period styles" if we are concerned with those features which distinguish, let us say, Egyptian art as a whole from Greek art. And within these broad period styles we in turn distinguish the styles of particular phases, such as the Old Kingdom; or, wherever it seems appropriate, we differentiate national or local styles within a period, until we arrive at the personal styles of individual artists. Even these may need to be subdivided further into the various phases of an artist's development. The extent to which we are able to categorize effectively depends on the degree of internal coherence, and on how much of a sense of continuity there is in the body of material we are dealing with.

Thus art, like language, requires that we learn the style and outlook of a country, period, and artist if we are to understand it properly. We are so accustomed to a naturalistic tradition of accurate reproductions that we expect art to imitate reality. But illusionism is only one vehicle for expressing an artist's understanding of reality. Truth, it seems, is indeed relative, for it is a matter not only of what our eyes tell us but also of the concepts through which our perceptions are filtered.

There is, then, no reason to place a premium on realistic representation for its own sake. Instead, style need only be appropriate to the intent of the work. The advantage of realism at face value is that it *seems* easier to understand. The disadvantage is that representational art, like prose, is always bound to the literal meaning and appearance of the everyday world, at least to some extent. Actually, realism is exceptional in the history of art and is not even necessary to its purposes. We must remember that any image is a separate and self-contained reality which has its own ends and responds to its own imperatives, for the artist is bound only to his creativity. Even the most convincing illusion is the product of the artist's imagination and understanding, so that we must always ask why he chose this subject and made it this way rather than some other way. Understanding the role of self-expression may provide some answers.

## Self-Expression and Audience

Most of us are familiar with the famous Greek myth of the sculptor Pygmalion, who carved such a beautiful statue of the nymph Galatea that he fell in love with it and embraced her when Venus made his sculpture come to life. The myth has been given a fresh interpretation by John De Andrea's *The Artist and His Model* (fig. 7), which tells us a good deal about creativity by reversing the roles. Now it is the artist, lost in thought, who is oblivious to the statue's gaze. Clearly based on a real woman rather than an ideal conception, the model is still in the process of "coming to life"; the artist has not finished painting her white legs. The illusion is so convincing that we wonder which figure is real and which one is dreaming of the other, the artist or the sculpture? De Andrea makes us realize that to the artist, the creative act is a "labor of love" that brings art to life through self-expression. But can we not also say that it is the work of art which gives birth to the artist?

The birth of a work of art is an intensely private experience (so much so that many artists can work only when completely alone and refuse to show their unfinished pieces to anyone), yet it must, as a final step, be shared by the public in order for the birth to be successful. The artist does not create merely for his own satisfaction, but wants his work validated by others. In fact, the creative process is not completed until the work has found an audience. In the end, works of art exist in order to be liked rather than to be debated.

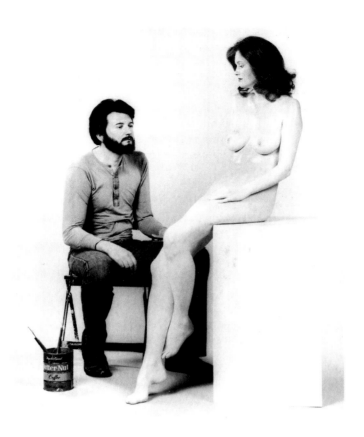

7. JOHN DE ANDREA. *THE ARTIST AND HIS MODEL.* 1980.
Polyvinyl, polychromed in oil; lifesize. Collection Foster Goldstrom,
Dallas and San Francisco. Courtesy O. K. Harris, New York

Perhaps we can resolve this seeming paradox once we understand what the artist means by "public." He is concerned not with *the* public as a statistical entity but with his particular public, his audience; quality rather than wide approval is what matters to him. At a minimum, this audience needs to consist of no more than one or two people whose opinions he values. Ordinarily, however, artists also need patrons among their audience who will purchase their work, thus combining moral and financial support. In contrast to a customer of applied art, for example, who knows from previous experience what he will get when he buys the products of craftsmanship, the "audience" for art merits such adjectives as critical, fickle, receptive, enthusiastic; it is uncommitted, free to accept or reject, so that anything placed before it is on trial—nobody knows in advance how it will receive the work. Hence, there is an emotional tension between artist and audience that has no counterpart in the relationship of craftsman and customer. It is this very tension, this sense of uncertainty and challenge, that the artist needs. He must feel that his work is able to overcome the resistance of the audience, otherwise he cannot be sure that what he has brought forth is a genuine creation, a work of art in fact as well as in intention. The more ambitious and original his work, the greater the tension and the more triumphant his sense of release after the response of the audience

has shown him that his leap of the imagination has been successful.

The audience whose approval looms so large in the artist's mind is a limited and special one; its members may be other artists as well as patrons, friends, critics, and interested beholders. The one quality they all have in common is an informed love of works of art—an attitude at once discriminating and enthusiastic that lends particular weight to their judgments. They are, in a word, experts, people whose authority rests on experience rather than theoretical knowledge. In reality, there is no sharp break, no difference in kind, between the expert and the layman, only a difference in degree.

## Tastes

Deciding what is art and rating a work of art are two separate problems; if we had an absolute method for distinguishing art from non-art, it would not necessarily enable us to measure quality. People tend to compound the two problems into one; quite often when they ask, "Why is that art?" they mean, "Why is that *good* art?" How often have we heard this question asked—or asked it ourselves, perhaps—in front of one of the strange, disquieting works that we are likely to find nowadays in museums or art exhibitions. There usually is an undertone of exasperation, for the question implies that *we* don't think we are looking at a work of art, but that the experts—the critics, museum curators, art historians—must suppose it to be one, or why else would they put it on public display? Clearly, their standards are very different from ours; we are at a loss to understand them and we wish they'd give us a few simple, clear-cut rules to go by. Then maybe we would learn to like what we see; we would know "why it is art." But the experts do not post exact rules, and the layman is apt to fall back upon his final line of defense: "Well, I don't know anything about art, but I know what I like."

It is a formidable roadblock, this stock phrase, in the path of understanding between expert and layman. Until not so very long ago, there was no great need for the two to communicate with each other; the general public had little voice in matters of art and therefore could not challenge the judgment of the expert few. Today both sides are aware of the barrier between them (the barrier itself is nothing new, although it may be greater now than at certain times in the past) and of the need to level it. That is why books like this one are written. Let us examine the roadblock and the various unspoken assumptions that buttress it.

Our puzzled layman might be willing to grant, on the basis of our discussion so far, that art is indeed a complex and in many ways mysterious human activity about which even the experts can hope to offer only tentative and partial conclusions; but he is also likely to take this as confirming his own belief that "I don't know anything about art." Are there really people who know nothing about art? If we except small children and people with certain mental disabilities, our answer must be no, for none of us can help knowing *something* about it, just as each of us knows something about politics and economics—no matter how indifferent we may be to the issues of the day. Art is so much a part of the fabric of human living that we encounter it all the time, even if our contacts with it are limited to magazine covers, advertising posters, war memorials, television, and the buildings where we live, work, and worship. Much of this art, to be sure, is pretty shoddy—art at third- and fourth-hand, worn out by endless repetition, representing the lowest common denominator of popular taste. Still, it is art of a sort; and since it is the only art most of us ever experience, it molds our ideas on art in general. When we say, "I know what I like," we may really mean, "I like what I know (and I reject whatever fails to match the things I am familiar with)." Such likes are not in truth ours at all, for they have been imposed by habit and culture without any personal choice. To like what we know and to distrust what we do not know is an age-old human trait. We always tend to think of the past as "the good old days," while the future seems fraught with danger.

But why should so many of us cherish the illusion of having made a personal choice in art when in fact we have not? There is another unspoken assumption at work here that goes something like this: "Since art is such an 'unruly' subject that even the experts keep disagreeing with each other, my opinion is as good as theirs—it's all a matter of subjective preference. In fact, my opinion may be *better* than theirs, because as a layman I react to art in a direct, straightforward

fashion, without having my view obstructed by a lot of complicated theories. There must be something wrong with a work of art if it takes an expert to appreciate it."

But if experts appreciate art more than the uninformed, why should we not emulate them? We have seen that the road to expertness is clear and wide, and that it invites anyone with an open mind and a capacity to absorb new experiences. As our understanding grows, we find ourselves liking a great many more things than we had thought possible at the start. We gradually acquire the courage of our own convictions, until we are able to say, with some justice, that we know what we like.

# LOOKING AT ART
## The Visual Elements

We live in a sea of images conveying the culture and learning of modern civilization. Fostered by an unprecedented media explosion, this "visual background noise" has become so much a part of our daily lives that we take it for granted. In the process, we have become desensitized to art as well. Anyone can buy cheap paintings and reproductions to decorate a room, where they often hang virtually unnoticed, perhaps deservedly so. It is small wonder that we look at the art in museums with equal casualness. We pass rapidly from one object to another, sampling them like dishes in a smorgasbord. We may pause briefly before a famous masterpiece that we have been told we are supposed to admire, then ignore the gallery full of equally beautiful and important works around it. We will have seen the art but not really looked at it. Looking at great art is not such an easy task, for art rarely reveals its secrets readily. While the experience of a work can be immediately electrifying, we sometimes do not realize its impact until time has let it filter through the recesses of our imaginations. It even happens that something that at first repelled or confounded us emerges only many years later as one of the most important artistic events of our lives. Because so much goes into art, it makes much the same demands on our faculties as it did on the person who created it. For that reason, we must be able to respond to it on many levels. If we are going to get the most out of art, we will have to learn how to look and think for ourselves in an intelligent way, which is perhaps the hardest task of all. After all, we will not always have someone at our side to help us. In the end, the confrontation of viewer and art remains a solitary act.

Understanding a work of art begins with a sensitive appreciation of its appearance. Art may be approached and appreciated for its purely visual elements: line, color, light, composition, form, and space. These may be shared by any work of art; their effects, however, vary widely according to medium (the physical materials of which the artwork is made) and technique, which together help to determine the possibilities and limitations of what the artist can achieve. For that reason, our discussion is merged with an introduction to four major arts: graphic arts, painting, sculpture, and architecture. (The technical aspects of the major media are treated in separate sections within the main body of the text

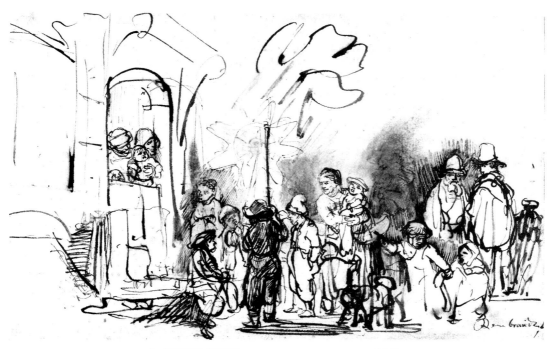

8. REMBRANDT. *THE STAR OF THE KINGS.* c. 1642.
Pen and bistre, wash, 8 × 12¾″ (20.3 × 32.4 cm). British Museum, London

and in the glossary toward the end of the book.) Just because line is discussed with drawing, however, does not mean that it is not equally important in painting and sculpture. And while form is introduced with sculpture, it is just as essential to painting, drawing, and architecture.

Visual analysis can help us to appreciate the beauty of a masterpiece, but we must be careful not to use a formulaic approach that would trivialize it. Every aesthetic "law" advanced so far has proven of dubious value, and usually gets in the way of our understanding. Even if a valid "law" were to be found—and none has yet been discovered—it would probably be so elementary as to prove useless in the face of art's complexity. We must also bear in mind that art appreciation is more than mere enjoyment of aesthetics. It is learning to understand the meaning (or iconography) of a work of art. And finally, let us remember that no work can be understood outside its historical context.

LINE. Line may be regarded as the most basic visual element. A majority of art is initially conceived in terms of contour line; its presence is often implied even when it is not actually used to describe form. And because children start out by scribbling, line is generally considered the most rudimentary component of art—although as anyone knows who has watched a youngster struggle to make a stick figure with pencil or crayon, drawing is by no means as easy as it seems. Line has traditionally been admired for its descriptive value, so that its expressive potential is easily overlooked. Yet line is capable of creating a broad range of effects.

Drawings represent line in its purest form. The appreciation of drawings as works of art dates from the Renaissance, when the artist's creative genius first came to be valued and paper began to be made in quantity. Drawing style can be as personal as handwriting. In fact, the term "graphic art," which designates drawings and prints, comes from the Greek word for writing, *graphos.* Collectors treasure drawings because they seem to reveal the artist's inspiration with unmatched freshness. Their role as records of artistic thought also makes drawings uniquely valuable to the art historian, for they help in documenting the evolution of a work from its inception to the finished piece.

Artists themselves commonly treat drawings as a form of note-taking. Some of these notes are discarded as fruitless, while others are tucked away to form a storehouse of motifs and studies for later use. Rembrandt was a prolific draftsman who was constantly jotting down observations of daily life and other ideas for further development. His use of line was highly expressive. Many of his sketches were done in pen and ink, a medium that captured his most intimate thoughts with admirable directness. In *The Star of the Kings* (fig. 8), one of his most elaborate sheets, Rembrandt rendered the essence of each pose and expression with remarkable succinctness—the dog, for example, consists of no more than a few strokes of the pen—yet every figure emerges as an individual character. Rembrandt's draftsmanship is so forceful that it allows us to mentally trace the movements of the master's hand with astonishing vividness.

Once a basic idea is established, an artist may develop it into a more complete study. Michelangelo's study (fig. 9) of the Libyan Sibyl for the Sistine Chapel ceiling is a drawing of compelling beauty. For this sheet, he chose the softer medium of red chalk over the scratchy line of pen and ink that he used in rough sketches; his chalk approximates the tex-

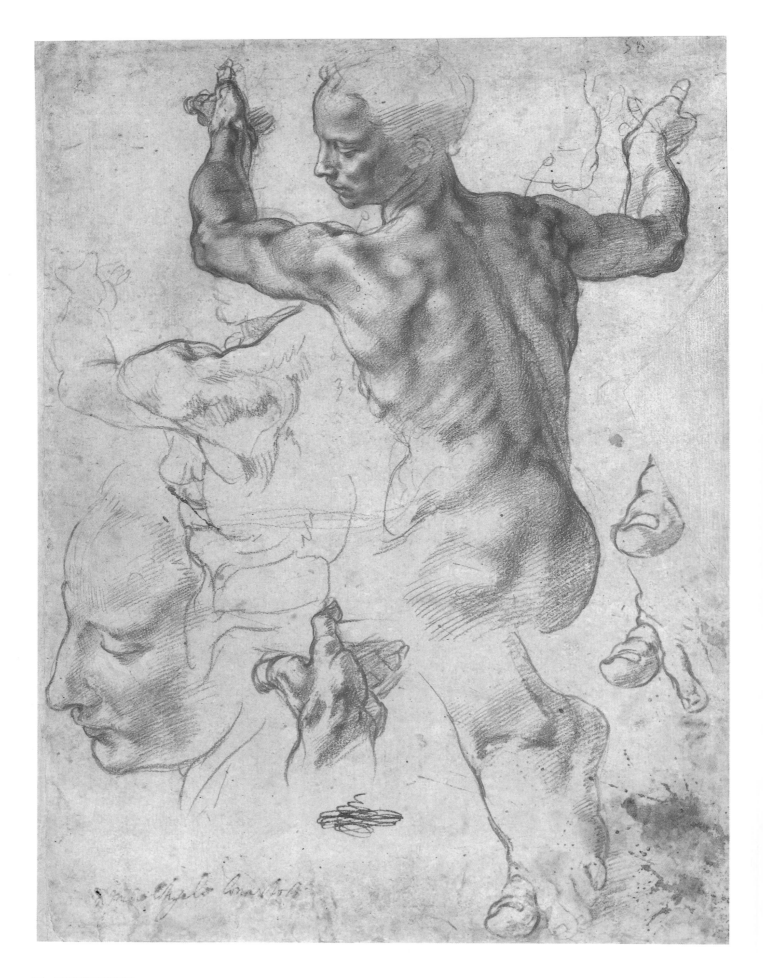

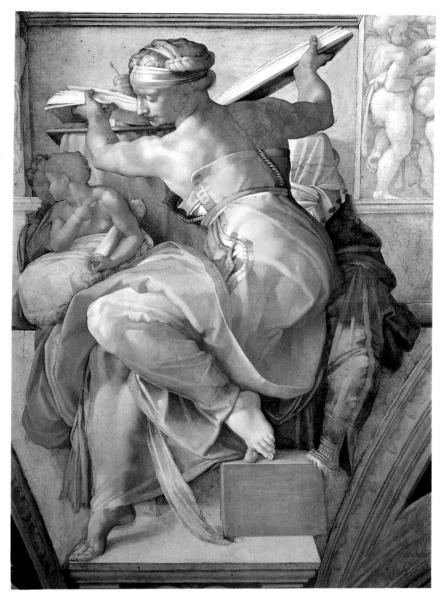

10. (*above*) MICHELANGELO. *LIBYAN SIBYL*, portion of the Sistine
Ceiling. 1508–12. Fresco. Sistine Chapel,
The Vatican, Rome

ture of flesh and captures the play of light and dark over the nude forms, giving the figure a greater sensuousness. The emphatic outline that defines each part of the form is so fundamental to the conceptual genesis and design process in all of Michelangelo's paintings and drawings that ever since his time line has been closely associated with the "intellectual" side of art.

It was Michelangelo's habit to base his female figures on male nudes drawn from life. To him, only the heroic male

nude possessed the physical monumentality necessary to express the awesome power of figures such as this mythical prophetess. In common with other sheets like this by him, Michelangelo's focus here is on the torso; he studied the musculature at length before turning his attention to details like the hand and toes. Since there is no sign of hesitation in the pose, we can be sure that the artist already had the conception firmly in mind; probably it had been established in a preliminary drawing. Why did he go to so much trouble when the finished sibyl is mostly clothed and must be viewed from a considerable distance below? Evidently Michelangelo believed that only by describing the anatomy completely could he be certain that the figure would be convincing. In the final painting (fig. 10) she communicates a superhuman strength, lifting her massive book of prophecies with the greatest ease.

9. (*opposite*) MICHELANGELO. *STUDY FOR THE LIBYAN SIBYL.*
c. 1511. Red chalk on paper, 11⅜ × 8⅜″ (28 × 21.3 cm).
The Metropolitan Museum of Art, New York.
Purchase, 1924, Joseph Pulitzer Bequest

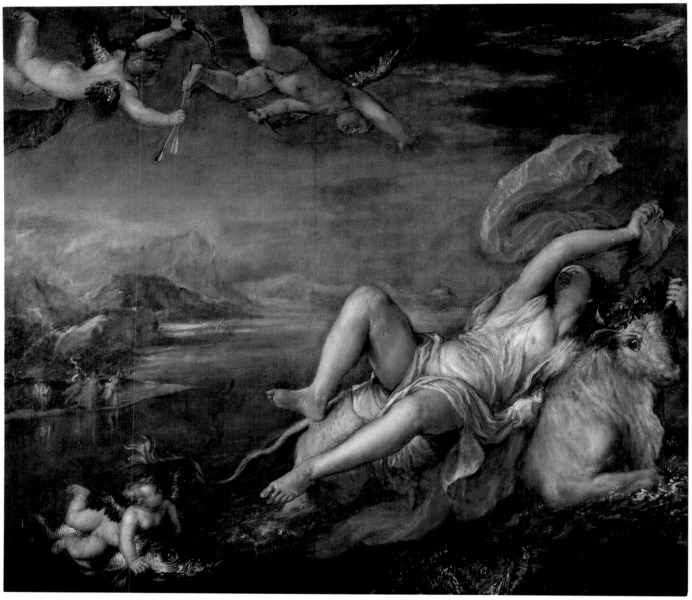

11. TITIAN. *THE RAPE OF EUROPA.*
1559–62. Oil on canvas, 70 × 80¾″ (178 × 205 cm).
Isabella Stewart Gardner Museum, Boston

COLOR. The world around us is alive with color, albeit even those of us who are not colorblind see only a relatively narrow band of the actual light spectrum. Whereas color is an adjunct element to graphics and sometimes sculpture, color is indispensable to virtually all forms of painting. This is true even of tonalism, which emphasizes dark, neutral hues like gray and brown. Of all the visual elements, color is undoubtedly the most expressive—as well as the most intractable. Perhaps for that reason, it has attracted the wide attention of researchers and theorists since the mid-nineteenth century. Along with the Post-Impressionists and, more recently, Op artists, color theorists have tried to set down their understanding of colors as perceptual and artistic laws equivalent to those of optical physics. Both Van Gogh and Seurat developed elaborate color systems, one entirely personal in its meaning, the other claiming to be "scientific." We often read that red seems to advance, while blue recedes; or that the former is a violent or passionate color, the latter a sad one. Like a recalcitrant child, however, color in art refuses to be governed by any rules; they work only when the painter consciously applies them.

Notwithstanding this large body of theory, the role of color in art rests primarily on its sensuous and emotive appeal, in contrast to the more cerebral quality generally associated with line. The merits of line versus color have been the subject of a debate that first arose between partisans of Michelangelo and Titian, his great contemporary in Venice. Titian himself was a fine draftsman and absorbed the influence of Michelangelo. He nevertheless stands at the head of the coloristic tradition that descends through Rubens and Van

Gogh to the Abstract Expressionists of the twentieth century. *The Rape of Europa* (fig. 11), painted toward the end of Titian's long career, shows the painterly application of sonorous color that is characteristic of his work. Though he no doubt worked out the essential features of the composition in preliminary drawings, none have survived. Nor evidently did he transfer the design onto the canvas but worked directly on the surface, making numerous changes as he went along. By varying the consistency of his pigments, the artist was able to capture the texture of Europa's flesh with uncanny accuracy, while distinguishing it clearly from her wind-swept dress and the shaggy coat of Zeus disguised as a bull. To convey these tactile qualities, Titian built up his surface in thin coats, known as glazes. The interaction between these layers produces a richness and complexity of color that are strikingly apparent in the orange drapery where it trails off into the green seawater, which has a delicious wetness. The medium is so filmy as to become nearly translucent in parts of the landscape background, which is painted with a deft, flickering brush.

Color is so potent that it does not need a system to work its magic in art. From the heavy outlines, it is apparent that Picasso must have originally conceived *Girl Before a Mirror* (fig. 12) in terms of form; yet the picture makes no sense in black and white. He has treated his shapes much like the enclosed, flat panes of a stained-glass window to create a lively decorative pattern. The motif of a young woman contemplating her beauty goes all the way back to antiquity, but rarely has it been depicted with such disturbing overtones. Picasso's girl is anything but serene. On the contrary, her face is divided into two parts, one with a somber expression, the other with a masklike appearance whose color nevertheless betrays passionate feeling. She reaches out to touch the image in the mirror with a gesture of longing and apprehension. Now, we all feel a jolt when we unexpectedly see ourselves in a mirror, which often gives back a reflection that upsets our self-conception. Picasso here suggests this visionary truth in several ways. Much as a real mirror introduces changes of its own and does not simply give back the simple truth, so this one alters the way the girl looks, revealing a deeper reality. She is not so much examining her physical appearance as exploring her sexuality. The mirror is a sea of conflicting emotions signified above all by the color scheme of her reflection. Framed by strong blue, purple, and green hues, her features stare back at her with fiery intensity. Clearly discernible is a tear on her cheek. But it is the masterstroke of the green spot, shining like a beacon in the middle of her forehead, that conveys the anguish of the girl's confrontation with her inner self. Picasso was probably aware of the theory that red and green are complementary colors which intensify each other. However, this "law" can hardly have dictated his choice of green to stand for the girl's psyche. That was surely determined as a matter of pictorial and expressive necessity.

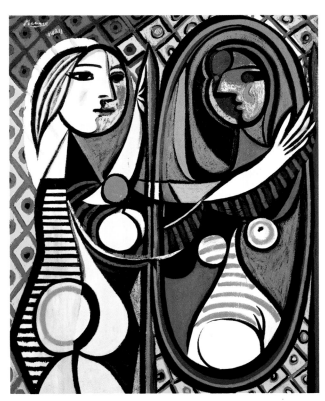

12. PABLO PICASSO. *GIRL BEFORE A MIRROR.*
March 1932. Oil on canvas, 64 × 51¼″ (162.6 × 130.2 cm).
Collection, The Museum of Modern Art, New York.
Gift of Mrs. Simon Guggenheim

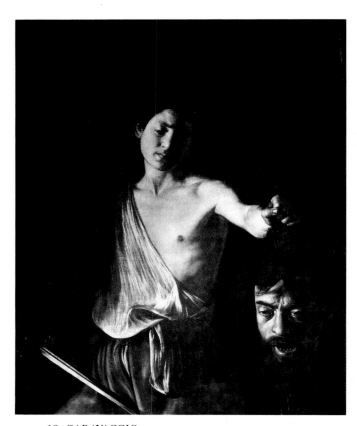

13. CARAVAGGIO. *DAVID WITH THE HEAD OF GOLIATH.*
1607 or 1609/10. Oil on canvas, 49¼ × 39⅜″ (125.1 × 100.1 cm).
Galleria Borghese, Rome

portrait, but although we may doubt the identification, this disturbing image communicates a tragic vision that was soon fulfilled. Not long after the David was painted, Caravaggio killed another man in a duel, which forced him to spend the rest of his short life on the run.

Light can also be implied through color. Piet Mondrian uses white and the three primary colors—red, yellow, and blue—to signify radiant light in *Broadway Boogie Woogie* (fig. 14), a painting that immortalizes his fascination with the culture he found in America after emigrating from his native Holland during World War II. The play of color evokes with stunning success the jaunty rhythms of light and music found in New York's nightclub district during the jazz age. *Broadway Boogie Woogie* is as flat as the canvas it is painted on. Mondrian has laid out his colored "tiles" along a grid system that appropriately resembles a city map. As in a medieval manuscript decoration (fig. 387), the composition relies entirely on surface pattern.

COMPOSITION. All art requires order. Otherwise its message would emerge as visually garbled. To accomplish this, the artist must control space within the framework of a unified composition. Moreover, pictorial space must work across the picture plane, as well as behind it. Since the Early Renaissance, we have become accustomed to experiencing paintings as windows onto separate illusionistic realities. The Renaissance invention of one-point perspective—also called linear or scientific perspective—provided a geometric system for the convincing representation of architectural and open-air settings. By having the orthogonals (shown as

LIGHT. Except for modern light installations such as laser displays, art is concerned with reflected light effects rather than with radiant light. Artists have several ways of representing radiant light. Divine light, for example, is sometimes indicated by golden rays, at other times by a halo or aura. A candle or torch may be depicted as the source of light in a dark interior or night scene. The most common method is not to show radiant light directly but to suggest its presence through a change in the value of reflected light from dark to light. Sharp contrast (known as *chiaroscuro*, the Italian word for light-dark) is identified with the Baroque artist Caravaggio, who made it the cornerstone of his style. In *David with the Head of Goliath* (fig. 13), he employed it to heighten the drama. An intense raking light from an unseen source at the left is used to model forms and create textures. The selective highlighting endows the lifesize figure of David and the gruesome head with a startling presence. Light here serves as a device to create the convincing illusion that David is standing before us. The pictorial space, with its indeterminate depth, becomes continuous with ours, despite the fact that the frame cuts off the figure. Thus, the foreshortened arm with Goliath's head seems to extend out to the viewer from the dark background. For all its obvious theatricality, the painting is surprisingly muted: David seems to contemplate Goliath with a mixture of sadness and pity. According to contemporary sources, the severed head is a self-

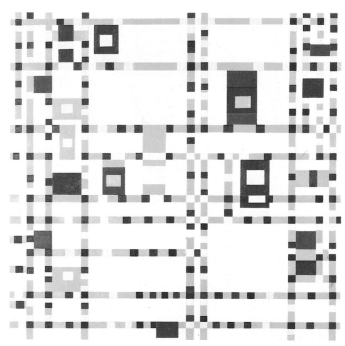

14. PIET MONDRIAN. *BROADWAY BOOGIE WOOGIE.*
1942–43. Oil on canvas, 50 × 50″ (127 × 127 cm).
Collection, The Museum of Modern Art,
New York. Given anonymously

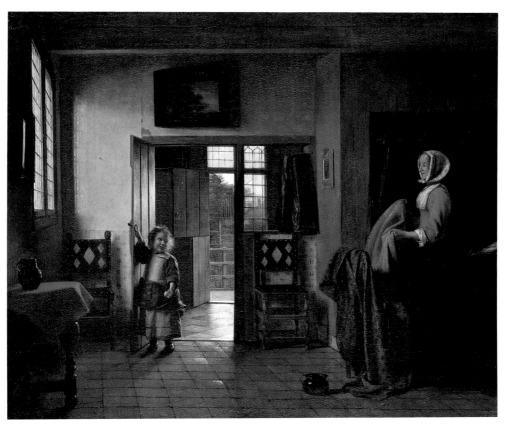

15. PIETER DE HOOCH. *THE BEDROOM.*
c. 1658–60. Oil on canvas, 20 × 23½″ (51 × 60 cm).
The National Gallery of Art, Washington, D.C. Widener Collection

diagonal lines) converge at a vanishing point on the horizon, it enabled the artist to gain command over every aspect of his composition, including the rate of recession and placement of figures. Pieter de Hooch, the Dutch Baroque artist, used one-point perspective in organizing *The Bedroom* (fig. 15). Nevertheless, the problems he faced in composing the three-dimensional space of his work were not so very different from those later confronted by Mondrian. (The surface geometry of De Hooch's painting is basically similar in design to *Broadway Boogie Woogie*.) Each part of the house is treated as a separate pocket of space and as a design element that is integrated into the scene as a whole.

The artist will usually dispense with aids like perspective and rely on his own eyes. This does not mean that he merely transcribes optical reality. *Blowing Bubbles* by the French painter Jean-Baptiste Chardin (fig. 16) depends in good measure on a satisfying composition for its success. The motif had been a popular one in earlier Dutch genre scenes, where bubbles symbolized life's brevity and, hence, the vanity of all earthly things. No such meaning can be attached to Chardin's picture, which is disarming in its simplicity. The interest lies solely in the seemingly insignificant subject and in the sense of enchantment imparted by the children's rapt attention to the moment. We know from a contemporary source that Chardin painted the youth "carefully from life and . . . tried hard to give him an ingenuous air." The results are anything but artless, however. The triangular shape of

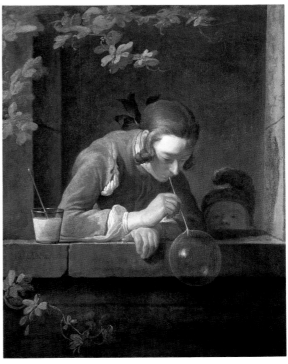

16. JEAN-BAPTISTE CHARDIN. *BLOWING BUBBLES.*
c. 1745. Oil on canvas, 36⅝ × 29⅜″ (93 × 74.6 cm).
The National Gallery of Art, Washington, D.C.
Gift of Mrs. John Simpson

the boy leaning on the ledge gives stability to the painting, which helps to suspend the fleeting instant in time. To fill out the composition, the artist includes the toddler peering intently over the ledge at the bubble, which is about the same size as his head. Chardin has carefully thought out every aspect of his arrangement. The honeysuckle in the upper left-hand corner, for example, echoes the contour of the adolescent's back, while the two straws are virtually parallel to each other. Even the crack in the stone ledge has a purpose: to draw attention to the glass of soap by setting it slightly apart.

Often the artist paints not what he sees but what he imagines. A wall painting from Thebes (fig. 17) presents a flattened view of a delightful garden in which everything is shown in profile except for the pond, which is seen from above. In order to provide the clearest, most complete idea of the scene, the Egyptian artist treated each element as an entity unto itself. Instead of using standard devices such as scale and overlapping, he treated space vertically, so that we read the trees at the bottom as being "closer" to us than those at the top, even though they are the same size. Despite the multiple vantage points and implausible bird's-eye view, the image works because it constitutes a self-contained reality. The picture, moreover, has an aesthetically satisfying decorative unity. The geometry underlying the composition reminds us once more of *Broadway Boogie Woogie*. At the same time, the presentation has such clarity that we feel as if we were seeing nature with open eyes for the first time.

Pictorial space need not conform to either conceptual or visual reality. El Greco's *Agony in the Garden* (fig. 18) uses contradictory, irrational space to help conjure up a mystical vision that instead represents a spiritual reality. Christ, isolated against a large rock that echoes His shape, is comforted by the angel bearing a golden cup, symbol of the Passion. The angel appears to kneel on a mysterious oval cloud, which envelops the sleeping disciples. In the distance to the right we see Judas and the soldiers coming to arrest the Lord. The composition is balanced by two giant clouds on either side. The entire landscape resounds with Christ's agitation, represented by the sweep of supernatural forces. The elongated forms, eerie moonlight, and expressive colors—other hallmarks of El Greco's style—help to heighten our sense of identification with Christ's suffering.

FORM. Every two-dimensional shape that we encounter in art is the counterpart to a three-dimensional form. There is nevertheless a vast difference between drawing or painting forms and sculpting them. The one transcribes, the other brings them to life, as it were. They require fundamentally different talents and attitudes toward material as well as subject matter. Although a number of artists have been competent in both painting and sculpture, only a handful managed to bridge the gap between them with complete success.

Sculpture is categorized according to whether it is carved or modeled and whether it is a relief or a free-standing

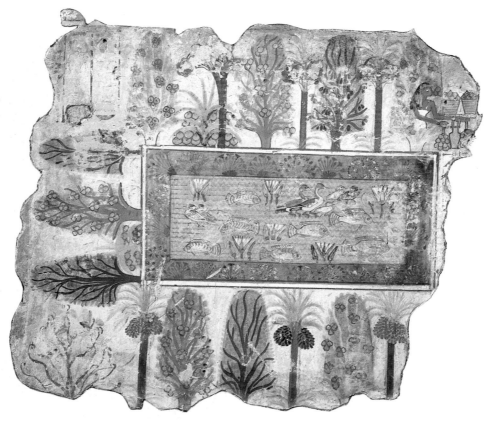

17. *A POND IN A GARDEN.* Fragment of a wall painting
from a tomb in Thebes. c. 1400 B.C. British Museum, London

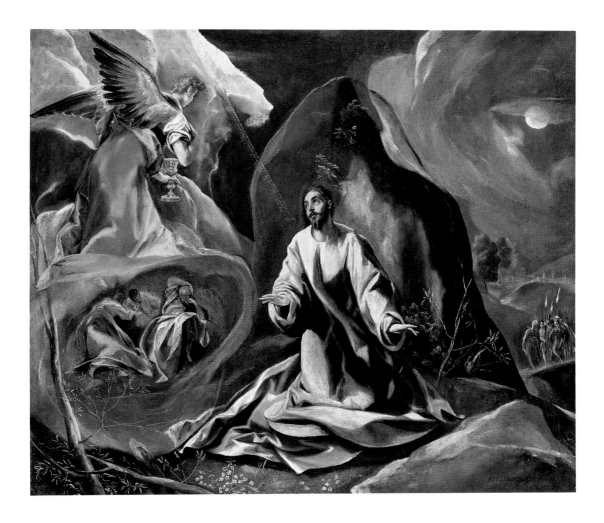

18. EL GRECO. *THE AGONY IN THE GARDEN*. 1597–1600.
Oil on canvas, 40¼ × 44¾″ (102.2 × 113.6 cm). Toledo Museum of Art,
Toledo, Ohio. Gift of Edward Drummond Libbey

19. *ALKESTIS LEAVING HADES*. Lower column drum from the Temple
of Artemis, Ephesus. c. 340 B.C. Marble, height 71″ (180.3 cm).
British Museum, London

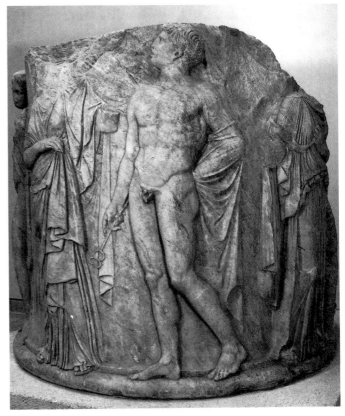

statue. Relief remains tied to the background, from which it only partially emerges, in contrast to free-standing sculpture, which is fully liberated from it. A further distinction is made between low (*bas*) relief and high (*alto*) relief, depending on how much the carving projects. However, since scale as well as depth must be taken into account, there is no single guideline, so that a third category, middle (*mezzo*) relief, is sometimes cited.

Low reliefs often share characteristics with painting. In Egypt, where low-relief carving attained unsurpassed subtlety, many reliefs were originally painted and included elaborate settings. High reliefs largely preclude this kind of pictorialism. The figures on a column drum from a Greek temple (fig. 19) have become so detached from the background that the addition of landscape or architecture elements would be both unnecessary and unconvincing. The neutral setting, moreover, is in keeping with the mythologi-

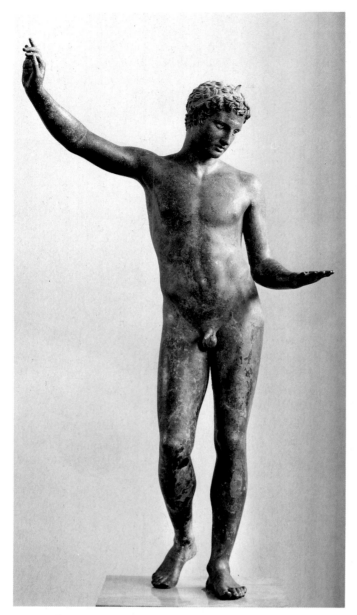

20. PRAXITELES (attr.). *STANDING YOUTH,* found in the sea off Marathon. c. 350–325 B.C. Bronze, height 51″ (129.5 cm). National Archeological Museum, Athens

attempting them in marble. In contrast to the figure of Hades on the column drum, the bronze youth in figure 20 is free to move about, lending him a lifelike presence that is further enhanced by his dancing pose. His inlaid eyes and soft patina, accentuated by oxidation and corrosion (he was found in the Aegean Sea off the coast of Marathon), make him even more credible in a way that marble statues, with their seemingly cold and smooth finish, rarely equal, despite their more natural color (compare fig. 21).

Carving is the very opposite of modeling. It is a subtractive process that starts with a solid block, usually stone, which is highly resistant to the sculptor's chisel. The brittleness of stone and the difficulty of cutting it tend to result in the compact, "closed" forms seen in Michelangelo's *St. Matthew* (fig. 3). One of the most daring attempts at overcoming the tyranny of mass over space is *Apollo and Daphne* by the Baroque sculptor Gianlorenzo Bernini (fig. 21). The dance-like pose of Apollo and graceful torsion of Daphne create the impression that they are moving in a carefully choreographed ballet. Time and motion have almost, but not quite, come to a standstill as the nymph begins to change into a tree rather than succumb to the god's amorous advances. The sculpture is an amazing technical achievement. Bernini is completely successful in distinguishing between the soft flesh of Daphne and the rough texture of the bark and leaves. The illusion of transformation is so convincing that we share Apollo's shock at the metamorphosis.

Like most monumental sculpture, *Apollo and Daphne* was commissioned for a specific site, which imposed severe restrictions. It was intended to be placed close to a wall and viewed across the room from a doorway slightly to the right. Bernini's ingenuity in solving this problem is confirmed by walking around the group, which is now displayed in the middle of the same room. The most characteristic view, illustrated here, corresponds to what would have been seen from the original vantage point, although the sculpture may be looked at profitably from other angles as well. The back side was never meant to be seen and provides little additional information, despite the fact that it is fully carved. As usual with this artist, however, the figures are not willing to accept these limitations and enliven the entire space around them.

SPACE. In our discussions of pictorial and sculptural space, we have repeatedly referred to architecture, for it is the principal means of organizing space. Of all the arts, it is also the most practical. Architecture's parameters are defined by utilitarian function and structural system, but there is almost always an aesthetic component as well, even when it consists of nothing more than a decorative veneer. A building proclaims the architect's concerns by the way in which it weaves these elements into a coherent program.

Architecture becomes memorable only when it expresses a transcendent vision, whether personal, social, or spiritual.

cal subject, which takes place in an indeterminate time and place. In compensation, the sculptor has treated the limited free space atmospherically; yet the figures remain imprisoned in stone.

Free-standing sculpture—that is, sculpture that is carved or modeled fully in the round—is made by either of two methods. One is modeling, an additive process using soft materials such as plaster, clay, or wax. Since these materials are not very durable, they are usually cast in a more lasting medium—anything that can be poured, including molten metal, cement, even plastic. Modeling encourages "open" forms with the aid of metal armatures to support their extension into space. This in conjunction with the development of lightweight hollow-bronze casting enabled the Greeks to experiment with daring poses in monumental sculpture before

21. *(opposite)* GIANLORENZO BERNINI. *APOLLO AND DAPHNE.* 1622–24. Marble, height 96″ (243.9 cm). Galleria Borghese, Rome

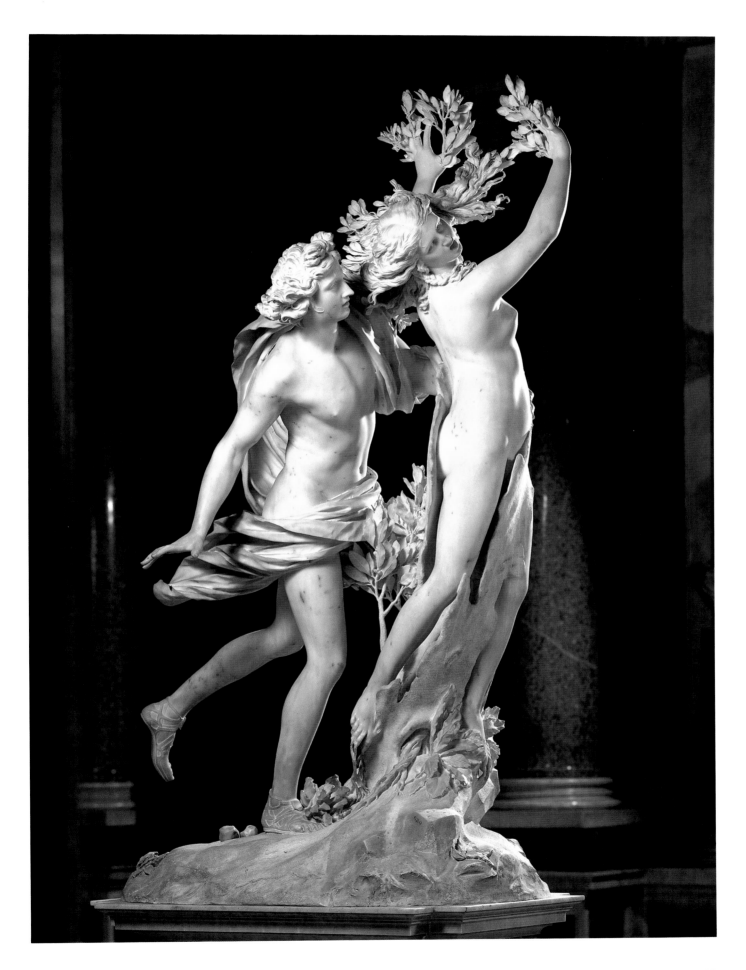

Such buildings are almost always important public places that require the marshaling of significant resources and serve the purpose of bringing people together to share common goals, pursuits, and values. Nowhere are these issues put in sharper relief than in the grandiose urban projects conceived by modern architects. They may be regarded as laboratory experiments which seek to redefine the role of architecture in shaping our lives. Limited by their very great scope, few of these ambitious proposals make it off the drawing board. Among the rare exceptions is Brasilia, the inland capital of Brazil built entirely since 1960. Presented with an unparalleled opportunity to design a major city from the ground up and with vast resources at its disposal, the design team, headed by Oscar Niemeyer, achieved undeniably spectacular results (fig. 22). Like most projects of this sort, Brasilia has a massive scale and insistent logic that make it curiously oppressive, so that despite its lavish display, Brasilia provides a chilling glimpse of the future.

Similar questions may be faced by architects of single buildings, only on a smaller scale. An extreme case is the Solomon R. Guggenheim Museum in New York by Frank Lloyd Wright. Scorned when it was first erected in the late 1950s, it is a brilliant, if idiosyncratic, creation by one of the most original architectural minds of the century. The sculptural exterior (fig. 23) announces that this can only be a museum, for it is self-consciously a work of art in its own right. As a piece of design, the Guggenheim Museum is remarkably willful. In shape it is as defiantly individual as the architect himself and refuses to conform to the boxlike apartments around it. From the outside, the structure looks like a gigantic snail, reflecting Wright's interest in organic shapes. The office area forming the "head" to the left is connected by a narrow passageway to the "shell" containing the main body of the museum.

The outside gives us some idea of what to expect inside (fig. 24), yet nothing quite prepares us for the extraordinary sensation of light and air in the main hall after being ushered through the unassuming entrance. The radical design makes it clear that Wright had completely rethought the purpose of an art museum. The exhibition area is a kind of inverted dome with a huge glass-covered eye at the top. The vast, fluid space creates an atmosphere of quiet harmony while actively shaping our experience by determining how art shall be displayed. After taking an elevator to the top of the building, one begins a leisurely descent down the gently sloping ramp. The continuous spiral provides for uninterrupted viewing, conducive to studying art. At the same time, the narrow confines of the galleries prevent us from becoming passive observers by forcing us into a direct confrontation with the works themselves. Sculpture takes on a heightened physical presence which demands that we look at it. Even paintings acquire a new prominence by protruding slightly from the curved walls, instead of receding into them. Viewing exhibitions at the Guggenheim is like being conducted through a predetermined stream of consciousness, where everything merges into a total unity. Whether one agrees with this approach or not, the building testifies to the strength of Wright's vision by precluding any other way of seeing the art.

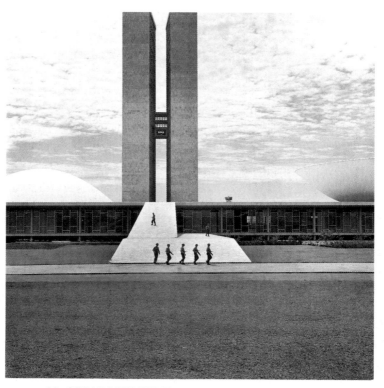

22. OSCAR NIEMEYER. Brasilia, Brazil. Completed 1960

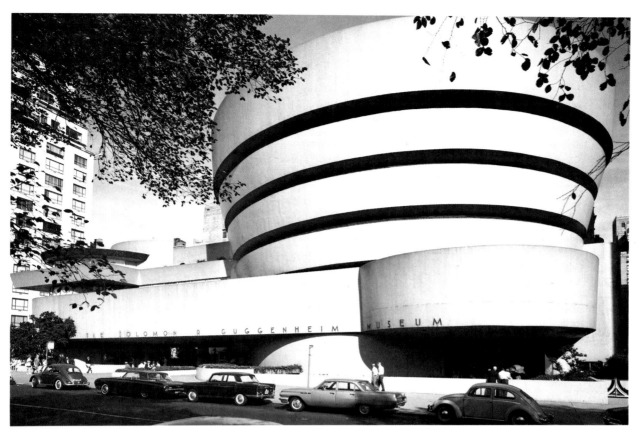

23. FRANK LLOYD WRIGHT. Solomon R. Guggenheim Museum, New York. 1956–59

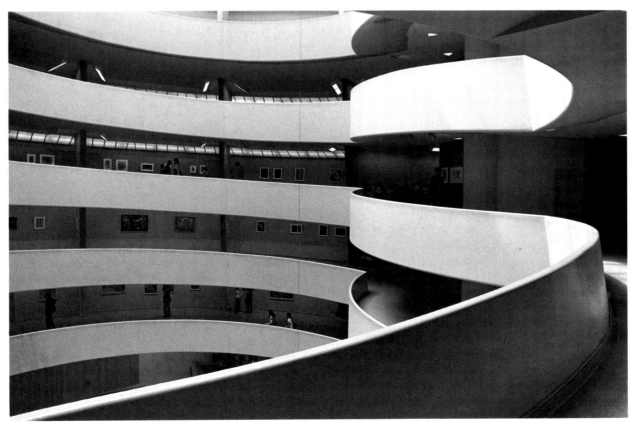

24. Interior. Solomon R. Guggenheim Museum

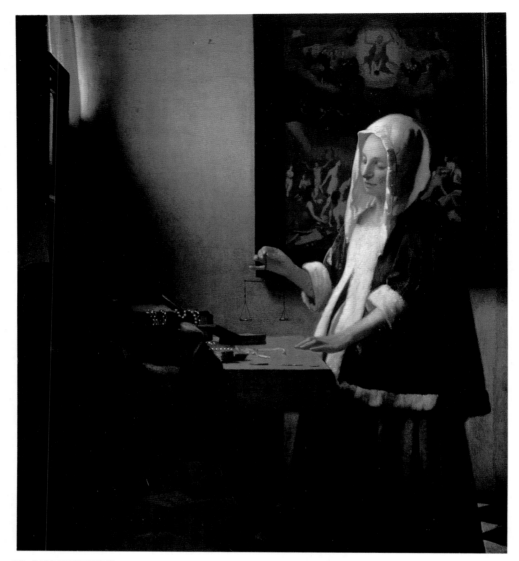

25. JAN VERMEER. *WOMAN HOLDING A BALANCE.* c. 1664. Oil on canvas, 16¾ × 15″ (42.5 × 38.1 cm).
The National Galley of Art, Washington, D.C. Widener Collection, 1942

## Meaning in Context

Art has been called a visual dialogue, for though the object itself is mute, it expresses its creator's intention just as surely as if he were speaking to us. For there to be a dialogue, however, our active participation is required. If we cannot literally talk to a work of art, we can learn how to respond to it and question it in order to fathom its meaning. Finding the right answers usually involves asking the right questions. Even if we aren't sure which question to ask, we can always start with, "What would happen if the artist had done it another way?" And when we are through, we must question our explanation according to the same test of adequate proof that applies to any investigation: have we taken into account *all* the available evidence—and arranged it in a logical and coherent way? There is, alas, no step-by-step method to guide us, but this does not mean that the process is entirely mysterious. We can illustrate it by looking at some examples together; the demonstration will help us gain courage to try the same analysis the next time we enter a museum.

The great Dutch painter Jan Vermeer has been called The Sphinx of Delft, and with good reason, for all his paintings have a degree of mystery. In *Woman Holding a Balance* (fig. 25), a young woman, richly dressed in at-home wear of the day and with strings of pearls and gold coins spread out on the table before her, is contemplating a balance in her hand. The canvas is painted entirely in gradations of cool, neutral tones, except for a bit of the red dress visible beneath her jacket. The soft light from the partly open window is concentrated on her face and the cap framing it. Other beads of light reflect from the pearls and her right hand. The serene atmosphere is sustained throughout the stable composition. Vermeer places us at an intimate distance within the relatively shallow space, which has been molded around the figure. The underlying grid of horizontals and verticals is modulated by the gentle curves of the woman's form and the heap of blue drapery, as well as by the oblique angles of the mirror. The design is so perfect that we cannot move a single element without upsetting the delicate balance.

The composition is controlled in part by perspective. The vanishing point of the diagonals formed by the top of the mirror and the right side of the table lies at the juncture of the woman's little finger and the picture frame. If we look carefully at the bottom of the frame, we see that it is actually lower on the right than on the left, where it lies just below her hand. The effect is so carefully calculated that the artist must have wanted to guide our eye to the painting in the background. Though difficult to read at first, it depicts Christ at the Last Judgment, when every soul is weighed. The parallel of this subject to the woman's activity tells us that, contrary to our initial impression, this cannot be simply a scene of everyday life. The meaning is nevertheless far from clear. Because Vermeer treated forms as beads of light, it was assumed until recently that the balance holds items of jewelry and that the woman is weighing the worthlessness of earthly possessions in the face of death; hence, the painting was generally called *The Pearl Weigher* or *The Gold Weigher*. If we look closely, however, we can see that the pans contain nothing. This is confirmed by infra-red photography, which also reveals that Vermeer changed the position of the balance: to make the picture more harmonious, he placed them parallel to the picture plane instead of allowing them to recede into space. What, then, is she doing? If she is weighing temporal against spiritual values, it can be only in a symbolic sense, because nothing about the figure or the setting betrays a sense of conflict. What accounts for this inner peace? Perhaps it is self-knowledge, symbolized here by the mirror. It may also be the promise of salvation through her faith. In *Woman Holding a Balance*, as in Caravaggio's *The Calling of St. Matthew* (fig. 739), light might therefore serve not only to illuminate the scene but also to represent religious revelation. In the end, we cannot be sure, because Vermeer's approach to his subject proves as subtle as his pictorial treatment. He avoids any anecdote or symbolism that might limit us to a single interpretation. There can be no doubt, however, about his fascination with light. Vermeer's mastery of light's expressive qualities elevates his concern for the reality of appearance to the level of poetry, and subsumes its visual and symbolic possibilities. Here, then, we have found the real "meaning" of Vermeer's art.

The ambiguity in *Woman Holding a Balance* serves to heighten our interest and pleasure, while the carefully organized composition expresses the artist's underlying concept with singular clarity. But what are we to do when a work deliberately seems devoid of ostensible meaning? Modern artists can pose a gap between their intention and the viewer's understanding. The gap is, however, often more apparent than real, for the meaning is usually intelligible to the imagination at some level. Still, we feel we must comprehend intellectually what we perceive intuitively. We can partially solve the personal code in Jasper Johns' *Target with Four Faces* (fig. 26) by treating it somewhat like a rebus. Where did he begin? Surely with the target, which stands alone as an object, unlike the long box at the top, particularly when its hinged door is closed. Why a target in the first place? The size, texture, and colors inform us that this is not to be interpreted as a real target. The design is never-

theless attractive in its own right, and Johns must have chosen it for that reason. When the wooden door is up, the assemblage is transformed from a neutral into a loaded image, bringing out the nascent connotations of the target. Johns has used the same plaster cast four times, which lends the faces a curious anonymity; then he cut them off at the eyes, "the windows of the soul," rendering them even more enigmatic; finally, he crammed them into their compartments, so that they seem to press urgently out toward us. The results are disquieting, aesthetically as well as expressively.

Something so disturbing cannot be without significance—but what? We may be reminded of prisoners trying to look out from small cell windows—or perhaps "blindfolded" targets of execution. Whatever our impression, the claustrophobic image radiates an aura of menacing danger. Unlike Picasso's joining of a bicycle seat and handlebars to form a bull's head, *Target with Four Faces* combines two disparate components in an open conflict that we cannot reconcile, no matter how hard we try. The intrusion of this ominous meaning creates an extraordinary tension with the

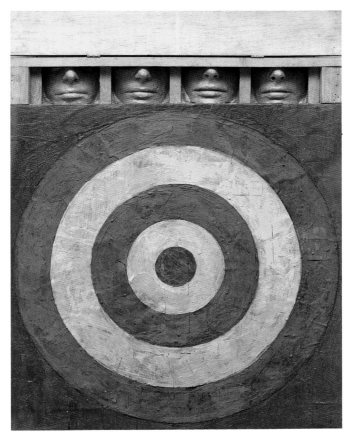

26. JASPER JOHNS. *TARGET WITH FOUR FACES*. 1955.
Assemblage: encaustic on newspaper and cloth over canvas,
26 × 26″ (66 × 66 cm) surmounted by four tinted plaster faces
in wood box with hinged front. Box, closed 3¾ × 26 × 3½″
(9.5 × 66 × 8.9 cm); overall dimensions with box open,
33⅝ × 26 × 3″ (85.3 × 66.7 × 6 cm).
Collection, The Museum of Modern Art, New York.
Gift of Mr. and Mrs. Robert C. Scull

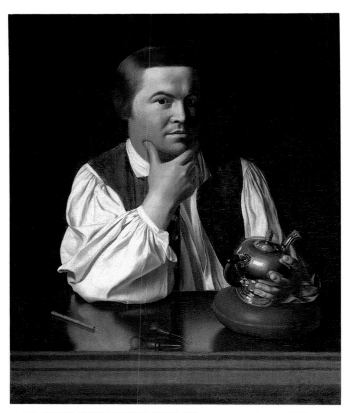

27. JOHN SINGLETON COPLEY. *PAUL REVERE*. c. 1768–70.
Oil on canvas, 38 × 28½″ (96.5 × 72.4 cm).
Museum of Fine Arts, Boston. Gift of Joseph W., William. B.,
and Edward H. R. Revere

of historical data can satisfy nearly as well. Our interest arises no doubt from the remnant of a primitive belief that an image captures not merely the likeness but also the soul of a sitter. In the age of photography, we have come to see portraits as mere likenesses and we readily forget that they call on all our skill to grasp their meaning. *Paul Revere*, painted by the American artist John Singleton Copley around 1770 (fig. 27), gives rise to questions we cannot solve with on-the-spot observations, so we must look elsewhere to answer them. The fruit of our investigation must agree with our observations; otherwise we cannot be sure that we are right.

Silversmith, printmaker, businessman, and patriot, Revere has acquired legendary status thanks to Henry Wadsworth Longfellow's long poem about his legendary midnight ride, and Copley's painting has become virtually an American icon. It has generally been treated as a workingman's portrait, so to speak. By rights, however, such a portrait ought to be much more straightforward than this and, hence, less memorable. Revere has a penetrating glance and thoughtful pose which are heightened by the sharp light, lending him an unusually forceful presence. He looks out at us with astonishing directness, as if he were reading us with the same intensity that we bring to bear on his strongly modeled features. Clearly, Revere is a thinker possessing an active intelligence, and we will recognize the pose of hand on chin as an old device used since antiquity to represent philosophers. This is certainly no ordinary craftsman here, and we may also wonder whether this is really his working outfit.

dispassionate investigation of the target's formal qualities. It is, then, this disparity between form and content that must have been Johns' goal.

How do we know we are right? After all, this is merely our "personal" interpretation, so we turn to the critics for help. We find them divided about the meaning of *Target with Four Faces*, although they agree it must have one. Johns, on the other hand, has insisted that there is none! Whom are we to believe, the critics or the artist himself? The more we think about it, the more likely it seems that both sides may be right. The artist is not always aware why he has made a work. That does not mean that there were no reasons, only that they were unconscious ones. Under these circumstances, the critic may well know the artist's mind better than he does and explain his creation more clearly. We can now understand that to Johns the leap of his imagination in *Target with Four Faces* remains as mysterious as it first seemed to us. Our account reconciles the artist's aesthetic concerns and the critics' search for meaning, and while we realize that no ultimate solution is possible, we have arrived at a satisfactory explanation by looking and thinking for ourselves.

It is all too easy to overlook the obvious, and this is especially true in looking at portraits. Those of famous people have a special appeal, for they seem to bridge a gap of time and place and to establish a personal link. In their faces we read a thousand insights about character which no amount

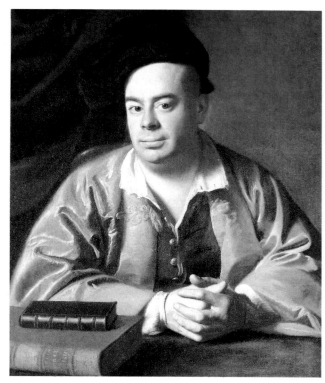

28. JOHN SINGLETON COPLEY. *NATHANIEL HURD*. c. 1765
Oil on canvas, 30 × 25½″ (76.2 × 64.8 cm).
The Cleveland Museum of Art. John Huntington Collection

Surely no silversmith would have carried out his craft in what are probably Revere's best business clothes. Simply by looking at the picture we have raised enough doubts to challenge the traditional view of this famous painting.

At this point, our questioning of the picture's surface comes to an end, for the portrait fails to yield up further clues. Once we have posed the problem of this "craftsman's" portrayal, we feel compelled to investigate it further. The more we pursue the matter, the more fascinating it becomes. Copley, we discover, had painted only a few years earlier a portrait of another Boston silversmith, Nathaniel Hurd (fig. 28). Yet this one is so different that we would never guess the sitter's trade. Hurd is wearing a casual robe and turban, and before him are two books, one of them devoted to heraldry from which he culled the coats of arms he needed for his work. Why, then, did Copley show Revere at a workbench with his engraving tools spread out before him, holding a teapot as the object of his contemplation and offering it to us for our inspection? In light of Hurd's portrait, Revere's work as a silversmith hardly explains these attributes and actions, natural as they seem. Oddly enough, the question has never been raised; yet surely the differences between the two paintings cannot be accidental.

Perhaps we can find the answer in the antecedents for each. Hurd's image can be traced back to informal portraits that originated in France in the early eighteenth century and soon became popular as well in England, where there was a rage for portraits of well-known men and women. This type of portrait was customarily reserved for artists, writers, and the like. In turn, the type gave rise to a distinctive offshoot that showed a sculptor at work in his studio with his tools prominently displayed (fig. 29). Sometimes an engraver is seen instead. There is another possible precedent: moralizing portraits, the descendants of pictures of St. Jerome, that show their subjects holding or pointing to skulls, much as Revere has the teapot in his hand. Copley was surely familiar with all of these kinds of images from the portrait engravings that we know he collected, but his exact sources for the Revere painting remain a mystery—and may never be discovered. For after 1765 Copley freely adapted and combined motifs from different prints in his paintings, often disguising their origins so completely that we cannot be certain which they were. It is likely that he conflated two or three in Revere's portrait. In any case, it is apparent that Copley has transformed Revere from a craftsman into an artist-philosopher.

Let us now look at this portrait in its larger historical and cultural context. In Europe, the craftsman's inferior position to the artist had been asserted since the Renaissance—except in England, where the newly founded Royal Academy first drew the distinction in 1768, about when Copley painted Hurd's portrait. But in the Colonies there was, as Copley himself complained, no distinction between the trades of artist and craftsman. Indeed, except for portraiture, it can be argued that the decorative arts *were* the fine arts of America.

It is significant that Copley's portrait probably dates from around the time of Revere's first efforts at making engravings, a form of art that arose, interestingly enough, out of silver- and goldsmith decorating during the late Middle

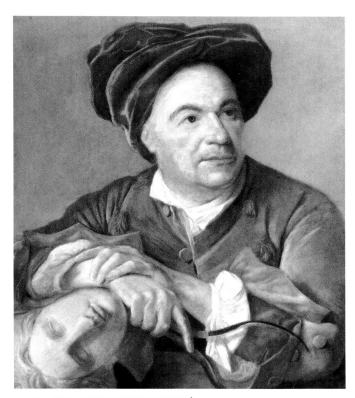

29. FRANCIS XAVIER VISPRÉ (attr.). *PORTRAIT OF LOUIS-FRANÇOIS ROUBILIAC*. c. 1750. Pastel, 24½ × 21½" (62.2 × 54.6 cm). Yale Center for British Art, New Haven, Connecticut. Paul Mellon Collection

Ages. Revere was then already involved with libertarianism, a cause which Copley himself did not share. This difference in their points of view did not prevent Copley from endowing Revere's portrait with an ingenious significance and penetrating seriousness of characterization. The painter and the silversmith must have known each other well. The portrait stands as Copley's compelling tribute to a fellow artist—and as an invaluable statement about the culture of the Colonial era.

Obviously, not everyone is in a position to undertake this kind of research—only the art historian and the occasional interested layman. But again, this does not mean that "there must be something wrong with a work of art if it takes an expert to appreciate it." On the contrary, our research serves only to affirm the portrait of Paul Revere as a masterpiece. Reacting to the portrait in "a direct, straightforward fashion," without the benefit of additional knowledge, deprives us of an understanding that is necessary for full appreciation. Critics, scholars, and curators are not our adversaries; in sharing their expertise and their knowledge of art's broader contexts with those who seek it, they expand the dimensions of our capacity for appreciating art, and they provide a model for our own find-and-seek experiences.

# PART ONE

# THE ANCIENT WORLD

Art history is more than a stream of art objects created over time. It is intimately related to history itself, that is, the recorded evidence of human events. For that reason, we must consider the *concept* of history, which, we are often told, begins with the invention of writing some 8,000 years ago. And indeed, the invention of writing was an early accomplishment of the "historic" civilizations of Mesopotamia and Egypt. Without writing, the growth we have known would have been impossible. We do not know the earliest phases of its development, but writing must have been several hundred years in the making—between 3300 and 3000 B.C., roughly speaking, with Mesopotamia in the lead—after the new societies were already past their first stage. Thus "history" was well under way by the time writing could be used to record events.

The invention of writing makes a convenient landmark, for the absence of written records is surely one of the key differences between prehistoric and historic societies. But as soon as we ask why this is so, we face some intriguing problems. First of all, how valid is the distinction between "prehistoric" and "historic"? Does it merely reflect a difference in our *knowledge* of the past? (Thanks to the invention of writing, we know a great deal more about history than about prehistory.) Or was there a genuine change in the way things happened—and of the kinds of things that happened—after "history" began? Obviously, prehistory was far from uneventful. Yet changes in the human condition that mark this road, decisive though they are, seem incredibly slow-paced and gradual when measured against the events of the last 5,000 years. The beginning of "history," then, means a sudden increase in the speed of events, a shifting from low gear into high gear, as it were. It also means a change in the *kind* of events. Historic societies quite literally make history. They not only bring forth "great individuals and great deeds"—one traditional definition of history—by demanding human effort on a large scale, but they make these achievements *memorable*. And for an event to be memorable, it must be more than "worth remembering"; it must also be accomplished quickly enough to be grasped by human memory, and not spread over many centuries. Collectively, memorable events have caused the ever-quickening pace of change during the past five millenniums, which begin with what we call the ancient world.

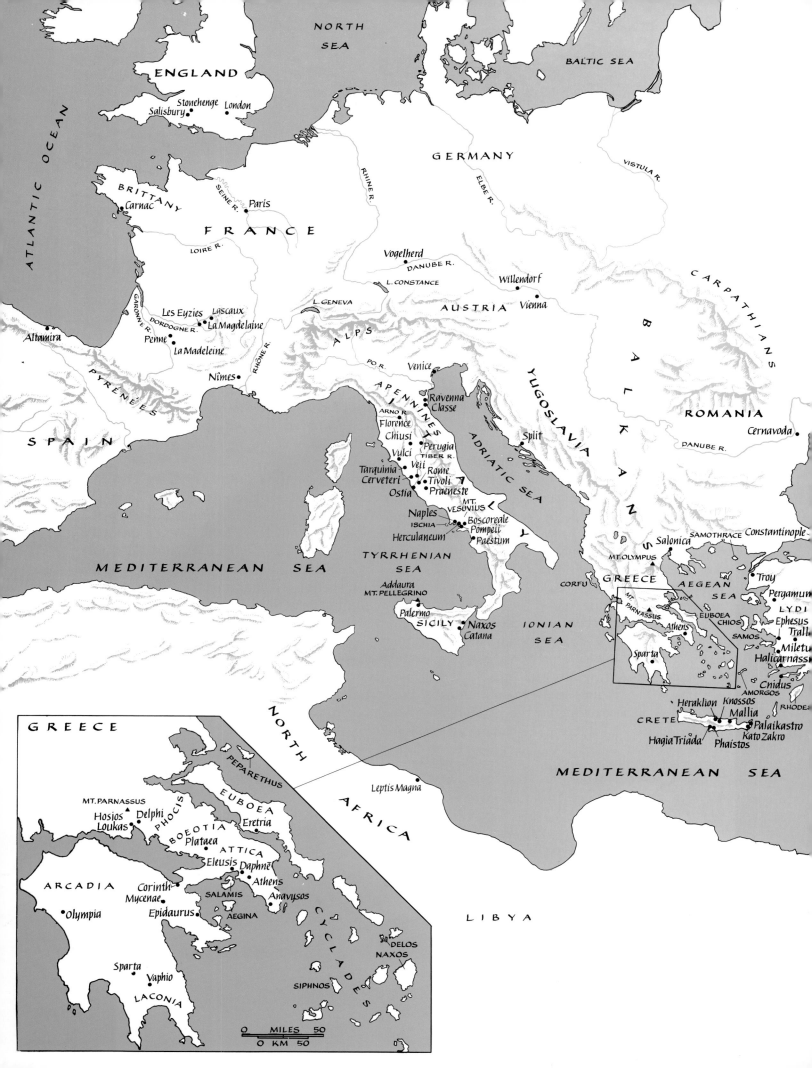

NORTH
SEA

BALTIC SEA

ENGLAND

Stonehenge London
Salisbury

GERMANY

VISTULA R.

ATLANTIC
OCEAN

BRITTANY
Carnac

SEINE R.
Paris

FRANCE

RHINE R.

ELBE R.

DANUBE R.

Vogelherd

CARPATHIANS

BALKANS

LOIRE R.

L. CONSTANCE

Willendorf

AUSTRIA
Vienna

L. GENEVA

Les Eyzies  Lascaux
DORDOGNE R. La Magdelaine
Penne
GARONNE R.
La Madeleine

ALPS

PO R.

Venice

ROMANIA

Cernavoda

Altamira

RHÔNE R.
Nîmes

APENNINES

ARNO R.

Ravenna
Classe

DANUBE R.

PYRÉNÉES

Florence
Chiusi

ADRIATIC
SEA

YUGOSLAVIA

Split

SPAIN

Vulci
Tarquinia  Veii
Cerveteri
Ostia

Perugia
TIBER R.
Rome
Tivoli
Praeneste

SAMOTHRACE

Constantinople

MT.
VESUVIUS

Salonica

Naples
ISCHIA
Herculaneum

Boscoreale
Pompeii
Paestum

MT.OLYMPUS

GREECE

AEGEAN
SEA

Troy

Pergamum

MEDITERRANEAN          SEA

TYRRHENIAN
SEA

CORFU

MT.
PARNASSUS

LYDIA
EUBOEA
CHIOS

Ephesus
Tralle

Addaura
MT. PELLEGRINO

Athens
Sparta

SAMOS

Miletu
Halicarnass

Palermo
SICILY

Naxos
Catana

IONIAN
SEA

Cnidus

AMORGOS

RHODE

Heraklion  Knossos
Hagia Triàda  Mallia
CRETE          Palaikastro
Phaistos  Kato Zakro

NORTH

AFRICA

Leptis Magna

MEDITERRANEAN          SEA

LIBYA

GREECE

PEPARETHUS

EUBOEA

MT. PARNASSUS
Hosios  Delphi  PHOCIS
Loukas

Eretria

BOEOTIA
Plataea

ATTICA

ARCADIA

Eleusis  Daphné
Athens

Corinth
Mycenae
Epidaurus

SALAMIS
Anavysos

AEGINA

CYCLADES

Olympia

DELOS
NAXOS

Sparta
Vaphio

SIPHNOS

LACONIA

0    MILES    50
0   KM   50

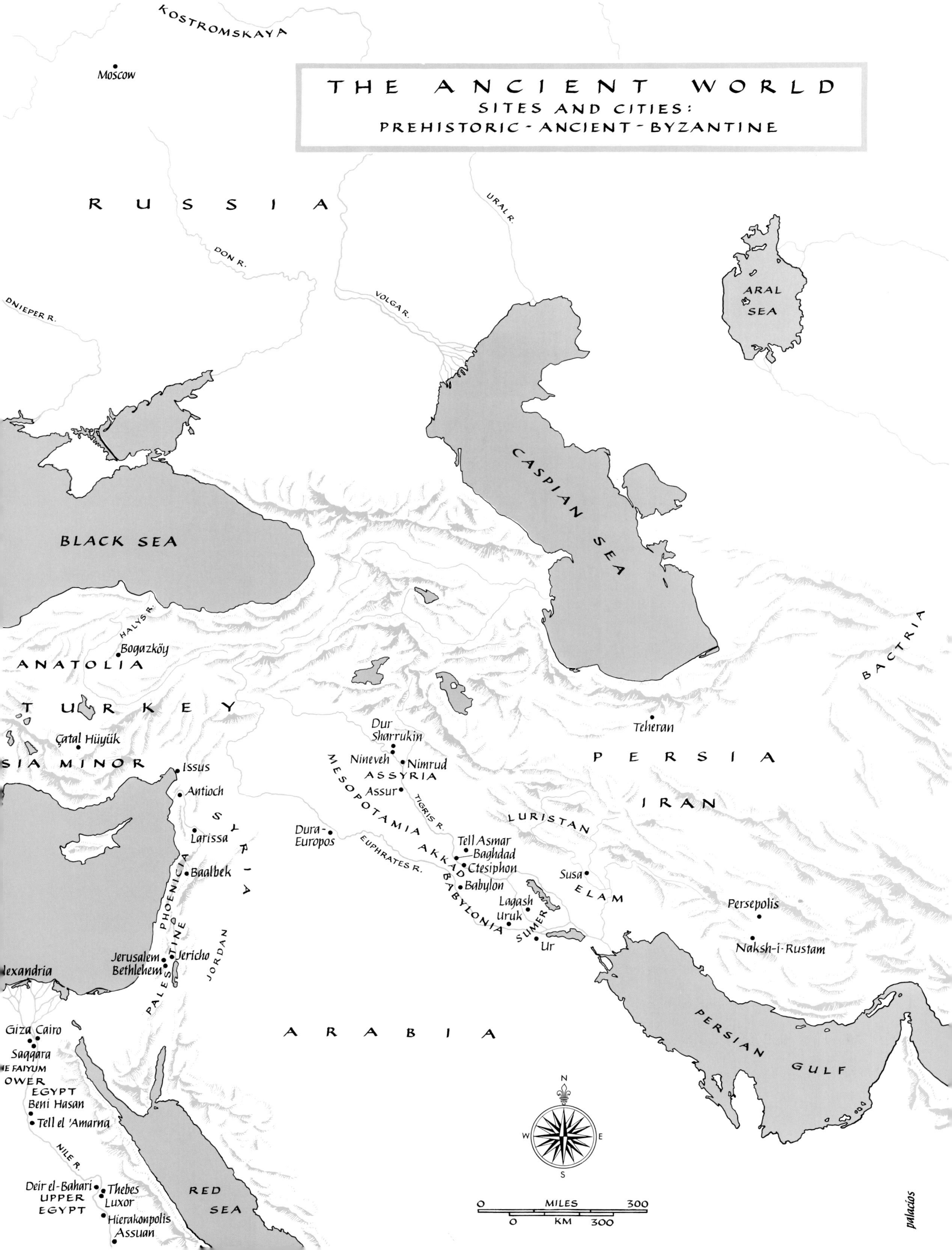

Moscow

# THE ANCIENT WORLD
## SITES AND CITIES:
### PREHISTORIC - ANCIENT - BYZANTINE

R U S S I A

DNIEPER R.

DON R.

VOLGA R.

URAL R.

ARAL SEA

BLACK SEA

CASPIAN SEA

HALYS R.

Bogazköy

ANATOLIA

BACTRIA

T U R K E Y

Çatal Hüyük

SIA MINOR

Issus

Antioch

S Y R I A

Larissa

Dura-Europos

Baalbek

PHOENICIA

PALESTINE

JORDAN

Jerusalem
Bethlehem

Jericho

lexandria

Dur Sharrukin

Nineveh • Nimrud

ASSYRIA

Assur

MESOPOTAMIA

TIGRIS R.

EUPHRATES R.

AKKAD

BABYLONIA

Tell Asmar
Baghdad
Ctesiphon

Babylon

Lagash
Uruk

SUMER

Ur

LURISTAN

Susa

ELAM

P E R S I A

I R A N

Teheran

Persepolis

Naksh-i-Rustam

Giza Cairo

Saqqara

E FAIYUM

OWER
EGYPT

Beni Hasan

Tell el 'Amarna

NILE R.

Deir el-Bahari • Thebes
UPPER      Luxor
EGYPT

Hierakonpolis
Assuan

RED SEA

A R A B I A

PERSIAN GULF

N

W        E

S

0        MILES        300

0        KM        300

palacios

*CHAPTER ONE*

# PREHISTORIC AND ETHNOGRAPHIC ART

## THE OLD STONE AGE

When did human beings start creating works of art? What prompted them to do so? What did these earliest works of art look like? Every history of art must begin with these questions—and with the admission that we cannot answer them. Our earliest ancestors began to walk the earth on two feet about four million years ago, but how they were using their hands remains unknown to us. More than two million years later we meet the earliest evidence of toolmaking. Humans must have been *using* tools all along; after all, even apes will pick up a stick to knock down a banana or a stone to throw at an enemy. The *making* of tools is a more complex matter. It demands first of all the ability to think of sticks or stones as "fruit knockers" or "bone crackers," not only when they are needed for such purposes but at other times as well.

Once people were able to do that, they gradually discovered that some sticks or stones had a handier shape than others, and they put them aside for future use. They selected and "appointed" certain sticks or stones as tools because they had begun to connect *form* and *function*. The sticks, of course, have not survived, but a few of the stones have; they are large pebbles or chunks of rock that show the marks of repeated use for the same operation—whatever that may have been. The next step was to try chipping away at these tools-by-appointment so as to improve their shape. This is the first craft of which we have evidence, and with it we enter a phase of human development known as the Paleolithic, or Old Stone Age.

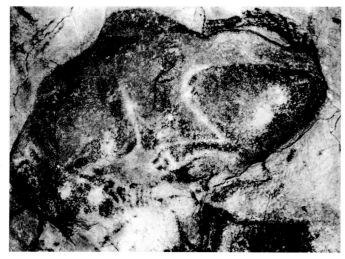

30. *WOUNDED BISON*. Cave painting. c. 15,000–10,000 B.C. Altamira, Spain

### Cave Art

It is during the last stage of the Paleolithic, which began about 35,000 years ago, that we meet the earliest works of art known to us. But these already show an assurance and refinement far removed from any humble beginnings. Unless we are to believe that they came into being in a single, sudden burst, we must assume that they were preceded by thousands of years of slow growth about which we know nothing at all. At that time the last Ice Age was drawing to a close in Europe (there had been at least three previous ones, alternating with periods of subtropical warmth, at intervals of about 25,000 years), and the climate between the Alps and Scandinavia resembled that of present-day Siberia or Alaska. Huge herds of reindeer and other large herbivores roamed the plains and valleys, preyed upon by the ferocious ancestors of today's lions and tigers—and by our own ancestors. These people liked to live in caves or in the shelter of overhanging rocks wherever they could find them. Many such sites have been discovered, mostly in Spain and in southwestern France; on the basis of differences among the tools and other remains found there, scholars have divided up the "cavemen" into several groups, each named after a characteristic site, and of these it is especially the so-called Aurignacians and Magdalenians who stand out for the gifted artists they produced and for the important role art must have played in their lives.

ALTAMIRA AND LASCAUX. The most striking works of Paleolithic art are the images of animals, incised, painted, or sculptured, on the rock surfaces of caves, such as the wonderful *Wounded Bison* from the cave at Altamira in northern Spain (fig. 30). The dying animal has collapsed on the ground, its legs no longer able to carry the weight of the body, its head lowered in defense. What a vivid, lifelike picture it is! We are amazed not only by the keen observation, the assured, vigorous outlines, and the subtly controlled shading that lends bulk and roundness to the forms, but even more perhaps by the power and dignity of this creature in its final agony. Equally impressive, if not quite as fine in detail, are the painted animals in the cave at Lascaux, in the Dordogne region of France (figs. 31 and 32). Bison, deer, horses, and cattle race across walls and ceiling in wild profusion, some of them simply outlined in black, others filled in with bright earth colors, but all showing the same uncanny sense of life.

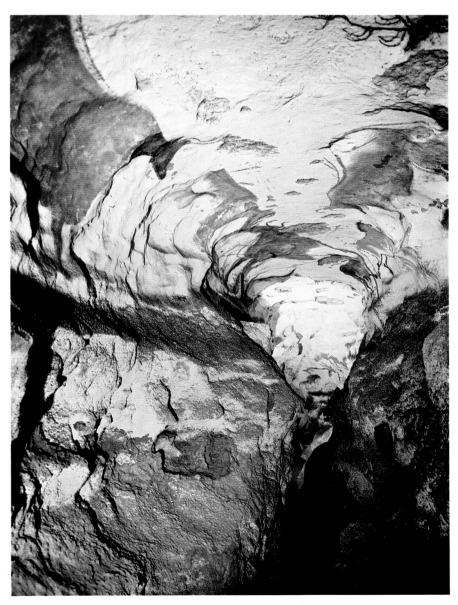

31. Axial Gallery, Lascaux (Montignac, Dordogne), France

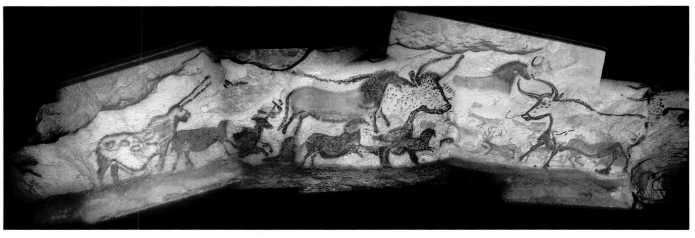

32. Cave paintings. 15,000–10,000 B.C. Lascaux

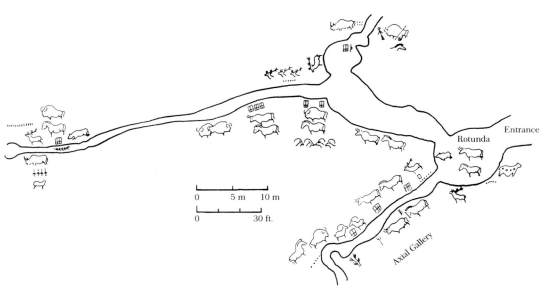

33. Schematic plan of Lascaux

How did this extraordinary art develop? What purpose did it serve? And how did it happen to survive intact over so many thousands of years? The last question can be answered easily enough—for the pictures never occur near the mouth of a cave, where they would be open to easy view (and destruction) but only in the darkest recesses, as far from the entrance as possible (fig. 33). Some can be reached only by crawling on hands and knees, and the path is so intricate that one would soon be lost without an expert guide. The cave at Lascaux, characteristically enough, was discovered purely by chance in 1940 by some neighborhood boys whose dog fell into a hole that led to the underground chamber.

Hidden away as they are in the bowels of the earth, to protect them from the casual intruder, these images must have served a purpose far more serious than mere decoration. There can be little doubt, in fact, that they were produced as part of a magic ritual, perhaps to ensure a successful hunt. We gather this not only from their secret location and from the lines meant to represent spears or darts that are sometimes found pointing at the animals, but also from the pecu-

liar, disorderly way the images are superimposed on one another (as in fig. 32). Apparently, people of the Old Stone Age made no clear distinction between image and reality; by making a picture of an animal they meant to bring the animal itself within their grasp, and in "killing" the image they thought they had killed the animal's vital spirit. Hence a "dead" image lost its potency after the killing ritual had been performed, and could be disregarded when the spell had to be renewed. The magic worked, too, we may be sure; hunters whose courage was thus fortified were bound to be more successful when slaying these formidable beasts with their primitive weapons. Nor has the emotional basis of this kind of magic been lost even today. We carry snapshots of those we love in our wallets because this gives us a sense of their presence, and people have been known to tear up the photograph of someone they have come to hate.

Even so, there remains a good deal that puzzles us about the cave paintings. Why do they have to be in such inaccessible places? Couldn't the hunting magic they serve have been performed just as well out in the open? And why are they so marvelously lifelike? Would not the magic have been equally effective if the "killing" had been practiced upon less realistic images? We know of countless later instances of magic which require only the crudest and most schematic kind of representation, such as two crossed sticks for a human figure.

Perhaps we should regard the Magdalenian cave pictures as the final phase of a development that began as simple killing magic at a time when big game was plentiful but shifted its meaning when the animals became scarce (there is evidence that the big herds withdrew northward as the climate of Central Europe grew warmer). At Altamira and Lascaux, then, the main purpose may no longer have been to "kill" but to "make" animals—to increase their supply, perhaps through seasonal rituals repeated year after year. In some of the weapons associated with the animals, images of plants have recently been recognized. Could it be that the Magdalenians practiced their fertility magic in the bowels of the earth because they thought of the earth itself as a living thing from whose womb all other life springs? Such a notion is familiar to us from the cults of earth deities of later times; it is not impossible that its origin goes back to the Old Stone Age. If it does, it would help to explain the admirable realism of the cave paintings, for an artist who believes that he is actually "creating" an animal is more likely to strive for this quality than one who merely sets up an image for the kill.

POSSIBLE ORIGINS. Some of the cave pictures may even provide a clue to the origin of this tradition of fertility magic; in a good many instances, the shape of the animal seems to have been suggested by the natural formation of the rock, so that its body coincides with a bump or its contour follows a vein or crack as far as possible. We all know how our imagination sometimes makes us see all sorts of images in chance formations such as clouds or blots. A Stone Age hunter, his mind filled with thoughts of the big game on which he depended for survival, would have been even more likely to recognize such animals as he stared at the rock surfaces of his cave and to attribute deep significance to his discovery. Perhaps at first he merely reinforced the outlines of such im-

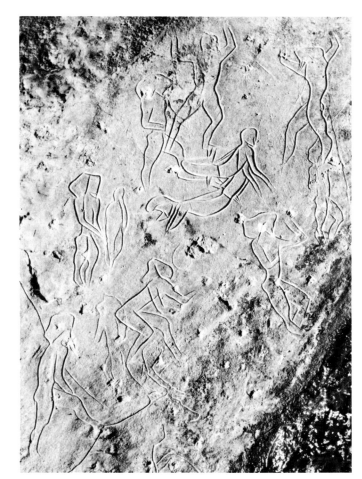

35. *RITUAL DANCE* (?). Rock engraving.
c. 10,000 B.C. Height of figures c. 10″ (25.4 cm).
Cave of Addaura, Monte Pellegrino (Palermo), Sicily

ages with a charred stick from the fire, so that others, too, could see what he had found. It is tempting to think that those who proved particularly good at finding such images were given a special status as artist-magicians and were relieved of the dangers of the real hunt so that they could perfect their image-hunting, until finally they learned how to make images with little or no aid from chance formations, though they continued to welcome such aid.

A striking example of this process of creation is the remarkable *Nude Woman* from the La Magdelaine Cave at Penne (fig. 34), one of the rare instances of the human figure in Paleolithic art (apparently human fertility was a less pressing problem than animal fertility). The legs and torso have been carved from natural ledges of the rock in such a way that the shapes seem to emerge almost imperceptibly from the stone. The right arm is barely visible and the head appears to have been omitted altogether, for lack of "cooperation" on the part of the natural surface. What kind of ritual may have centered on this figure we can only guess. Yet the existence of cave rituals relating to both human and animal fertility would seem to be confirmed by a unique group of Paleolithic drawings found in the 1950s on the walls of the cave of Addaura near Palermo in Sicily (fig. 35).

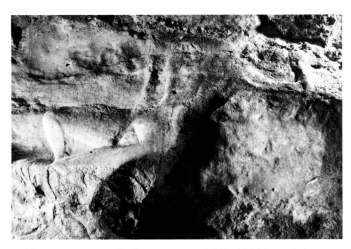

34. *NUDE WOMAN*. Rock carving. c. 15,000–10,000 B.C. Lifesize.
La Magdelaine Cave, Penne (Tarn), France

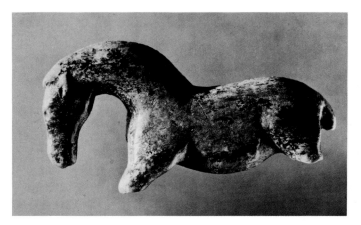

36. *HORSE,* from Vogelherd Cave. c. 28,000 B.C.
Mammoth ivory, length 2½" (6.4 cm). Shown 120 percent actual size.
Private collection (Photograph copyright Alexander Marshack)

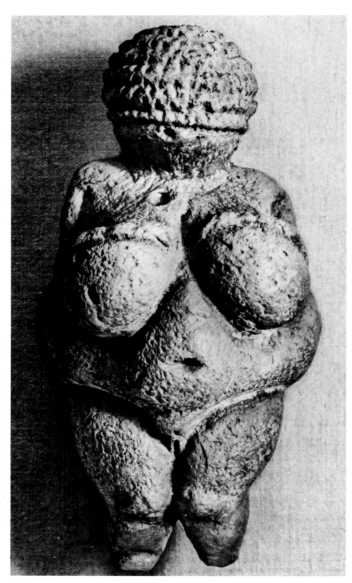

37. *VENUS OF WILLENDORF.* c. 25,000–20,000 B.C. Stone, height 4⅜" (11 cm).
Shown 137 percent actual size. Naturhistoriches Museum, Vienna

These images, incised into the rock with quick and sure lines, show human figures in dancelike movements, along with some animals; and here, as at Lascaux, we again find several layers of images superimposed on one another.

## Carved and Painted Objects

Apart from large-scale cave art, the people of the Upper Paleolithic also produced small, hand-sized drawings and carvings in bone, horn, or stone, skillfully cut by means of flint tools. The earliest of these found so far are small figures of mammoth ivory from a cave in southwestern Germany, made 30,000 years ago. Even they, however, are already so accomplished that they must be the fruit of an artistic tradition many thousands of years old. The graceful, harmonious curves of the running horse (fig. 36) could hardly be improved upon by a more recent sculptor. Many years of handling have worn down some details of the tiny animal; but the two converging lines on the shoulder, indicating a dart or wound, were not part of the original design. In the end, then, this horse too has been "killed" or "sacrificed."

Some of these carvings suggest that the objects may have originated with the recognition and elaboration of some chance resemblance. At an earlier stage, it seems, Stone Age people were content to collect pebbles (as well as less durable small specimens) in whose natural shape they saw something that rendered them "magic"; echoes of this approach can sometimes be felt in later, more fully worked pieces. Thus the so-called *Venus of Willendorf* in Austria (fig. 37), one of many such female fertility figurines, has a bulbous roundness of form that recalls an egg-shaped "sacred pebble"; her navel, the central point of the design, is a natural cavity in the stone. And the masterful *Bison* (fig. 38) of reindeer horn owes its compact, expressive outline in part to the contours of the palm-shaped piece of antler from which it was carved. It is not an unworthy companion to the splendid beasts at Altamira and Lascaux.

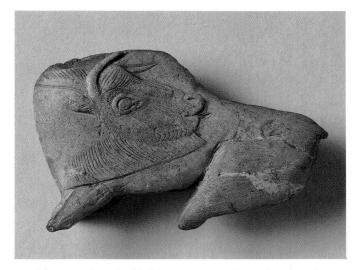

38. *BISON*, from La Madeleine near Les Eyzies (Dordogne). c. 15,000–10,000 B.C. Reindeer horn, length 4″ (10.15 cm). Musée des Antiquités Nationales, St.-Germain-en-Laye, France

The art of the Old Stone Age in Europe as we know it today marks the highest achievements of a way of life that began to decline soon after. Adapted almost perfectly to the special conditions of the receding Ice Age, it could not survive beyond them. In other parts of the world, the Old Stone Age gave way to new developments between c. 10,000 and 5000 B.C., except for a few particularly inhospitable areas where the Old Stone Age way of life continued because there was nothing to challenge or disturb it. The Bushmen of South Africa and the aborigines of Australia are—or were, until very recently—the last remnants of this primeval phase of human development. Even their art has decidedly Paleolithic features; the painting on tree bark from North Australia (fig. 39), while far less skillful than the cave pic-

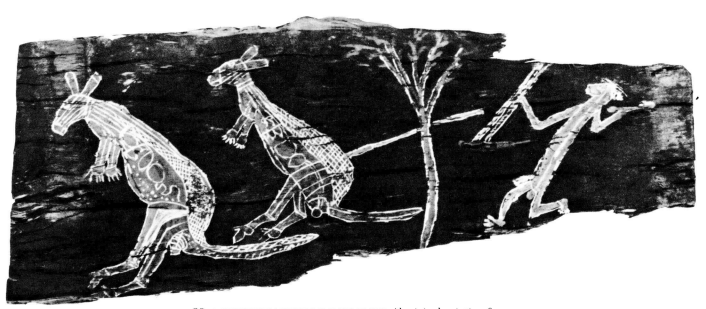

39. *A SPIRIT MAN SPEARING KANGAROOS*. Aboriginal painting from Western Arnhem Land, North Australia. c. 1900 A.D. Tree bark

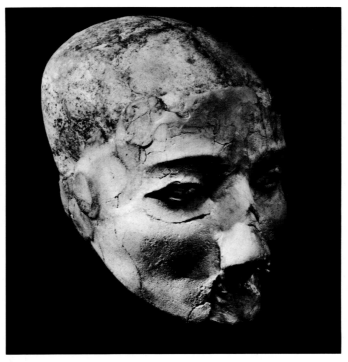

40. Neolithic plastered skull, from Jericho. c. 7000 B.C.
Lifesize. Archaeological Museum, Amman, Jordan

tures of Europe, shows a similar interest in movement and a keen observation of detail (including an "X-ray view" of the inner organs), only here it is kangaroos rather than bison on which the hunting magic is being worked.

# THE NEW STONE AGE

What brought the Old Stone Age to a close has been termed the Neolithic Revolution. And a revolution it was indeed, although its course extended over several thousand years. It began in the Near East sometime about 8000 B.C., with the first successful attempts to domesticate animals and food grains—one of the truly epoch-making achievements of human history. People in Paleolithic societies had led the unsettled life of the hunter and food gatherer, reaping where nature sowed and thus at the mercy of forces that they could neither understand nor control. But now, having learned how to assure a food supply by their own efforts, men and women settled down in permanent village communities; a new discipline and order entered their lives. There is, then, a very basic difference between the New Stone Age, or Neolithic, and the Old, or Paleolithic, despite the fact that all still depended on stone as the material of their main tools and weapons. The new mode of life brought forth a number of important new crafts and inventions long before the earliest appearance of metals: pottery, weaving and spinning, basic methods of architectural construction in wood, brick, and stone.

We know all this from the tangible remains of Neolithic settlements that have been uncovered by excavation. Unfortunately, these remains tell us very little, as a rule, of the spiritual condition of Neolithic culture; they include stone implements of ever greater technical refinement and beauty of shape, and an infinite variety of clay vessels covered with abstract ornamental patterns, but hardly anything comparable to the painting and sculpture of the Paleolithic. Yet the changeover from hunting to husbandry must have been accompanied by profound changes in the people's view of themselves and the world, and it seems impossible to believe that these did not find expression in art. There may be a vast chapter in the development of art here that is lost to us simply because Neolithic artists worked in wood or other impermanent materials. Or perhaps excavations in the future will help to fill the gap.

JERICHO. A tantalizing glimpse of what lies in store for us is provided by the discoveries at prehistoric Jericho, which include a group of impressive sculptured heads dating from about 7000 B.C. (fig. 40). They are actual human skulls whose faces have been "reconstituted" in tinted plaster, with pieces of seashell for the eyes. The subtlety and precision of the modeling, the fine gradation of planes and ridges, the feeling for the relationship of flesh and bone would be remarkable enough in themselves, quite apart from the amazingly early date. The features, moreover, do not conform to a single type; each has a strongly individual cast. Mysterious as they are, those Neolithic heads clearly point forward to Mesopotamian art (compare fig. 110); they are the first harbingers of a tradition of portraiture that will continue unbroken until the collapse of the Roman Empire.

Unlike Paleolithic art, which had grown from the perception of chance images, the Jericho heads are not intended to "create" life but to perpetuate it beyond death by replacing the transient flesh with a more enduring substance. From the circumstances in which these heads were found, we gather that they were displayed above ground while the rest of the body was buried beneath the floor of the house; presumably they belonged to venerated ancestors whose beneficent presence was thus assured.

Paleolithic societies, too, had buried their dead, but we do not know what ideas they associated with the grave: was death merely a return to the womb of mother earth, or did they have some conception of the beyond? The Jericho heads, on the other hand, suggest that people of the Neolithic era believed in a spirit or soul, located in the head, that could survive the death of the body and assert its power over the fortunes of later generations, and thus had to be appeased or controlled. The preserved heads, apparently, were "spirit traps" designed to keep the spirit in its original dwelling place. They express in visible form the sense of tradition, of family or clan continuity, that sets off the settled life of husbandry from the roving existence of the hunter. And Neolithic Jericho was a settled community of the most emphatic sort: the people who treasured the skulls of their forebears lived in stone houses with neat plaster floors, within a fortified town protected by walls and towers of rough but strong masonry construction (fig. 41). Yet, amazingly enough, they had no pottery; the technique of baking clay in a kiln, it seems, was not invented until later.

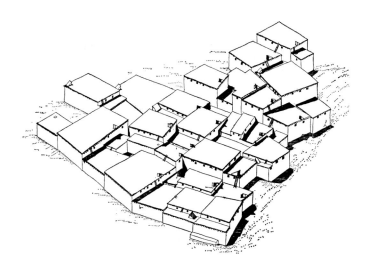

42. Houses and shrines in terraces. Çatal Hüyük, Turkey (schematic reconstruction of Level VI after Mellaart). c. 6000 B.C.

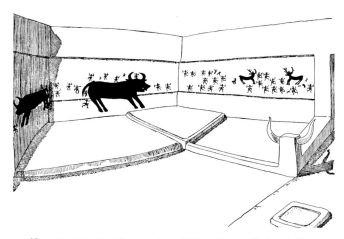

43. *ANIMAL HUNT.* Restoration of Main Room, Shrine A.III.1, Çatal Hüyük (after Mellaart). c. 6000 B.C. 27 × 65″ (68.5 × 165 cm)

ÇATAL HÜYÜK. Excavations at Çatal Hüyük in Anatolia brought to light another Neolithic town, roughly a thousand years younger than Jericho. Its inhabitants lived in houses built of mud bricks and timber, clustered around open courtyards (fig. 42). There were no streets, since the houses had no doors; people apparently entered through the roof. The settlement included a number of religious shrines—the earliest found so far—and on their plaster-covered walls we encounter the earliest paintings on a man-made surface. Animal hunts, with small running figures surrounding huge bulls or stags (fig. 43), evoke echoes of the Old Stone Age, an indication that the Neolithic Revolution must have been a recent event at the time. But the balance has already shifted; these hunts have the character of rituals honoring the male deity to whom the bull and stag were sacred, rather than of an everyday activity necessary for survival.

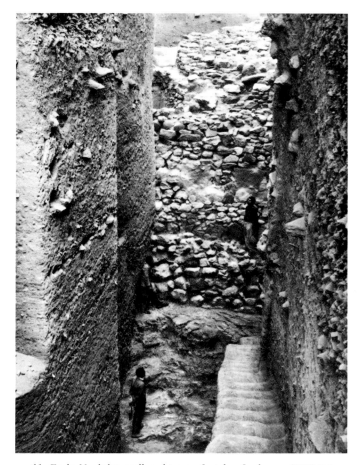

41. Early Neolithic wall and tower, Jericho, Jordan. c. 7000 B.C.

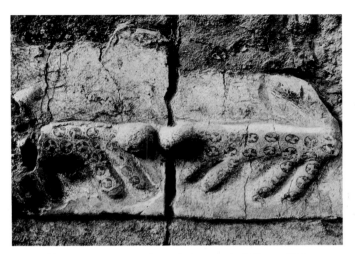

44. *TWIN LEOPARDS*. Painted plaster relief, Shrine VI.A.,
Çatal Hüyük. c. 6000 B.C. 27×65″ (68.5×165 cm)

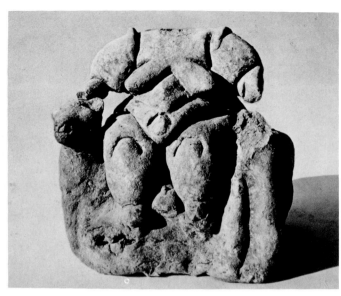

45. *FERTILITY GODDESS*, from Shrine A.II.1, Çatal Hüyük.
c. 6000 B.C. Baked clay, height 8″ (20.3 cm).
Archaeological Museum, Ankara, Turkey

Compared to the animals of the cave paintings, these at Çatal Hüyük are simplified and immobile; it is the hunters who are in energetic motion. Animals associated with female deities display an even more rigid discipline; the two symmetrically opposed leopards (fig. 44) are mirror images of each other, and another pair of leopards forms the sides of the throne of a fertility goddess (fig. 45), one of the many baked clay statuettes that betray their descent from the *Venus of Willendorf* (compare fig. 37). Among the wall paintings at Çatal Hüyük, the most surprising one is a view of the town itself, with the twin cones of an erupting volcano above it (figs. 46 and 47). The densely packed rectangles of the houses are seen from above, while the mountain is shown in profile, its slope covered with dots representing blobs of lava. Such a volcano is still visible today from Çatal Hüyük. Its eruption must have been a terrifying event for the inhabi-

tants; how could they have viewed it except as a manifestation of a diety's power? Nothing less could have brought forth this image, halfway between a map and a landscape.

## Neolithic Europe

While the Near East became the cradle of civilization (to be civilized, after all, means to live as a citizen, a town dweller), the Neolithic Revolution progressed at a very much slower pace in Europe. About 3000 B.C., Near Eastern influences began to spread to the northern shore of the Mediterranean. Baked clay figurines of fertility goddesses found in the Balkans, such as the very striking one from Cernavoda (figs. 48 and 49), have their closest relatives in Asia Minor. What makes the Cernavoda *Fertility Goddess* so memorable is the

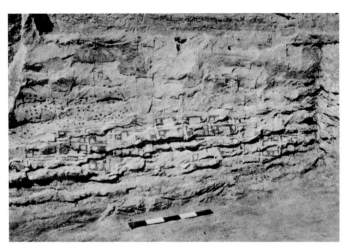

46. *VIEW OF TOWN AND VOLCANO*. Wall painting, Shrine VII.14,
Çatal Hüyük. c. 6000 B.C.

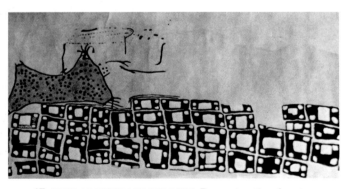

47. *VIEW OF TOWN AND VOLCANO*. Reconstruction drawing

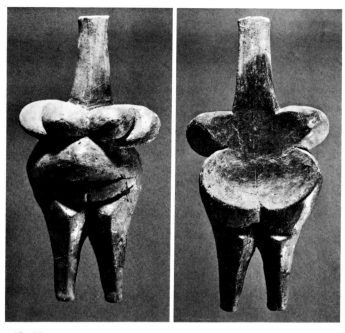

48, 49. *FERTILITY GODDESS,* from Cernavoda, Romania. c. 5000 B.C.
Baked clay, height 6¼" (16 cm). National Museum, Bucharest
(Photographs copyright Alexander Marshack)

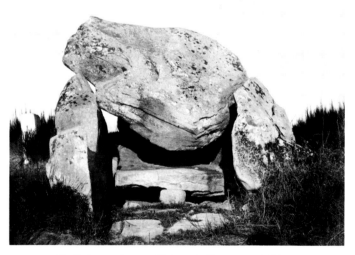

50. Dolmen, Carnac (Brittany), France. c. 1500 B.C.

sculptor's ability to simplify the shapes of a woman's body and yet retain its salient features (which, to him, did not include the face). The smoothly concave back sets off the ballooning convexity of the front—thighs, belly, arms, and breasts—in a way that would do honor to any twentieth-century sculptor.

DOLMENS AND CROMLECHS. North of the Alps, Near Eastern influence cannot be detected until a much later time. In Central and Northern Europe, a sparse population continued to lead the simple tribal life of small village communities even after the introduction of bronze and iron, until a few hundred years before the birth of Christ. Thus

Neolithic Europe never reached the level of social organization that produced the masonry architecture of Jericho or the dense urban community of Çatal Hüyük. Instead we find there monumental stone structures of a different kind, called megalithic because they consist of huge blocks or boulders placed upon each other without mortar. Their purpose was religious, rather than civic or utilitarian; apparently, the sustained and co-ordinated effort they required could be compelled only by the authority of religious faith—a faith that almost literally demanded the moving of mountains. Even today these megalithic monuments have an awe-inspiring, superhuman air about them, as if they were the work of a forgotten race of giants. Some, known as dolmens,

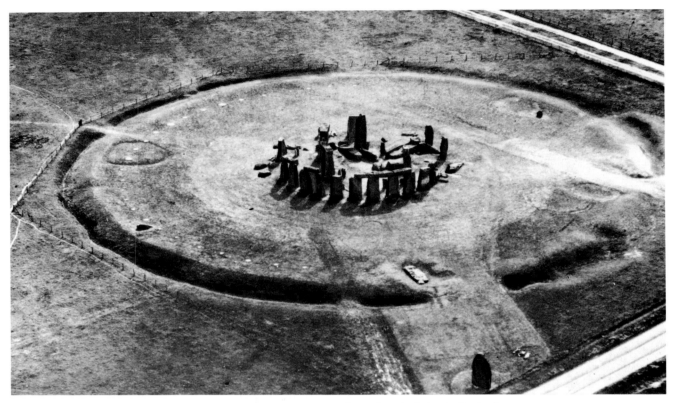

51. Stonehenge (aerial view), Salisbury Plain (Wiltshire), England.
c. 2000 B.C. Diameter of circle 97′ (29.6 m)

are tombs, "houses of the dead" with upright stones for walls and a single giant slab for a roof (fig. 50).

Others, the so-called cromlechs, form the setting of religious observances. Stonehenge in southern England (figs. 51 and 52) has a great outer circle of evenly spaced uprights supporting horizontal slabs (lintels) and two inner circles similarly marked, with an altarlike stone at the center (fig. 53). The entire structure is oriented toward the exact point at which the sun rises on the day of the summer solstice, and therefore it must have served a sun-worshiping ritual.

Whether a monument such as this should be termed architecture is a matter of definition: nowadays, we tend to think of architecture in terms of enclosed interiors, yet we also have landscape architects, the designers of gardens, parks, and playgrounds; nor would we want to deny the status of architecture to open-air theaters or sports stadiums. Perhaps we ought to consult the ancient Greeks, who coined the term. To them, "archi-tecture" meant something higher than ordinary "tecture" (that is, "construction" or "building")—much as an archbishop ranks above a bishop or an archfiend above a fiend—a structure distinguished from the merely practical, everyday kind by its scale, order, permanence, or solemnity of purpose. A Greek, therefore, would certainly have acknowledged Stonehenge as architecture. And we, too, shall have no difficulty in doing so once we understand that it is not necessary to *enclose* space in order to define or articulate it. If architecture is "the art of shaping space to human needs and aspirations," then Stonehenge more than meets the test.

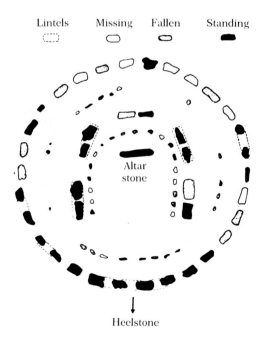

52. (*opposite*) Stonehenge

53. (*above*) Diagram of original arrangement of stones at Stonehenge (after F. Hoyle)

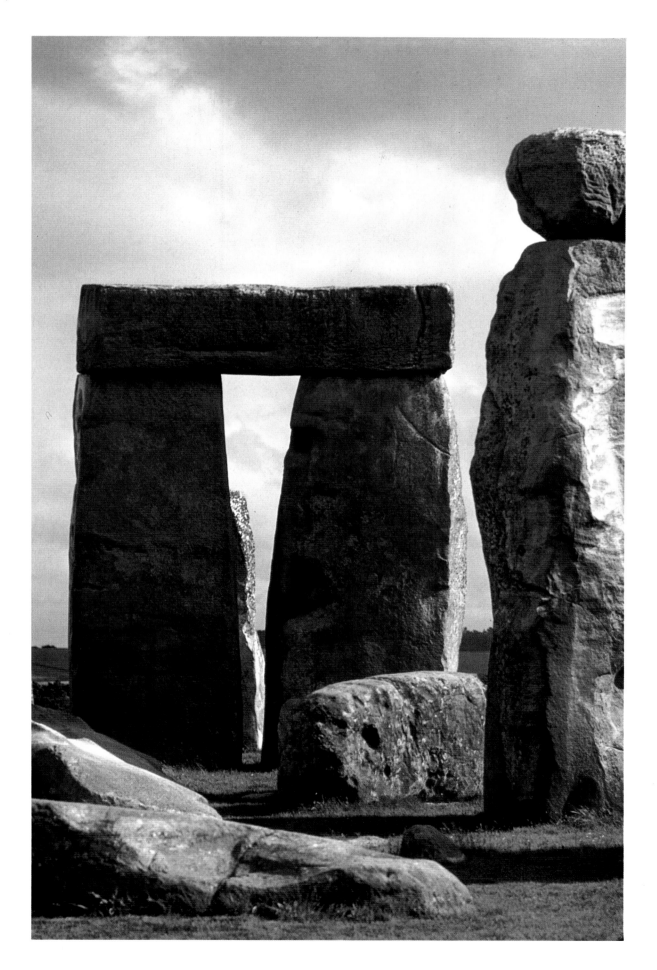

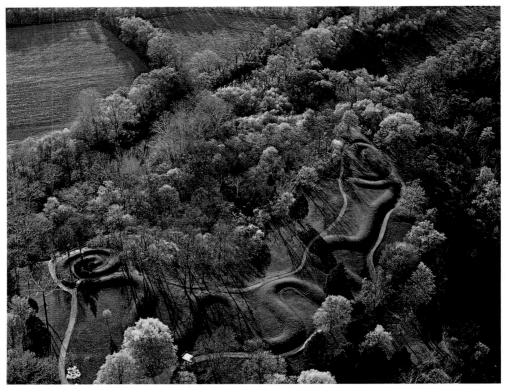

54. Great Serpent Mound, Adams County, Ohio. c. 300 B.C.–400 A.D.
Length 1400′ (426.7 m). © Tony Linck, Fort Lee, New Jersey

### Neolithic America

Comparable to the megalithic monuments of Europe in terms of the effort involved is the "earth art" of the prehistoric Indians of North America, the so-called Mound Builders. The term is misleading, since these mounds vary greatly in shape and purpose as well as in date, ranging from about 2000 B.C. to the time of the Europeans' arrival. Of particular interest are the "effigy mounds" in the shape of animals—presumably the totems of the tribes that produced them. The most spectacular is the Great Serpent Mound (fig. 54), a snake some 1,400 feet long that slithers along the crest of a ridge by a small river in southern Ohio. The huge head, its center marked by a heap of stones that may once have been an altar, occupies the highest point. Evidently it was the natural formation of the terrain that inspired this extraordinary work of landscape architecture, as mysterious and moving in its way as Stonehenge.

# ETHNOGRAPHIC ART

There are, as we have seen, a few human groups for whom the Old Stone Age lasted until the present day. Modern survivors of the Neolithic are far easier to find. They include all the so-called primitive societies of tropical Africa, the islands of the South Pacific, and the Americas. "Primitive" is a somewhat unfortunate word: it suggests—quite wrongly—that these societies represent the original human condition, and has thus come to be burdened with many conflicting emotional overtones. The term "ethnographic" will serve us better. It stands for a way of life that has passed through the Neolithic Revolution but shows no signs of evolving in the direction of the "historic" civilizations. What this means is that ethnographic societies are essentially rural and self-sufficient; their social and political units are the village and the tribe, rather than the city and the state; they perpetuate themselves by custom and tradition, without the aid of written records: hence they depend on oral tradition for their own history.

The entire pattern of ethnographic life is static rather than dynamic, without the inner drive for change and expansion that we take for granted in ours. Ethnographic societies tend to be strongly isolationist and defensive toward outsiders; they represent a stable but precarious balance of human beings and their environment, ill-equipped to survive contact with urban civilizations. Most of them have proved tragically helpless against encroachment by "civilized" societies. Yet at the same time the cultural heritage of ethnographic societies has enriched our own: their customs and beliefs, their folklore, and their music have been recorded by ethnologists, and ethnographic art is being avidly collected and admired throughout the Western world.

ANCESTOR SPIRITS. The rewards of this concern with the world of ethnographic societies have been manifold. Among them is a better understanding of the origins of our own culture in the Neolithic of the Near East and Europe.

Though the materials on which we base our knowledge of ethnographic peoples and their ways are almost invariably of quite recent date—very few of them go back beyond the seventeenth century—they offer striking analogies with the Neolithic of the distant past; and, of course, they are infinitely richer. Thus the meaning of the cult of skulls at Jericho (fig. 40) is illuminated by countless parallels in primitive art.

The closest parallel is to be found in the Sepik River district of New Guinea, where until quite recently the skulls of ancestors (and of important enemies) were given features in much the same fashion, including the use of seashells for

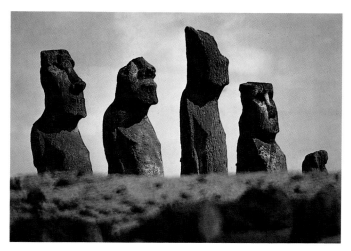

57. Stone images, Akivi, Easter Island.
17th century or earlier. Height c. 30′ (9.1 m)

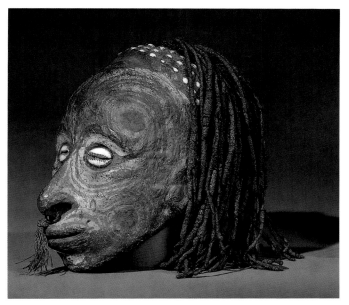

55. Plastered skull, from the Sepik River, New Guinea.
19th century. British Museum, London

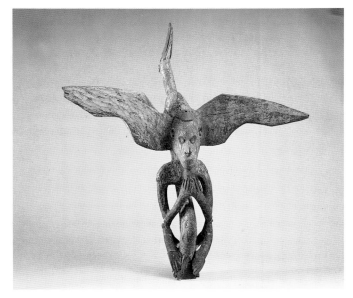

56. *MALE FIGURE SURMOUNTED BY A BIRD,* from the Sepik River, New Guinea. 19th–20th century. Wood, height 48″ (122 cm).
Washington University Gallery of Art, St. Louis.
University Purchase, Kende Sale Fund, 1945

eyes (fig. 55). And here we *know* that the purpose was to "trap" and thereby to gain power over the spirit of the dead. On the other hand, the Jericho cult probably differed from the New Guinea version in some significant respects, for the sculptured skulls from the Sepik River lack the delicate, realistic modeling of those from Jericho; the painted status markings on the faces, rather than any actual portrait resemblance, establishes the identity of the deceased. Their savagery of expression makes it hard for us to think of these heads as works of art, yet they embody the same belief as the splendid wood carvings of ancestral figures produced in that area, such as the one in figure 56. The entire design is centered on the head, with its intensely staring shell eyes, while the body—as in ethnographic art generally—has been reduced to the role of a mere support. The limbs suggest the embryo position in which so many such peoples like to bury their dead.

The bird emerging from behind the head with its great wings outspread represents the ancestor's vital spirit or life force; from its appearance, it must be a frigate bird or some other sea bird noted for its powers of flight. Its soaring movement, contrasted with the rigidity of the human figure, forms a compelling image—and a strangely familiar one: for our own tradition, too, includes the "soul bird," from the dove of the Holy Spirit to the albatross of the Ancient Mariner, so that we find ourselves responding to a work of art that at first glance might seem to be both puzzling and disconcerting.

GUARDIANS. Ancestor rituals are the most persistent feature of early religions and the strongest cohesive force in ethnographic societies, but since the "primitive" world consists of countless isolated tribal groups, it can take an almost infinite variety of forms, and its artistic expression varies even more. On Easter Island, for instance, we find huge ancestral figures carved from volcanic rock. Lined up on raised platforms like giant guardians, they must have cast a powerful protective spell (fig. 57). Here the carver's effort has again centered on the elongated, craggy features of the face, and the back of the head is suppressed entirely. These figures seem to reflect an impulse akin to that behind the megalithic monuments of Europe.

Among the native tribes of Gabon in Equatorial Africa, the skulls of ancestors used to be collected in large containers that were protected by a carved guardian figure, a sort of communal dwelling place of the ancestral spirits. Figure 58 shows such a guardian in the form traditional among the Kota. This tribe, like a number of others along the west coast of Central Africa, was familiar with nonferrous metals to some extent, so that its artists were able to sheathe their guardian images in polished brass, thus endowing them with special importance. This figure is a remarkable example of the geometric abstraction that occurs, to a greater or

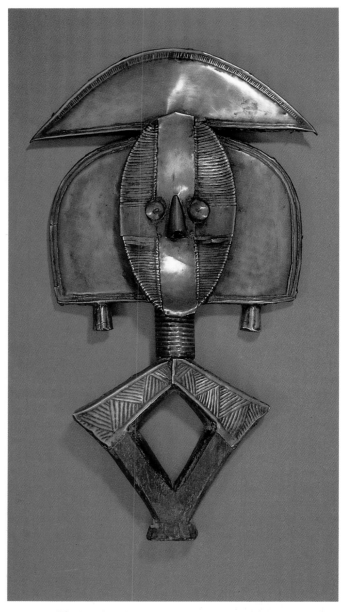

58. Guardian figure, from the Kota area, Gabon.
19th–20th century. Wood and copper, height 30″ (76.3 cm).
Musée Ethnographie, Geneva.
Gift of Dr. Graz, 1929

lesser extent, throughout the realm of primitive art. Except for the head, the entire design has been flattened into a single plane; body and limbs are contracted to a hollow diamond shape, and the headdress consists of two segments of circles. The face, in contrast, is a concave oval within which two spherical eyes and a pyramidlike nose nestle as they would in the center of a dish. The effect of the whole is extraordinarily calm, disciplined, and harmonious—a finely balanced sequence of shapes so unaggressive that one might almost mistake it for mere decoration. Surely this guardian could not have been meant to frighten anybody.

Tribal secrets are not readily betrayed, hence the available accounts do not tell us very much about the exact significance of the Kota guardians. It seems reasonable, however, to explain their extreme remoteness from nature—and the abstract tendency of ethnographic art generally—as an effort to convey the "otherness" of the spirit world, to divorce it as strictly as the artist's imagination would allow from the world of everyday appearances. Well and good—but how are we to account for the varying *degrees* of abstraction in primitive art? Must we assume that the more abstract its form, the more "spiritual" its meaning? If so, does the difference between the Kota and Sepik River figures reflect an equally great difference in the kinds of ancestor worship from which they spring, or are there perhaps other factors to be taken into account as well?

As it happens, the Kota guardians provide a good test for these assumptions. They have been collected in considerable numbers, and the differences among them are notable, even though they all clearly belong to a single type and must have been employed for exactly the same purpose. Our second example (fig. 59) is almost identical with the first, except for the head, which in comparison seems almost gruesomely realistic; its shape is strongly convex rather than concave, and every detail has an unmistakably representational meaning. This face, with its open mouth full of pointed teeth, seems designed to frighten. Here, we feel, is a guardian figure that does indeed live up to its function. Yet the members of the tribe failed to share our reaction, for they found the more abstract guardian figure equally acceptable.

What, then, is the relation between the two guardians? They were probably made at different times, but the interval could not have been more than a century or two, inasmuch as wooden sculpture does not survive for long under tropical conditions, and European travelers, so far as we know, did not begin to bring back any Kota guardians until the eighteenth century. In any event, given the rigidly conservative nature of this society, we can hardly believe that the ancestor cult of the Kota underwent any significant change during the time span that separates figure 58 from figure 59. Which of them came first, or—to put the question more cautiously—which represents the older, more nearly original version? Figure 59 surely is, since we cannot imagine how its realistic features could have evolved from the spare geometry of figure 58. The line of development thus leads from figure 59 to figure 58, from representation to abstraction (we also have a good many intermediate examples). This change seems to have taken place while the religious meaning re-

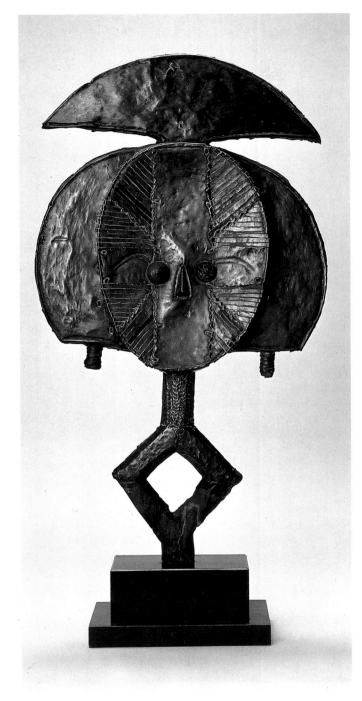

59. Guardian figure, from the Kota area, Gabon.
19th–20th century. Metal hammered on wood, height 23″ (58.4 cm).
The Heard Museum, Phoenix, Arizona

mained the same. Must we then credit the artist and his public with an interest in abstraction for its own sake? That hardly sounds plausible. There is, in fact, a far easier explanation: the increasingly abstract quality of the Kota guardians resulted from endless repetition.

We do not know how many such figures were in use at the same time, but the number must have been considerable, since each guardian presided over a container of not more than a dozen skulls. Their life expectancy being limited, they had to be replaced at frequent intervals, and the conser-

vative temper of such a society demanded that every new guardian follow the pattern of its predecessor. Yet, as we know, no copy is ever completely faithful to its model; so long as he repeated the basic outlines of the traditional design, the Kota carver enjoyed a certain latitude, for no two of the many surviving guardian figures have exactly the same facial structure. Maybe these slight variations were even expected of him, so as to distinguish the newly created guardian from the one it replaced. Any gesture or shape that is endlessly repeated tends to lose its original character—it becomes ground down, simplified, more abstract. We see a good example of this in the ideographs of Chinese writing, which started out as tiny pictures but before long lost all trace of their representational origin and became mere signs. The same kind of transformation, although not nearly as far-reaching, can be traced among the Kota guardians: they grew simpler and more abstract, since this was the only direction in which they could develop.

We have discussed the process at such length because it is a fundamental characteristic of Neolithic and ethnographic art, though we cannot often observe it as clearly as in the case of the Kota figures. But let us be careful not to take a negative view of this abstraction. It has its dangers, to be sure, but it also leads to the creation of an infinite variety of new and distinctive designs. Finally, we should note that transformation has its ultimate source in the artist's concern with the otherness of the spirit world; for it is this concern that makes him repeat the same designs over and over again. After all, if he sets out to create a guardian of ancestral skulls, the only model he can use is another such guardian figure, and he cannot know whether he has succeeded unless the two resemble each other.

RULERS. The strong traditionalism in ethnographic art can be interrupted in two ways: there may be a cross-fertilization of different cultures as the consequence of migration or conquest, or conditions may develop that favor a return to the world of visible appearances. Such conditions prevailed for a time along the coast of Equatorial Africa a few hundred miles northwest of Gabon. There, through contact with the historic civilizations of the Mediterranean, a number of native kingdoms arose, but none of them proved very enduring. A king, unlike a tribal chieftain, bases his authority on the claim that it has been given to him by supernatural forces; he rules "by the grace of God," embodying the divine will in his own person, or he may even assume the status of a deity himself. There are thus no inherent limits, ethnic, linguistic, or otherwise, to royal authority. Every king is, at least in theory, all-conquering. Hence his domain is not only larger and more complex than that of the tribal chief; he also has to exact far greater obedience from his subjects. He does so with the aid of a favored ruling elite, the aristocracy, to whom he delegates some of his authority. They enforce security and order among the rest of the population, which in return must support the aristocracy and the royal court by contributing a share of its goods and services.

The institution of kingship, then, demands a society divided into classes, rather than the loose association of family or clan groups that makes up a tribe. It means the victory of the

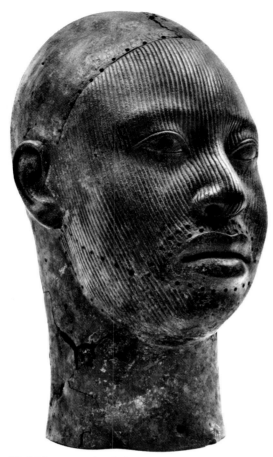

60. Male portrait head, from Ife, Nigeria. 12th century.
Bronze, height 13½″ (34.3 cm). Collection the Oni of Ife

At the time this head was produced, the twelfth century A.D., nothing of comparable character can be found in Europe. Only the tribal scars on the face, and the holes for attaching hair and beard, relate it to ethnographic art elsewhere; these, and the purpose for which it was made, ancestor ritual. Our head, together with its companions, must have formed part of a long series of portraits of dead rulers, and the use of real hair—probably hair taken from the person represented—strongly suggests that these heads were prepared as "traps" for the spirits of the deceased. But since the rulers each had individual importance, their spirits, unlike those of the tribal ancestors, could not be merged into an impersonal collective entity; in order to be an effective trap, every head had to be an authentic, clearly distinguishable portrait. It is possible, in fact, that these heads were made (if not of bronze, then at least of terracotta) while their subjects were still alive, and became spirit traps only after the ruler's death, through the addition of his hair. Clearly, each of these heads is unique and irreplaceable. It had to last forever, hence it was executed in laborious bronze rather than wood. It is no accident, then, that the Ife heads bear a closer resemblance to the Jericho skulls than to the ancestor figures of primitive art, for the rulers of Ife had indeed recaptured something of the urban quality of the Jericho ancestor cult.

The bronze technique of Ife was handed on to the kingdom of Benin, which arose in the same area and did not disappear until the early eighteenth century. In addition to ancestor heads, the artists of Benin produced a vast variety of works that had nothing to do with the spirit world but served to glorify the ruler and his court. The *Hornblower* (fig. 61) is characteristic of this art for display. By the standards of ethnographic sculpture as a whole, it seems exceptionally realistic, but when measured against the art of Ife it betrays its close kinship with tribal wood carvings in the emphasis on the head and the geometric simplification of every detail.

ANIMISM. That ethnographic peoples should prefer to think of the spirits of their ancestors collectively, as did the Kota, rather than in terms of separate individuals, is a result of the animism that underlies their religious beliefs. Such religious beliefs have been termed animism, for to these people a spirit exists in every living thing. An animist will feel that he must appease the spirit of a tree before he cuts it down, but the spirit of any particular tree is also part of a collective "tree spirit" which in turn merges into a general "life spirit." Other spirits dwell in the earth, in rivers and lakes, in the rain, in the sun and moon; still others demand to be appeased in order to promote fertility or cure disease.

Their dwelling places may be given the shape of human figures, in which case such spirits sometimes achieve enough of a stable identity to be viewed as rudimentary de-

town over the countryside, and thus runs counter to the rural tenor of ethnographic society. The African kingdoms never quite achieved this victory, so their instability is perhaps not surprising. The decisive factor may have been their failure to develop or adopt a system of writing. They existed, as it were, along the outer edge of the historic civilizations, and their rise and fall, therefore, are known to us only in fragmentary fashion.

Artistically, the most impressive remains of these vanished native kingdoms are the portrait heads excavated at Ife, Nigeria, somewhat to the west of the lower course of the Niger River. Some are of terracotta; others, such as the splendid example in figure 60, of bronze. The casting technique, called the cire-perdue (lost-wax) process, surely had been imported from the Mediterranean, but it was used here with great skill: the actual modeling is done in wax over an earthen core, another layer of earth is firmly packed around the head, the whole is then heated to melt out the wax, and molten bronze is poured into the hollow form thus created. Even more astonishing than its technical refinement, however, is the subtle and assured realism of our Ife head. The features are thoroughly individual, yet so harmonious and noble in expression as to recall the classical art of Greece and Rome (see figs. 231 and 295).

61. *(opposite)* HORNBLOWER, from Benin. Late 16th–early 18th century. Bronze, height 24⅞″ (63.3 cm). The Metropolitan Museum of Art, New York. The Michael C. Rockefeller Memorial Collection. Gift of Nelson A. Rockefeller, 1972

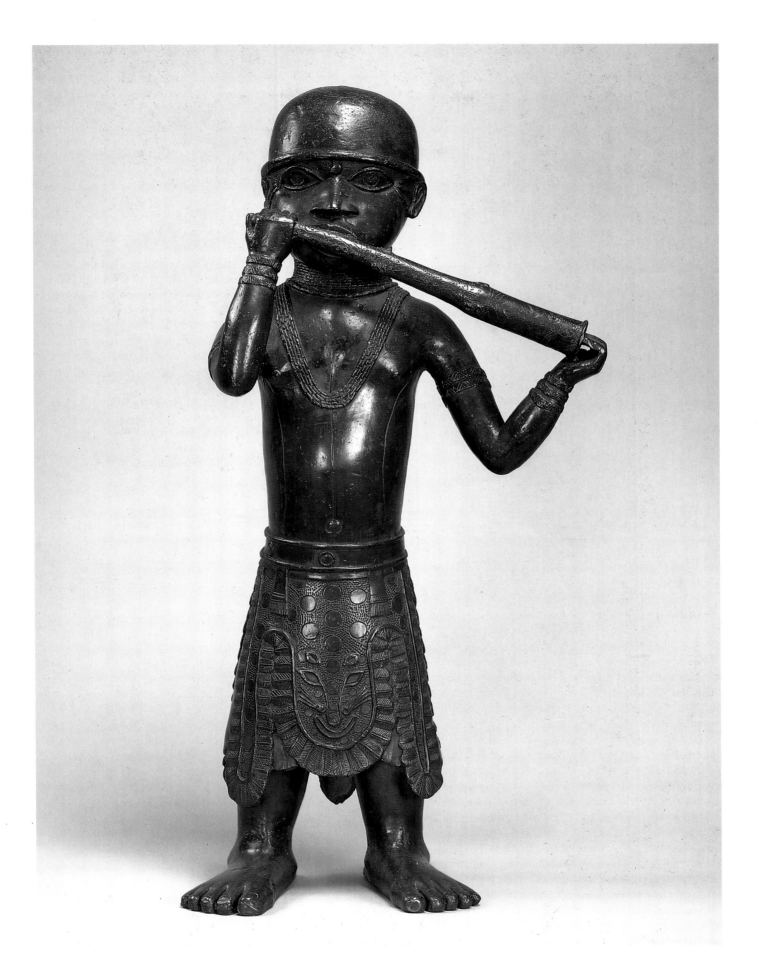

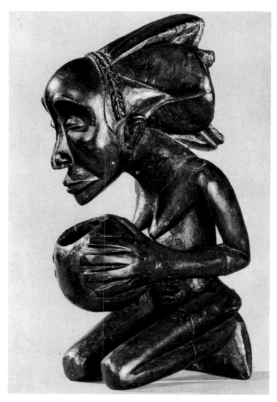

62. *KNEELING WOMAN,* from the Baluba area, Kinshasa, Zaire.
19th–20th century. Wood, height 18½″ (47 cm).
Koninklijk Museum for Midden-Afrika, Tervuren, Belgium

Masks form by far the richest chapter in "primitive" art; the proliferation of shapes, materials, and functions is almost limitless. Even the manner of wearing them varies surprisingly: some cover only the face, others the entire head; some rest on the shoulders; some may be worn above the head, attached to a headdress or atop a pole. There are masks of human faces, ranging from the realistic to the most fantastic, and animal masks or combinations of both in every conceivable form. There are also masks that are not made to be worn at all but to be displayed independently as images complete in themselves.

The few samples reproduced here can convey no more than the faintest suggestion of the wealth of the available material. Their meaning, more often than not, is impossible to ascertain; the ceremonies they served usually had elements of secrecy that were jealously guarded from the uninitiated, especially if the performers themselves formed a secret society. This emphasis on the mysterious and spectacular not only heightened the dramatic impact of the ritual, it also permitted the makers of masks to strive for imaginative new effects, so that masks in general are less subject to traditional restrictions than other kinds of "primitive" sculpture.

ities. This seems to be true of the very fine *Kneeling Woman* (fig. 62), produced by the Baluba tribe of the Congo region, though little is known about her ritual significance. The figure is among the gentlest and least abstract of all tribal carvings, and her trancelike expression, as well as the hollow bowl, suggests a ceremonial of incantation or divination.

MASKS. In dealing with the spirit world, people were not content to perform rituals or to present offerings before their spirit traps; they needed to act out their relations with the spirit world through dances and similar dramatic ceremonials in which they could themselves temporarily assume the role of the spirit trap by disguising themselves with elaborate masks and costumes. The origin of these dance rituals goes back as far as the Old Stone Age (see fig. 35), and there are indications that animal disguises were worn even then. In these early societies, the acting-out ceremonials assumed a vast variety of patterns and purposes; and the costumes, always with a mask as the central feature, became correspondingly varied and elaborate. Nor has the fascination of the mask died out to this day. We still feel the thrill of a real change of identity when we wear one at Halloween or carnival time, and among the folk customs of the European peasantry there were, until recently, certain survivals of pre-Christian ceremonies in which the participants impersonated demons by means of carved masks of truly primitive character (fig. 63).

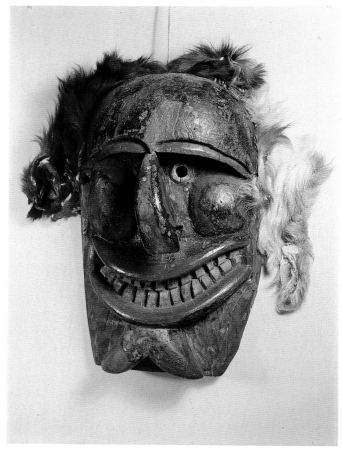

63. Mask, from Kippel, Lötschental, Switzerland.
19th century. Wood, height 18″ (45.7 cm).
Rietberg Museum, Zurich. E.v.d. Heydt Collection

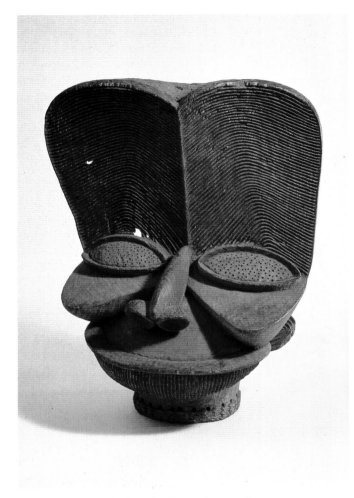

64. Mask, from the Bamenda area, Cameroon.
19th–20th century. Wood, height 26½″ (67.3 cm).
Rietberg Museum, Zurich. E.v.d. Heydt Collection

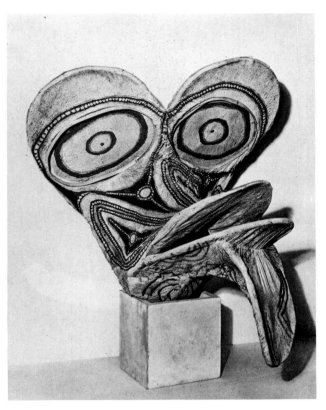

65. Mask, from the Gazelle Peninsula, New Britain.
19th–20th century. Bark cloth, height 18″ (45.7 cm).
Museo Nacional de Antropología, Mexico City

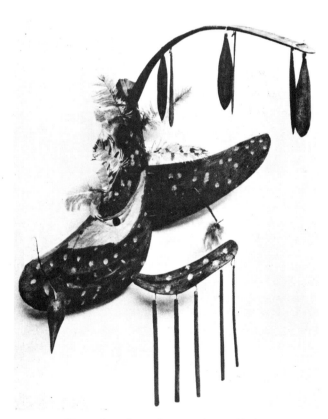

66. Mask. Eskimo, from southwest Alaska.
Early 20th century. Wood, height 22″ (56 cm).
Museum of the American Indian, Heye Foundation, New York

African masks, such as the one in figure 64, are distinguished for symmetry of design and the precision and sharpness of their carving. In our example, the features of the human face have not been rearranged but restructured, so to speak, with the tremendous eyebrows rising above the rest like a protective canopy. The solidity of these shapes becomes strikingly evident as we turn to the fluid, ghostly features of the mask from the Gazelle Peninsula on the island of New Britain in the South Pacific made of bark cloth over a bamboo frame (fig. 65). It is meant to represent an animal spirit, said to be a crocodile, and was worn in nocturnal ceremonies by dancers carrying snakes. Even stranger is the Eskimo mask from southwest Alaska (fig. 66), with its non-symmetrical design of seemingly unrelated elements, especially the dangling "leaves" or sticks attached to curved "branches." The single eye and the mouth full of teeth are the only recognizable details to the outsider, yet to those who know how to "read" this assembly of shapes it is the condensed representation of a tribal myth about a swan that drives white whales to the hunters. Such radical displacement of facial details is characteristic of Eskimo masks generally, though it is seldom carried as far as here.

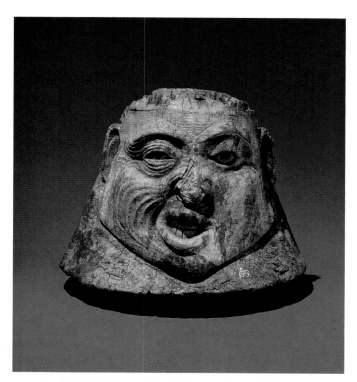

67. War helmet. Tlingit, from southeast Alaska.
Early 19th century. Wood, height 12″ (30.5 cm).
The American Museum of Natural History, New York

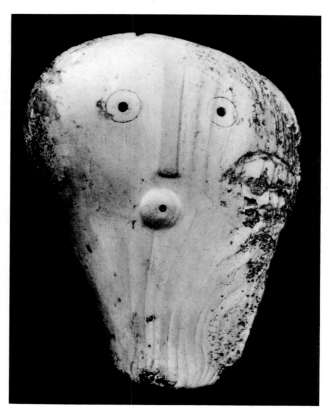

68. Mask, from the Brakebill Mound, Tennessee.
c. 1000–1600 A.D. Ocean shell, height 8⅝″ (22 cm).
Peabody Museum of Harvard University,
Cambridge, Massachusetts

The wooden war helmet from southeast Alaska (fig. 67), in contast, strikes us by its powerful realism, which may be due not only to the fact that this is a work of American Indian rather than Eskimo origin, but also to its function. It, too, is a kind of mask, a second face intended to disconcert the enemy by its fierce expression. Our final example, one of the most fascinating of all, comes from an Indian burial mound in Tennessee (fig. 68). It has been estimated as being between 400 and 1,000 years old. The material is a single large seashell, whose rim has been smoothed and whose gently convex outer surface has been transformed into a face by simple but strangely evocative carving and drilling. Shell masks such as this seem to have been placed in graves for the purpose of providing the dead with a second, permanent face to trap his spirit underground.

PAINTING. Compared to sculpture, painting plays a subordinate role in ethnographic societies. Though the technique was widely known, its use was restricted in most areas to the coloring of wood carvings or of the human body sometimes with intricate ornamental designs (see fig. 56). As an independent art, however, painting could establish itself only when exceptional conditions provided suitable surfaces. Thus the Nootka Indians on Vancouver Island, off the northwest coast of North America, developed fairly large wooden houses with walls of smooth boards which they liked to decorate with scenes of tribal legends. Figure 69 shows a section of such a wall, representing a thunder bird on a killer whale flanked by a lightning snake and a wolf. The animals are clearly recognizable, but they do not form a meaningful scene unless we happen to know the context of the story. The owner of the house obviously did, so the painter's main concern was how to combine the four creatures into an effective pattern filling the area at his disposal.

It is apparent that these animals, which play important parts in the tribal mythology, must have been represented countless times before; each of them is assembled in accordance with a well-established traditional formula made up of fixed ingredients—small, firmly outlined pieces of solid color that look as if they have been cut out separately and laid down one by one. The artist's pattern-consciousness goes so far that any overlapping of forms embarrasses him; where he cannot avoid it, he treats the bodies of the animals as transparent, so that the outline of the whale's back can be seen continuing right through the lower part of the bird's body, and the feathers of the right wing reveal the front legs of the wolf.

SAND PAINTING. Formal and abstract as the Nootka wall painting may seem in comparison with the animals of the Paleolithic, it becomes downright realistic if we judge it by the standards of the sand painting visible in figure 70. That unique art grew up among the Indian tribes inhabiting the arid Southwest of the United States; its main practitioners today are the Navajo of Arizona and New Mexico. The technique, which demands considerable skill, consists of pouring powdered rock or earth of various colors on a flat bed of sand. Despite (or perhaps because of) the fact that they are impermanent and must be made fresh for each occasion

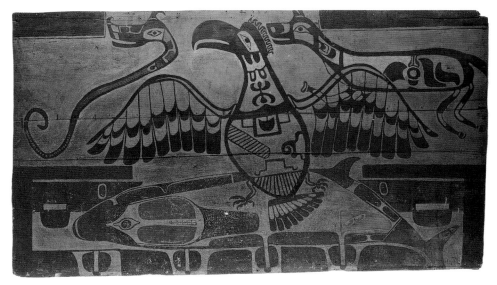

69. *LIGHTNING SNAKE, WOLF, AND THUNDER BIRD ON KILLER WHALE.* Nootka. c. 1850. Wood, 5'8" × 8'10" (1.7 × 2.7 m). The American Museum of Natural History, New York

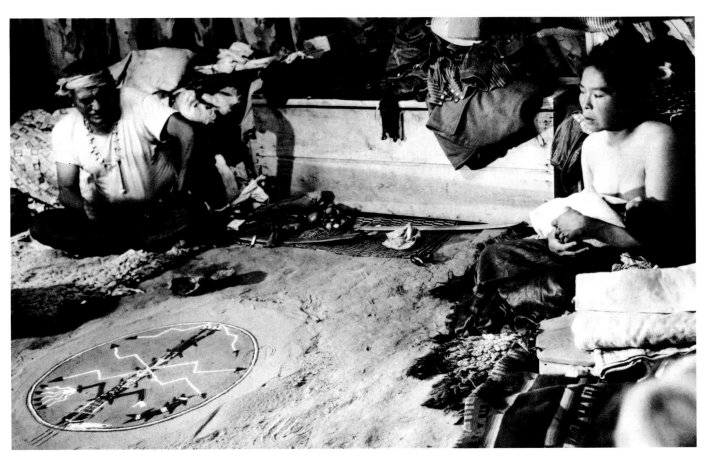

70. Sand painting ritual for a sick child. Navajo. Arizona

that demands them, the designs are rigidly fixed by tradition. The various compositions are rather like recipes, prescribed by the medicine man and "filled" under his supervision by the painter, for the main use of sand paintings is in ceremonies of healing.

That these ceremonies are sessions of great emotional intensity on the part of both doctor and patient is well attested by our illustration. Such a close union—or even, at times, identity—of priest, healer, and artist may be difficult to understand in modern Western terms. But for people trying to bend nature to their needs by magic and ritual, the functions appear as different aspects of a single process. And the success or failure of this process is to them virtually a matter of life and death.

# CHAPTER TWO
# EGYPTIAN ART

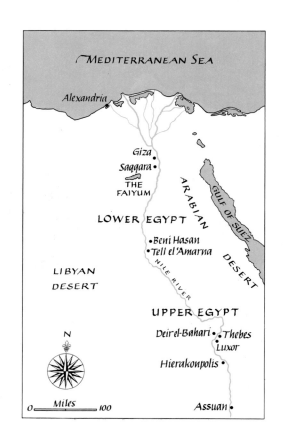

MEDITERRANEAN SEA

Alexandria

Giza •
Saqqara •
THE
FAIYUM

LOWER EGYPT

• Beni Hasan
• Tell el 'Amarna

LIBYAN
DESERT

ARABIAN

GULF OF SUEZ

DESERT

NILE RIVER

UPPER EGYPT

Deir el-Bahari • • Thebes
Luxor
Hierakonpolis •

N

0 ___ Miles ___ 100

Assuan •

## From Prehistoric to Historic

The road from hunting to husbandry is a long and arduous one. The problems and pressures faced by historic societies are very different from those that confronted peoples in the Paleolithic or Neolithic eras. Prehistory was a phase of evolution during which humans as a species learned how to maintain themselves against a hostile environment; their achievements were responses to threats of physical extinction. With the domestication of animals and edible plants, people had won a decisive victory in this battle, assuring our survival on this planet. But the Neolithic Revolution placed us on a level at which we might well have remained indefinitely: the forces of nature—at least during that geological era—would never again challenge men and women as they had Paleolithic peoples. And in many parts of the globe, as we saw in the previous chapter, people were content to stay on a "Neolithic plateau."

In a few places, however, the Neolithic balance of humans and nature was upset by a new threat, a threat posed not by nature but by people themselves. The earliest monument to that threat is seen in the fortifications of Neolithic Jericho (see fig. 41), constructed almost 9,000 years ago. What was the source of the human conflict that made them necessary? Competition for grazing land among tribes of herdsmen or for arable soil among farming communities? The basic cause, we suspect, was that the Neolithic Revolution had been too successful in this area, permitting the local population to grow beyond the available food supply. This situation might have been resolved in a number of ways: constant tribal warfare could have reduced the population; or the people could have united in larger and more disciplined social units for the sake of ambitious group efforts that no loosely organized tribal society would have been able to achieve. The fortifications at Jericho were an enterprise of this kind, requiring sustained and specialized labor over a long period. We do not know the outcome of the struggle in that region (future excavations may tell us how far the urbanizing process extended) but about 3,000 years later, similar conflicts, on a larger scale, arose in the Nile valley and that of the Tigris and Euphrates, and there these conflicts generated enough pressure to produce a new kind of society, very much more complex and efficient than had ever existed before.

First in Egypt and Mesopotamia, somewhat later in neighboring areas, and in the Indus valley and along the Yellow River in China, people were to live in a more dynamic world, where their capacity to survive was challenged not by the forces of nature but by human forces—by tensions and conflicts arising either within society or as the result of competition between societies. These efforts to cope with human environment have proved a far greater challenge than the earlier struggle with nature.

# THE OLD KINGDOM

Egyptian civilization has long been regarded as the most rigid and conservative ever. Plato said that Egyptian art had not changed in 10,000 years. Perhaps "enduring" and "continuous" are better terms for it, although at first glance all Egyptian art between 3000 and 500 B.C. does tend to have a certain sameness. There is a kernel of truth in this: the basic pattern of Egyptian institutions, beliefs, and artistic ideas was formed during the first few centuries of that vast span of years and kept reasserting itself until the very end. We shall see, however, that as time went on this basic pattern went through ever more severe crises that challenged its ability to survive; had it been as inflexible as supposed, it would have succumbed long before it finally did. Egyptian art alternates between conservatism and innovation, but is never static. Some of its great achievements had a decisive influence on Greek and Roman art, and thus we can still feel ourselves linked to the Egypt of 5,000 years ago by a continuous, living tradition.

DYNASTIES. The history of Egypt is divided into dynasties of rulers, in accordance with ancient Egyptian practice, beginning with the First Dynasty, shortly after 3000 B.C. (the dates of the earliest rulers are difficult to translate exactly into our calendar). The transition from prehistory to the First Dynasty is known as the predynastic period. The Old Kingdom forms the first major division after that, ending about 2155 B.C. with the overthrow of the Sixth Dynasty. This method of counting historic time conveys at once the strong Egyptian sense of continuity and the overwhelming importance of the pharaoh (king), who was not only the supreme ruler but a god. We have had occasion to mention the main features of kingship before (see page 89); the pharaoh transcended them all, for his kingship was not a duty or privilege derived from a superhuman source, but was absolute, divine. This belief remained the key feature of Egyptian civilization and largely determined the character of Egyptian art. We do not know exactly the steps by which the early pharaohs established their claim to divinity, but we know their historic achievements: molding the Nile valley from the first cataract at Assuan to the Delta into a single, effective state, and increasing its fertility by regulating the river waters through dams and canals.

TOMBS AND RELIGION. Of these vast public works nothing remains today, and very little has survived of ancient Egyptian palaces and cities. Our knowledge of Egyptian civilization rests almost entirely on the tombs and their contents. This is no accident, since these tombs were built to last forever. Yet we must not make the mistake of concluding that the Egyptians viewed life on this earth mainly as a road to the grave. Their preoccupation with the cult of the dead is a link with the Neolithic past, but the meaning they gave it was quite new and different: the dark fear of the spirits of the dead which dominates primitive ancestor cults seems entirely absent. Instead, the Egyptian attitude was that each person must provide for his own happy afterlife. The ancient Egyptians would equip their tombs as a kind of shadowy replica of their daily environment for their spirits (*ka*) to enjoy, and would make sure that the *ka* had a body to dwell in (their own mummified corpse or, if that should become destroyed, a statue of themselves).

There is a curious blurring of the sharp line between life and death here, and perhaps that was the essential impulse

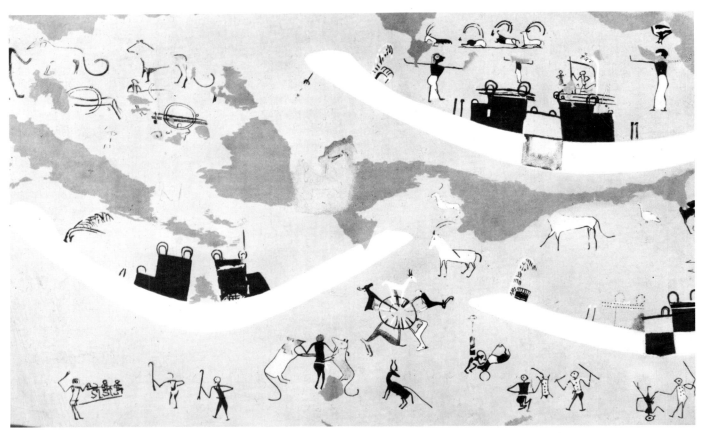

71. *PEOPLE, BOATS, AND ANIMALS.* Wall painting in predynastic tomb. c. 3200 B.C. Hierakonpolis, Egypt

behind these mock households; a man who knew that after death his *ka* would enjoy the same pleasures he did, and who had provided these pleasures in advance by his own efforts, could look forward to an active and happy life without being haunted by fear of the great unknown. In a sense, then, the Egyptian tomb was a kind of life insurance, an investment in peace of mind. Such, at least, is the impression one gains of Old Kingdom tombs. Later on, the serenity of this concept of death was disturbed by a tendency to subdivide the spirit or soul into two or more separate identities, and by the introduction of a sort of judgment, a weighing of souls; and it is only then that we also find expressions of the fear of death.

HIERAKONPOLIS. An early stage in the development of Egyptian funerary customs—and of Egyptian art—can be seen in the fragment of a wall painting from Hierakonpolis (fig. 71). The design is still decidedly primitive in its character—an even scattering of forms over the entire surface. It is instructive to note, however, that the human and animal figures tend to become standardized, abbreviated "signs," almost as if they were on the verge of turning into hieroglyphics (such as we see in fig. 105). The large white shapes are boats; their significance here seems to be that of funeral barges or "vehicles of the soul," since that is their role in later tombs. The black-and-white figures above the topmost boat are mourning women, their arms spread out in a ges-

ture of grief. For the rest, the picture does not appear to have any coherence as a scene or any symbolic import; perhaps we ought to view it as an early attempt at those typical scenes of daily life that we meet several centuries later in Old Kingdom tombs (figs. 89 and 90).

## Egyptian Style and the Palette of King Narmer

At the time of the Hierakonpolis mural—about 3200 B.C.—Egypt was in process of learning the use of bronze tools. The country, we may assume, was ruled by a number of local sovereigns not too far removed from the status of tribal chiefs. The fight scenes between black-bodied and white-bodied men in the painting probably reflect local wars or raids. Out of these emerged two rival kingdoms, Upper and Lower Egypt. The struggle between them was ended when certain Upper Egyptian kings conquered Lower Egypt and combined the two realms.

One of these was King Narmer, who appears on the impressive object in figures 72 and 73, a ceremonial slate palette celebrating a victory over Lower Egypt (note the different crowns worn by the king). It, too, comes from Hierakonpolis, but otherwise it has little in common with the wall painting. In many ways, the Narmer palette can claim to be the oldest historic work of art we know: not only is it the earliest surviving image of a historic personage identified by name, but its character is clearly no longer primitive; in fact, it already shows most of the features of late Egyptian art. If only we had enough preserved material to trace step-by-step the evolution that led from the wall painting to this palette!

Let us first "read" the scenes on both sides. The fact that we are able to do so is another indication that we have left prehistoric art behind. For the meaning of these reliefs is made clear and explicit not only by means of hieroglyphic labels, but also through the use of a broad range of visual symbols conveying precise messages to the beholder and—most important of all—through the disciplined, rational orderliness of the design. In figure 72 Narmer has seized a fallen enemy by the hair and is about to slay him with his mace; two more defeated enemies are placed in the bottom compartment (the small rectangular shape next to the man on the left stands for a fortified town or citadel). Facing the king in the upper right we see a complex bit of picture writing: a falcon standing above a clump of papyrus plants holds a tether attached to a human head that "grows" from the same soil as the plants. This composite image actually repeats the main scene on a symbolic level; the head and papyrus plant stand for Lower Egypt, while the victorious falcon

is Horus, the local god of Upper Egypt. The parallel is plain: Horus and Narmer are the same; a god triumphs over human foes. Hence, Narmer's gesture must not be taken as representing a real fight; the enemy is helpless from the very start, and the slaying is a ritual rather than a physical effort. We gather this from the fact that Narmer has taken off his sandals (the court official behind him carries them in his right hand), an indication that he is standing on holy ground.

On the other side of the palette (fig. 73), he again appears barefoot, followed by the sandal carrier, as he marches in solemn procession behind a group of standard-bearers to inspect the decapitated bodies of prisoners. (The same notion recurs in the Old Testament, apparently as the result of Egyptian influence, when the Lord commands Moses to remove his shoes before He appears to him in the burning bush.) The bottom compartment re-enacts the victory once again on a symbolic level, with the pharaoh represented as a strong bull trampling an enemy and knocking down a citadel. (A bull's tail hanging down from his belt is shown in both images of Narmer; it was to remain a part of pharaonic ceremonial garb for the next 3,000 years.) Only the center section fails to convey an explicit meaning; the two long-

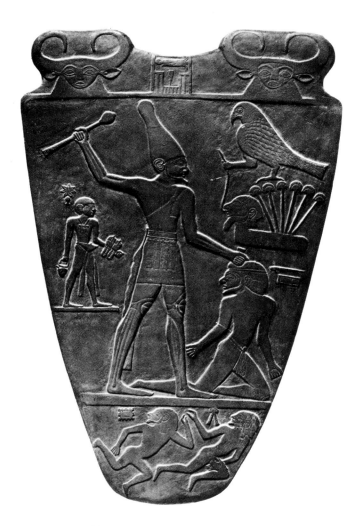
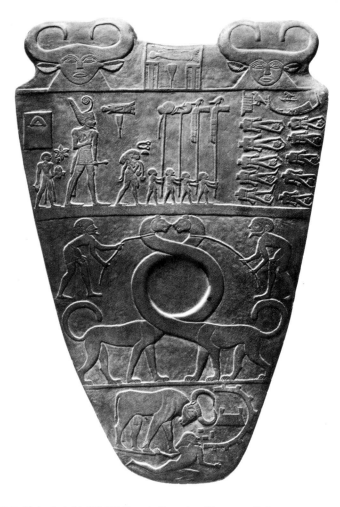

72, 73. *PALETTE OF KING NARMER*, from Hierakonpolis. c. 3000 B.C. Slate, height 25″ (63.5 cm). Egyptian Museum, Cairo

necked beasts and their attendants have no identifying attributes and may well be a carry-over from earlier, purely ornamental palettes. In any event, they do not reappear in Egyptian art.

LOGIC OF EGYPTIAN STYLE.  The new inner logic of the Narmer palette's style becomes readily apparent in contrast to the predynastic wall painting. What strikes us first is its strong sense of order: the surface of the palette has been divided into horizontal bands (or registers), and each figure stands on a line or strip denoting the ground. The only exceptions are the attendants of the long-necked beasts, whose role seems mainly ornamental; the hieroglyphic signs, which belong to a different level of reality; and the dead enemies. The latter are seen from above, whereas the standing figures are seen from the side. Obviously, the modern notion of representing a scene as it would appear to a single observer at a single moment is as alien to the Egyptian artist as it had been to his Neolithic predecessor; he strives for clarity, not illusion, and therefore he picks the most telling view in each case.

But he imposes a strict rule on himself: when he changes his angle of vision, he must do so by 90 degrees, as if he were sighting along the edges of a cube. As a consequence, he acknowledges only three possible views: full face, strict profile, and vertically from above. Any intermediate position embarrasses him (note the oddly rubberlike figures of the fallen enemies; fig. 73, bottom). Moreover, he is faced with the fact that the standing human figure, unlike that of an animal, does not have a single main profile but two competing profiles, so that, for the sake of clarity, he must combine these views. His method of doing this—a method that was to survive unchanged for 2,500 years—is clearly shown in the large figure of Narmer in figure 72: eye and shoulders in

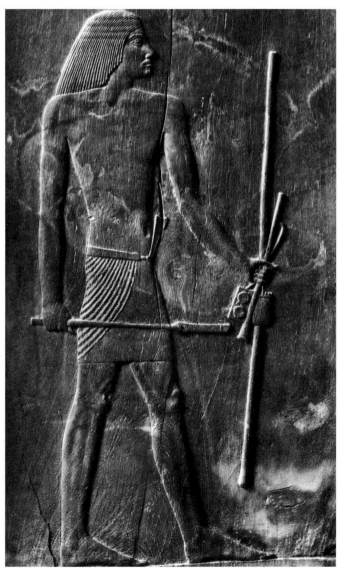

74. *PORTRAIT PANEL OF HESY-RA,* from Saqqara.
c. 2660 B.C. Wood, height 45″ (114.3 cm). Egyptian Museum, Cairo

frontal view, head and legs in profile. Apparently this formula was worked out so as to show the pharaoh (and all persons of significance who move in the penumbra of his divinity) in the most complete way possible. And since the scenes depict solemn and, as it were, timeless rituals, our artist did not have to concern himself with the fact that this method of representing the human body made almost any kind of movement or action practically impossible. In fact, the frozen quality of the image would seem especially suited to the divine nature of the pharaoh; ordinary mortals *act*, he simply *is*.

Whenever physical activity demanding any sort of effort or strain must be depicted, the Egyptian artist does not hesitate to abandon the composite view if necessary, for such activity is always performed by underlings whose dignity does not have to be preserved; thus, in our palette the two animal trainers and the four men carrying standards are shown in strict profile throughout (except for the eyes). The Egyptian style of representing the human figure, then, seems to have been created specifically for the purpose of conveying in visual form the majesty of the divine king; it must have originated among the artists working for the royal court. And it never lost its ceremonial, sacred flavor, even when, in later times, it had to serve other purposes as well.

## Third Dynasty

The full beauty of the style which we saw in the Narmer palette does not become apparent until about three centuries later, during the Third Dynasty, and especially under the reign of King Zoser, who was its greatest figure. From the tomb of Hesy-ra, one of Zoser's high officials, comes the masterly wooden relief (fig. 74) showing the deceased with the emblems of his rank. (These include writing materials, since the position of scribe was a highly honored one.) The view of the figure corresponds exactly to that of Narmer on

the palette, but the proportions are far more balanced and harmonious, and the carving of the physical details shows keen observation as well as great delicacy of touch.

TOMBS. When we speak of the Egyptians' attitude toward death and afterlife as expressed in their tombs, we must be careful to make it clear that we do not mean the attitude of the average Egyptian but only that of the small aristocratic caste clustered around the royal court. The tombs of the members of this class of high officials (who were often relatives of the royal family) are usually found in the immediate neighborhood of the pharaohs' tombs, and their shape and contents reflect, or are related to, the funerary monuments of the divine kings. We still have a great deal to learn about the origin and significance of Egyptian tombs, but there is reason to believe that the concept of afterlife we find in the so-called private tombs did not apply to ordinary mortals but only to the privileged few because of their association with the immortal pharaohs.

MASTABAS. The standard form of these tombs was the mastaba, a squarish mound faced with brick or stone, above the burial chamber, which was deep underground and linked to the mound by a shaft (figs. 75 and 76). Inside the

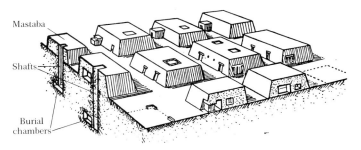

75. Group of mastabas (after A. Badawy). 4th Dynasty

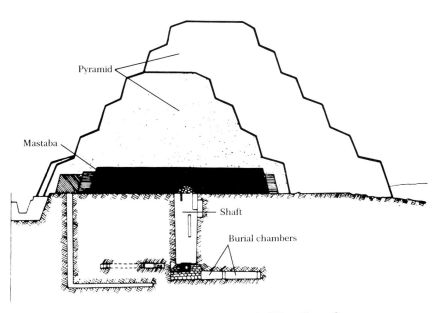

76. Transverse section of the Step Pyramid of King Zoser, Saqqara

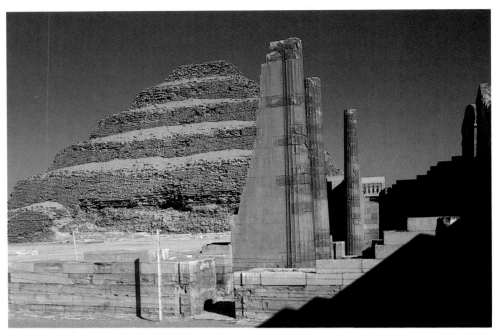

77. Step Pyramid of King Zoser, Saqqara. 3rd Dynasty. c. 2600 B.C.

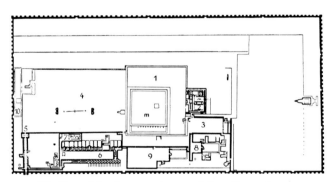

78. Plan of the funerary district of King Zoser, Saqqara
(M. Hirmer after J. P. Lauer). 1) pyramid (m = mastaba);
2) funerary temple; 3, 4, 6) courts; 5) entrance hall;
7) small temple; 8) court of North Palace;
9) court of South Palace; 10) southern tomb

pharaoh's lifetime as well as after. The most elaborate of these is the funerary district around the Step Pyramid of Zoser (fig. 78): enough of its architecture has survived to make us understand why its creator, Imhotep, came to be deified in later Egyptian tradition. He is the first artist whose name has been recorded in history, and deservedly so, since his achievement is most impressive even today.

COLUMNS. Egyptian architecture had begun with structures made of mud bricks, wood, reeds, and other light materials. Imhotep used cut-stone masonry, but his repertory of architectural forms still reflected shapes or devices developed for less enduring materials. Thus we find columns of several kinds—always "engaged" rather than free-standing—which echo the bundles of reeds or the wooden supports that used to be set into mud-brick walls in order to

mastaba is a chapel for offerings to the *ka* and a secret cubicle for the statue of the deceased. Royal mastabas grew to conspicuous size as early as the First Dynasty, and their exteriors could be elaborated to resemble a royal palace. During the Third Dynasty, they developed into step pyramids; the best known (and probably the first) is that of King Zoser (fig. 77), built over a traditional mastaba (see figs. 76 and 78). The pyramid itself, unlike later examples, is a completely solid structure whose only purpose seems to have been to serve as a great landmark.

FUNERARY DISTRICTS. The modern imagination, enamored of "the silence of the pyramids," is apt to create a false picture of these monuments. They were not erected as isolated structures in the middle of the desert, but as part of vast funerary districts, with temples and other buildings that were the scene of great religious celebrations during the

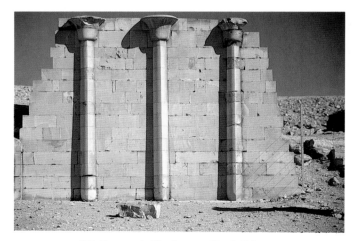

79. Papyrus half-columns, North Palace,
Funerary district of King Zoser, Saqqara

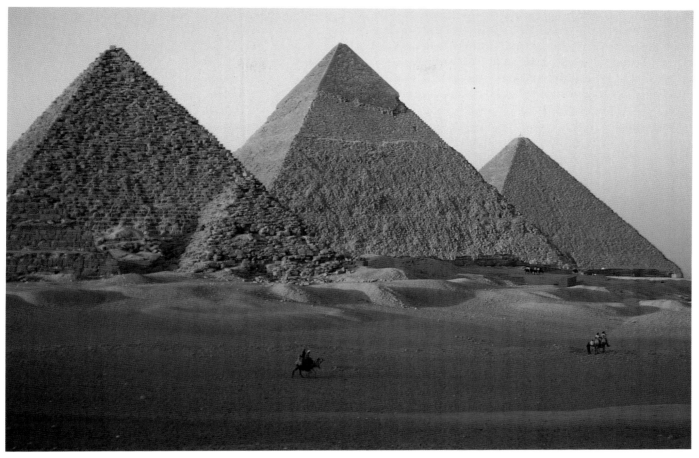

80. The Pyramids of Mycerinus (c. 2470 B.C.), Chefren (c. 2500 B.C.), and Cheops (c. 2530 B.C.), Giza

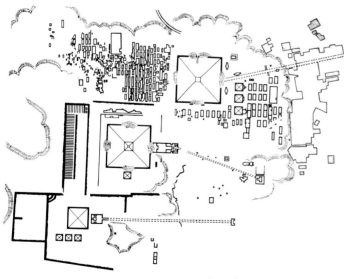

81. Plan of the pyramids at Giza

these forms have a clear-cut structural service to perform (such as supporting or enclosing), they are mere surface decoration. But let us look at the slender, tapering, fluted columns in figure 77, or the papyrus-shaped half-columns in figure 79: these do not simply decorate the walls to which they are attached, but interpret them and give them life, as it were. Their proportions, the feeling of strength or resilience they convey, their spacing, the degree to which they project, all share in this task.

We shall learn more about their expressive role when we discuss Greek architecture, which took over the Egyptian stone column and developed it further. For the time being, let us note one additional factor that may enter into the design and use of such columns: announcing the symbolic purpose of the building. The papyrus half-columns in figure 79 are linked with Lower Egypt (compare the papyrus plants in fig. 72); hence they appear in the North Palace of Zoser's funerary district. The South Palace has columns of different shape to evoke its association with Upper Egypt.

## Fourth Dynasty

PYRAMIDS OF GIZA. The development of the pyramid reaches its climax during the Fourth Dynasty in the famous triad of great pyramids at Giza (figs. 80 and 81), all of them of the familiar, smooth-sided shape. They originally had an

strengthen them. But the very fact that these members no longer had their original functional purpose made it possible for Imhotep and his fellow architects to redesign them so as to make them serve a new, *expressive* purpose. The notion that architectural forms can express anything may seem difficult to grasp at first; today we tend to assume that unless

outer casing of carefully dressed stone, which has disappeared except near the top of the Pyramid of Chefren. Each of the three differs slightly from the others in details of design and construction; the essential features are shown in the section of the earliest and largest, that of Cheops (fig. 82): the burial chamber is now near the center of the structure, rather than below ground as in the Step Pyramid of Zoser. Clustered about the three great pyramids are several smaller ones and a large number of mastabas for members of the royal family and high officials, but the unified funerary district of Zoser has given way to a simpler arrangement; adjoining each of the great pyramids to the east is a funerary temple, from which a processional causeway leads to a second temple at a lower level, in the Nile valley, at a distance of about a third of a mile.

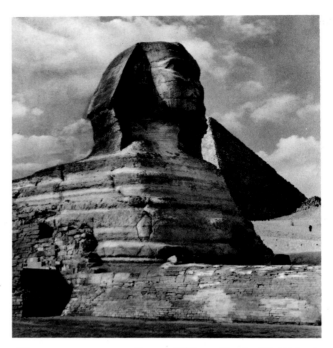

83. *THE GREAT SPHINX*, Giza. c. 2500 B.C. Height 65′ (19.8 m)

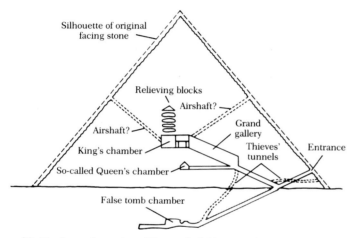

82. North-south section of Pyramid of Cheops (after L. Borchardt)

THE GREAT SPHINX. Next to the valley temple of the Pyramid of Chefren stands the Great Sphinx carved from the live rock (fig. 83), perhaps an even more impressive embodiment of divine kingship than the pyramids themselves. The royal head rising from the body of a lion towers to a height of 65 feet and once bore, in all probability, the features of Chefren (damage inflicted upon it during Islamic times has obscured the details of the face). Its awesome majesty is such that a thousand years later it could be regarded as an image of the sun-god.

Enterprises of this huge scale mark the high point of pharaonic power. After the end of the Fourth Dynasty (less than two centuries after Zoser) they were never attempted again, although pyramids on a much more modest scale continued to be built. The world has always marveled at the sheer size of the great pyramids as well as at the technical accomplishment they represent; but they have also come to be regarded as symbols of slave labor—thousands of men forced by cruel masters to serve the aggrandizement of absolute rulers. Such a picture may well be unjust: certain records have been preserved indicating that the labor was paid

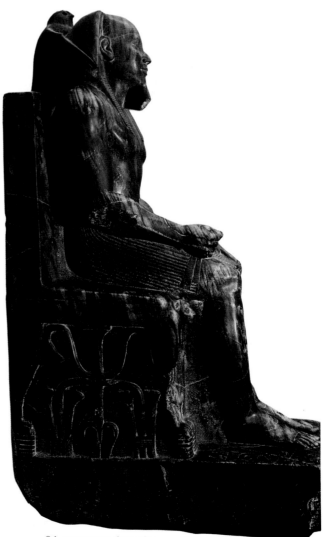

84. *CHEFREN*, from Giza. c. 2500 B.C. Diorite, height 66″ (167.7 cm). Egyptian Museum, Cairo

for, so that we are probably nearer the truth if we regard these monuments as vast public works providing economic security for a good part of the population.

PORTRAITURE. Apart from its architectural achievements, the chief glories of Egyptian art, during the Old Kingdom and later, are the portrait statues recovered from funerary temples and tombs. One of the finest is that of Chefren, from the valley temple of his pyramid (fig. 84). Carved of diorite, a stone of extreme hardness, it shows the king enthroned, with the falcon of the god Horus enfolding the back of the head with its wings (we encountered the association, in different form, in the Narmer palette, fig. 72). Here the Egyptian sculptor's "cubic" view of the human

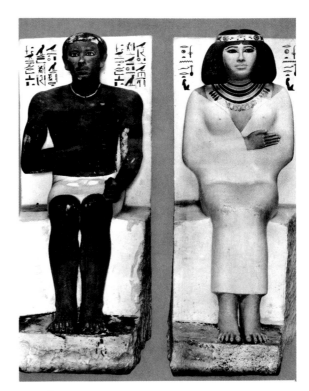

86. *PRINCE RAHOTEP AND HIS WIFE NOFRET.*
c. 2580 B.C. Painted limestone, height 47¼" (120 cm).
Egyptian Museum, Cairo

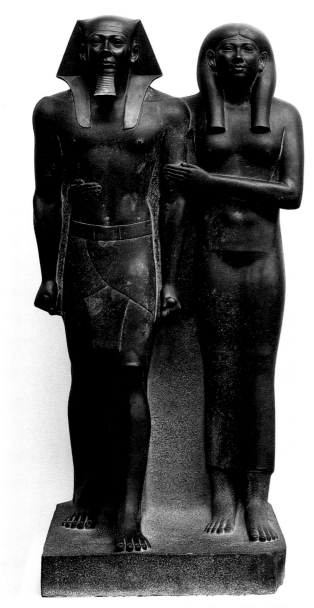

85. *MYCERINUS AND HIS QUEEN,* from Giza. 2599–2571 B.C.
Slate, height 54½" (142.3 cm).
Courtesy of Museum of Fine Arts, Boston

form appears in full force: clearly, the sculptor prepared the statue by drawing its front and side views on the faces of a rectangular block and then worked inward until these views met. The result is a figure almost overpowering in its three-dimensional firmness and immobility. Truly it is a magnificent vessel for the spirit! The body, well proportioned and powerfully built, is completely impersonal; only the face suggests some individual traits, as will be seen if we compare it with that of Mycerinus (fig. 85), Chefren's successor and the builder of the third and smallest pyramid at Giza.

Mycerinus, accompanied by his queen, is standing. Both have the left foot placed forward, yet there is no hint of a forward movement. Since the two are almost of the same height, they afford an interesting comparison of male and female beauty as interpreted by one of the finest of Old Kingdom sculptors, who knew not only how to contrast the structure of the two bodies but also how to emphasize the soft, swelling forms of the queen through her light and close-fitting gown.

The sculptor who carved the statues of Prince Rahotep and his wife Nofret (fig. 86) was less subtle in this respect. They owe their strikingly lifelike appearance to their vivid coloring, which they must have shared with other such statues but which has survived completely intact only in a few instances. The darker body color of the prince has no individual significance; it is the standard masculine complexion in Egyptian art. The eyes have been inlaid with shining quartz to make them look as alive as possible, and the portrait character of the faces is very pronounced.

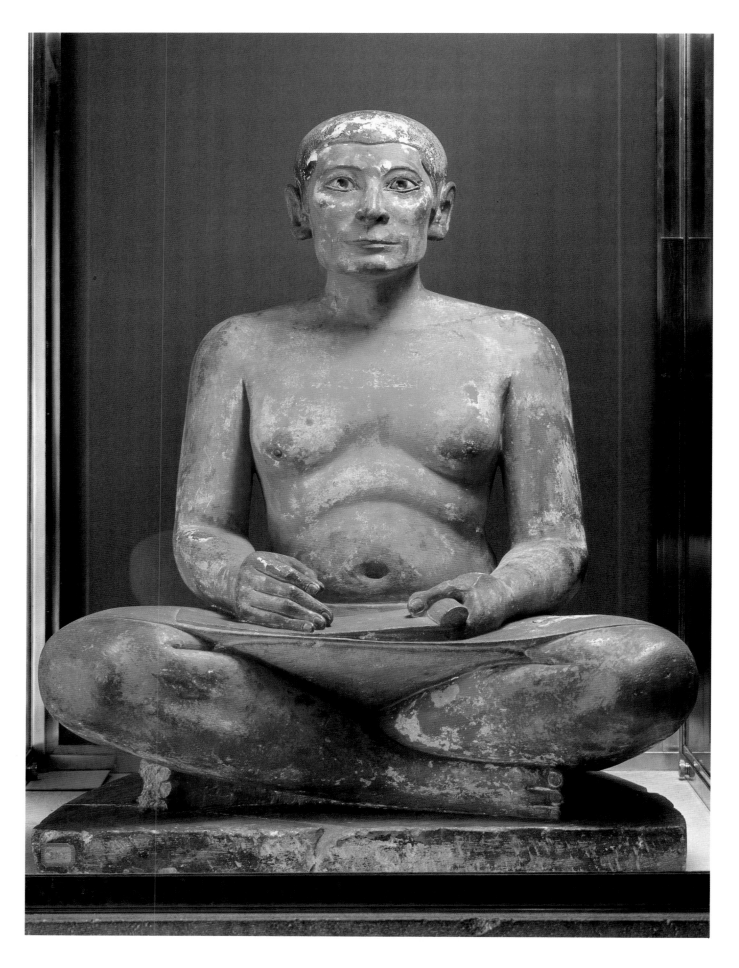

Standing and seated figures comprise the basic repertory of Egyptian large-scale sculpture in the round. At the end of the Fourth Dynasty, a third pose was added, as symmetrical and immobile as the first two: that of the scribe squatting cross-legged on the ground. The finest of these scribes dates from the beginning of the Fifth Dynasty (fig. 87). The name of the sitter (in whose tomb at Saqqara the statue was found) is unknown, but we must not think of him as a lowly secretary waiting to take dictation; rather, the figure represents a high court official, a "master of sacred—and secret—letters," and the solid, incisive treatment of form bespeaks the dignity of his station (which in the beginning seems to have been restricted to the sons of pharaohs). Our example stands out not only for the vividly alert expression of the face, but also for the individual handling of the torso, which records the somewhat flabby body of a man past middle age.

Another invention of Old Kingdom art was the portrait bust, a species of sculpture so familiar that we tend to take it for granted. Yet its origin is puzzling: was it simply an abbreviated statue, a cheaper substitute for a full-length figure? Or did it have a distinct purpose of its own, perhaps as a remote echo of the Neolithic custom of keeping the head of the deceased separate from the rest of his body (see page 81)? Be that as it may, the earliest of these busts (fig. 88) is also the finest—indeed, one of the great portraits of all time. In this noble head, we find a memorable image of the sitter's individual character as well as a most subtle differentiation between the solid, immutable shape of the skull and its soft, flexible covering of flesh.

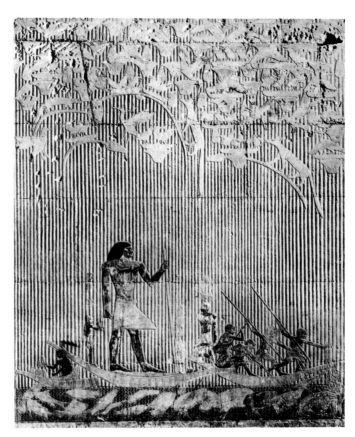

89. *TI WATCHING A HIPPOPOTAMUS HUNT.*
Painted limestone relief. c. 2400 B.C. Tomb of Ti, Saqqara

87. *(opposite) SEATED SCRIBE,* from Saqqara. c. 2400 B.C. Limestone, height 21″ (53.3 cm). Musée du Louvre, Paris

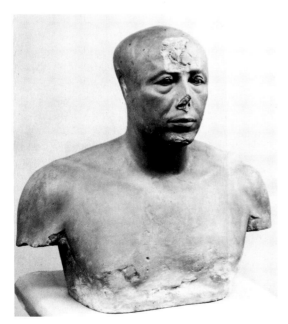

88. *BUST OF PRINCE ANKH-HAF,* from Giza. c. 2520 B.C. Limestone, lifesize. Museum of Fine Arts, Boston

TOMB DECORATION. Before we leave the Old Kingdom, let us look briefly at some of the scenes of daily life from the offering chambers of nonroyal tombs, such as that of the architectural overseer Ti at Saqqara. The hippopotamus hunt in figure 89 is of special interest to us because of its landscape setting. The background of the relief is formed by a papyrus thicket; the stems of the plants make a regular, rippling pattern that erupts in the top zone into an agitated scene of nesting birds menaced by small predators. The water in the bottom zone, marked by a zigzag pattern, is equally crowded with struggling hippopotamuses and fish. All these, as well as the hunters in the first boat, are acutely observed and full of action; only Ti himself, standing in the second boat, is immobile, as if he belonged to a different world. His pose is that of the funerary portrait reliefs and statues (compare fig. 74), and he towers above the other men, since he is more important than they.

His size also lifts him out of the context of the hunt—he neither directs nor supervises it, but simply observes. His passive role is characteristic of the representations of the deceased in all such scenes from the Old Kingdom. It seems to be a subtle way of conveying the fact that the body is dead but the spirit is alive and aware of the pleasures of this world, though the man can no longer participate in them directly. We should also note that these scenes of daily life do not represent the dead man's favorite pastimes; if they did, he would be looking back, and such nostalgia is quite alien

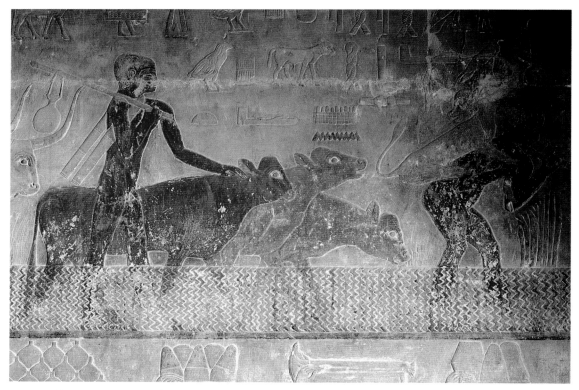

90. *CATTLE FORDING A RIVER.* Detail of a painted limestone relief. c. 2400 B.C. Tomb of Ti, Saqqara

to the spirit of Old Kingdom tombs. It has been shown, in fact, that these scenes form a seasonal cycle, a sort of perpetual calendar of recurrent human activities for the spirit of the deceased to watch year in and year out. For the artist, on the other hand, these scenes offered a welcome opportunity to widen his powers of observation, so that in details we often find astounding bits of realism.

Another relief from the tomb of Ti shows some cattle fording a river (fig. 90); one of the herders carries a newborn calf on his back to keep it from drowning, and the frightened animal turns its head to look back at its mother, who answers with an equally anxious glance. Such sympathetic portrayal of an emotional relationship is as delightful as it is unexpected in Old Kingdom art. It will be some time before we encounter anything similar in the human realm. But eventually we shall even see the deceased abandoning his passive, timeless stance to participate in scenes of daily life.

# THE MIDDLE KINGDOM

After the collapse of centralized pharaonic power at the end of the Sixth Dynasty, Egypt entered a period of political disturbances and ill fortune that was to last almost 700 years. During most of this time, effective authority lay in the hands of local or regional overlords, who revived the old rivalry of North and South. Many dynasties followed one another in rapid succession, but only two, the Eleventh and Twelfth, are worthy of note. The latter constitute the Middle Kingdom (2134–1785 B.C.), when a series of able rulers managed to reassert themselves against the provincial nobility. How-

ever, the spell of divine kingship, having once been broken, never regained its old effectiveness, and the authority of the Middle Kingdom pharaohs tended to be personal rather than institutional. Soon after the close of the Twelfth Dynasty, the weakened country was invaded by the Hyksos, a western Asiatic people of somewhat mysterious origin, who seized the Delta area and ruled it for 150 years until their expulsion by the princes of Thebes about 1570 B.C.

PORTRAITURE. The unquiet spirit of the times is well reflected in Middle Kingdom art. We find it especially in the new type of royal portrait that marks the Twelfth Dynasty, such as the one in figure 91. There is a real sense of shock on first encountering this strangely modern face; the serene assurance of the Old Kingdom has given way to a brooding, troubled expression that bespeaks a new level of self-awareness. Deprived of its royal trappings, our fragment displays so uncompromising a realism, physical as well as psychological, that at first glance the link with the sculptural tradition of the past seems broken entirely. Here is another enduring achievement of Egyptian art, destined to live on in Roman portraiture and in the portraiture of the Renaissance.

PAINTING AND RELIEF. A loosening of established rules also makes itself felt in Middle Kingdom painting and relief, where it leads to all sorts of interesting departures from convention. They occur most conspicuously in the decoration of the tombs of local princes at Beni Hasan, which have survived destruction better than most Middle Kingdom monu-

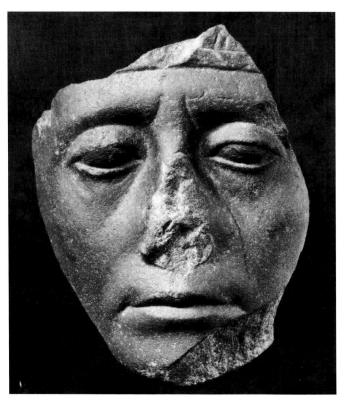

91. *PORTRAIT OF SESOSTRIS III.* c. 1850 B.C.
Quartzite, height 6⅛″ (15.7 cm). The Metropolitan
Museum of Art, New York. Gift of Edward S. Harkness, 1926

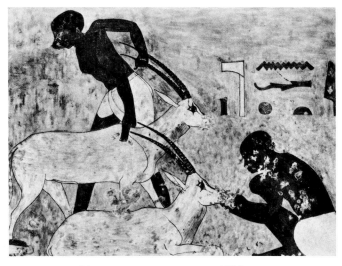

92. *FEEDING THE ORYXES.* c. 1920 B.C.
Tomb of Khnum-hotep, Beni Hasan

ments because they are carved into the living rock. The mural *Feeding the Oryxes* (fig. 92) comes from one of these rock-cut tombs, that of Khnum-hotep. (As the emblem of the prince's domain, the oryx antelope seems to have been a sort of honored pet in his household.) According to the standards of Old Kingdom art, all the figures ought to share the same ground-line, or the second oryx and its attendant ought to be placed above the first; instead, the painter has introduced a secondary ground-line only slightly higher than the primary one, and as a result the two groups are related in a way that closely approximates normal appearances. His interest in exploring spatial effects can also be seen in the awkward but quite bold foreshortening of the shoulders of the two attendants. If we cover up the hieroglyphic signs, which emphasize the flatness of the wall, we can "read" the forms in depth with surprising ease.

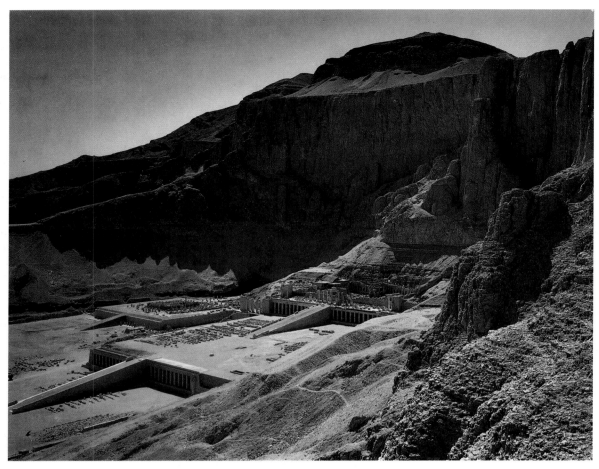

93. Funerary Temple of Hatshepsut, Deir el-Bahari. 18th Dynasty, c. 1480 B.C.

# THE NEW KINGDOM

The five hundred years following the expulsion of the Hyksos, and comprising the Eighteenth, Nineteenth, and Twentieth dynasties, represent a third Golden Age of Egypt. The country, once more united under strong and efficient kings, extended its frontiers far to the east, into Palestine and Syria (hence this period is also known as the Empire). During the climactic period of power and prosperity, between c. 1500 and the end of the reign of Ramesses III in 1162 B.C., tremendous architectural projects were carried out, centering on the region of the new capital, Thebes, while the royal tombs reached unequaled material splendor.

The divine kingship of the pharaohs was now asserted in a new way: by association with the god Amun, whose identity had been fused with that of the sun-god Ra, and who became the supreme deity, ruling the lesser gods much as the pharaoh towered above the provincial nobility. But this very development produced an unexpected threat to royal authority; the priests of Amun grew into a caste of such wealth and power that the pharaoh could maintain his position only with their consent. Amenhotep IV, the most remarkable figure of the Eighteenth Dynasty, tried to defeat them by proclaiming his faith in a single god, the sun disk Aten. He changed his name to Akhenaten, closed the Amun temples,

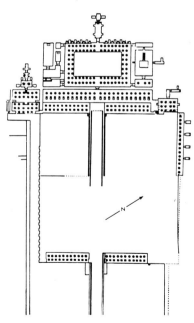

94. Plan of Funerary Temple of Queen Hatshepsut (after Lange)

and moved the capital to central Egypt, near the modern Tell el'Amarna. His attempt to place himself at the head of a new monotheistic faith, however, did not outlast his reign (1365–1347 B.C.), and under his successors orthodoxy was speedily restored. During the long decline that began about 1000 B.C., the country became increasingly priest-ridden, until, under Greek and Roman rule, Egyptian civilization came to an end in a welter of esoteric religious doctrines.

New Kingdom art covers a vast range of styles and quality, from rigid conservatism to brilliant inventiveness, from oppressively massive ostentation to the most delicate refinement. Like the art of Imperial Rome fifteen hundred years later, it is almost impossible to summarize in terms of a representative sampling. Different strands are interwoven into a fabric so complex that any choice of monuments is bound to seem arbitrary. All we can hope to accomplish is to convey some of the flavor of its variety.

## Architecture

TEMPLE OF HATSHEPSUT. Among the architectural enterprises that have survived from the early years of the New Kingdom, the outstanding one is the Funerary Temple of Queen Hatshepsut, built about 1480 B.C. against the rocky cliffs of Deir el-Bahari (figs. 93 and 94) and dedicated to Amun and several other deities. The worshiper is led toward the holy of holies—a small chamber driven deep into the rock—through three large courts on ascending levels, linked by ramps among long colonnades: a processional road reminiscent of those at Giza, but with the mountain instead of a pyramid at the end. It is this magnificent union of architecture and nature—note how ramps and colonnades echo the shape of the cliff—that makes Hatshepsut's temple the rival of any of the Old Kingdom monuments.

TEMPLE AT LUXOR. The later rulers of the New Kingdom continued to build funerary temples, but an ever greater share of their architectural energies was devoted to huge imperial temples of Amun, the supreme god whom the reigning monarch traditionally claimed as his father. The temple at Luxor, across the Nile from Thebes, dedicated to Amun, his wife Mut, and their son Khonsu, was begun about 1390 B.C. by Amenhotep III but was extended and completed more than a century later. Its plan is characteristic of the general pattern of later Egyptian temples. The façade consists of two massive walls, with sloping sides, flanking the entrance; this unit is known as the gateway or pylon (fig. 95, far left, and fig. 96) and leads to the court (fig. 97, A). The court, in this case, is a parallelogram, because

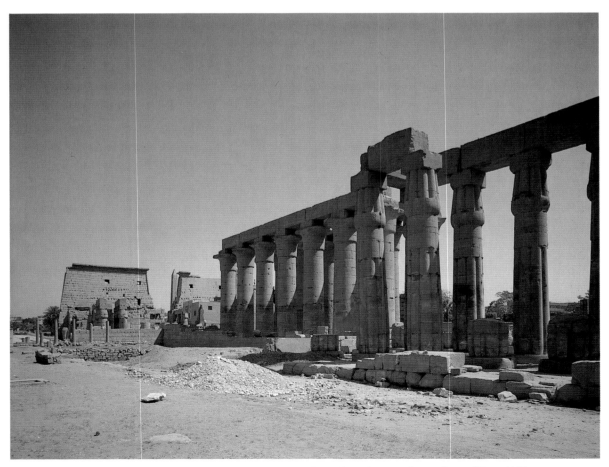

95. Court and pylon of Ramesses II, c. 1260 B.C.; colonnade and court of Amenhotep III, c. 1390 B.C.
Temple of Amun-Mut-Khonsu, Luxor

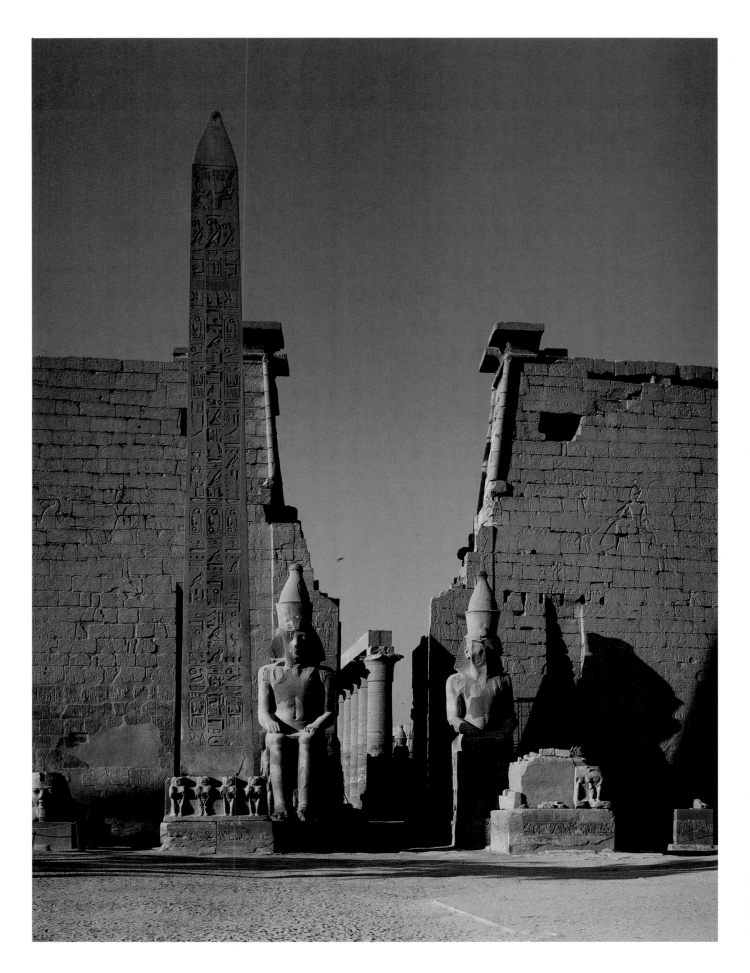

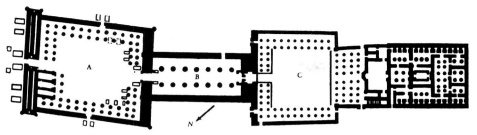

97. Plan of the Temple of Amun-Mut-Khonsu, Luxor
(after N. de Garis Davies)

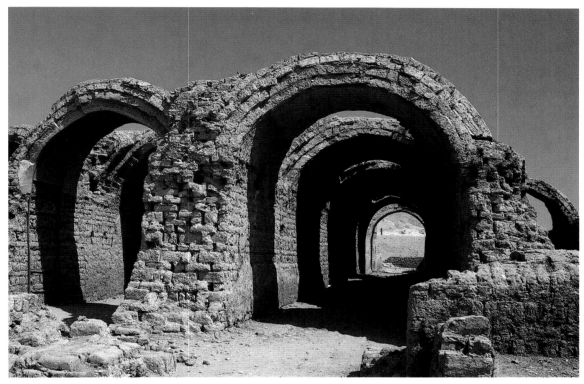

98. Brick storehouses, Mortuary Temple of Ramesses II,
West Thebes. c. 1260 B.C.

Ramesses II, who added it to the temple that had been planned under Amenhotep III, changed the axis of his court slightly, so as to conform with the direction of the Nile. We then enter a pillared hall, which brings us to the second court (fig. 97, B and C; fig. 95, center and right). On its far side we find another pillared hall. Beyond it, the temple proper begins: a series of symmetrically arranged halls and chapels shielding the holy of holies, a square room with four columns (fig. 97, extreme right).

The entire sequence of courts, halls, and temple was enclosed by high walls that shut off the outside world. Except

96. (*opposite*) Pylon of Ramesses II,
Temple of Amun-Mut-Khonsu, Luxor. c. 1260 B.C.

for the monumental façade (fig. 96), such a structure is designed to be experienced from within; ordinary worshipers were confined to the courts and could but marvel at the forest of columns that screened the dark recesses of the sanctuary. The columns had to be closely spaced, for they supported the stone lintels of the ceiling, and these had to be short to keep them from breaking under their own weight. Yet the architect has consciously exploited this condition by making the columns far heavier than they need be. As a result, the beholder feels almost crushed by their sheer mass. The overawing effect is certainly impressive, but also rather vulgar when measured against the earlier masterpieces of Egyptian architecture. We need only compare the papyrus columns of the colonnade of Amenhotep III with their remote ancestors in Zoser's North Palace (fig. 79) in order to realize how little of the genius of Imhotep has survived at Luxor.

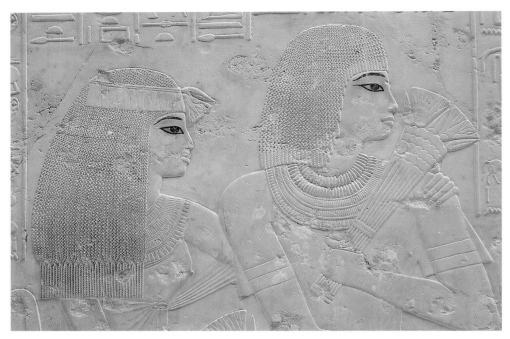

99. *MAI AND HIS WIFE UREL.* Detail of a limestone relief. c. 1375 B.C. Tomb of Ramose, Thebes

BRICK ARCHITECTURE. The massive vastness of their tombs and temples makes us think that the Egyptians built mainly in stone. Yet, except where absolute durability was essential for religious reasons, they used sun-dried mud bricks, a cheaper and more convenient material. The achievements of Egyptian brick architecture have attracted comparatively little interest so far, and much of the work has been destroyed, but the few well-preserved structures, such as the storehouses attached to the mortuary temple of Ramesses II (fig. 98), show a masterful command of brick building techniques. These barrel vaults, with a span of over 13 feet, anticipate the engineering skill of the Romans.

## Akhenaten

Of the great projects built by Akhenaten hardly anything remains above ground. He must have been a revolutionary not only in his religious beliefs but in his artistic tastes as well, consciously fostering a new style and a new ideal of beauty in his choice of masters. The contrast with the past becomes strikingly evident if we compare a head in low relief from the Tomb of Ramose, done at the end of the reign of Amenhotep III (fig. 99), with a low-relief portrait of Akhenaten that is only about ten years later in date (fig. 100). Figure 99 shows the traditional style at its best; the wonderful subtlety of the carving—the precision and refinement of its lines—makes the head of Akhenaten seem at first glance like a brutal caricature. And the latter work is indeed an extreme statement of the new ideal, with its oddly haggard features and over-emphatic, undulating outlines. Still, we can perceive its kinship with the justly famous bust of Akhenaten's queen, Nofretete (fig. 101), one of the masterpieces of the "Akhenaten style."

What distinguishes this style is not greater realism so much as a new sense of form that seeks to unfreeze the traditional immobility of Egyptian art; not only the contours

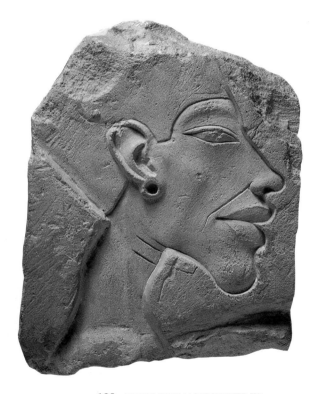

100. *AKHENATEN (AMENHOTEP IV).*
c. 1360 B.C. Limestone, height 3⅛″ (8.1 cm).
Ägyptisches Museum, Staatliche Museen, Berlin

but the plastic shapes, too, seem more pliable and relaxed, anti-geometric, as it were. We find these qualities again in the delightful fragment of a wall painting showing the daughters of Akhenaten (fig. 102). Their playful gestures and informal poses seem in defiance of all rules of pharaonic dignity.

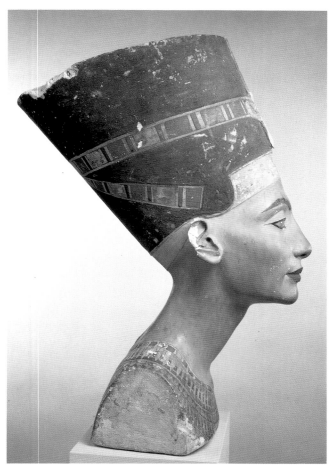

101. *QUEEN NOFRETETE*. c. 1360 B.C. Limestone, height 19″ (50 cm).
Ägyptisches Museum, Staatliche Museen, Berlin

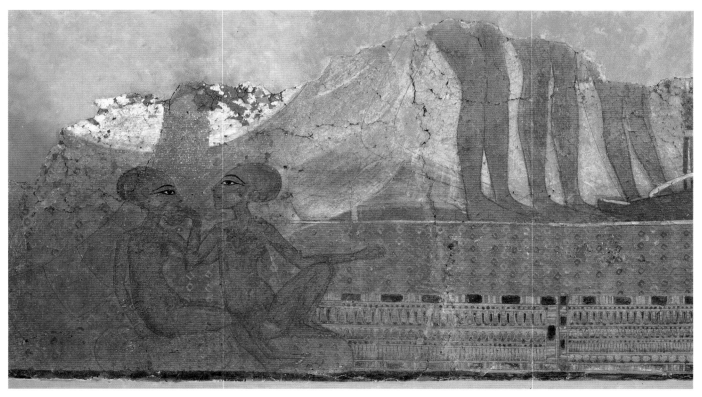

102. *THE DAUGHTERS OF AKHENATEN*. c. 1360 B.C. 11¾ × 16″ (30 × 40.7 cm). The Oriental Institute, University of Chicago

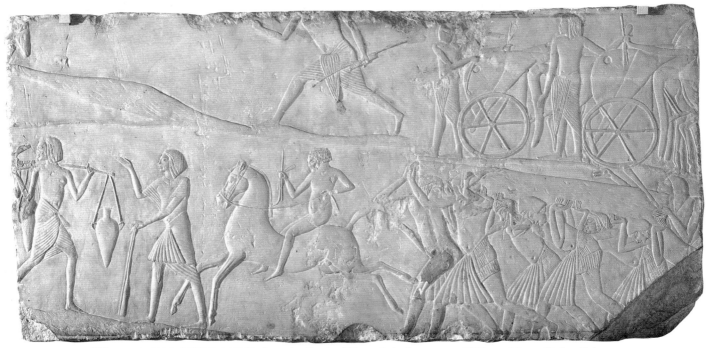

103. *WORKMEN CARRYING A BEAM,* from the Tomb of Horemheb, Saqqara. c. 1325 B.C. Museo Civico, Bologna

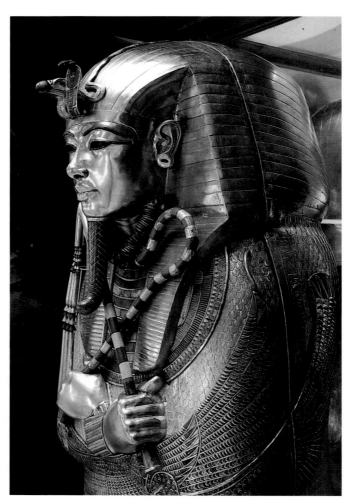

104. Cover of the coffin of Tutankhamen. c. 1340 B.C.
Gold, inlaid with enamel and semiprecious stones,
height of whole 72⅞" (185 cm). Egyptian Museum, Cairo

The old religious tradition was quickly restored after Akhenaten's death, but the artistic innovations he encouraged could be felt in Egyptian art for some time to come. The scene of workmen struggling with a heavy beam (fig. 103), from the Tomb of Horemheb at Saqqara, shows a freedom and expressiveness that would have been unthinkable in earlier times.

## Tutankhamen

Even the face of Akhenaten's successor, Tutankhamen, as it appears on his gold coffin cover, betrays an echo of the Akhenaten style (fig. 104). Tutankhamen, who died at the age of eighteen, owes his fame entirely to the accident that his is the only pharaonic tomb discovered in our times with most of its contents undisturbed. The sheer material value of the tomb (Tutankhamen's gold coffin alone weighs 250 pounds) makes it understandable that grave robbing has been practiced in Egypt ever since the Old Kingdom. To us, the exquisite workmanship of the coffin cover, with the rich play of colored inlays against the polished gold surfaces, is even more impressive.

As unique in its way as the gold coffin is a painted chest from the same tomb, showing the youthful king in battle and hunting scenes (fig. 105). These had been traditional subjects since the late years of the Old Kingdom, but here they are done with astonishing freshness, at least so far as the animals are concerned. While the king and his horse-drawn chariot remain frozen against the usual blank background filled with hieroglyphs, the same background in the right-hand half of the scene suddenly turns into a desert; the surface is covered with stippled dots to suggest sand, desert plants are strewn across it in considerable variety, and the animals stampede over it helter-skelter, without any ground-lines to impede their flight.

Here is an aspect of Egyptian painting that we rarely see on the walls of tombs; perhaps this lively scattering of forms against a landscape background existed only on the miniature scale of the scenes on Tutankhamen's chest, and even there it became possible only as a result of the Akhenaten style. How these animals-in-landscape survived in later Egyptian painting we do not know, but they must have survived somehow, for their resemblance to Islamic miniatures done more than 2,000 years later is far too striking to be ignored.

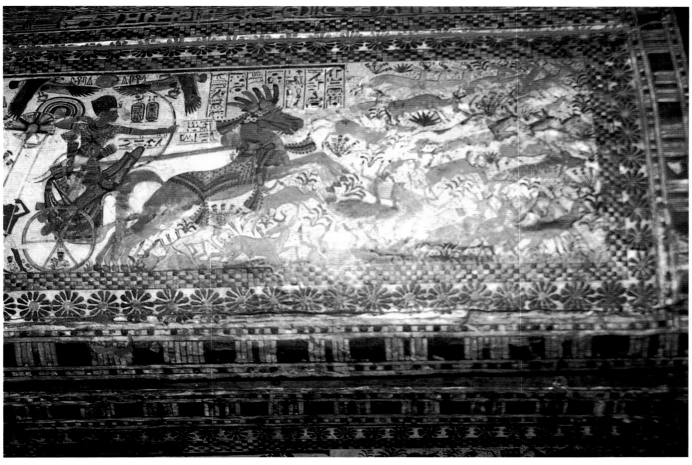

105. *TUTANKHAMEN HUNTING*, from a painted chest found in the king's tomb, Thebes. c. 1340 B.C. Length of scene c. 20″ (50.7 cm). Egyptian Museum, Cairo

# CHAPTER THREE
# ANCIENT NEAR EASTERN ART

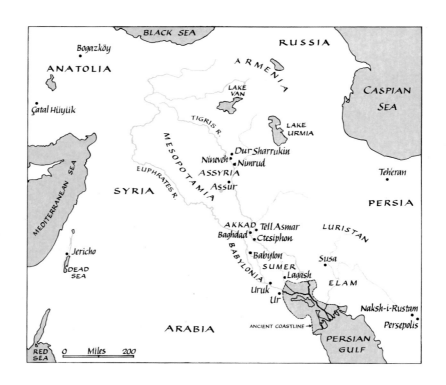

# SUMERIAN ART

It is an odd and astonishing fact that human civilization should have emerged into the light of history in two separate places at just about the same time. Between 3500 and 3000 B.C., when Egypt was being united under pharaonic rule, another great civilization arose in Mesopotamia, the "land between the rivers." And for close to 3,000 years, the two rival centers retained their distinct character, even though they had contact with each other from their earliest beginnings and their destinies were interwoven in many ways. The pressures that forced the inhabitants of both regions to abandon the pattern of Neolithic village life may well have been the same (see fig. 41). But the valley of the Tigris and Euphrates rivers, unlike that of the Nile, is not a narrow fertile strip protected by deserts on either side; it resembles a wide, shallow trough with few natural defenses, crisscrossed by two great rivers and their tributaries, and easily encroached upon from any direction.

Thus the facts of geography tended to discourage the idea of uniting the entire area under a single head. Rulers who had this ambition did not appear, so far as we know, until about a thousand years after the beginnings of Mesopotamian civilization, and they succeeded in carrying it out only for brief periods and at the cost of almost continuous warfare. As a consequence, the political history of ancient Mesopotamia has no underlying theme of the sort that divine kingship provides for Egypt; local rivalries, foreign incursions, the sudden upsurge and equally sudden collapse of military power—these are its substance. Against such a disturbed background, the continuity of cultural and artistic traditions seems all the more remarkable. This common heritage is very largely the creation of the founders of Mesopotamian civilization, whom we call Sumerians after the region of Sumer, which they inhabited, near the confluence of the Tigris and Euphrates.

The origin of the Sumerians remains obscure. Their language is unrelated to any other known tongue. Sometime before 4000 B.C., they came to southern Mesopotamia from Persia, and there, within the next thousand years, they founded a number of city-states and developed their distinctive form of writing in cuneiform (wedge-shaped) characters on clay tablets. This transitional phase, corresponding to the predynastic period in Egypt, is called "protoliterate"; it leads to the early dynastic period, from about 3000 to 2340 B.C. The first evidence of Bronze Age culture is seen in Sumer around 4000 B.C.

ARCHAEOLOGICAL CONDITIONS. Unfortunately, the tangible remains of Sumerian civilization are extremely scanty compared to those of ancient Egypt; building stone being unavailable in Mesopotamia, the Sumerians used mud brick and wood, so that almost nothing is left of their architecture except the foundations. Nor did they share the Egyptians' concern with the hereafter, although some richly endowed tombs—in the shape of vaulted chambers below ground—of the early dynastic period have been found in the city of Ur. Our knowledge of Sumerian civilization thus depends very largely on chance fragments brought to light by excavation, including vast numbers of inscribed clay tablets.

Yet we have learned enough to form a general picture of the achievements of this vigorous, inventive, and disciplined people.

RELIGION. Each Sumerian city-state had its own local god, who was regarded as its "king" and owner. It also had a human ruler, the steward of the divine sovereign, who led the people in serving the deity. The local god, in return, was expected to plead the cause of his subjects among his fellow deities who controlled the forces of nature such as wind and weather, water, fertility, and the heavenly bodies. Nor was the idea of divine ownership treated as a mere pious fiction; the god was quite literally believed to own not only the territory of the city-state but also the labor power of the population and its products. All these were subject to his commands, transmitted to the people by his human steward. The result was an economic system that has been dubbed "theocratic socialism," a planned society whose administrative center was the temple. It was the temple that controlled the pooling of labor and resources for communal enterprises, such as the building of dikes or irrigation ditches, and it collected and distributed a considerable part of the harvest. All this required the keeping of detailed written records. Hence we need not be surprised to find that the texts of early Sumerian inscriptions deal very largely with economic and administrative rather than religious matters, although writing was a priestly privilege.

ARCHITECTURE. The dominant role of the temple as the center of both spiritual and physical existence is strikingly conveyed by the layout of Sumerian cities. The houses clustered about a sacred area that was a vast architectural complex embracing not only shrines but workshops, storehouses, and scribes' quarters as well. In their midst, on a raised platform, stood the temple of the local god. These platforms soon reached the height of true mountains, comparable to the pyramids of Egypt in the immensity of effort required and in their effect as great landmarks that tower above the featureless plain. They are known as ziggurats.

The most famous of them, the biblical Tower of Babel, has been completely destroyed, but a much earlier example, built shortly before 3000 B.C. and thus several centuries older than the first of the pyramids, survives at Warka, the site of the Sumerian city of Uruk (called Erech in the Bible). The mound, its sloping sides reinforced by solid brick masonry, rises to a height of 40 feet; stairs and ramps lead up to the platform on which stands the sanctuary, called the "White Temple" because of its whitewashed brick exterior (figs. 106 and 107). Its heavy walls, articulated by regularly spaced projections and recesses, are sufficiently well preserved to suggest something of the original appearance of the structure. The main room, or cella (fig. 108), where sacrifices were offered before the statue of the god, is a narrow hall that runs the entire length of the temple and is flanked by a series of smaller chambers. But the main entrance to the cella is on the southwest side, rather than on the side facing the stairs or on one of the narrow sides of the temple, as one might expect. In order to understand the reason for this, we must view the ziggurat and temple as a whole: the entire

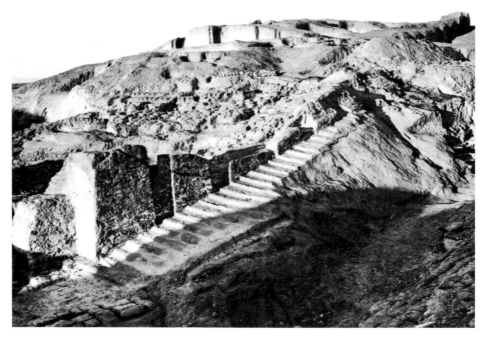

106. The "White Temple" on its ziggurat, Uruk (Warka), Iraq. c. 3500–3000 B.C.

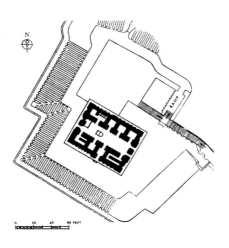

107. Plan of the "White Temple" on its ziggurat (after H. Frankfort)

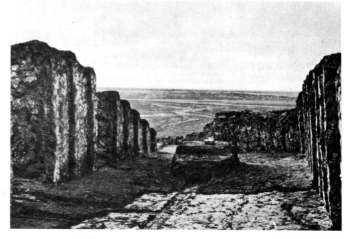

108. Interior of the cella, "White Temple"

complex is planned in such a way that the worshiper, starting at the bottom of the stairs on the east side, is forced to go around as many corners as possible before he reaches the cella. The processional path, in other words, resembles a sort of angular spiral.

This "bent-axis approach" is a fundamental characteristic of Mesopotamian religious architecture, in contrast to the straight, single axis of Egyptian temples (see fig. 97). During the following 2,500 years, it was elaborated into ever taller and more towerlike ziggurats rising in multiple stages. The one built by King Urnammu at Ur about 2500 B.C. (fig. 109) had three levels. Little is left of the upper two stages, but the bottom one, some 50 feet high, has survived fairly well, and its facing of brick has been restored. What was the impulse behind these structures? Certainly not the kind of pride attributed to the builders of the Tower of Babel in the

Old Testament. They reflect, rather, the widespread belief that mountaintops are the dwelling places of the gods (we need only think of the Mount Olympus of the Greeks). The Sumerians felt they could provide a fit residence for a deity only by creating their own artificial mountains.

STONE SCULPTURE. The image of the god to whom the "White Temple" was dedicated is lost—it was probably Anu, the god of the sky—but a splendid female head of white marble from the same period at Uruk (Warka) may well have belonged to another cult statue (fig. 110). The eyes and eyebrows were originally inlaid with colored materials, and the hair was covered with a "wig" of gold or copper. The rest of the figure, which must have been close to lifesize, probably consisted of wood. As an artistic achievement, this head is on the level of the finest works of Egyptian Old Kingdom

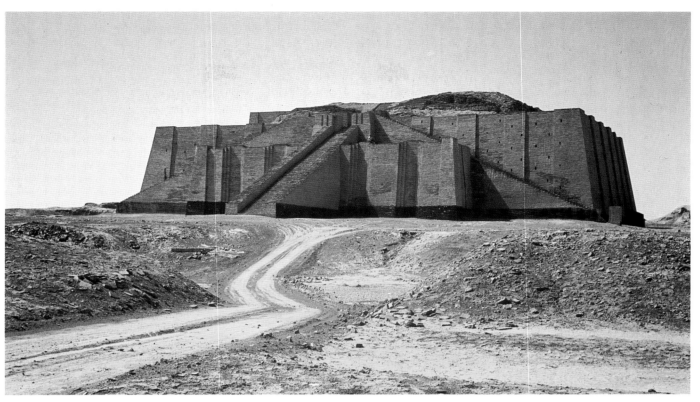

109. Ziggurat of King Urnammu, Ur (El Muqeiyar), Iraq. c. 2500 B.C.

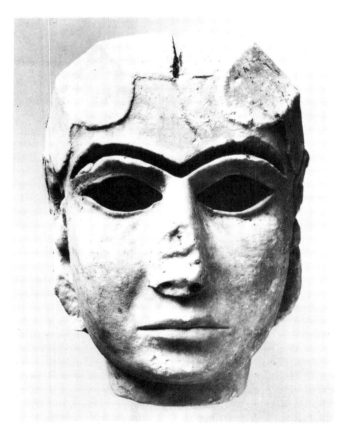

110. *FEMALE HEAD*, from Uruk (Warka). c. 3500–3000 B.C.
Marble, height 8″ (20.3 cm). Iraq Museum, Baghdad

sculpture. The softly swelling cheeks, the delicate curves of the lips, combined with the steady gaze of the huge eyes, create a balance of sensuousness and severity that seems worthy of any goddess.

It was the geometric and expressive aspects of the Uruk head, rather than the realistic ones, that survived in the stone sculpture of the early dynastic period, as seen in a group of figures from Tell Asmar (fig. 111) carved about five centuries later than the head. The tallest, about 30 inches high, represents Abu, the god of vegetation; the second largest, a mother goddess; the others, priests and worshipers. The two deities are distinguished from the rest not only by their size but by the larger diameter of the pupils of their eyes, although the eyes of all the figures are enormous. Their insistent stare is emphasized by colored inlays, which are still in place. The entire group must have stood in the cella of the Abu temple, the priests and worshipers confronting the two gods and communicating with them through their eyes.

"Representation" here had a very direct meaning: the gods were believed to be present in their images, and the statues of the worshipers served as stand-ins for the persons they portrayed, offering prayers or transmitting messages to the deity in their stead. Yet none of them indicates any attempt to achieve a real likeness. The bodies as well as the faces are rigorously simplified and schematic, in order to avoid distracting attention from the eyes, "the windows of the soul." If the Egyptian sculptor's sense of form was essentially cubic, that of the Sumerian was based on the cone and cylinder. Arms and legs have the roundness of pipes, and the long skirts worn by all these figures are as smoothly curved as if they had been turned on a lathe. Even in later times, when Mesopotamian sculpture had acquired a far richer repertory of shapes, this quality asserted itself again and again.

BRONZE OR ASSEMBLED SCULPTURE. The conic-cylindrical simplification of the Tell Asmar statues is characteristic of the carver, who works by cutting his forms out of a solid block. A far more flexible and realistic style prevails among the Sumerian sculpture that was made by addition rather than subtraction (that is, either modeled in soft materials for casting in bronze or put together by combining such varied substances as wood, gold leaf, and lapis lazuli). Some pieces of the latter kind, roughly contemporary with the Tell Asmar figures, have been found in the tombs at Ur which we had occasion to mention earlier. They include the fascinating object shown in figure 112, an offering stand in the shape of a ram rearing up against a flowering tree. The animal, marvelously alive and energetic, has an almost demonic power of expression as it gazes at us from between the branches of the symbolic tree. And well it might, for it is sacred to the god Tammuz and thus embodies the male principle in nature.

Such an association of animals with deities is a carry-over from prehistoric times; we find it not only in Mesopotamia

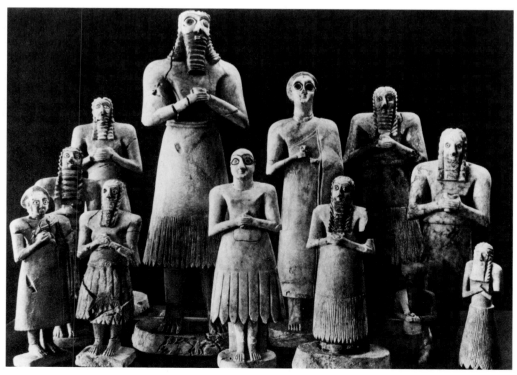

111. Statues, from the Abu Temple, Tell Asmar. c. 2700–2500 B.C. Marble, height of tallest figure c. 30″ (76.3 cm). Iraq Museum, Baghdad, and The Oriental Institute, University of Chicago

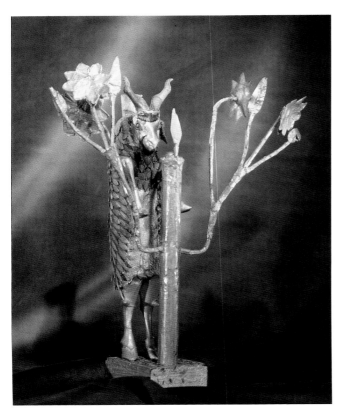

112. *RAM AND TREE.* Offering stand from Ur. c. 2600 B.C.
Wood, gold, and lapis lazuli, height 20″ (50.7 cm).
The University Museum, Philadelphia

in the West from Aesop to La Fontaine. At least one of them, the ass with the harp, survived as a fixed image, and we encounter it almost 4,000 years later in medieval sculpture.

## Akkadian

Toward the end of the early dynastic period, the theocratic socialism of the Sumerian city-states began to decay. The local "stewards of the god" had in practice become reigning monarchs, and the more ambitious among them attempted to enlarge their domain by conquering their neighbors. At the same time, the Semitic inhabitants of northern Mesopotamia drifted south in ever larger numbers, until they outweighed the Sumerian stock in many places. They had adopted Sumerian civilization but were less bound to the tradition of the city-state. So it is perhaps not surprising that in Sargon of Akkad and his successors (2340–2180 B.C.) they produced the first Mesopotamian rulers who openly called themselves kings and proclaimed their ambition to rule the entire earth.

Under these Akkadians, Sumerian art faced a new task—the personal glorification of the sovereign. The most impressive work of this kind that has survived is a magnificent roy-

but in Egypt as well (see the falcon of Horus in figs. 72 and 74). What distinguishes the sacred animals of the Sumerians is the active part they play in mythology. Much of this lore, unfortunately, has not come down to us in written form, but tantalizing glimpses of it can be caught in pictorial representations such as those on an inlaid panel from a harp (fig. 113) that was recovered together with the offering stand at Ur. The hero embracing two human-headed bulls in the top compartment was so popular a subject that its design has become a rigidly symmetrical, decorative formula; the other sections, however, show animals performing a variety of human tasks in surprisingly animated and precise fashion: the wolf and the lion carry food and drink to an unseen banquet, while the ass, bear, and deer provide musical entertainment (the bull-headed harp is the same type as the instrument to which the inlaid panel was attached). At the bottom, a scorpion-man and a goat carry some objects they have taken from a large vessel.

The skillful artist who created these scenes was far less constrained by rules than his contemporaries in Egypt; even though he, too, places his figures on ground-lines, he is not afraid of overlapping forms or foreshortened shoulders. We must be careful, however, not to misinterpret his intention—what strikes the modern eye as delightfully humorous was probably meant to be viewed with perfect seriousness. If we only knew the context in which these actors play their roles! Nevertheless, we are entitled to regard them as the earliest known ancestors of the animal fable that flourished

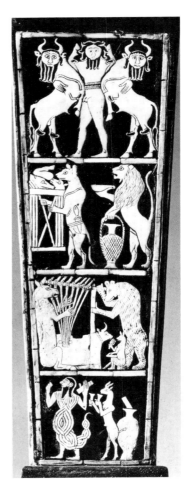

113. Inlay panel from the soundbox of a lyre,
from Ur. c. 2600 B.C. Shell and bitumen,
12¼ × 4½″ (31.1 × 11.3 cm).
The University Museum, Philadelphia

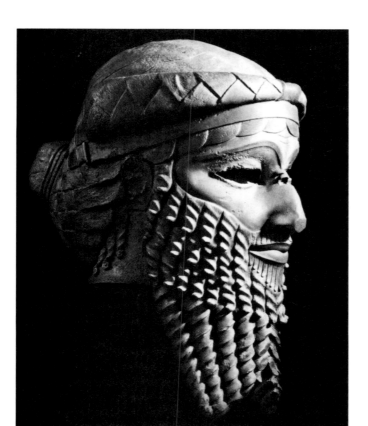

114. *HEAD OF AN AKKADIAN RULER,* from Nineveh (Kuyunjik), Iraq. c. 2300–2200 B.C. Bronze, height 12″ (30.7 cm). Iraq Museum, Baghdad

al portrait head in bronze from Nineveh (fig. 114). Despite the gouged-out eyes (once inlaid with precious materials), it remains a persuasive likeness, majestic and humanly moving at the same time. Equally admirable is the richness of the surfaces framing the face; the plaited hair and the finely curled strands of the beard are shaped with incredible precision, yet without losing their organic character and becoming mere ornament. The complex technique of casting and chasing has been handled with an assurance that bespeaks true mastery. This head could hold its own in the company of the greatest works of any period.

STELE OF NARAM-SIN. Sargon's grandson, Naram-Sin, had himself and his victorious army immortalized in relief on a large stele (fig. 115)—an upright stone slab used as a marker—which owes its survival to the fact that at a later time it was carried off as booty to Susa, where modern archaeologists discovered it. Here rigid ground-lines have been discarded; we see the king's forces advancing among the trees on a mountainside. Above them, Naram-Sin alone stands triumphant, as the defeated enemy soldiers plead for mercy. He is as vigorously active as his men, but his size and his isolated position endow him with superhuman status. Moreover, he wears the horned crown hitherto reserved for the gods. Nothing appears above him except the mountaintop and the celestial bodies, his "good stars." This is the earliest known monument to the glory of a conqueror.

# Ur

The rule of the Akkadian kings came to an end when tribesmen from the northeast descended into the Mesopotamian plain and gained mastery of it for more than half a century. They were driven out in 2125 B.C. by the kings of Ur, who reestablished a united realm that was to last a hundred years.

GUDEA. During the period of foreign dominance, Lagash (the modern Telloh), one of the lesser Sumerian city-states, managed to retain local independence. Its ruler, Gudea, was careful to reserve the title of king for the city-god, whose cult he promoted by an ambitious rebuilding of his temple. Of this architectural enterprise nothing remains today, but Gu-

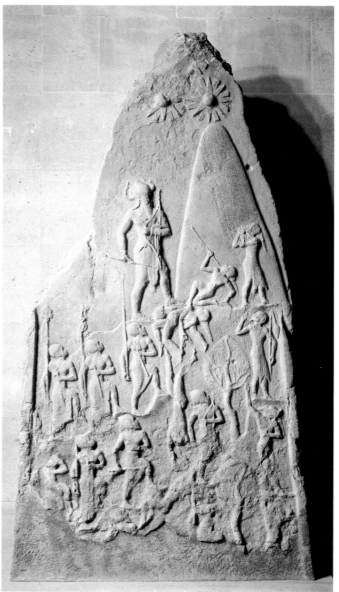

115. *VICTORY STELE OF NARAM-SIN.* c. 2300–2200 B.C. Stone, height 6′6″ (2 m). Musée du Louvre, Paris

merian carver has rounded off all the corners to emphasize the cylindrical quality of the forms. Equally characteristic is the muscular tension in Gudea's bare arm and shoulder, compared with the passive, relaxed limbs of Egyptian statues.

## Babylonian

The second millennium B.C. was a time of almost continuous turmoil in Mesopotamia. The ethnic upheaval that brought the Hyksos to Egypt had an even more disruptive effect on the valley of the Tigris and Euphrates. Central power by native rulers prevailed only from about 1760 to 1600 B.C., when Babylon assumed the role formerly played by Akkad and Ur. Hammurabi (c. 1955–1913 B.C.), the founder of the Babylonian dynasty, is by far the greatest figure of the age: combining military prowess with a deep respect for Sumerian tradition, he saw himself as "the favorite shepherd" of the sun god Shamash, whose mission it was "to cause justice to

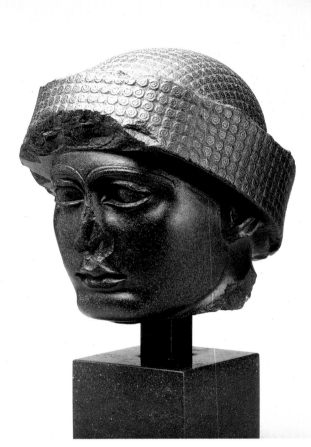

116. *HEAD OF GUDEA*, from Lagash (Telloh), Iraq. c. 2150 B.C.
Diorite, height 9″ (23 cm). Courtesy of
Museum of Fine Arts, Boston.
Frances Bartlett Donation

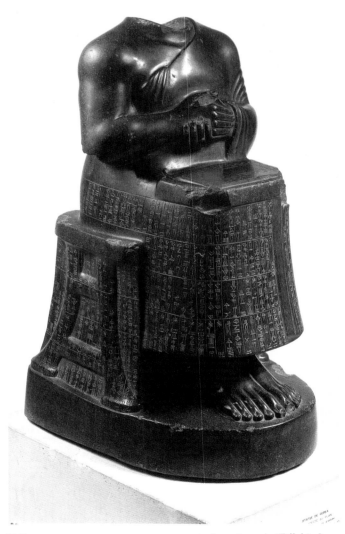

117. *GUDEA WITH ARCHITECTURAL PLAN*, from Lagash (Telloh), Iraq.
c. 2150 B.C. Diorite, height 29″ (73.7 cm). Musée du Louvre, Paris

dea also had numerous statues of himself placed in the shrines of Lagash, and some twenty examples, all obviously of the same general type, have been found so far. Carved of diorite, the extremely hard stone favored by Egyptian sculptors, they are much more ambitious works than their predecessors from Tell Asmar. Even Gudea, however devoted he was to the traditional pattern of the Sumerian city-state, seems to have inherited something of the sense of personal importance that we felt in the Akkadian kings, although he prided himself on his intimate relations with the gods rather than on secular power.

His portrait head (fig. 116) appears far less distinctly individualized when compared with the Akkadian ruler, yet its fleshy roundness is far removed from the geometric simplicity of the Tell Asmar statues. The stone has been worked to a high and subtly accented finish, inviting a wonderful play of light upon the features. The seated statue (fig. 117) represents Gudea with an architectural plan on his lap (perhaps the enclosing wall of a temple district), which he is offering for the god's approval; there are six entrances framed by towerlike projections, and the walls show regularly spaced buttresses of the kind we saw in the "White Temple" at Uruk (Warka). The figure makes an instructive contrast with such Egyptian statues as in figures 84 and 86—the Su-

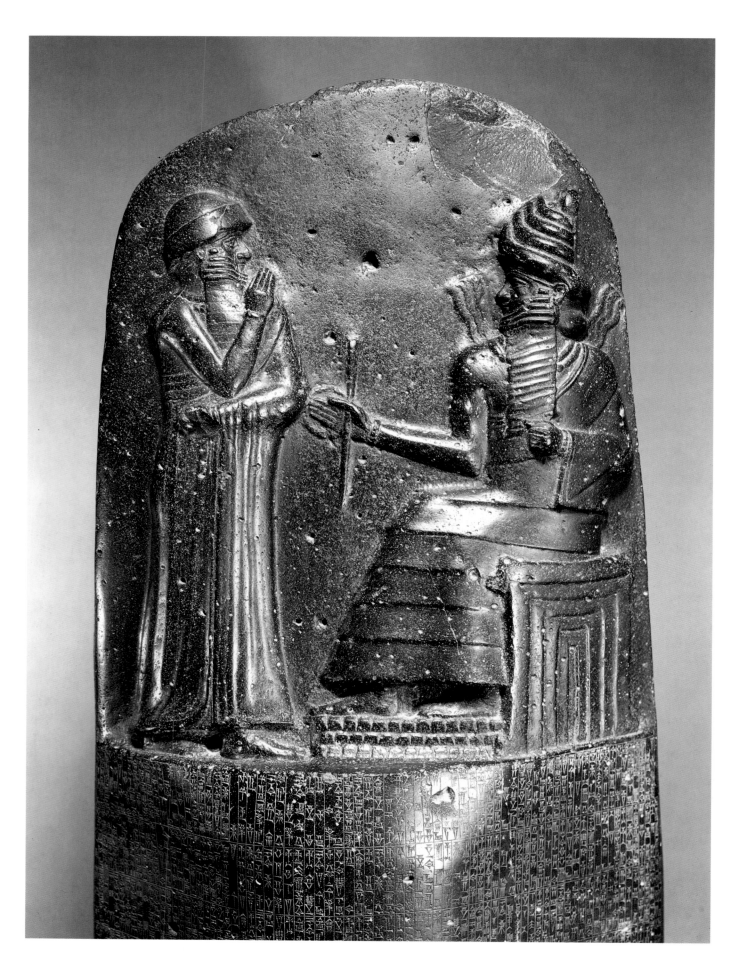

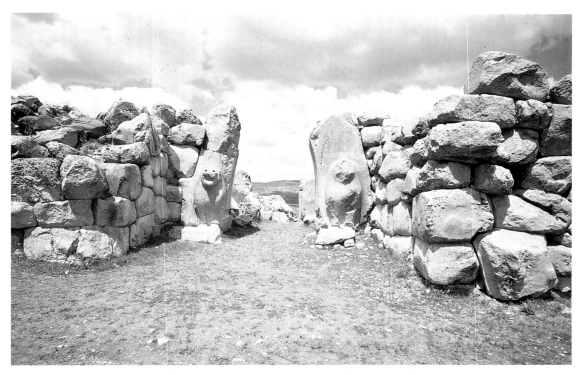

119. The Lion Gate, Bogazsköy, Anatolia, Turkey. c. 1400 B.C.

prevail in the land." Under him and his successors, Babylon became the cultural center of Sumer. The city was to retain this prestige for more than a thousand years after its political power had waned.

CODE OF HAMMURABI. Hammurabi's most memorable achievement is his law code, justly famous as the earliest uniform written body of laws and amazingly rational and humane in conception. He had it engraved on a tall diorite stele whose top shows Hammurabi confronting the sun god (fig. 118). The ruler's right arm is raised in a speaking gesture, as if he were reporting his work of codification to the divine king. Although this scene was carved four centuries after the Gudea statues, it is strongly related to them in both style and technique. In fact, the relief here is so high that the two figures almost give the impression of statues sliced in half when we compare them with the pictorial treatment of the Naram-Sin stele. As a result, the sculptor has been able to render the eyes in the round, so that Hammurabi and Shamash gaze at each other with a force and directness unique in representations of this kind. They make us recall the statues from Tell Asmar, whose enormous eyes indicate an attempt to establish the same relationships between man and god in an earlier phase of Sumerian civilization.

118. (opposite) Upper part of stele inscribed with the Law Code of Hammurabi. c. 1760 B.C. Diorite, height of stele c. 7' (2.1 m); height of relief 28" (71 cm). Musée du Louvre, Paris

# ASSYRIAN ART

The city-state of Assur on the upper course of the Tigris owed its rise to power to a strange chain of events. During the earlier half of the second millennium B.C., Asia Minor had been invaded from the east by people of Indo-European language. One group, the Mitannians, created an independent kingdom in Syria and northern Mesopotamia, including Assur, while another, the Hittites, established themselves farther north on the rocky plateau of Anatolia. Their capital, near the present-day Turkish village of Bogazköy, was protected by impressive fortifications built of large, roughly cut stones; the gates were flanked by snarling lions or other guardian figures protruding from the enormous blocks that formed the jambs of the doorway (fig. 119).

About 1360 B.C., the Hittites attacked the Mitannians, who were allies of the Egyptians. But the latter, because of the internal crisis provoked by the religious reforms of Akhenaten (see pages 114–16), could send no effective aid; the Mitannians were defeated and Assur regained its independence. Under a series of able rulers, the Assyrian domain gradually expanded until it embraced not only Mesopotamia proper but the surrounding regions as well. At the height of its power, from about 1000 to 612 B.C., the Assyrian empire stretched from the Sinai peninsula to Armenia; even Lower Egypt was successfully invaded in 671 B.C.

## Palaces and Their Decoration

The Assyrians, it has been said, were to the Sumerians what the Romans were to the Greeks. Assyrian civilization drew on the achievements of the south but reinterpreted them to

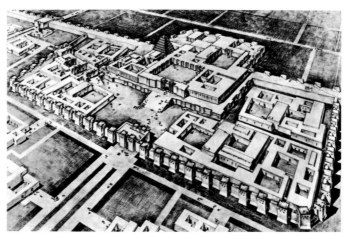

120. Citadel of Sargon II, Dur Sharrukin
(Khorsabad), Iraq. 742–706 B.C. (reconstruction by Charles Altman)

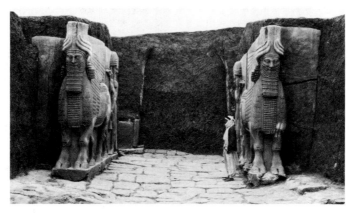

121. Gate of the Citadel of Sargon II (during excavation)

fit its own distinctive character. Thus the temples and ziggurats they built were adapted from Sumerian models while the palaces of Assyrian kings grew to unprecedented size and magnificence.

DUR SHARRUKIN. One of these, that of Sargon II (died 705 B.C.) at Dur Sharrukin (the modern Khorsabad), dating from the second half of the eighth century B.C., has been explored sufficiently to permit a reconstruction (fig. 120). It was surrounded by a citadel with turreted walls that shut it off from the rest of the town. Figure 121 shows one of the two gates of the citadel in the process of excavation. Although the Assyrians, like the Sumerians, built in brick, they liked to line gateways and the lower walls of important interiors with great slabs of stone (which were less difficult to procure in northern Mesopotamia). These slabs were either decorated with low reliefs or, as in our case, elaborated into guardian demons that are an odd combination of relief and sculpture in the round. They must have been inspired by Hittite examples such as the Lion Gate at Bogazköy (fig. 119). Awesome in size and appearance, the gates were meant to impress the visitor with the power and majesty of the king.

Inside the palace, the same impression was reinforced by long series of reliefs illustrating the conquests of the royal armies. Every campaign is described in detail, with inscriptions supplying further data. The Assyrian forces, relentlessly efficient, always seem to be on the march, meeting the enemy at every frontier of the overextended empire, destroying his strong points and carrying away booty and prisoners. There is neither drama nor heroism in these scenes—the outcome of the battle is never in doubt—and they are often depressingly repetitious. Yet, as the earliest large-scale efforts at narrative in the history of art, they represent an achievement of great importance. To describe the progress of specific events in time and space had been outside the scope of both Egyptian and Sumerian art; even the scene on the stele of Naram-Sin is symbolic rather than historic. The Assyrian artist thus had to develop an entirely new set of devices in order to cope with the requirements of pictorial story-telling.

NINEVEH. If the artist's results can hardly be called beautiful, they achieve their main purpose—to be clearly readable. This is certainly true of our example (fig. 122), from the Palace of Ashurbanipal (died 626? B.C.), at Nineveh (now

Kuyunjik), which shows the sack of the Elamite city of Hamanu in the main register: Assyrian soldiers with pickaxes and crowbars are demolishing the fortifications—notice the falling timbers and bricks in mid-air—after they have set fire to the town itself; others are marching away from it, down a wooded hill, laden with booty. The latter group poses a particularly interesting problem in representation, for the road on which they walk widens visibly as it approaches the foreground, as if the artist had meant to render it in perspective, yet the same road also serves as a curved band that frames the marchers. An odd mixture of modes—but an effective device for linking foreground and background. Below the main scene, we observe the soldiers at camp, relaxing with food and drink, while one of them stands guard.

LION HUNTS. The mass of descriptive detail in the reliefs of military campaigns often leaves little room for the personal glorification of the king. This purpose is served more directly by another recurrent subject, the royal lion hunts. These were more in the nature of ceremonial combats than actual hunts: the animals were released from cages within a hollow square formed by troops with shields for the king to kill. (Presumably, at a much earlier time, the hunting of lions in the field had been an important duty of Mesopotamian rulers as the "shepherds" of the communal flocks.) Here the Assyrian relief sculptor rises to his greatest heights; in figure 123, from the Palace of Ashurnasirpal II (died 860? B.C.) at Nimrud (Calah), the lion attacking the royal chariot from the rear is clearly the hero of the scene. Of magnificent strength and courage, the wounded animal seems to embody all the dramatic emotion that we miss in the pictorial accounts of war. The dying lion on the right is equally impressive in its agony. How differently the Egyptian artist (see fig. 105) had interpreted the same composition! We need only compare the horses—the Assyrian ones are less graceful but very much more energetic and alive as

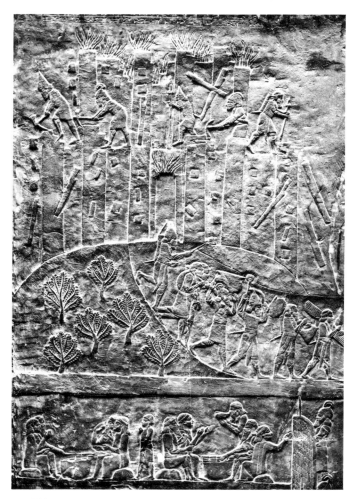

122. *THE SACK OF THE CITY OF HAMANU BY ASHURBANIPAL,* from the Palace of Ashurbanipal, Nineveh (Kuyunjik), Iraq. c. 650 B.C. Limestone, 36 × 24½″ (92.7 × 62.2 cm). British Museum, London

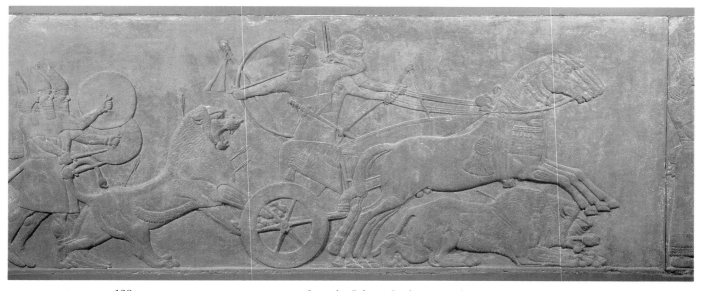

123. *ASHURNASIRPAL II KILLING LIONS,* from the Palace of Ashurnasirpal II, Nimrud (Calah), Iraq. c. 850 B.C. Limestone, 3′3″ × 8′4″ (1 × 2.5 m). British Museum, London

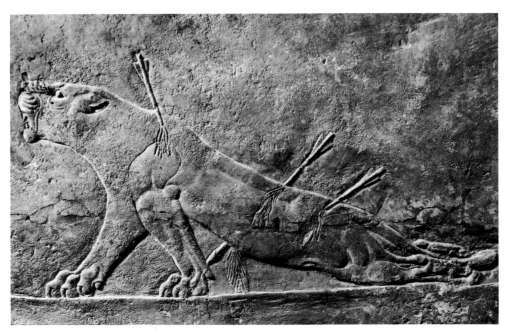

124. *DYING LIONESS*, from Nineveh (Kuyunjik), Iraq. c. 650 B.C.
Limestone, height of figure 13¾″ (35 cm). British Museum, London

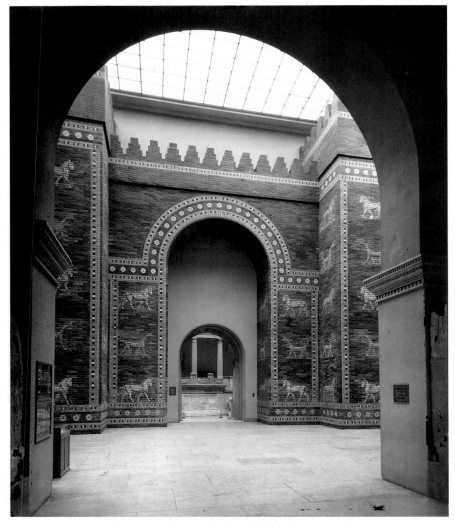

125. Ishtar Gate (restored), from Babylon, Iraq. c. 575 B.C.
Glazed brick. Vorderasiatisches Museum der Staatlichen Museen, Berlin

they flee from the attacking lion, their ears folded back in fear. The lion hunt reliefs from Nineveh, about two centuries later than those of Nimrud, are the finest of all. Despite the shallowness of the actual carving, the bodies have a greater sense of weight and volume because of the subtle gradations of the surface. Images such as the dying lioness (fig. 124) have an unforgettable tragic grandeur.

## Neo-Babylonian

The Assyrian empire came to an end in 612 B.C. when Nineveh fell before the combined onslaught of Medes and Scythians from the east. At that time the commander of the Assyrian army in southern Mesopotamia made himself king of Babylon; under him and his successors the ancient city had a final brief flowering between 612 and 539 B.C., before it was conquered by the Persians. The best known of these Neo-Babylonian rulers was Nebuchadnezzar (died 562 B.C.), the builder of the Tower of Babel. That famous structure represented only one part of a very large architectural complex comparable to the Citadel of Sargon II at Dur Sharrukin.

Whereas the Assyrians had used carved stone slabs, the Neo-Babylonians (who were farther removed from the sources of such slabs) substituted baked and glazed brick. This technique, too, had been developed in Assyria, but now it was used on a far larger scale, both for surface ornament and for architectural reliefs. Its very distinctive effect becomes evident if we compare the gate of Sargon's citadel (fig. 121) with the Ishtar Gate of Nebuchadnezzar's sacred precinct in Babylon, which has been rebuilt from the thousands of individual glazed bricks that covered its surface (fig. 125). The stately procession of bulls, dragons, and other animals of molded brick within a framework of vividly colored ornamental bands has a grace and gaiety far removed from the ponderous guardian monsters of the Assyrians. Here, for the last time, we sense again that special genius of ancient Mesopotamian art for the portrayal of animals, which we noted in early dynastic times.

# PERSIAN ART

Persia, the mountain-fringed high plateau to the east of Mesopotamia, takes its name from the people who occupied Babylon in 539 B.C. and became the heirs of what had been the Assyrian empire. Today the country is called Iran, its older and more suitable name, since the Persians, who put the area on the map of world history, were latecomers who had arrived on the scene only a few centuries before they began their epochal conquests. Inhabited continuously since prehistoric times, Iran always seems to have been a gateway for migratory tribes from the Asiatic steppes to the north as well as from India to the east. The new arrivals would settle down for a while, dominating or intermingling with the local population, until they in turn were forced to move on—to Mesopotamia, to Asia Minor, to southern Russia—by the next wave of migrants. These movements form a shadowy area of historical knowledge; all available information is vague and uncertain. Since nomadic tribes leave

no permanent monuments or written records, we can trace their wanderings only by a careful study of the objects they buried with their dead. Such objects, of wood, bone, or metal, represent a distinct kind of portable art which we call the nomad's gear: weapons, bridles for horses, buckles, fibulas and other articles of adornment, cups, bowls, and the like. They have been found over a vast area, from Siberia to Central Europe, from Iran to Scandinavia. They have in common not only a jewellike concentration of ornamental design but also a repertory of forms known as the "animal style." And one of the sources of this animal style appears to be ancient Iran.

ANIMAL STYLE. Its main feature, as the name suggests, is the decorative use of animal motifs in a rather abstract and imaginative manner. We find its earliest ancestors on the prehistoric painted pottery of western Iran, such as the fine beaker in figure 126, which shows an ibex (a wild mountain goat) reduced to a few sweeping curves, so that the body of the animal becomes a mere appendage of the huge horns.

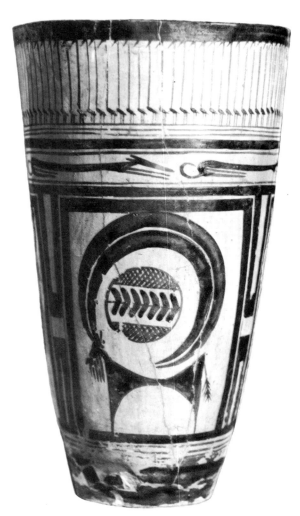

126. Painted beaker, from Susa. c. 5000–4000 B.C. Height 11¼" (28.3 cm). Musée du Louvre, Paris

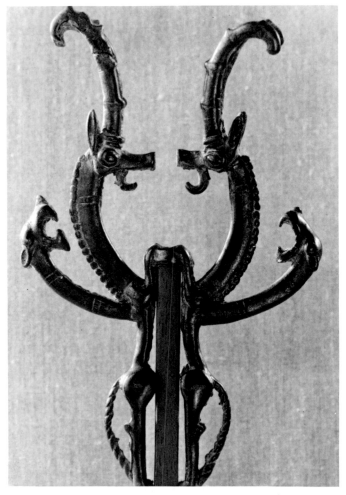

127. Pole-top ornament, from Luristan. 9th–7th century B.C. Bronze, height 7½″ (19 cm). British Museum, London

animal's body here shows far less arbitrary distortion, and the smoothly curved sections divided by sharp ridges have no counterpart among Luristan bronzes, yet the way the antlers have been elaborated into an abstract openwork ornament betrays a similar feeling for form.

Whether or not this typically Scythian piece reflects Central Asiatic sources independent of the Iranian tradition, the Scythians surely learned a good deal from the bronze casters of Luristan during their stay in Iran. They belonged to a group of nomadic Indo-European tribes, including the Medes and the Persians, that began to filter into the country soon after 1000 B.C. An alliance of Medes and Scythians, it will be recalled, had crushed Nineveh in 612 B.C. The Persians at that time were vassals of the Medes, but only sixty years later, under Cyrus the Great of the family of the Achaemenids, they reversed this situation.

## Achaemenid

After conquering Babylon in 539 B.C., Cyrus (c. 600–529 B.C.) assumed the title King of Babylon along with the ambitions of the Assyrian rulers. The empire he founded continued to expand under his successors; Egypt as well as Asia Minor fell to them, and Greece escaped the same fate only by the narrowest of margins. At its high tide, under Darius I (c. 550–486 B.C.) and Xerxes (519–465 B.C.), the Persian empire was far larger than its Egyptian and Assyrian predecessors together. Moreover, this vast domain endured for two centuries—it was toppled by Alexander the Great (356–323 B.C.) in 331 B.C.—and during most of its life it was ruled both efficiently and humanely. For an obscure tribe of nomads to have achieved all this is little short of miraculous. Within a single generation, the Persians not only mastered the complex machinery of imperial administration but also evolved a monumental art of remarkable originality to express the grandeur of their rule.

Despite their genius for adaptation, the Persians retained their own religious belief drawn from the prophecies of Zoroaster; this was a faith based on the dualism of Good and Evil, embodied in Ahuramazda (Light) and Ahriman (Dark-

The racing hounds above the ibex are little more than horizontal streaks, and on closer inspection the striations below the rim turn out to be long-necked birds. In the historic art of Sumer, this style soon gave way to an interest in the organic unity of animal bodies (see figs. 112 and 113), but in Iran it survived despite the powerful influence of Mesopotamia.

Several thousand years later, in the ninth to seventh centuries B.C., the style reappears in the small bronzes of the Luristan region, nomad's gear of a particularly resourceful kind. The pole-top ornament (fig. 127) consists of a symmetrical pair of rearing ibexes, with vastly elongated necks and horns; originally, we suspect, they were pursued by a pair of lions, but the bodies of the latter have been absorbed into those of the ibexes, whose necks have been pulled out to dragonlike slenderness. By and for whom the Luristan bronzes were produced remains something of a mystery. There can be little doubt, however, that they are somehow linked with the animal-style metalwork of the Asiatic steppes, such as the splendid Scythian gold stag from southern Russia, which is only slightly later in date (fig. 128). The

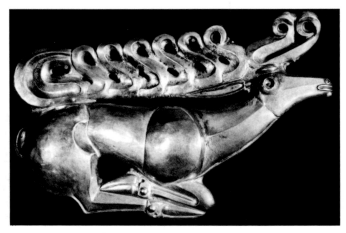

128. STAG, from Kostromskaya. Scythian. 7th–6th century B.C. Chased gold, height c. 12″ (30.5 cm). Hermitage Museum, Leningrad

ness). Since the cult of Ahuramazda centered on fire altars in the open air, the Persians had no religious architecture. Their palaces, on the other hand, were huge and impressive structures.

PERSEPOLIS. The most ambitious palace, at Persepolis, was begun by Darius I in 518 B.C.; its general layout is shown in figure 129—a vast number of rooms, halls, and courts assembled on a raised platform—recalls the royal residences of Assyria (see fig. 120), and Assyrian traditions are the strongest single element throughout. Yet they do not determine the character of the building, for they have been combined with influences from every corner of the empire in such a way that the result is a new, uniquely Persian style. Thus, at Persepolis columns are used on a grand scale.

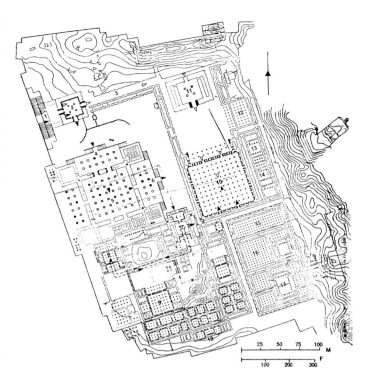

129. Plan of the Palace of Darius and Xerxes, Persepolis. 1) Great entrance stairway; 2) Gatehouse of Xerxes; 3) Audience Hall of Darius and Xerxes; 4) Throne Hall of Xerxes; 5) Palace of Darius; 6) Palace, probably rebuilt by Ataxerxes; 7) Palace of Xerxes; 8) Council Hall; 9) Restored area of the "Harem"; 10) Treasury; 11) Section of northern fortifications; 12) Royal tomb, probably of Ataxerxes

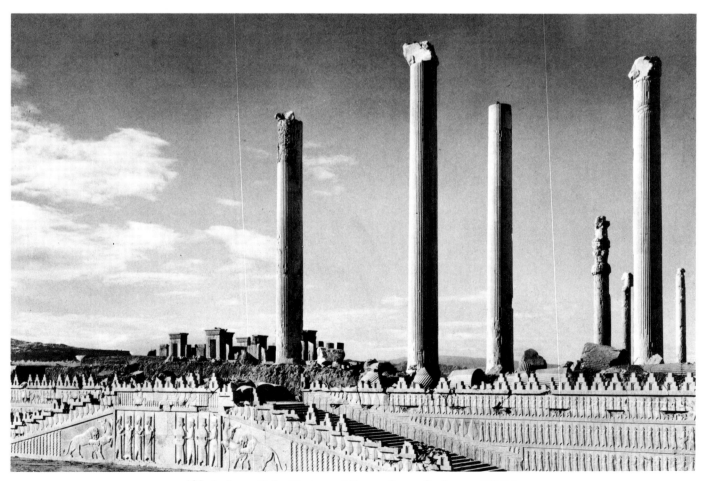

130. Audience Hall of Darius and Xerxes, Persepolis, Iran. c. 500 B.C.

The Audience Hall of Darius, a room 250 feet square, had a wooden ceiling supported by 36 columns 40 feet tall, a few of which are still standing (fig. 130). Such a massing of columns suggests Egyptian architecture (compare fig. 95), and Egyptian influence does indeed appear in the ornamental detail of the bases and capitals, but the slender, fluted shaft of the Persepolis columns is derived from the Ionian Greeks in Asia Minor, who are known to have furnished artists to the Persian court. Entirely without precedent in earlier architecture is the strange "cradle" for the beams of the ceiling, composed of the front parts of two bulls or similar creatures, that crowns the Persepolis columns (fig. 131); while the animals themselves are of Assyrian origin, the way they are combined suggests nothing so much as an enormously enlarged version of the pole-top ornaments of Luristan. This seems to be the only instance of Persian architects' drawing upon their native artistic heritage of nomad's gear (fig. 127).

The double stairway leading up to the Audience Hall is decorated with long rows of solemnly marching figures in low relief (fig. 130). Their repetitive, ceremonial character emphasizes a subservience to the architectural setting that is typical of all Persian sculpture. We find it even in scenes of special importance, such as *Darius and Xerxes Giving Audience* (fig. 132); the expressive energy and narrative skill of Assyrian relief have been deliberately rejected.

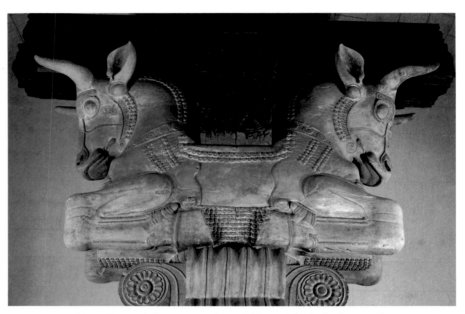

131. Bull capital, from Persepolis. c. 500 B.C. Musée du Louvre, Paris

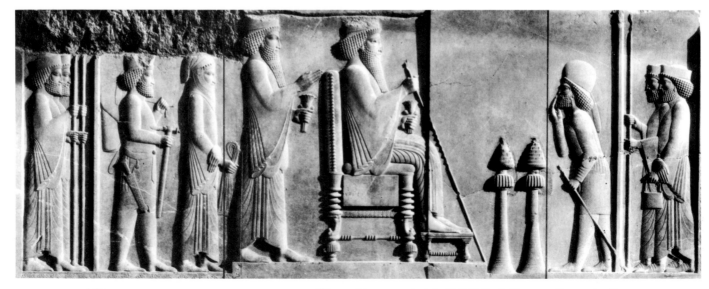

132. *DARIUS AND XERXES GIVING AUDIENCE.* c. 490 B.C. Limestone, height 8′4″ (2.5 m). Treasury, Persepolis, Iran

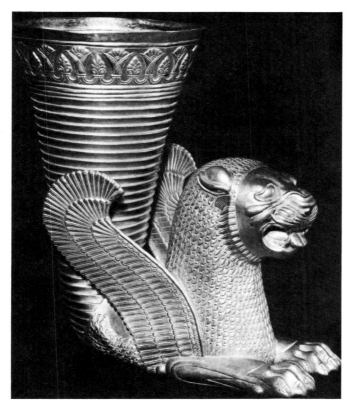

133. Gold rhyton. Achaemenid. 5th–3rd century B.C.
Archaeological Museum, Teheran

PERSIAN STYLE. The style of these Persian carvings seems at first glance to be only a softer and more refined echo of the Mesopotamian tradition. Even here, however, we discover that the Assyrian-Babylonian heritage has been enriched in one important respect: there is no precedent in Near Eastern sculpture for the layers of overlapping garments, for the play of finely pleated folds such as we see in the Darius and Xerxes relief. Another surprising effect is the way the arms and shoulders of these figures press through the fabric of the draperies. These innovations stem from the Ionian Greeks, who had created them in the course of the sixth century B.C.

Persian art under the Achaemenids, then, is a remarkable synthesis of many diverse elements. Yet it lacked a capacity for growth; the style formulated under Darius I about 500 B.C. continued without significant change until the end of the empire. The main reason for this failure, it seems, was the Persians' preoccupation with decorative effects regardless of scale, a carry-over from their nomadic past that they never discarded. There is no essential difference between the bull capital of figure 131 and the fine goldsmith's work (fig. 133), textiles, and other portable art of Achaemenid Persia. The latter tradition, unlike that of monumental architecture and sculpture, somehow managed to survive the more than 500 years during which the Persian empire was under Greek and Roman domination, so that it could flower

once more when Persia regained its independence and seized Mesopotamia from the Romans.

## Sassanian

The rulers who accomplished this feat were of the house of the Sassanians; their greatest figure, Shapur I (died 272 B.C.) had the political and artistic ambitions of Darius. At Naksh-i-Rustam, the burial place of the Achaemenid kings not far from Persepolis, he commemorated his victory over two Roman emperors in an enormous relief hewn into the living rock (fig. 134). The formal source of this scene of triumph is a well-known composition in Roman sculpture—with the emperors now in the role of the humiliated barbarians—but the flattening of the volumes and the ornamental elaboration of the draperies indicate a revival of Persian qualities. The two elements hold each other in balance, and that is what makes the relief so strangely impressive. A blending of Roman and Near Eastern elements can also be observed in Shapur's palace at Ctesiphon, near Babylon, with its enormous brick-vaulted audience hall (fig. 135); the blind arcades of the façade again emphasize decorative surface pattern.

But monumental art under Sassanian rule proved as incapable of further evolution as it had under the Achaemenids. Metalwork and textiles, on the other hand, continued to flourish. The chief glory of Sassanian art—and a direct

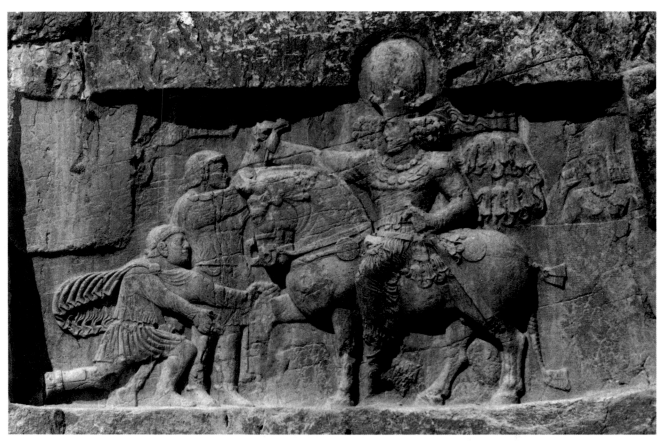

134. *SHAPUR I TRIUMPHING OVER THE EMPERORS PHILIPPUS THE ARAB AND VALERIAN*. 260–72 A.D. Naksh-i-Rustam (near Persepolis), Iran

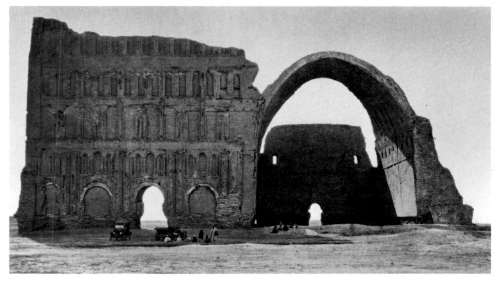

135. Palace of Shapur I, Ctesiphon, Iraq. 242–72 A.D.

echo of the ornamental tradition reaching back more than a thousand years to the Luristan bronzes—is its woven silks, such as the splendid sample in figure 136. They were copiously exported both to Constantinople and to the Christian West, and we shall see that their wealth of colors and patterns exerted an important stimulus upon the art of the Middle Ages. And since their manufacture was resumed after the Sassanian realm fell to the Arabs in the mid-seventh century, they provided an essential treasury of design motifs for Islamic art as well.

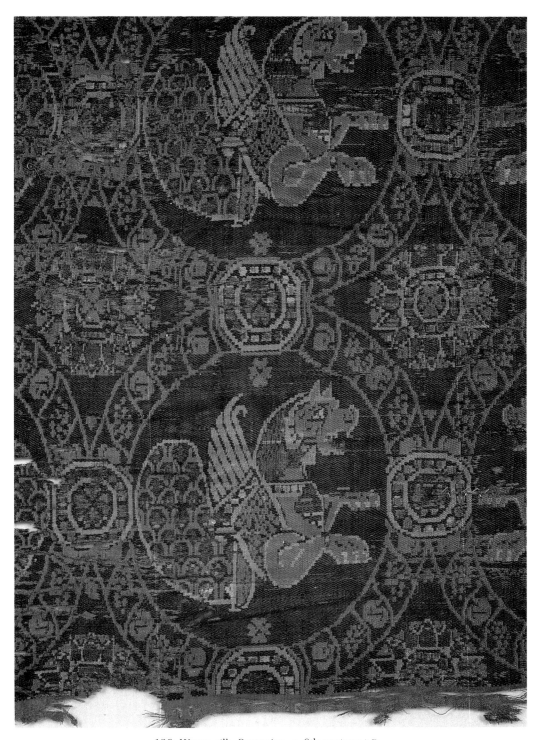

136. Woven silk. Sassanian. c. 6th century A.D.
Museo Nazionale del Bargello, Florence. Franchetti Collection

# CHAPTER FOUR
# AEGEAN ART

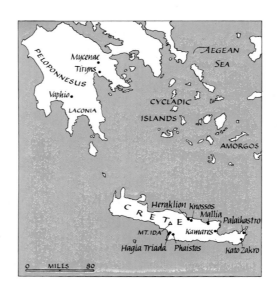

If we sail from the Nile Delta northwestward across the Mediterranean, our first glimpse of Europe will be the eastern tip of Crete. Beyond it, we find a scattered group of small islands, the Cyclades, and, a little farther on, the mainland of Greece, facing the coast of Asia Minor across the Aegean Sea. To archaeologists, "Aegean" is not merely a geographical term; they have adopted it to designate the civilizations that flourished in this area during the third and second millenniums B.C., before the development of Greek civilization proper. There are three of these, closely interrelated yet distinct from each other: that of Crete, called Minoan after the legendary Cretan King Minos; that of the small islands north of Crete (Cycladic); and that of the Greek mainland (Helladic), which includes Mycenaean civilization. Each of them has in turn been divided into three phases, Early, Middle, and Late, which correspond, very roughly, to the Old, Middle, and New Kingdoms in Egypt. The most important remains, and the greatest artistic achievements, date from the latter part of the Middle phase and from the Late phase.

Aegean civilization was long known only from Homer's account of the Trojan War in the *Iliad* and from Greek legends centering on Crete. The earliest excavations (by Heinrich Schliemann during the 1870s in Asia Minor and Greece and by Sir Arthur Evans in Crete shortly before 1900) were undertaken to test the factual core of these tales. Since then, a great amount of fascinating material has been brought to light—far more than the literary sources would lead us to expect—but our knowledge of Aegean civilization even now is very much more limited than our knowledge of Egypt or the ancient Near East. Unfortunately, our reading of the archaeological evidence has so far received almost no aid at all from the written records of the Aegeans.

MINOAN SCRIPT AND LINEAR B. In Crete a system of writing was developed about 2000 B.C.; a late form of this Minoan script, called Linear B, which was in use about six centuries later both in Crete and on the Greek mainland, was deciphered in the early 1950s. The language of Linear B is Greek, yet this apparently was not the language for which Minoan script was used before the fifteenth century B.C., so that being able to read Linear B does not help us to understand the great mass of earlier Minoan inscriptions. Moreover, the Linear B texts are largely palace inventories and administrative records, which reveal very little about the history and religion of the people who composed them. We thus lack a great deal of the background knowledge necessary for an understanding of Aegean art. Its forms, although linked both to Egypt and the Near East on the one hand and to later Greek art on the other, are no mere transition between these two worlds; they have a haunting beauty of their own that belongs to neither. Among the many strange qualities of Aegean art, and perhaps the most puzzling, is its air of freshness and spontaneity, which makes us forget how little we know of its meaning.

## CYCLADIC ART

The people who inhabited the Cycladic Islands between about 2600 and 1100 B.C. have left hardly any trace apart from their modest stone tombs. The things they buried with their dead are remarkable in one respect only: they include a large number of marble idols of a peculiarly impressive kind. Almost all of them represent a standing nude female figure with arms folded across the chest, presumably the mother and fertility goddess known to us from Asia Minor and the ancient Near East, whose ancestry reaches far back to the Old Stone Age (see figs. 37, 48, and 49). They also share a distinctive shape, which at first glance recalls the angular, abstract qualities of Paleolithic and Neolithic sculpture: the flat, wedge shape of the body, the strong, columnar neck, and the tilted, oval shield of the face, featureless except for the long, ridgelike nose. Within this narrowly defined and stable type, however, the Cycladic idols show wide variations in scale (from a few inches to lifesize) as well as form. The best of them, such as that in figure 137, have a disciplined refinement utterly beyond the range of Paleolithic or ethnographic art.

The longer we study this piece, the more we come to realize that its qualities can only be defined as "elegance" and "sophistication," however incongruous such terms may seem in context. What an extraordinary feeling for the organic structure of the body there is in the delicate curves of the outline, in the hints of convexity marking the knees and abdomen. Even if we discount its deceptively modern look, the figure seems a bold departure from anything we have seen before. There is no dearth of earlier fertility idols, but almost all of them betray their descent from the bulbous, heavy-bodied "Venus" figurines of the Old Stone Age; in fact, the earliest Cycladic idols, too, were of that type. What, then, made the Cycladic sculptors suppress the traditional fertility aspects of their female idols until they arrived at the lithe, "girlish" ideal of figure 137? Was there perhaps a radical change in the meaning or the ritual purposes of these statues?

We cannot even venture a guess to explain the mystery. Suffice it to say that the Cycladic sculptors of the second millennium B.C. produced the oldest lifesize figures of the female nude we know, and that for many hundreds of years they were the only ones to do so. In Greek art, we find very few nude female statues until the middle of the fourth century B.C., when Praxiteles and others began to create cult images of the nude Venus. It can hardly be coincidence that the most famous of these Venuses were made for sanctuaries on the Aegean islands or the coast of Asia Minor, the region where the Cycladic idols had flourished.

## MINOAN ART

Minoan civilization is by far the richest, as well as the strangest, of the Aegean world. What sets it apart, not only from Egypt and the Near East but also from the Classical civilization of Greece, is a lack of continuity that appears to have deeper causes than archaeological accident. In surveying the main achievements of Minoan art, we cannot really speak of growth or development; they appear and disappear so abruptly that their fate must have been determined by external forces—sudden violent changes affecting the entire

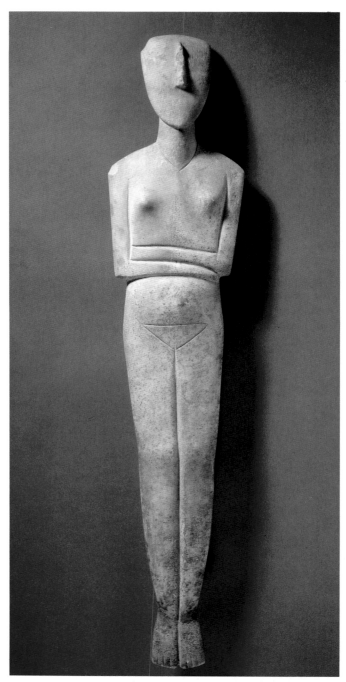

137. Idol from Amorgos. 2500–1100 B.C.
Marble, height 30″ (76.3 cm). The Ashmolean Museum, Oxford

writing but an urban civilization as well, centering on several great palaces. At least three of them, at Knossos, Phaistos, and Mallia, were built in short order. Hardly anything is left today of this sudden spurt of large-scale building activity, for the three palaces were all destroyed at the same time, about 1700 B.C.; after an interval of a hundred years, new and even larger structures began to appear on the same sites, only to suffer destruction, in their turn, about 1500 B.C.

It is these "new" palaces that are our main source of information on Minoan architecture. The one at Knossos, called the Palace of Minos, was the most ambitious, covering a vast territory and composed of so many rooms that it survived in Greek legend as the labyrinth of the Minotaur. It has been carefully excavated and partly restored. We cannot recapture the appearance of the building as a whole, but we can assume that the exterior probably did not look impressive compared with Assyrian or Persian palaces (see figs. 120 and 130). There was no striving for unified, monumental effect. The individual units are generally rather small and the ceilings low (figs. 138 and 139), so that even those parts of the structure that were several stories high could not have seemed very tall.

Nevertheless, the numerous porticoes, staircases, and air shafts must have given the palace a pleasantly open, airy quality; and some of the interiors, with their richly decorated walls, retain their atmosphere of intimate elegance to this day. The masonry construction of Minoan palaces is excellent throughout, but the columns were always of wood. Although none has survived, their characteristic form (the smooth shaft tapering downward, topped by a wide, cushion-shaped capital) is known from representations in painting and sculpture. About the origins of this type of column, which in some contexts could also serve as a religious symbol, or about its possible links with Egyptian architecture, we can say nothing at all.

Who were the rulers that built these palaces? We do not know their names or deeds (except for the legendary Minos), but the archaeological evidence permits a few conjectures: they were not warrior princes, since no fortifications have been found anywhere in Minoan Crete, and military subjects are almost unknown in Minoan art; nor is there any hint that they were sacred kings on the Egyptian or Mesopotamian model, although they may well have presided at religious festivals (the only parts of Minoan palaces that can be identified as places of worship are small chapels, suggesting that religious ceremonies took place out of doors). On the other hand, the many storerooms, workshops, and "offices" at Knossos indicate that the palace was not only a royal residence but a great center of administrative and commercial activity. Since shipping and trade formed an important part of Minoan economic life (to judge from elaborate harbor installations and from Cretan export articles found in Egypt and elsewhere), perhaps the king should be viewed as the head of a merchant aristocracy.

## Sculpture

The religious life of Minoan Crete is even harder to define than the political or social order. It centered on certain sacred places, such as caves or groves; and its chief deity (or

island—about which we know little or nothing. Yet the character of Minoan art, which is gay, even playful, and full of rhythmic motion, conveys no hint of such threats.

## Architecture

The first of these unexpected shifts occurred about 2000 B.C. Until that time, during the eight centuries of the Early Minoan era, the Cretans had not advanced much beyond the Neolithic level of village life, even though they seem to have engaged in some overseas trade that brought them contact with Egypt. Then they created not only their own system of

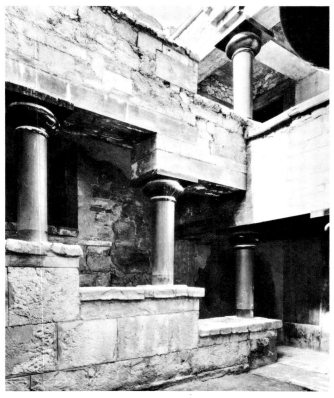

138. Staircase, east wing, Palace of Minos, Knossos, Crete. c. 1500 B.C.

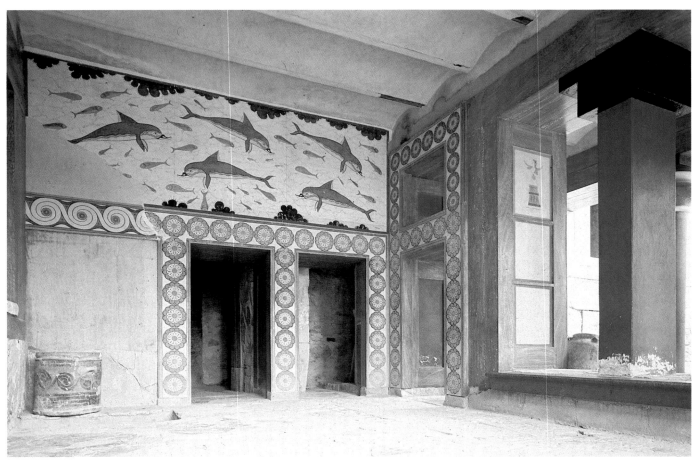

139. The Queen's Megaron, Palace of Minos, Knossos, Crete

deities?) was female, akin to the mother and fertility goddesses we have encountered before. Since the Minoans had no temples, we are not surprised to find that they lacked large cult statues as well, but even on a small scale, religious subjects in Minoan art are few in number and of uncertain significance. Two terracotta statuettes of c. 1600 B.C. from Knossos may represent the goddess in one of her several identities; one of them (fig. 140) shows her with three long snakes wound around her arms, body, and headdress. The meaning would seem to be clear: snakes are associated with earth deities and male fertility in many ancient religions, just as the bared breasts of our statuette suggest female fertility.

But is she really a cult image? Her rigid, frontal stance would be equally fitting for a votive figure, and the snakes may represent a ritual of snake-handling rather than a divine attribute. Perhaps, then, our figure is a queen or priestess. She seems oddly lacking in awesomeness, and the emphasis on the costume endows her with a secular, "fash-

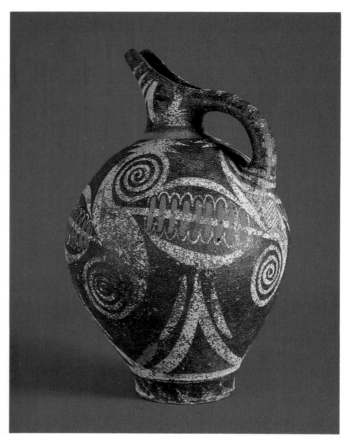

141. Beaked jug (Kamares Style), from Phaistos. c. 1800 B.C. Height 10⅝" (27 cm). Museum, Heraklion, Crete

ionable" air. Another paradox is the fact that Crete has few snakes, so that its snake cult was probably imported, not home-grown, yet no snake goddesses have so far been discovered outside Crete. Only the style of the statuette hints at a possible foreign source: the emphatically conical quality of the figure and the large eyes and heavy, arched eyebrows suggest a kinship—remote and indirect, perhaps through Asia Minor—with Mesopotamian art.

## Paintings, Pottery, and Reliefs

Our snake goddess dates from the beginning of the brief period between 1600 and 1450 B.C. that produced almost everything we have of Minoan architecture, sculpture, and painting. After the catastrophe that had wiped out the earlier palaces, and a century of slow recovery, there was what seems to our eyes an explosive increase in wealth and an equally remarkable outpouring of creative energy.

The most surprising aspect of this sudden efflorescence, however, is its great achievement in painting. At the time of the earlier palaces, between 2000 and 1700 B.C., Crete had developed a type of pottery famous for its technical perfection and its dynamic, swirling ornament (fig. 141), but in no way preparing us for the "naturalistic" murals that covered the walls of the new palaces. Unfortunately, these paintings have survived only in small fragments, so that we hardly ever have a complete composition, let alone the design of an entire wall.

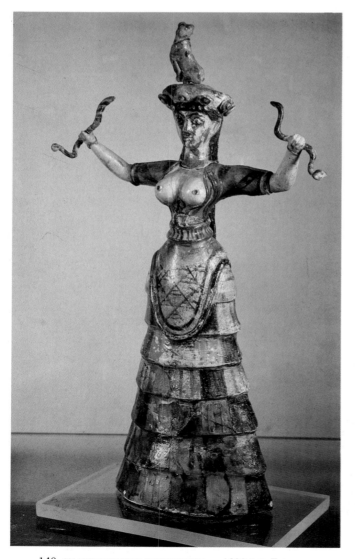

140. SNAKE GODDESS (PRIESTESS?). c. 1600 B.C. Faience, height 11⅝" (29.5 cm). Museum, Heraklion, Crete

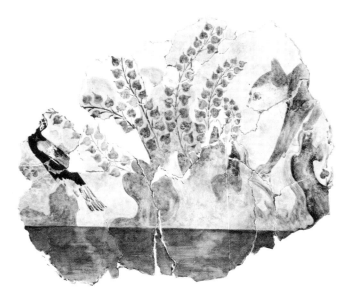

142. *CAT STALKING A PHEASANT.* Mural fragment, from Hagia Triada. c. 1600–1580 B.C. Height 21″ (53.3 cm). Museum, Heraklion, Crete

A great many of them were scenes from nature showing animals and birds among luxuriant vegetation, or the creatures of the sea. In the remarkable fragment in figure 142, we see a cat cautiously stalking a pheasant behind a bush. The flat forms, silhouetted against a background of solid color, recall Egyptian painting, and the acute observation of plants and animals also suggests Egyptian art. But if Minoan wall painting owes its origin to Egyptian influence, it betrays an attitude of mind, a sense of beauty, very different

from that of the Nile valley: instead of permanence and stability, we find a passion for rhythmic, undulating movement, and the forms themselves have an oddly weightless quality—they seem to float, or sway, in a world without gravity, as if the scene took place under water.

Marine life (as seen in the fish and dolphin fresco in fig. 139) was a favorite subject of Minoan painting, and the marine feeling pervades everything else as well; we sense it even in *The Toreador Fresco,"* the largest and most dynamic Minoan mural recovered so far (fig. 143); the darker patches are the original fragments on which the restoration is based. The conventional title should not mislead us: what we see here is not a bullfight but a ritual game in which the performers vault over the back of the animal. Two of the slim-waisted athletes are girls, differentiated (as in Egyptian art) mainly by their lighter skin color. That the bull was a sacred animal, and that bull-vaulting played an important role in Minoan religious life, is beyond doubt; scenes such as this still echo in the Greek legend of the youths and maidens sacrificed to the minotaur. If we try, however, to "read" the fresco as a description of what actually went on during these performances, we find it strangely ambiguous. Do the three figures show successive phases of the same action? How did the youth in the center get onto the back of the bull, and in what direction is he moving? Scholars have even consulted rodeo experts without getting clear answers to these questions. All of which does not mean that the Minoan artist was deficient—it would be absurd to blame him for failing to accomplish what he never intended to do in the first place— but that fluid, effortless ease of movement was more important to him than factual precision or dramatic power. He

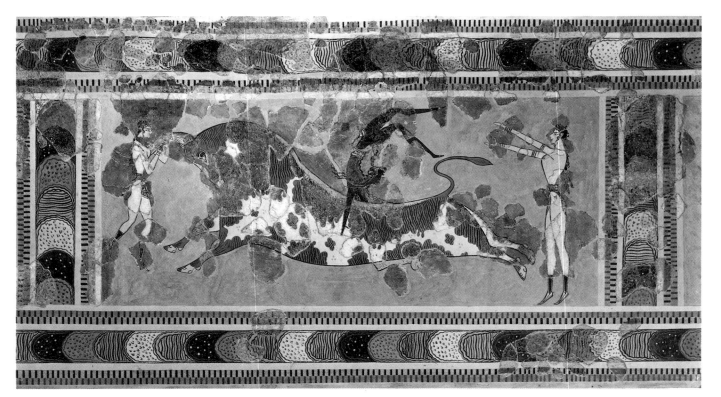

143. *"THE TOREADOR FRESCO."* c. 1500 B.C. Height including upper border c. 24½″ (62.3 cm). Museum, Heraklion, Crete

has, as it were, idealized the ritual by stressing its harmonious, playful aspect to the point that the participants behave like dolphins gamboling in the sea.

The floating world of Minoan wall painting was an imaginative creation so rich and original that its influence can be felt throughout Minoan art during the era of the new palaces. In painted pottery, the abstract patterns of old (fig. 141) gave way to a new repertory of designs drawn from plant and animal life. Some vessels are covered entirely with fish, shells, and octopuses, as if the ocean itself had been caught within them (fig. 144). Monumental sculpture, had there been any, might have retained its independence, but the small-scale works to which the Minoan sculptor was confined are often closely akin to the style of the murals; the splendidly observed mountain goat carved on a stone vase (fig. 145) leaps in the same "flying" movement as the bull of *The Toreador Fresco.* These mountain goats, too, were sacred animals.

Even more vivid is the relief on the so-called *Harvester Vase* (fig. 146; the lower part is lost): a procession of slim, muscular men, nude to the waist, carrying long-handled implements that look like a combination of scythe and rake. A harvest festival? Quite probably, although here again the lively rhythm of the composition takes precedence over descriptive clarity. Our view of the scene includes three singers led by a fourth who is swinging a sistrum (a rattle of Egyptian origin); they are bellowing with all their might, especially the "choirmaster," whose chest is so distended that the ribs press through the skin. What makes the entire relief so remarkable—in fact, unique—is its emphasis on physical strain, its energetic, raucous gaiety, which combines sharp observation with a consciously humorous intent. How many

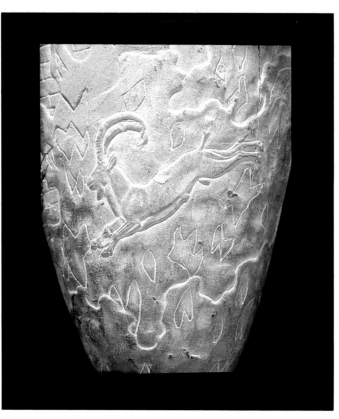

145. *LEAPING MOUNTAIN GOAT,* on a vase from the palace at Kato Zakro. c. 1500 B.C. Limestone, originally covered with gold foil, length of goat c. 4″ (10.3 cm). Museum, Heraklion, Crete

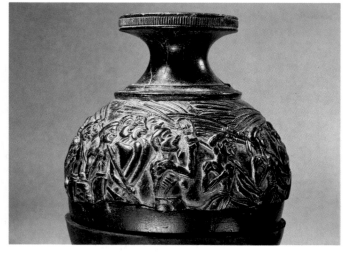

146. *HARVESTER VASE,* from Hagia Triada. c. 1550–1500 B.C. Steatite, width 4½″ (11.3 cm). Museum, Heraklion, Crete

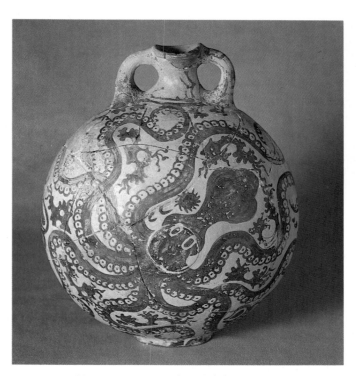

144. *"OCTOPUS VASE,"* from Palaikastro, Crete. c. 1500 B.C. Height 11″ (28 cm). Museum, Heraklion, Crete

works of this sort, we wonder, did Minoan art produce? Only once have we met anything at all like it: in the relief of workmen carrying a beam (see fig. 103), carved almost two centuries later under the impact of the Akhenaten style (see pages 114–16). Is it possible that pieces similar to the *Harvester Vase* stimulated Egyptian artists during that brief but important period?

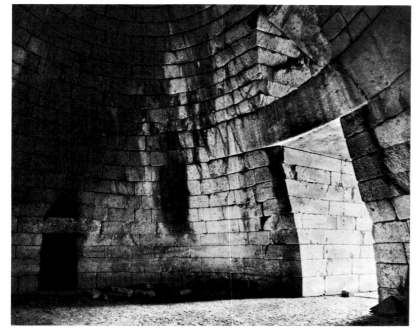

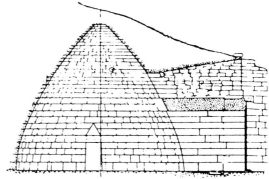

147. Interior, Treasury of Atreus,
Mycenae, Greece. c. 1300–1250 B.C.

148. Section, Treasury of Atreus

## MYCENAEAN ART

Along the southeastern shores of the Greek mainland there were during Late Helladic times (c. 1600–1100 B.C.) a number of settlements that corresponded in many ways to those of Minoan Crete. They, too, were grouped around palaces. Their inhabitants have come to be called Mycenaeans, after Mycenae, the most important of these settlements. Since the works of art unearthed there by excavation often showed a strikingly Minoan character, the Mycenaeans were at first regarded as having come from Crete, but it is now agreed that they were the descendants of the earliest Greek tribes, who had entered the country soon after 2000 B.C.

### Tombs and Their Contents

For some four hundred years, these people had led an inconspicuous pastoral existence in their new homeland; their modest tombs have yielded only simple pottery and a few bronze weapons. Toward 1600 B.C., however, they suddenly began to bury their dead in deep shaft graves and, a little later, in conical stone chambers, known as beehive tombs. This development reached its height toward 1300 B.C. in such impressive structures as the one shown in figures 147 and 148, built of concentric layers of precisely cut stone blocks. Its discoverer thought it far too ambitious for a tomb and gave it the misleading name "Treasury of Atreus." Burial places as elaborate as this can be matched only in Egypt during the same period.

The Treasury of Atreus had been robbed of its contents long ago, but other Mycenaean tombs were found intact, and what they yielded up caused even greater surprise: alongside the royal dead were placed masks of gold or silver, presumably to cover their faces. If so, these masks were similar in purpose (if not in style) to the masks found in pharaonic tombs of the Middle and New Kingdoms (compare fig. 104). There was considerable personal equip-

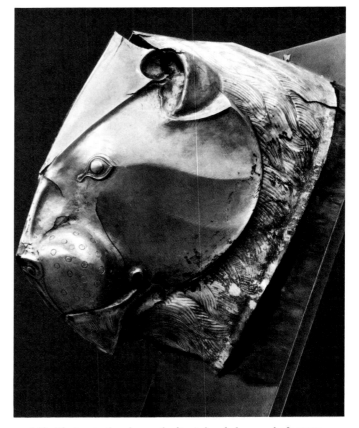

149. Rhyton in the shape of a lion's head, from a shaft grave
at Mycenae. c. 1550 B.C. Gold, height 8″ (20.3 cm).
National Archeological Museum, Athens

ment—drinking vessels, jewelry, weapons—much of it gold and exquisite in workmanship. Some of these pieces, such as the magnificent gold vessel in the shape of a lion's head (fig. 149), show a boldly expressive style of smooth planes

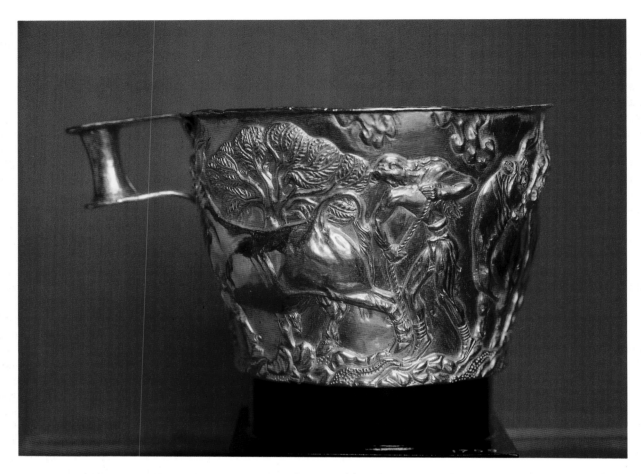

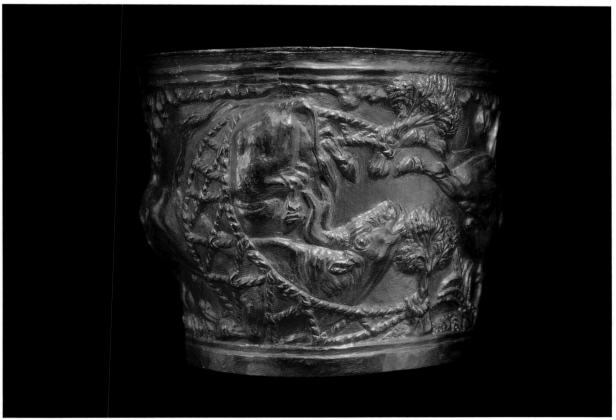

150, 151. *VAPHIO CUPS.* c. 1500 B.C. Gold, heights 3″; 3½″ (7.5; 9 cm).
Shown actual size. National Archeological Museum, Athens

bounded by sharp ridges which suggests contact with the Near East, while others are so Minoan in flavor that they might be imports from Crete.

Of the latter kind are the two famous gold cups from a tomb at Vaphio (figs. 150 and 151); they must have been made about 1500 B.C., a few decades after the lion vessel, but where, for whom, and by whom? Here the problem "Minoan or Mycenaean?" becomes acute. The dispute is not as idle as it may seem, for it tests our ability to differentiate between the two neighboring cultures. It also forces us to consider every aspect of the cups: do we find anything in their style or content that is un-Minoan? Our first impulse, surely, is to note the similarity of the human figures to those on the *Harvester Vase*, and the similarity of the bulls to the animal in *"The Toreador Fresco."* On the other hand, we cannot overlook the fact that the men on the *Vaphio Cups* are not engaged in the Cretan bull-vaulting game but in the far more mundane business of catching the animals on the range, a subject that does not occur in Minoan art, though we do find it in Mycenae. Once we realize this, we are also apt to notice that the design on the cups does not quite match the continuous rhythmic movement of Minoan compositions, and that the animals, for all their physical power, have the look of cattle rather than of sacred animals. It would seem, then, that the cups are a Mycenaean adaptation of Minoan forms, either by a mainland artist or by a Cretan working for Mycenaean patrons.

MYCENAE, CRETE, AND EGYPT. In the sixteenth century B.C., Mycenae thus presents a strange picture: what appears to be an Egyptian influence on burial customs is combined with a strong artistic influence from Crete and with an extraordinary material wealth as expressed in the lavish use of gold. Did the Mycenaeans perhaps conquer the Minoans, causing the destruction of the "new" palaces there about 1500 B.C.? This idea has now been discarded; the new palaces, it seems, were destroyed by a natural catastrophe (earthquakes and tidal waves following the eruption of a volcano). In any event, it does not account for the puzzling connection with Egypt.

What we need is a triangular explanation that involves the Mycenaeans with Crete as well as Egypt about a century before the destruction of the new palaces; and such a theory—fascinating and imaginative, if hard to confirm in detail—has been taking shape in recent years. It runs about as follows: between 1700 and 1580 B.C., the Egyptians were trying to rid themselves of the Hyksos, who had seized the Nile Delta (see page 110). For this they gained the aid of warriors from Mycenae, who returned home laden with gold (of which Egypt alone had an ample supply) and deeply impressed with Egyptian funerary customs. The Minoans, not military but famous as sailors, ferried the Mycenaeans back and forth, so that they, too, had a new and closer contact with Egypt (which may help to account for their sudden prosperity toward 1600 B.C. as well as for the rapid development of naturalistic wall painting at that time). The close relations between Crete and Mycenae, once established, were to last a long time; toward 1400 B.C., when Linear B script began to appear, the Mycenaeans were the rulers of

Crete, either by conquest or through dynastic marriage. In any event, their power rose as that of the Minoans declined; the great monuments of Mycenaean architecture were all built between 1400 and 1200 B.C.

## Architecture

Apart from such details as the shape of the columns or decorative motifs of various sorts, Mycenaean architecture owes little to the Minoan tradition. The palaces on the mainland were hilltop fortresses surrounded by defensive walls of huge stone blocks, a type of construction quite unknown in Crete but similar to the Hittite fortifications at Bogazköy (see fig. 119). The Lion Gate at Mycenae (fig. 152) is the most impressive remnant of these massive ramparts, which inspired such awe in the Greeks of later times that they were regarded as the work of the Cyclopes (a mythical race of one-eyed giants). Even the Treasury of Atreus, although built of smaller and more precisely shaped blocks, has a Cyclopean lintel (see fig. 147).

Another aspect of the Lion Gate foreign to the Minoan tradition is the great stone relief over the doorway. The two lions flanking a symbolic Minoan column have the same grim, heraldic majesty as the golden lion's head we encountered in figure 149. Their function as guardians of the gate, their tense, muscular bodies, and their symmetrical design again suggest an influence from the ancient Near East. We may at this point recall the Trojan War, which brought the Mycenaeans to Asia Minor soon after 1200 B.C.; it seems likely, however, that they began to sally eastward across the Aegean, for trade or war, much earlier than that.

The center of the palace, at Mycenae and other mainland sites, was the royal audience hall, called the megaron. Only its plan is known for certain: a large rectangular room with a round hearth in the middle and four columns to support the roof beams (fig. 153). It was entered through a deep porch with two columns and an antechamber. This design is in essence no more than an enlarged version of the simple houses of earlier generations; its ancestry can be traced back to Middle Helladic times. There must have been a rich decorative scheme of wall paintings and ornamental carvings to stress its dignity as the king's abode.

## Sculpture

No trace has been found of Mycenaean temple architecture—if it ever existed. The palaces did, however, include modest shrines, as in Crete. What gods were worshiped there is a matter of dispute; Mycenaean religion surely included Minoan elements but also influences from Asia Minor, as well as deities of Greek origin inherited from their own forebears. But gods have an odd way of merging or exchanging their identities, so that the religious images in Mycenaean art are extremely hard to interpret.

What, for instance, are we to make of the exquisite little ivory group (fig. 154) unearthed at Mycenae in 1939? The style of the piece—its richly curved shapes and easy, flexible body movements—still echoes Minoan art, but the subject is strange indeed. Two kneeling women, closely united, tend a single child; whose is he? The natural interpretation would be to regard the now headless figure as the mother,

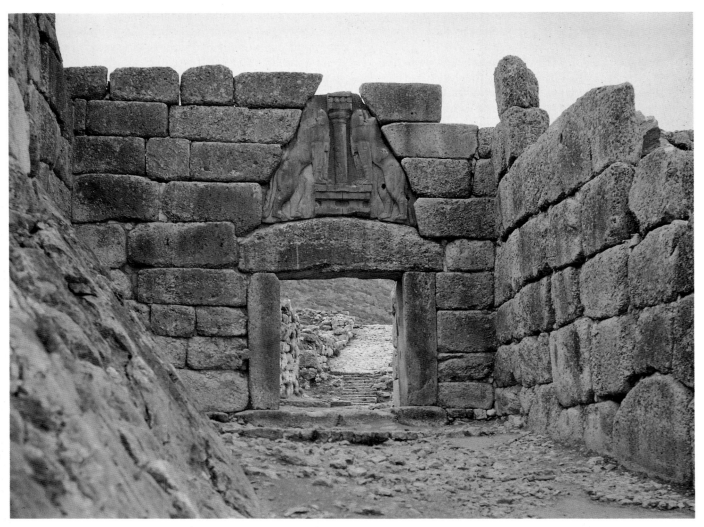

152. The Lion Gate, Mycenae, Greece. 1250 B.C.

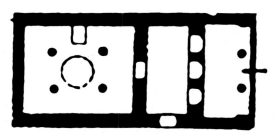

153. Plan of a Mycenaean megaron

since the child clings to her arm and turns toward her; the second woman, whose left hand rests on the other's shoulder, would then be the grandmother. Such three-generation family groups are a well-known subject in Christian art, in which we often find St. Anne, the Virgin Mary, and the Infant Christ combined in similar fashion.

It is the memory of these later works that colors our view of the Mycenaean ivory. Yet we search in vain for a subject in ancient religion that fits our reading of the group. On the other hand, there is a very widespread myth about the divine child (his name varies from place to place) who is aban-

doned by his mother and reared by nymphs, goddesses, or even animals. We are thus forced to conclude—rather reluctantly—that our ivory in all likelihood shows a motherless child god with his nurses. The real mystery, however, lies deeper; it is the tender play of gestures, the intimate human feeling, that binds the three figures together. Nowhere in the entire range of ancient art before the Greeks do we find gods—or people, for that matter—expressing affection with such warmth and eloquence.

Something quite basically new is reflected here, a familiar view of divine beings that makes even the Minoan snake goddess (fig. 140) seem awesome and remote. Was this change of attitude, and the ability to express it in art, a Mycenaean achievement? Or did they inherit it from the Minoans? However that may be, our ivory group opens up a dimension of experience that had never been accessible to Egypt or Mesopotamia.

154. (*opposite*) *THREE DEITIES* , from Mycenae.
c. 1500–1400 B.C. Ivory, height 3″ (7.5 cm).
Shown 250 percent actual size.
National Archeological Museum, Athens

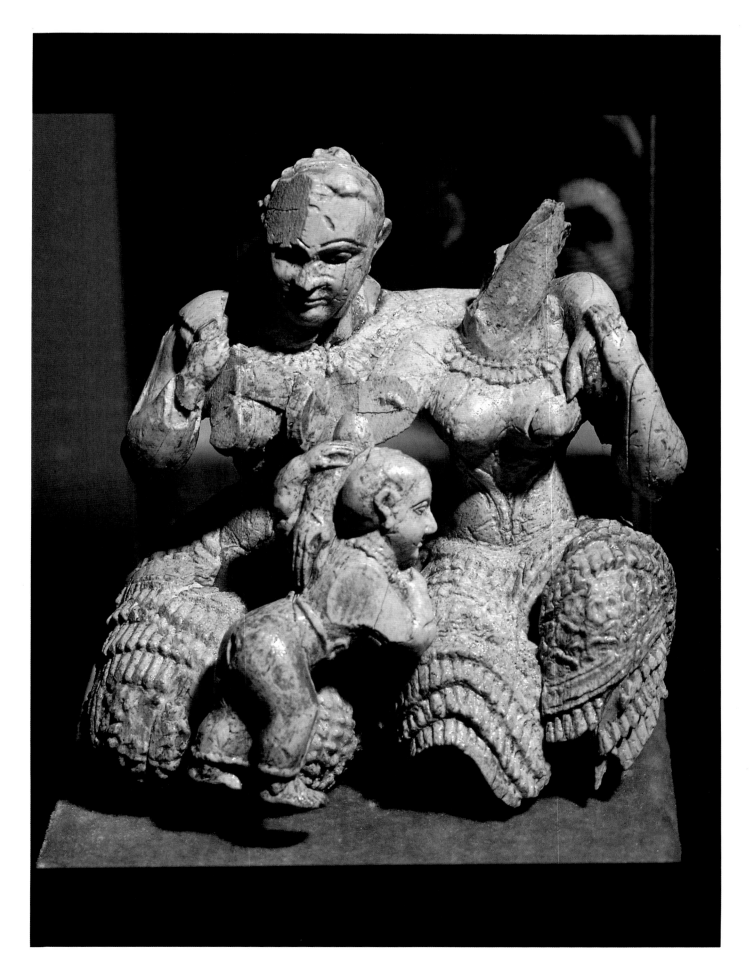

# CHAPTER FIVE
# GREEK ART

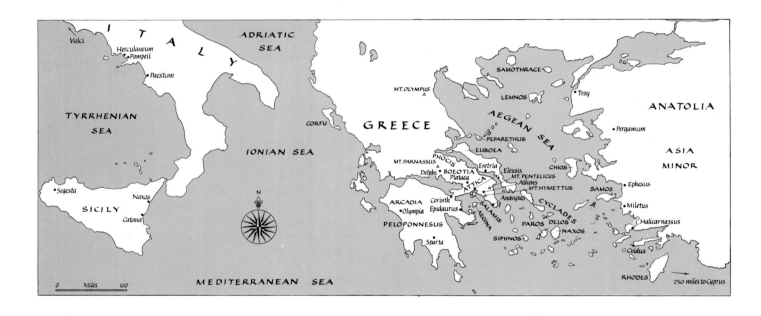

The works of art we have come to know so far are like fascinating strangers: we approach them fully aware of their alien background and of the "language difficulties" they present. If it turns out that, after all, we can understand something of what they have to say, we are surprised and grateful. As soon as we reach the Greeks, our attitude undergoes a change: they are not strangers but relatives, we feel, older members of our own family whom we recognize immediately. A Greek temple will remind us at a glance of the bank around the corner, a Greek statue will bring to mind countless other statues we have seen somewhere, a Greek coin will make us want to reach for the small change in our own pockets. But this air of familiarity is not an unmixed blessing. We would do well to keep in mind that the continuous tradition that links us with the Greeks is a handicap as well as an advantage. If we are to get an unhampered view of Greek architecture, we must take care not to be swayed by our memories of banks and offices, and in judging Greek sculpture we had better forget its latter-day descendants in public parks.

Another complication peculiar to the study of Greek art arises from the fact that we have three separate, and sometimes conflicting, sources of information on the subject. There are, first of all, the monuments themselves, a reliable but often woefully inadequate source. Then we have various copies made in Roman times that tell us something about important Greek works that would otherwise be lost to us entirely. These copies, however, always pose a problem: some are of such high quality that we cannot be sure that they really *are* copies; others make us wonder how faithfully they follow their model (especially if we have several copies, all slightly different, of the same lost original).

Finally, there are the literary sources. The Greeks were the first people in history to write at length about their own artists, and their accounts were eagerly collected by the Romans, who handed them down to us. From them we learn what the Greeks themselves considered their most important achievements in architecture, sculpture, and painting. This written testimony has helped us to identify some celebrated artists and monuments, but much of it deals with works of which no visible trace remains today, while other works, which do survive and which strike us as among the greatest masterpieces of their time, are not mentioned at all. To reconcile the literary evidence with that of the copies and that of the original monuments, and to weave these strands into a coherent picture of the development of Greek art, is a difficult task indeed, despite the vast amount of work that has been done since the beginnings of archaeological scholarship some two hundred and twenty-five years ago.

Who were the Greeks? We have met some of them before, such as the Mycenaeans, who had come to Greece about 2,000 B.C. Other Greek-speaking tribes entered the peninsula from the north, toward 1100 B.C., overwhelmed and absorbed the Mycenaean stock, and gradually spread to the Aegean islands and Asia Minor. It was these tribes who during the following centuries created the great civilization for which we now reserve the name Greek. We do not know how many separate tribal units there were in the beginning,

but two main groups stand out: the Dorians, who settled mostly on the mainland, and the Ionians, who inhabited the Aegean islands and the nearby coast of Asia Minor and thus had closer contacts with the ancient Near East. Some centuries later, the Greeks also spread westward, founding important settlements in Sicily and southern Italy.

Despite a strong sense of kinship based on language and common beliefs, expressed in such traditions as the four great Panhellenic (all-Greek) festivals, the Greeks remained divided into many small, independent city-states. The pattern may be viewed as an echo of age-old tribal loyalties, as an inheritance from the Mycenaeans, or as a response to the geography of Greece, whose mountain ranges, narrow valleys, and jagged coastline would have made political unification difficult in any event. Perhaps all of these factors reinforced one another. The intense rivalry of these states— military, political, and commercial—undoubtedly stimulated the growth of ideas and institutions.

Our own thinking about government continues to make use of a number of key terms of Greek origin which reflect the evolution of the city-state: *monarchy, aristocracy, tyranny, democracy,* and, most important, *politics* (derived from *polites,* the citizen of the *polis,* or city-state). In the end, however, the Greeks paid dearly for their inability to broaden the concept of the state beyond the local limits of the *polis.* The Peloponnesian War (431–404 B.C.), in which the Spartans and their allies defeated the Athenians, was a catastrophe from which Greece never recovered.

## Geometric Style

The formative phase of Greek civilization embraces about four hundred years, from c. 1100 to 700 B.C. Of the first three centuries of this period we know very little, but after about 800 B.C. the Greeks rapidly emerge into the full light of history. The earliest specific dates that have come down to us are from that time: 776 B.C., the founding of the Olympic Games and the starting point of Greek chronology, as well as several slightly later dates recording the foundation of various cities. That time also saw the full development of the oldest characteristically Greek style in the fine arts, the so-called Geometric. We know it only from painted pottery and small-scale sculpture (monumental architecture and sculpture in stone did not appear until the seventh century).

Greek potters quickly developed a considerable variety of shapes (the basic ones are shown in fig. 155). Chief among these was the amphora, a two-handled vase used for storing wine and oil, which provided artists with a generous field. Each type, however, presented unique challenges, and some painters became specialists at decorating certain types of vases.

DIPYLON VASE. At first the pottery had been decorated only with abstract designs—triangles, checkers, concentric circles—but toward 800 B.C. human and animal figures began to appear within the geometric framework, and in the most mature examples these figures could form elaborate scenes. Our specimen (fig. 156), from the Dipylon cemetery in Athens, belongs to a group of very large vases that served

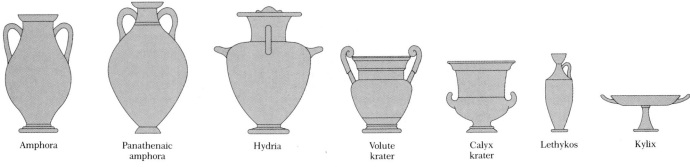

Amphora    Panathenaic    Hydria    Volute    Calyx    Lethykos    Kylix
           amphora                  krater    krater

155. Greek vase shapes

as grave monuments; its bottom has holes through which liquid offerings could filter down to the dead below. On the body of the vessel we see the deceased lying in state, flanked by figures with their arms raised in a gesture of mourning, and a funeral procession of chariots and warriors on foot.

The most remarkable thing about this scene is that it contains no reference to an afterlife; its purpose is purely commemorative. Here lies a worthy man, it tells us, who was mourned by many and had a splendid funeral. Did the Greeks, then, have no conception of a hereafter? They did, but the realm of the dead to them was a colorless, ill-defined region where the souls, or "shades," led a feeble and passive existence without making any demands upon the living. When Odysseus, in the Homeric poem, conjures up the shade of Achilles, all the dead hero can do is mourn his own demise: "Speak not conciliatorily of death, Odysseus. I'd rather serve on earth the poorest man . . . than lord it over all the wasted dead." If the Greeks nevertheless marked and tended their graves, and even poured libations over them, they did so in a spirit of pious remembrance, rather than to satisfy the needs of the dead. Clearly, they had refused to adopt the elaborate burial customs of the Mycenaeans (see page 145). Nor is the Geometric style an outgrowth of the Mycenaean tradition but a fresh—and in some respects quite primitive—start.

Given his limited repertory of shapes, the artist who painted our vase has achieved an astonishingly varied effect. The spacing of the bands, their width and density show a rather subtle relationship to the structure of the vessel. His interest in representation, however, is as yet very limited: the figures or groups, repeated at regular intervals, are little more than another kind of ornament, part of the same over-all texture, so that their size varies in accordance with the area to be filled. Organic and geometric elements still coexist in the same field, and the distinction between them is often difficult: lozenges indicate legs, whether of a man, a chair, or a bier; circles with dots may or may not be human heads; and the chevrons, boxed triangles, and so on between the figures may be decorative or descriptive—we cannot tell.

Much the same could be said of figure 157, a shipwreck scene from another Geometric vase which makes an instructive contrast with the Minoan view of marine life (see fig. 144); if it were not for the fact that the boat is upside

down and that the biggest fish has seized the head of one of the men, we would read the design simply as a pattern, rather than as a disaster at sea. And what of the swastikas? Are they ornamentalized starfish or abstract space fillers?

Geometric pottery has been found not only in Greece but in Italy and the Near East as well, a clear indication that Greek traders were well established throughout the eastern

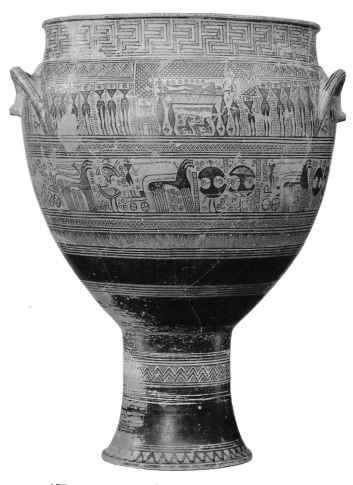

156. *DIPYLON VASE*. 8th century B.C. 42⅝" (108.2 cm).
The Metropolitan Museum of Art,
New York. Rogers Fund, 1914

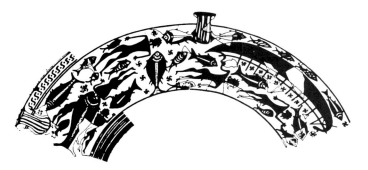

157. *SHIPWRECK*. Drawing after a Geometric vase
in the Museum at Ischia, Greece. 8th century B.C.

Mediterranean in the eighth century B.C. What is more, they had already adopted the Phoenician alphabet and reshaped it for their own use, as we know from the inscriptions on these same vases. The greatest Greek achievements of this era, however, are the two Homeric epics, the *Iliad* and the *Odyssey*. The scenes on Geometric vases contain barely a hint of the narrative power of these poems; if our knowledge of eighth-century Greece were based on the visual arts alone, we would inevitably think of it as a far simpler and more provincial society than the literary evidence suggests.

There is a paradox here that needs to be resolved. Perhaps, at this particular time, Greek civilization was so language-minded that painting and sculpture played a less important role than they were to assume in the following centuries. In that event, the Geometric style may well have been something of an anachronism in the eighth century, a conservative tradition about to burst at the seams. In the shipwreck scene, its rigid order already seems to be dissolving; representation and narrative demand greater scope than the style can provide. Toward 700 B.C., the dam finally bursts; new forms come flooding in, and Greek art enters another phase, which we call the Orientalizing style.

## Orientalizing Style

As its name implies, the new style reflects powerful influences from Egypt and the Near East, stimulated by increasing trade with these regions. Between c. 725 and 650 B.C. Greek art absorbed a host of Oriental motifs and ideas, and was profoundly transformed in the process. The change becomes very evident if we compare the large amphora from Eleusis (fig. 158) with the *Dipylon Vase* of a hundred years earlier (fig. 156).

ELEUSIS AMPHORA. Geometric ornament has not disappeared from this vase altogether, but it is confined to the peripheral zones—the foot, the handles, and the lip; new, curvilinear motifs—such as spirals, interlacing bands, palmettes and rosettes—are conspicuous everywhere; on the shoulder of the vessel we see a frieze of fighting animals, derived from the repertory of Near Eastern art. The major areas, however, are given over to narrative, which has become the dominant element.

Narrative painting tapped a nearly inexhaustible source of subjects from Greek myths and legends. These tales were the result of mixing local Doric and Ionic deities and heroes into the pantheon of Olympian gods and Homeric sagas. They also represent a comprehensive attempt to understand the world. The Greeks grasped the internal meaning of events in terms of fate and human character rather than as

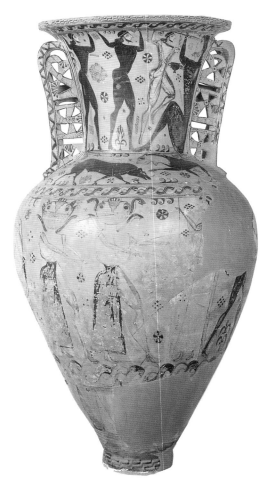

158. *THE BLINDING OF POLYPHEMUS* and *GORGONS*, on
a Proto-Attic amphora. c. 675–650 B.C.
Height 56″ (142.3 cm). Archaeological Museum, Eleusis

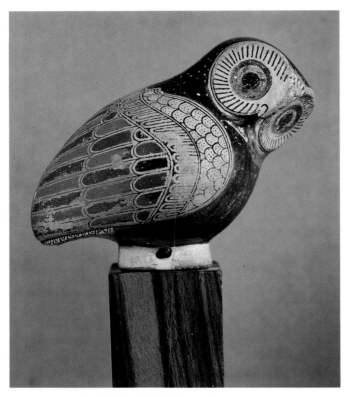

159. Proto-Corinthian perfume vase.
c. 650 B.C. Height 2″ (5 cm). Musée du Louvre, Paris

the accidents of history, in which they had little interest before about 500 B.C. The main focus was on explaining why the legendary heroes of the past seemed incomparably greater than men of the present. Some were historical figures—Herakles, for example, was the king of Mycenaean Tiryns—but all were believed to be descendants of the gods, themselves often very human in behavior, who had had children with mortals. This lineage explained the hero's extraordinary powers.

Such an outlook also helps us to understand the strong appeal exerted on the Greek imagination by Oriental lions and monsters. These terrifying creatures embodied the unknown forces of life faced by the hero. This fascination is clearly seen on the Eleusis amphora. The figures have gained so much in size and descriptive precision that the decorative patterns scattered among them can no longer interfere with their actions; ornament of any sort now belongs to a separate and lesser realm, clearly distinguishable from that of representation.

As a result, the blinding of the giant Polyphemus by Odysseus and his companions—the scene on the neck of the amphora—is enacted with memorable directness and dramatic force. If these men lack the beauty we expect of epic heroes, their movements have an expressive vigor that makes them seem thoroughly alive. The slaying of another monstrous creature is depicted on the body of the vase, the main part of which has been badly damaged, so that only two figures have survived intact; they are Gorgons, the sisters of the snake-haired, terrible-faced Medusa whom Perseus killed

with the aid of the gods. Even here we notice an interest in the articulation of the body far beyond the limits of the Geometric style.

The Eleusis vase belongs to a group called Proto-Attic, the ancestors of the great tradition of vase painting that was soon to develop in Attica, the region around Athens. A second family of Orientalizing vases is known as Proto-Corinthian, since it points toward the later pottery production of Corinth. These vessels, noted for their spirited animal motifs, show particularly close links with the Near East. Some of them, such as the perfume vase in figure 159, are molded in the shape of animals. The enchanting little owl, "streamlined" to fit the palm of a lady's hand and yet so animated in pose and expression, helps us to understand why Greek pottery came to be in demand throughout the Mediterranean world.

## ARCHAIC VASE PAINTING

The Orientalizing phase of Greek art was a period of experiment and transition, in contrast to the stable and consistent Geometric style. Once the new elements from the East had been fully assimilated, there emerged another style, as well defined as the Geometric but infinitely greater in range: the Archaic, which lasted from the later seventh century to about 480 B.C., the time of the famous Greek victories over the Persians at Salamis and Plataea. During the Archaic period, we witness the unfolding of the artistic genius of Greece not only in vase painting but also in monumental architecture and sculpture. While Archaic art lacks the balance, the sense of perfection of the Classical style of the later fifth century, it has a freshness that gives it particularly strong appeal for the modern beholder. It is difficult to argue with those who regard it as the most vital phase in the development of Greek art.

Greek architecture and sculpture on a large scale must have begun to develop long before the mid-seventh century. Until that time, however, both were mainly of wood, and nothing of them has survived except the foundations of a few buildings. The desire to build and sculpt in stone, for the sake of permanence, was the most important new idea that entered Greece during the Orientalizing period. Moreover, the revolution in material and technique must have brought about decisive changes of style as well, so that we cannot safely reconstruct the appearance of the lost wooden temples or statues on the basis of later works. In vase painting, on the other hand, there was no such break in continuity. It thus seems best to deal with Archaic vases before we turn to the sculpture and architecture of the period.

The significance of Archaic vase painting is in some ways completely unique. Decorated pottery, however great its value as an archaeologist's tool, rarely enters into the mainstream of the history of art; we think of it, in general, as a craft or industry. This remains true even of Minoan vases, despite their exceptional beauty and technical refinement, and the same may be said of the vast bulk of Greek pottery. Yet if we study such pieces as the *Dipylon Vase* or the amphora from Eleusis, impressive not only by virtue of their sheer size but as vehicles of pictorial effort, we cannot escape the feeling that they are among the most ambitious works of art of their day.

There is no way to prove this, of course—far too much has been lost—but it seems obvious that these are objects of highly individual character, rather than routine ware produced in quantity according to set patterns. Archaic vases are generally a good deal smaller than their predecessors, since pottery vessels no longer served as grave monuments (which were now made of stone). Their painted decoration, however, shows a far greater emphasis on pictorial subjects (fig. 162); scenes from mythology, legend, and everyday life appear in endless variety, and the artistic level is often very high indeed, especially among Athenian vases.

How greatly the Greeks themselves valued the beauty of these vessels is evident from figure 160, which shows Athena and two Victories bestowing wreaths on a vase painter and two male assistants, presumably because he was the winner of a contest. The scene also includes a female assistant (on the extreme right), the earliest depiction we know of a woman artist at work. She was, we may assume, a member of a family workshop. Unlike Sappho, the greatest of early Greek lyric poets, women artists in Greece never achieved individual fame; yet even the subordinate role played by our female vase painter must be significant of women's participation in the arts.

After the middle of the sixth century, the finest vases frequently bear the signatures of the artists who made them. This indicates not only that individual artists—potters as well as painters—took pride in their work, but also that they could become famous for their personal style. To us, such signatures in themselves do not mean a great deal; they are no more than convenient labels unless we know enough of an artist's work to gain some insight into his personality. And, remarkably enough, that is possible with a good many Archaic vase painters. Some of them have so distinctive a style that their artistic "handwriting" can be recognized even without the aid of a signature; and in a few cases we are lucky enough to have dozens (in one instance, over two hundred) of vases by the same hand, so that we can trace one master's development over a considerable period. Archaic vase painting thus introduces us to the first clearly defined personalities in the entire history of art. For while it is true that signatures occur in Archaic sculpture and architecture as well, they have not helped us to identify the personalities of individual masters.

Archaic Greek painting was, of course, not confined to vases. There were murals and panels, too. Although nothing has survived of them except a few poorly preserved fragments, we can form a fair idea of what they looked like from the wall paintings in Etruscan tombs of the same period (see figs. 242 and 243). How, we wonder, were these large-scale works related to the vase pictures? We do not know—but one thing seems certain: *all* Archaic painting was essentially drawing filled in with solid, flat color, and therefore murals could not have been very different in appearance from vase pictures.

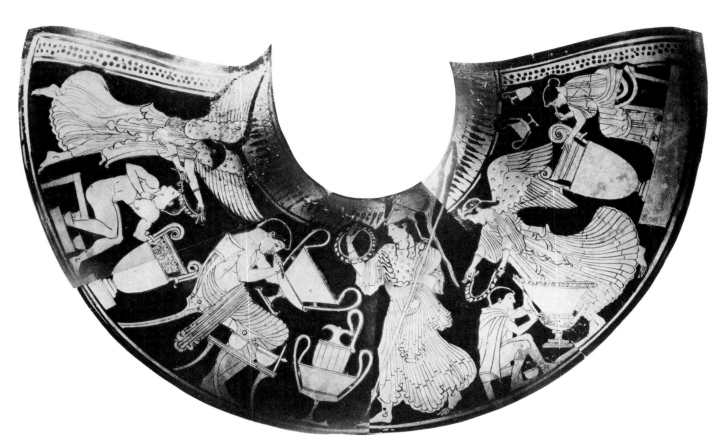

160. *A VASE PAINTER AND ASSISTANTS, CROWNED BY ATHENA AND VICTORIES.*
Detail from an Attic red-figured hydria (composite photograph). c. 450 B.C. Private collection

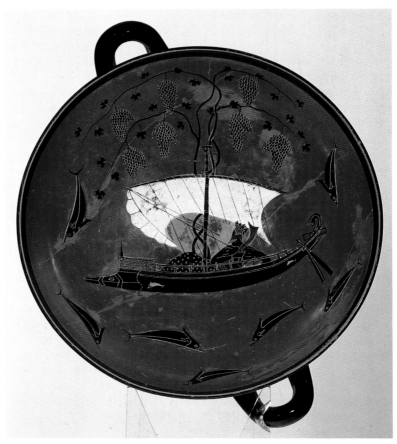

161. EXEKIAS. *DIONYSUS IN A BOAT.* Interior of an Attic black-figured kylix. c. 540 B.C.
Diameter 12″ (30.5 cm). Staatliche Antikensammlungen, Munich

According to the literary sources, Greek wall painting did not come into its own until after the Persian wars (c. 475–450 B.C.), through the gradual discovery of modeling and spatial depth. From that time on, vase painting became a lesser art, since depth and modeling were beyond its limited technical means; by the end of the fifth century, its decline was obvious. The great age of vase painting, then, was the Archaic era. Until about 475 B.C., good vase painters enjoyed as much prestige as other artists. Whether or not their work directly reflects the lost wall paintings, it deserves to be viewed as a major achievement.

BLACK-FIGURED STYLE. The difference between Orientalizing and Archaic vase painting is one of artistic discipline. In the amphora from Eleusis (fig. 158), the figures are shown partly as solid silhouettes, partly in outline, or as a combination of both. Toward the end of the seventh century, Attic vase painters resolved these inconsistencies by adopting the "black-figured" style, which means that the entire design is silhouetted in black against the reddish clay; internal details are scratched in with a needle, and white and purple may be added on top of the black to make certain areas stand out. The virtues of this procedure, which favors a decorative, two-dimensional effect, are apparent in figure 161, a kylix (drinking cup) of c. 540 B.C. by Exekias. The slender, sharp-edged forms have a lacelike delicacy, yet also

resilience and strength, so that the composition adapts itself to the circular surface without becoming mere ornament. Dionysus reclines in his boat (the sail was once entirely white); it moves with the same ease as the dolphins, whose light forms are counterbalanced by the heavy clusters of grapes. But why is he at sea? What does the happy poetry of Exekias' image mean?

According to a Homeric hymn, the god of wine had once been abducted by pirates, whereupon he caused vines to grow all over the ship and frightened his captors until they jumped overboard and were turned into dolphins. We see him here on his return journey (an event to be gratefully recalled by every Greek drinker), accompanied by seven dolphins and seven bunches of grapes for good luck.

If the spare elegance of Exekias seems to retain something of the spirit of Geometric pottery (see fig. 157 for an instructive comparison), the work of the slightly younger Psiax seems more akin to the forceful Orientalizing style of the blinding of Polyphemus in the Eleusis amphora. The scene of Herakles killing the lion, on an amphora attributed to Psiax (fig. 162), is all grimness and violence. The two

162. (*opposite*) PSIAX. *HERAKLES STRANGLING THE NEMEAN LION,*
on an Attic black-figured amphora from Vulci, Italy. c. 525 B.C.
Height 19½″ (49.5 cm). Museo Civico, Brescia

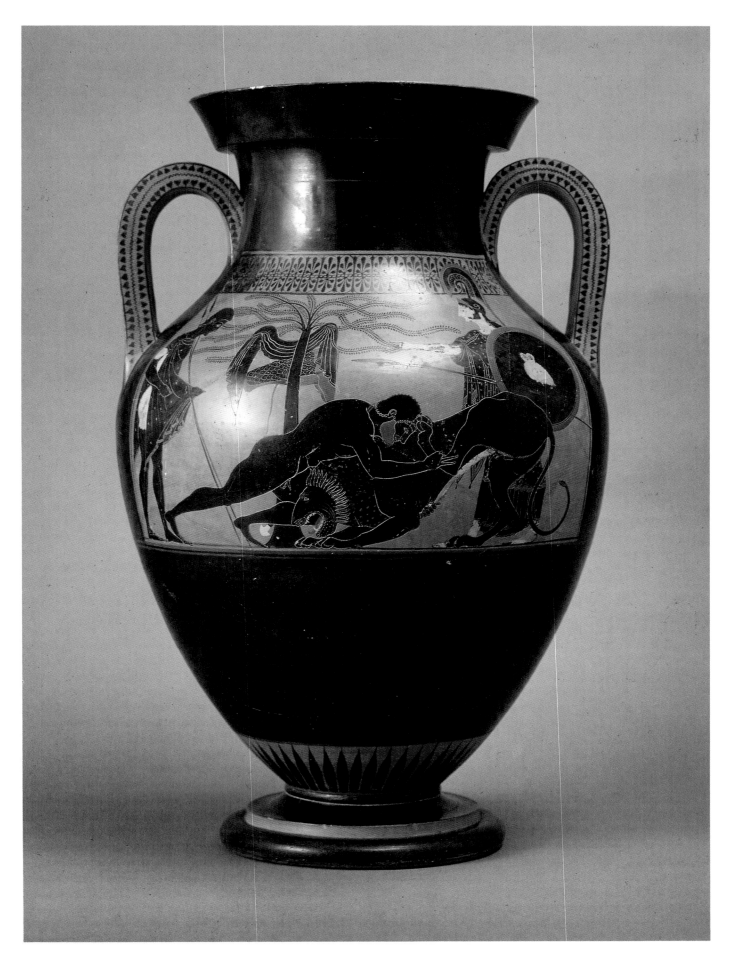

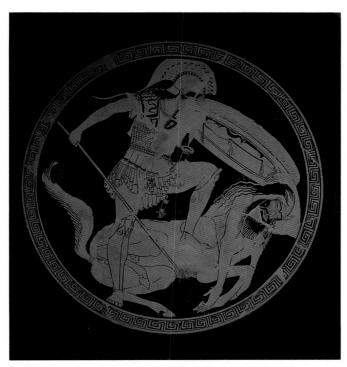

163. THE "FOUNDRY PAINTER." *LAPITH AND CENTAUR.*
Interior of an Attic red-figured kylix. c. 490–480 B.C.
Staatliche Antikensammlungen, Munich

heavy bodies are truly locked in combat, so that they almost grow together into a single, compact unit. Incised lines and subsidiary colors have been added with utmost economy in order to avoid breaking up the massive expanse of black. Yet Psiax succeeds to an extraordinary degree in conveying the three-dimensional quality of these figures; his knowledge of body structure, his ability to use foreshortening—note the way the abdomen and shoulders of Herakles are rendered—seem little short of amazing when measured against anything we have seen before. Only in such details as the eye of Herakles do we still find the traditional combination of front and profile views.

RED-FIGURED STYLE. Psiax must have felt that the silhouettelike black-figured technique made the study of foreshortening unduly difficult, for in some of his vases he tried the reverse procedure, leaving the figures red and filling in the background. This red-figured technique gradually replaced the older method toward 500 B.C. Its advantages are well shown in figure 163, a kylix of c. 490–480 B.C. by an unknown master nicknamed the "Foundry Painter." The details of the *Lapith and Centaur* are now freely drawn with the brush, rather than laboriously incised, so the artist depends far less on the profile view than before; instead, he exploits the internal lines of communication that permit him to show boldly foreshortened and overlapping limbs, precise details of costume (note the pleated skirt), and interest in facial expressions. He is so fascinated by all these new effects that he has made the figures as large as he possibly could. They almost seem to burst from their circular frame, and a piece of the Lapith's helmet has actually been cut off.

A similar striving for monumental effect, but with more harmonious results, may be seen in the *Eos and Memnon* by Douris (fig. 164), one of the masterpieces of late Archaic vase painting. It shows the goddess of dawn holding the body of her son, who had been killed and despoiled of his armor by Achilles. In this moving evocation of grief, Greek art touches a mood that seems strangely prophetic of the Christian *Pietà* (see fig. 505). Notable too is the expressive freedom of the draftsmanship; the lines are as flexible as if they had been done with a pen. Douris knows how to trace the contours of limbs beneath the drapery, how to contrast vigorous, dynamic outlines with thinner and more delicate secondary strokes, such as those indicating the anatomical details of Memnon's body. This vase also has a special interest because of its elaborate inscription, which includes the signatures of both painter and potter as well as a dedication ("Hermogenes is beautiful").

# ARCHAIC SCULPTURE

The new motifs that distinguish the Orientalizing style from the Geometric—fighting animals, winged monsters, scenes of combat—had reached Greece mainly through the importation of ivory carvings and metalwork from Phoenicia or Syria, pieces that reflected Mesopotamian as well as Egyptian influences. Such objects have actually been found on Greek soil, so that we can regard this channel of transmission as well established. They do not help us, however, to explain the rise of monumental architecture and sculpture in stone about 650 B.C., which must have been based on acquaintance with Egyptian works that could be studied only on the spot. We know that small colonies of Greeks existed in Egypt at the time, but why, we wonder, did Greece sud-

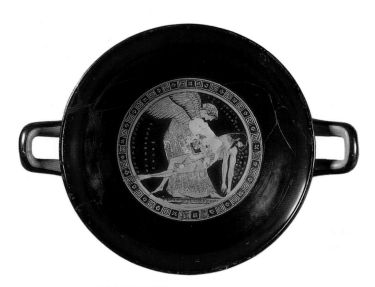

164. DOURIS. *EOS AND MEMNON.*
Interior of an Attic red-figured kylix. c. 490–480 B.C.
Diameter 10½" (26.7 cm). Musée du Louvre, Paris

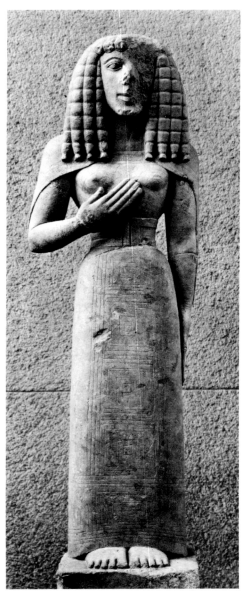

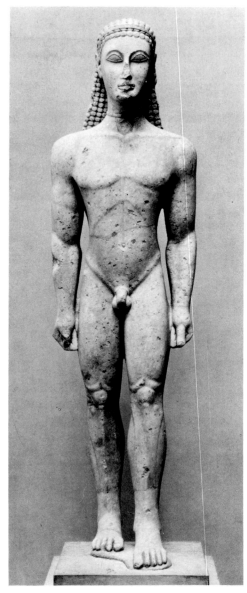

165. *FEMALE FIGURE,* c. 650 B.C. Limestone, height 24½″ (62.3 cm). Musée du Louvre, Paris

166. *STANDING YOUTH (KOUROS).* c. 600 B.C. Marble, height 6′1½″ (1.9 m). The Metropolitan Museum of Art, New York. Fletcher Fund, 1932

denly develop a taste for monumentality, and how did her artists acquire so quickly the Egyptian mastery of stone carving? The mystery may never be cleared up, for the oldest surviving Greek stone sculpture and architecture show that the Egyptian tradition had already been well assimilated and Hellenized, though their link with Egypt is still clearly visible.

## Kouros and Kore

Let us consider two very early Greek statues, a female figure of c. 650–625 B.C. (fig. 165) and a nude youth of c. 600 B.C. (fig. 166), and compare them with their Egyptian predecessors (fig. 85). The similarities are certainly striking: we note the block-conscious, cubic character of all four statues, the

slim, broad-shouldered silhouette of the male figures, the position of their arms, their clenched fists, the way they stand with the left leg forward, the emphatic rendering of the kneecaps. The formalized, wiglike treatment of the hair, the close-fitting garment of the female figure, and her raised arm are further points of resemblance. Judged by Egyptian standards, the Archaic statues seem somewhat "primitive"—rigid, oversimplified, awkward, less close to nature. Whereas the Egyptian sculptor allows the legs and hips of the female figure to press through the skirt, the Greek shows a solid, undifferentiated mass from which only the toes protrude.

But the Greek statues also have virtues of their own that cannot be measured in Egyptian terms. First of all, they are

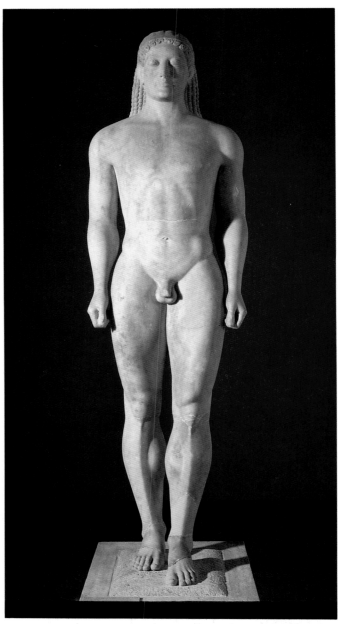

167. *KROISOS (KOUROS FROM ANAVYSOS)*. c. 525 B.C. Marble, height 6'4" (1.9 m). National Archaeological Museum, Athens

ceptions are the tiny bridges between the fists and the thighs of the nude youth). Apparently it is of the greatest importance to him that a statue consist only of stone that has representational meaning within an organic whole; the stone must be transformed. It cannot be permitted to remain inert, neutral matter.

This is not, we must insist, a question of technique but of artistic intention. The act of liberation achieved in our two figures endows them with a spirit basically different from that of any of the Egyptian statues. While the latter seem becalmed by a spell that has released them from every strain for all time to come, the Greek images are tense, full of hidden life. The direct stare of their huge eyes offers the most telling contrast to the gentle, faraway gaze of the Egyptian figures.

Whom do they represent? We call the female statues by the general name of Kore (Maiden), the male ones by that of Kouros (Youth)—noncommittal terms that gloss over the difficulty of identifying them further. Nor can we explain why the Kouros is always nude while the Kore is clothed. Whatever the reason, both types were produced in large numbers throughout the Archaic era, and their general outlines remained extraordinarily stable. Some are inscribed with the names of artists ("So-and-so made me") or with dedications to various deities. These, then, were votive offerings; but whether they represent the donor, the deity, or a divinely favored person such as a victor in athletic games remains uncertain in most cases. Others were placed on graves, yet they can be viewed as representations of the deceased only in the broadest (and completely impersonal) sense. This odd lack of differentiation seems part of the essential character of these figures; they are neither gods nor mortals but something in between, an ideal of physical perfection and vitality shared by mortal and immortal alike, just as the heroes of the Homeric epics dwell in the realms of both history and mythology.

If the type of Kouros and Kore is narrowly circumscribed, its artistic interpretation shows the same inner dynamic we have traced in Archaic vase painting. The pace of this development becomes strikingly clear from a comparison of the Kouros of figure 166 with another carved some seventy-five years later (fig. 167) and identified by the inscription on its base as the funerary statue of Kroisos, who had died a hero's death in the front line of battle. Like all such figures, it was originally painted; traces of color can still be seen in the hair and the pupils of the eyes. Instead of the sharply contoured, abstract planes of the older statue, we now find swelling curves. The whole body displays a greater awareness of massive volumes, but also a new elasticity, and countless anatomical details are more functionally rendered than before. The style of the *Kroisos* thus corresponds exactly to that of Psiax's Herakles (fig. 162); we witness the transition from black-figured to red-figured in sculptural terms.

There are numerous statues from the middle years of the sixth century marking previous way stations along the same road, such as the magnificent *Calf-Bearer* of c. 570 B.C. (fig. 168), a votive figure representing the donor with the sacrificial animal he is offering to Athena. Needless to say, it is not a portrait, any more than the *Kroisos* is, but it shows a

truly free-standing—the earliest large stone images of the human form in the entire history of art of which this can be said. The Egyptian carver had never dared to liberate such figures completely from the stone; they remain immersed in it to some degree, as it were, so that the empty spaces between the legs and between the arms and the torso (or between two figures in a double statue, as in fig. 85) always remain partly filled. There are never any holes in Egyptian stone figures. In that sense, they do not rank as sculpture in the round but as an extreme case of high relief. The Greek carver, on the contrary, does not mind holes in the least; he separates the arms from the torso and the legs from each other (unless they are encased in a skirt), and goes to great lengths to cut away every bit of dead material (the only extype: the beard indicates a man of mature years. The *Calf-Bearer* originally had the Kouros standing pose (the legs are badly damaged), and the body conforms to the Kouros ideal of physical perfection; its vigorous, compact forms are emphasized, rather than obscured, by the thin cloak, which fits them like a second skin, detaching itself only momentarily at the elbows. The face, effectively framed by the soft curve of the animal, no longer has the masklike quality of the early Kouros; the features have, as it were, caught up with the rest of the body in that they, too, are permitted a gesture, a movement expressive of life: the lips are drawn up in a smile. We must be careful not to impute any psychological meaning to this "Archaic smile," for the same radiant expression occurs throughout sixth-century Greek sculpture (even on the face of the dead hero Kroisos). Only after 500 B.C. does it gradually fade out.

One of the most famous instances of this smile is the wonderful *Rampin Head* (fig. 169), which probably belonged to the body of a horseman. Slightly later than the *Calf-Bearer*, it shows the black-figured phase of Archaic sculpture at its highest stage of refinement. Hair and beard have the appearance of richly textured beaded embroidery that sets off the subtly accented planes of the face.

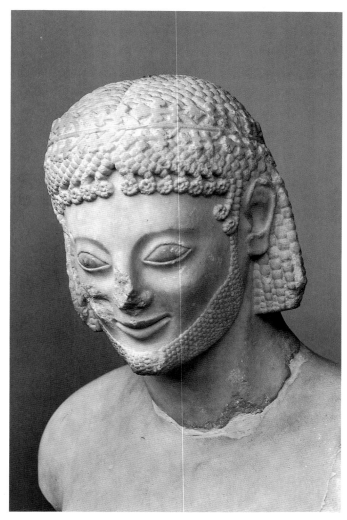

169. *THE RAMPIN HEAD*. c. 560 B.C. Marble, height 11½″ (29.3 cm). Musée du Louvre, Paris

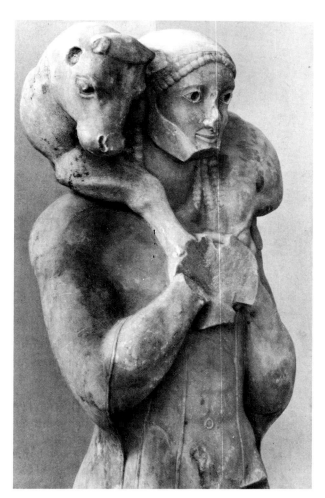

168. *CALF-BEARER*, upper portion. c. 570 B.C. Marble, height of entire statue 65″ (165 cm). Acropolis Museum, Athens

The Kore type is somewhat more variable than that of the Kouros, although it follows the same pattern of development. A clothed figure by definition, it poses a different problem—how to relate body and drapery. It is also likely to reflect changing habits or local differences of dress. Thus, the impressive statue in figure 170, carved about the same time as the *Calf-Bearer*, does not represent a more evolved stage of the Kore in figure 165 but an alternative approach to the same basic task. She was found in the Temple of Hera on the island of Samos and may well have been an image of the goddess because of her great size as well as her extraordinary dignity. If the earlier Kore echoes the planes of a rectangular slab, the "*Hera*" seems like a column come to life. Instead of clear-cut accents, such as the nipped-in waist in figure 165, we find here a smooth, continuous flow of lines uniting limbs and body. Yet the majestic effect of the statue depends not so much on its abstract quality as on the way the abstract form blossoms forth into the swelling softness of a living body. The great upward sweep of the lower third of the figure gradually subdivides to reveal several separate layers of garments, and its pace is slowed further (but never fully stopped) as it encounters the protruding shapes of arms, hips, and torso. In the end, the drapery, so completely architectonic up to the knee region, turns into a second skin, the kind we have seen in the *Calf-Bearer*.

The Kore of figure 171, in contrast, seems a linear descendant of our first Kore, even though she was carved a full century later. She, too, is blocklike rather than columnar, with a strongly accented waist. The simplicity of her garments, however, is new and sophisticated; the heavy cloth forms a distinct, separate layer over the body, covering but not concealing the solidly rounded shapes beneath. And the left hand, which originally was extended forward, proffering a votive gift of some sort, must have given the statue a spatial quality quite beyond the two earlier Kore figures we have discussed. Equally new is the more organic treatment of the hair, which falls over the shoulders in soft, curly strands, as compared with the massive, rigid wig in figure 165. Most

noteworthy of all, perhaps, is the full, round face with its enchantingly gay expression—a softer, more natural smile than any we have seen hitherto. Here, as in the *Kroisos*, we sense the approaching red-figured phase of Archaic art.

Our final Kore (fig. 172), about a decade later, has none of the severity of figure 171, though both were found on the Acropolis of Athens. In many ways she seems more akin to the "*Hera*" from Samos: in fact, she probably came from Chios, another island of Ionian Greece. The architectural grandeur of her ancestress, though, has given way to an ornate, perhaps overly refined grace. The garments still loop around the body in soft diagonal curves, but the play of richly differentiated folds, pleats, and textures has almost become an end in itself. Color must have played a particularly important role in such works, and we are fortunate that so much of it survives in this example.

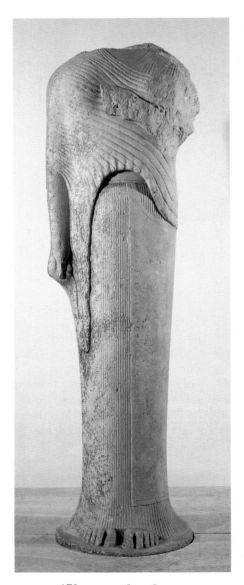 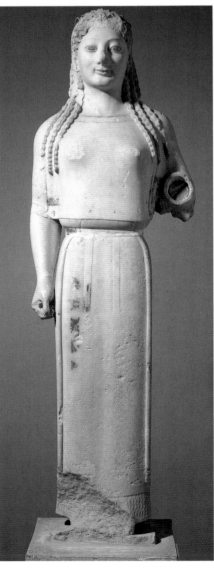 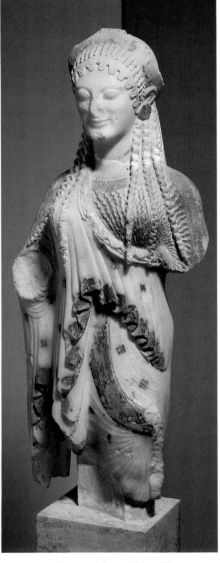

170. *"HERA,"* from Samos.
c. 570–560 B.C. Marble,
height 6′4″ (1.9 m). Musée du Louvre, Paris

171. *KORE IN DORIAN PEPLOS.*
c. 530 B.C. Marble, height 48″ (122 cm).
Acropolis Museum, Athens

172. *KORE,* from Chios (?).
c. 520 B.C. Marble, height 21⅞″ (55.3 cm).
Acropolis Museum, Athens

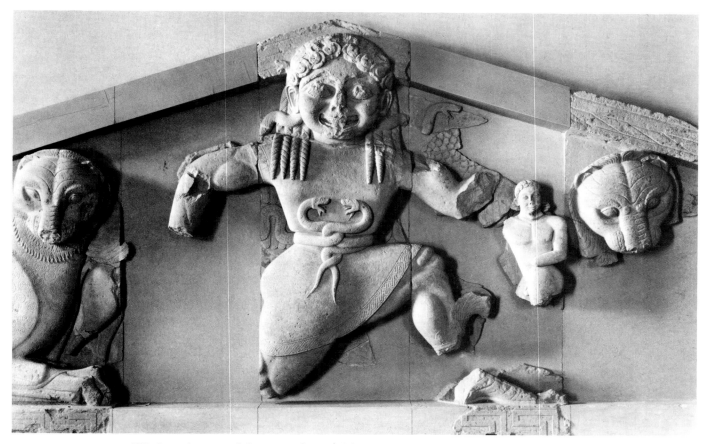

173. Central portion of the west pediment of the Temple of Artemis at Corfu. c. 600–580 B.C.
Limestone, height 9′2″ (2.8 m). Archaeological Museum, Corfu

## Architectural Sculpture

When the Greeks began to build their temples in stone, they also fell heir to the age-old tradition of architectural sculpture. The Egyptians had been covering the walls (and even the columns) of their buildings with reliefs since the time of the Old Kingdom, but these carvings were so shallow (for example, figs. 89 and 103) that they left the continuity of the wall surface undisturbed; they had no weight or volume of their own, so that they were related to their architectural setting only in the same limited sense as Egyptian wall paintings (with which they were, in practice, interchangeable). This is also true of the reliefs on Assyrian, Babylonian, and Persian buildings (for example, figs. 123 and 132). There existed, however, another kind of architectural sculpture in the ancient Near East, originated, it seems, by the Hittites: the great guardian monsters protruding from the blocks that framed the gateways of fortresses or palaces (see figs. 119 and 121). This tradition must have inspired, although perhaps indirectly, the carving over the Lion Gate at Mycenae (see fig. 152). We must nevertheless note one important feature that distinguishes the Mycenaean guardian figures from their predecessors: although they are carved in high relief on a huge slab, this slab is thin and light compared to the enormously heavy, Cyclopean blocks around it. In building the gate, the Mycenaean architect left an empty triangular space above the lintel, for fear that the weight of the wall above would crush it, and then filled the hole with the com-

paratively lightweight relief panel. Here, then, we have a new kind of architectural sculpture—a work integrated with the structure yet also a separate entity rather than a modified wall surface or block.

TEMPLE OF ARTEMIS, CORFU. The Lion Gate relief is indeed the direct ancestor of Greek architectural sculpture, as will become evident when we compare it with the façade of the early Archaic Temple of Artemis on the island of Corfu, erected soon after 600 B.C. (figs. 173 and 174). Here again

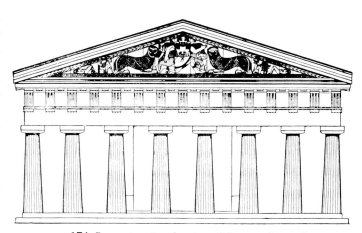

174. Reconstruction drawing of the west front of
the Temple of Artemis at Corfu (after Rodenwaldt)

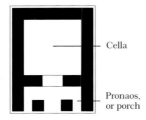

175. Plan of the Treasury of the Siphnians

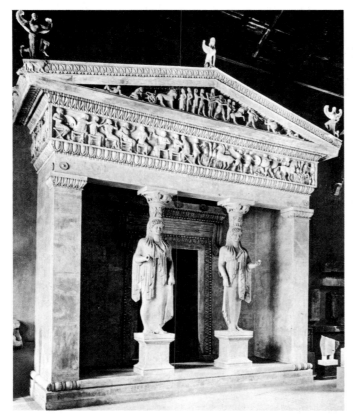

176. Reconstruction of the façade of the Treasury of
the Siphnians in the Sanctuary of Apollo at Delphi. c. 525 B.C.
Archeological Museum, Delphi

the sculpture is confined to a zone that is framed by structural members but is itself structurally empty: the triangle between the horizontal ceiling and the sloping sides of the roof. This area, called the pediment, need not be filled in at all except to protect the wooden rafters behind it against moisture; it demands not a wall but merely a thin screen. And it is against this screen that the pedimental sculpture is displayed.

Technically, these carvings are in high relief, like the guardian lions at Mycenae. Characteristically enough, however, the bodies are strongly undercut, so as to detach them from the background. Even at this early stage of development, the Greek sculptor wanted to assert the independence

of his figures from their architectural setting. The head of the central figure actually overlaps the frame. Who is this frightening creature? Not Artemis, surely, although the temple was dedicated to that goddess. As a matter of fact, we have met her before: she is a Gorgon, a descendant of those on the Eleusis amphora (fig. 158). Her purpose here was to serve as a guardian, along with the two huge lions, warding off evil from the temple and the sacred image of the goddess within. (The other pediment, of which only small fragments survive, had a similar figure.) She might be defined, therefore, as an extraordinarily monumental—and still rather frightening—hex sign. On her face, the Archaic smile appears as a hideous grin; and to emphasize further how alive and real she is, she has been represented running, or rather flying, in a pinwheel stance that conveys movement without locomotion.

The symmetrical, heraldic arrangement of the Gorgon and the two animals reflects an Oriental scheme which we know not only from the Lion Gate at Mycenae but from many earlier examples as well (see fig. 71, bottom center, and fig. 113, top). Because of its ornamental character, it fits the shape of the pediment to perfection. Yet the early Archaic designer was not content with that; he also wanted the pediment to contain narrative scenes; therefore he has added a number of smaller figures in the spaces left between or behind the huge main group. The design of the whole thus shows two conflicting purposes in uneasy balance. As we might expect, narrative will soon win out over heraldry.

Aside from the pediment, there were not many places that the Greeks deemed suitable for architectural sculpture. They might put free-standing figures—often of terracotta—above the ends and the center of the pediment to break the severity of its outline. And they often placed reliefs in the zone immediately below the pediment. In Doric temples such as that at Corfu (fig. 174), this "frieze" consists of alternating triglyphs (blocks with three vertical markings) and metopes. The latter were originally the empty spaces between the ends of the ceiling beams; hence they, like the pediment, could be filled with sculpture. In Ionic architecture, the triglyphs were omitted, and the frieze became what the term usually conveys to us, a continuous band of painted or sculptured decoration. The Ionians would also sometimes elaborate the columns of a porch into female statues—not a very surprising development in view of the columnar quality of the "Hera" from Samos (fig. 170).

SIPHNIAN TREASURY, DELPHI. All these possibilities are combined in the Treasury (a miniature temple for storing votive gifts) erected at Delphi shortly before 525 B.C. by the inhabitants of the Ionian island of Siphnos. Although the building itself is not standing any longer, it has been convincingly reconstructed on the basis of the preserved fragments (figs. 175 and 176). Of its lavish sculptural décor, the most impressive part is the splendid frieze. The detail reproduced here (fig. 177) shows part of the battle of the Greek gods against the giants: on the extreme left, two lions (who pull the chariot of Cybele) are tearing apart an anguished giant; in front of them, Apollo and Artemis advance together, shooting their arrows; a dead giant, despoiled of his ar-

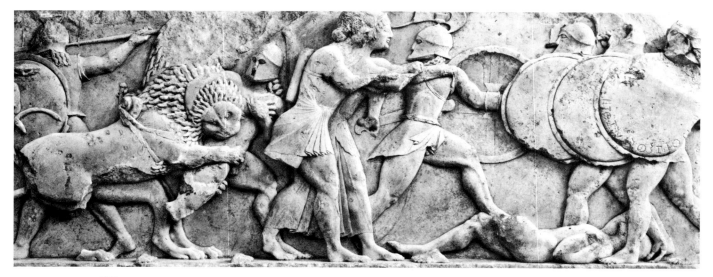

177. *BATTLE OF THE GODS AND GIANTS,* from the north frieze of the Treasury of the Siphnians. c. 530 B.C.
Marble, height 26″ (66 cm). Archeological Museum, Delphi

mor, lies at their feet, while three others enter from the right.

The high relief, with its deep undercutting, recalls the Corfu pediment, but the Siphnian sculptor has taken full advantage of the spatial possibilities offered by this technique. He uses the projecting ledge at the bottom of the frieze as a stage on which he can place his figures in depth. The arms and legs of those nearest the beholder are carved completely in the round; in the second and third layer, the forms become shallower, yet even those farthest removed from us are never permitted to merge with the background. The result is a limited and condensed but very convincing space that permits a dramatic relationship between the figures such as we have never seen before in narrative reliefs. Any comparison with older examples (such as figs. 90, 122, 146, and 150) will show us that Archaic art has indeed conquered a new dimension here, not only in the physical but also in the expressive sense.

TEMPLE OF APHAIA, AEGINA. Meanwhile, in pedimental sculpture, relief has been abandoned altogether. Instead, we find separate statues placed side by side in complex dramatic sequences designed to fit the triangular frame. The most ambitious ensemble of this kind, that of the east pediment of the Temple of Aphaia at Aegina, was created about 490 B.C., and thus brings us to the final stage in the evolution of Archaic sculpture. The figures were found in pieces on the ground and are now in Munich, stripped of their nineteenth-century restorations. The position of each within the pediment, however, can be determined almost exactly, since their height (but not their scale) varies with the sloping sides of the triangle (fig. 178). The center is accented by the standing goddess Athena, who calmly presides, as it were, over the battle between Greeks and Trojans that rages to either side of her in symmetrically diminishing fashion.

The correspondence in the poses of the fighters on the two halves of the pediment makes for a balanced and orderly design, yet it also forces us to see the statues as elements in an ornamental pattern and thus robs them of their individuality to some extent. They speak most strongly to us when viewed one by one. Among the most impressive are the fallen warrior from the left-hand corner (fig. 179) and the kneeling Herakles—who once held a bronze bow—from the right-hand half (fig. 180); both are lean, muscular figures whose bodies seem marvelously functional and organic. That in itself, however, does not explain their great beauty, much as we may admire the artist's command of the human form in action. What really moves us is their nobility of spirit, whether in the agony of dying or in the act of killing. These men, we sense, are suffering—or carrying out—what fate has decreed, with tremendous dignity and resolve. And this communicates itself to us in the very feel of the magnificently firm shapes of which they are composed.

# ARCHITECTURE

## Orders and Plans

In architecture, the Greek achievement has been identified since ancient Roman times with the creation of the three classical architectural orders, Doric, Ionic, and Corinthian. Actually, there are only two, the Corinthian being a variant of the Ionic. The Doric (so named because its home is the Greek mainland) may well claim to be the basic order, since it is older and more sharply defined than the Ionic, which developed on the Aegean islands and the coast of Asia Minor.

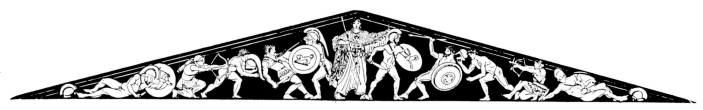

178. Reconstruction drawing of the east pediment of the Temple of Aphaia, Aegina (after Furtwängler)

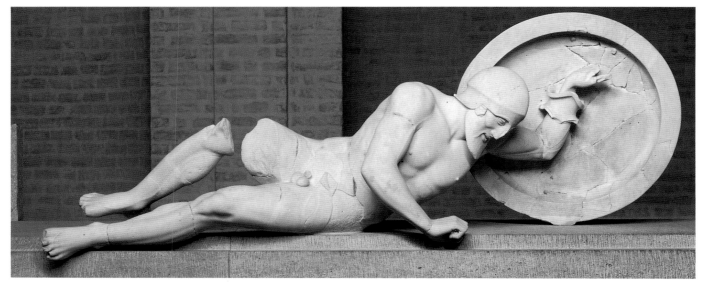

179. *DYING WARRIOR*, from the east pediment of the Temple of Aphaia, Aegina. c. 490 B.C.
Marble, length 72″ (183 cm). Staatliche Antikensammlungen, Munich

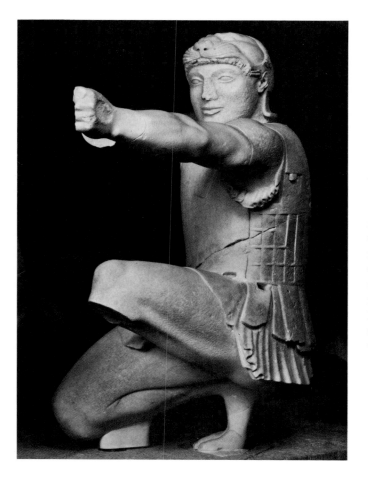

What do we mean by "architectural order"? By common agreement, the term is used for Greek architecture only (and its descendants); and rightly so, for none of the other architectural systems known to us produced anything like it. Perhaps the simplest way to make clear the unique character of the Greek orders is this: there is no such thing as "the Egyptian temple" or "the Gothic church"—the individual buildings, however much they may have in common, are so varied that we cannot distill a generalized type from them—while "the Doric temple" is a real entity that inevitably forms in our minds as we examine the monuments themselves. We must be careful, of course, not to think of this abstraction as an ideal that permits us to measure the degree of perfection of any given Doric temple; it simply means that the elements of which a Doric temple is composed are extraordinarily constant in number, in kind, and in their relation to one another. As a result of this narrowly circumscribed repertory of forms, Doric temples all belong to the same clearly recognizable family, just as the Kouros statues do; like the Kouros statues, they show an internal consistency, a mutual adjustment of parts, that gives them a unique quality of wholeness and organic unity.

180. *HERAKLES,* from the east pediment of the Temple of Aphaia, Aegina. c. 490 B.C. Marble, height 31″ (78.7 cm). Staatliche Antikensammlungen, Munich

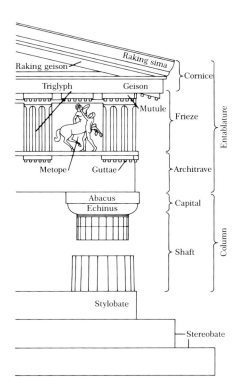
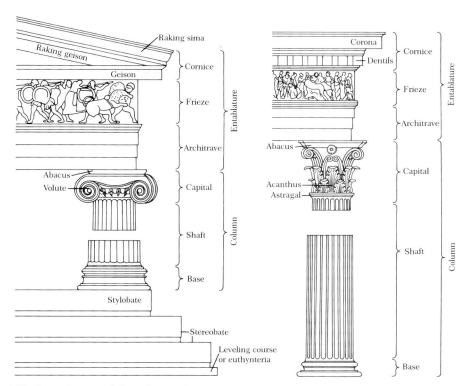

181. Doric, Ionic, and Corinthian orders

DORIC ORDER. The term Doric order refers to the standard parts, and their sequence, constituting the exterior of any Doric temple. Its general outlines are already familiar to us from the façade of the Temple of Artemis at Corfu (fig. 174): the diagram in figure 181 shows it in detail, along with names of all the parts. To the nonspecialist, the detailed terminology may seem something of a nuisance, yet a good many of these terms have become part of our general architectural vocabulary, to remind us of the fact that analytical thinking, in architecture as in countless other fields, originated with the Greeks. Let us first look at the three main divisions: the stepped platform, the columns, and the entablature (which includes everything that rests on the columns). The Doric column consists of the shaft, marked by shallow vertical grooves known as flutes, and the capital, which is made up of the flaring, cushionlike echinus and a square tablet called the abacus. The entablature is the most complex of the three major units. It is subdivided into the architrave (a series of stone blocks directly supported by the columns), the frieze with its triglyphs and metopes, and the projecting cornice. On the long sides of the temple, the cornice is horizontal, while on the short sides (or façades), it is split open in such a way as to enclose the pediment between its upper and lower parts.

The entire structure is built of stone blocks fitted together without mortar; they had to be shaped with extreme precision to achieve smooth joints. Where necessary, they were fastened together by means of metal dowels or clamps. Columns, with very rare exceptions, are composed of sections, called drums (clearly visible in fig. 184). The roof consisted of terracotta tiles supported by wooden rafters, and wooden beams were used for the ceiling; thus the threat of fire was constant.

TEMPLE PLANS. The plans of Greek temples are not directly linked to the orders (which, as we have seen, concern the elevation only). They may vary according to the size of the building or regional preferences, but their basic features are so much alike that it is useful to study them from a generalized "typical" plan (fig. 182). The nucleus is the cella or naos (the room in which the image of the deity is placed) and the porch (pronaos) with its two columns flanked by pilasters (antae). The Siphnian Treasury shows this minimal

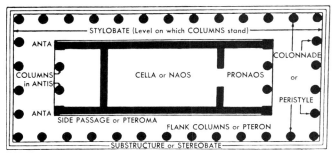

182. Ground plan of a typical Greek peripteral temple (after Grinnell)

plan (see fig. 175). Often we find a second porch added behind the cella, to make the design more symmetrical. In the larger temples, this central unit is surrounded by a colonnade, called the peristyle, and the structure is then known as peripteral. The very largest temples of Ionian Greece may even have a double colonnade.

## Doric Temples

How did the Doric originate? What factors shaped the rigid and precise vocabulary of the Doric order? This is an important and fascinating problem that has occupied archaeologists for many years but that even now can be answered only in part, for we have hardly any remains from the time when the system was still in process of formation. The earliest stone temples known to us, such as that of Artemis at Corfu, show that the essential features of the Doric order were already well established soon after 600 B.C. How these features developed, individually and in combination, why they congealed into a system as rapidly as they seem to have done, remains a puzzle to which we have few reliable clues.

The early Greek builders in stone apparently drew upon three distinct sources of inspiration: Egypt, Mycenae, and pre-Archaic Greek architecture in wood and mud brick. The Mycenaean contribution is the most tangible, although probably not the most important, of these. The central unit of the Greek temple, the cella and porch, clearly derives from the megaron (see fig. 153), either through a continuous tradition or by way of revival. There is something oddly symbolic about the fact that the Mycenaean royal hall should have been converted into the dwelling place of the Greek gods; for the entire Mycenaean era had become part of Greek mythology, as attested by the Homeric epics, and the walls of the Mycenaean fortresses were believed to be the work of mythical giants, the Cyclopes. The religious awe the Greeks felt before these remains also helps us to understand the relationship between the Lion Gate relief at Mycenae and the sculptured pediments on Doric temples. Finally, the flaring, cushionlike capital of the Minoan-Mycenaean column is a good deal closer to the Doric echinus and abacus than is any Egyptian capital. The shaft of the Doric column, on the other hand, tapers upward, not downward as does the Minoan-Mycenaean column, and this definitely points to Egyptian influence.

Perhaps we will recall now—with some surprise—the fluted columns (or rather half-columns) in the funerary district of Zoser at Saqqara (see fig. 79) that had approximated the Doric shaft more than 2,000 years before its appearance in Greece. Moreover, the very notion that temples ought to be built of stone, and that they required large numbers of columns, must have come from Egypt. It is true, of course, that the Egyptian temple is designed to be experienced from the inside, while the Greek temple is arranged so that the impressive exterior matters most (few were allowed to enter the dimly lit cella, and religious ceremonies usually took place at altars erected out-of-doors, with the temple façade as a backdrop). But might a peripteral temple not be interpreted as the columned court of an Egyptian sanctuary turned inside-out? The Greeks also must have acquired much of their stonecutting and masonry techniques from the Egyptians, along with architectural ornament and the knowledge of geometry they needed in order to lay out their temples and to fit the parts together. Yet we cannot say just how they went about all this, or exactly what they took over, technically and artistically, although there can be little doubt that they owed more to the Egyptians than to the Minoans or the Mycenaeans.

FORM FOLLOWS FUNCTION? The problem of origins becomes acute when we consider a third factor: to what extent can the Doric order be understood as a reflection of wooden structures. Those historians of architecture who believe that form follows function—that an architectural form will inevitably reflect the purpose for which it was devised— have pursued this line of approach at great length, especially in trying to explain the details of the entablature. Up to a point, their arguments are convincing; it seems plausible to assume that at one time the triglyphs did mask the ends of wooden beams, and that the droplike shapes below, called guttae (see fig. 181), are the descendants of wooden pegs. The peculiar vertical subdivisions of the triglyphs are perhaps a bit more difficult to accept as an echo of three half-round logs. And when we come to the flutings of the column, our doubts continue to rise: were they really developed from adz marks on a tree trunk, or did the Greeks take them over ready-made from the "proto-Doric" stone columns of Egypt?

As a further test of the functional theory, we would have to ask how the Egyptians came to put flutes in their columns. They, too, after all, had once had to translate architectural forms from impermanent materials into stone. Perhaps it was they who turned adz marks into flutes? But the predynastic Egyptians had so little timber that they seem to have used it only for ceilings; the rest of their buildings consisted of mud brick, fortified by bundles of reeds. And since the proto-Doric columns at Saqqara are not free-standing but are attached to walls, their flutings might represent a sort of abstract echo of bundles of reeds (there are also columns at Saqqara with convex rather than concave flutes that come a good deal closer to the notion of a bundle of thin staves). On the other hand, the Egyptians may have developed the habit of fluting without reference to any earlier building techniques at all; perhaps they found it an effective way to disguise the horizontal joints between the drums and to stress the continuity of the shaft as a vertical unit. Even the Greeks did not flute the shafts of their columns drum by drum, but waited until the entire column was assembled and in position. Be that as it may, fluting certainly enhances the expressive character of the column. A fluted shaft looks stronger, more energetic and resilient, than a smooth one; and this, rather than its manner of origin, accounts for the persistence of the habit.

Why then did we enter at such length into an argument that seems at best inconclusive? Mainly in order to suggest the complexity—and the limitations—of the technological approach to problems of architectural form. The question, always a thorny one, of how far stylistic features can be explained on a functional basis will face us again and again. Obviously, the history of architecture cannot be fully under-

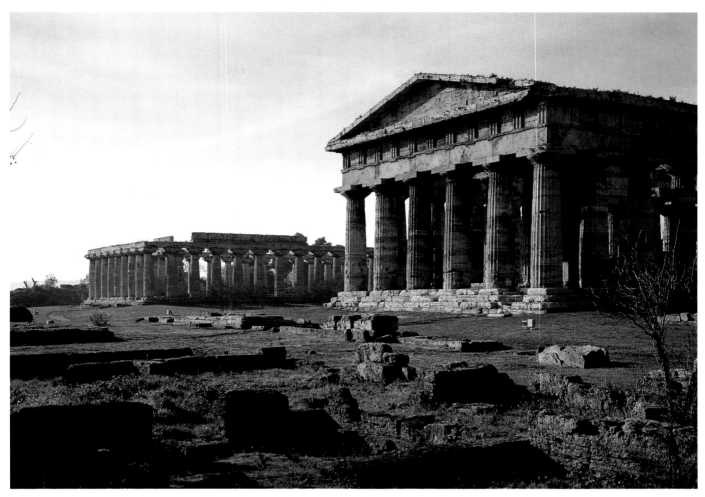

183. The "Basilica," c. 550 B.C.; and the "Temple of Poseidon," c. 460 B.C. Paestum, Italy

stood if we view it only as an evolution of style in the abstract, without considering the actual purposes of building or its technological basis. But we must likewise be prepared to accept the purely aesthetic impulse as a motivating force. At the very start, Doric architects certainly imitated in stone some features of wooden temples, if only because these features were deemed necessary in order to identify a building as a temple. When they enshrined them in the Doric order, however, they did not do so from blind conservatism or force of habit, but because the wooden forms had by now been so thoroughly transformed that they were an organic part of the stone structure.

TEMPLES AT PAESTUM. We must confront the problem of function once more when we consider the best-preserved sixth-century Doric temple, the so-called "Basilica" at Paestum in southern Italy (fig. 183, left; fig. 184), in relation to its neighbor, the so-called "Temple of Poseidon" (fig. 183, right), which was built almost a century later. Both are Doric, but we at once note striking differences in their proportions. The "Basilica" seems low and sprawling (and not only because so much of the entablature is missing), while the "Temple of Poseidon" looks tall and compact. Even the columns themselves are different: those of the older temple taper far more emphatically, their capitals are larger and more flaring. Why the difference?

The peculiar shape of the columns of the "Basilica" (peculiar, that is, compared to fifth-century Doric) has been explained as being due to overcompensation: the architect, not yet fully familiar with the properties of stone as compared with wood, exaggerated the taper of the shaft for greater stability and enlarged the capitals so as to narrow the gaps to be spanned by the blocks of the architrave. Maybe so—but if we accept this interpretation in itself as sufficient to account for the design of these Archaic columns, do we not judge them by the standards of a later age? To label them simply primitive, or awkward, would be to disregard the particular expressive effect that is theirs—and theirs alone.

The "Basilica's" columns seem to be more burdened by their load than those of the "Temple of Poseidon," so that the contrast between the supporting and supported members of the order is dramatized rather than harmoniously balanced, as in the later building. Various factors contribute to this impression; the echinus of the "Basilica's" capitals is not only larger than its counterpart in the "Temple of Poseidon," it seems more elastic and hence more distended by the weight

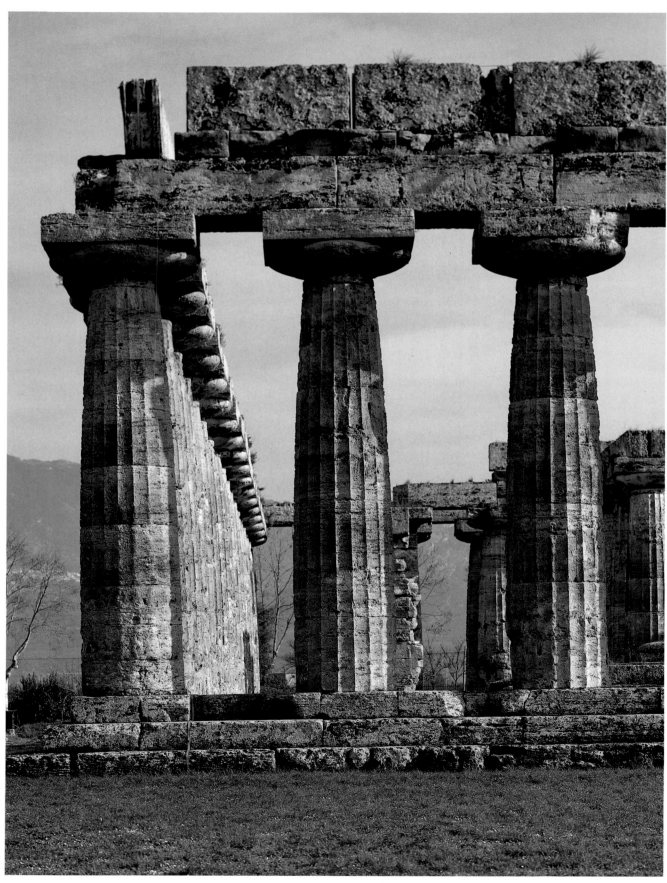

184. Corner of the "Basilica," Paestum. c. 550 B.C.

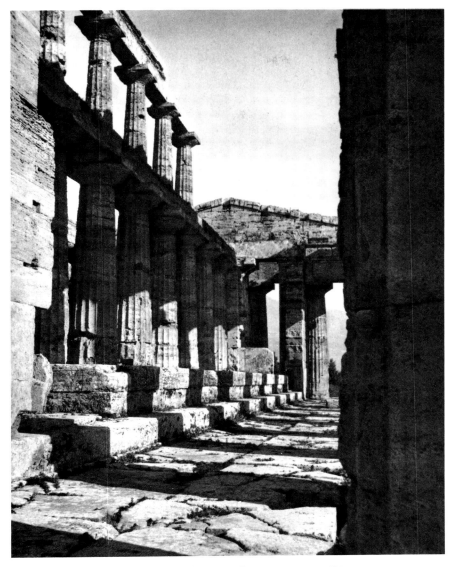

185. Interior, "Temple of Poseidon," Paestum. c. 460 B.C.

it carries, almost as if it were made of rubber. And the shafts not only show a more pronounced taper but also a particularly strong bulge or curve along the line of taper, so that they, too, convey a sense of elasticity and compression compared with the rigidly geometric blocks of the entablature. (This curve, called "entasis," is a basic feature of the Doric column; although it may be very slight, it endows the shaft with a "muscular" quality quite unknown in Egyptian or Minoan-Mycenaean columns.)

The "Temple of Poseidon" (figs. 183, 185, and 186)—it was probably dedicated to Hera—was begun c. 475 B.C. and finished fifteen years later; it is also among the best preserved of all Doric sanctuaries. Of special interest are the interior supports of the cella ceiling (fig. 185), two rows of columns, each supporting a smaller set of columns in a way that makes the tapering seem continuous despite the architrave in between. Such a two-story interior, which became a practical necessity for the cellas of the larger Doric temples,

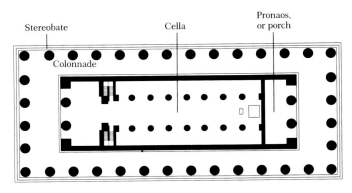

186. Plan of the "Temple of Poseidon"

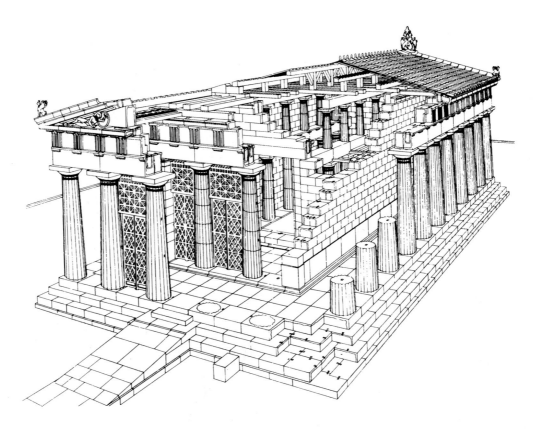

187. Sectional view (restored) of the Temple of Aphaia, Aegina

is first found at the Temple of Aphaia at Aegina around the beginning of the fifth century, shown here in a reconstruction drawing to illustrate its construction scheme (fig. 187).

ATHENS, PERICLES, AND THE PARTHENON. In 480 B.C., shortly before their defeat, the Persians had destroyed the temple and statues on the Acropolis, the sacred hill above Athens which had been a fortified site since Mycenaean times. (For modern archaeologists, this disaster has turned out to be a blessing in disguise, since the debris, which was subsequently used as fill, has yielded many fine Archaic pieces, such as those in figures 168, 169, 171, and 172 that would hardly have survived otherwise.) The rebuilding of the Acropolis under the leadership of Pericles during the later fifth century, when Athens was at the height of her power, was the most ambitious enterprise in the history of Greek architecture, as well as its artistic climax. Individually and collectively, these structures represent the Classical phase of Greek art in full maturity.

The greatest temple, and the only one to be completed before the Peloponnesian War (431–404 B.C.), is the Parthenon (figs. 188 and 189), dedicated to the virginal Athena, the patron deity in whose honor Athens was named. Built of gleaming white marble on the most prominent site along the southern flank of the Acropolis, it dominates the entire city and the surrounding countryside, a brilliant landmark against the backdrop of mountains to the north of it. The history of the Parthenon is as extraordinary as its artistic significance—it is the only sanctuary we know that has served four different faiths in succession. The architects Ictinus and Callicrates erected it in 448–432 B.C., an amazingly brief span of time for a project of this size. In order to meet the huge expense of building the largest and most lavish temple on the Greek mainland, Pericles delved into funds collected from states allied with Athens for mutual defense against the Persians. He may have felt that the danger was no longer a real one, and that Athens, the chief victim and victor at the climax of the Persian War in 480–478 B.C., was justified in using the money to rebuild what the Persians had destroyed. His act did weaken the position of Athens, however (Thucydides openly reproached him for adorning the city "like a harlot with precious stones, statues, and temples costing a thousand talents"), and contributed to the disastrous outcome of the Peloponnesian War. In Christian times, the Virgin Mary displaced the virginal Athena; the Parthenon became first a Byzantine church, then a Catholic cathedral; finally, under the Turks, it was a mosque. It has been a ruin since 1687, when a store of gunpowder the Turks had put into the cella exploded during a siege. Much of the sculpture was removed during the years 1801–1803 by Lord Elgin; the Elgin Marbles are today the greatest treasure of the British Museum.

As the perfect embodiment of Classical Doric architecture, the Parthenon makes an instructive contrast with the "Temple of Poseidon" (fig. 183). Despite its greater size, it seems far less massive. Rather, the dominant impression it creates is one of festive, balanced grace within the austere scheme of the Doric order. This has been achieved by a gen-

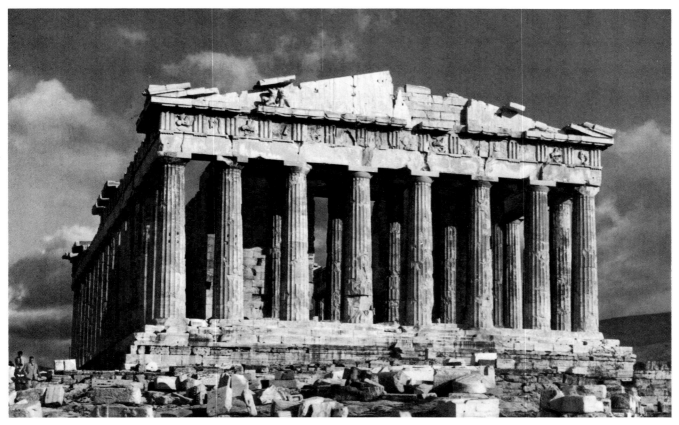

188. ICTINUS and CALLICRATES. The Parthenon (view from the west), Acropolis, Athens. 448–432 B.C.

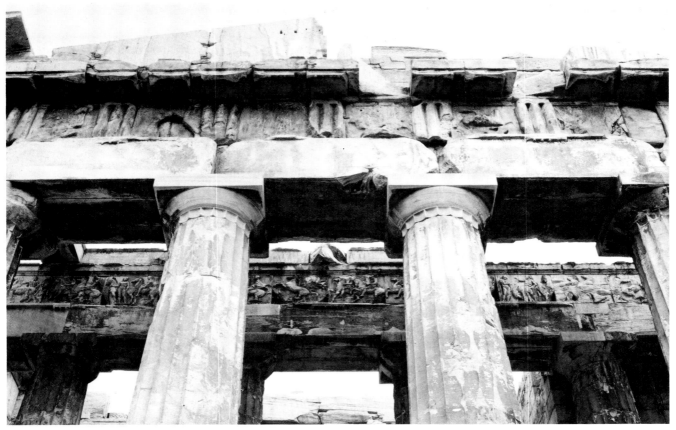

189. Frieze above the western entrance of the cella of the Parthenon (see also fig. 209)

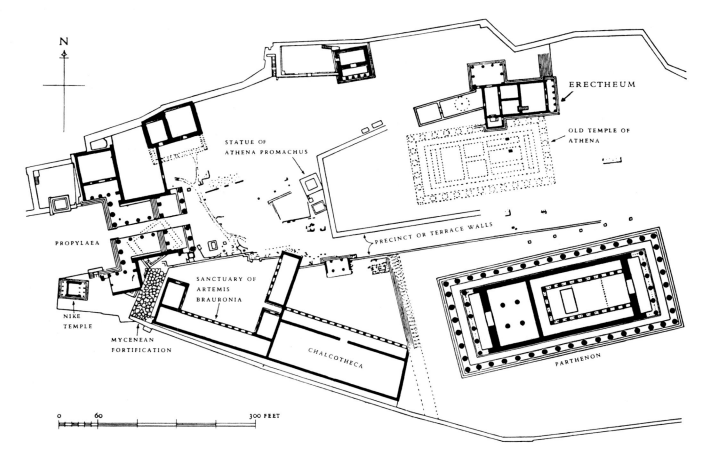

190. Plan of the Acropolis at Athens in 400 B.C. (after A. W. Lawrence)

eral lightening and readjustment of the proportions: the entablature is lower in relation to its width and to the height of the columns; the cornice projects less; and the columns themselves are a good deal more slender, their tapering and entasis less pronounced and the capitals smaller and less flaring; yet the spacing of the columns has become wider. We might say that the load carried by the columns has decreased, and as a consequence the supports can fulfill their task with a new sense of ease.

THE PARTHENON'S REFINEMENTS. These so-called refinements, intentional departures from the strict geometric regularity of the design for aesthetic reasons, are another feature of the Classical Doric style that can be observed in the Parthenon better than anywhere else. Thus the stepped platform and the entablature are not absolutely straight but slightly curved, so that the center is a bit higher than the ends; the columns lean inward; and the interval between the corner column and its neighbors is smaller than the standard interval adopted for the colonnade as a whole.

A great deal has been written about these deviations from mechanical exactitude. That they are planned rather than accidental is beyond doubt, but why did the architects go to the enormous trouble of carrying them through? (Every capital of the colonnade is slightly distorted to fit the curving architrave.) They used to be regarded as optical corrections designed to produce the illusion of absolutely straight horizontals and verticals. Unfortunately, however, this functional explanation does not work: if it did, we should be unable to perceive the deviations except by careful measurement; yet the fact is that, though unobtrusive, they are visible to the naked eye, even in photographs such as our figure 188. Moreover, in temples that do not have these refinements, the columns do not give the appearance of leaning outward, nor do the horizontal lines look "dished." Plainly, then, the deviations were built into the Parthenon because they were thought to add to its beauty; they are a positive element that is meant to be noticed. And they do indeed contribute—in ways that are hard to define—to the integral, harmonious quality of the structure.

The cella of the Parthenon (see plan, fig. 190) is unusually wide and somewhat shorter than in other temples, so as to accommodate a second room behind it. The pronaos and its counterpart at the western end have almost disappeared, but there is an extra row of columns in front of either entrance. The architrave above these columns is more Ionic than Doric, since it has no triglyphs and metopes but a continuous sculptured frieze that encircles the entire cella (fig. 189).

PROPYLAEA. Immediately after the completion of the Parthenon, Pericles commissioned another splendid and expensive edifice, the monumental entry gate at the western end of the Acropolis, called the Propylaea (see plan, fig. 190). It was begun in 437 B.C., under the architect Mnesicles, who completed the main part in five years; the remainder had to be abandoned because of the Peloponnesian War. Again the entire structure was built of marble and included refinements comparable to those of the Parthenon. Its main fascination for us consists in the manner in which the elements of a Doric temple have here been adapted to another task, on an irregular and steeply rising site. Mnesicles has indeed acquitted himself nobly; his design not only fits the difficult terrain but also transforms it, so that a rude passage among rocks becomes a splendid overture to the sacred precinct on which it opens.

Of the two porches (or façades) at either end, only the eastern one is in fair condition today (fig. 191); it resembles a Classical Doric temple front, except for the wide opening between the third and fourth columns. The western porch was flanked by two wings (figs. 192 and 193). The one to the north, considerably larger than its companion, included a picture gallery (*pinakotheke*), the first known instance of a room especially designed for the display of paintings. Along the central roadway that passes through the Propylaea, we find two rows of columns which are Ionic rather than Doric. Apparently at that time the trend in Athenian architecture was toward using Ionic elements inside Doric structures (we recall the sculptured frieze of the Parthenon cella).

## Ionic Temples

Athens, with its strong Aegean orientation, had shown itself hospitable to the eastern Greek style of building from the mid-fifth century on, and the finest surviving examples of the Ionic order are to be found among the structures of the Acropolis. The previous development of the order is known only in very fragmentary fashion; of the huge Ionic temples that were erected in Archaic times on Samos and at Ephesus, little has survived except the plans. Its vocabulary, however, seems to have remained fairly fluid, with strong affinities to the Near East (see figs. 130 and 131), and it did not really become an order in the strict sense until the Classical period. Even then it continued to be rather more flexible than the Doric order. Its most striking feature is the Ionic column, which differs from the Doric not only in body but also, as it were, in spirit (see fig. 181). It rests on an ornately profiled base of its own; the shaft is more slender, and there is less tapering and entasis; the capital shows a large double scroll, or volute, between the echinus and abacus, which projects strongly beyond the width of the shaft.

That these details add up to an entity very distinct from the Doric column becomes clear as soon as we turn from the diagram to an actual building (fig. 196). How shall we define it? The Ionic column is, of course, lighter and more graceful than its mainland cousin; it lacks the latter's muscular quality. Instead, it evokes the echo of a growing plant,

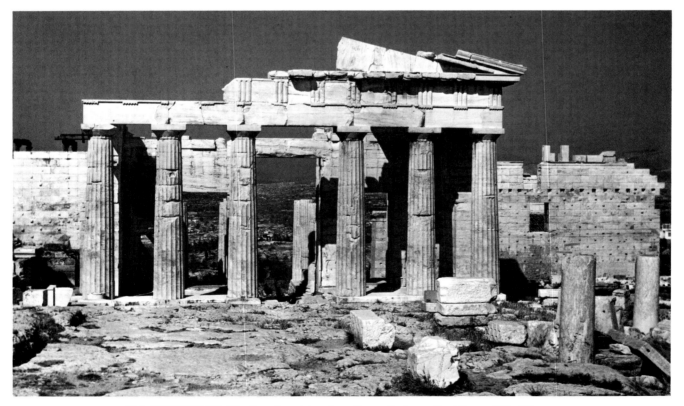

191. MNESICLES. The Propylaea (view from the east), Acropolis, Athens. 437–432 B.C.

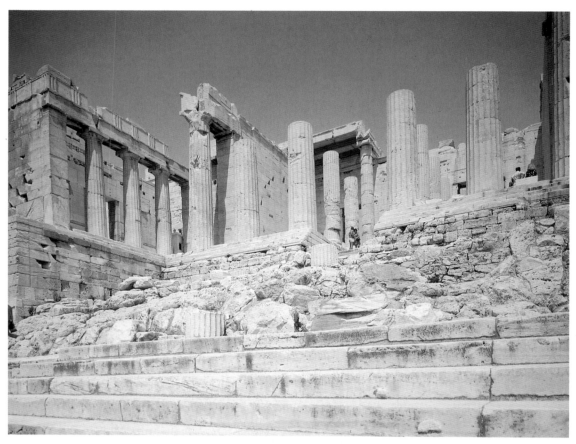

192. The Propylaea (with *pinakotheke*), western entrance

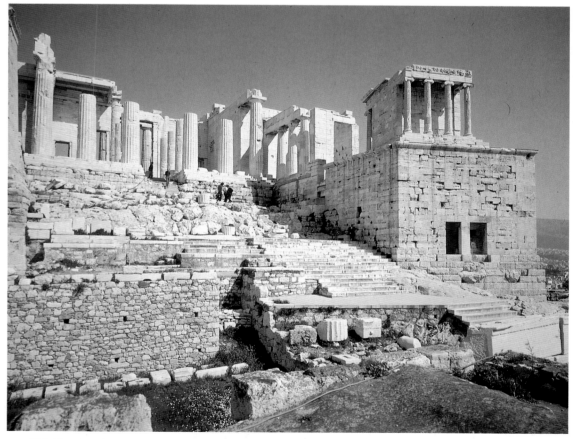

193. The Propylaea (view from the west) and the Temple of Athena Nike (427–424 B.C.), Acropolis, Athens

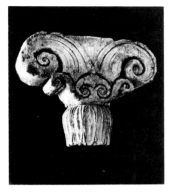

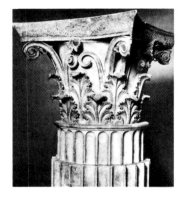

194. (*far left*) Aeolian capital, from Larissa. c. 600 B.C. Archaeological Museum, Istanbul

195. (*left*) Corinthian capital, from the Tholos at Epidaurus. c. 350 B.C. Museum, Epidaurus

196. (*below*) The Erechtheum (view from the south), Acropolis, Athens. 421–405 B.C.

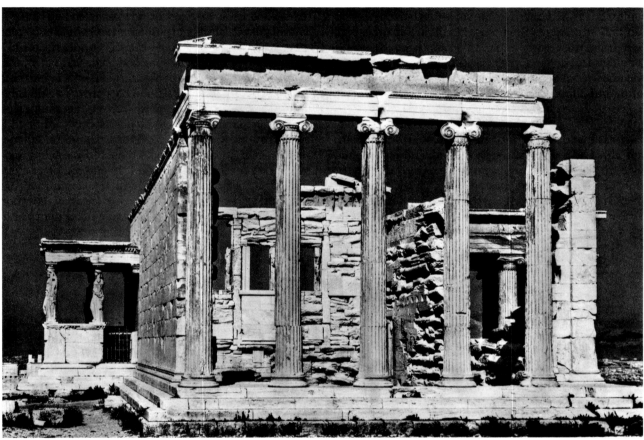

of something like a formalized palm tree. And this vegetal analogy is not sheer fancy, for we have early ancestors, or relatives, of the Ionic capital that bear it out (fig. 194). If we were to pursue these plantlike columns all the way back to their point of origin, we would eventually find ourselves at Saqqara, where we not only encounter "proto-Doric" supports but the wonderfully graceful papyrus half-columns of figure 79, with their curved, flaring capitals. It may well be, then, that the Ionic column, too, had its ultimate source in Egypt, but instead of reaching Greece by sea, as we suppose the proto-Doric column did, it traveled a slow and tortuous path by land through Syria and Asia Minor.

In pre-Classical times, the only Ionic structures on the Greek mainland had been the small treasuries built by eastern Greek states at Delphi in the regional styles (see fig.

176). Hence the Athenian architects who took up the Ionic order about 450 B.C. thought of it, at first, as suitable only for small temples of simple plan. Such a building is the little Temple of Athena Nike on the southern flank of the Propylaea (fig. 193), probably built 427–424 B.C. from a design prepared twenty years earlier by Callicrates.

ERECHTHEUM. Larger and more complex is the Erechtheum (fig. 196 and plan, fig. 190), on the northern edge of the Acropolis opposite the Parthenon. It was erected in 421–405 B.C., perhaps by Mnesicles, for, like the Propylaea, it is masterfully adapted to an irregular, sloping site. The area had various associations with the mythical founding of Athens, so that the Erechtheum was actually a "portmanteau" sanctuary with several religious functions. Its

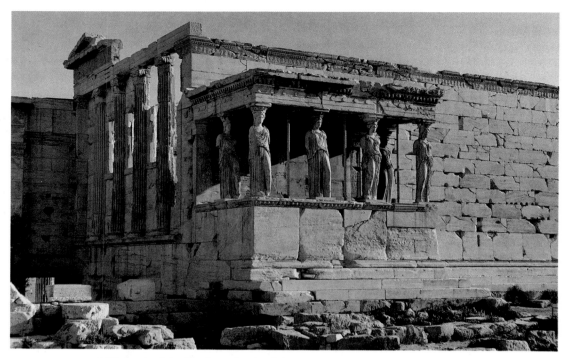

197. Porch of the Maidens, the Erechtheum, Acropolis, Athens. 421–405 B.C.

name derives from Erechtheus, a legendary king of Athens; the eastern room was dedicated to Athena Polias (Athena the city goddess); and it may also have covered the spot where a contest between Athena and Poseidon was believed to have taken place. (Apparently there were four rooms, in addition to a basement on the western side, but their exact purpose is under dispute.)

Instead of a west façade, the Erechtheum has two porches attached to its flanks, a very large one facing north and a small one toward the Parthenon. The latter is the famous Porch of the Maidens (fig. 197), its roof supported by six female figures (caryatids) on a high parapet, instead of regular columns (compare fig. 176). One wonders whether these statues were the reason why a Turkish governor chose the building to house his harem two thousand years later. We cannot altogether blame him, for here the exquisite refinement of the Ionic order does indeed convey a "feminine" quality, compared with the "masculinity" of the Parthenon across the way. Apart from the caryatids, sculptural decoration on the Erechtheum was confined to the frieze (of which very little survives). The pediments remained bare, perhaps for lack of funds at the end of the Peloponnesian War. However, the ornamental carving on the bases and capitals of the columns, and on the frames of doorways and windows, is extraordinarily delicate and rich; its cost, according to the accounts inscribed on the building, was higher than that of figure sculpture.

CORINTHIAN CAPITAL. Such emphasis on ornament seems characteristic of the late fifth century. It was at this time that the Corinthian capital was invented as an elaborate substitute for the Ionic (for a comparison of Doric, Ionic, and Corinthian capitals, see fig. 181); its shape is that of

an inverted bell covered with the curly shoots and leaves of the acanthus plant, which seem to sprout from the top of the column shaft (fig. 195). At first, Corinthian capitals were used only for interiors. Not until a century later do we find them replacing Ionic capitals on the exterior. The earliest known instance is the Monument of Lysicrates in Athens (fig. 198), built soon after 334 B.C. It is not really a building in the full sense of the term—the interior, though hollow, has no entrance—but an elaborate support for a tripod won by Lysicrates in a contest. The round structure, resting on a tall base, is a miniature version of a tholos, a type of circular building of which several earlier examples are known to have existed. The columns here are engaged (set into the wall) rather than free-standing, to make the monument more compact. Soon after, the Corinthian capital came to be employed on the exteriors of large buildings as well, and in Roman times it was the standard capital for almost any purpose.

TOWN PLANNING AND THEATERS. During the three centuries between the end of the Peloponnesian War and the Roman conquest, Greek architecture shows little further development. Even before the time of Alexander the Great, the largest volume of building activity was to be found in the Greek cities of Asia Minor. There we do encounter some structures of a new kind, often under Oriental influence, such as the huge Tomb of Mausolus at Halicarnassus (see figs. 216–18) and the Altar of Zeus at Pergamum (see figs. 226–28); town planning on a rectangular grid pattern, first introduced at Miletus in the mid-fifth century, assumed new importance, as did the municipal halls (stoas) lining the market places where the civic and commercial life of Greek towns was centered; private houses, too, became larger and

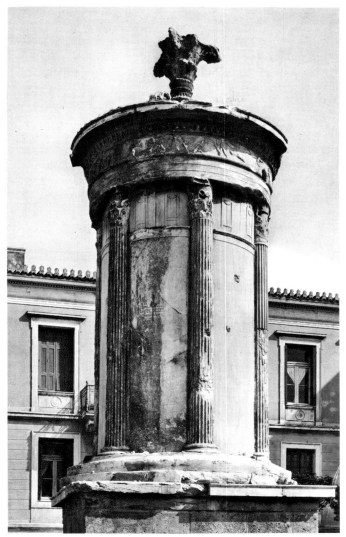

198. The Monument of Lysicrates, Athens. c. 334 B.C.

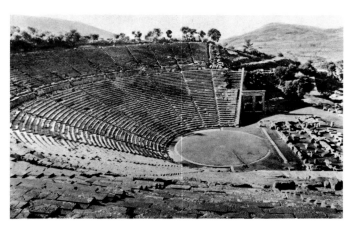

199. The Theater, Epidaurus. c. 350 B.C.

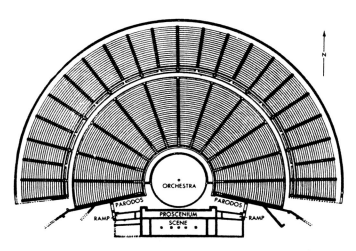

200. Plan of the Theater, Epidaurus (after Picard-Cambridge)

more ornate than before. Yet the architectural vocabulary, aesthetically as well as technically, remained essentially that of the temples of the late fifth century.

The basic repertory of Greek architecture was increased in one respect only: the open-air theater achieved a regular, defined shape. Before the fourth century, the auditorium had simply been a natural slope, preferably curved, equipped with stone benches; now the hillside was provided with concentric rows of seats, and with staircase-aisles at regular intervals, as at Epidaurus (figs. 199–200). At the center is the orchestra, where most of the action took place. At the extreme right we see the remains of a hall-like building that formed the backdrop and supported the scenery.

## Limitations of Greek Architecture

How are we to account for the fact that Greek architecture did not grow significantly beyond the stage it had reached at the time of the Peloponnesian War? After all, neither intellectual life nor the work of sculptors and painters show any tendency toward staleness during the last three hundred years of Greek civilization. Are we perhaps misjudging her architectural achievements after 400 B.C.? Or were there inherent limitations that prevented Greek architecture from continuing the pace of development it had maintained in Archaic and Classical times? A number of such limitations come to mind: the concern with monumental exteriors at the expense of interior space; the concentration of effort on temples of one particular type; the lack of interest in any structural system more advanced than the post-and-lintel (uprights supporting horizontal beams). Until the late fifth century, these had all been positive advantages; without them, the great masterpieces of the Periclean age would have been unthinkable. But the possibilities of the traditional Doric temple were nearly exhausted by then, as indicated by the attention lavished on expensive refinements.

What Greek architecture needed after the Peloponnesian War was a breakthrough, a revival of the experimental spirit of the seventh century, that would create an interest in new building materials, vaulting, and interior space. What prevented the breakthrough? Could it have been the architec-

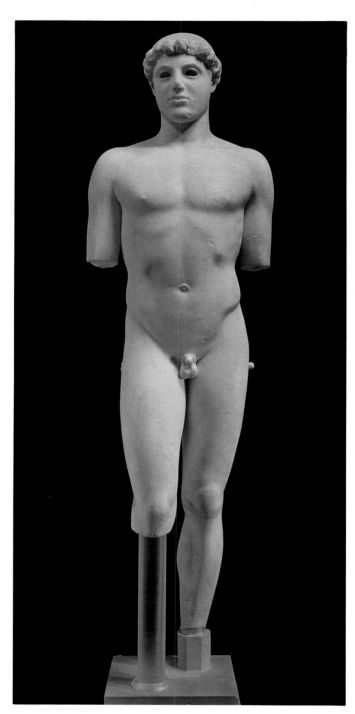

201. *STANDING YOUTH (KRITIOS BOY)*. c. 480 B.C.
Marble, height 34″ (86.3 cm). Acropolis Museum, Athens

# CLASSICAL SCULPTURE

KRITIOS BOY. Among the statues excavated from the debris the Persians had left behind on the Acropolis, there is one Kouros (fig. 201) that stands apart from the rest. It must have been carved very shortly before the fateful year 480 B.C. This remarkable work, which some have attributed to the Athenian sculptor Kritios and which therefore has come to be known as the *Kritios Boy,* differs subtly but importantly from the Archaic Kouros figures we discussed above (figs. 166 and 167): it is the first statue we know that *stands* in the full sense of the word. Of course, the earlier figures also stand, but only in the sense that they are in an upright position, and are not reclining, sitting, kneeling, or running; their stance is really an arrested walk, with the weight of the body resting evenly on both legs. The *Kritios Boy,* too, has one leg placed forward, yet we never doubt for an instant that he is standing still. Why this is so becomes evident when we compare the left and right half of his body, for we then discover that the strict symmetry of the Archaic Kouros has now given way to a calculated nonsymmetry: the knee of the forward leg is lower than the other, the right hip is thrust down and inward, the left hip up and outward; and if we trace the axis of the body, we realize that it is not a straight vertical line but a faint, S-like curve (or, to be exact, a reversed S-curve). Taken together, all these small departures from symmetry tell us that the weight of the body rests mainly on the left leg, and that the right leg plays the role of an elastic prop or buttress to make sure that the body keeps its balance.

CONTRAPPOSTO. The *Kritios Boy,* then, not only stands, he stands at ease. And the artist has masterfully observed the balanced nonsymmetry of this relaxed natural stance. To describe it, we use the Italian word *contrapposto* (counterpoise); the leg that carries the main weight is commonly called the engaged leg; the other, the free leg. These terms are a useful shorthand, for from now on we shall have frequent occasion to mention *contrapposto.* It was a very basic discovery. Only by learning how to represent the body at rest could the Greek sculptor gain the freedom to show it in motion. But is there not plenty of motion in Archaic art? There is indeed (see figs. 173, 176, 179, and 180), but it is somewhat mechanical and inflexible in kind; we read it from the poses without really feeling it. In the *Kritios Boy,* on the other hand, we sense for the first time not only a new repose but an animation of the body structure that evokes the experience we have of our own body. Life now suffuses the entire figure, hence the Archaic smile, the "sign of life," is no longer needed. It has given way to a serious, pensive expression characteristic of the early phase of Classical sculpture (or, as it is often called, the Severe Style).

The new articulation of the body that appears in the *Kritios Boy* was to reach its full development within half a century in the mature Classical style of the Periclean era. The most famous Kouros statue of that time, the *Doryphorus (Spear Bearer)* by Polyclitus (fig. 202), is known to us only through Roman copies whose hard, dry forms convey little of the beauty of the original. Still, it makes

tural orders, or rather the cast of mind that produced them? The suspicion will not go away that it was the very coherence and rigidity of these orders which made it impossible for Greek architects to break from the established pattern. What had been their great strength in earlier days became a tyranny. It remained for later ages to adapt the Greek orders to brick and concrete, to arched and vaulted construction, for such adaptation necessitated doing a certain amount of violence to the original character of the orders, and the Greeks, it seems, were incapable of that.

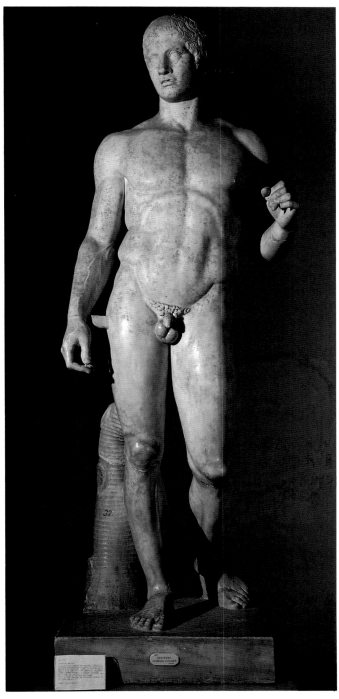

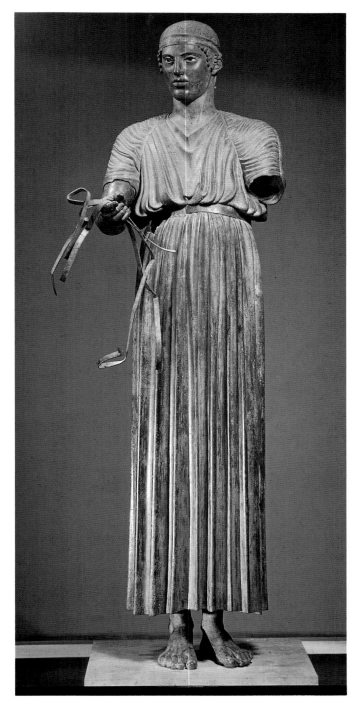

202. *DORYPHORUS (SPEAR BEARER)*. Roman copy after
an original of c. 450–440 B.C. by POLYCLITUS. Marble,
height 6'6" (2 m). Museo Archeologico Nazionale, Naples

203. *CHARIOTEER*, from the Sanctuary of Apollo
at Delphi. c. 470 B.C. Bronze, height 71" (28 cm).
Archeological Museum, Delphi

an instructive comparison with the *Kritios Boy.* The *contrapposto* (with the engaged leg in the forward position) has now become much more emphatic; the differentiation between the left and right halves of the body can be seen in every muscle, and the turn of the head, barely hinted at in the *Kritios Boy,* is equally pronounced. This studied poise, the precise, if overexplicit, anatomical detail, and above all the harmonious proportions of the figure made the *Doryphorus* renowned as the standard embodiment of the Classi-

cal ideal of human beauty. According to one ancient writer, it was known simply as the Canon (rule, measure), so great was its authority.

SEVERE STYLE. But let us return to the Severe Style. The reason why this term was chosen to describe the character of Greek sculpture during the years between c. 480 and 450 B.C. becomes clear to us as we look at the splendid *Charioteer* from Delphi (fig. 203), one of the earliest extant large

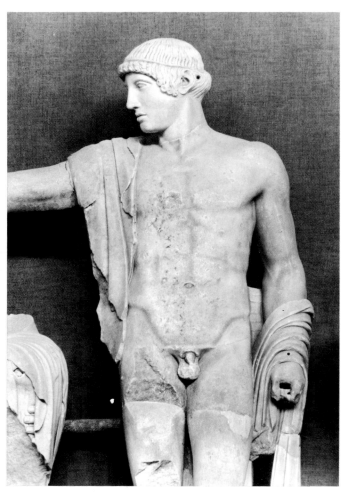

204. *APOLLO* (portion), from the west pediment of
the Temple of Zeus at Olympia. c. 460 B.C.
Marble, over lifesize. Archaeological Museum, Olympia

TEMPLE OF ZEUS, OLYMPIA. The greatest sculptural ensemble of the Severe Style is the pair of pediments of the Temple of Zeus at Olympia, carved c. 460 B.C. and now reassembled in the local museum. In the west pediment, the more mature of the two, we see the victory of the Lapiths over the Centaurs under the aegis of Apollo, who forms the center of the composition (fig. 204). His commanding figure is part of the drama and yet above it; the outstretched right arm and the strong turn of the head show his active intervention—he *wills* the victory but, as befits a god, does not physically help to achieve it. Nevertheless, there is a tenseness, a gathering of forces, in this powerful body that makes its outward calm doubly impressive. The forms themselves are massive and simple, with soft contours and undulating, continuous surfaces. Apollo's glance is directed at a Centaur who has seized Hippodamia, bride of the king of the Lapiths (fig. 205). Here we witness another achievement of the Severe Style: the passionate struggle is expressed not only through action and gesture but through the emotions mirrored in the faces—revulsion on the face of the girl, pain and desperate effort on that of the Centaur. Nor would an Archaic artist have known how to combine the two figures into a group so compact, so full of interlocking movements.

MOVEMENT IN STATUES. Strenuous action had already been investigated in pedimental sculpture of the Late Archaic period (see figs. 179 and 180). Such figures, however, although technically carved in the round, are not free-standing; they represent, rather, a kind of super-relief, since they

bronze statues in Greek art. It must have been made about a decade later than the *Kritios Boy,* as a votive offering after a race; the young victor originally stood on a chariot drawn by four horses. Despite the long, heavy garment, we sense a hint of *contrapposto* in the body—the feet are carefully differentiated so as to inform us that the left leg is the engaged one, and the shoulders and head turn slightly to the right. The garment is severely simple, yet compared with Archaic drapery the folds seem softer and more pliable; we feel (probably for the first time in the history of sculpture) that they reflect the behavior of real cloth. Not only the body but the drapery, too, has been transformed by a new understanding of functional relationships, so that every fold is shaped by the forces that act upon it—the downward pull of gravity, the shape of the body underneath, and the belts or straps that constrict its flow. The face has the pensive, somewhat faraway look we saw in the *Kritios Boy,* but the color inlay of the eyes, fortunately preserved in this instance, as well as the slightly parted lips, give it a more animated expression. The bearing of the entire figure conveys the solemnity of the event commemorated, for chariot races and similar contests at that time were competitions for divine favor, not sporting events in the modern sense.

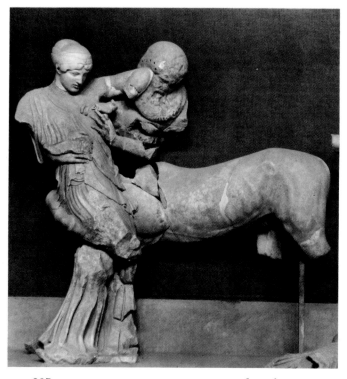

205. *HIPPODAMIA ATTACKED BY A CENTAUR,* from the west
pediment of the Temple of Zeus at Olympia. c. 460 B.C. Marble,
slightly over lifesize. Archaeological Museum, Olympia

are designed to be seen against a background and from one direction only. To infuse the same freedom of movement into genuinely free-standing statues was a far greater challenge; not only did it run counter to an age-old tradition that denied mobility to these figures, but the unfreezing had to be done in such a way as to safeguard their all-around balance and self-sufficiency. The problem could not really be tackled until the concept of *contrapposto* had been established, but once this was done, the solution no longer presented serious difficulties. Large, free-standing statues in motion are the most important achievement of the Severe Style. The finest figure of this kind was recovered from the sea near the coast of Greece (fig. 206): a magnificent nude bronze Poseidon (or Zeus?), almost seven feet tall, in the act of hurling his trident (or thunderbolt?). The pose is that of an athlete, yet it does not strike us as the arrested phase of a continuous succession of movements but as an awe-inspiring gesture that reveals the power of the god. Hurling a weapon is a divine attribute here, rather than a specific performance aimed at a particular adversary.

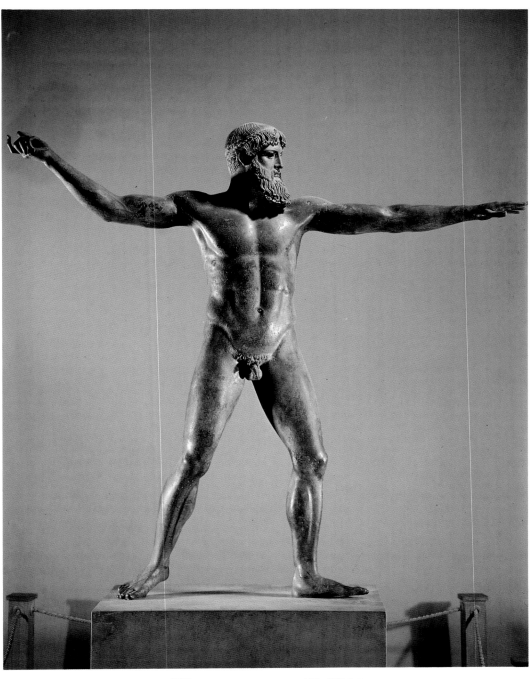

206. *POSEIDON (ZEUS?)*. c. 460–450 B.C.
Bronze, height 6′10″ (2.1 m).
National Archeological Museum, Athens

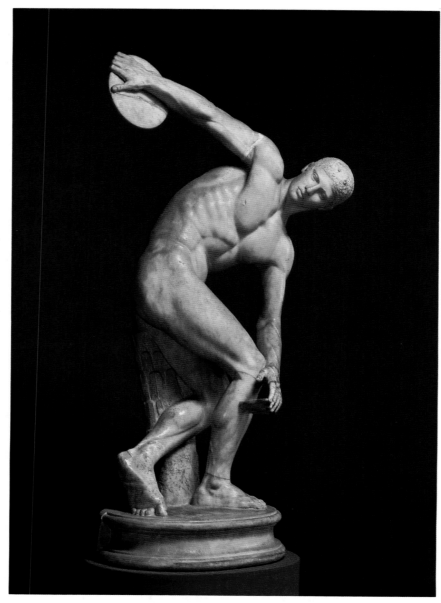

207. *DISCOBOLUS (DISCUS THROWER)*. Roman marble copy
after a bronze original of c. 450 B.C. by MYRON.
Lifesize. Museo delle Terme, Rome

Some years after the *Poseidon,* about 450 B.C., Myron created his famous bronze statue of the *Discobolus (Discus Thrower),* which came to enjoy a reputation comparable to that of the *Doryphorus.* Like the latter, it is known to us only from Roman copies (fig. 207). Here the problem of how to condense a sequence of movements into a single pose without freezing it is a very much more complex one, involving a violent twist of the torso in order to bring the action of the arms into the same plane as the action of the legs. We wonder whether the copy does not make the design seem harsher and less poised than it was in the original.

CLASSICAL STYLE. The *Discobolus* brings us to the threshold of the second half of the century, the era of the mature Classical style. The conquest of movement in a free-standing statue now exerted a liberating influence on pedimental sculpture as well, endowing it with a new spaciousness, fluidity, and balance. The *Dying Niobid* (fig. 208), a work of the 440s, was carved for the pediment of a Doric temple but is so richly three-dimensional, so self-contained, that we hardly suspect her original context. Niobe, according to legend, had humiliated the mother of Apollo and Artemis by boasting of her seven sons and seven daughters, whereupon the two gods killed all of Niobe's children. Our Niobid has been shot in the back while running; her strength broken, she sinks to the ground while trying to extract the fatal arrow. The violent movement of her arms has made her garment slip off; her nudity is thus a dramatic device, rather than a necessary part of the story. The artist's primary motive in devising it, however, was to display a beautiful female body in the kind of strenuous action hitherto reserved for the male nude. (The *Niobid* is the earliest known large female nude in Greek art.) Still, we must not misread the artist's intention: it was not a detached interest in the physical aspect of the event alone but the desire to unite motion and emotion and thus to make the beholder experience the suffering of this victim of a cruel fate. Looking at the face of the Niobid, we feel that here, for the first time, human feeling is expressed as eloquently in the features as in the rest of the figure.

A brief glance backward at the wounded warrior from Aegina (fig. 179) will show us how very differently the agony of death had been conceived only half a century before. What separates the *Niobid* from the world of Archaic art is a quality summed up in the Greek word *pathos*, which means suffering, but particularly suffering conveyed with nobility and restraint so that it touches rather than horrifies us. Late Archaic art may approach it now and then, as in the Eos and Memnon group (fig. 164), yet the full force of pathos can be felt only in Classical works such as the *Niobid*. Perhaps, in

order to measure the astonishing development we have witnessed since the beginnings of Greek monumental sculpture less than two centuries before, we ought to compare the *Niobid* with the earliest pedimental figure we came to know, the Gorgon from Corfu (fig. 173); and as we do so, we suddenly realize that these two, worlds apart as they may be, belong to the same artistic tradition, for the *Niobid*, too, shows the pinwheel stance, even though its meaning has been radically reinterpreted. Once we recognize the ancient origin of her pose, we understand better than before why the Niobid, despite her suffering, remains so monumentally self-contained.

PHIDIAS AND THE PARTHENON. The largest, as well as the greatest, group of Classical sculptures at our disposal consists of the remains of the marble decoration of the Parthenon, most of them, unfortunately, in battered and fragmentary condition. The centers of both pediments are gone completely, and of the figures in the corners only those from the east pediment are sufficiently well preserved to convey

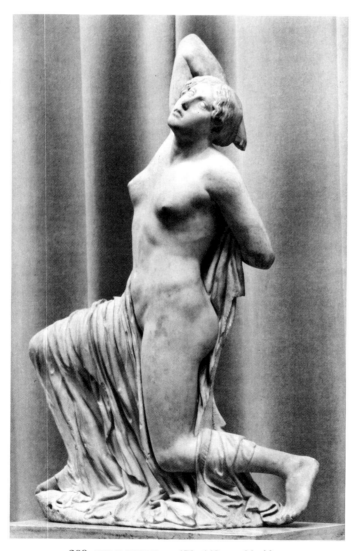

208. *DYING NIOBID.* c. 450–440 B.C. Marble,
height 59″ (150 cm). Museo delle Terme, Rome

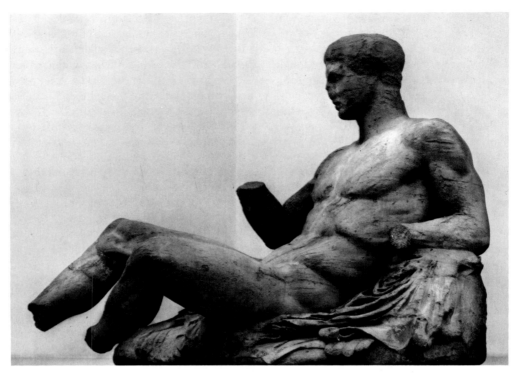

209. *DIONYSUS,* from the east pediment of the Parthenon. c. 438–432 B.C.
Marble, over lifesize. British Museum, London

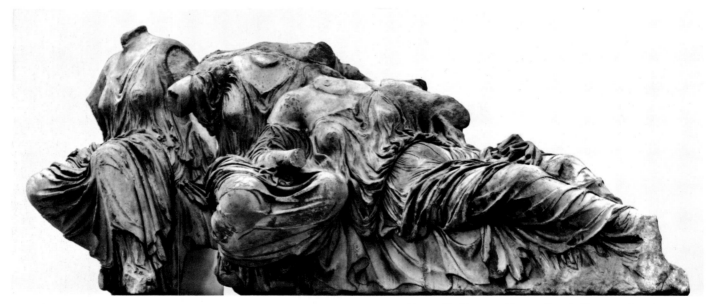

210. *THREE GODDESSES,* from the east pediment of the Parthenon. c. 438–432 B.C. Marble, over lifesize. British Museum, London

something of the quality of the ensemble. They represent various deities, most in sitting or reclining poses, witnessing the birth of Athena from the head of Zeus (figs. 209 and 210). Here, even more than in the case of the *Dying Niobid,* we marvel at the spaciousness, the complete ease of movement of these statues. There is neither violence nor pathos in them, indeed no specific action of any kind, only a deeply felt poetry of being. We find it equally in the relaxed masculine body of Dionysus and in the soft fullness of the three goddesses, enveloped in thin drapery that seems to share the

qualities of a liquid substance as it flows and eddies around the forms underneath.

The figures are so freely conceived in depth that they create their own aura of space, as it were. How, we wonder, did they ever fit into the confined shape of a pediment? Might they not have looked a bit incongruous, as if they had been merely shelved there? The great master who designed them must have felt something of the sort, for the composition as a whole suggests that he refused to accept the triangular field as more than a purely physical limit. In the sharp angles at

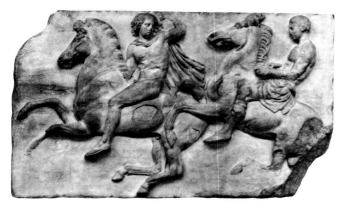

211. *HORSEMEN,* from the west frieze of the Parthenon.
c. 440 B.C. Marble, height 43″ (109.3 cm).
British Museum, London (see also fig. 287)

the corners, at the feet of Dionysus and the reclining goddesses, he has placed two horses' heads; they are meant to
represent the chariots of the rising sun and the waning
moon emerging into (and dipping below) the pedimental
space, but visually the heads are merely two fragments arbi-
trarily cut off by the frame. Clearly, we are approaching the
moment when the pediment will be rejected altogether as
the focal point of Greek architectural sculpture.

The frieze of the Parthenon, a continuous band 525 feet
long (fig. 189), shows a procession honoring Athena in the
presence of the other Olympic gods. It is of the same high
rank as the pedimental sculptures. In a somewhat different
way it, too, suffered from its subordination to the architectural setting, for it must have been poorly lit and difficult to
see, placed as it was immediately below the ceiling. The
depth of the carving and the concept of relief are not radically different from the frieze of the Siphnian Treasury (figs.
176 and 177), although the illusion of space and of rounded
form is now achieved with sovereign ease. The most remarkable quality of the Parthenon frieze is the rhythmic grace of
the design, particularly striking in the spirited movement of
the groups of horsemen (fig. 211).

Who was responsible for this magnificent array of sculptures? They have long been associated with the name of
Phidias, the chief overseer of all artistic enterprises sponsored by Pericles. According to ancient writers, Phidias was
particularly famous for a huge ivory-and-gold statue of Athena he made for the cella of the Parthenon, a colossal Zeus in
the same technique for the temple of that god in Olympia,
and an equally large bronze statue of Athena that stood on
the Acropolis facing the Propylaea. None of these survives,
and small-scale representations of them in later times are utterly inadequate to convey anything of the artist's style. It is,
in any event, hard to imagine that enormous statues of this
sort, burdened with the requirements of cult images and the
demands of a difficult technique, shared the vitality of the
Elgin Marbles. The admiration they elicited could have been
due in large part to their size, the preciousness of the materials, and the aura of religious awe surrounding them. Phidias' personality thus remains oddly intangible; he may have
been a great genius, or simply a very able coordinator and
supervisor. The term "Phidian style" used to describe the

Parthenon sculptures is no more than a generic label, justified by its convenience but of questionable accuracy. Undoubtedly a large number of masters were involved, since
the frieze and the two pediments were executed in less than
ten years (c. 440–432 B.C.). The metopes, which we have
omitted here, date from the 440s.

PHIDIAN STYLE. It is hardly surprising that the Phidian
style should have dominated Athenian sculpture until the
end of the fifth century and beyond, even though large-scale
sculptural enterprises gradually came to a halt because of
the Peloponnesian War. The last of these was the balustrade
erected around the small temple of Athena Nike c. 410–407
B.C. Like the Parthenon frieze, it shows a festive procession,
but the participants are winged Nike figures (personifications of victory) rather than citizens of Athens. One Nike
(fig. 212) is taking off her sandals, in conformity with an

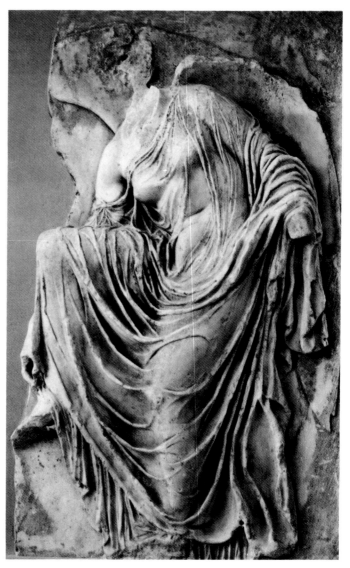

212. *NIKE,* from the balustrade of the Temple of
Athena Nike. c. 410–407 B.C. Marble, height 42″ (106.7 cm).
Acropolis Museum, Athens

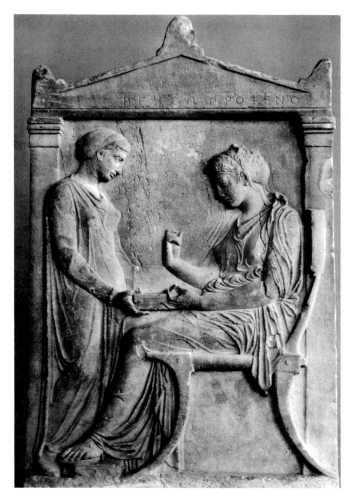

213. *GRAVE STELE OF HEGESO.* c. 410–400 B.C. Marble,
height 59″ (150 cm). National Archeological Museum, Athens

age-old tradition, indicating that she is about to step on holy ground (see page 99). Her wings—one open, the other closed—are effectively employed to help her keep her balance, so that she performs with consummate elegance of movement what is ordinarily a rather awkward act. Her figure is more strongly detached from the relief ground than are those on the Parthenon frieze, and her garments, with their deeply cut folds, cling to the body as if they were wet (we have seen an earlier phase of this treatment of drapery in the *Three Goddesses* of the Parthenon, fig. 210).

"Phidian," too, and also from the last years of the century, is the beautiful *Grave Stele of Hegeso* (fig. 213). Memorials of this kind were produced in large numbers by Athenian sculptors, and their export must have helped to spread the Phidian style throughout the Greek world. Few of them, however, can match the harmonious design and the gentle melancholy of our example. The deceased is represented in a simple domestic scene; she has picked a necklace from the box held by the girl servant and seems to be contemplating it as if it were a keepsake. The delicacy of the carving can be seen especially well in the forms farthest removed from the beholder, such as the servant's left arm supporting the lid of the jewel box, or the veil behind Hegeso's right shoulder. Here the relief merges almost imperceptibly with the back-

ground, so that the ground no longer appears as a solid surface but assumes something of the transparency of empty space. This novel effect was probably inspired by the painters of the period, who, according to the literary sources, had achieved a great breakthrough in mastering illusionistic space.

## CLASSICAL PAINTING

Unhappily, we have no murals or panels to verify that the Greeks had mastered illusionistic space; and vase painting by its very nature could echo the new concept of pictorial space only in rudimentary fashion. Still, there are vessels that form an exception to this general rule; we find them mostly in a special class of vases, the lekythoi (oil jugs) used as funerary offerings. These had a white coating on which the painter could draw as freely, and with the same spatial effect, as his modern successor using pen and paper. The white ground, in both cases, is treated as empty space from which the sketched forms seem to emerge—if the draftsman knows how to achieve this.

Not many lekythos painters were capable of bringing off the illusion. Foremost among them is the unknown artist, nicknamed the "Achilles Painter," who drew the woman in figure 214. Although some twenty-five years older than the Hegeso stele, this vase shows exactly the same scene: here, too, a standing maidservant holds a box from which the deceased has just taken a piece of jewelry. There is the same mood of "Phidian" reverie, and even the chairs match almost exactly. This scene, then, was a standard subject for painted or sculptured memorials of young women.

Our chief interest, however, is in the masterly draftsmanship; with a few lines, sure, fresh, and fluid, the artist not only creates a three-dimensional figure but reveals the body beneath the drapery as well. How does he manage to persuade us that these shapes exist in depth rather than merely on the surface of the vase? First of all, by his command of foreshortening. But the "internal dynamics" of the lines are equally important, their swelling and fading, which make some contours stand out boldly while others merge with one another or disappear into the white ground. However, we must not assume that the carver of the Hegeso stele actually

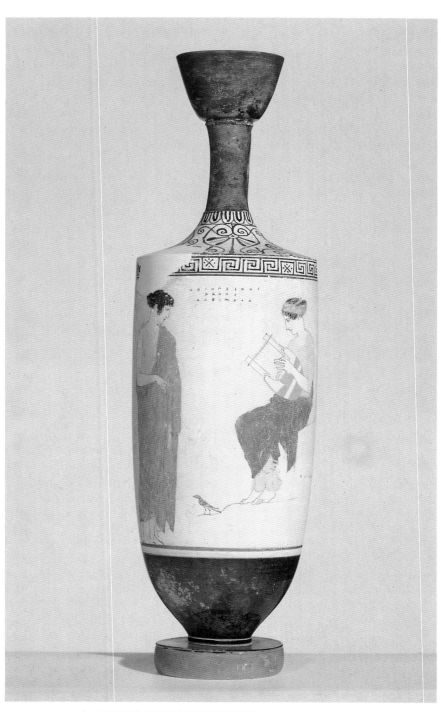

214. THE "ACHILLES PAINTER". *MUSE AND MAIDEN,*
on an Attic white-ground lekythos. c. 440–430 B.C.
Height 16″ (40.7 cm). Staatliche Antikensammlungen, Munich

knew our lekythos: more likely, they both derive from a common ancestor, which may have been a marble stele like that of Hegeso but with a *painted* representation of the jewel-box scene.

Considering its artistic advantages, we might expect a more general adoption of the white-ground technique. Such, however, was not the case. Instead, from the mid-fifth century on, the impact of monumental painting gradually transformed vase painting as a whole into a satellite art that tried to reproduce large-scale compositions in a kind of shorthand dictated by its own limited technique. The result, more often than not, was spotty and overcrowded.

Even the finest examples suffer from this defect, as we can see in figure 215, which is taken from a vase produced in central Italy—probably by a Greek master—not very long after 400 B.C. It shows Thetis, who was about to bathe under a fountain, being abducted by Peleus as her two girl servants flee in panic. Our artist, the "Aurora Painter," has placed three of the figures on a rocky slope (the fourth, intended to be farther away, seems suspended in mid-air) in order to suggest the spatial setting of the scene; he even shows the fountain, in the shape of two pipes coming out of a rock in the upper right-hand corner. Yet the effect remains sil-

houettelike, because of the obtrusive black background. He has also tried to enlarge his color range: the body of Thetis has a lighter tint than the other figures, and some details have been added in white. This expedient, too, fails to solve his problem, since his medium does not permit him to shade or model. He thus must rely on creating a maximum of dramatic excitement to hold the scene together; and, being a spirited draftsman, he almost succeeds. Still, it is a success at second hand, for the composition must have been inspired by a mural or panel picture. He is, as it were, battling for a lost cause; in another hundred years, vase painting was to disappear altogether.

# FOURTH-CENTURY SCULPTURE

There is, unfortunately, no single word, like Archaic or Classical, that we can use to designate the third phase in the development of Greek art from c. 400 to the first century B.C. The seventy-five-year span between the end of the Peloponnesian War and the rise of Alexander the Great used to be labeled "Late Classical," and the remaining two centuries and a half, "Hellenistic," a term meant to convey the spread of Greek civilization southeastward through Asia Minor and

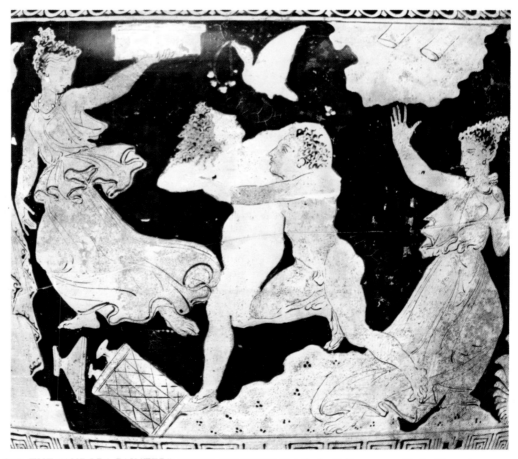

215. THE "AURORA PAINTER". *PELEUS AND THETIS*. Detail of a Faliscan vase. Early 4th century B.C.
Museo Nazionale di Villa Giulia, Rome

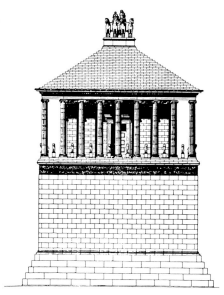

216. Reconstruction drawing of the Mausoleum
at Halicarnassus (after F. Krischen)

Mesopotamia, Egypt, and the borders of India. It was perhaps natural to expect that the world-shaking conquests of Alexander in 333–323 B.C. would also effect an artistic revolution, but the history of style is not always in tune with political history, and we have come to realize that there was no decisive break in the tradition of Greek art at the end of the fourth century. The art of the Hellenistic era is the direct outgrowth of developments that occurred, not at the time of Alexander, but during the preceding fifty years.

Here, then, is our dilemma: "Hellenistic" is a concept so closely linked with the political and cultural consequences of Alexander's conquest that we cannot very well extend it backward to the early fourth century, although there is wide agreement now that the art of the years 400–325 B.C. can be far better understood if we view it as pre-Hellenistic rather than as Late Classical. Until the right word is found and wins general acceptance, we shall have to make do with the existing terms as best we can, always keeping in mind the essential continuity of the "third phase" that we are about to examine.

THE MAUSOLEUM AT HALICARNASSUS. The contrast between Classical and pre-Hellenistic is strikingly demonstrated by the only project of the fourth century that corresponds to the Parthenon in size and ambition. It is not a temple but a huge tomb—so huge, in fact, that its name, Mausoleum, has become a generic term for all outsized funerary monuments. It was erected at Halicarnassus in Asia Minor just before and after 350 B.C. by Mausolus, who was ruler of the area as a satrap of the Persians, and by his widow Artemisia. The structure itself is completely destroyed, but its dimensions and general appearance can be reconstructed on the basis of ancient descriptions and the excavated fragments (including a good deal of sculpture). The drawing

in figure 216 does not pretend to be exact in detail; it probably shows fewer statues than were actually there. We do know, however, that the building rose in three stages to a height of about 160 feet. A tall rectangular base 117 feet wide and 82 feet deep supported a colonnade of Ionic columns 40 feet tall, and above this rose a pyramid crowned by a chariot with statues of the deceased. The sculptural program consisted of three friezes showing Lapiths battling Centaurs, Greeks fighting Amazons, and chariot races; their combined length was twice that of the Parthenon frieze. There were also rows of carved guardian lions and an unknown number of large statues, including portraits of the deceased and their ancestors.

The commemorative and retrospective character of the monument, based on the idea of human life as a glorious struggle or chariot race, is entirely Greek, yet we immediately notice the un-Greek way it has been carried out. The huge size of the tomb, and more particularly the pyramid, derive from Egypt; they imply an exaltation of the ruler far beyond ordinary human status. His kinship with the gods may have been hinted at. Apparently Mausolus took this view of himself as a divinely ordained sovereign from the Persians, who in turn had inherited it from the Assyrians and Egyptians, although he seems to have wanted to glorify his individual personality as much as his high office. The structure embodying these ambitions must have struck his contemporaries as impressive and monstrous at the same time, with its multiple friezes and the receding faces of a pyramid in place of pediments above the colonnade.

SCOPAS. According to ancient sources, the sculpture on each of the four sides of the monument was entrusted to a different master, chosen from among the best of the time. Scopas, the most famous, did the main side, the one to the east. His dynamic style has been recognized in some portions of the Amazon frieze, such as the portion in figure 217. The Parthenon tradition can still be felt here, but there is also a decidedly un-Classical violence, physical as well as emotional, conveyed through strained movements and passionate facial expressions (deep-set eyes are a hallmark of Scopas' style). As a consequence, we no longer find the rhythmic flow of the Parthenon frieze; continuity and harmony have been sacrificed so that each figure may have greater scope for sweeping, impulsive gestures. Clearly, if we are to do justice to this explosive energetic style we must not judge it by Classical standards.

The "pre-Hellenistic" flavor is even more pronounced in the portrait statue presumed to represent Mausolus himself (fig. 218). The colossal figure must be the work of a man younger than Scopas and even less encumbered by Classical standards, probably Bryaxis, the master of the north side. We know, through Roman copies, of some Greek portraits of Classical times, but they seem to represent types rather than individuals, whereas the *Mausolus* is both the earliest Greek portrait to have survived in the original and the first to show a clear-cut personal character. This very fact links it with the future rather than the past, for individual likenesses were to play an important part in Hellenistic times. Nor is it merely the head, with its heavy jaws and small, sensuous mouth, that records the sitter's appearance; the thick neck and the broad, fleshy body seem equally individual. The massiveness of the forms is further emphasized by the sharp-edged and stiff-textured drapery, which might be said to *encase,* rather than merely clothe, the body. The great volumes of folds across the abdomen and below the left arm seem designed for picturesque effect more than for functional clarity.

PRAXITELES. Some of the features of the Mausoleum sculpture recur in other important works of the period. Foremost among these is the wonderful seated figure of Demeter from the temple of that goddess at Cnidus (fig. 219), a work only slightly later in date than the *Mausolus.* Here again the drapery, though more finely textured, has an impressive volume of its own; motifs such as the S-curve of folds across the chest form an effective counterpoint to the shape of the body beneath. The deep-set eyes gaze into the distance with an intensity that suggests the influence of Scopas. The modeling of the head, on the other hand, has a veiled softness that points to an altogether different source: Praxiteles, the master of feminine grace and sensuous evocation of flesh.

As it happens, Praxiteles' most acclaimed statue, an Aphrodite (fig. 220), was likewise made for Cnidus, although probably some years later than the *Demeter.* But his reputation was well established even earlier, so that the unknown sculptor who carved the *Demeter* would have had no difficulty incorporating some Praxitelean qualities into his own work. The *Cnidian Aphrodite* by Praxiteles achieved such proverbial fame that she is often referred to in ancient literature as a synonym for absolute perfection. To what extent her renown was based on her beauty, or on the fact that she was (so far as we know) the first completely nude cult image of the goddess, is difficult to say, for the statue is known to us only through Roman copies that can be no more than pal-

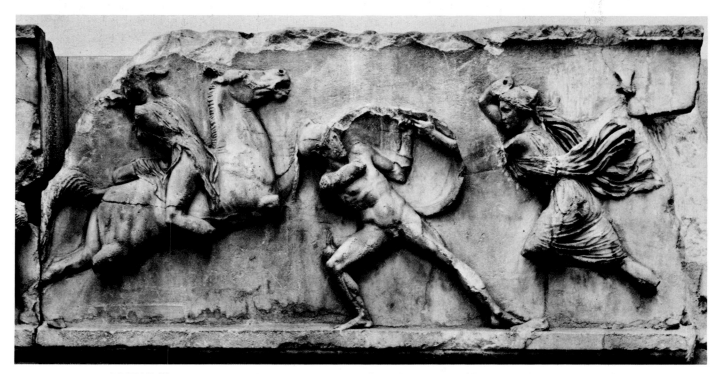

217. SCOPAS (?). *BATTLE OF THE GREEKS AND AMAZONS,* from the east frieze of the Mausoleum, Halicarnassus.
359–351 B.C. Marble, height 35″ (89 cm). British Museum, London

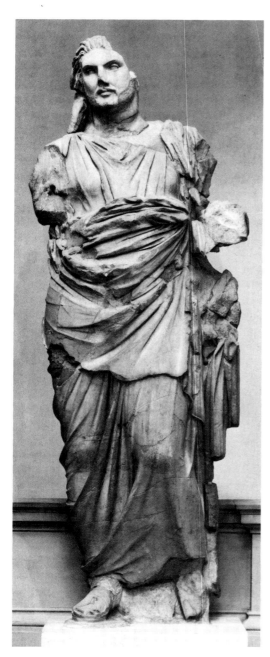

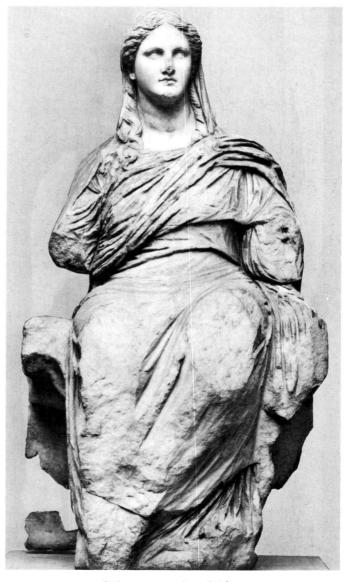

218. *MAUSOLUS*, from the Mausoleum at
Halicarnassus. 359–351 B.C. Marble,
height 9′10″ (3.1 m). British Museum, London

219. *DEMETER*, from Cnidus.
c. 340–330 B.C. Marble, height 60″ (152.3 cm).
British Museum, London

lid reflections of the original. She was to have countless descendants in Hellenistic and Roman art.

A more faithful embodiment of Praxitelean beauty is the group of Hermes with the infant Bacchus at Olympia (fig. 221); it is of such high quality that it was long regarded as Praxiteles' own work. Today some scholars believe it to be a very fine Greek copy made some three centuries later. The dispute is of little consequence for us, except perhaps in one respect: it emphasizes the unfortunate fact that we do not have a single undisputed original by any of the famous sculptors of Greece. Nevertheless, the *Hermes* is the most completely Praxitelean statue we know. The lithe propor-

tions, the sinuous curve of the torso, the play of gentle curves, the sense of complete relaxation (enhanced by the use of an outside support for the figure to lean against), all these agree well enough with the character of the *Cnidian Aphrodite*. We also find many refinements here that are ordinarily lost in a copy, such as the caressing treatment of the marble, the faint smile, the meltingly soft, "veiled" modeling of the features; even the hair, left comparatively rough for contrast, shares the silky feel of the rest of the work. The bland, lyrical charm of the *Hermes* makes it easy to believe that the *Cnidian Aphrodite* was the artist's most successful accomplishment.

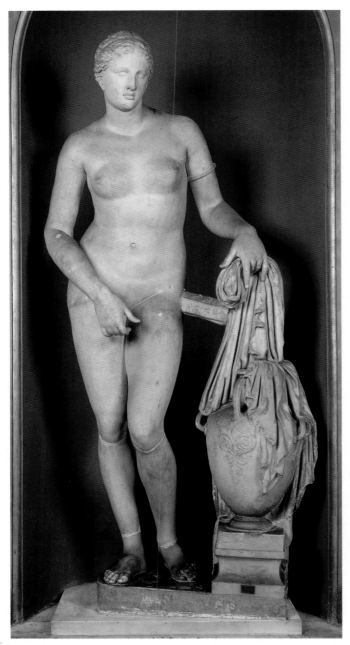

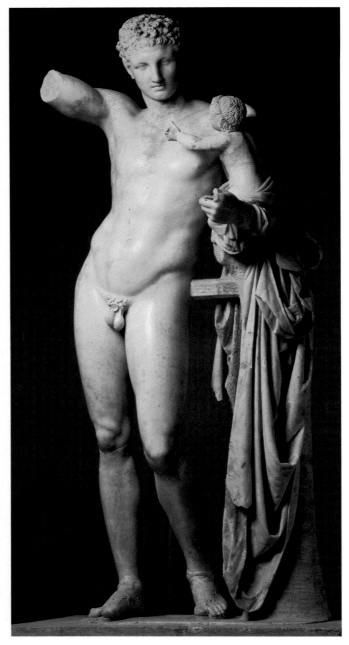

220. *CNIDIAN APHRODITE*. Roman copy after an original
of c. 300 B.C. by PRAXITELES. Marble, height 6′8″ (2 m).
Vatican Museums, Rome

221. PRAXITELES. *HERMES*. c. 300–320 B.C. (or copy?).
Marble, height 7′1″ (2.2 m). Archaeological Museum, Olympia

APOLLO BELVEDERE.  The same qualities recur in many other statues, all of them Roman copies of Greek works in a more or less Praxitelean vein. The best known—one is tempted to say the most notorious—is the *Apollo Belvedere* (fig. 222); it interests us less for its own sake than because of its tremendous popularity during the eighteenth and nineteenth centuries. Johann Joachim Winckelmann, Goethe, and other champions of the Greek Revival (see page 619) found it the perfect exemplar of Classical beauty; plaster casts or reproductions of it were thought indispensable for all museums, art academies, or liberal arts colleges, and generations of students grew up in the belief that it em-

bodied the essence of the Greek spirit. This enthusiasm tells us a good deal—not about the qualities of the *Apollo Belvedere* but about the character of the Greek Revival. Although our own time takes a less enthusiastic view of the statue, we had better refrain from scoffing at the naïveté of our forefathers. Who knows whether the tide of taste may not turn some day? Let us not discount the possibility that the *Apollo Belvedere* may again hold a message for our grandchildren.

LYSIPPUS.  Besides Scopas and Praxiteles, there is yet another great name in pre-Hellenistic sculpture: Lysippus, whose long career may have begun as early as c. 370 B.C. and continued to the end of the century. The main features of his personal style, however, are more difficult to grasp than those of his two famous contemporaries, because of the contradictory evidence of the Roman copies that are assumed to reproduce his work. Ancient authors praised him for replacing the canon of Polyclitus with a new set of proportions that produced a more slender body and a smaller head. His realism, too, was proverbial: he is said to have had no master other than nature itself. But these statements describe little more than a general trend toward the end of the fourth century. Certainly the proportions of Praxiteles' statues are Lysippic rather than "Polyclitan," nor could Lysippus have been the only artist of his time to conquer new aspects of reality.

Even in the case of the *Apoxyomenos*, the statue most insistently linked with his name, the evidence is far from conclusive (fig. 223). It shows a young athlete cleaning himself with a scraper, a motif often represented in Greek art from Classical times on. Our version, of which only a single copy has turned up so far, is distinguished from all the others by the fact that the arms are horizontally extended in front of the body. This bold thrust into space, at the cost of obstructing the view of the torso, is a noteworthy feat, whether or not we credit it to Lysippus; it endows the figure with a new capacity for spontaneous three-dimensional movement. A similar freedom is suggested by the diagonal line of the free leg. Even the unruly hair reflects the new trend toward spontaneity.

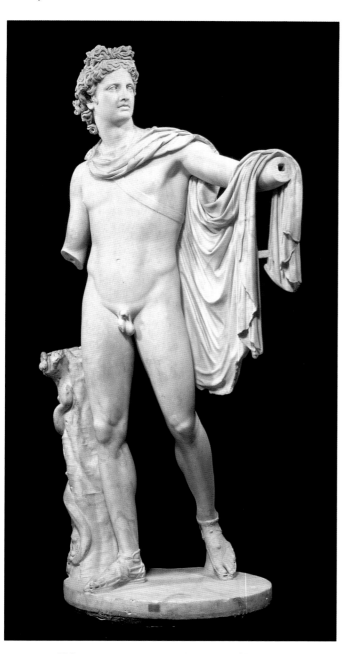

222. *APOLLO BELVEDERE*. Roman marble copy, probably of a Greek original of the late 4th (or 1st) century B.C. Height 7'4" (2.3 m). Vatican Museums, Rome

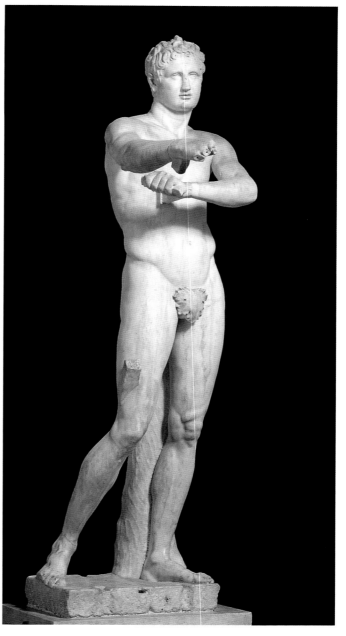

223. *APOXYOMENOS (SCRAPER)*. Roman marble copy, probably after a bronze original of c. 330 B.C. by LYSIPPUS. Height 6'9" (2.1 m). Vatican Museums, Rome

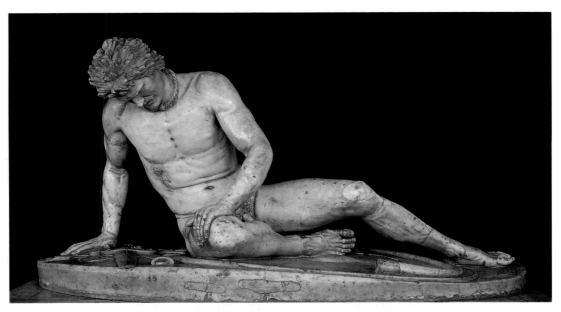

224. *DYING GAUL*. Roman copy after a bronze original of c. 230–220 B.C. from Pergamum, Turkey.
Marble, lifesize. Museo Capitolino, Rome

# HELLENISTIC SCULPTURE

Of the artistic enterprises sponsored by Alexander the Great, such as the numerous portraits of the great conqueror by Lysippus, no direct evidence survives. In fact, we know very little of the development of Greek sculpture as a whole during the first hundred years of the Hellenistic era. Even after that, we have few fixed points of reference; of the large number of works at our disposal only a small fraction can be securely identified as to date and place of origin. Moreover, Greek sculpture was now being produced throughout a vast territory, and the interplay of local and international currents must have formed a complex pattern, a pattern of which we can trace only some isolated strands. One of these is represented by the bronze groups dedicated by Attalus I of Pergamum (a city in northwestern Asia Minor) between c. 240 and 200 B.C. to celebrate his victories over the Gauls. The Gauls were a Celtic tribe that had entered Asia Minor and kept raiding the Greek states there until Attalus forced them to settle down; we meet them a few centuries later as the Galatians in St. Paul's Epistle.

DYING GAUL. The statues commemorating the Gauls' defeat were reproduced in marble for the Romans (who may have had a special interest in them because of their troubles with Celtic tribes in northwestern Europe), and a number of these copies have survived, including the famous *Dying Gaul* (fig. 224). The sculptor who conceived the figure must have known the Gauls well, for he has carefully rendered the ethnic type in the facial structure and in the bristly shock of hair. The torque around the neck is another characteristically Celtic feature. Otherwise, however, the Gaul shares the heroic nudity of Greek warriors, such as those on the Aegina pediments (see fig. 179); and if his agony seems infinitely more realistic in comparison, it still has considerable dignity and pathos. Clearly, the Gauls were not considered unworthy foes. "They knew how to die, barbarians though they were," is the thought conveyed by the statue. Yet we also sense something else, an animal quality that had never before been part of Greek images of men. Death, as we witness it here, is a very concrete physical process: no longer able to move his legs, the Gaul puts all his waning strength into his arms, as if to prevent some tremendous invisible weight from crushing him against the ground.

BARBERINI FAUN. A similar exploration of uncontrolled bodily responses may be seen in the *Barberini Faun* (fig. 225), probably a very fine Roman copy after a Hellenistic work of the late third century B.C., contemporary with the *Dying Gaul*. A drunken satyr is sprawled on a rock, asleep in the heavy-breathing, unquiet manner of the inebriated. He is obviously dreaming, and the convulsive gesture of the right arm and the troubled expression of the face betray the passionate, disturbing nature of his dream. Here again we witness a partial uncoupling of body and mind, no less persuasive than in the *Dying Gaul*.

PERGAMUM ALTAR. Some decades later, we find a second sculptural style flourishing at Pergamum. About 180 B.C., the son and successor of Attalus I had a mighty altar erected on a hill above the city to commemorate his father's victories. Much of the sculptural decoration has been recovered by excavation, and the entire west front of the altar is to be seen in Berlin (fig. 226). It is an impressive structure indeed. The altar proper occupies the center of a rectangular court surrounded by an Ionic colonnade which rises on a tall base about 100 feet square; a monumental flight of stairs leads to the court on the west side (fig. 227). Altar structures of such great size seem to have been an Ionian tradition since Archaic times, but the Pergamum Altar is the most

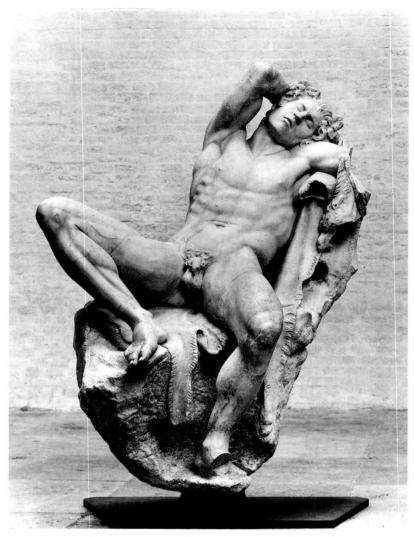

225. *BARBERINI FAUN*. Roman copy of a Greek original
of c. 220 B.C. Marble, over lifesize.
Staatliche Antikensammlungen, Munich

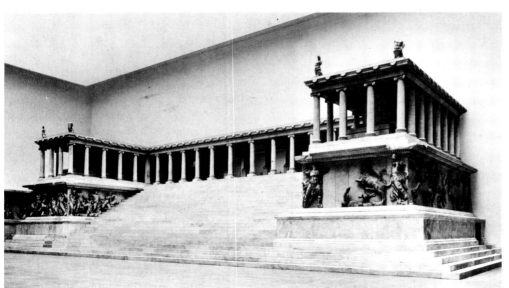

226. The west front of the Altar of Zeus at Pergamum (restored).
Pergamonmuseum, Berlin

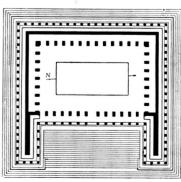

227. Plan of the Altar of Zeus at
Pergamum (after J. Schrammen)

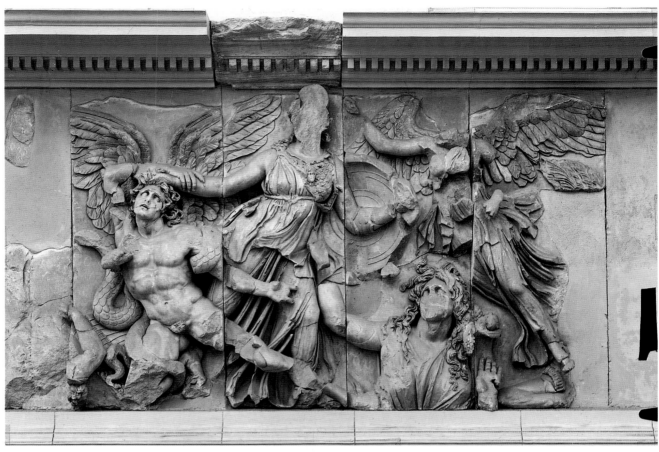

228. *ATHENA AND ALCYONEUS,* from the east side of the Great Frieze of the Altar of Zeus at Pergamum.
c. 180 B.C. Marble, height 7′6″ (2.3 m). Pergamonmuseum, Berlin

elaborate of all, as well as the only one of which considerable portions have survived. Its boldest feature is the great frieze covering the base, 400 feet long and between 7 and 8 feet tall. The huge figures, carved to such a depth that they are almost detached from the background, have the scale and weight of pedimental statues without the confining triangular frame—a unique compound of two separate traditions that represents a thundering climax in the development of Greek architectural sculpture (fig. 228).

The subject, the battle of the gods and giants, is a traditional one for Ionic friezes; we saw it before on the Siphnian Treasury (compare fig. 177). At Pergamum, however, it has a novel significance, since the victory of the gods is meant to symbolize the victories of Attalus I. Such a translation of history into mythology had been an established device in Greek art for a long time; victories over the Persians were habitually represented in terms of Lapiths battling Centaurs or Greeks fighting Amazons. But to place Attalus I in analogy with the gods themselves implies an exaltation of the ruler that is Oriental rather than Greek in origin. Since the time of Mausolus, who may have been the first to introduce it on Greek soil, the idea of divine kingship had been adopted by Alexander the Great and it continued to flourish among the lesser sovereigns who divided his realm, such as the rulers of Pergamum.

The carving of the frieze, though not very subtle in detail, has tremendous dramatic force; the heavy, muscular bodies rushing at each other, the strong accents of light and dark, the beating wings and wind-blown garments are almost overwhelming in their dynamism. A writhing movement pervades the entire design, down to the last lock of hair, linking the victors and the vanquished in a single continuous rhythm. It is this sense of unity that disciplines the physical and emotional violence of the struggle and thus keeps it—but just barely—from exploding its architectural frame.

NIKE OF SAMOTHRACE. Equally dramatic in its impact is another great victory monument of the early second century B.C., the *Nike of Samothrace* (fig. 229). The goddess has just descended to the prow of a ship; her great wings spread wide, she is still partly air-borne by the powerful head wind against which she advances. This invisible force of onrushing air here becomes a tangible reality; it not only balances the forward movement of the figure but also shapes every fold of the wonderfully animated drapery. As a result, there is an active relationship—indeed, an interdependence—between the statue and the space that envelops it, such as we have never seen before. Nor shall we see it again for a long time to come. The *Nike of Samothrace* deserves all of her fame as the greatest masterpiece of Hellenistic sculpture.

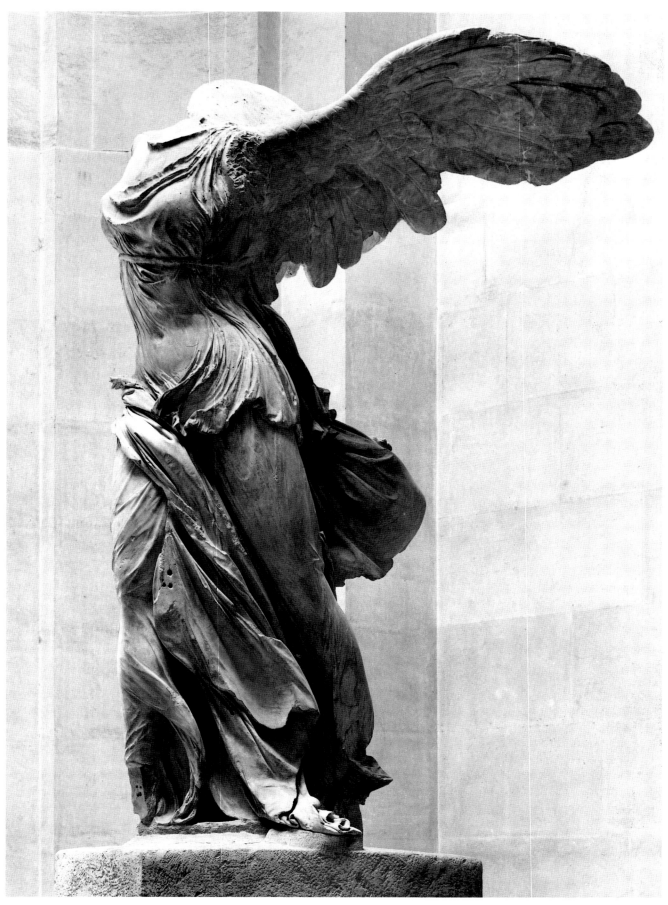

229. *NIKE OF SAMOTHRACE.* c. 200–190 B.C. Marble, height 8′ (2.4 m). Musée du Louvre, Paris

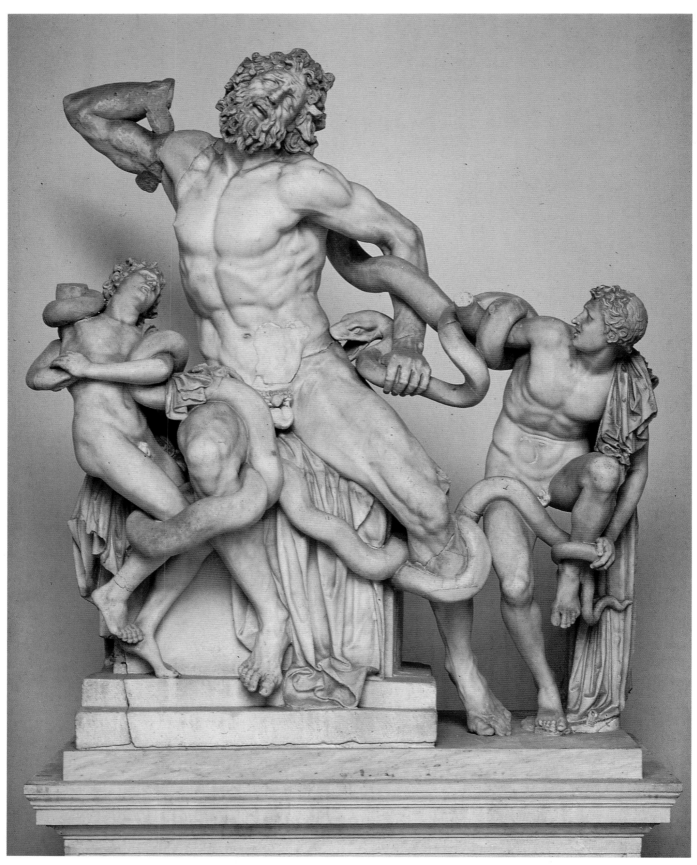

230. *THE LAOCOÖN GROUP.* Roman copy, perhaps after
AGESANDER, ATHENODORUS, and POLYDORUS OF RHODES
(present state, former restorations removed). 1st century A.D.
Marble, height 7′ (2.1 m). Vatican Museums, Rome

LAOCOÖN. Until the *Nike* was discovered over a hundred years ago, the most admired work of Hellenistic statuary had been a group showing the death of Laocoön and his two sons (fig. 230). It had been found in Rome as early as 1506 and had made a tremendous impression on Michelangelo and countless others. The history of its fame is rather like that of the *Apollo Belvedere*; the two were treated as complementary, the *Apollo* exemplifying harmonious beauty, the *Laocoön* sublime tragedy. Today we tend to find the pathos of the group somewhat calculated and rhetorical; its meticulous surface finish strikes us as a display of virtuoso technique. In style, including the relieflike spread of the three figures, it clearly descends from the Pergamum frieze, although its dynamism has become uncomfortably self-conscious. It was long accepted as a Greek original and identified with a group by Agesander, Athenodorus, and Polydorus of Rhodes that the Roman writer Pliny mentions in the palace of the Emperor Titus; now it is thought to be a Roman copy or reconstruction of a late Hellenistic work. For the Romans, the subject must have held a special meaning: the divine punishment meted out to Laocoön and his sons forewarned Aeneas of the fall of Troy and caused him to flee that city in time. Since Aeneas was believed to have come to Italy and to have been the ancestor of Romulus and Remus, the death of Laocoön could be viewed as the first link in a chain of events that ultimately led to the founding of Rome.

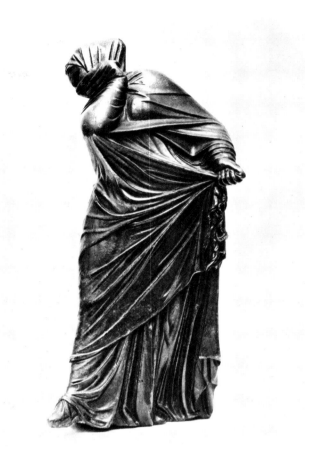

232. *VEILED DANCER*. c. 200 B.C.? Bronze statuette, height 8½″ (22 cm). Collection Walter C. Baker, New York

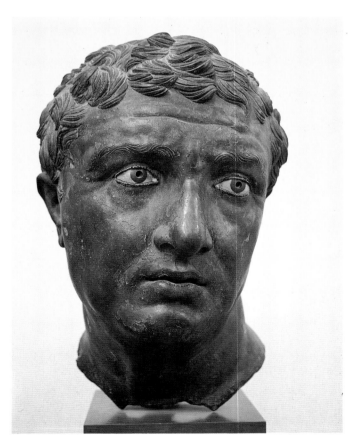

231. *PORTRAIT HEAD,* from Delos. c. 80 B.C. Bronze, height 12¾″ (32 cm). National Archeological Museum, Athens

PORTRAITS. Portraiture, an important branch of Greek sculpture since the fourth century, continued to flourish in Hellenistic times. Its achievements, however, are known to us only indirectly, for the most part through Roman copies. One of the few originals is the very vivid bronze head from Delos, a work of the early first century B.C. (fig. 231). It was not made as a bust but, in accordance with Greek custom, as part of a full-length statue. The identity of the sitter is unknown. Whoever he was, we get an intensely private view of him that immediately captures our interest. The fluid modeling of the somewhat flabby features, the uncertain, plaintive mouth, the unhappy eyes under furrowed brows reveal an individual beset by doubts and anxieties, an extremely human, unheroic personality. There are echoes of Greek pathos in these features, but it is a pathos translated into psychological terms. Men of these particular character traits had surely existed earlier in the Greek world, just as they exist today. Yet it is significant that the inner complexity of such men could be conveyed by a work of art only when Greek independence, culturally as well as politically, was about to come to an end.

STATUETTES. Before we leave Hellenistic sculpture, we must cast at least a passing glance at another aspect of it, represented by the enchanting bronze statuette of a veiled dancer (fig. 232). She introduces us to the vast variety of

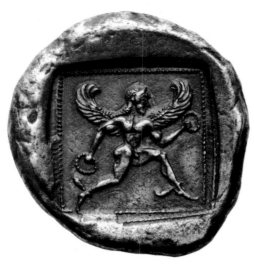

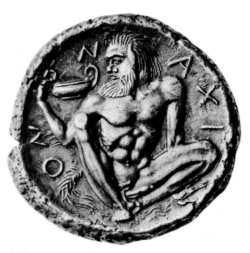

233. *WINGED GOD.* Silver coin from Peparethus. c. 500 B.C.
Diameter 1½″ (3.7 cm). British Museum, London

234. *SILENUS.* Silver coin from Naxos. c. 460 B.C.
Diameter 1¼″ (3.3 cm). British Museum, London

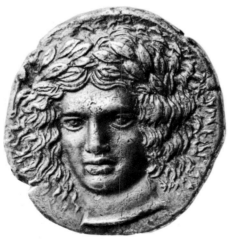

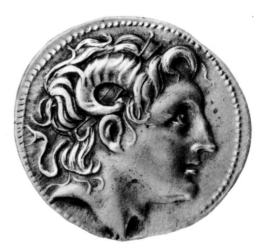

235. *APOLLO.* Silver coin from Catana. c. 415–400 B.C.
Diameter 1⅛″ (3 cm). British Museum, London

236 . *ALEXANDER THE GREAT WITH AMUN HORNS.* Four-drachma
silver coin issued by Lysimachus. c. 300 B.C. Diameter 1⅛″ (3 cm)

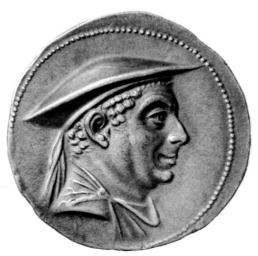

237. *ANTIMACHUS OF BACTRIA.* Silver coin. c. 185 B.C.
Diameter 1¼″ (3.3 cm). British Museum, London

small-scale works produced for private ownership. Such pieces were collected in much the same way as painted vases had been in earlier times; and, like vase pictures, they show a range of subject matter far broader than that of monumental sculpture. Besides the familiar mythological themes we encounter a wealth of everyday subjects: beggars, street entertainers, peasants, young ladies of fashion. The grotesque, the humorous, the picturesque—qualities that rarely enter into Greek monumental art—play a conspicuous role here. At their best, as in our example, these small figures have an imaginative freedom rarely matched on a larger scale. The bold spiral twist of the veiled dancer, reinforced by the diagonal folds of the drapery, creates a multiplicity of interesting views that practically forces the beholder to turn the statuette in his hands. No less extraordinary is the rich interplay of concave and convex forms, the intriguing contrast between the compact silhouette of the figure and the mobility of the body within. If we only knew when and where this little masterpiece was made!

# COINS

We rarely think of coins as works of art, and the great majority of them do not encourage us to do so. The study of their history and development, known as numismatics, offers many rewards, but visual delight is the least of these. If many Greek coins form an exception to this general rule, it is not simply because they are the earliest (the idea of stamping metal pellets of standard weight with an identifying design originated in Ionian Greece sometime before 600 B.C.); after all, the first postage stamps were no more distinguished than their present-day descendants. The reason, rather, is the persistent individualism of Greek political life. Every city-state had its own coinage, adorned with its particular emblem, and the designs were changed at frequent intervals so as to take account of treaties, victories, or other occasions for local pride. As a consequence, the number of coins struck at any one time remained relatively small, while the number of coinages was large.

The constant demand for new designs produced highly skilled specialists who took such pride in their work that they sometimes even signed it. Greek coins thus are not only an invaluable source of historical knowledge but an authentic expression of the changing Greek sense of form. Within their own compass, they illustrate the development of Greek sculpture from the sixth to the second century B.C. as faithfully as the larger works we have examined. And since they form a continuous series, with the place and date of almost every item well established, they reflect this development more fully in some respects than do the works of monumental art.

Characteristically enough, the finest coins of Archaic and Classical Greece were usually produced not by the most powerful states such as Athens, Corinth, or Sparta, but by the lesser ones along the periphery of the Greek world. Our first example (fig. 233), from the Aegean island of Peparethus, reflects the origin of coinage: a square die deeply embedded in a rather shapeless pellet, like an impression in sealing wax. The winged god, his pinwheel stance so perfectly adapted to the frame, is a summary-in-miniature of Archaic art, down to the ubiquitous smile. On the coin from Naxos in Sicily (fig. 234), almost half a century later, the die fills the entire area of the coin; the drinking Silenus fits it as tightly as if he were squatting inside a barrel. An astonishingly monumental figure, he shows the articulation and organic vitality of the Severe Style. Our third coin (fig. 235) was struck in the Sicilian town of Catana toward the end of the Peloponnesian War. It is signed with the name of its maker, Herakleidas, and it well deserves to be, for it is one of the true masterpieces of Greek coinage. Who would have thought it possible to endow the full-face view of a head in low relief with such plasticity! This radiant image of Apollo has all the swelling roundness of the mature Classical style. Its grandeur completely transcends the limitations of the tiny scale of a coin.

From the time of Alexander the Great onward, coins began to show profile portraits of rulers. The successors of Alexander at first put his features on their coins to emphasize their link with the deified conqueror. Such a piece is shown in figure 236; Alexander here displays the horns identifying him with the ram-headed Egyptian god Amun. His "inspired" expression, conveyed by the half-open mouth and the upward-looking eyes, is as characteristic of the emotionalism of Hellenistic art as are the fluid modeling of the features and the agitated, snakelike hair. As a likeness, this head can have only the most tenuous relation to the way Alexander actually looked; yet this idealized image of the all-conquering genius projects the flavor of the new era more eloquently than do the large-scale portraits of Alexander.

Once the Hellenistic rulers started putting themselves on their coins, the likenesses became more individual. Perhaps the most astonishing of these (fig. 237) is the head of Antimachus of Bactria (present-day Afghanistan), which stands at the opposite end of the scale from the Alexander-Amun. Its mobile features show a man of sharp intelligence and wit, a bit skeptical perhaps about himself and others, and, in any event, without any desire for self-glorification. This penetratingly human portrait seems to point the way to the bronze head from Delos (fig. 231) a hundred years later. It has no counterpart in the monumental sculpture of its own time, and thus helps to fill an important gap in our knowledge of Hellenistic portraiture.

# CHAPTER SIX

# ETRUSCAN ART

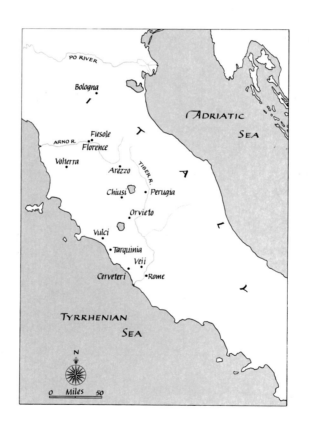

The Italian peninsula did not emerge into the light of history until fairly late. The Bronze Age, which emerged first in Mesopotamia around 4000 B.C., came to an end in the Italian peninsula only in the eighth century B.C., about the time the earliest Greeks began to settle along the southern shores of Italy and in Sicily. Even earlier, if we are to believe the Classical Greek historian Herodotus, another great migration had taken place: the Etruscans had left their homeland of Lydia in Asia Minor and settled in the area between Florence and Rome, which to this day is known as Tuscany, the country of the Tusci or Etrusci. Who were the Etruscans? Did they really come from Asia Minor? Strange as it may seem, Herodotus' claim is still the subject of lively debate among scholars. We know that the Etruscans borrowed their alphabet from the Greeks toward the end of the eighth century, but their language—of which our understanding is as yet very limited—has no kin among any known tongues.

Culturally and artistically, the Etruscans are strongly linked with Asia Minor and the ancient Near East, yet they also show many traits for which no parallels can be found anywhere. Might they not, then, be a people whose presence on Italian soil goes back to before the Indo-European migrations of about 2000–1200 B.C. that brought the Mycenaeans and the Dorian tribes to Greece and the ancestors of the Romans to Italy? If so, the sudden flowering of Etruscan civilization from about 700 B.C. onward could have resulted from a fusion of this prehistoric Italian stock with small but powerful groups of seafaring invaders from Lydia in the course of the eighth century. Interestingly enough, such a hypothesis comes very close to the legendary origin of Rome; the Romans believed that their city had been founded in 753 B.C. by the descendants of refugees from Troy (see page 201) in Asia Minor. Was this perhaps an Etruscan story which the Romans later made their own, along with a great many other things they took from their predecessors?

What the Etruscans themselves believed about their origin we do not know. The only Etruscan writings that have come down to us are brief funerary inscriptions and a few somewhat longer texts relating to religious ritual, though Roman authors tell us that a rich Etruscan literature once existed. We would, in fact, know practically nothing about the Etruscans at first hand were it not for their elaborate tombs, which the Romans did not molest when they destroyed or rebuilt Etruscan cities and which therefore have survived intact until modern times.

Italian Bronze Age burials had been of the modest sort found elsewhere in prehistoric Europe: the remains of the deceased, contained in a pottery vessel or urn, were placed in a simple pit along with the equipment they required in afterlife (weapons for men, jewelry and household tools for women). In Mycenaean Greece, this primitive cult of the dead had been elaborated under Egyptian influence, as shown by the monumental beehive tombs. Something very similar happened eight centuries later in Tuscany. Toward 700 B.C., Etruscan tombs began to imitate, in stone, the interiors of actual dwellings, covered by great conical mounds of earth; they could be roofed by vaults or domes built of horizontal, overlapping courses of stone blocks, as was the Treasury of Atreus at Mycenae (see fig. 147). And at the same time, the pottery urns gradually took on human shape: the lid grew into the head of the deceased, and body markings appeared on the vessel itself, which could be placed on a sort of throne to indicate high rank (fig. 238). Alongside the modest beginnings of funerary sculpture, we find sudden evidence of great wealth in the form of exquisite goldsmith's work decorated with motifs familiar from the Orientalizing Greek vases of the same period (see fig. 159), intermingled with precious objects imported from the ancient Near East.

The seventh and sixth centuries B.C. saw the Etruscans at the height of their power. Their cities rivaled those of the Greeks, their fleet dominated the western Mediterranean and protected a vast commercial empire competing with the Greeks and Phoenicians, and their territory extended as far as Naples in the south and the lower Po valley in the north. Rome itself was ruled by Etruscan kings for about a century, until the establishing of the Republic in 510 B.C. The kings threw the first defensive wall around the seven hills, drained the swampy plain of the Forum, and built the original temple on the Capitoline Hill, thus making a city out of what had been little more than a group of villages before.

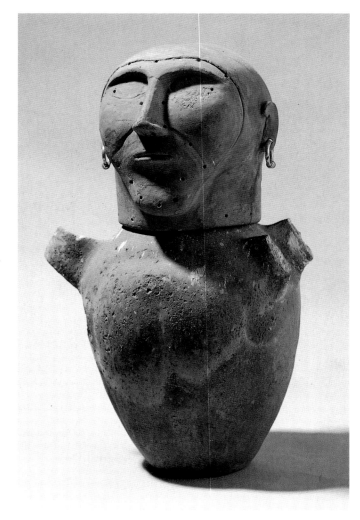

238. Human-headed cinerary urn.
c. 675–650 B.C. Terracotta, height 25½″ (64.7 cm).
Museo Etrusco, Chiusi, Italy

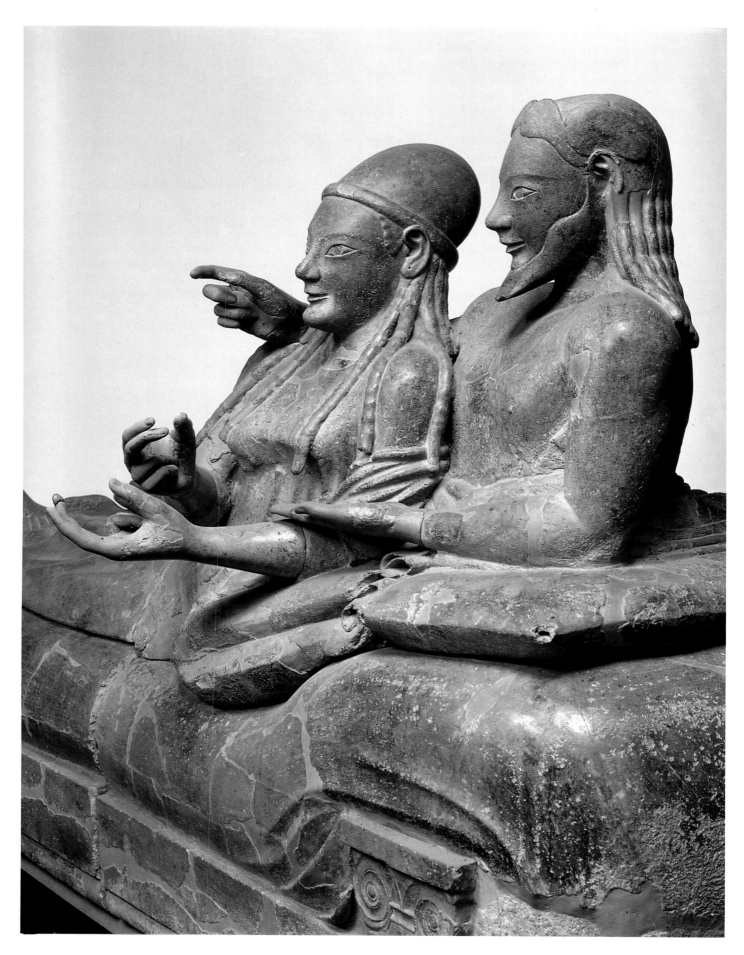

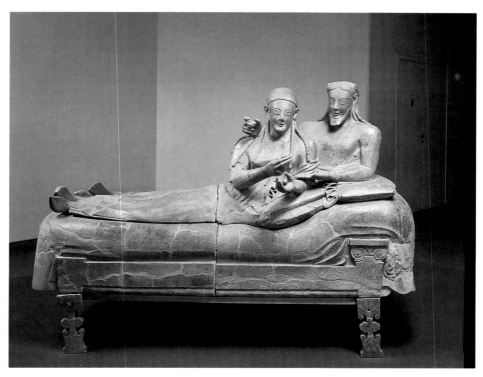

240. Sarcophagus, from Cerveteri. c. 520 B.C. Terracotta,
length 6'7" (2 m). Museo Nazionale di Villa Giulia, Rome

But the Etruscans, like the Greeks, never formed a unified nation; they were no more than a loose federation of individual city-states given to quarreling among themselves and slow to unite against a common enemy. During the fifth and fourth centuries B.C., one Etruscan city after another succumbed to the Romans; by the end of the third, all of them had lost their independence, although many continued to prosper, if we are to judge by the richness of their tombs during the period of political decline.

## Tombs and Their Decoration

The flowering of Etruscan civilization thus coincides with the Archaic age in Greece. It was during this period, especially near the end of the sixth and early in the fifth century B.C., that Etruscan art showed its greatest vigor. Greek Archaic influence had displaced the Orientalizing tendencies—many of the finest Greek vases have been found in Etruscan tombs of that time—but Etruscan artists did not simply imitate their Hellenic models. Working in a very different cultural setting, they retained their own clear-cut identity.

One might expect to see the Etruscan cult of the dead wane under Greek influence, but that was by no means the case. On the contrary, the tombs and their equipment grew more elaborate as the capacities of the sculptor and painter expanded. The deceased themselves could now be represented full-length, reclining on the lids of sarcophagi shaped like couches, as if they were participants in a festive repast, an Archaic smile about their lips. The monumental example in figures 239 and 240 shows a husband and wife side by side, strangely gay and majestic at the same time. The entire work is of terracotta and was once painted in bright colors. The smoothly rounded, elastic forms betray the Etruscan sculptor's preference for modeling in soft materials, in contrast to the Greek love of stone carving; there is less formal discipline here but an extraordinary directness and vivacity.

EARLY FUNERARY BELIEFS. We do not know precisely what ideas the Archaic Etruscans held about the afterlife. Effigies such as our reclining couple, which for the first time in history represent the deceased as thoroughly alive and enjoying themselves, suggest that they regarded the tomb as an abode not only for the body but for the soul as well (in contrast to the Egyptians, who thought of the soul as roaming freely and whose funerary sculpture therefore remained "inanimate"). Or perhaps the Etruscans believed that by filling the tomb with banquets, dancing, games, and similar pleasures they could induce the soul to stay put in the city of the dead and therefore not haunt the realm of the living. How else are we to understand the purpose of the wonderfully rich array of murals in these funerary chambers? Since nothing of the sort has survived in Greek territory, they are uniquely important, not only as an Etruscan achievement but also as a possible reflection of Greek wall painting.

239. (opposite) Detail of sarcophagus, from Cerveteri. c. 520 B.C.
Terracotta. Museo Nazionale di Villa Giulia, Rome

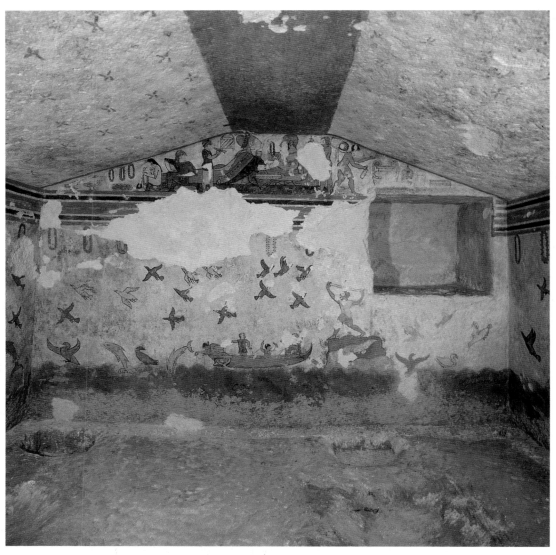

241. Tomb of Hunting and Fishing, Tarquinia, Italy. c. 520 B.C.

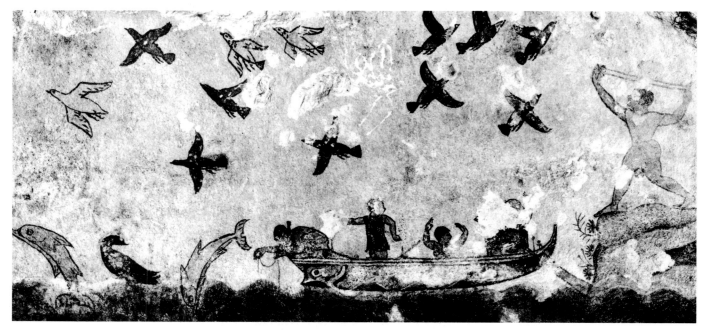

242. Wall painting, detail. c. 520 B.C. Tomb of Hunting and Fishing, Tarquinia, Italy

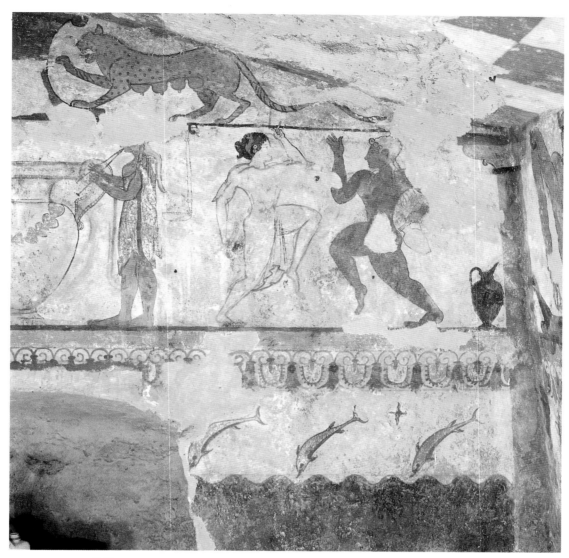

243. *MUSICIANS AND TWO DANCERS.* Detail of a wall painting. c. 480–470 B.C.
Tomb of the Lionesses, Tarquinia, Italy

TOMB OF HUNTING AND FISHING. Perhaps the most astonishing of murals all are found in the Tomb of Hunting and Fishing at Tarquinia of c. 520 B.C. Figure 241 shows the great marine panorama at one end of the low chamber: a vast, continuous expanse of water and sky in which the fishermen, and the hunter with his slingshot, play only an incidental part (fig. 242). The free, rhythmic movement of birds and dolphins is strangely reminiscent of Minoan painting of a thousand years earlier (see fig. 139), but the weightless, floating quality of Cretan art is absent. We might also recall Exekias' *Dionysus in a Boat* (see fig. 161) as the closest Greek counterpart to our scene. The differences here, however, are as revealing as the similarities, and one wonders if any Greek Archaic artist knew how to place human figures in a natural setting as effectively as the Etruscan painter did. Could the mural have been inspired by Egyptian scenes of hunting in the marshes, such as the one in figure

89? They seem the most convincing precedent for the general conception of our subject. If so, the Etruscan artist has brought the scene to life, just as the reclining couple in figure 240 has been brought to life compared with Egyptian funerary statues.

TOMB OF THE LIONESSES. A somewhat later example from another tomb in Tarquinia (fig. 243) shows a pair of ecstatic dancers; the passionate energy of their movements again strikes us as characteristically Etruscan rather than Greek in spirit. Of particular interest is the transparent garment of the woman, which lets the body shine through; in Greece, this differentiation appears only a few years earlier, in the final phase of Archaic vase painting. The contrasting body color of the two figures continues a practice introduced by the Egyptians more than two thousand years before (see fig. 86).

LATER FUNERARY BELIEFS. During the fifth century, the Etruscan view of the hereafter must have become a good deal more complex and less festive. We notice the change immediately if we compare the group in figure 244, a cinerary container carved of soft local stone soon after 400 B.C., with its predecessor in figure 240. The woman now sits at the foot of the couch, but she is not the wife of the young man; her wings indicate that she is the demon of death, and the scroll in her left hand records the fate of the deceased. The young man is pointing to it as if to say, "Behold, my time has come." The thoughtful, melancholy air of the two figures may be due to some extent to the influence of Classical Greek art which pervades the style of our group. At the same time, however, a new mood of uncertainty and regret is reflected: human destiny is in the hands of inexorable supernatural forces; death is the great divide rather than a continuation, albeit on a different plane, of life on earth.

In later tombs, the demons of death gain an ever more fearful aspect; other, more terrifying demons enter the scene, often battling against benevolent spirits for possession of the soul of the deceased. One of these demons appears in the center of figure 245, a tomb of the third century B.C. at Cerveteri, richly decorated with stucco reliefs rather than paintings. The entire chamber, cut into the live rock, closely imitates the interior of a house, including the beams of the roof. The sturdy pilasters (note the capitals, which recall the Aeolian type from Asia Minor; fig. 194), as well as the wall surfaces between the niches, are covered with exact reproductions of weapons, armor, household implements, small domestic animals, and busts of the deceased. In such a setting, the snake-legged demon and his three-headed hound (whom we recognize as Cerberus, the guardian of the infernal regions) seem particularly disquieting.

## Temples and Their Decoration

Only the stone foundations of Etruscan temples have survived, since the buildings themselves were built of wood. Apparently the Etruscans, although they were masters of masonry construction for other purposes, rejected for religious reasons the use of stone in temple architecture. The design of their sanctuaries bears a general resemblance to the simpler Greek temples (fig. 246), but with several distinctive features, some of these later perpetuated by the Romans. The entire structure rests on a tall base, or podium, that is no wider than the cella and has steps only on the south side; these lead to a deep porch, supported by two rows of four columns each, and to the cella beyond. The cella is generally subdivided into three compartments, for Etruscan religion was dominated by a triad of gods, the predecessors of the Roman Juno, Jupiter, and Minerva. The Etruscan temple, then, must have been of a squat, squarish shape compared to the graceful Greek sanctuaries, and more closely linked with domestic architecture. Needless to say, it provided no place for stone sculpture; the plastic decoration usually consisted of terracotta plaques covering the architrave and the edges of the roof. Only after 400 B.C. do we occasionally find large-scale terracotta groups designed to fill the pediment above the porch.

VEII. We know, however, of one earlier attempt—and an astonishingly bold one—to find a place for monumental sculpture on the exterior of an Etruscan temple. The so-called Temple of Apollo at Veii, not very far north of Rome, a structure of standard type in every other respect, had four lifesize terracotta statues on the ridge of its roof (seen also in the reconstruction model, fig. 246). They formed a dramatic group of the sort we might expect in Greek pedimental

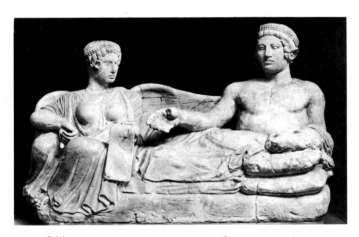

244. *YOUTH AND DEMON OF DEATH.* Cinerary container.
Early 4th century B.C. Stone (pietra fetida),
length 47″ (119.4 cm). Museo Archeologico Nazionale, Florence

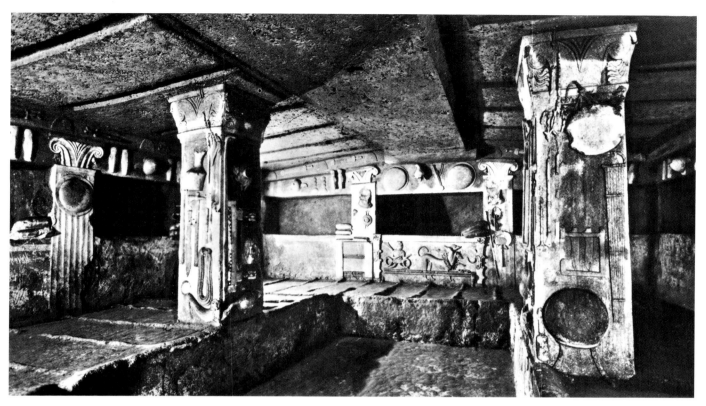

245. Burial chamber. Tomb of the Reliefs, Cerveteri, Italy. 3rd century B.C.

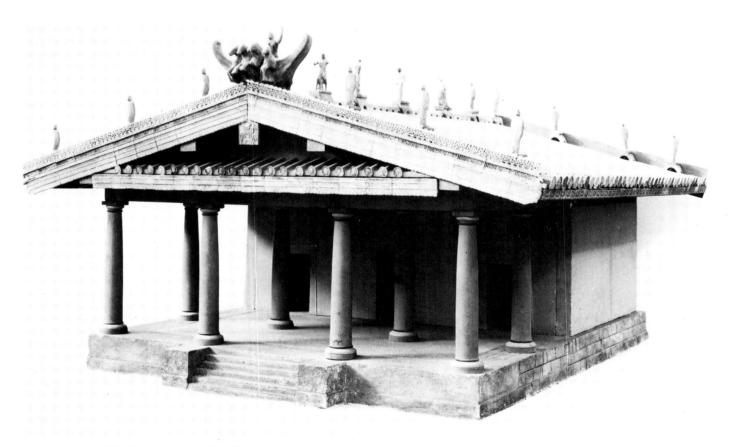

246. Reconstruction of an Etruscan temple. Istituto di Etruscologia e Antichità Italiche, University of Rome

sculpture: the contest of Hercules and Apollo for the sacred hind, in the presence of other deities. The best preserved of these figures is the *Apollo* (fig. 247), acknowledged to be the masterpiece of Etruscan Archaic sculpture. His massive body, completely revealed beneath the ornamental striations of the drapery; the sinewy, muscular legs; the hurried, purposeful stride—all these betray an expressive power that has no counterpart in free-standing Greek statues of the same date.

That Veii was indeed a sculptural center at the end of the sixth century seems to be confirmed by the Roman tradition that the last of the Etruscan rulers of the city called on a master from Veii to make the terracotta image of Jupiter for the temple on the Capitoline Hill. This image has disappeared, but an even more famous symbol of Rome, the bronze figure of the she-wolf that nourished Romulus and Remus, is still in existence (fig. 248). The two babes are Renaissance additions, and the early history of the statue is ob-

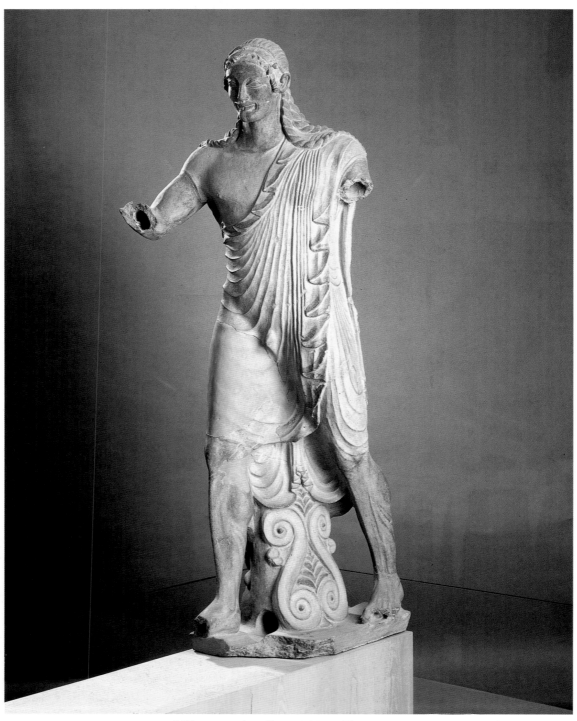

247. *APOLLO*, from Veii. c. 510 B.C. Terracotta, height 69″ (175.3 cm). Museo Nazionale di Villa Giulia, Rome

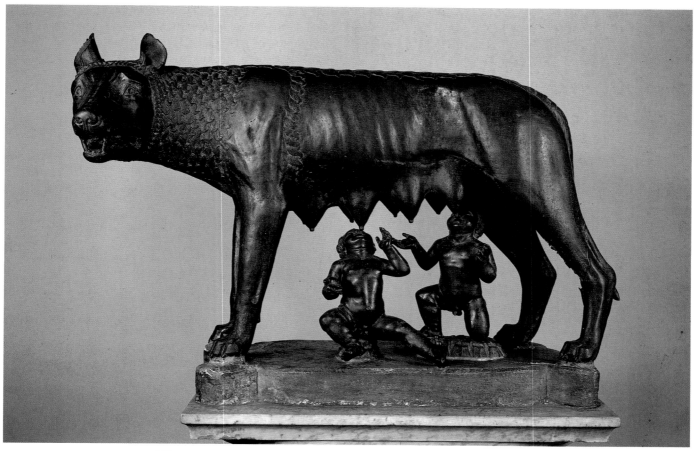

248. *SHE-WOLF.* c. 500 B.C. Bronze, height 33½″ (85 cm). Museo Capitolino, Rome

scure; some scholars, therefore, have even suspected it of being a medieval work. Nevertheless, it is almost surely an Etruscan Archaic original, for the wonderful ferocity of expression, the latent physical power of the body and legs, have the same awesome quality we sense in the *Apollo* from Veii. In any event, the she-wolf as the totemic animal of Rome has the strongest links with Etruscan mythology, in which wolves seem to have played an important part from very early times.

## Portraiture and Metalwork

The Etruscan concern with effigies of the deceased might lead us to expect an early interest in individual portraiture. Yet the features of such funerary images as those in figures 240 and 244 are entirely impersonal, and it was only toward 300 B.C., under the influence of Greek portraiture, that individual likenesses began to appear in Etruscan sculpture. The finest of them are not funerary portraits, which tend to be rather crude and perfunctory, but the heads of bronze statues. *Portrait of a Boy* (fig. 249) is a real masterpiece of its kind; the firmness of modeling lends a special poignancy to the sensitive mouth and the gentle, melancholy eyes.

No less impressive is the very high quality of the casting and finishing, which bears out the ancient fame of the

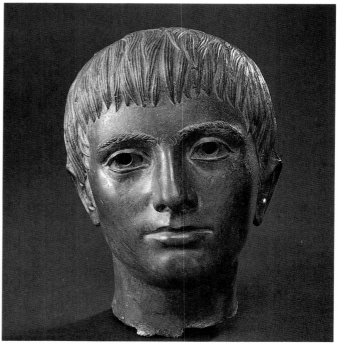

249. *PORTRAIT OF A BOY.* Early 3rd century B.C. Bronze, height 9″ (23 cm). Museo Archeologico Nazionale, Florence

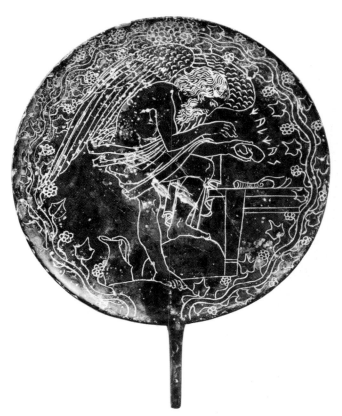

250. Engraved back of a mirror. c. 400 B.C.
Bronze, diameter 6″ (15.3 cm). Vatican Museums, Rome

Etruscans as master craftsmen in metal. Their ability in this respect was of long standing, for the wealth of Etruria was founded on the exploitation of copper and iron deposits. From the sixth century on, they produced vast quantities of bronze statuettes, mirrors, and such, both for export and domestic consumption. The charm of these small pieces is well displayed by the engraved design on the back of a mirror done soon after 400 B.C. (fig. 250). Within an undulating wreath of vines, we see a winged old man, identified as Chalchas, examining a roundish object. The draftsmanship is so beautifully balanced and assured that we are tempted to assume that Classical Greek art was the direct source of inspiration.

DIVINATION. So far as the style of our piece is concerned, this may well be the case, but the subject is uniquely Etruscan, for the winged genius is gazing at the liver of a sacrificial animal.

We are witnessing a practice that loomed as large in the lives of the Etruscans as the care of the dead: the search for omens or portents. The Etruscans believed that the will of the gods manifested itself through signs in the natural world, such as thunderstorms or the flight of birds, and that by reading them people could find out whether the gods smiled or frowned upon their enterprises. The priests who knew the secret language of these signs enjoyed enormous prestige; even the Romans were in the habit of consulting them before any major public or private event. Divination (as the Romans called the art of interpreting omens) can be traced back to ancient Mesopotamia—the practice was not unknown in Greece—but the Etruscans carried it further than any of their predecessors. They put especial trust in the livers of sacrificial animals, on which, they thought, the gods had inscribed the hoped-for divine message. In fact, they viewed the liver as a sort of microcosm, divided into regions that corresponded, in their minds, to the regions of the sky. Weird and irrational as they were, these practices became part of our cultural heritage, and echoes of them persist to this day. True, we no longer try to tell the future by watching the flight of birds or examining animal livers, but tea leaves and horoscopes are still prophetic to many people; and we speak of auspicious events, that is, of events indicating a favorable future, unaware that "auspicious" originally referred to a favorable flight of birds. Perhaps we do not believe very seriously that four-leaf clovers bring good luck and black cats bad luck, yet a surprising number of us admit to being superstitious.

## The Architecture of Cities

According to Roman writers, the Etruscans were masters of architectural engineering, and of town planning and surveying. That the Romans learned a good deal from them can hardly be doubted, but exactly how much the Etruscans contributed to Roman architecture is difficult to say, since hardly anything of Etruscan or early Roman architecture remains standing above ground. Roman temples certainly retained many Etruscan features, and the atrium, the central hall of the Roman house (see fig. 275), likewise originated in Etruria. In town planning and surveying, too, the Etruscans have a good claim to priority over the Greeks. The original homeland of the Etruscans, Tuscany, was too hilly to encourage geometric schemes; however, when they colonized the flatlands south of Rome in the sixth century, they laid out their newly founded cities as a network of streets centering on the intersection of two main thoroughfares, the *cardo* (which ran north and south) and the *decumanus* (which ran east and west). The four quarters thus obtained could be further subdivided or expanded, according to need. This system, which the Romans adopted for the new cities they were to found throughout Italy, western Europe, and North Africa, may have been derived from the plan of Etruscan military camps. Yet it also seems to reflect the religious beliefs that made the Etruscans divide the sky into regions according to the points of the compass and place their temples along a north-south axis.

The Etruscans must also have taught the Romans how to build fortifications, bridges, drainage systems, and aqueducts, but very little remains of their vast enterprises in these fields. The only truly impressive surviving monument is the Porta Augusta in Perugia, a fortified city gate of the second century B.C. (fig. 251). The gate itself, recessed between two massive towers, is not a mere entry but an architectural façade. The tall opening is spanned by a semicircular arch framed by a molding; above it is a balustrade of dwarf pilasters alternating with round shields, a pattern ob-

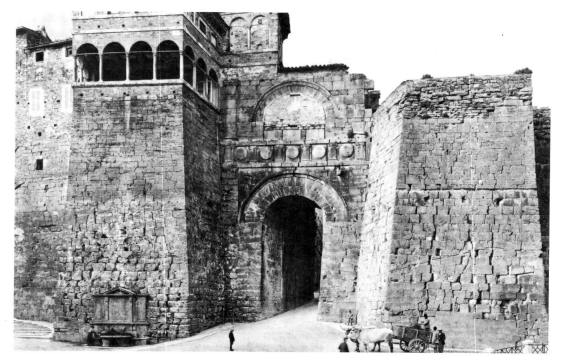

251. Porta Augusta, Perugia. 2nd century B.C.

viously derived from the triglyphs and metopes of the Doric frieze; it supports a second arched opening (now filled in) flanked by two larger pilasters.

THE ARCH. The arches here are true, which means they are constructed of wedge-shaped blocks, called voussoirs, each pointing toward the center of the semicircular opening (see fig. 252). Such an arch is strong and self-sustaining, in contrast to the "false" arch composed of horizontal courses of masonry or brickwork (like the opening above the lintel of the Lion Gate at Mycenae, fig. 152). The true arch, and its extension, the barrel vault, had been discovered in Egypt as early as c. 2700 B.C., but the Egyptians had used it mainly in underground tomb structures and in utilitarian buildings (see fig. 98), never in temples. Apparently they thought it unsuited to monumental architecture. In Mesopotamia, the true arch was used for city gates (see fig. 121) and perhaps elsewhere as well—to what extent we cannot determine for lack of preserved examples. The Greeks knew the principle from the fifth century on, but they confined the use of the true arch to underground structures or to simple gateways, refusing to combine it with the elements of the architectural orders. And herein lies the importance of the Porta Augusta: it is the first instance we know in which arches were integrated with the vocabulary of the Greek orders into a monumental whole. The Romans were to develop this combination in a thousand ways, but the merit of having invented it, of having made the arch respectable, seems to belong to the Etruscans.

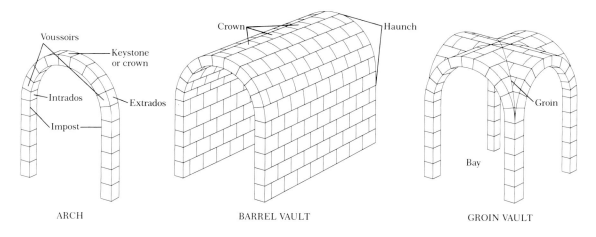

252. Arch, barrel vault, and groin vault

# CHAPTER SEVEN

# ROMAN ART

Among the civilizations of the ancient world, that of the Romans is far more accessible to us than any other. The growth of the Roman domain from city-state to empire; its military and political struggles, its changing social structure, the development of its institutions; the public and private lives of its leading personalities—all these we can trace with a wealth of detail that never ceases to amaze us. Nor is this a matter of chance. The Romans themselves seem to have wanted it that way. Articulate and posterity-conscious, they have left us a vast literary legacy, from poetry and philosophy to humble inscriptions recording everyday events, and an equally huge mass of visible monuments that were scattered throughout their Empire, from England to the Persian Gulf, from Spain to Romania.

Yet, paradoxically, there are few questions more embarrassing to the art historian than "What is Roman art?" The Roman genius, so clearly recognizable in every other sphere of human activity, becomes oddly elusive when we ask whether there was a characteristic Roman style in the fine arts. Why is this so? The most obvious reason is the great admiration the Romans had for Greek art of every period and variety. Not only did they import originals of earlier date— Archaic, Classical, and Hellenistic—by the thousands, and have them copied in even greater numbers; their own production was clearly based on Greek sources, and many of their artists, from Republican times to the end of the Empire, were of Greek origin. Moreover, Roman authors show little concern with the art of their own time. They tell us a good deal about the development of Greek art as described in Greek writings on the subject, or they speak of artistic production during the early days of the Roman Republic, of

which not a trace survives today, but rarely about contemporary works. While anecdotes or artists' names may be mentioned incidentally in other contexts, the Romans never developed a rich literature on the history, theory, and criticism of art such as had existed among the Greeks. Nor do we hear of Roman artists who enjoyed individual fame, although the great names of Greek art—Polyclitus, Phidias, Praxiteles, Lysippus—were praised as highly as ever.

One might well be tempted to conclude, therefore, that the Romans themselves looked upon the art of their time as being in decline compared with the great Greek past, whence all important creative impulses had come. This, indeed, was the prevalent attitude among scholars until not very long ago. Roman art, they claimed, is essentially Greek art in its final decadent phase—Greek art under Roman rule; there is no such thing as Roman style, there is only Roman subject matter. Yet the fact remains that, as a whole, the art produced under Roman auspices does look distinctly different from Greek art; otherwise our problem would not have arisen. If we insist on evaluating this difference by Greek standards, it will appear as a process of decay. If, on the other hand, we interpret it as expressing different, un-Greek intentions, we are likely to see it in a less negative light; and once we admit that art under the Romans had positive un-Greek qualities, we cannot very well regard these innovations as belonging to the final phase of Greek art, no matter how many artists of Greek origin we may find in Roman records. Actually, the Greek names of these men do not signify much; most of the artists, it seems, were thoroughly "Romanized." The Empire was a cosmopolitan society in which national or regional traits were soon absorbed

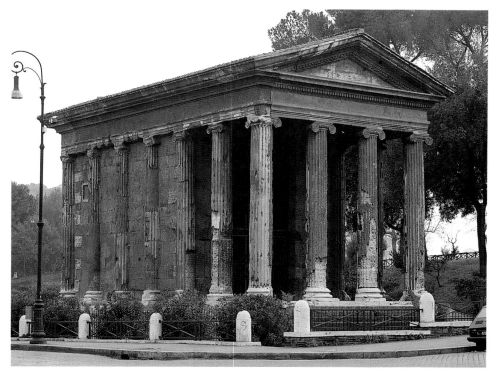

253. "Temple of Fortuna Virilis," Rome. Late 2nd century B.C.

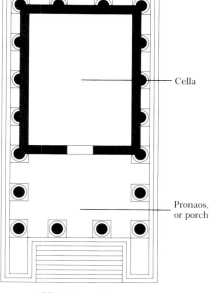

Cella

Pronaos, or porch

254. Plan of the "Temple of Fortuna Virilis"

into the common all-Roman pattern set by the capital, the city of Rome. In any event, the great majority of Roman works of art are unsigned, and their makers, for all we know, may have come from any part of the far-flung Roman domain.

But Roman society from the very start proved astonishingly tolerant of alien traditions; the all-Roman pattern had a way of accommodating them all, so long as they did not threaten the security of the state. The populations of newly conquered provinces were not forced into a uniform straitjacket but, rather, were put into a fairly low-temperature melting pot. Law and order, and a token reverence for the symbols of Roman rule, were imposed on them; at the same time, however, their gods and sages were hospitably received in the capital, and eventually they themselves would be given the rights of citizenship. Roman civilization—and Roman art—thus acquired not only the Greek heritage but, to a lesser extent, that of the Etruscans and of Egypt and the Near East as well. All this made for an extraordinarily complex and open society, homogeneous and diverse at the same time. The sanctuary of Mithras accidentally unearthed in the center of London offers a striking illustration of the cosmopolitan character of Roman society: the god is Persian in origin but he had long since become a Roman "citizen," and his sanctuary, now thoroughly and uniquely Roman in form, can be matched by hundreds of others throughout the Empire.

Under such conditions, it would be little short of a miracle if Roman art were to show a consistent style such as we found in Egypt, or the clear-cut evolution that distinguishes the art of Greece. Its development—to the extent that we understand it today—might be likened to a counterpoint of divergent tendencies that may exist side by side, even within a single monument, and none of them ever emerges as overwhelmingly dominant. The "Roman-ness" of Roman art must be found in this complex pattern, rather than in a single and consistent quality of form.

# ARCHITECTURE

If the autonomy of Roman sculpture and painting has been questioned, Roman architecture is a creative feat of such magnitude as to silence all doubts of this sort. Its growth, moreover, from the very start reflected a specifically Roman way of public and private life, so that whatever elements had been borrowed from Etruscans or Greeks were soon marked with an unmistakable Roman stamp. These links with the past are strongest in the temple types developed during the final century of the Republican period (510–60 B.C.), the heroic age of Roman expansion.

## Religious Architecture

"TEMPLE OF FORTUNA VIRILIS." The delightful small "Temple of Fortuna Virilis" (the name is sheer fancy, for the sanctuary seems to have been dedicated to the Roman god of harbors, Portunus) is the oldest well-preserved example of its kind (fig. 253). Built in Rome during the last years of the second century B.C., it suggests, in the elegant proportions of its Ionic columns and entablature, the wave of Greek influence following the Roman conquest of Greece in 146. Yet it is no mere copy of a Greek temple, for we recognize a number of Etruscan elements: the high podium, the deep

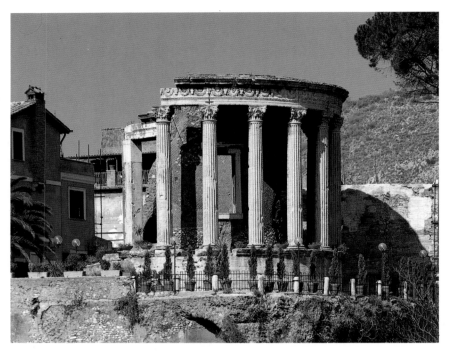

255. "Temple of the Sibyl," Tivoli. Early 1st century B.C.

porch, and the wide cella, which engages the columns of the peristyle. On the other hand, the cella is no longer subdivided into three compartments as it had been under the Etruscans; it now encloses a single unified space (fig. 254). The Romans needed spacious temple interiors, since they used them not only for the image of the deity but also for the display of trophies (statues, weapons, etc.) brought back by their conquering armies. The "Temple of Fortuna Virilis" thus represents a well-integrated new type of temple designed for Roman requirements, not a haphazard cross of Etruscan and Greek elements. It was to have a long life; numerous examples of it, usually large and with Corinthian columns, can be found as late as the second century A.D., both in Italy and in the provincial capitals of the Empire.

TEMPLE OF THE SIBYL. Another type of Republican temple is seen in the so-called Temple of the Sibyl at Tivoli (figs. 255 and 256), erected a few decades later than the "Temple of Fortuna Virilis." It, too, was the result of the merging of two separate traditions. Its original ancestor was a structure in the center of Rome in which the sacred flame of the city was kept. This building at first had the shape of the traditional round peasant huts in the Roman country-side; later on it was redesigned in stone, under the influence of Greek structures of the tholos type (see page 178), and thus became the model for the round temples of late Republican times. Here again we find the high podium, with steps only opposite the entrance, and a graceful Greek-inspired exterior.

As we look closely at the cella, however, we notice that while the door and window frames are of cut stone, the wall is built in a technique we have not encountered before. It is made of concrete—a mixture of mortar and gravel with rub-

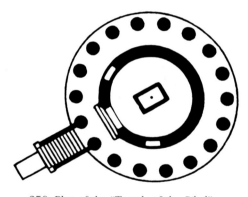

256. Plan of the "Temple of the Sibyl"

ble (that is, small pieces of building stone and brick)—and, in this case, faced with small, flat pieces of stone. Concrete construction had been invented in the Near East more than a thousand years earlier but had been used mainly for fortifications; it was the Romans who developed its potentialities until it became their chief building technique. Its advantages are obvious: strong, cheap, and flexible, it alone made possible the vast architectural enterprises that are still the chief mementos of "the grandeur that was Rome." The Romans knew how to hide the unattractive concrete surface behind a facing of brick, stone, or marble, or by covering it with smooth plaster. Today, this decorative skin has disappeared from the remains of most Roman buildings, leaving the concrete core exposed and thus depriving these ruins of the appeal that Greek ruins have for us. They speak to us in other ways, through massive size and boldness of conception.

SANCTUARY OF FORTUNA PRIMIGENIA. The oldest monument in which these qualities are fully in evidence is the Sanctuary of Fortuna Primigenia at Palestrina, in the foothills of the Apennines east of Rome. Here, in what had once been an important Etruscan stronghold, a strange cult had been established since early times, dedicated to Fortuna (Fate) as a mother deity and combined with a famous oracle. The Roman sanctuary dates from the early first century B.C.; its size and shape were almost completely hidden by the medieval town that had been built over it, until a bombing attack in 1944 destroyed most of the later houses and thus laid bare the remains of the huge ancient temple precinct, which has been thoroughly explored during the past decades. A series of ramps and terraces (clearly visible in fig. 257) lead up to a great colonnaded court, from which we ascend, on a flight of steps arranged like the seats of a Greek theater, to the semicircular colonnade that crowned the entire structure (fig. 258). Arched openings, framed by engaged columns and entablatures, play an important part in the elevation, just as semicircular recesses do in the plan. One

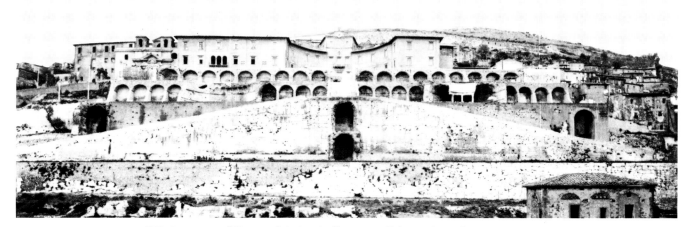

257. Sanctuary of Fortuna Primigenia, Praeneste (Palestrina). Early 1st century B.C.

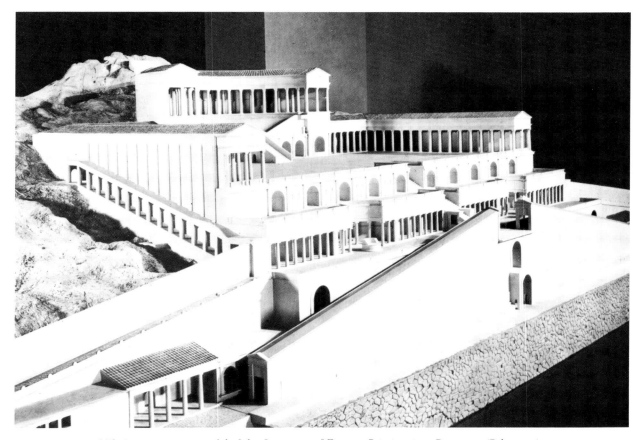

258. Reconstruction model of the Sanctuary of Fortuna Primigenia at Praeneste (Palestrina).
Museo Archeologico Nazionale, Palestrina, Italy

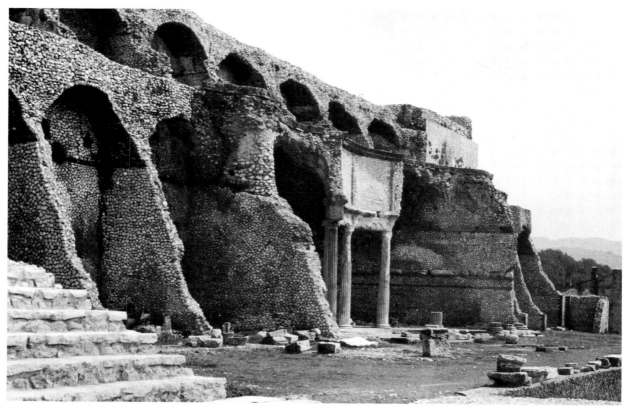

259. Lower terraces, Sanctuary of Fortuna Primigenia at Praeneste (Palestrina)

of these openings appears in our view of the lower terrace (fig. 259); it is covered by a barrel vault, another characteristic feature of the Roman architectural vocabulary. Except for the columns and architraves, all the surfaces now visible are of concrete, like the cella of the round temple at Tivoli, and it is indeed hard to imagine how a complex as vast as this could have been constructed otherwise.

What makes the sanctuary at Palestrina so imposing, however, is not merely its scale but the superb way it fits the site. An entire hillside, comparable to the Acropolis of Athens in its commanding position, has been transformed and articulated so that the architectural forms seem to grow out of the rock, as if human beings had simply completed a design laid out by nature herself. Such a molding of great open spaces had never been possible—or even desired—in the Classical Greek world; the only comparable projects are found in Egypt (see the Temple of Hatshepsut, figs. 93 and 94). Nor did it express the spirit of the Roman Republic. Significantly enough, the Palestrina sanctuary dates from the time of Sulla, whose absolute dictatorship (82–79 B.C.) marked the transition from Republican government to the one-man rule of Julius Caesar and his Imperial successors. Since Sulla had won a great victory against his enemies in the civil war at Palestrina, it is tempting to assume that he personally ordered the sanctuary built, both as a thanks-offering to Fortuna and as a monument to his own fame.

FORUMS. If Sulla did order it, the Palestrina complex perhaps inspired Julius Caesar, who near the end of his life sponsored a project planned on a similar scale in Rome itself: the Forum Julium, a great architecturally framed square adjoining the Temple of Venus Genetrix, the mythical ancestress of Caesar's family. Here the merging of religious cult and personal glory is even more overt. This Forum of Caesar set the pattern for all the later Imperial forums, which were linked to it by a common major axis (fig. 260), forming the most magnificent architectural sight of the Roman world. Unfortunately, nothing is left of the forums today but a stubbly field of ruins that conveys little of their original splendor.

## Secular Architecture

The arch and vault, which we encountered at Palestrina as an essential part of Roman monumental architecture, also formed the basis of construction projects such as sewers, bridges, and aqueducts, designed for efficiency rather than beauty. The first enterprises of this kind were built to serve the city of Rome as early as the end of the fourth century B.C.; only traces of them survive today. There are, however, numerous others of later date throughout the Empire, such as the exceptionally well-preserved aqueduct at Nîmes in southern France known as the Pont du Gard (fig. 261). Its rugged, clean lines that span the wide valley are a tribute not

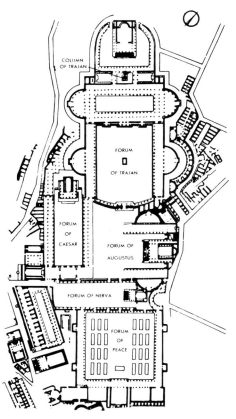

260. Plan of the Forums, Rome

only to the high quality of Roman engineering but also to the sense of order and permanence that inspired these efforts.

COLOSSEUM. The qualities we met here impress us again in the Colosseum, the enormous amphitheater for gladiatorial games in the center of Rome (figs. 262–64). Completed in 80 A.D., it is, in terms of mass, one of the largest single buildings anywhere; when intact, it accommodated more than 50,000 spectators. The concrete core, with its miles of vaulted corridors and stairways, is a masterpiece of engineering efficiency to ensure the smooth flow of traffic to and from the arena. It utilizes both the familiar barrel vault and a more complex form, the groined vault (see fig. 252), that results from the interpenetration of two barrel vaults at right angles. The exterior, dignified and monumental, reflects the interior articulation of the structure but clothes and accentuates it in cut stone. There is a fine balance between vertical and horizontal elements in the framework of engaged columns and entablatures that contains the endless series of arches. The three Classical orders are superimposed according to their intrinsic "weight": Doric, the oldest and most severe, on the ground floor, followed by Ionic and Corinthian. The lightening of the proportions, however, is barely noticeable; the orders, in their Roman adaptation, are almost alike. Structurally, they have become ghosts, yet their aesthetic function continues unimpaired, for it is through them that this enormous façade becomes related to the human scale.

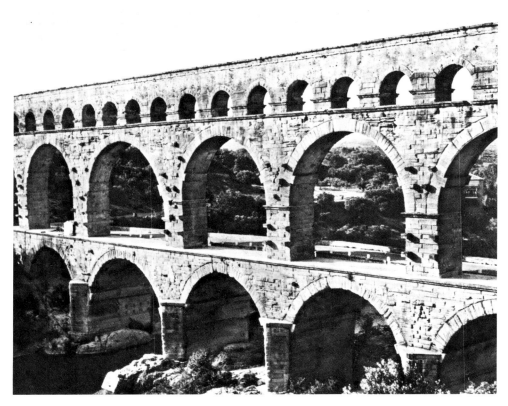

261. Pont du Gard, Nîmes, France.
Early 1st century A.D.

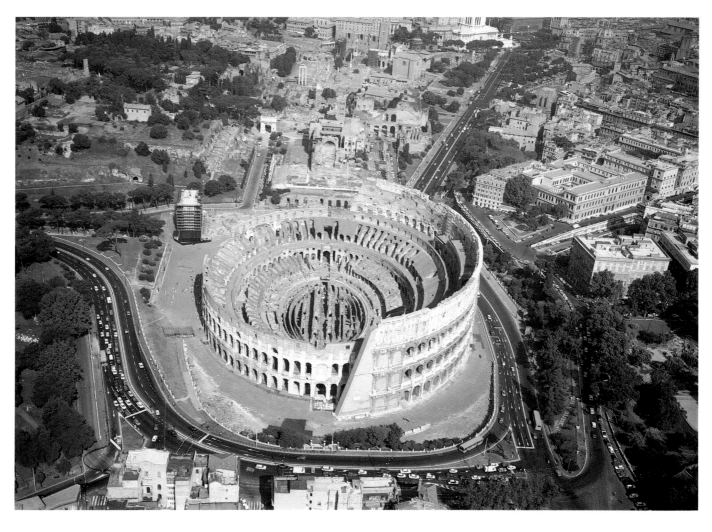

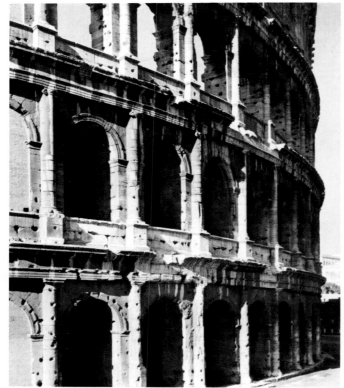

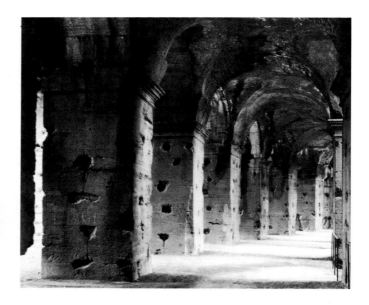

262. (*above*) The Colosseum (aerial view), Rome. 72–80 A.D.

263. (*left*) View of the outer wall of the Colosseum

264. (*below*) Interior, second floor of the Colosseum

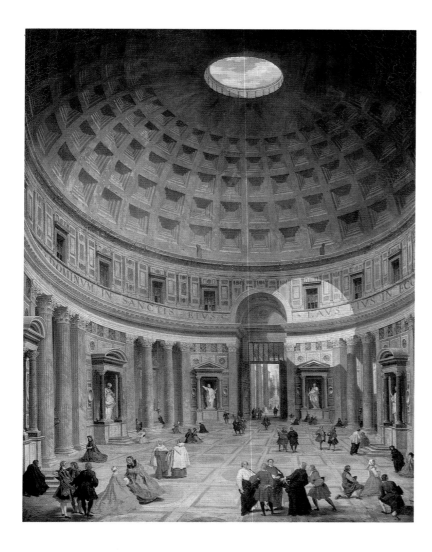

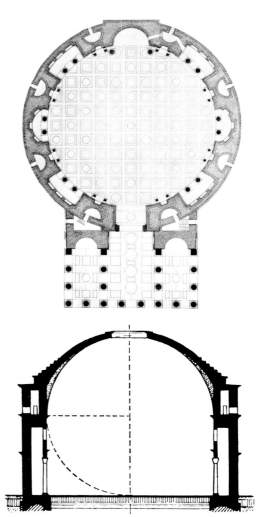

## Interiors

Arches, vaults, and the use of concrete permitted the Romans, for the first time in the history of architecture, to create vast interior spaces. These were explored especially in the great baths, or thermae, which had become important centers of social life in Imperial Rome. The experience gained there could then be applied to other, more traditional types of buildings, sometimes with revolutionary results.

PANTHEON. Perhaps the most striking example of this process is the famous Pantheon in Rome, a very large round temple of the early second century A.D. whose interior is the best preserved as well as the most impressive of any surviving Roman structure (figs. 265–68). There had been round temples long before that time, but their shape, well represented by the "Temple of the Sibyl" (see figs. 255 and 256), is so different from that of the Pantheon that the latter could not possibly have been derived from them. On the outside, the cella of the Pantheon appears as an unadorned cylindrical drum, surmounted by a gently curved dome; the entrance is emphasized by a deep porch of the kind familiar to us from Roman temples of the standard type (see figs. 253 and 254). The junction of these two elements seems rather abrupt, but we must remember that we no longer see the

265. (upper left) THE INTERIOR OF THE PANTHEON. Painting by Giovanni Paolo Pannini, c. 1740. The National Gallery of Art, Washington, D.C. Samuel H. Kress Collection

266. (top) Plan of the Pantheon

267. (above) Transverse section of the Pantheon

268. (below) The Pantheon, Rome. 118–25 A.D.

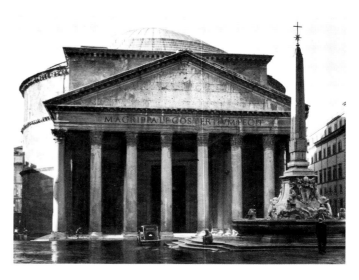

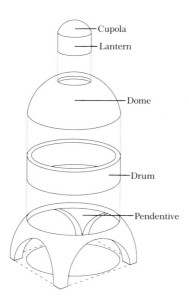

269. Parts of a dome

building as it was meant to be seen. Today the level of the surrounding streets is a good deal higher than it was in antiquity, so that the steps leading up to the porch are now submerged; moreover, the porch was designed to form part of a rectangular, colonnaded forecourt, which must have had the effect of detaching it from the rotunda. So far as the cella is concerned, therefore, the architect apparently discounted the effect of the exterior, putting all the emphasis on the great domed space that opens before us with dramatic suddenness as we step through the entrance.

The impact of this interior, awe-inspiring and harmonious at the same time, is impossible to convey in photographs; even the painting we have chosen (fig. 266) renders it only imperfectly. In any event, the effect is quite different from what the rather forbidding exterior would lead us to expect. The dome is not shallow, but is a true hemisphere; and the circular opening in its center admits an ample—and wonderfully even—flow of light. This "eye" is 143 feet above the floor, and that is also the diameter of the interior (fig. 268); dome and drum, also of equal heights, are in exact balance. On the exterior, this balance could not be achieved, for the outward thrust of the dome had to be contained by making its base considerably heavier than the top (the thickness of the dome decreases upward from 20 feet to 6 feet). Another surprise are the niches, which show that the weight of the dome does not rest uniformly on the drum but is concentrated on eight wide "pillars" (see fig. 269). The niches, of course, are closed in back, but with their screen of columns they give the effect of openings that lead to adjoining rooms and thus prevent us from feeling imprisoned inside the Pantheon. The columns, the colored marble paneling of the wall surfaces, and the floor remain essentially as they were in Roman times: the recessed coffers of the dome, too, are original, but the gilt that covered them has disappeared.

As its name suggests, the Pantheon was dedicated to "all the gods" or, more precisely, to the seven planetary gods (there are seven niches). It seems reasonable, therefore, to assume that the golden dome had a symbolic meaning, that it represented the Dome of Heaven. Yet this solemn and splendid structure grew from rather humble antecedents. The Roman architect Vitruvius, writing more than a century earlier, describes the domed steam chamber of a bathing establishment that anticipates (undoubtedly on a very much smaller scale) the essential features of the Pantheon: a hemispherical dome, a proportional relationship of height and width, and the circular opening in the center (which could be closed by a bronze shutter on chains, to adjust the temperature of the steam room).

BASILICAS. The Basilica of Constantine, of the early fourth century A.D., is a similar example, for, unlike other basilicas, of which we speak below, it derives its shape from the main hall of the public baths built by two earlier emperors, Caracalla and Diocletian. But it is built on an even vaster scale. It must have been the largest roofed interior in all of Rome. Today only the north aisle—three huge barrel-vaulted compartments—is still standing (fig. 270). The center tract, or nave, covered by three groined vaults (figs. 271 and 272), rose a good deal higher. Since a groined vault resembles a canopy, with all the weight and thrust concentrated at the four corners (see fig. 252), the upper walls of the nave (called the clerestory) could be pierced by large windows, so that the interior of the basilica must have had a light and airy quality despite its enormous size. We shall meet its echoes in many later buildings, from churches to railway stations.

Basilicas, long halls serving a variety of civic purposes, had first been developed in Hellenistic Greece. Under the Romans, they became a standard feature of every major town, where one of their chief functions was to provide a dignified setting for the courts of law that dispensed justice in the name of the emperor. Rome itself had a number of basilicas, but very little remains of them today. Those in the provinces have fared somewhat better. An outstanding one is that at Leptis Magna in North Africa (figs. 273 and 274), which has most of the characteristics of the standard type. The long nave terminates in a semicircular niche, or apse, at either end; its walls rest on colonnades that give access to the side aisles. These are generally lower than the nave to permit clerestory windows in the upper part of the nave wall.

These basilicas had wooden ceilings instead of masonry vaults, for reasons of convenience and tradition rather than technical necessity. They were thus subject to destruction by fire; the one at Leptis Magna, sadly ruined though it is, counts among the best-preserved examples. The Basilica of Constantine in Rome was a daring attempt to create a novel, vaulted type, but the design seems to have met with little public favor; it had no direct successors. Perhaps people felt that it lacked dignity because of its obvious resemblance to the public baths. In any event, the Christian basilicas of the fourth century were modeled on the older, wooden-roofed type (see fig. 318). Not until seven hundred years later did vaulted basilican churches become common in western Europe.

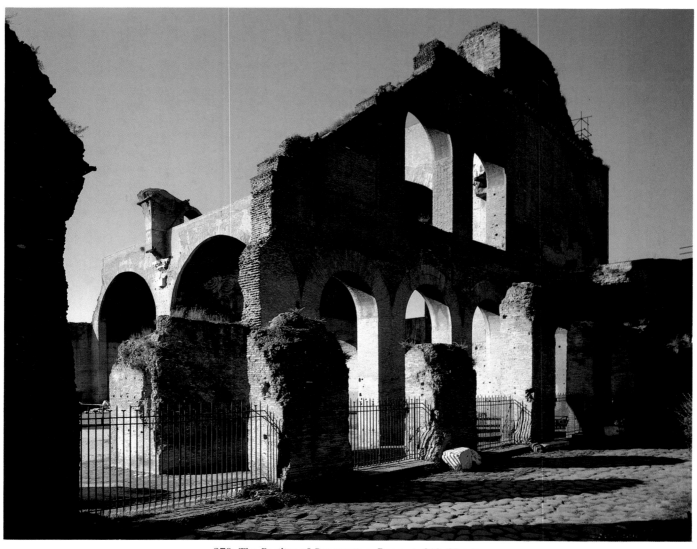

270. The Basilica of Constantine, Rome. c. 310–20 A.D.

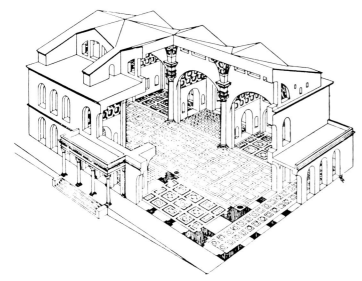

271. Reconstruction drawing of the Basilica of
Constantine (after Huelsen)

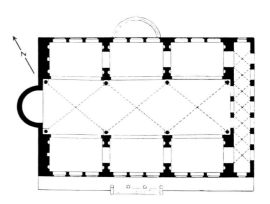

272. Plan of the Basilica of Constantine

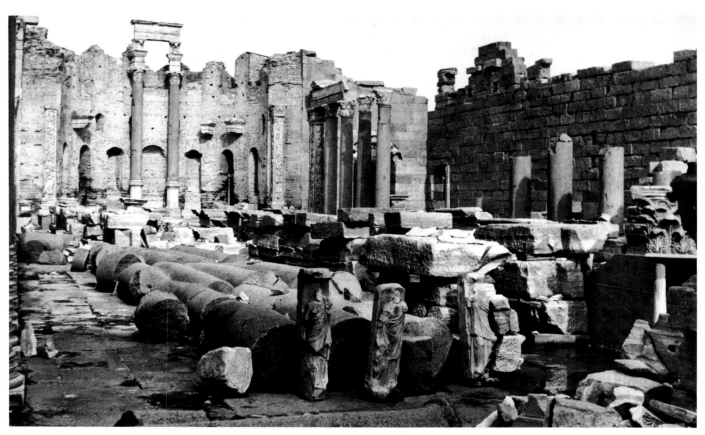

273. Basilica, Leptis Magna, Libya. Early 3rd century A.D.

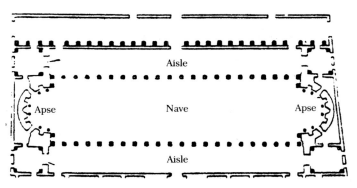

274. Plan of the Basilica, Leptis Magna

## Domestic Architecture

One of the delights in studying Roman architecture is that it includes not only great public edifices but also a vast variety of residential dwellings, from Imperial palaces to the quarters of the urban poor. If we disregard the extremes of this scale, we are left with two basic types that account for most of the domestic architecture that has survived. The *domus* is a single-family house based on ancient Italic tradition. Its distinguishing feature is the atrium, a square or oblong central hall lighted by an opening in the roof, around which the other rooms are grouped. In Etruscan times, it had been a rural dwelling, but the Romans "citified" and elaborated it into the typical home of the well-to-do.

Many examples of the domus, in various stages of development, have come to light at Herculaneum and Pompeii, the two famous towns near Naples that were buried under volcanic ash during an eruption of Mount Vesuvius in 79 A.D. Let us enter the so-called House of the Silver Wedding at Pompeii. The view in figure 275 is taken from the vestibule, along the main axis of the domus. Here the atrium has become a room of impressive size; the four Corinthian columns at the corners of the opening in the roof give it something of the quality of an enclosed court. There is a shallow basin in the center to catch the rain water (the roof slants inward). The atrium was the traditional place for keeping portrait images of the ancestors of the family. At its far end we see a recess, the *tablinum*, and beyond it the garden, surrounded by a colonnade, the peristyle. In addition to the chambers grouped around the atrium, there may be further rooms attached to the back of the house. The entire establishment is shut off from the street by windowless walls; obviously, privacy and self-sufficiency were important to the wealthy Roman.

Less elegant than the domus, and decidedly urban from the very start, is the *insula*, or city block, which we find mainly in Rome itself and in Ostia, the ancient port of Rome near the mouth of the Tiber. The insula anticipates many features of the modern apartment house; it is a good-sized concrete-and-brick building (or a chain of such buildings) around a small central court, with shops and taverns open to the street on the ground floor and living quarters for numer-

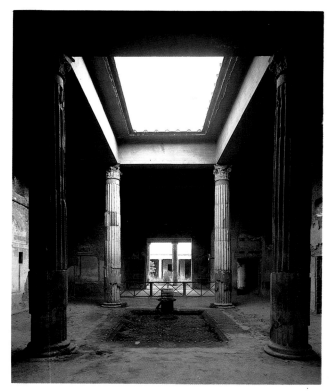

275. Atrium, House of the Silver Wedding,
Pompeii. Early 1st century A.D.

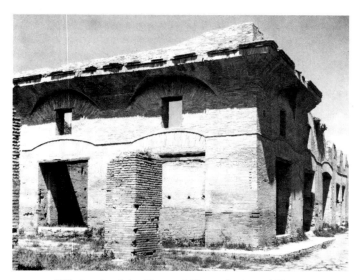

276. Insula of the House of Diana, Ostia. c. 150 A.D.

ous families above. Some insulae had as many as five stories, with balconies above the second floor (fig. 276). The daily life of the craftsmen and shopkeepers who inhabited such an insula was oriented toward the street, as it still is to a large extent in modern Italy. The privacy of the domus was reserved for the minority that could afford it.

## Late Roman Architecture

In discussing the new forms based on arched, vaulted, and domed construction, we have noted the Roman architect's continued allegiance to the Classical Greek orders. If he no longer relied on them in the structural sense, he remained faithful to their spirit, acknowledging the aesthetic authority of the post-and-lintel system as an organizing and articulating principle. Column, architrave, and pediment might be merely superimposed on a vaulted brick-and-concrete core, but their shape, as well as their relationship to each other, was still determined by the original grammar of the orders.

This orthodox, reverential attitude toward the architectural vocabulary of the Greeks prevailed, generally·speaking, from the Roman conquest of Greece until the end of the first century A.D. After that, we find increasing evidence of a con-

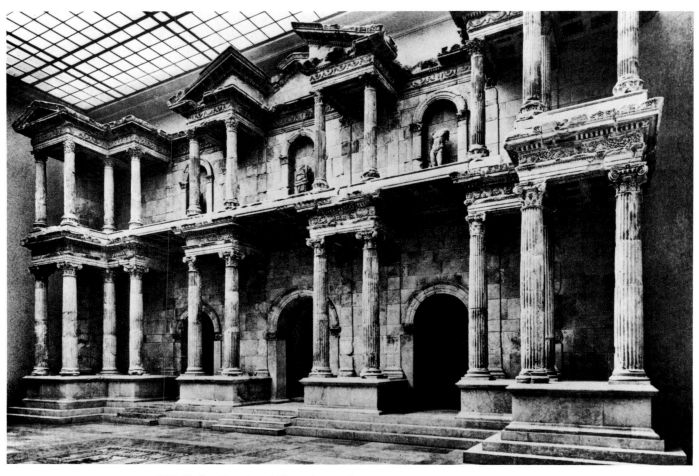

277. Market Gate from Miletus (restored). c. 160 A.D. Staatliche Museen, Berlin

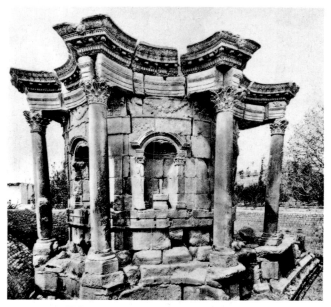

278. Temple of Venus, Baalbek, Lebanon
First half of the 3rd century A.D.

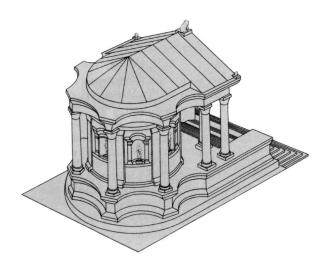

279. Schematic reconstruction of
Temple of Venus, Baalbek

trary trend, of a taste for imaginative, "ungrammatical" transformations of the Greek vocabulary. Just when and where it began is still a matter of dispute; there is some evidence that it may go back to late Hellenistic times in the Near East. The tendency certainly was most pronounced in the Asiatic and African provinces of the Empire. A characteristic example is the Market Gate from Miletus, c. 160 A.D. (rebuilt in the state museums in Berlin; fig. 277). One might refer to it as display architecture in terms both of its effect and of its ancestry, for the picturesque façade, with its alternating recesses and projections, derives from the architectural stage backgrounds of the Roman theater. The continuous in-and-out rhythm has even seized the pediment above the central doorway, breaking it into three parts. Equally astonishing is the small Temple of Venus at Baalbek, probably built in the early second century A.D. and refurbished in the third (figs. 278 and 279). The convex curve of the cella is effectively counterbalanced by the concave niches and the scooped-out base and entablature, introducing a new play of forces into the conventional ingredients of the round temple (compare figs. 255 and 256).

By the late third century, unorthodox ideas such as these had become so well established that the traditional "gram-mar" of the Greek orders was in process of dissolution everywhere. In the peristyle of the Palace of Diocletian (fig. 280) at Spalato (Split), the architrave between the two center columns is curved, echoing the arch of the doorway below, and on the left we see an even more revolutionary device—a series of arches resting directly on columns. A few isolated instances of such an arcade can be found earlier, but it was only now, on the eve of the victory of Christianity, that the marriage of arch and column became fully legitimate. The union, indispensable to the future development of architecture, seems so natural to us that we can hardly understand why it was ever opposed.

## SCULPTURE

The dispute over the question "Is there such a thing as a Roman style?" has centered largely on the field of sculpture, and for quite understandable reasons. Even if we discount the wholesale importing and copying of Greek originals, the reputation of the Romans as imitators seems borne out by vast quantities of works that are obviously—or at least probably—adaptations and variants of Greek models of every period. While the Roman demand for sculpture was tremen-

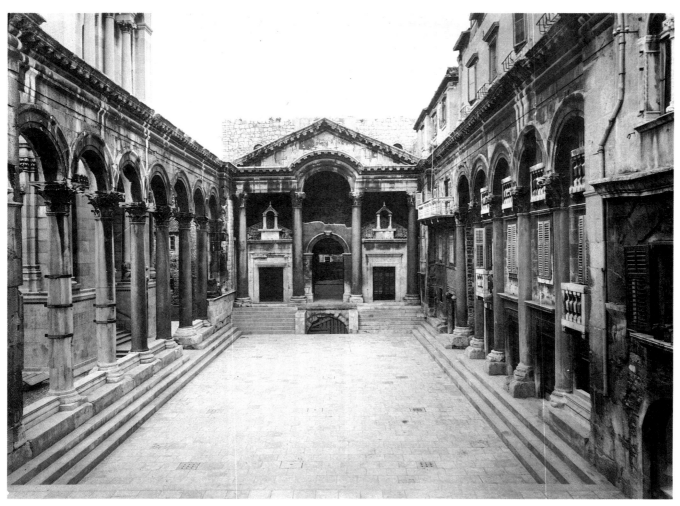

280. Peristyle, Palace of Diocletian, Spalato (Split), Yugoslavia. c. 300 A.D.

dous, a good deal of it may be attributed to antiquarianism, both the learned and the fashionable variety, and to a taste for sumptuous interior decoration. There are thus whole categories of sculpture produced under Roman auspices that deserve to be classified as "deactivated" echoes of Greek creations, emptied of their former meaning and reduced to the status of highly refined works of craftsmanship. At times this attitude extended to Egyptian sculpture as well, creating a vogue for pseudo-Egyptian statuary. On the other hand, there can be no doubt that some kinds of sculpture had serious and important functions in ancient Rome. They represent the living sculptural tradition, in contradistinction to the antiquarian-decorative trend. We shall concern ourselves here mainly with those aspects of Roman sculpture that are most conspicuously rooted in Roman society: portraiture and narrative relief.

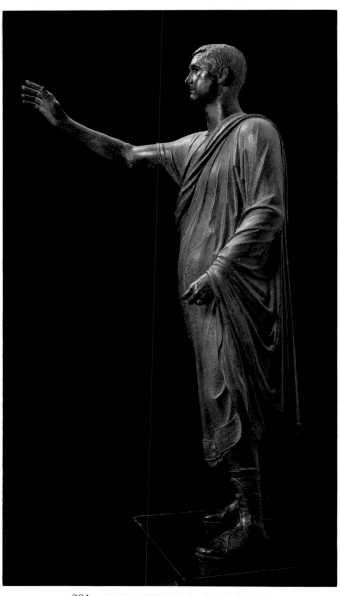

281. *AULUS METELLUS (L'ARRINGATORE)*.
Early 1st century B.C. Bronze, height 71″ (280 cm).
Museo Archeologico Nazionale, Florence

## Republican

We know from literary accounts that, from early Republican times on, meritorious political or military leaders were honored by having their statues put on public display. The habit was to continue until the end of the Empire a thousand years later. Its beginnings may well have derived from the Greek custom of placing votive statues of athletic victors and other important individuals in the precincts of such sanctuaries as Delphi and Olympia (see fig. 203). Unfortunately, the first four hundred years of this Roman tradition are a closed book to us; not a single Roman portrait has yet come to light that can be dated before the first century B.C. with any degree of confidence. How were those early statues related to Etruscan or Greek sculpture? Did they ever achieve any specifically Roman qualities? Were they individual likenesses in any sense, or were their subjects identified only by pose, costume, attributes, and inscriptions?

L'ARRINGATORE. Our sole clue in answer to these questions is the lifesize bronze statue called *L'Arringatore* (fig. 281), once assigned to the second century B.C. but now generally placed in the early years of the first. It comes from southern Etruscan territory and bears an Etruscan inscription that includes the name Aule Metele (Aulus Metellus in Latin), presumably the name of the official represented. He must have been a Roman, or at least a Roman-appointed official. The workmanship is evidently Etruscan, as indicated by the inscription, but the gesture, which denotes both address and salutation, recurs in hundreds of Roman statues of the same sort, and the costume, too, is Roman—an early kind of toga. One suspects, therefore, that our sculptor tried to conform to an established Roman type of portrait statue, not only in these externals but in style as well. For we find very little here of the Hellenistic flavor characteristic of the later Etruscan tradition. What makes the figure remarkable is its serious, prosaically factual quality, down to the neatly tied shoelaces. The term "uninspired" suggests itself, not as a criticism but as a way to describe the basic attitude of the artist in contrast to the attitude of Greek or Etruscan portraitists.

PORTRAITS. That seriousness was consciously intended as a positive value becomes clear when we familiarize ourselves with Roman portrait heads of the years around 75 B.C., which show it in its most pronounced form. Apparently the creation of a monumental, unmistakably Roman portrait style was achieved only in the time of Sulla, when Roman architecture, too, came of age (see page 219). We see it at its most impressive perhaps in the features of the unknown Roman of figure 282, contemporary with the fine Hellenistic portrait from Delos in figure 231. A more telling contrast could hardly be imagined; both are extremely persuasive likenesses, yet they seem worlds apart. Whereas the Hellenistic head impresses us with its subtle grasp of the sitter's psychology, the Roman may strike us at first glance as nothing but a detailed record of facial topography—the sitter's character emerges only incidentally, as it were. And yet this is not really the case: the wrinkles are true to life, no doubt, but the carver has nevertheless treated them with a selective

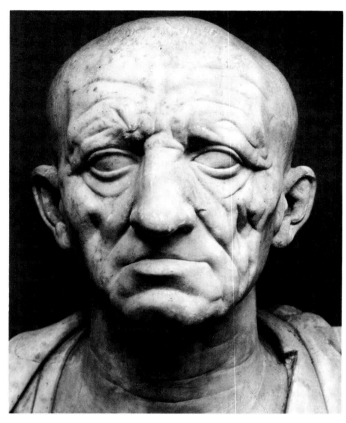

282. *PORTRAIT OF A ROMAN.* c. 80 B.C. Marble,
lifesize. Palazzo Torlonia, Rome

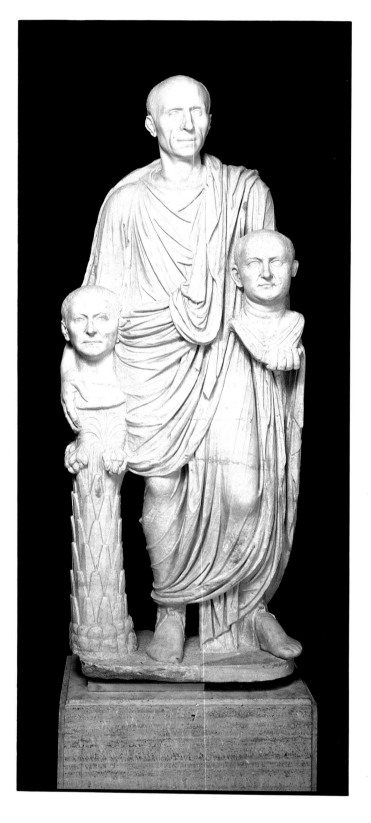

283. *A ROMAN PATRICIAN WITH BUSTS OF HIS ANCESTORS.*
Late 1st century B.C. Marble, lifesize.
Museo Capitolino, Rome

emphasis designed to bring out a specifically Roman personality—stern, rugged, iron-willed in its devotion to duty. It is
a "father image" of frightening authority, and the minutely
observed facial details are like individual biographical data
that differentiate this father image from others.

Its peculiar flavor reflects a patriarchal Roman custom of
considerable antiquity; at the death of the head of the family, a waxen image was made of his face, which was then
preserved in a special shrine, or family altar. At funerals,
these ancestral images were carried in the procession. We
have seen the roots of this kind of ancestor worship in
"primitive" societies (compare figs. 40 and 55–60); the patrician families of Rome clung to it tenaciously well into Imperial times. The images were, of course, records rather
than works of art, and because of the perishability of wax
they probably did not last more than a few decades. Thus the
desire to have them duplicated in marble seems natural
enough, yet the demand did not arise until the early first
century B.C.; perhaps the patricians, feeling their traditional
position of leadership endangered, wanted to make a greater
public display of their ancestors, as a way of emphasizing
their ancient lineage.

That display certainly is the purpose of the statue in figure
283, carved about half a century later than our previous example. It shows an unknown Roman holding two busts of
his ancestors, presumably his father and grandfather. The
work has little distinction, yet the "father-image" spirit can

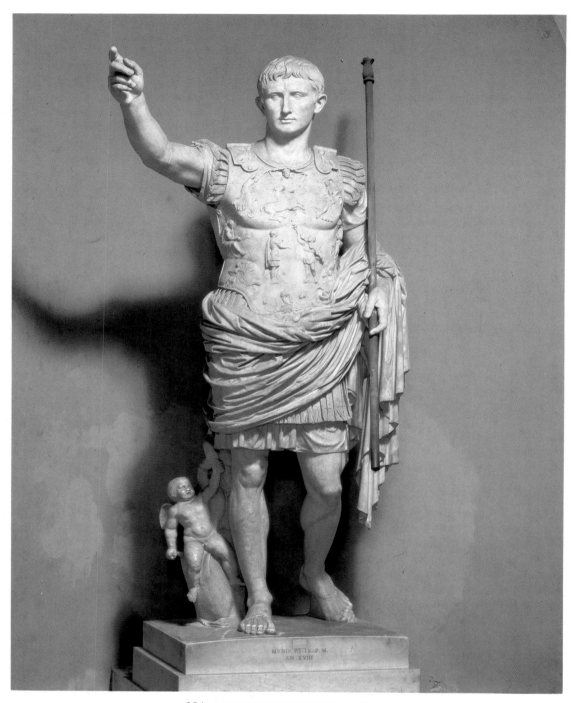

284. *AUGUSTUS OF PRIMAPORTA*. c. 20 B.C.
Marble, 6'8" (2 m). Vatican Museums, Rome

be felt even here. Needless to say, this quality was not present in the wax images themselves; it came to the fore when they were translated into marble, a process that not only made the ancestral images permanent but monumentalized them in the spiritual sense as well. Nevertheless, the marble heads retained the character of records, of visual documents, which means that they could be freely duplicated; what mattered was only the facial "text," not the "handwriting" of the artist who recorded it. The impressive head in figure 282 is itself a copy, made some fifty years later than the lost original, and so are the two ancestors in figure 283 (differences in style and in the shape of the bust indicate that the original of the head on the left is about thirty years older than that of its companion). Perhaps this Roman lack of feeling for the uniqueness of the original, understandable enough in the context of their ancestor cult, also helps to explain why they developed so voracious an appetite for copies of famous Greek statues.

# Imperial

PORTRAITS. As we approach the reign of the Emperor Augustus (27 B.C.–14 A.D.), we find a new trend in Roman portraiture that reaches its climax in the images of Augustus himself, as, for example, in the splendid statue from Primaporta (fig. 284). At first glance, we may well be uncertain of whether it represents a god or a human being; this doubt is entirely appropriate, for the figure is meant to be both. Here, on Roman soil, we meet a concept familiar to us from Egypt and the ancient Near East: that of the divine ruler. It had entered the Greek world in the fourth century B.C. (see fig. 218); Alexander the Great had made it his own, and so did his successors, who modeled themselves after him. The latter, in turn, transmitted it to Julius Caesar and the Roman emperors, who at first encouraged the worship of themselves only in the eastern provinces, where belief in a divine ruler was a long-established tradition.

The idea of attributing superhuman stature to the emperor, thus enhancing his authority, soon became official policy, and while Augustus did not carry it as far as his successors, the Primaporta statue clearly shows him enveloped in an air of divinity. Still, despite its heroic, idealized body, the statue has an unmistakably Roman flavor; the Emperor's gesture is familiar from *Aulus Metellus* (fig. 281); the costume, including the rich allegorical program on the breastplate, has a concreteness of surface texture that conveys the actual touch of cloth, metal, and leather. The head, too, is idealized, or, better perhaps, "Hellenized"; small physiognomic details are suppressed, and the focusing of attention on the eyes gives it something of the "inspired" look we find in portraits of Alexander the Great (compare fig. 236). Nevertheless, the face is a definite likeness, elevated but clearly individual, as we can determine by comparison with the numerous other portraits of Augustus. All Romans would have recognized it immediately, for they knew it from coins and countless other representations. In fact, the emperor's image soon came to acquire the symbolic significance of a national flag. As a consequence of such mass production, artistic quality was rarely very high, except when portraits were produced under the ruler's direct patronage. That must have been true of the Primaporta statue, which was found in the villa of Augustus' wife, Livia.

NARRATIVE RELIEF. Imperial art, however, was not confined to portraiture. The emperors also commemorated their outstanding achievements in narrative reliefs on monumental altars, triumphal arches, and columns. Similar scenes are familiar to us from the ancient Near East (see figs. 115, 122 and 132) but not from Greece. Historic events—that is, events which occurred only once, at a specific time and in a particular place—had not been dealt with in Classical Greek sculpture; if a victory over the Persians was to be commemorated, it would be represented indirectly, as a combat of Lapiths and Centaurs, or Greeks and Amazons—a mythical event outside any space-time context. Even in Hellenistic times, this attitude persisted, although not quite as absolutely; when the kings of Pergamum celebrated their victories over the Gauls, the latter were represented faithfully (see fig. 224) but in typical poses of defeat rather than in the framework of a particular battle.

Greek painters, on the other hand, had depicted historic subjects such as the battle of Salamis as early as the mid-fifth century, although we do not know how specific these pictures were in detail. According to the Roman writer Pliny, Philoxenus of Eretria at the end of the fourth century painted the victory of Alexander the Great over Darius at Issus; an echo of that work may survive in a famous Pompeian mosaic (see fig. 302). In Rome, too, historic events had been depicted from the third century B.C. on; a victorious military leader would have his exploits painted on panels that were carried in his triumphal procession, or he would show such panels in public places. These pictures seem to have had the fleeting nature of posters advertising the hero's achievements. None has survived. Sometime during the late years of the Republic—we do not know exactly when—the temporary representations of such events began to assume more monumental and permanent form, no longer painted, but carved and attached to structures intended to last indefinitely. They were thus a ready tool for the glorification of Imperial rule, and the emperors did not hesitate to use them on a large scale.

ARA PACIS. Since the leitmotif of his reign was peace, Augustus preferred to appear in his monuments as the "Prince of Peace" rather than as the all-conquering military hero. The most important of these monuments was the Ara Pacis (the Altar of Peace), voted by the Roman Senate in 13 B.C. and completed four years later. It is probably identical with the richly carved Augustan altar that bears this name today. (Parts of it were found as early as the sixteenth century A.D., but their reintegration was not achieved until 1938.) The entire structure (fig. 285) recalls the Pergamum Altar, though on a much smaller scale (compare figs. 226 and 228). On the wall that screens the altar proper, a monumental frieze depicts allegorical and legendary scenes as well as a solemn procession led by the emperor himself.

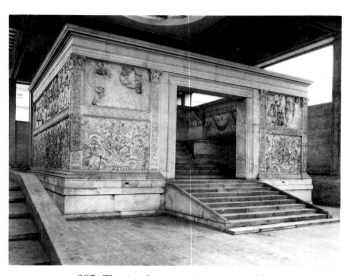

285. The Ara Pacis. c. 13–9 B.C. Marble, width of altar c. 35'. Museum of the Ara Pacis, Rome

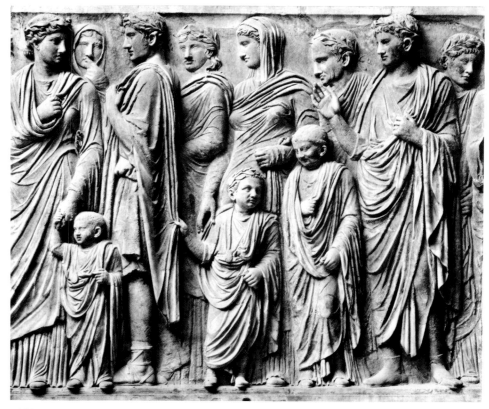

286. *IMPERIAL PROCESSION,* a portion of the frieze of the Ara Pacis. Marble, height 63″ (160 cm)

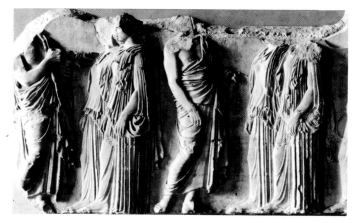

287. *PROCESSION,* a portion of the east frieze, Parthenon. c. 440 B.C.
Marble, height 43″ (109.3 cm). Musée du Louvre, Paris

Here the "Hellenic," classicizing style we noted in the Primaporta statue reaches fullest expression. It is instructive, therefore, to compare the Ara Pacis frieze (fig. 286) with that of the Parthenon (figs. 189 and 287). Only a direct confrontation of the two will show how different they really are, despite all surface similarities. The Parthenon frieze belongs to an ideal, timeless world; it shows a procession that took place in the remote, mythic past, beyond living memory. What holds it together is the great formal rhythm of the ritual itself, not its variable particulars. On the Ara Pacis, in contrast, we see a procession in celebration of one particular recent event—probably the founding of the altar in 13 B.C.—idealized to evoke something of the solemn air that surrounds the Parthenon procession, yet filled with concrete details of a remembered event. The participants, at least so far as they belong to the Imperial family, are meant to be identifiable as portraits, including those of children dressed in miniature togas but too young to grasp the significance of the occasion: note how the little boy in the center of our group is tugging at the mantle of the young man in front of him while the somewhat older child to his left smilingly tells him to behave. The Roman artist also shows a greater concern with spatial depth than his Classical Greek predecessor: the softening of the relief background, which we first observed in the *Grave Stele of Hegeso* (fig. 213), has been carried so far that the figures farthest removed from us seem partly immersed in the stone (such as the woman on the left whose face emerges behind the shoulder of the young mother in front of her).

The same interest in space appears even more strongly in the allegorical panel in figure 288, showing Mother Earth as the embodiment of human, animal, and plant fertility, flanked by two personifications of winds. Here the figures are placed in a real landscape setting of rocks, water, and vegetation, and the blank background clearly stands for the empty sky. Whether this pictorial treatment of space is a Hellenistic or Roman invention remains a matter of dispute. There can be no question, however, about the Hellenistic look of the three personifications, which represent not only a different level of reality but also a different—and less distinctly Roman—style from the Imperial procession. The acanthus ornament on the pilasters and the lower part of the wall, on the other hand, has no counterpart in Greek art, although the acanthus motif as such derives from Greece. The plant forms are wonderfully graceful and alive, yet the design as a whole, with its emphasis on bilateral symmetry, never violates the discipline of surface decoration and thus serves as an effective foil for the spatially conceived reliefs above.

Much the same contrast of flatness and depth occurs in the stucco decoration of a Roman house, a casual but enchanting product of the Augustan era (fig. 289). The modeling, as suits the light material, is delicate and sketchy throughout, but the meaning of the blank surfaces to which it is applied varies a great deal. On the bottom strip of our illustration, there are two winged genii with plant ornament; here depth is carefully eschewed, since this zone belongs to the framework. Above it, we see that which is being framed; it can only be described as a "picture painted in relief," an idyllic landscape of great charm and full of atmospheric depth, despite the fact that its space is merely suggested rather than clearly defined. The whole effect echoes that of painted room decorations (see fig. 304).

ARCH OF TITUS. The spatial qualities of the Ara Pacis reliefs reached their most complete development in the two large narrative panels on the triumphal arch erected in 81 A.D. to commemorate the victories of the Emperor Titus. One

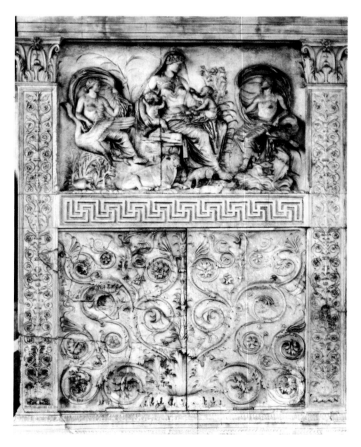

288. Allegorical and ornamental panels of the Ara Pacis

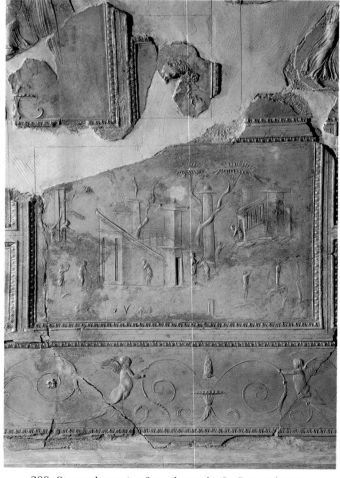

289. Stucco decoration from the vault of a Roman house. Late 1st century B.C. Museo delle Terme, Rome

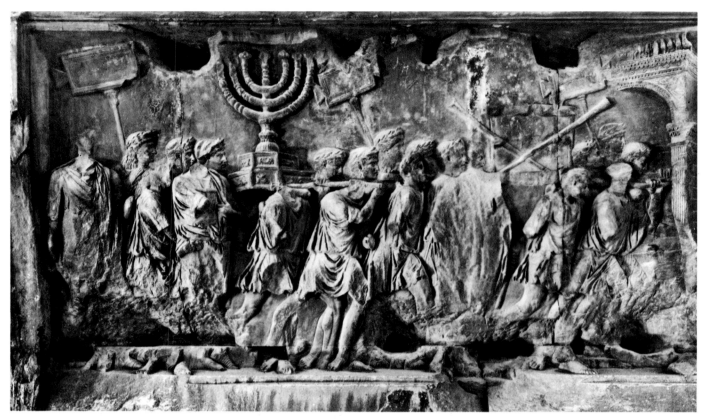

290. *SPOILS FROM THE TEMPLE IN JERUSALEM.* Relief in passageway, Arch of Titus, Rome. 81 A.D. Marble, height 7'10" (2.4 m)

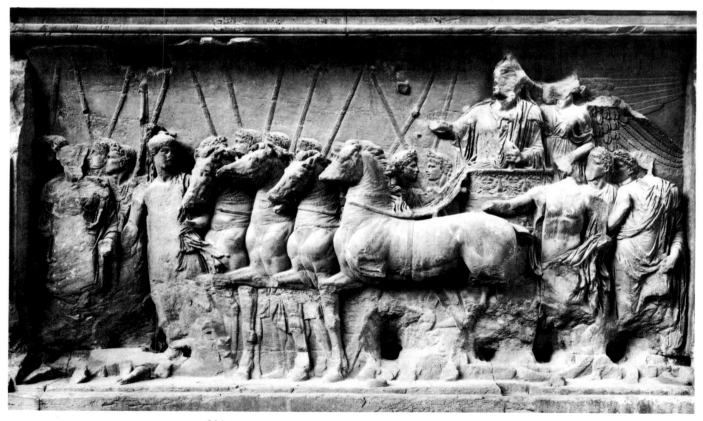

291. *TRIUMPH OF TITUS.* Relief in passageway, Arch of Titus

of them (fig. 290) shows part of the triumphal procession celebrating the conquest of Jerusalem; the booty displayed includes the seven-branched candlestick and other sacred objects. Despite the mutilated surface, the movement of a crowd of figures in depth still appears strikingly successful. On the right, the procession turns away from us and disappears through a triumphal arch placed obliquely to the background plane so that only the nearer half actually emerges from the background—a radical but effective device.

The companion panel (fig. 291) avoids such experiments, although the number of layers of relief is equally great here. We also sense that its design has an oddly stationary quality, despite the fact that this is simply another part of the same procession. The difference must be due to the subject, which is the emperor himself in his chariot, crowned by the winged Victory behind him. Apparently the sculptor's first concern was to display this set image, rather than to keep the procession moving. Once we try to read the Imperial chariot and the surrounding figures in terms of real space, we become aware of how strangely contradictory the spatial relationships are: four horses, shown in strict profile view, move in a direction parallel to the bottom edge of the panel, but the chariot is not where it ought to be if they were really pulling it. Moreover, the bodies of the emperor and of most of the other figures are represented in frontal view, rather than in profile. These seem to be fixed conventions for representing the triumphant emperor which our artist felt constrained to respect, though they were in conflict with his desire to create the kind of consistent movement in space he achieved so well in figure 290.

COLUMN OF TRAJAN. That the purposes of Imperial art, narrative or symbolic, were sometimes incompatible with a realistic treatment of space becomes fully evident in the Column of Trajan, erected in 106–113 A.D. to celebrate that emperor's victorious campaigns against the Dacians (the ancient inhabitants of Romania). Single, free-standing columns had been used as commemorative monuments from Hellenistic times on; their ultimate source may have been the obelisks of Egypt. The Column of Trajan is distinguished not only by its great height (125 feet, including the base) but by the continuous spiral band of relief covering its surface (fig. 292) and recounting, in epic breadth, the history of the Dacian wars. The column was crowned by a statue of the emperor (destroyed in the Middle Ages) and the base served as a burial chamber for his ashes. If we could unwind the relief band, we would find it to be 656 feet long, two-thirds the combined length of the three friezes of the Mausoleum at Halicarnassus and a good deal longer than the Parthenon frieze. In terms of the number of figures and the density of the narrative, however, our relief is by far the most ambitious frieze composition attempted up to that time. It is also the most frustrating, for beholders must "run around in circles like a circus horse" (to borrow the apt description of one scholar) if they want to follow the narrative; once above the fourth or fifth turn, they find themselves defeated by the wealth of detail unless equipped with field glasses.

One wonders for whose benefit this elaborate pictorial account was intended. In Roman times, the monument formed the center of a small court flanked by public buildings at least two stories tall, but even that does not quite answer our question. Nor does it explain the evident success of our column, which served as the model for several others of the same type. But let us take a closer look at the scenes visible in our figure 292: in the center of the bottom strip, we see the upper part of a large river god representing the Danube; to the left, there are some river boats laden with supplies, and a Roman town on the rocky bank; to the right, the Roman army crosses the river on a pontoon bridge. The second strip shows Trajan addressing his soldiers (to the left) and the building of fortifications; the third, the construction of a garrison camp and bridge as Roman cavalry (on the right) sets out on a reconnaissance mission. In the fourth strip, Trajan's foot soldiers are crossing a mountain stream (center); on the right, the emperor addresses his troops in front of a Dacian fortress. These scenes are a fair sampling; among the more than a hundred fifty separate episodes, ac-

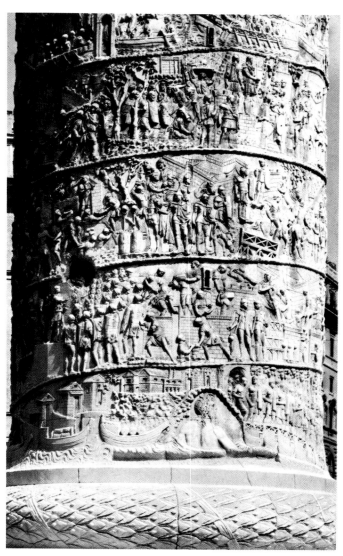

292. Lower portion of the Column of Trajan, Rome.
106–13 A.D. Marble, height of relief band c. 50″ (127 cm)

tual combat occurs only rarely, while the geographic, logistic, and political aspects of the campaign receive detailed attention, much as they do in Julius Caesar's famous account of his conquest of Gaul.

Only at one other time have we seen this matter-of-fact visualization of military operations—in Assyrian reliefs such as that in figure 122. Was there an indirect link between the two? And, if so, of what kind? The question is difficult to answer, especially since there are no extant copies of the Roman antecedents for our reliefs: the panels showing military conquests that were carried in triumphal processions (see page 233). At any rate, the spiral frieze on the Column of Trajan was a new and demanding framework for historic narrative which imposed a number of difficult conditions upon the sculptor: since there could be no clarifying inscriptions, the pictorial account had to be as self-sufficient and explicit as possible, which meant that the spatial setting of each episode had to be worked out with great care; visual continuity had to be preserved without destroying the inner coherence of the individual scenes; and the actual depth of the carving had to be much shallower than in reliefs such as those on the Arch of Titus, otherwise the shadows cast by the projecting parts would make the scenes unreadable from below.

Our artist has solved these problems with conspicuous success, but at the cost of sacrificing all but the merest rem-

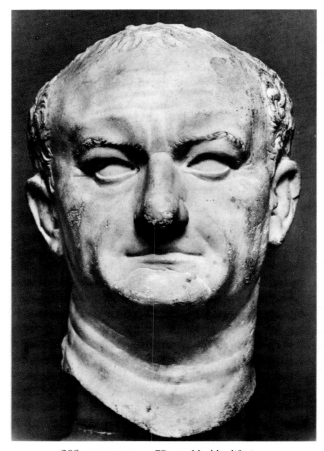

293. *VESPASIAN.* c. 75 A.D. Marble, lifesize, with damaged chin repaired. Museo delle Terme, Rome

nants of illusionistic spatial depth. Landscape and architecture are reduced to abbreviated "stage sets," and the ground on which the figures stand is tilted upward. All these devices had already been employed in Assyrian narrative reliefs; here they asserted themselves once more, against the tradition of foreshortening and perspective space. In another two hundred years, they were to become dominant, and we shall find ourselves at the threshold of medieval art. In this respect, the relief band on the Column of Trajan is curiously prophetic of both the end of one era and the beginning of the next.

PORTRAITS. The Ara Pacis, the Arch of Titus, and the Column of Trajan are monuments of key importance for the art of Imperial Rome at the height of its power. To single out equally significant works among the portraits of the same period is very much more difficult; their production was vast, and the diversity of types and styles mirrors the ever more complex character of Roman society. If we regard the Republican ancestral image tradition and the Greek-inspired *Augustus of Primaporta* as opposite ends of the scale, we can find almost any variety of interbreeding between the two. The fine head of the Emperor Vespasian, of c. 75 A.D., is a case in point (fig. 293): he was the first of the Flavian emperors, a military man who came to power after the Julio-Claudian (Augustan) line had died out and who must have viewed the idea of emperor worship with considerable skepticism. (When he was dying, he is reported to have said, "It seems I am about to become a god.") His humble origin and simple tastes may be reflected in the anti-Augustan, Republican flavor of his portrait. The soft, veiled quality of the carving, on the other hand, with its emphasis on the texture of skin and hair, is so Greek that it immediately recalls the seductive marble technique of Praxiteles and his school. A similar refinement can be felt in the surfaces of the slightly later bust of a lady (fig. 294), probably the subtlest portrait of a woman in all of Roman sculpture. The graceful tilt of the head and the glance of the large eyes convey a gentle mood of reverie; and how effectively the silky softness of skin and lips is set off by the many corkscrew curls of the fashionable coiffure.

The wonderful head of Trajan (fig. 295), of c. 100 A.D., is another masterpiece of portraiture. Its firm, rounded forms recall the *Augustus of Primaporta*, as does the commanding look of the eyes, dramatized by the strongly projecting brows. The face radiates a strange emotional intensity that is difficult to define—a kind of Greek pathos transmuted into Roman nobility of character.

Trajan still conformed to age-old Roman custom by being clean-shaven. His successors, in contrast, adopted the Greek fashion of wearing beards as an outward sign of admiration for the Hellenic heritage. It is not surprising, therefore, to find a strong neo-Augustan, classicistic trend, often of a peculiarly cool, formal sort, in the sculpture of the second century A.D., especially during the reigns of Hadrian and Marcus Aurelius, both of them introspective men deeply interested in Greek philosophy. We can sense this quality in the equestrian bronze statue of Marcus Aurelius (fig. 296), which is remarkable not only as the sole survivor of this class

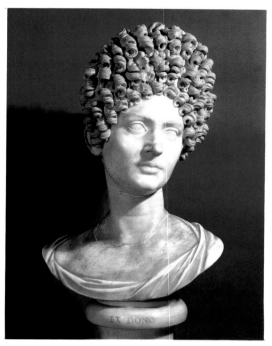

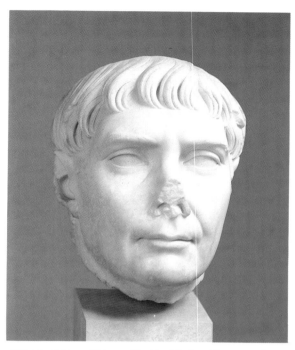

294. *PORTRAIT OF A LADY.* c. 90 A.D. Marble, lifesize. Museo Capitolino, Rome

295. *TRAJAN.* c. 100 A.D. Marble, lifesize. Museum, Ostia

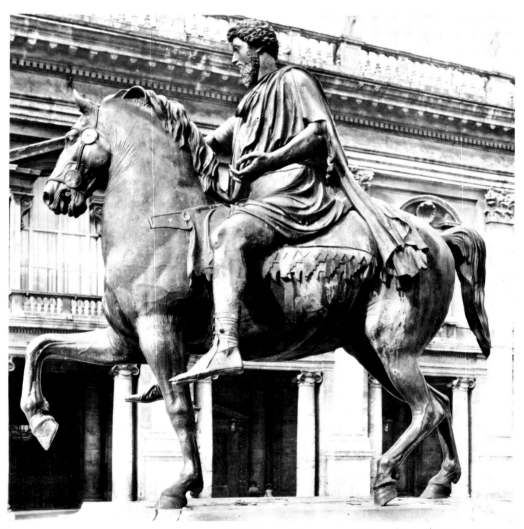

296. *EQUESTRIAN STATUE OF MARCUS AURELIUS.* 161–180 A.D. Bronze, over lifesize. Piazza del Campidoglio, Rome

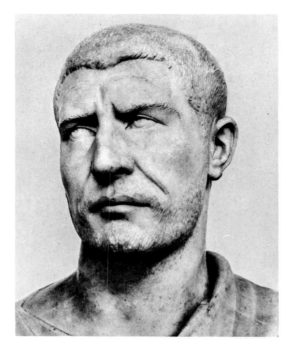

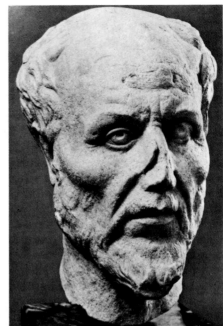

297. *(above) PHILIPPUS THE ARAB.* 244–49 A.D.
Marble, lifesize. Vatican Museums, Rome

298. *(above right) PORTRAIT HEAD* (probably Plotinus). Late 3rd
century A.D. Marble, lifesize. Museum, Ostia

of monument but as one of the few Roman statues that remained on public view throughout the Middle Ages. The equestrian image of the emperor, displaying him as the all-conquering lord of the earth, had been a firmly established tradition ever since Julius Caesar had permitted such a statue of himself to be erected in the Forum Julium. That of Marcus Aurelius, too, was meant to characterize the emperor as ever victorious, for beneath the right front leg of the horse (according to medieval accounts) there once crouched a small figure of a bound barbarian chieftain. The wonderfully spirited and powerful horse expresses this martial spirit. But the emperor himself, without weapons or armor, presents a picture of stoic detachment—a bringer of peace rather than a military hero. And so indeed he saw himself and his reign (161–180 A.D.).

It was the calm before the storm. The third century saw the Roman Empire in almost perpetual crisis. Barbarians endangered its far-flung frontiers while internal conflicts undermined the authority of the Imperial office. To retain the throne became a matter of naked force, succession by murder a regular habit; the "soldier emperors"—mercenaries from the outlying provinces of the realm—followed one another at brief intervals. The portraits of some of these men, such as Philippus the Arab (fig. 297; see fig. 134), who reigned from 244 to 249 A.D., are among the most powerful likenesses in all of art. Their facial realism is as uncompromising as that of Republican portraiture, but its aim is expressive rather than documentary: all the dark passions of the human mind—fear, suspicion, cruelty—suddenly stand revealed here, with a directness that is almost unbelievable.

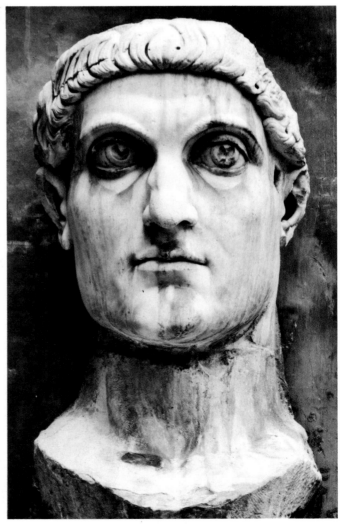

299. *CONSTANTINE THE GREAT.* Early 4th century A.D.
Marble, height 8′ (2.4 m). Palazzo dei Conservatori, Rome

The face of Philippus mirrors all the violence of the time. Yet in a strange way it also moves us to pity; there is a psychological nakedness about it that recalls a brute creature doomed and cornered. Clearly, the agony of the Roman world was not only physical but spiritual. That Roman art should have been able to create an image of a man embodying this crisis is a tribute to its continued vitality.

Let us note the new plastic means through which the impact of these portraits is achieved: we are struck, first of all, by the way expression centers on the eyes, which seem to gaze at some unseen but powerful threat. The engraved outline of the iris and the hollowed-out pupils, devices alien to earlier portraits, serve to fix the direction of the glance. The hair, too, is rendered in thoroughly un-Classical fashion as a close-fitting, textured cap; and the beard has been replaced by a peculiar unshaven look that results from roughing up the surfaces of the lower part of the face with short chisel strokes.

A somewhat later portrait, probably that of the late Greek philosopher Plotinus, suggests a different aspect of the third-century crisis (fig. 298). Plotinus' thinking—abstract, speculative, and strongly tinged with mysticism—marked a retreat from concern with the outer world that seems closer to the Middle Ages than to the Classical tradition of Greek philosophy. It sprang from the same mood that, on a more popular level, expressed itself in the spread of Oriental mystery cults throughout the Roman empire. How trustworthy a likeness our head represents is hard to say; the ascetic features, the intense eyes and tall brow, may well portray inner

qualities more accurately than outward appearance. According to his biographer, Plotinus was so contemptuous of the imperfections of the physical world that he refused to have any portrait made of himself. The body, he maintained, was an awkward enough likeness of the true, spiritual self; why then go to the bother of making an even more awkward "likeness of a likeness"?

Such a view presages the end of portraiture as we have known it so far. If a physical likeness is worthless, a portrait becomes meaningful only as a visible symbol of the spiritual self. It is in these terms that we must view the head of Constantine the Great, the first Christian emperor and reorganizer of the Roman state (fig. 299). Originally, it belonged to a colossal statue which stood in the Basilica of Constantine. We may call it superhuman, not only because of its enormous size, but even more so perhaps as an image of Imperial majesty. The huge, radiant eyes, the massive, immobile features do not tell us much about Constantine's actual appearance; they tell us a great deal about how he viewed himself and his exalted office.

ARCH OF CONSTANTINE. Constantine's conception of his role is clearly reflected in his triumphal arch (fig. 300), erected near the Colosseum 312–315 A.D. One of the largest and most elaborate of its kind, it is decorated for the most part with sculpture taken from earlier Imperial monuments. This procedure has often been viewed as dictated by haste and by the poor condition of the sculptural workshops of Rome at that time. These may have been contributory fac-

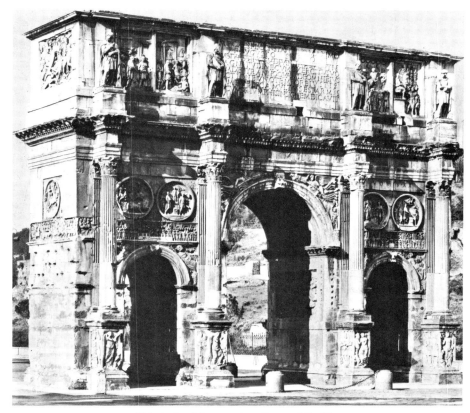

300. Arch of Constantine, Rome. 312–15 A.D.

tors, but there appears to be a conscious and carefully considered plan behind the way the earlier pieces were chosen and employed. All of them come from a related group of monuments, those dedicated to Trajan, Hadrian, and Marcus Aurelius, and the portraits of these emperors have been systematically reworked into likenesses of Constantine. Does this not convey Constantine's view of himself as the restorer of Roman glory, the legitimate successor of the "good emperors" of the second century?

The arch also contains a number of reliefs made especially for it, however, such as the friezes above the lateral openings, and these show the new Constantinian style in full force. If we compare the medallions of figure 301, carved in Hadrian's time, with the relief immediately below them, the contrast is such that they seem to belong to two different worlds. The scene represents Constantine, after his entry into Rome in 312 A.D., addressing the Senate and the people from the rostrum in the Forum.

The first thing we notice here is the avoidance of all the numerous devices developed since the fifth century B.C. for creating spatial depth; we find no oblique lines, no foreshortening, and only the barest ripple of movement in the listening crowds. The architecture has been flattened out against the relief background, which thus becomes a solid, impenetrable surface. The rostrum and the people on or beside it form a second, equally shallow layer—the second row

of figures appears simply as a series of heads above those of the first. The figures themselves have an oddly doll-like quality: the heads are very large, while the bodies seem not only dwarfish (because of the thick, stubby legs) but also lacking in articulation. The mechanism of *contrapposto* has disappeared completely, so that these figures no longer stand freely and by their own muscular effort; rather, they seem to dangle from invisible strings.

All the characteristics we have described so far are essentially negative, judged from the Classical point of view: they represent the loss of many hard-won gains—a throwback to earlier, more primitive levels of expression. Yet such an approach does not really advance our understanding of the new style. The Constantinian panel cannot be explained as the result of a lack of ability, for it is far too consistent within itself to be regarded as no more than a clumsy attempt to imitate earlier Roman reliefs. Nor can it be viewed as a return to Archaic art, since there is nothing in pre-Classical times that looks like it. No, the Constantinian sculptor must have had a positive new purpose of his own. Perhaps we can approach it best by stressing one dominant feature of our relief: its sense of self-sufficiency.

The scene fills the available area, and fills it completely (note how all the background buildings are made to have the same height), but any suggestion that it continues beyond the frame is carefully avoided. It is as if our artist had asked

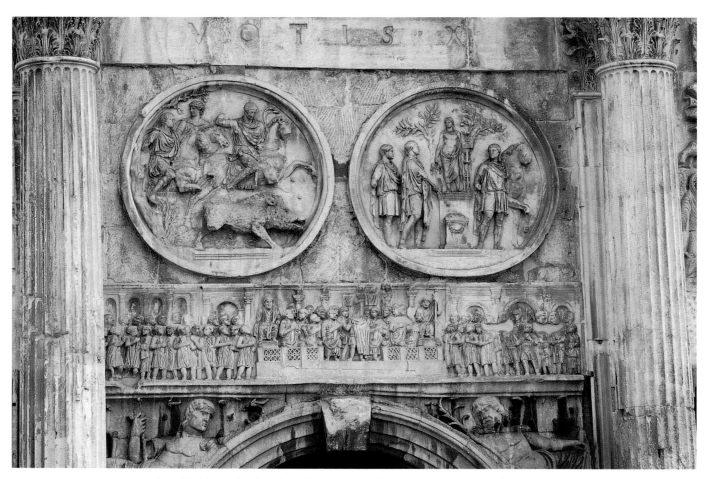

301. Medallions (117–138 A.D.) and frieze (early 4th century), Arch of Constantine

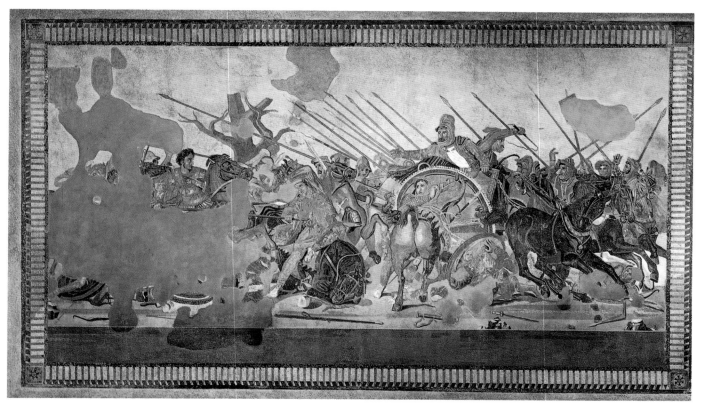

302. *THE BATTLE OF ISSUS* or *BATTLE OF ALEXANDER AND THE PERSIANS.* Mosaic copy from Pompeii, 1st century B.C., of a Hellenistic painting. 8'11" × 16'9½" (2.7 × 5.1 m). Museo Archeologico Nazionale, Naples

himself, "How can I get *all* of this complicated ceremonial event into my panel?" In order to do so, he has imposed an abstract order upon the world of appearances: the middle third of the strip is given over to the rostrum with Constantine and his entourage, the rest to the listeners and the buildings that identify the Roman Forum as the scene of the action (they are all quite recognizable, even though their scale and proportions have been drastically adjusted). The symmetrical design also permits him to make clear the unique status of the emperor. Constantine not only occupies the exact center; he is shown full-face (his head, unfortunately, has been knocked off), while all the other figures turn their heads toward him to express their dependent relationship. That the frontal pose is indeed a position of majesty reserved for sovereigns, human or divine, is nicely demonstrated by the seated figures at the corners of the rostrum, the only ones besides Constantine to face us directly: these figures are statues of emperors—the same "good emperors" we met elsewhere on the arch, Hadrian and Marcus Aurelius. Looked at in this way, our relief reveals itself as a bold and original creation. It is the harbinger of a new vision that will become basic to the development of Christian art.

# PAINTING

The modern beholder, whether expert or amateur, is apt to find painting the most exciting as well as the most baffling aspect of art under Roman rule—exciting because it represents the only large body of ancient painting subsequent to

the Etruscan murals and because much of it, having come to light only in modern times, has the charm of the unfamiliar; baffling because we know infinitely less about it than we do about Roman architecture or sculpture. The surviving material, with very few exceptions, is severely limited in range; almost all of it consists of wall paintings, and the great majority of these come from Pompeii, Herculaneum, and other settlements buried by the eruption of Mount Vesuvius in 79 A.D., or from Rome and its environs. Their dates cover a span of less than two hundred years, from the end of the first century B.C. to the late first century A.D.; what happened before or after remains largely a matter of guesswork. And since we have no Classical Greek or Hellenistic wall paintings, the problem of singling out the Roman element as against the Greek is far more difficult than in sculpture or architecture.

## Greek Sources

That there was copying of Greek designs, that Greek paintings as well as painters were imported, nobody will dispute. But the number of instances in which this can be demonstrated is small indeed. Let us consider two of these. At an earlier point, we mentioned Pliny's reference to a Greek picture of the late fourth century B.C. representing the battle of Issus (see page 233). The same subject—or, at any rate, another battle of Alexander's war against the Persians—is shown in an exceptionally large and technically accomplished floor mosaic from a Pompeian house of the first century B.C. Figure 302 illustrates the center and right half, with

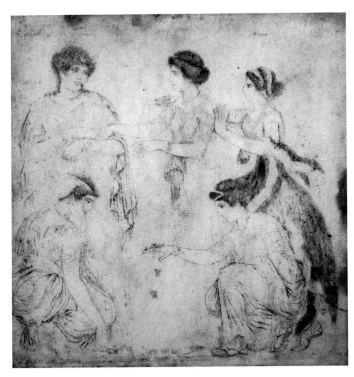

303. ALEXANDROS OF ATHENS. *THE KNUCKLEBONE PLAYERS.*
1st century B.C. Marble panel, 16½ × 15″ (42 × 38 cm).
Museo Archeologico Nazionale, Naples

Darius and the fleeing Persians, and the badly damaged left-hand portion, with the figure of Alexander. While there is no special reason to link this mosaic with Pliny's account, we can hardly doubt that it is a copy—and an astonishingly proficient one—of a Hellenistic painting. But a Hellenistic painting of what date? The crowding, the air of frantic excitement, the powerfully modeled and foreshortened forms, the precise cast shadows—when did all these qualities reach this particular stage of development? We do not know, for even the great frieze of Pergamum seems restrained in comparison.

Our second instance is the very opposite of the first. A small marble panel from Herculaneum painted in a delicate linear style, it shows a group of five women, two of them engaged in a game of knucklebones (fig. 303). An inscription tells us that Alexandros of Athens painted this. The style plainly recalls that of the late fifth century B.C. (compare the Attic white-ground lekythos in fig. 214), yet the execution seems so much weaker than the conception that it must be a copy or, better perhaps, an imitation in the Classical manner, comparable to the copies or adaptations of Classical Greek statues manufactured for the Roman market. It belongs to a special class of "collector's items" that is no more representative of Roman painting as a whole than the Alexander mosaic. We wonder, moreover, whether anything as attenuated as this actually existed in Classical Athenian art. Was it perhaps a late "neo-Attic" invention meant to cater to the taste of some particular group of Roman connoisseurs?

## Roman Illusionism

The earliest phase of Roman wall painting, known from a few examples of the second century B.C., does show a clear connection with the Hellenistic world, since it has also been found in the eastern Mediterranean. Unfortunately, it is not very informative for us, as it consists entirely of the imitation of colored marble paneling. About 100 B.C., this so-called First Style began to be displaced by a far more ambitious and elaborate style that sought to push back or open up the flat surface of the wall by means of illusionistic architectural perspectives and "window effects," including landscapes and figures. Three phases of this more elaborate style have been distinguished, known as the Second, Third, and Fourth Styles, but the differences between them are not always clear, and there seems to have been considerable overlapping in their sequence, so that we can largely disregard this classification here. The Fourth Style, which prevailed at the time of the eruption of Mount Vesuvius in 79 A.D., is the most intricate of all; our example, a corner of the Ixion Room in the House of the Vettii at Pompeii (fig. 304), combines imitation marble paneling, conspicuously framed mythological scenes intended to give the effect of panel pictures set into the wall, and fantastic architectural vistas seen through make-believe windows. This architecture has a strangely unreal and picturesque quality that is believed to

304. (*opposite*) The Ixion Room, House of the Vettii,
Pompeii. 63–79 A.D.

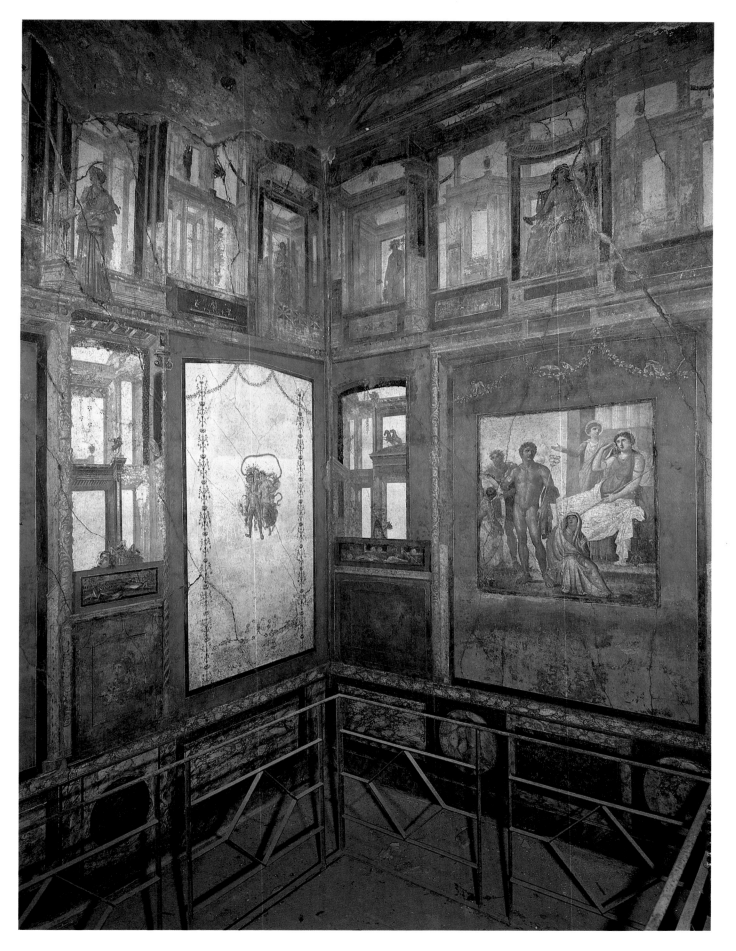

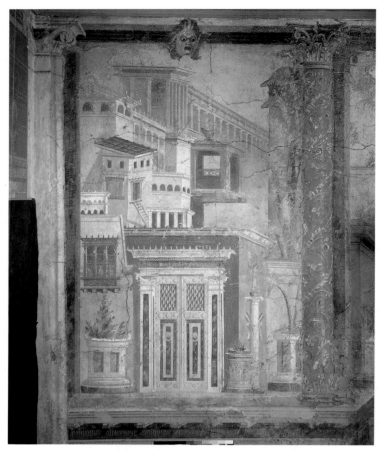

305. *ARCHITECTURAL VIEW.* Wall painting from a villa at Boscoreale,
near Naples. 1st century B.C. The Metropolitan Museum of Art,
New York. Rogers Fund, 1903

reflect the architectural backdrops of the theaters of the
time; it often anticipates effects such as that of the Market
Gate of Miletus (see fig. 277).

The architectural vistas of the Second Style, as represented by our figure 305, are a good deal more substantial and
thus provide a better measure of the illusionistic devices by
which the Roman painter achieved these breakthroughs.
He is clearly a master of modeling and surface textures; the
forms framing the vista—the lustrous, richly decorated columns, the moldings, the mask at the top—have an extraordinary degree of three-dimensional reality. They effectively
set off the distant view of buildings, which is flooded with
light to convey a sense of free, open-air space. But as soon as
we try to penetrate this architectural maze, we find ourselves lost; the individual structures cannot be disentangled
from each other, their size and relationship are obscure. And
we quickly realize that the Roman painter has no systematic
grasp of spatial depth, that his perspective is haphazard and
inconsistent within itself. Apparently he never intended us
to enter the space he has created; like a promised land, it
remains forever beyond us.

When landscape takes the place of architectural vistas,
exact foreshortening becomes less important, and the virtues of the Roman painter's approach outweigh his limita-

tions. This is most strikingly demonstrated by the famous
Odyssey Landscapes, a continuous stretch of landscape
subdivided into eight compartments by a framework of pilasters. Each section illustrates an episode of the adventures of
Odysseus (Ulysses). One of the adventures with the Laestrygonians is reproduced (fig. 306). The airy, bluish tones
create a wonderful feeling of atmospheric, light-filled space
that envelops and binds together all the forms within this
warm Mediterranean fairyland, where the human figures
seem to play no more than an incidental role. Only upon further reflection do we realize how frail the illusion of coherence is even here: if we were to try mapping this landscape,
we would find it just as ambiguous as the architectural perspective discussed above. Its unity is not structural but poetic, like that of the stucco landscape in figure 289.

The Odyssey Landscapes contrast with another approach
to nature, which we know from the murals in a room of the
Villa of Livia at Primaporta (fig. 307). Here the architectural
framework has been dispensed with altogether; the entire
wall is given over to a view of a delightful garden full of
flowers, fruit trees, and birds. These charming details have
the same tangible quality, the same concreteness of color
and texture as the architectural framework of figure 305,
and their apparent distance from the beholder is also about

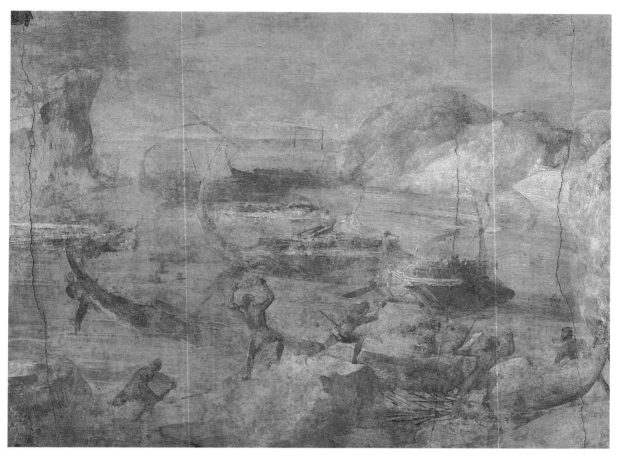

306. *THE LAESTRYGONIANS HURLING ROCKS AT THE FLEET OF ODYSSEUS.*
Wall painting from a house on the Esquiline Hill, Rome. Late 1st century B.C. Vatican Museums, Rome

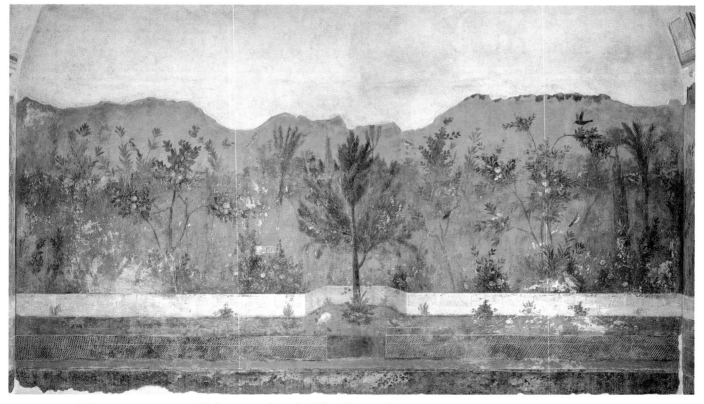

307. *VIEW OF A GARDEN.* Wall painting from the Villa of Livia at Primaporta. c. 20 B.C. Museo delle Terme, Rome

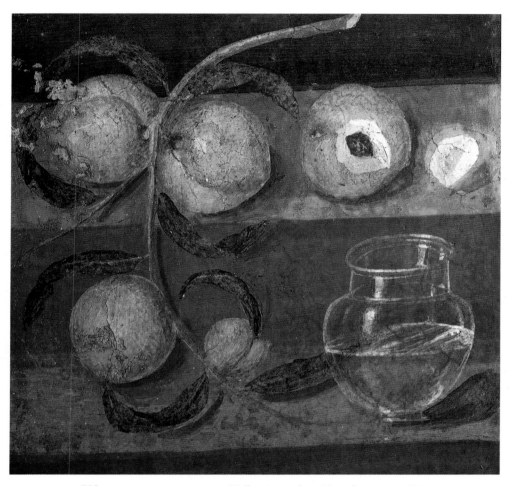

308. *PEACHES AND GLASS JAR*. Wall painting from Herculaneum. c. 50 A.D.
Museo Archeologico Nazionale, Naples

the same—they seem to be within arm's reach. At the bottom, there is a low trellis, beyond it a narrow strip of lawn with a tree in the center, then a low wall, and immediately after that the garden proper begins. Oddly enough, however, we cannot enter it; behind the front row of trees and flowers lies an opaque mass of greenery that shuts off our view as effectively as a dense hedge. This garden, then, is another promised land made only for looking. The wall has not really been opened up but merely pushed back a few feet and replaced by a wall of plants. It is this very limitation of spatial depth that endows our mural with its unusual degree of coherence.

On a large scale, such restraint does not occur often in Roman mural decoration. We do find it, though, in the still lifes that sometimes make their appearance within the intricate architectural schemes. These usually take the form of make-believe niches or cupboards, so that the objects, which are often displayed on two levels, remain close to us. Our example (fig. 308) is particularly noteworthy for the rendering of the translucent glass jar half filled with water. The reflections are so acutely observed that we feel the painter must have copied them from an actual jar illuminated in just this way. But if we try to determine the source and direction of the light in the picture, we find that this cannot

be done, because the shadows cast by the various objects are not consistent with each other. Nor do we have the impression that the jar stands in a stream of light; instead, the light seems to be imprisoned within the jar. Clearly, the Roman artist, despite his striving for illusionistic effects, is no more systematic in his approach to the behavior of light than in his handling of perspective. However sensuously real the details, his work nearly always lacks a basic unifying element in its overall structure. In the finest examples, this lack is amply compensated for by other qualities, so that our observation must not be regarded as condemning him to an inferior status. The absence of a consistent view of the visible world should be thought of instead as a fundamental barrier that differentiates Roman painting from that of the Renaissance or of modern times.

The illusionistic tendencies that gained the upper hand in Roman murals during the first century B.C. may have been anticipated to some extent by Hellenistic painters, but in the form in which we know them they seem to be a specifically Roman development, as against the reproductive or imitative works we had examined before. Echoes of the latter persist in the mythological panels that occur like islands within an elaborate architectural framework (see fig. 304). While these scenes hardly ever give the impression of straightforward copies after Hellenistic originals, they often have the somewhat disjointed character of compilations of motifs from various sources.

A characteristic example is the picture of Hercules discovering the infant Telephus in Arcadia, from the basilica at Herculaneum (fig. 309). What stamps this as the handiwork of a Roman painter is its oddly unstable style; almost everything here has the look of a "quotation," so that not only the forms, but even the brushwork varies from one figure to the next. Thus the personification of Arcadia, seated in the center, seems as cold, immobile, and tightly modeled as a statue, whereas Hercules, although his pose is equally statuesque, exhibits a broader and more luminous technique. Or compare the lion, painted in sketchy, agitated dabs, with the precise and graceful outlines of the doe. The sparkling highlights on the basket of fruit are derived from yet another source: still lifes such as figure 308. And the mischievously smiling young Pan in the upper–left-hand corner is composed of quick, feathery brushstrokes that have a character all their own.

VILLA OF THE MYSTERIES. There exists, however, one monument whose sweeping grandeur of design and coherence of style are unique in Roman painting: the great frieze in one of the rooms in the Villa of the Mysteries just outside Pompeii (fig. 310). Like the garden view from the Villa of

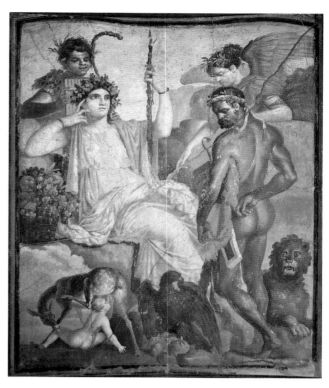

309. *HERCULES AND TELEPHUS.* Wall painting from Herculaneum. c. 70 A.D. Museo Archeologico Nazionale, Naples

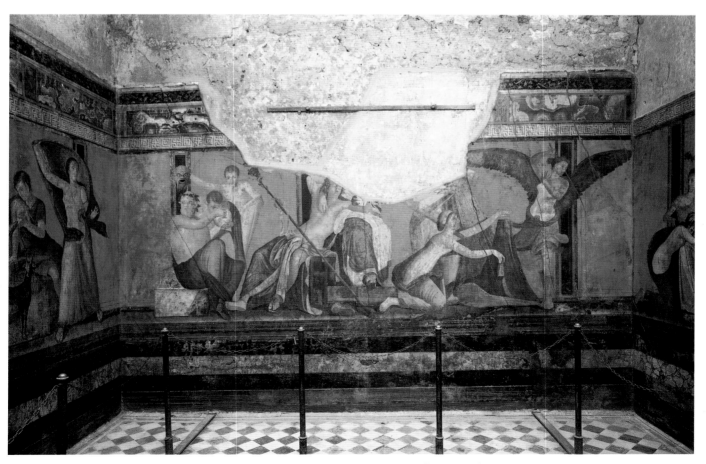

310. *SCENES OF A DIONYSIAC MYSTERY CULT.* Wall painting frieze. c. 50 B.C. Villa of the Mysteries, Pompeii

Livia, it dates from the latter part of the first century B.C., when the Second Style was at its height. So far as the treatment of the wall space is concerned, the two works have more in common with each other than with other Second Style murals, for both of them are conceived in terms of rhythmic continuity and arm's-length depth.

The artist who created the frieze in the Villa of the Mysteries has placed his figures on a narrow ledge of green against a regular pattern of red panels separated by strips of black, a kind of running stage on which they enact their strange and solemn ritual. Who are they, and what is the meaning of the cycle? Many details remain puzzling, but the program as a whole represents various aspects of the Dionysiac Mysteries, a semisecret cult of very ancient origin that had been brought to Italy from Greece. The sacred rites are performed in the presence of Dionysus and Adriadne, with their train of satyrs and sileni, so that human and mythical reality tend to merge into one.

We sense the blending of these two spheres in the qualities all the figures have in common—their dignity of bearing and expression, the wonderful firmness of body and drapery, the rapt intensity with which they participate in the drama of the ritual (fig. 311). Many of the poses and gestures are taken from the repertory of Classical Greek art, yet they lack the studied and self-conscious quality we call classicism. An artist of exceptional greatness of vision has filled these forms with new life. Whatever his relation to the famous masters of Greek painting whose works are lost to us forever, he was their legitimate heir in the same sense that the finest Latin poets of the Augustan age were the legitimate heirs to the Greek poetic tradition.

PORTRAITS. Portrait painting, according to Pliny, was an established custom in Republican Rome, serving the ancestor cult as did the portrait busts discussed earlier (see pages 230–33). None of these panels has survived, and the few portraits found on the walls of Roman houses in Pompeii may well derive from a different, a Hellenistic, tradition. The only coherent group of painted portraits at our disposal, strangely enough, comes from the Faiyum district in Lower Egypt. The earliest of them found so far seem to date from the second century A.D. We owe them to the survival—or revival—of an ancient Egyptian custom, that of attaching a portrait of the deceased to the wrapped, mummified body. Originally, these portraits had been sculptured (compare fig. 104), but became replaced in Roman times by painted ones such as the very fine and well-preserved wooden panel reproduced in figure 312.

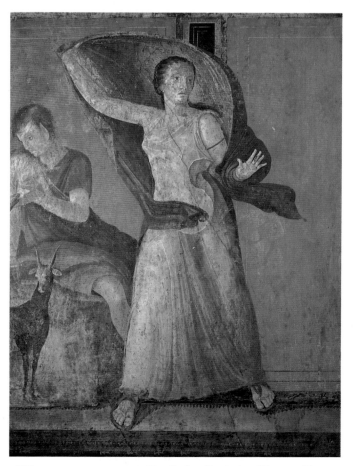

311. *WOMAN WITH A VEIL*. Detail of wall painting frieze. c. 50 B.C. Villa of the Mysteries, Pompeii

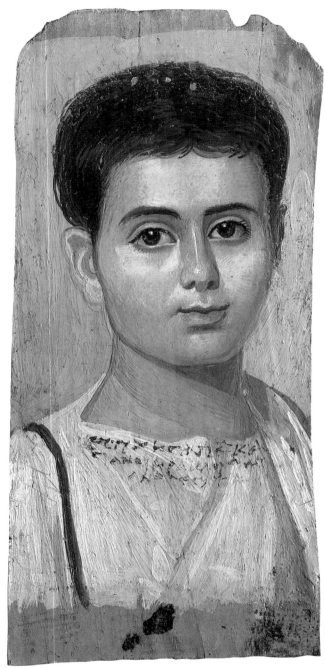

312. *PORTRAIT OF A BOY*, from the Faiyum,
Lower Egypt. 2nd century A.D. Encaustic on panel,
13 × 7¼″ (33 × 18.3 cm).
The Metropolitan Museum of Art, New York.
Gift of Edward S. Harkness, 1918

The amazing freshness of its colors is due to the fact that it was done in a technique of great durability called encaustic, which means that the pigments are suspended in hot wax. The mixture can be opaque and creamy, like oil paint, or thin and translucent. At their best, these portraits have an immediacy and sureness of touch that have rarely been surpassed; our dark-haired boy is as solid, sparkling, and lifelike a piece of reality as anyone might wish. The style of the picture—and it does have style, otherwise we could not tell it from a snapshot—becomes apparent only when we compare it with other Faiyum portraits. Since they were produced quickly and in large numbers, they tend to have many elements in common, such as the emphasis on the eyes, the placing of the highlights and shadows, the angle from which the face is seen. In the later examples, these conventional elements stiffen more and more into a fixed type, while in ours they merely furnish a flexible mold within which to cast the individual likeness.

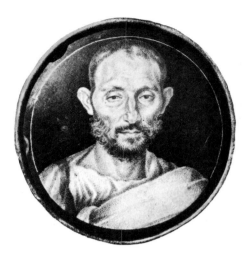

313. *PORTRAIT OF A MAN.* c. 250 A.D. Glass,
diameter c. 2″ (5 cm).
Archaeological Museum, Arezzo, Italy

Whether to call this style Roman or Hellenistic is an idle question. We do know, however, that it was not confined to Egypt, since it can be linked with some portrait miniatures on glass apparently done in Italy during the third century A.D. The finest of them is the medallion shown in its actual size in figure 313. Its power of characterization, superior to that of any Faiyum portrait, represents the same climax of Roman portraiture that produced the marble bust of Philippus the Arab (see fig. 297).

## Eastern Religions

In discussing the crisis of the Roman world in the third century A.D. (see page 240), we mentioned as characteristic of the mood of the times the spread of Oriental mystery religions. They were of various origins—Egyptian, Persian, Semitic—and their early development naturally centered in their home territory, the southeastern provinces and border regions of the Roman Empire. Although based on traditions in effect long before the conquest of these ancient lands by Alexander the Great, the cults had been strongly influenced by Greek ideas during the Hellenistic period; it was, in fact, to this fusion of Oriental and Greek elements that they owed their vitality and appeal.

The names of most of these cults, and their doctrines, are today remembered only by specialists, even though they were powerful rivals of Christianity during the early centuries of our era. In those days, the Near East was a vast religious and cultural melting pot where all the competing faiths, including Judaism, Christianity, Mithraism, Manichaeism, Gnosticism, and many more, tended to influence each other, so that they had an astonishing number of things in common, whatever their differences of origin, ritual, or nomenclature. Most of them shared such features as an emphasis on revealed truth, the hope of salvation, a chief prophet or messiah, the dichotomy of good and evil, a ritual of purification or initiation (baptism), and the duty to seek converts among the "unbelievers." The last and, in Near

Eastern terms, the most successful product of this cross-breeding process was Islam, which still dominates the entire area to this day (see pages 290–91).

The growth of the Graeco-Oriental religions under Roman rule is as yet very incompletely understood, since much of it was part of an underground movement which has left few tangible traces. Besides, the area where it took place has been a theater of war and destruction so many times that important discoveries, such as of the Dead Sea Scrolls, are rare events indeed. There is mounting evidence, however, that the new faiths also gave birth to a new style in art, and that this style, too, resulted from a fusion of Graeco-Roman and Oriental elements. The artists who struggled with the task of coining images to express the contents of these faiths were not among the most gifted of their time; they were provincial craftsmen of modest ambition who drew upon whatever visual sources happened to be available to them, adapting, combining, and reshaping these as best they could. Their efforts are often clumsy, yet it is here that we find the beginnings of a tradition that was to become of basic importance for the development of medieval art.

DURA-EUROPOS. The most telling illustrations of this new compound style have been found in the Mesopotamian town of Dura-Europos on the upper Euphrates, a Roman frontier station that was captured by the resurgent Persians under Shapur I about 256 A.D. and abandoned by its population soon after. Its ruins have yielded the remains of sanctuaries of several religions, decorated with murals which all show essentially the same Graeco-Oriental character. The best preserved are those from the assembly hall of a synagogue, painted about 250 A.D.; of their numerous compartments, we illustrate the one representing the consecration of the tabernacle (fig. 314).

It is characteristic of the melting-pot conditions described above that even Judaism should have been affected by them. Momentarily, at least, the age-old injunction against images was relaxed so that the walls of the assembly hall could be covered with a richly detailed visual account of the history of the Chosen People and their Covenant with the Lord. The new attitude seems to have been linked with a tendency to change Judaism from a national to a universal faith by missionary activity among the non-Jewish population; interestingly, some of the inscriptions on the murals (such as the name Aaron in fig. 314) are in Greek. In any event, we may be sure that the artists who designed these pictures faced an unaccustomed task, just as did the painters who worked for the earliest Christian communities; they had to cast into visible form what had hitherto been expressed only in words. How did they go about it? Let us take a closer look at our illustration: we can read the details—animals, human beings, buildings, cult objects—without trouble, but their relationship eludes us. There is no action, no story, only an assembly of forms and figures confronting us in the expectation that we will be able to establish the proper links between them. The frieze in the Villa of the Mysteries presents a similar difficulty—there, too, the beholder is supposed to know—yet it strikes us as very much less puzzling, for the figures have an eloquence of gesture and expression that makes them meaningful even though we may not understand the context of the scenes.

If the synagogue painter fails to be equally persuasive, must we attribute this to his lack of competence, or are there other reasons as well? The question is rather like the one we faced when discussing the Constantinian relief in figure 301, which resembles the Dura-Europos mural in a number of ways. The synagogue painter exhibits the same sense of self-sufficiency, of condensation for the sake of completeness, but his subject is far more demanding: he had to represent a historical event of vast religious importance (the consecration of the tabernacle and its priests, which began the reconciliation of humanity and God) as described in detail in the Holy Scriptures, and he had to represent it in such a way as to suggest that it was also a timeless, recurrent ritual. Thus his picture is burdened with a wealth of significance far greater and more rigidly defined than that of the Dionysiac frieze or the Constantinian relief. Nor did he have a well-established tradition of Jewish religious painting at his disposal to help him visualize the tabernacle and the consecration ceremony.

No wonder he has fallen back on a sort of symbolic shorthand composed of images borrowed from other, older traditions. The tabernacle itself, for instance, is shown as a Classical temple simply because our artist could not imagine it, in accordance with the biblical description, as a tentlike construction of poles and goat's-hair curtains. The attendant and red heifer in the lower–left-hand corner are derived from Roman scenes of animal sacrifice, hence they show remnants of foreshortening not found among the other figures. Other echoes of Roman painting appear in the perspective view of the altar table next to the figure of Aaron, in the perfunctory modeling here and there, and in the rudimentary cast shadows attached to some of the figures. Did the painter still understand the purpose of these shadows?

They seem to be mere empty gestures, since the rest of the picture betrays no awareness of either light or space in the Roman sense. Even the occasional overlapping of forms appears largely accidental. The sequence of things in space is conveyed by other means: the seven-branched candlestick, the two incense burners, the altar, and Aaron are to be understood as behind, rather than on top of, the crenellated wall that shields the precinct of the tabernacle. Their size, however, is governed by their importance, not by their position in space. Aaron, as the principal figure, is not only larger than the attendants but also more rigid and abstract. His costume, because of its ritual significance, is diagramed in detail, at the cost of obliterating the body underneath. The attendants, on the other hand, still show a residue of mobility and three-dimensional existence. Their garments, surprisingly enough, are Persian, an indication not only of the odd mixture of civilizations in this border area but of possible artistic influences from Persia.

Our synagogue mural, then, combines—in none-too-skillful a fashion—a considerable variety of formal elements whose only common denominator is the religious message of the whole. In the hands of a great artist, this message might have been a stronger unifying force, but even then the shapes and colors would have been no more than a humble, imperfect simile of the spiritual truth they were meant to serve. That, surely, was the outlook of the authorities who supervised the execution of the mural cycle and controlled its program. The essential quality of these pictures can no longer be understood in the framework of ancient art; they express an attitude that seems far closer to the Middle Ages. If we were to sum up their purpose in a single phrase, we could hardly do better than to quote a famous dictum justifying the pictorial representation of Christian themes: *Quod legentibus scriptura, hoc idiotis...pictura*—translated freely: painting conveys the Word of God to the unlettered.

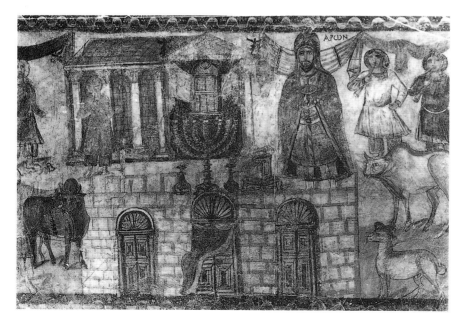

314. *THE CONSECRATION OF THE TABERNACLE AND ITS PRIESTS,* from the Assembly Hall of the Synagogue at Dura-Europos. 245–56 A.D. Mural, 4'8¼" × 7'8¼" (1.4 × 2.3 m). National Museum, Damascus, Syria

*CHAPTER EIGHT*

# EARLY CHRISTIAN AND BYZANTINE ART

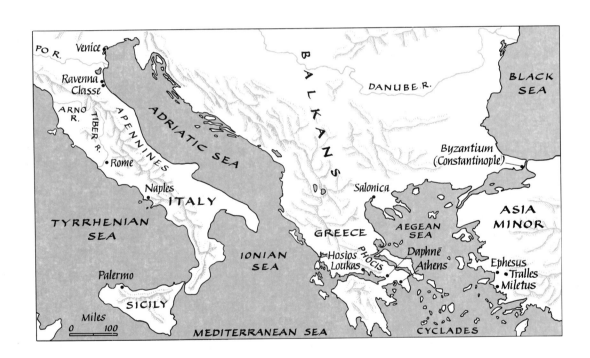

In 323 A.D. Constantine the Great made a fateful decision, the consequences of which are still felt today—he resolved to move the capital of the Roman Empire to the Greek town of Byzantium, which henceforth was to be known as Constantinople, and today, as Istanbul. Six years later, after an energetic building campaign, the transfer was officially completed. In taking this step, the Emperor acknowledged the growing strategic and economic importance of the eastern provinces (a development that had been going on for some time). The new capital also symbolized the new Christian basis of the Roman state, since it was in the heart of the most thoroughly Christianized region of the Empire.

Constantine could hardly have foreseen that shifting the seat of Imperial power would result in splitting the realm, yet within less than a hundred years the division had become an accomplished fact, even though the emperors at Constantinople did not relinquish their claim to the western provinces. The latter, ruled by western Roman emperors, soon fell prey to invading Germanic tribes—Visigoths, Vandals, Ostrogoths, Lombards. By the end of the sixth century, the last vestige of centralized authority had disappeared. The eastern, or Byzantine, Empire, in contrast, survived these onslaughts, and under Justinian (527–565) reached new power and stability. With the rise of Islam a hundred years later, the African and Near Eastern parts of the Empire were overrun by conquering Arab armies: in the eleventh century, the Turks occupied a large part of Asia Minor, while the last Byzantine possessions in the West (in southern Italy) fell to the Normans. Yet the Empire, with its domain reduced to the Balkans and Greece, held on until 1453, when the Turks finally conquered Constantinople itself.

The division of the Roman Empire soon led to a religious split as well. At the time of Constantine, the bishop of Rome, deriving his authority from St. Peter, was the acknowledged head, the pope, of the Christian Church. His claim to pre-eminence, however, soon came to be disputed by the patriarch of Constantinople, differences in doctrine began to develop, and eventually the division of Christendom into a Western, or Catholic, and an Eastern, or Orthodox, Church, became all but final. The differences between them went very deep; Roman Catholicism maintained its independence from Imperial or any other state authority and became an international institution reflecting its character as the Universal Church, while the Orthodox Church was based on the union of spiritual and secular authority in the person of the emperor, who appointed the patriarch. It thus remained dependent on the power of the State, exacting a double allegiance from the faithful and sharing the vicissitudes of political power. We will recognize this pattern as the Christian adaptation of a very ancient heritage, the divine kingship of Egypt and the Near East; if the Byzantine emperors, unlike their pagan predecessors, could no longer claim the status of gods, they retained an equally unique and exalted role by placing themselves at the head of the Church as well as of the State. Nor did the tradition die with the fall of Constantinople. The tsars of Russia claimed the mantle of the Byzantine emperors, Moscow became "the third Rome," and the Russian Orthodox Church was as closely tied to the State as was its Byzantine parent body.

"EARLY CHRISTIAN" AND "BYZANTINE." It is the religious even more than the political separation of East and West that makes it impossible to discuss the development of Christian art in the Roman Empire under a single heading. "Early Christian" does not, strictly speaking, designate a style; it refers, rather, to any work of art produced by or for Christians during the time prior to the splitting off of the Orthodox Church—or, roughly, the first five centuries of our era. "Byzantine art," on the other hand, designates not only the art of the eastern Roman Empire but a specific quality of style as well. Since this style grew out of certain tendencies that can be traced back to the time of Constantine or even earlier, there is no sharp dividing line between Early Christian and Byzantine art. Thus the reign of Justinian has been termed the First Golden Age of Byzantine art, yet Justinian himself was a man of strongly western, Latin orientation who almost succeeded in reuniting the Constantinian domain; and the monuments he sponsored, especially those on Italian soil, may be viewed as either Early Christian or Byzantine, depending on which frame of reference we select.

Soon after, it is true, the political and religious cleavage between East and West became an artistic cleavage as well. In western Europe, Celtic and Germanic peoples fell heir to the civilization of late antiquity, of which Early Christian art had been a part, and transformed it into that of the Middle Ages. The East, in contrast, experienced no such break; in the Byzantine Empire, late antiquity lived on, although the Greek and Oriental elements came increasingly to the fore at the expense of the Roman heritage. As a consequence, Byzantine civilization never became wholly medieval. "The Byzantines may have been senile," one historian has observed, "but they remained Greeks to the end." The same sense of tradition, of continuity with the past, determines the development of Byzantine art. We can understand it best, therefore, if we see it in the context of the final, Christian phase of antiquity rather than in the context of the Middle Ages.

# EARLY CHRISTIAN ART

When and where the first Christian works of art were produced remain a matter of conjecture. Of the surviving monuments, none can be dated earlier than about 200 A.D.; therefore, we lack all direct knowledge of art in the service of Christianity before that time. In fact, there is little we know for certain about Christian art until we reach the reign of Constantine the Great, because the third century, too, is poorly represented. The painted decorations of the Roman catacombs, the underground burial places of the Christians, provide the only sizable and coherent body of material, but these are merely one among various possible kinds of Christian art.

Before Constantine's reign, Rome did not embody the faith; older and larger Christian communities existed in the great cities of North Africa and the Near East, such as Alexandria and Antioch. They had probably developed separate artistic traditions of their own. The extraordinary murals of the synagogue at Dura-Europos (see fig. 314) suggest that

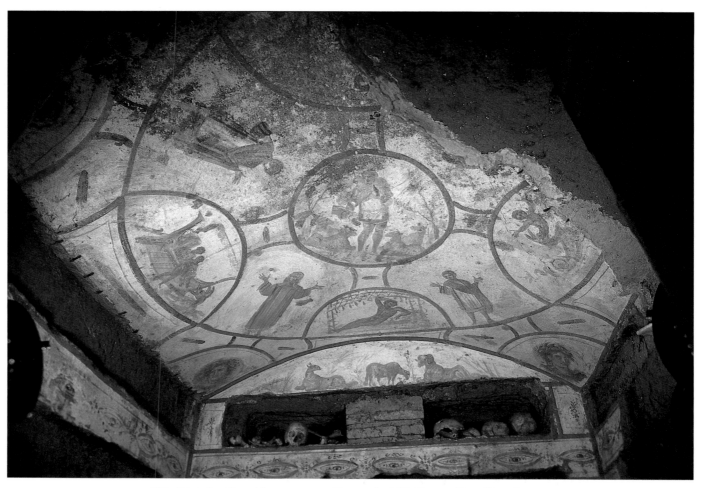

315. Painted ceiling. 4th century A.D. Catacomb of SS. Pietro e Marcellino, Rome

paintings similarly orientalizing in style may have decorated the walls of Christian places of worship in Syria and Palestine, since the earliest Christian congregations were formed by dissident members of the Jewish community. Alexandria, the home of a large and thoroughly Hellenized Jewish colony, during the first or the second century A.D. may have produced illustrations of the Old Testament in a style akin to that of Pompeian murals. We meet echoes of such scenes in Christian art later on, but we cannot be sure when or where they originated, or by what paths they entered the Christian tradition.

## Catacombs

If the dearth of material from the eastern provinces of the Empire makes it difficult to judge the position of the catacomb paintings within the early development of Christian art, the paintings nevertheless tell us a good deal about the spirit of the communities that sponsored them. The burial rite and the safeguarding of the tomb were of vital concern to the early Christian, whose faith rested on the hope of eternal life in paradise. The imagery of the catacombs, as can be seen in the painted ceiling in figure 315, clearly expresses this otherworldly outlook, although the forms are in essence still those of pre-Christian mural decoration. Thus we recog-

nize the division of the ceiling into compartments as a late and highly simplified echo of the illusionistic architectural schemes in Pompeian painting, and the modeling of the figures, as well as the landscape settings, betray their descent from the same Roman idiom, which here, in the hands of an artist of very modest ability, has become debased by endless repetition. But the catacomb painter has used this traditional vocabulary to convey a new, symbolic content, and the original meaning of the forms is of little interest to him. Even the geometric framework shares in this task, for the great circle suggests the Dome of Heaven, inscribed with the cross, the basic symbol of the faith. In the central medallion we see a youthful shepherd, with a sheep on his shoulders, in a pose that can be traced back as far as Greek Archaic art (compare fig. 168); he stands for Christ the Saviour, the Good Shepherd who gives His life for His sheep.

The semicircular compartments tell the story of Jonah: on the left he is cast from the ship, on the right he emerges from the whale, and at the bottom he is safe again on dry land, meditating upon the mercy of the Lord. This Old Testament miracle, often juxtaposed with New Testament miracles, enjoyed immense favor in Early Christian art as proof of the Lord's power to rescue the faithful from the jaws of death. The standing figures represent members of the

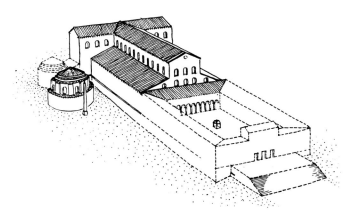

316. Reconstruction of Old St. Peter's, Rome,
Begun c. 333 A.D. (after Frazer)

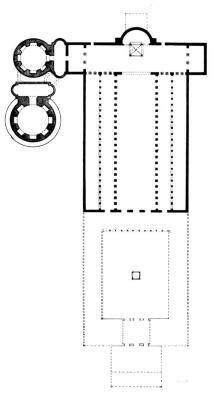

317. Plan of Old St. Peter's (after Frazer)

Church, with their hands raised in prayer, pleading for divine help. The entire scheme, though small in scale and unimpressive in execution, has a coherence and clarity that set it apart from its pagan ancestors as well as from the synagogue murals of Dura-Europos (see fig. 314). Here is, if not the reality, at least the promise of a truly monumental new form (compare fig 349).

## Architecture

Constantine's decision to make Christianity the state religion of the Roman Empire had a profound impact on Christian art. Until that time, congregations had been unable to meet for worship in public; services were held covertly in the houses of the wealthier members. Now, almost overnight, an impressive architectural setting had to be created for the new official faith, so that the Church might be visible to all. Constantine himself devoted the full resources of his office to this task, and within a few years an astonishing number of large, Imperially sponsored churches arose, not only in Rome but also in Constantinople, in the Holy Land, and at other important sites.

THE BASILICA. These structures were a new type, now called the Early Christian basilica, that provided the basic model for the development of church architecture in western Europe. Unfortunately, none of them has survived in its original form, but the plan of the greatest Constantinian church, Old St. Peter's in Rome, is known with considerable accuracy (figs. 316 and 317). For an impression of the interior, we must draw upon the slightly later basilica of St. Paul Outside the Walls, built on the same pattern, which remained essentially intact until it was wrecked by fire in 1823 (fig. 318). The Early Christian basilica, as exemplified in these two monuments, is a synthesis of assembly hall, temple, and private house. It also has the qualities of an original creation that cannot be wholly explained in terms of its sources. What it owes to the Imperial basilicas of pagan times becomes obvious when we compare the plan of St. Peter's with that of the basilica at Leptis Magna, erected a hundred years earlier (fig. 274): the long nave flanked by aisles and lit by clerestory windows, the apse, the wooden roof are

familiar features of the earlier structure. The pagan basilica was indeed a uniquely suitable model for Constantinian churches, since it combined the spacious interior demanded by Christian ritual with Imperial associations that proclaimed the privileged status of Christianity as the new state religion.

But a church had to be more than an assembly hall; in addition to enclosing the community of the faithful, it was the sacred House of God, the Christian successor to the temples of old. In order to express this function, the design of the pagan basilica had to be given a new focus, the altar,

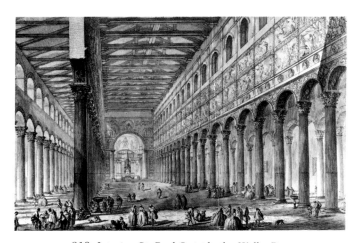

318. Interior, St. Paul Outside the Walls, Rome.
Begun 386 A.D. (etching by G. B. Piranesi, 1749)

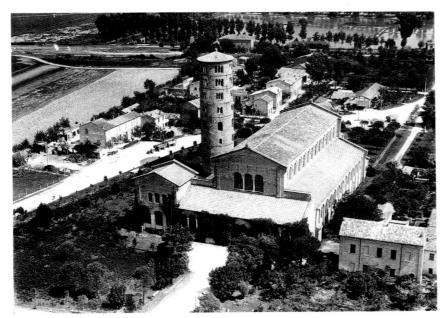

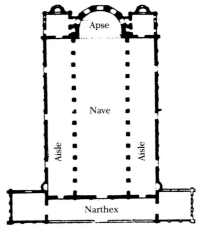

319. S. Apollinare in Classe, Ravenna. 533–49 A.D.

320. Plan of S. Apollinare in Classe
(after De Angelis d'Ossat)

which was placed in front of the apse at the eastern end of the nave, and the entrances, which in pagan basilicas had usually been on the flanks, were shifted to the western end. The Christian basilica was thus oriented along a single, longitudinal axis that is curiously reminiscent of the layout of Egyptian temples (compare fig. 97). Before entering the church proper, we traverse a colonnaded court, the atrium (see page 226), the far side of which forms an entrance hall, the narthex. Only when we step through the nave portal do we gain the view presented in figure 318. The steady rhythm of the nave arcade pulls us toward the great arch at the eastern end (called the triumphal arch), which frames the altar and the vaulted apse beyond. As we come closer, we realize that the altar stands in a separate compartment of space placed at right angles to the nave and aisles, the transept (in the lesser basilican churches, this feature is frequently omitted).

One essential aspect of Early Christian religious architecture has not yet emerged from our discussion: the contrast between exterior and interior. It is strikingly demonstrated in the sixth-century church of S. Apollinare in Classe near Ravenna, which still retains its original appearance for the most part. The plain brick exterior (figs. 319 and 320) remains conspicuously unadorned; it is merely a shell whose shape reflects the interior space it encloses—the exact opposite of the Classical temple. (Our view, taken from the west, shows the narthex but not the atrium, which was torn down a long time ago; the round bell tower, or campanile, is a medieval addition.) This ascetic, antimonumental treatment of the exterior gives way to the utmost richness as we enter the church (fig. 321). Here, having left the everyday world behind, we find ourselves in a shimmering realm of light and color where precious marble surfaces and the brilliant glitter of mosaics evoke the spiritual splendor of the Kingdom of God.

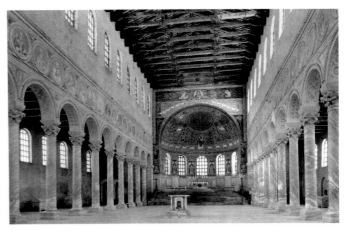

321. Interior (view toward the apse),
S. Apollinare in Classe, Ravenna. 533–49 A.D.

DOMED STRUCTURES. Before dealing with these mosaic decorations at greater length, we must take note of another type of structure that entered the tradition of Christian architecture in Constantinian times: round or polygonal buildings crowned with a dome. They had been developed, we will recall, as part of the elaborate Roman baths; the design of the Pantheon was derived from that source (see page 224). Similar structures had been built to serve as monumental tombs, or mausoleums, by the pagan emperors. In the fourth century, this type of building is given a Christian meaning in the baptisteries (where the bath becomes a sacred rite) and the funerary chapels linked with basilican churches. The finest surviving example is Sta. Costanza (figs. 322–24), the mausoleum of Constantine's daughter

322. (*opposite*) Interior, Sta. Costanza, Rome. c. 350 A.D.

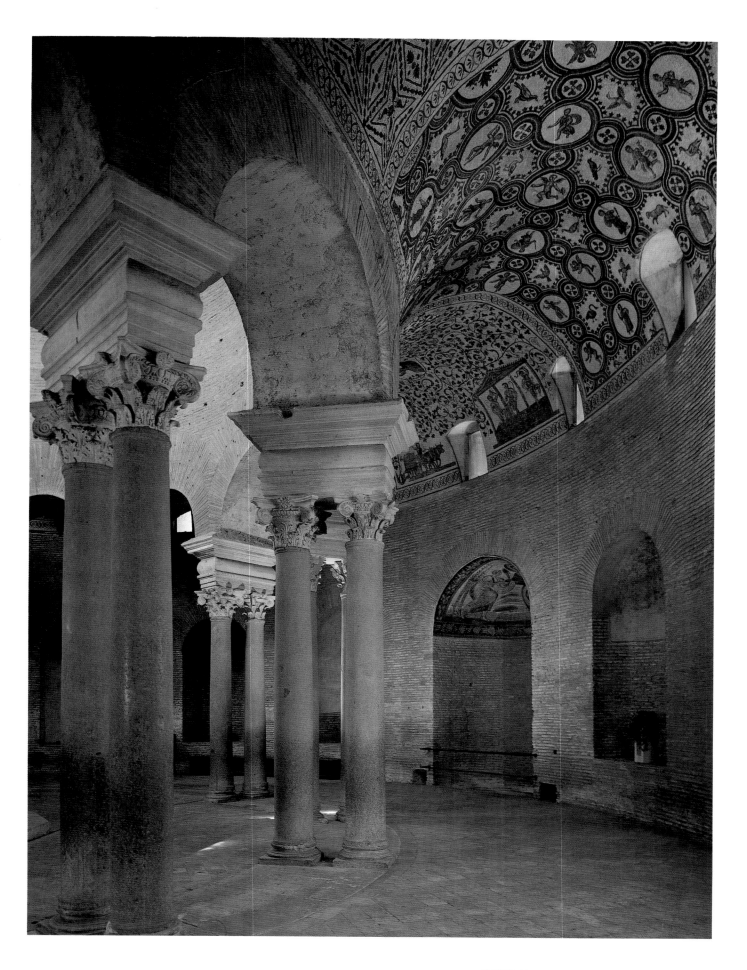

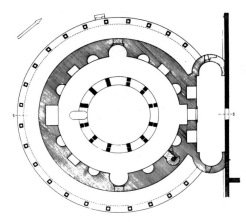

323. Plan of Sta. Costanza

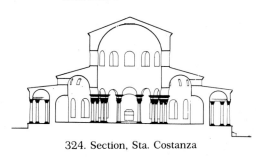

324. Section, Sta. Costanza

Constantia, originally attached to the (now ruined) Roman church of St. Agnes Outside the Walls. In contrast to its pagan predecessors, it shows a clear articulation of the interior space into a domed cyclindrical core lit by clerestory windows—the counterpart of the nave of a basilican church—and a ring-shaped "aisle" or ambulatory covered by a barrel vault. Here again the mosaic decoration plays an essential part in setting the mood of the interior.

## Painting and Mosaic

The rapid growth of Christian architecture on a large scale must have had an almost revolutionary effect on the development of Early Christian painting. All of a sudden, huge wall surfaces had to be covered with images worthy of their monumental framework. Who was equal to this challenge? Certainly not the humble artists who had decorated the catacombs with their limited stock of types and subjects. They were superseded by masters of greater ability, recruited, we may suppose, under Imperial auspices, as were the architects of the new basilicas. Unfortunately, so little has survived of the decoration of fourth-century churches that its history cannot be traced in detail. Apparently, great pictorial cycles were spread over the nave walls, the triumphal arch, and the apse from the very start. These cycles must have drawn upon a great variety of earlier sources, reflecting the whole range of Graeco-Roman painting. The heritage of the past, however, was not only absorbed but transformed so as to make it fit its new environment, physical and spiritual.

WALL MOSAICS. Out of this process, there emerged a great new art form, the Early Christian wall mosaic, which to a large extent replaced the older and cheaper technique of mural painting. Mosaics—designs composed of small pieces of colored material set in plaster—had been used by the Sumerians as early as the third millennium B.C. to embellish architectural surfaces. The Hellenistic Greeks and the Romans, employing small cubes of marble called tesserae, had refined the technique to the point that it could reproduce paintings, as in *The Battle of Issus* (see fig. 302). But these were mostly floor mosaics, and the color scale, although rich in gradations, lacked brilliance, since it was limited to the various kinds of colored marble found in nature. The Romans would also produce wall mosaics occasionally, but only for special purposes and on a limited scale.

The vast and intricate wall mosaics of Early Christian art thus are essentially without precedent. The same is true of their material, for they consist of tesserae made of colored glass. These, too, were not entirely unknown to the Romans, yet their special virtues had never been exploited before; they offered colors of far greater range and intensity than marble tesserae, including gold, but lacked the fine gradations in tone necessary for imitating painted pictures. Moreover, the shiny (and slightly irregular) faces of glass tesserae act as tiny reflectors, so that the over-all effect is that of a glittering, immaterial screen rather than of a solid, continuous surface. All these qualities made glass mosaic the ideal complement of the new architectural aesthetic that confronts us in Early Christian basilicas.

CONTRASTS WITH GRAECO-ROMAN PAINTING. The guiding principle of Graeco-Roman architecture, we recall, had been to express a balance of opposing forces, rather like the balance within the *contrapposto* of a classical statue—a muscular, physical display of active and passive, supporting and supported members, whether these were structurally real or merely superimposed on a concrete core. Viewed in such terms, Early Christian architecture is strangely inexpressive, even antimonumental. The tangible, material structure has become subservient to the creation and definition of immaterial space; walls and vaults have the quality of weightless shells, their actual thickness and solidity hidden rather than emphasized as before. The brilliant color, the light-filled, transparent brightness of gold, the severe geometric order of the images in a mosaic complex such as that of S. Apollinare in Classe (fig. 321) fit the spirit of these interiors to perfection. One might say, in fact, that Early Christian and Byzantine churches *demand* mosaics the way Greek temples demand architectural sculpture.

Roman mural painting had developed elaborate illusionistic devices in order to suggest a reality beyond the surface of the wall. In Early Christian mosaics the flatness of the wall surface is also denied, but for the purpose of achieving an "illusion of unreality," a luminous realm peopled by celestial beings or symbols. The difference in aim becomes particularly striking whenever these mosaics make use of the old formulas of spatial illusionism. Such is the case in figure 325, which shows a section of the magnificent dome mosaics from the church of St. George at Salonica, done at the end of the fourth century. Two saints, their hands raised in prayer, stand against a background that clearly betrays its descent from the perspective vistas of "stage architecture"

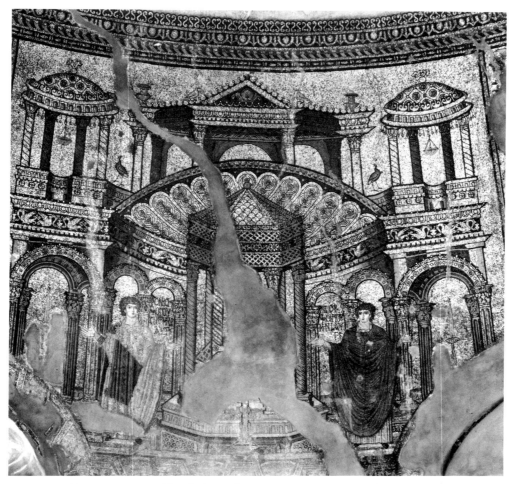

325. Dome mosaic (detail). Late 4th century A.D. St. George, Salonica, Greece

in Pompeian painting; the foreshortening, to be sure, seems somewhat askew, but a surprising amount of it survives intact. Even so, the structure no longer seems real, for it lacks all physical substance: its body consists of the same gold as the background (other colors, mainly purple, blue, and green, are used only in the shaded portions and the ornament), so that the entire building becomes translucent. This is not a stage set but a piece of symbolic, otherworldly architecture meant to evoke such concepts as the Heavenly Jerusalem, or the City of God.

STA. MARIA MAGGIORE, ROME. In narrative scenes, too, we see the illusionistic tradition of ancient painting being transformed by new content. Long sequences of scenes, selected from the Old and New Testaments, adorned the nave walls of Early Christian basilicas. *The Parting of Lot and Abraham* (fig. 326) is taken from the oldest surviving cycle of this kind, executed about 430 in the church of Sta. Maria Maggiore in Rome. Abraham, his son Isaac, and the rest of his family occupy the left half of the composition; Lot and his clan, including his two small daughters, turn toward the city of Sodom on the right.

The task of the artist who designed our panel is comparable to that faced by the sculptors of the Column of Trajan (see fig. 292): how to condense complex actions into a visual

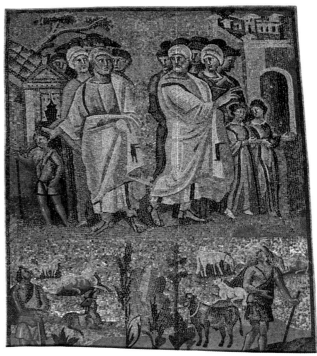

326. *THE PARTING OF LOT AND ABRAHAM*. Mosaic.
c. 430 A.D. Sta. Maria Maggiore, Rome

form that would permit them to be read at a distance. He has, in fact, employed many of the same "shorthand" devices, such as the abbreviative formulas for house, tree, and city, or the trick of showing a crowd of people as a "grape-cluster of heads" behind the foreground figures. But in the Trajanic reliefs, these devices could be used only to the extent that they were compatible with the realistic aim of the scenes, which re-create actual historic events. "Look, this is what happened in the Dacian wars," we are told. The mosaics in Sta. Maria Maggiore, on the other hand, depict the history of salvation; the reality they illustrate is the living word of the Scriptures (in our instance, Genesis 13), which is a *present* reality shared by artist and beholder alike, rather than something that happened only once in the space-and-time context of the external world.

Our panel does not tell us, "This is what happened in Genesis 13" (we are expected to know that already), but "Behold the working of the Lord's will." Hence the artist need not clothe the scene with the concrete details of historic narrative; glances and gestures are becoming more important to him than dramatic movement or three-dimensional form. The symmetrical composition, with its cleavage in the center, makes clear the symbolic significance of this parting: the way of Abraham, which is that of righteousness and the Covenant, as against the way of Lot, destined for divine vengeance. And the contrasting fate of the two groups is further emphasized by the juxtaposition of Isaac and the daughters of Lot, whose future roles are thus called to mind.

## Roll, Book, and Illustration

From what source did the designers of narrative mosaic cycles such as that of Sta. Maria Maggiore derive their compositions? Were they the first to illustrate scenes from the Bible in extensive fashion? For certain subjects, they could have found models among the catacomb murals, but their most important prototypes may have come from illustrated manuscripts, especially of the Old Testament. As a scriptural religion, founded on the Word of God as revealed in Holy Writ, the early Christian Church must have sponsored the duplicating of the sacred text on a vast scale; and every copy of it was handled with a reverence quite unlike the treatment of any book in Graeco-Roman civilization. But when did these copies become works of pictorial art as well? And what did the earliest Bible illustrations look like?

Books, unfortunately, are frail things; thus, their history in the ancient world is known to us largely from indirect evidence. It begins in Egypt—we do not know exactly when—with the discovery of a suitable material, paperlike but rather more brittle, made from the papyrus plant. Books of papyrus were in the form of rolls; they remained in use throughout antiquity. Not until late Hellenistic times did a better substance become available: parchment or vellum, thin, bleached animal hide, far more durable than papyrus. It was strong enough to be creased without breaking, and thus made possible the kind of bound book we know today, technically called a codex.

Between the first and the fourth century A.D., the vellum codex gradually replaced the roll, whether vellum or papyrus. This technological change must have had an important effect on the growth of book illustration. As long as the roll form prevailed, illustrations seem to have been mostly line drawings, since layers of pigment would soon have cracked and come off in the process of rolling and unrolling; only the vellum codex permitted the use of rich colors, including gold, that was to make book illustration—or, as we usually say, illumination—the small-scale counterpart of murals, mosaics, and panel pictures. When, where, and at what pace the development of pictorial book illumination took place, whether biblical or classical subjects were primarily depicted, how much of a carry-over there might have been from roll to codex—all these are still unsettled problems.

VATICAN VERGIL. There can be little question, however, that the earliest illuminations, whether Christian, Jewish, or pagan, were done in a style strongly influenced by the illusionism of Hellenistic-Roman painting of the sort we met at Pompeii. One of the oldest illustrated manuscript books known, the *Vatican Vergil,* probably made in Italy about the time of the Sta. Maria Maggiore mosaics, reflects this tradition, although the quality of the miniatures is far from inspired (fig. 327); the picture, separated from the rest of the page by a heavy frame, has the effect of a window, and in the landscape we find remnants of deep space, perspective, and the play of light and shade.

The oldest illustrated Bible manuscripts so far discovered apparently belong to the early sixth century (except for one fragment of five leaves that seems related to the *Vatican Vergil*); they, too, contain echoes of the Hellenistic-Roman style, in various stages of adaptation to religious narrative, often with a Near Eastern flavor that at times recalls the Dura-Europos murals (see fig. 314).

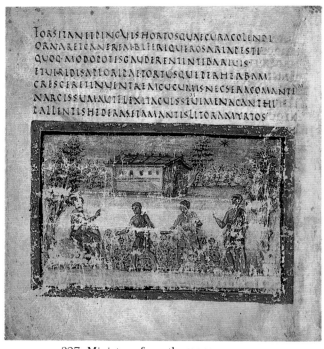

327. Miniature from the *VATICAN VERGIL.*
Early 5th century A.D. Biblioteca Apostolica Vaticana, Rome

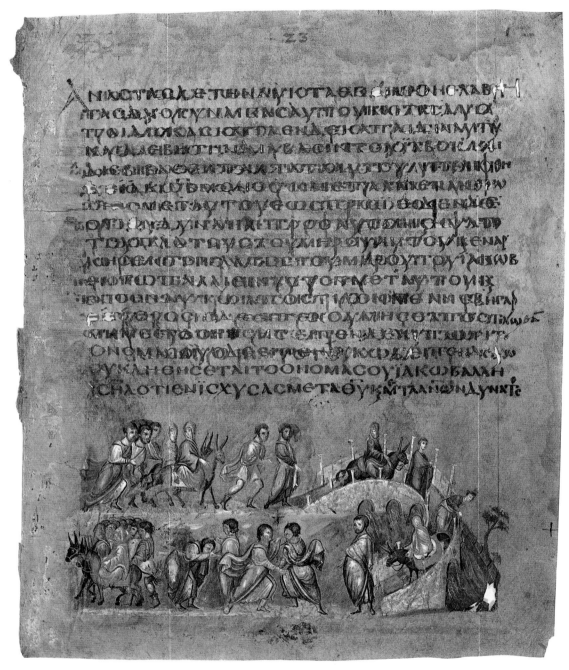

328. Page with *JACOB WRESTLING THE ANGEL,* from the *VIENNA GENESIS.* Early 6th century A.D. 13¼ × 9½″ (33.6 × 24 cm). Österreichische Nationalbibliothek, Vienna

VIENNA GENESIS. The most important example, the *Vienna Genesis,* is a far more striking work than the *Vatican Vergil.* Written in silver (now turned black) on purple vellum and adorned with brilliantly colored miniatures, it achieves a sumptuous effect not unlike that of the mosaics we have seen. Figure 328 shows a part of the story of Jacob; in the foreground, we see him wrestling with the angel and receiving the angel's benediction. The picture, then, does not show a single event but a whole sequence, strung out along a single U-shaped path, so that progression in space becomes progression in time. This method, known as continuous narration, has a complex—and much debated—history going back as far as ancient Egypt and Mesopotamia; its appearance in miniatures such as ours may reflect earlier illustrations made for books in roll form. (Our picture certainly looks like a frieze turned back upon itself.)

For manuscript illustration, the continuous method offers the advantage of spatial economy; it permits the painter to pack a maximum of narrative content into the area at his disposal. Our artist apparently thought of his picture as a running account to be read like lines of text, rather than as a window demanding a frame. The painted forms are placed directly on the purple background that holds the letters, emphasizing the importance of the page as a unified field.

## Sculpture

Compared to painting and architecture, sculpture played a secondary role in Early Christian art. The biblical prohibition of graven images was thought to apply with particular force to large cult statues, the idols worshiped in pagan temples; if religious sculpture was to avoid the pagan taint of idolatry, it had to eschew lifesize representations of the human figure. It thus developed from the very start in an anti-monumental direction: away from the spatial depth and massive scale of Graeco-Roman sculpture toward shallow, small-scale forms and lacelike surface decoration. The earliest works of Christian sculpture are marble sarcophagi, which were produced from the middle of the third century on for the more important members of the Church. Before the time of Constantine, their decoration consisted mostly of the same limited repertory of themes familiar from catacomb murals—the Good Shepherd, Jonah and the Whale, and so forth—but within a framework borrowed from pagan sarcophagi. Not until a century later do we find a significantly broader range of subject matter and form.

SARCOPHAGUS OF JUNIUS BASSUS. A key example for those years is the richly carved *Sarcophagus of Junius Bassus*, a prefect of Rome, who died in 359 (figs. 329 and 330). Its colonnaded front, divided into ten square compartments, shows a mixture of Old and New Testament scenes: in the upper row (left to right), the Sacrifice of Isaac, St. Peter Taken Prisoner, Christ Enthroned between SS. Peter and Paul, Christ before Pontius Pilate (two compartments); in the lower, the Misery of Job, the Fall of Man, Christ's Entry into Jerusalem, Daniel in the Lions' Den, and St. Paul Led to His Martyrdom. This choice, somewhat strange to the modern beholder, is highly characteristic of the Early Christian way of thinking, which stresses the divine rather than the human nature of Christ. Hence His suffering and death are merely hinted at; He appears before Pilate as a youthful, long-haired philosopher expounding the true wisdom (note the scroll), and the martyrdom of the two apostles is represented in the same discreet, nonviolent fashion. The two central scenes are devoted to Christ the King: as Ruler of the Universe He sits enthroned above the personification of the firmament, and as an earthly sovereign He enters Jerusalem in triumph. Adam and Eve, the original sinners, denote the burden of guilt redeemed by Christ, the Sacrifice of Isaac is the Old Testament prefiguration of Christ's sacrificial death, while Job and Daniel carry the same message as Jonah— they fortify the hope of salvation.

When measured against the anti-Classical style of the frieze on the Arch of Constantine, carved almost half a century before (see fig. 301), the *Sarcophagus of Junius Bassus* seems decidedly classicistic. The figures in their deeply recessed niches betray a conscious attempt to recapture the statuesque dignity of the Greek tradition. Yet beneath this superimposed quality we sense a basic kinship to the Constantinian style in the doll-like bodies, the large heads, the oddly becalmed, passive air of scenes calling for dramatic action. The events and personages confronting us are no longer intended to tell their own story, physically or emotionally, but to call to our minds a higher, symbolic meaning that binds them together.

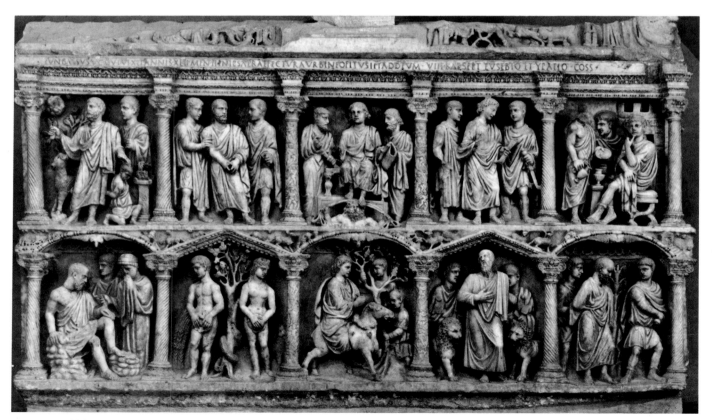

329. *SARCOPHAGUS OF JUNIUS BASSUS.* c. 359 A.D. Marble, 3'10½" × 8' (1.2 × 2.4 m). Museo Petriano, St. Peter's, Rome

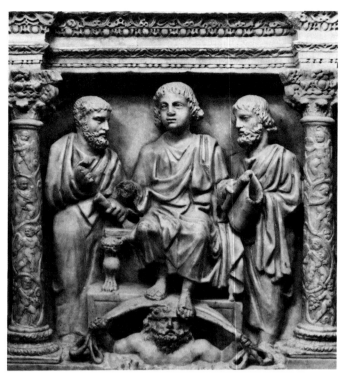

330. *CHRIST ENTHRONED* (detail of fig. 329)

CLASSICISM. Classicizing tendencies of this sort seem to have been a recurrent phenomenon in Early Christian sculpture from the mid-fourth to the early sixth century. Their causes have been explained in various ways. On the one hand, during this period paganism still had many important adherents who may have fostered such revivals as a kind of rear-guard action; recent converts (such as Junius Bassus himself, who was not baptized until shortly before his death) often kept their allegiance to values of the past, artistic and otherwise. There were also important leaders of the Church who favored a reconciliation of Christianity with the heritage of Classical antiquity; the imperial courts, too, both East and West, always remained aware of their institutional links with pre-Christian times, and could thus become centers for revivalist impulses. Whatever its roots in any given instance, classicism had its virtues in this age of transition, for it preserved—and thus helped to transmit to the future—a treasury of forms and an ideal of beauty that might have been irretrievably lost without it.

IVORY DIPTYCHS. All this holds true particularly for a class of objects whose artistic importance far exceeds their physical size: the ivory panels and other small-scale reliefs in precious materials. Designed for private ownership and meant to be enjoyed at close range, they often mirror a collector's taste, a refined aesthetic sensibility not found among the large, official enterprises sponsored by Church or State. Such a piece is the ivory leaf (fig. 331) forming the right half of a hinged diptych that was carved about 390–400, probably on the occasion of a wedding among the Nicomachi and

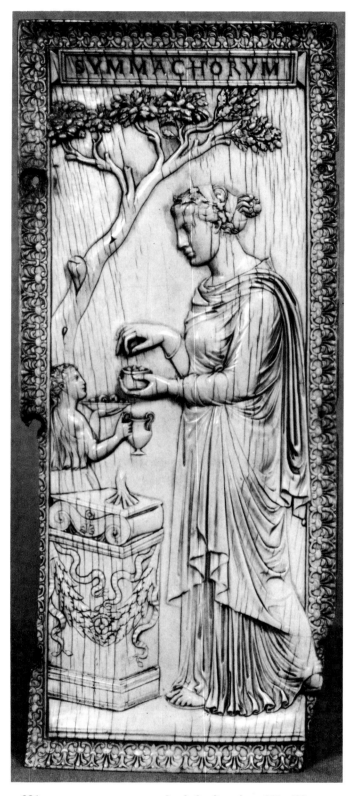

331. *PRIESTESS OF BACCHUS*. Leaf of a diptych. c. 390–400 A.D. Ivory, 11¾ × 5½" (30 × 14 cm). Victoria & Albert Museum, London (Crown copyright reserved)

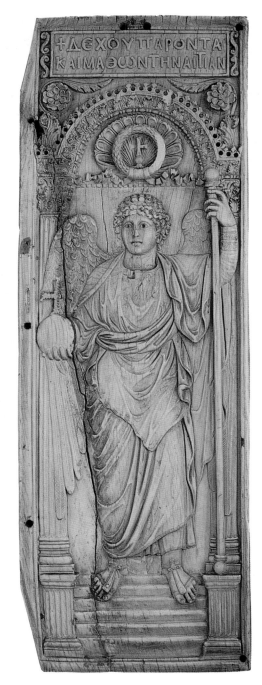

332. *THE ARCHANGEL MICHAEL*. Leaf of a diptych.
Early 6th century A.D. Ivory, 17 × 5½″ (43.3 × 14 cm).
British Museum, London

many centuries later; its cool perfection had an appeal for the Middle Ages as well.

Our second ivory (fig. 332), done soon after 500 in the eastern Roman Empire, shows a classicism that has become an eloquent vehicle of Christian content. The majestic archangel is clearly a descendant of the winged Victories of Graeco-Roman art, down to the richly articulated drapery. Yet the power he heralds is not of this world; nor does he inhabit an earthly space. The architectural niche against which he appears has lost all three-dimensional reality; its relationship to him is purely symbolic and ornamental, so that he seems to hover rather than to stand (notice the position of the feet on the steps). It is this disembodied quality, conveyed through classically harmonious forms, that gives him so compelling a presence.

PORTRAITURE. If monumental statuary was discouraged by the Church, it retained, for a while at least, the patronage of the State. Emperors, consuls, and high officials continued the old custom of erecting portrait statues of themselves in public places as late as the reign of Justinian, and sometimes later than that (the last recorded instance is in the late eighth century). Here, too, we find retrospective tendencies during the latter half of the fourth century and the early years of the fifth, with a revival of pre-Constantinian types and a renewed interest in individual characterization. From about 450 on, however, the outward likeness gives way to the image of a spiritual ideal, sometimes intensely expressive, but increasingly impersonal; there were not to be any more portraits, in the Graeco-Roman sense of the term, for almost a thousand years to come.

Symmachi, two aristocratic Roman families. Their conservative outlook is reflected not only in the pagan subject (a priestess of Bacchus and her assistant before an altar of Jupiter) but also in the design, which harks back to the era of Augustus (compare fig. 286). At first glance, we might well mistake it for a much earlier work, until we realize, from small spatial incongruities such as the priestess' right foot overlapping the frame, that these forms are quotations, reproduced with loving care but no longer fully understood. Significantly enough, the pagan theme did not prevent our panel from being incorporated into the shrine of a saint

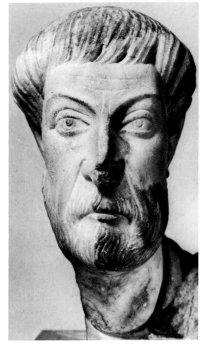

333. *PORTRAIT OF EUTROPIOS*. c. 450 A.D. Marble,
height 12½″ (31.7 cm). Kunsthistorisches Museum, Vienna

The process is strikingly exemplified by the head of Eutropios from Ephesus (fig. 333), one of the most memorable of its kind. It reminds us of the strangely sorrowful features of "Plotinus" (see fig. 298) and of the masklike colossal head of Constantine (see fig. 299), but both of these have a physical concreteness that seems almost gross compared to the extreme attentuation of Eutropios. The face is frozen in visionary ecstasy, as if the sitter were a hermit saint; it looks, in fact, more like that of a specter than of a being of flesh and blood. The avoidance of solid volumes has been carried so far that the features are for the most part indicated only by thin ridges or shallow engraved lines. Their smooth curves emphasize the elongated oval of the head and thus reinforce its abstract, otherworldly character. Not only the individual person but the human body itself has ceased to be a tangible reality here; and with that the Greek tradition of sculpture in the round has reached the end of the road.

# BYZANTINE ART

There is no clear-cut line of demarcation between Early Christian and Byzantine art. It could be argued that a Byzantine style (that is, a style associated with the imperial court of Constantinople) becomes discernible within Early Christian art as early as the beginning of the fifth century, soon after the effective division of the Empire. We have avoided making this distinction, for East Roman and West Roman—or, as some scholars prefer to call them, Eastern and Western Christian—characteristics are often difficult to separate before the sixth century. Until that time, both areas contributed to the development of Early Christian art, al-though the leadership tended to shift more and more to the East as the position of the West declined. During the reign of Justinian (527–565) this shift was completed; Constantinople not only reasserted its political dominance over the West but became the undisputed artistic capital as well. Justinian himself was an art patron on a scale unmatched since Constantine's day; the works he sponsored or promoted have an Imperial grandeur that fully justifies the acclaim of those who have termed his era a golden age. They also display an inner coherence of style which links them more strongly with the future development of Byzantine art than with the art of the preceding centuries.

## Architecture and Decoration of the First Golden Age

Ironically enough, the richest array of monuments of the First Golden Age (526–726 A.D.) survives today not in Constantinople (where much has been destroyed) but on Italian soil, in the town of Ravenna. Originally a naval station on the Adriatic, it had become the capital of the West Roman emperors in 402 and, at the end of the century, of Theodoric, king of the Ostrogoths, whose tastes were patterned after those of Constantinople. Under Justinian, Ravenna was the main stronghold of Byzantine rule in Italy.

S. VITALE, RAVENNA. The most important church of that time, S. Vitale, built in 526–547, is of a type derived mainly from Constantinople. We recognize its octagonal plan, with the domed central core (figs. 334–37), as a descendant of the mausoleum of Sta. Costanza in Rome (see figs. 322–24), but the intervening development seems to have taken place

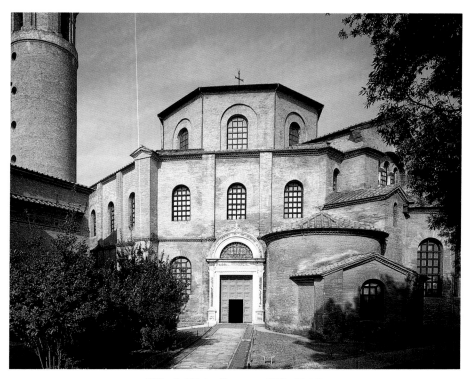

334. S. Vitale, Ravenna, 526–47 A.D.

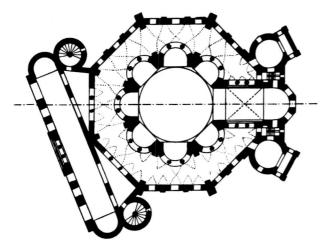

335. Plan of S. Vitale

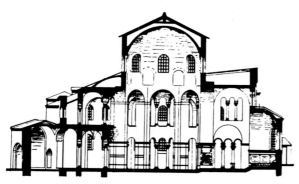

336. Transverse section of S. Vitale

may be relevant, yet, if the truth be told, they fall short of a really persuasive explanation. In any event, from the time of Justinian, domed, central-plan churches were to dominate the world of Orthodox Christianity as thoroughly as the basilican plan dominated the architecture of the medieval West.

As for S. Vitale, its link with the Byzantine court is evidenced by the two famous mosaics flanking the altar (figs. 338 and 339), whose design must have come directly from the Imperial workshop. Here Justinian and his empress, Theodora, accompanied by officials, the local clergy, and ladies-in-waiting, attend the service as if this were a palace chapel. In these large panels, made shortly before the consecration of the church, we find an ideal of human beauty quite distinct from the squat, large-headed figures we encountered in the art of the fourth and fifth centuries; occasionally (figs. 315, 331 and 332) we had caught a glimpse of this emerging new ideal, but only now do we see it complete: extraordinarily tall, slim figures, with tiny feet, small al-

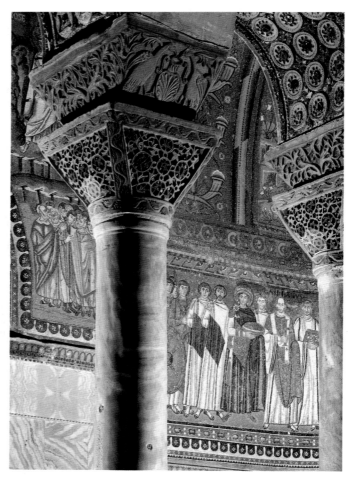

337. (above) Interior (view from the apse into the choir), S. Vitale

338. (opposite top) EMPEROR JUSTINIAN AND HIS ATTENDANTS. Mosaic. c. 547 A.D. S. Vitale

339. (opposite bottom) EMPRESS THEODORA AND HER ATTENDANTS. Mosaic. c. 547 A.D. S. Vitale

in the East, where domed churches of various kinds had been built during the previous century. Compared to Sta. Costanza, S. Vitale is both larger in scale and very much richer in its spatial effect; below the clerestory, the nave wall turns into a series of semicircular niches that penetrate into the aisle and thus link it to the nave in a new and intricate way. The aisle itself has been given a second story (the galleries were reserved for women). A new economy in the construction of the vaulting permits large windows on every level, which flood the interior with light. We find only the merest remnants of the longitudinal axis of the Early Christian basilica: a cross-vaulted compartment for the altar, backed by an apse, toward the east, and a narthex on the other side (its odd, nonsymmetrical placement has never been fully accounted for).

Remembering S. Apollinare in Classe (see figs. 319–21), built at the same time on a straightforward basilican plan, we are particularly struck by the alien character of S. Vitale. How did it happen that the East favored a type of church building (as distinct from baptisteries and mausoleums) so radically different from the basilica and—from the Western point of view—so ill-adapted to Christian ritual? After all, had not the design of the basilica been backed by the authority of Constantine himself? Many different reasons have been suggested—practical, religious, political. All of them

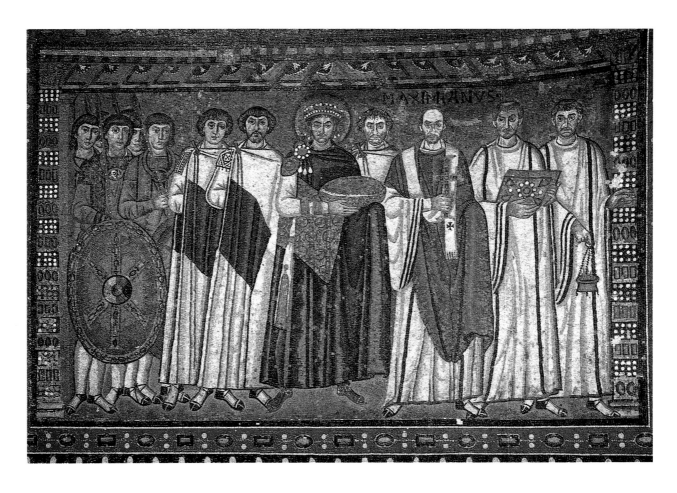

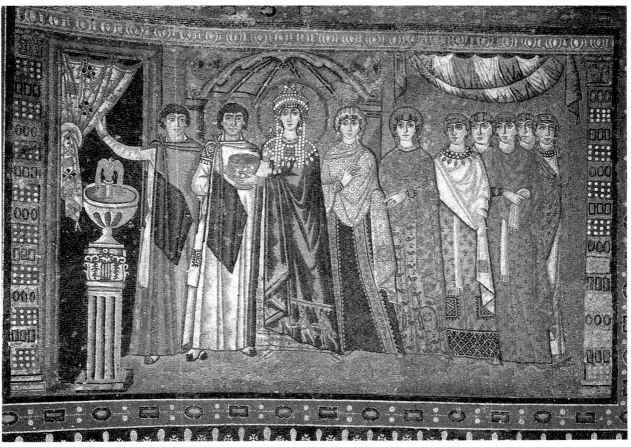

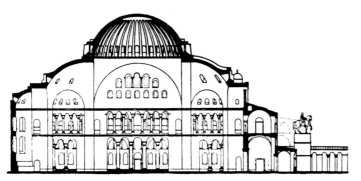

340. Section of Hagia Sophia. 532–35 A.D. (after Gurlitt)

341. Plan of Hagia Sophia (after v. Sybel)

mond-shaped faces dominated by their huge, staring eyes, and bodies that seem to be capable only of slow ceremonial gestures and the display of magnificently patterned costumes. Every hint of movement or change is carefully excluded—the dimensions of time and earthly space have given way to an eternal present amid the golden translucency of Heaven, and the solemn, frontal images seem to present a celestial rather than a secular court. This union of political and spiritual authority accurately reflects the "divine kingship" of the Byzantine emperor. We are, in fact, invited to see Justinian and Theodora as analogous to Christ and the Virgin: on the hem of Theodora's mantle (just visible in figure 339) is conspicuous embroidery showing the three Magi carrying their gifts to Mary and the newborn King; and Justinian is flanked by twelve companions—the Imperial equivalent of the twelve apostles (six are soldiers, crowded behind a shield with the monogram of Christ).

If we turn from these mosaics to the interior space of the church, we discover that it, too, shares the quality of dematerialized, soaring slenderness that endows the figures with their air of mute exaltation. Justinian, Theodora, and their immediate neighbors were surely intended to be individual likenesses, and their features are indeed differentiated to a degree (those of the archbishop, Maximianus, more so than the rest), but the ideal type has molded the faces as well as the bodies, so that they all have a curious family resemblance. We shall meet the same large dark eyes under curved brows, the same small mouths and long, narrow, slightly aquiline noses countless times from now on in Byzantine art.

HAGIA SOPHIA, ISTANBUL. Among the surviving monuments of Justinian's reign in Constantinople, the most important by far is Hagia Sophia (the Church of Holy Wisdom), the architectural masterpiece of that age and one of the great creative triumphs of any age (figs. 340–44). Built in 532–537, it achieved such fame that the names of the architects, too, were remembered—Anthemius of Tralles and Isidorus of Miletus. After the Turkish conquest in 1453, it became a mosque (the four minarets were added then) and the mosaic decoration was largely hidden under whitewash. Some of the mosaics were uncovered in our cen-

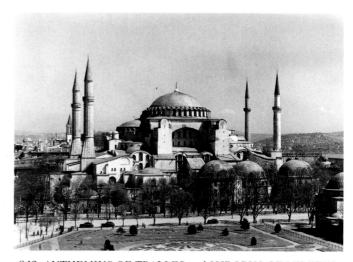

342. ANTHEMIUS OF TRALLES and ISIDORUS OF MILETUS. Hagia Sophia, Istanbul

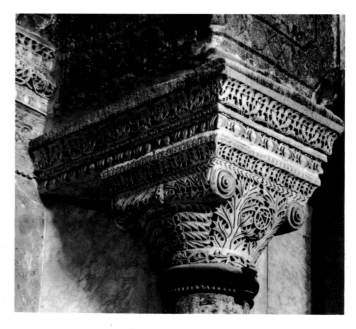

343. (above) Capital, Hagia Sophia

344. (opposite) Interior, Hagia Sophia

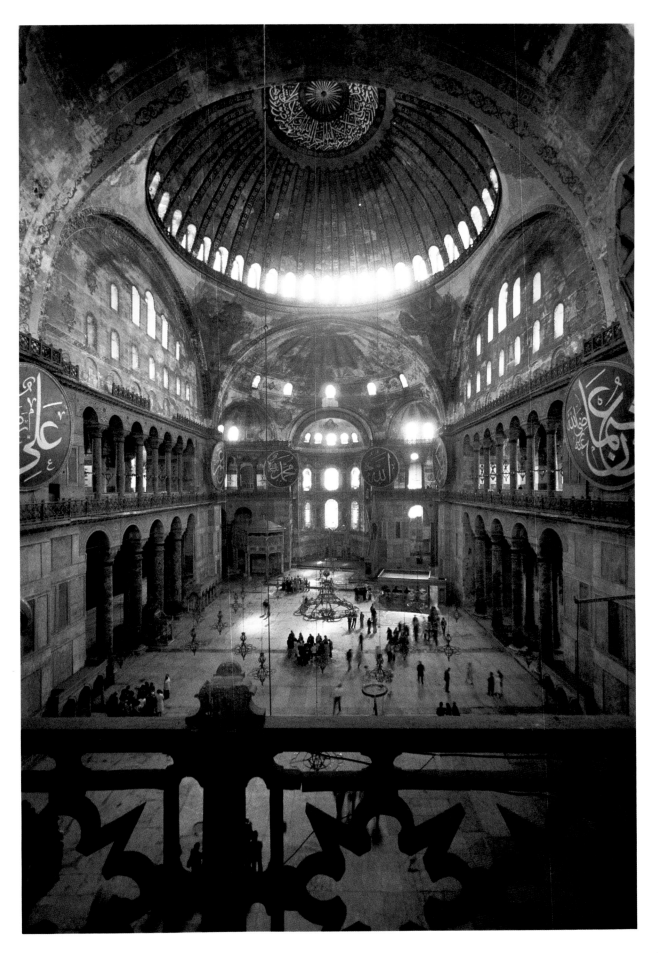

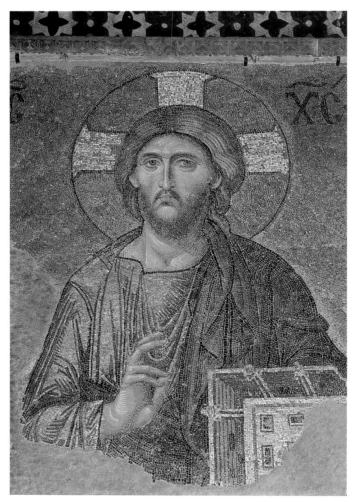

345. *CHRIST,* from *DEËSIS* mosaic. 13th century. Hagia Sophia, Istanbul

tury (fig. 345), since the building was turned into a museum.

The design of Hagia Sophia presents a unique combination of elements: it has the longitudinal axis of an Early Christian basilica, but the central feature of the nave is a square compartment crowned by a huge dome and abutted at either end by half domes, so that the nave becomes a great oval. Attached to these half domes are semicircular niches with open arcades, similar to those in S. Vitale; one might say, then, that the dome of Hagia Sophia has been inserted between the two halves of a central-plan church. The dome rests on four arches that carry its weight to the great piers at the corners of the square, so that the walls below the arches have no supporting function at all. The transition from the square formed by these arches to the circular rim of the dome is achieved by spherical triangles called pendentives (see fig. 269); hence we speak of the entire unit as a dome on pendentives. This device permits the construction of taller, lighter, and more economical domes than the older method (as seen in the Pantheon, Sta. Costanza, and S. Vitale) of placing the dome on a round or polygonal base. Where or when the dome on pendentives was invented we do not know; Hagia Sophia is the earliest case we have of its use on a monumental scale, and its example must have been of epoch-making importance, for from that time on the dome on pendentives became a basic feature of Byzantine architecture and, somewhat later, of Western architecture as well.

There is, however, still another element that entered into the design of Hagia Sophia. The plan, the buttressing of the main piers, and the vast scale of the whole recall the Basilica

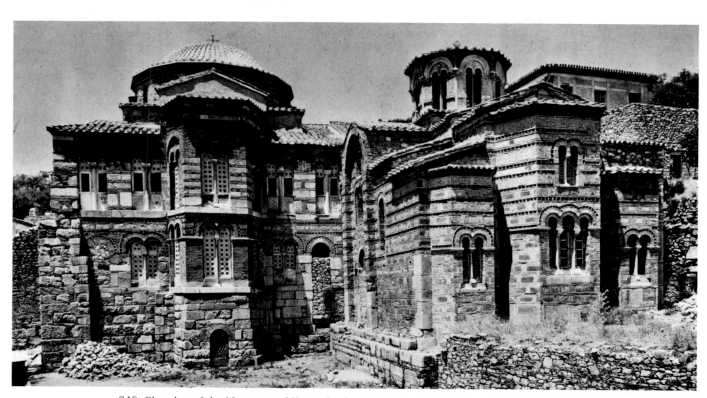

346. Churches of the Monastery of Hosios Loukas (St. Luke of Stiris), Greece. Early 11th century

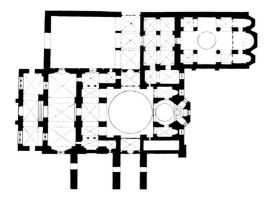

347. Plan of churches of the Monastery of
Hosios Loukas (after Diehl)

cross with arms of equal length) contained in a square, with a narthex added on one side and an apse (sometimes with flanking chapels) on the other. The central feature is a dome on a square base; it often rests on a cylindrical drum with tall windows, which raises it high above the rest of the building, as in both churches of the Monastery of Hosios Loukas in Greece (figs. 346–48). They also show other characteristics of later Byzantine architecture: a tendency toward more elaborate exteriors, in contrast to the extreme severity we observed earlier (compare fig. 334), and a preference for elongated proportions. The full impact of this verticality, however, strikes us only when we enter the church (fig. 348 shows the interior of the Katholikon, on the left in figs. 346 and 347). The tall, narrow space compartments produce a sense of crowdedness, almost of compression, which is dramatically relieved as we raise our glance toward the luminous pool of space beneath the dome.

of Constantine (figs. 270–72), the most ambitious achievement of Imperial Roman vaulted architecture and the greatest monument associated with a ruler for whom Justinian had particular admiration. Hagia Sophia thus unites East and West, past and future, in a single overpowering synthesis. Its massive exterior, firmly planted upon the earth like a great mound, rises by stages to a height of 184 feet—41 feet higher than the Pantheon—and therefore its dome, although its diameter is somewhat smaller (112 feet), stands out far more boldly.

Once we are within, all sense of weight disappears, as if the material, solid aspects of the structure had been banished to the outside; nothing remains but an expanding space that inflates, like so many sails, the apsidal recesses, the pendentives, and the dome itself. Here the architectural aesthetic we saw taking shape in Early Christian architecture (see pages 257–60) has achieved a new, magnificent dimension. Even more than previously, light plays a key role: the dome seems to float—"like the radiant heavens," according to a contemporary description of the building— because it rests upon a closely spaced ring of windows, and the nave walls are pierced by so many openings that they have the transparency of lace curtains.

The golden glitter of the mosaics must have completed the "illusion of unreality." We can sense the new aesthetic even in ornamental details such as moldings and capitals (fig. 343). The motifs—scrolls, acanthus foliage, and such—all derive from classical architecture, but their effect is radically different; instead of actively cushioning the impact of heavy weight upon the shaft of the column, the capital has become a sort of openwork basket whose delicate surface pattern belies the strength and solidity of the stone.

## Architecture and Decoration of the Second Golden Age

Byzantine architecture never produced another structure to match Hagia Sophia. The churches of the Second Golden Age (from the late ninth to the eleventh century) and after were modest in scale, and monastic rather than imperial in spirit. Their usual plan is that of a Greek cross (that is, a

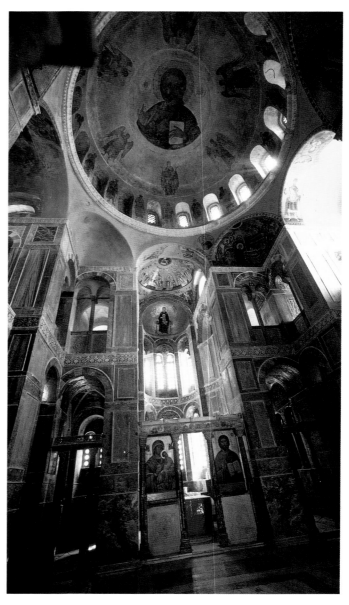

348. Interior, Katholikon, Hosios Loukas

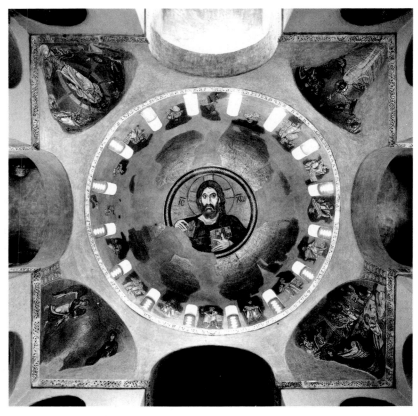

349. Dome mosaics. 11th century.
Monastery Church, Daphnē, Greece

Figure 349 shows this view as it presents itself to us in the Greek monastery church of Daphnē, where the pictorial decoration of the dome is better preserved than in the Katholikon of Hosios Loukas. Staring down from the center of the dome is an awesome mosaic image of Christ the Pantocrator (Ruler of the Universe) against a gold background, its huge scale emphasized by the much smaller figures of the sixteen Old Testament prophets between the windows. In the corners, we see four scenes revealing the divine and human natures of Christ—the Annunciation (bottom left) followed in counterclockwise order by the Birth, Baptism, and Transfiguration. The entire cycle represents a theological program so perfectly in harmony with the geometric relationship of the images that we cannot say whether the architecture has been shaped by the pictorial scheme or vice versa. A similarly strict order governs the distribution of subjects throughout the rest of the interior.

The largest and most lavishly decorated church of the Second Golden Age surviving today is St. Mark's in Venice, begun in 1063. The Venetians had long been under Byzantine sovereignty and remained artistically dependent on the East well after they had become politically and commercially powerful in their own right. St. Mark's, too, has the Greek-cross plan inscribed within a square, but here each arm of the cross is emphasized by a dome of its own (figs. 350 and 351). These domes are not raised on drums; instead, they

have been encased in bulbous wooden helmets covered by gilt copper sheeting and topped by ornate lanterns, to make them appear taller and more conspicuous at a distance. They make a splendid landmark for the seafarer. The spacious interior, famous for its mosaics, shows that it was meant to receive the citizenry of a large metropolis, and not just a small monastic community as at Daphnē or Hosios Loukas.

During the Second Golden Age, Byzantine architecture also spread to Russia, along with the Orthodox faith. There the basic type of the Byzantine church underwent an amazing transformation through the use of wood as a structural material. The most famous product of this native trend is the Cathedral of St. Basil adjoining the Kremlin in Moscow (fig. 352). Built during the reign of Ivan the Terrible, it seems as unmistakably Russian as that extraordinary ruler. The domes, growing in amazing profusion, have become fantastic towerlike structures whose vividly patterned helmets may resemble anything from mushrooms and berries to Oriental turbans. These huge ice-cream cones have the gay unreality of a fairy tale, yet their total effect is oddly impressive; keyed as they are to the imagination of faithful peasants (who must have stared at them in open-mouthed wonder on their rare visits to the capital), they nevertheless convey a sense of the miraculous that is derived from the more austere miracles of Byzantine architecture.

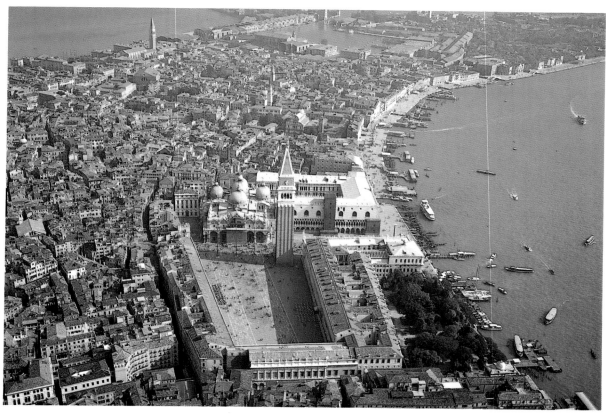

350. St. Mark's (aerial view), Venice. Begun 1063

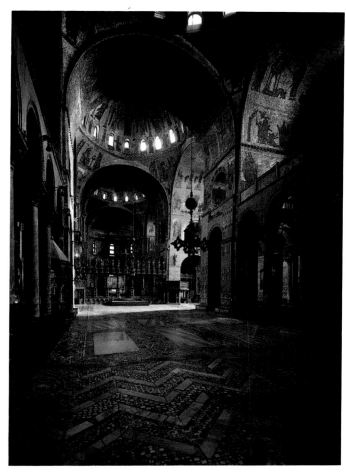

351. Interior, St. Mark's, Venice. Begun 1063

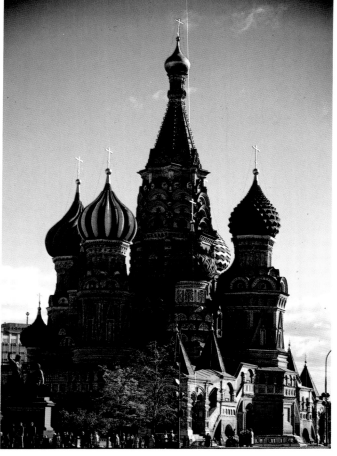

352. Cathedral of St. Basil, Moscow. 1554–60

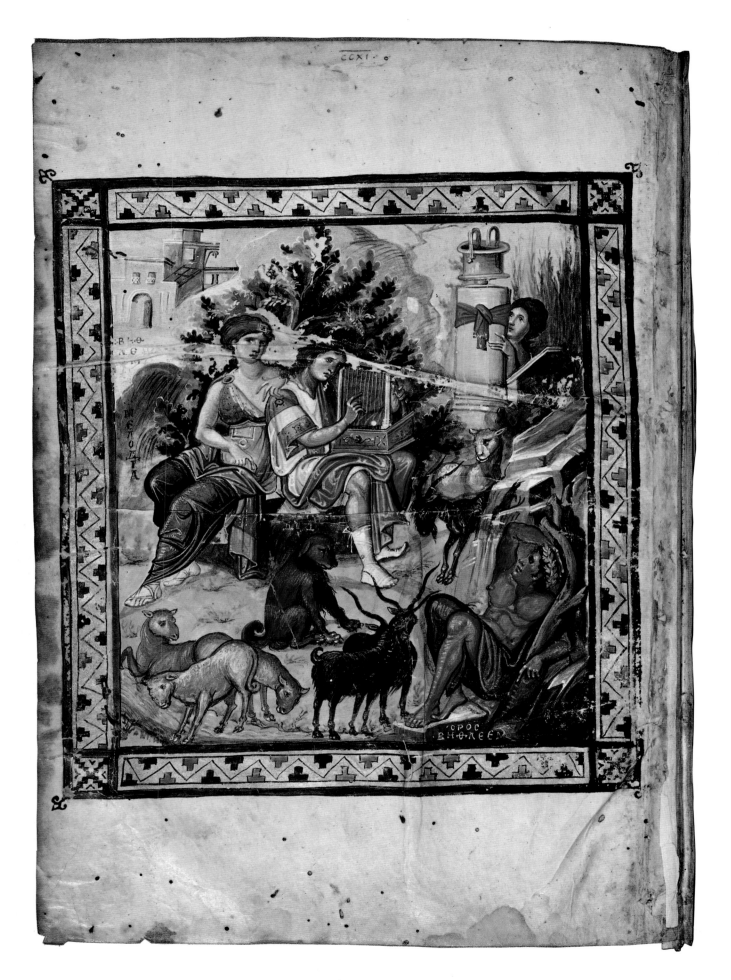

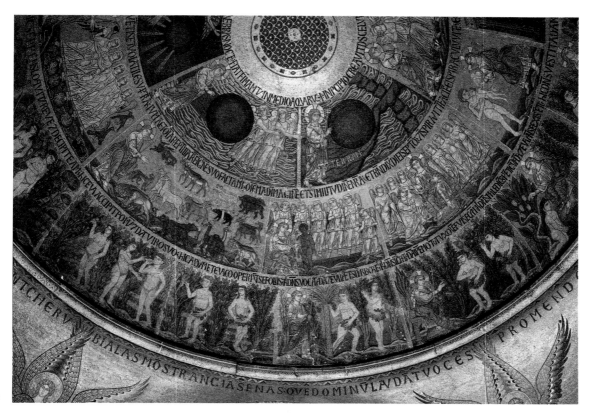

354. Scenes from Genesis. Mosaic. c. 1200. St. Mark's, Venice

ICONOCLASTS AND ICONOPHILES. The development of Byzantine painting and sculpture after the age of Justinian was disrupted by the Iconoclastic Controversy, which began with an Imperial edict of 726 prohibiting religious images. It raged for more than a hundred years, dividing the population into two hostile groups. The image-destroyers (Iconoclasts), led by the emperor and supported mainly in the eastern provinces of the realm, insisted on a literal interpretation of the biblical ban against graven images as conducive to idolatry; they wanted to restrict religious art to abstract symbols and plant or animal forms. Their opponents, the Iconophiles, were led by the monks and centered in the western provinces, where the imperial edict remained ineffective for the most part. The roots of the conflict went very deep: on the plane of theology they involved the basic issue of the relationship of the human and the divine in the person of Christ; socially and politically, they reflected a power struggle between State and Church. The Controversy also marked the final break between Catholicism and the Orthodox faith.

Had the edict been enforceable throughout the Empire, it might well have dealt Byzantine religious art a fatal blow. It did succeed in reducing the production of sacred images very greatly, but failed to wipe it out altogether, so that there was a fairly rapid recovery after the victory of the Icono-

philes in 843. While we know little for certain about how the Byzantine artistic tradition managed to survive from the early eighth to the mid-ninth century, Iconoclasm seems to have brought about a renewed interest in secular art, which was not affected by the ban.

CLASSICAL REVIVAL. This interest may help to explain the astonishing reappearance of Late Classical motifs in the art of the Second Golden Age, as in *David Composing the Psalms* from the so-called *Paris Psalter* (fig. 353). It was probably illuminated about 900, although the temptation to put it earlier is almost irresistible. Not only do we find a landscape that recalls Pompeian murals, but the figures, too, obviously derive from Classical models. David himself could well be mistaken for Orpheus charming the beasts with his music, and his companions prove even more surprising, since they are allegorical figures that have nothing at all to do with the Bible: the young woman next to David is Melody, the one coyly hiding behind a pillar is Echo, and the male figure with a tree trunk personifies the mountains of Bethlehem. The late date of the picture is evident only from certain qualities of style such as the abstract zigzag pattern of the drapery covering Melody's legs.

Another fascinating reflection of an early source is the sequence of scenes from Genesis among the mosaics of St. Mark's in Venice (fig. 354), which must have been adapted from an Early Christian illuminated manuscript. The squat, large-headed figures recall the art of the fourth century, as

353. *(opposite) DAVID COMPOSING THE PSALMS,* from the *Paris Psalter*
c. 900 A.D. 14⅛ × 10¼" (36 × 26 cm). Bibliothèque Nationale, Paris

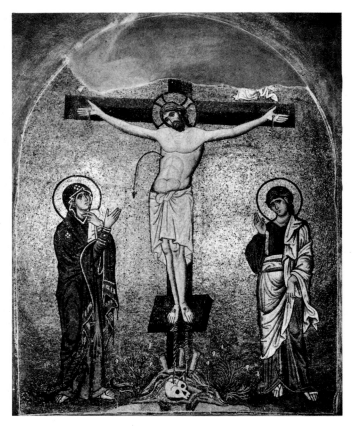

355. *THE CRUCIFIXION*. Mosaic. 11th century.
Monastery Church, Daphnē, Greece

does the classical young philosopher type representing the Lord (compare fig. 330), which had been long since replaced in general usage by the more familiar bearded type (see fig. 349). Of particular interest is the scene in the upper–right-hand corner. Ancient art had visualized the human soul as a tiny nude figure with butterfly wings; here this image reappears—or survives, rather—under Christian auspices as the spirit of life that the Lord breathes into Adam.

The *Paris Psalter* and the Genesis mosaics in St. Mark's betray an almost antiquarian enthusiasm for the traditions of Classical art. Such direct revivals, however, are extreme cases. The finest works of the Second Golden Age show a classicism that has been harmoniously merged with the spiritualized ideal of human beauty we encountered in the art of Justinian's reign. Among these, the *Crucifixion* mosaic at Daphnē (fig. 355) enjoys special fame. Its Classical qualities are more fundamental, and more deeply felt, than those of the *Paris Psalter*, yet are also completely Christian: there is no attempt to re-create a realistic spatial setting, but the composition has a balance and clarity that are truly monumental as against the cluttered Pompeian landscape of the David miniature. Classical, too, is the statuesque dignity of the figures, which seem extraordinarily organic and graceful compared to those of the Justinian mosaics at S. Vitale (figs. 338 and 339).

The most important aspect of these figures' Classical heritage, however, is emotional rather than physical; it is the gentle pathos conveyed by their gestures and facial expressions, a restrained and noble suffering of the kind we first met in Greek art of the fifth century B.C. (see pages 184–87). Early Christian art had been quite devoid of this quality. Its view of Christ stressed the Saviour's divine wisdom and power, rather than His sacrificial death, so that the Crucifixion was depicted only rarely and in a notably unpathetic spirit. The image of the Pantocrator as we saw it on the *Sarcophagus of Junius Bassus* and above the apse of S. Apollinare in Classe (figs. 330 and 321) retained its importance throughout the Second Golden Age—the majestic dome mosaic at Daphnē stems from that tradition—but alongside it we now find a new emphasis on the Christ of the Passion.

When and where this human interpretation of the Saviour made its first appearance we cannot say for sure; it seems to have developed in the wake of the Iconoclastic Controversy. There are few examples of it earlier than the Daphnē *Crucifixion,* and none of them has so powerful an appeal to the emotions of the beholder. To have introduced this compassionate quality into sacred art was perhaps the greatest achievement of the Second Golden Age, even though its full possibilities were to be exploited not in Byzantium but in the medieval West at a later date. Yet Byzantine art, too, preserved and developed the human view of Christ in the centuries to come. The wonderful mosaic fragment from Hagia Sophia (fig. 345), probably of the thirteenth century, no longer has the forbidding severity of the Daphnē *Pantocrator*; instead, we find an expression of gentle melancholy, along with a subtlety of modeling and color that perpetuates the best Classical tradition of the Second Golden Age.

## Late Byzantine Painting

In 1204 Byzantium sustained an almost fatal defeat when the armies of the Fourth Crusade, instead of warring against the Turks, assaulted and took the city of Constantinople. For over fifty years, the core of the Eastern Empire remained in Latin hands. Byzantium, however, survived this catastrophe; in 1261, it once more regained its sovereignty, and the fourteenth century saw a last efflorescence of Byzantine painting, with a distinct and original flavor of its own, before the Turkish conquest in 1453.

Because of the impoverished state of the greatly shrunken Empire, mural painting often took the place of mosaics, as in the recently uncovered wall decoration of a mortuary chapel attached to the Kariye Camii (the former Church of the Saviour in Chora) in Istanbul. From this impressive cycle of pictures, done about 1310–20, we reproduce the *Anastasis* (Greek word for resurrection), in figure 356. The scene actually depicts the event just before the Resurrection—Christ's Descent into Limbo. Surrounded by a radiant gloriole, the Saviour has vanquished Satan and battered down the gates of Hell (note the bound Satan at His feet, in the midst of an incredible profusion of hardware), and is raising

Adam and Eve from the dead. What amazes us about this central group is its dramatic force, a quality we would hardly expect to find on the basis of what we have seen of Byzantine art so far. Christ here moves with extraordinary physical energy, tearing Adam and Eve from their graves, so that they appear to fly through the air—a magnificently expressive image of divine triumph. Such dynamism had been unknown in the earlier Byzantine tradition. Coming in the fourteenth century, it shows that eight hundred years after Justinian, Byzantine art still had its creative powers.

ICONS. During the Iconoclastic Controversy, one of the chief arguments in favor of sacred images was the claim that Christ Himself had permitted St. Luke to paint His portrait, and that other portraits of Christ or of the Virgin had miraculously appeared on earth by divine fiat. These original, "true" sacred images were supposedly the source for the later, man-made ones. Such pictures, or icons, had developed in early Christian times out of Graeco-Roman portrait panels (such as fig. 312). Little is known about their origins, for examples antedating the Iconoclastic Controversy are extremely scarce.

Of the few discovered so far, perhaps the most important is the *Madonna* from Sta. Francesca Romana in Rome, brought to light some years ago by the cleaning of a much-

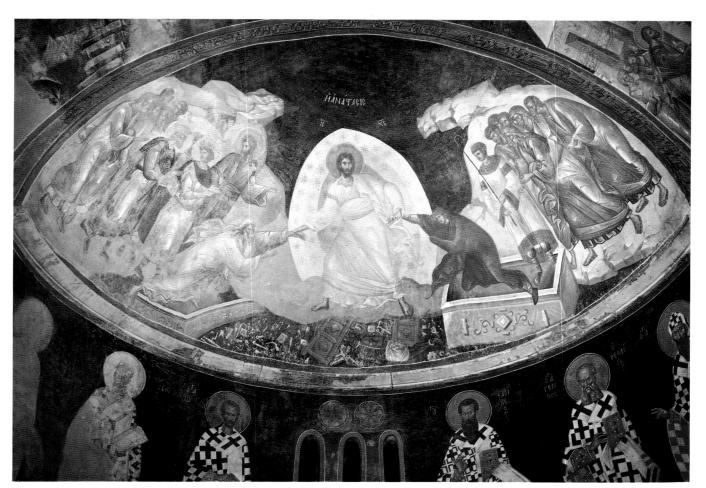

356. *ANASTASIS.* Fresco. c. 1310–20. Kariye Camii (Church of the Saviour in Chora), Istanbul

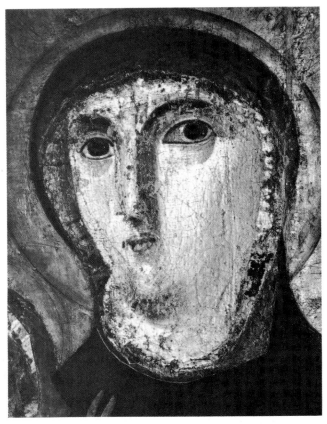

357. *MADONNA* (detail). 6th–7th century A.D.
Encaustic on wood. Sta. Francesca Romana, Rome

repainted panel. Only the Virgin's face still shows the original surface in fair condition (fig. 357). Its link with Graeco-Roman portraiture is evident not only from the painting medium, which is encaustic (see page 251), a technique that went out of use after the Iconoclastic Controversy, but also from the fine gradations of light and shade. The forms themselves, however—the heart-shaped outline of the face, the tiny mouth, the long, narrow nose, the huge eyes under strongly arched brows—reflect an ideal of human beauty as spiritualized as that of the S. Vitale mosaics, while retaining a far higher degree of three-dimensional solidity. What makes this image so singularly impressive is the geometric severity of the design, which endows the features with a monumental grandeur such as we never encounter again in Early Christian or Byzantine art. Where and when was it produced? In the sixth or seventh century, we must assume, but whether in Italy or the East we cannot say, for lack of comparable material. Be that as it may, it is a work of extraordinary power that makes us understand how people came to believe in the superhuman origin of sacred pictures.

Because of the veneration in which they were held, icons had to conform to strict formal rules, with fixed patterns repeated over and over again. As a consequence, the majority of them are more conspicuous for exacting craftsmanship than for artistic inventiveness. The *Madonna Enthroned* (fig. 358) is a work of this kind; although painted in the thirteenth century, it reflects a type of several hundred years earlier. Echoes of the Classicism of the Second Golden Age

abound: the graceful pose, the rich play of drapery folds, the tender melancholy of the Virgin's face, the elaborate, architectural perspective of the throne (which looks rather like a miniature replica of the Colosseum). But all these elements have become oddly abstract. The throne, despite its foreshortening, no longer functions as a three-dimensional object, and the highlights on the drapery resemble ornamental sunbursts, in strange contrast to the soft shading of hands and faces. The total effect is neither flat nor spatial but transparent, somewhat like that of a stained-glass window; the shapes look as if they were lit from behind. And this is almost literally true, for they are painted in a thin film on a highly reflective gold surface that forms the highlights, the halos, and the background, so that even the shadows never seem wholly opaque.

This all-pervading celestial radiance, we will recall, is a quality first encountered in Early Christian mosaics. Panels such as ours, therefore, should be viewed as the aesthetic equivalent, on a smaller scale, of mosaics, and not simply as the descendants of the ancient panel painting tradition. In fact, the most precious Byzantine icons are miniature mosaics done on panels, rather than paintings.

Along with the Orthodox faith, icon painting spread throughout the Balkans and Russia, where it continued to flourish even after the disappearance of the Byzantine Empire. The shifting of the creative impulses within this tradition to the outlying areas of the Orthodox world is signalized by the work of Andrei Rublev, the finest Russian icon painter and a great artist by any standard. Figure 359 shows his famous panel *Old Testament Trinity*, done about 1410–20. (The title refers to the three angels who visited Abraham at Mamre.) Although parts of it are poorly preserved—most of the background has disappeared—the picture reveals a harmonious beauty of design and a depth of lyrical feeling that vie with the most Classical products of the Second Golden Age. Rublev must have been thoroughly acquainted with the best that Byzantine art had to offer, either through contact with Greek painters in Russia or through a sojourn in Constantinople. The most individual element—and also the most distinctively Russian—is the color scale, brighter, more complex, and different in key from that of any Byzantine work. In the hands of a lesser master, such combinations as orange, vermilion, and turquoise might easily have a primitive garishness of the sort we often find in folk art; here, the controlled intensity of these tones is an essential part of the composition.

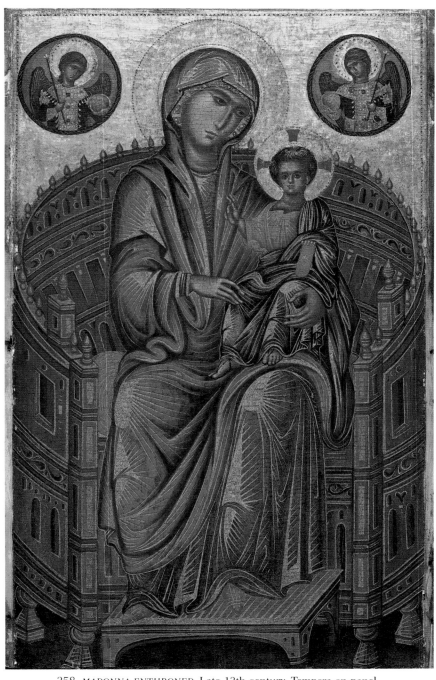

358. *MADONNA ENTHRONED.* Late 13th century. Tempera on panel,
32⅛ × 19⅜″ (81.9 × 49.3 cm). The National Gallery of Art,
Washington, D.C. Andrew Mellon Collection, 1937

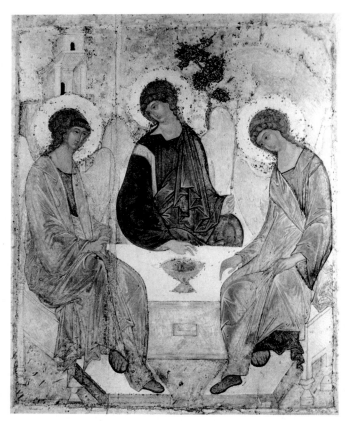

359. ANDREI RUBLEV. *OLD TESTAMENT TRINITY.* c. 1410–20.
Panel, 55½ × 44½″ (141 × 113 cm). Tretyakov Gallery, Moscow

## Sculpture

Monumental sculpture, as we saw earlier, tended to disappear completely from the fifth century on. In Byzantine art, large-scale statuary died out with the last Imperial portraits, and stone carving was confined almost entirely to architectural ornament (see fig. 343). But small-scale reliefs, especially in ivory and metal, continued to be produced throughout the Second Golden Age and beyond.

Their extraordinary variety of content, style, and purpose is suggested by the two samples shown here, both of them dating from the tenth century. One is a triptych—a small portable altar shrine with two hinged wings—of the kind a high dignitary might carry for his private devotions while traveling (fig. 360); in the upper half of the center panel we see Christ Enthroned, flanked by St. John the Baptist and the Virgin—who plead for divine mercy on behalf of humanity—and five apostles below. The exquisite refinement of this icon-in-miniature recalls the style of the Daphnē *Crucifixion* (fig. 355).

Our second panel, representing the Sacrifice of Iphigenia (fig. 361), belongs to an ivory casket meant for wedding gifts that, rather surprisingly, is decorated with scenes of Greek mythology. Even more than the miniatures of the *Paris Psalter*, it illustrates the antiquarian aspects of Byzantine Classicism after the Iconclastic Controversy, for the subject is that of a famous Greek drama by Euripides; and our composition (which is curiously shallow, despite the deep undercutting of the relief) probably derives from an illustrated Euripides manuscript, rather than from a sculptural source. Though drained of all tragic emotion and reduced to a level of ornamental playfulness, these knobby little figures form a coherent visual quotation from ancient art. It was through channels such as this that the Graeco-Roman heritage entered the mainstream of Byzantine tradition.

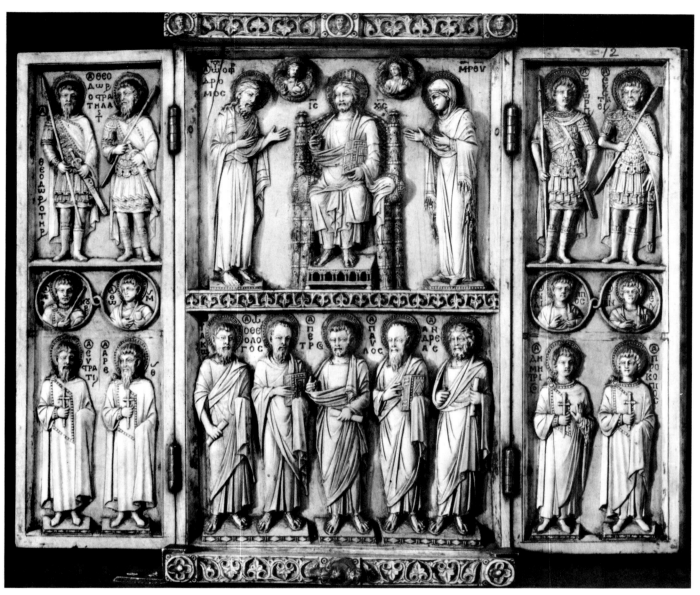

360. *THE HARBAVILLE TRIPTYCH.* Late 10th century. Ivory, 9½ × 11″ (24 × 28 cm). Musée du Louvre, Paris

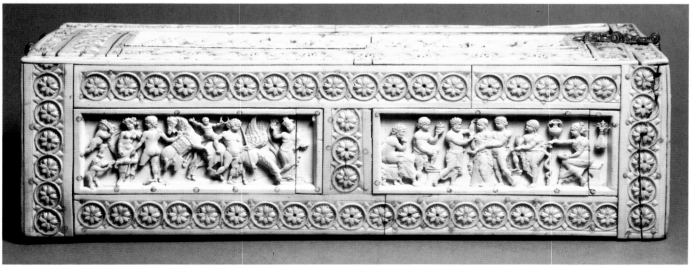

361. *THE SACRIFICE OF IPHIGENIA.* Detail of ivory casket. 10th century.
Victoria & Albert Museum, London (Crown copyright reserved)

# ILLUSTRATED TIME CHART I

| POLITICAL HISTORY, RELIGION | LITERATURE, SCIENCE, TECHNOLOGY |

B.C. 7000

6000

4000

Sumerians settle in lower Mesopotamia
Predynastic period in Egypt; Menes
   unites Upper and Lower Egypt c. 3100

"White Temple"
and ziggurat, Uruk

Pictographic writing, Sumer, c. 3500
Wheeled carts, Sumer, c. 3500–3000
Sailboats used on Nile c. 3500
Potter's wheel, Sumer, c. 3250

3000

Old Kingdom, Egypt (dynasties I–VI)
   c. 3100–2185
Divine Kingship of the Pharaoh
Early dynastic period, Sumer, c. 3000–
   2340; Akkadian Kings 2340–2180;
   Gudea c. 2150
Theocratic socialism in Sumer

Hieroglyphic writing, Egypt, c. 3000
Cuneiform writing, Sumer, c. 2900
First bronze tools and weapons, Sumer
Plows drawn by oxen

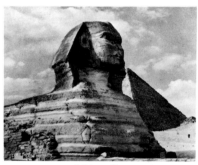

Sphinx, Giza

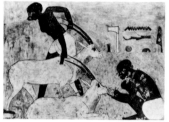

Tomb of Khnum-hotep, Beni Hasan

2000

Middle Kingdom, Egypt 2133–1786
Hammurabi founds Babylonian dynasty
   c. 1760, writes Code of Hammurabi
Hittites conquer Babylon c. 1600
Flowering of Minoan civilization
   c. 1700–1500
New Kingdom, Egypt, c. 1580–1085
Monotheism of Akhenaten (r. 1372–
   1358)
Dorians invade Greece c. 1100

Bronze tools and weapons in Egypt
Canal from Nile to Red Sea
Mathematics and astronomy flourish in
   Babylon under Hammurabi
Hittites employ iron tools and weapons
*Book of the Dead*, first papyrus book,
   XVIII dynasty
Hyksos bring horses and wheeled vehi-
   cles to Egypt c. 1725
China develops silk production c. 1500

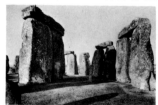

Stonehenge, England

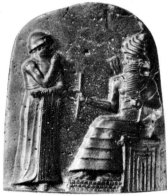

Stele of Hammurabi

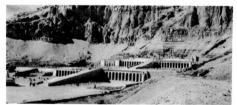

Funerary temple of Hatshepsut, Deir el-Bahari

1000

Hebrews accept monotheism
Jerusalem capital of Palestine; rule of
   David; of Solomon (died 926)
Assyrian Empire c. 1000–612
Zoroaster, Persian prophet (born c. 660)
Nebuchadnezzar destroys Jerusalem 586
Gautama Buddha (563–483), India
Confucius (551–479), Chinese philos-
   opher
Persians conquer Babylon 539; Egypt
   525
Athenians expel tyrants, establish de-
   mocracy 510
Romans revolt against Etruscans, set up
   republic 509

Phoenicians develop alphabetic writing
   c. 1000; Greeks adopt it c. 800
Earliest iron tools and weapons in China
Ideographic writing in China
First Olympic games 776
Homer (fl. c. 750–700), *Iliad* and *Odyssey*
Coinage invented in Lydia (Asia Minor)
   c. 700–650; soon adopted by Greeks
Thales of Miletus calculates solar eclipse
   585; Anaximander of Miletus designs
   geographic map and celestial globe c. 560
Aeschylus, Greek playwright (525–456)
Pythagoras, Greek philosopher (fl. c. 520)

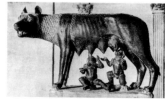

*She-Wolf* from Rome

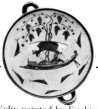

Kylix painted by Exekias

500

Fortifications and Sculpture, Jericho, Jordan

Houses, Shrine, and Wall Painting, Çatal Hüyük

Painted beaker, Susa
Female Head from Uruk
"White Temple" and ziggurat, Uruk
Mural, Hierakonpolis

Plaster skull, Jericho

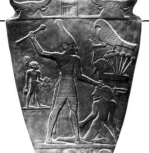

Palette of Narmer

Palette of Narmer
Statues from Abu temple, Tell Asmar
Step pyramid and funerary district of Zoser,
    Saqqara, by Imhotep
Harp and offering stand from Ur
*Rahotep and Nofret*
Sphinx, Giza
Pyramids at Giza
Cycladic Idol from Amorgos
Ziggurat of King Urnammu
Tomb of Ti, Saqqara
Stele of Naram-Sin
Gudea statues from Lagash

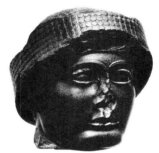

Gudea statue from Lagash

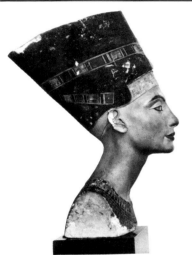

Nofretete

Tomb of Khnum-hotep, Beni Hasan
*Sesostris III*
Stonehenge, England
Stele of Hammurabi
*Cat Stalking Pheasant*, Hagia Triada
Snake goddess, Crete
*"Toreador Fresco"*
Harvester Vase from Hagia Triada
Vaphio Cups
Palace of Minos, Knossos, Crete
Funerary temple of Hatshepsut, Deir el-Bahari
Lion Gate, Bogazköy
Temple of Amun-Mut-Khonsu, Luxor
Akhenaten and Nofretete
Tomb of Tutankhamen
Treasure of Atreus, Mycenae
Lion Gate, Mycenae

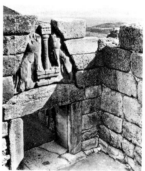

Lion Gate, Mycenae

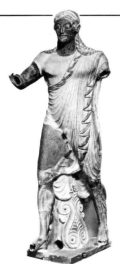

*Apollo* from Veii

Dipylon vase
Citadel of Sargon II, Dur Sharrukin
Stag, Scythian
Reliefs from Nimrud and Nineveh
Temple of Artemis, Corfu
Ishtar Gate, Babylon
*"Hera"* from Samos
"Basilica," Paestum
Kylix painted by Exekias
*"Peplos Kore"*
Siphnian Treasury and sculpture, Delphi
Tomb of Hunting and Fishing, Tarquinia
Kore from Chios
Sarcophagus from Cerveteri
*Apollo* from Veii
*She-Wolf* from Rome

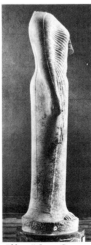

*"Hera"* from Samos

7000 B.C.
6000
4000
3000
2000
1000
500

500

Persian Wars in Greece 499–478
Periclean Age in Athens c. 460–429
Peloponnesian War, Sparta against Athens, 431–404
Alexander the Great (356–323)
   occupies Egypt 333; defeats Persia
   331; conquers Near East
Rome defeats Carthage in First Punic
   War 264–241; acquires Spain 201
Gauls invade eastern Greek states; repulsed 240, 200

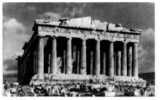

Parthenon

Travels of Herodotus, Greek historian
   c. 460–440
Sophocles, Greek tragic playwright
   (496–406)
Euripides, Greek tragic playwright (died 406)
Hippocrates, Greek physician (born 469)
Socrates, philosopher (died 399)
Plato, philosopher (427–347); founds
   Academy 386
Aristotle (384–322)
Theophrastus of Athens, botanist (fl. c. 300)
Euclid's books on geometry (fl. c. 300–280)
Archimedes, physicist and inventor
   (287–212)
Eratosthenes of Cyrene measures the
   globe c. 240
Plautus, Roman comedies (255–184)

*Charioteer*, Delphi

200

Rome dominates Asia Minor and Egypt;
   annexes Macedonia (and thereby
   Greece) 147; destroys Carthage 146

Invention of paper, China
Carneades of Cyrene, head of Academy,
   brings delegation of Greek
   philosophers to Rome 156
Terence, Roman comedies (died 159)

100

Sulla, dictator of Rome 82–79
Julius Caesar conquers Gaul 58–49;
   dictator of Rome 49–44
Emperor Augustus (r. 27 B.C.–14 A.D.)

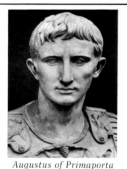

Golden Age of Roman literature: Cicero,
   Catullus, Vergil, Horace, Ovid, Livy
Earliest water wheels
Vitruvius' *De architectura*

*Augustus of Primaporta*

A.D. 1

Crucifixion of Jesus c. 30
Jewish rebellion against Rome 66–70;
   destruction of Jerusalem by Emperor
   Titus
Paul (died c. 65) spreads Christianity to
   Asia Minor and Greece
Eruption of Mt. Vesuvius buries Pompeii,
   Herculaneum 79

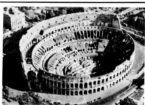

Colosseum, Rome

Pliny the Elder, *Natural History*, dies in
   Pompeii 79
Varieties of glass blowing
Tacitus, *Germania*
Seneca, Roman statesman

100

Emperor Trajan (r. 98–117) rules
   Roman Empire at its largest extent
Emperor Marcus Aurelius (r. 161–180),
   author of *Meditations*

Ptolemy, geographer and astronomer
   (died 160)
Galen, physician and anatomist (died
   201)

200

Shapur I (r. 242–272), Sassanian king of Persia
Persecution of Christians in Roman
   Empire 250–302
Emperor Diocletian (r. 284–305) divides
   Empire
Mithraism spreads in Roman Empire

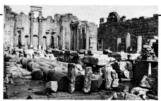

Basilica, Leptis Magna

Plotinus,
Neo-Platonist
philosopher (died 270)

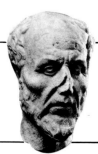

Plotinus

300

500

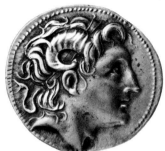

Alexander the Great

Palace, Persepolis
East pediment from Aegina
Tomb of Lionesses, Tarquinia
*Charioteer*, Delphi
Pediments, Temple of Zeus, Olympia
"Temple of Poseidon," Paestum
*Doryphorus* by Polyclitus
Temples on Acropolis, Athens:
    Parthenon, Propylaea, Temple of
    Athena Nike, Erechtheum
Parthenon sculpture by Phidias
Mausoleum, Halicarnassus
Theater, Epidaurus
Monument of Lysicrates, Athens
*Aphrodite* and *Hermes* by Praxiteles
*Apoxyomenos* by Lysippus

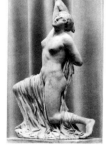

Dying Niobid

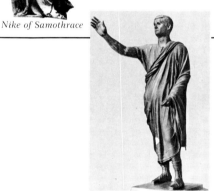

Nike of Samothrace

200

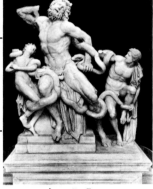

*Laocoön* Group

*Nike of Samothrace*
Pergamum Altar
Porta Augusta, Perugia
*Laocoön* Group
"Temple of Fortuna Virilis," Rome

100

*Aulus Metellus*
"Temple of the Sibyl," Tivoli
Sanctuary of Fortuna, Praeneste
Portrait head from Delos
Villa of the Mysteries, Pompeii
Forum of Caesar, Rome
Villa of Livia, Primaporta
*Augustus of Primaporta*
Odyssey Landscapes
Ara Pacis (Altar of Peace), Rome

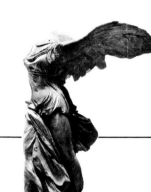

Aulus Metellus

1 A.D.

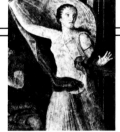

Villa of the Mysteries, Pompeii

House of the Silver Wedding, Pompeii
House of the Vettii, Pompeii
*Hercules and Telephus*, Herculaneum
Colosseum, Rome
*Vespasian*
Arch of Titus, Rome

100

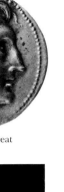

Equestrian statue of
Marcus Aurelius, Rome

Column of Trajan, Rome
Pantheon, Rome
Insula of House of Diana, Ostia
Market Gate, Miletus
Equestrian statue of Marcus Aurelius,
    Rome
Portrait of a boy, Faiyum
Temple of Venus, Baalbek

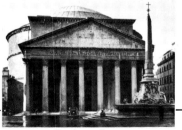

Pantheon, Rome

200

Palace of Shapur I, Ctesiphon; *Triumph
    of Shapur I*, Naksh-i-Rustam
Basilica, Leptis Magna
*Philippus the Arab*
Synagogue, Dura-Europos

300

300

Christianity legalized by Edict of Milan
  313; state religion 395
Emperor Constantine the Great (r. 324–
  337) moves capital to Byzantium
  (renamed Constantinople) 330;
  recognizes Christianity; baptized on
  deathbed
St. Ambrose (340–397); St. Jerome
  (c. 347–420); St. Augustine (354–430)
Roman Empire split into eastern and
  western branches 395

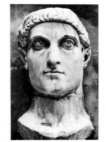

Colossal statue of Constantine

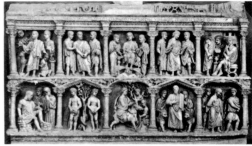

Sarcophagus of Junius Bassus

400

Rome sacked by Visigoths 410
St. Patrick (died c. 461) founds Celtic
  Church in Ireland 432
Western Roman Empire falls to Goths 476
Theodoric founds Ostrogoth kingdom in
  Ravenna c. 493
"Golden Age" of Justinian 527–565
St. Gregory (540–604)
St. Benedict (died 543) founds
  Benedictine order
Lombard kingdom in north Italy 568

Invention of the stirrup in China
Silk cultivation brought to eastern
  Mediterranean from China
Oldest illustrated Bible manuscripts,
  early 6th cent.

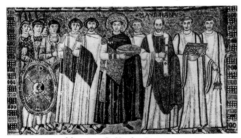

Mosaics, S. Vitale, Ravenna

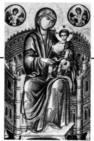

*Archangel Michael*, diptych leaf

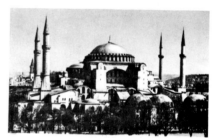

Hagia Sophia, Istanbul

600

Mohammed (570–632); Hegira 622, beginning
  of Moslem chronology
Byzantium loses Near Eastern and
  African provinces to Moslems 642–732;
  to Seljuk Turks 1071
Moslems conquer Spain 711
Iconoclastic controversy 726–843
Conversion of Russia to Orthodox Church c. 990

Koran 652

1200

Latin empire in Constantinople 1204–61
Mongols conquer China 1234–79

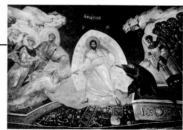

*Madonna Enthroned*, icon        Fresco, Kariye Camii, Istanbul

1400

Constantinople conquered by Ottoman
  Turks 1453; Moscow assumes
  leadership of Orthodox Church

300

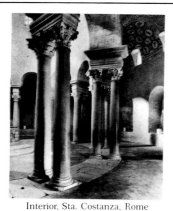

Palace of Diocletian, Split
Arch of Constantine, Rome
Colossal statue of Constantine
Basilica of Constantine, Rome
Old St. Peter's, Rome
Sta. Costanza, Rome
Sarcophagus of Junius Bassus
St. Paul Outside the Walls, Rome
Catacomb of Santi Pietro e Marcellino,
    Rome
Dome mosaic, St. George, Salonica

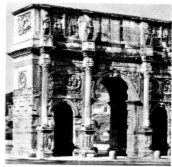

Arch of Constantine, Rome

*Interior, Sta. Costanza, Rome*

400

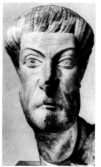

Mosaics, Sta. Maria Maggiore, Rome
*Eutropios*
*Vatican Vergil*
Mosaics, S. Apollinare in Classe and
    S. Vitale, Ravenna
S. Vitale, Ravenna
Hagia Sophia, Istanbul
*Vienna Genesis*
*Archangel Michael*, diptych leaf

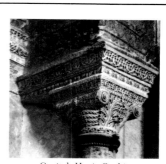

Capital, Hagia Sophia

*Portrait of Eutropios*

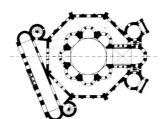

Plan of S. Vitale, Ravenna

600

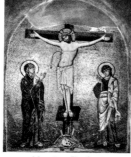

*Madonna*, Sta. Francesca
    Romana, Rome
St. Mark's, Venice
Harbaville Triptych
*Paris Psalter*
Monastery churches,
    Hosios Loukas
Mosaics, Daphnē
*The Sacrifice of Iphigenia*

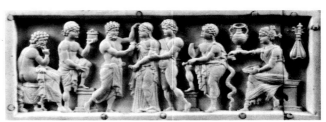

*The Sacrifice of Iphigenia*

Mosaics, Daphnē

1200

Mosaics, St. Mark's, Venice
Fresco, Kariye Camii, Istanbul
*Madonna Enthroned*, icon

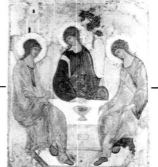

1400

*Old Testament Trinity* by Andrei Rublev
Cathedral of St. Basil, Moscow

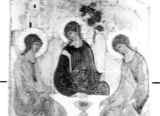

*Old Testament Trinity* by Andrei Rublev

# PART TWO

# THE MIDDLE AGES

When we think of the great civilizations of our past, we tend to do so in terms of visible monuments that have come to symbolize the distinctive character of each: the pyramids of Egypt, the ziggurats of Babylon, the Parthenon of Athens, the Colosseum, Hagia Sophia. The Middle Ages, in such a review of climactic achievements, would be represented by a Gothic cathedral—Notre-Dame in Paris, perhaps, or Chartres, or Salisbury. We have many to choose from, but whichever one we pick, it will be well north of the Alps, although in territory that formerly belonged to the Roman Empire. And if we were to spill a bucket of water in front of the cathedral of our choice, this water would eventually make its way to the English Channel, rather than to the Mediterranean.

Here, then, we have the most important single fact about the Middle Ages: the center of gravity of European civilization has shifted to what had been the northern boundaries of the Roman world. The

Mediterranean, for so many centuries the great highway of commercial and cultural exchange binding together all the lands along its shores, has become a barrier, a border zone.

We have already observed some of the events that paved the way for this shift—the removal of the imperial capital to Constantinople, the growing split between the Catholic and Orthodox faiths, the decay of the western half of the Roman Empire under the impact of invasions by Germanic tribes. Yet these tribes, once they had settled down in their new environment, accepted the framework of late Roman, Christian civilization, however imperfectly; the local kingdoms they founded—the Vandals in North Africa, the Visigoths in Spain, the Franks in Gaul, the Ostrogoths and Lombards in Italy—were all Mediterranean-oriented, provincial states on the periphery of the Byzantine Empire, subject to the pull of its military, commercial, and cultural power. As late as 630, after the Byzantine armies had recovered Syria, Palestine, and Egypt from the Sassanid Persians, the reconquest of the lost Western provinces remained a serious possibility.

Ten years later, the chance had ceased to exist, for meanwhile a tremendous and completely unforeseen new force had made itself felt in the East: the Arabs, under the banner of Islam, were overrunning the Near Eastern and African provinces of Byzantium. By 732, within a century after the death of Mohammed, they had swallowed all of North Africa as well as Spain, and threatened to add southwestern France to their conquests.

It would be difficult to exaggerate the impact of the lightninglike advance of Islam upon the Christian world. The Byzantine Empire, deprived of its western Mediterranean bases, had to concentrate all its efforts on keeping Islam at bay in the East. Its impotence in the West (where it retained only a precarious foothold on Italian soil) left the European shore of the western Mediterranean, from the Pyrenees to Naples, exposed to Arabic raiders from North Africa or Spain. Western Europe was thus forced to develop its own resources, political, economic, and spiritual. The Church in Rome broke its last ties with the East and turned for support to the Germanic north, where the Frankish kingdom, under the energetic leadership of the Carolingian dynasty, rose to the status of imperial power during the eighth century.

When the pope, in the year 800, bestowed the title of emperor upon Charlemagne, he solemnized the new order of things by placing himself and all of Western Christianity under the protection of the king of the Franks and Lombards. He did not, however, subordinate himself to the newly created Catholic emperor, whose legitimacy depended on the pope, whereas hitherto it had been the other way around (the emperor in Constantinople had formerly ratified the newly elected pope). This interdependent dualism of spiritual and political authority, of Church and State, was to distinguish the West from both the Orthodox East and the Islamic South. Its outward symbol was the fact that though the emperor had to be crowned in Rome, he did not reside there; Charlemagne built his capital at the center of his effective power, in Aachen, close to France, Belgium, and the Netherlands, and in Germany on the present-day map of Europe.

Meanwhile, Islam had created a new civilization stretching from Spain in the west to the Indus Valley in the east, a civilization that reached its highest point far more rapidly than did that of the medieval West. Baghdad on the Tigris, the capital city of Charlemagne's great contemporary, Harun al-Rashid, rivaled the splendor of Byzantium. Islamic art, learning, and craftsmanship were to have a far-ranging influence on the European Middle Ages, from arabesque ornament, the manufacture of paper, and Arabic numerals to the transmission of Greek philosophy and science through the writings of Arabic scholars. (Our language records this debt in such words of Arabic origin as algebra and alcohol.) It is well, therefore, that we acquaint ourselves with some of the artistic achievements of Islam before we turn to medieval art in western Europe.

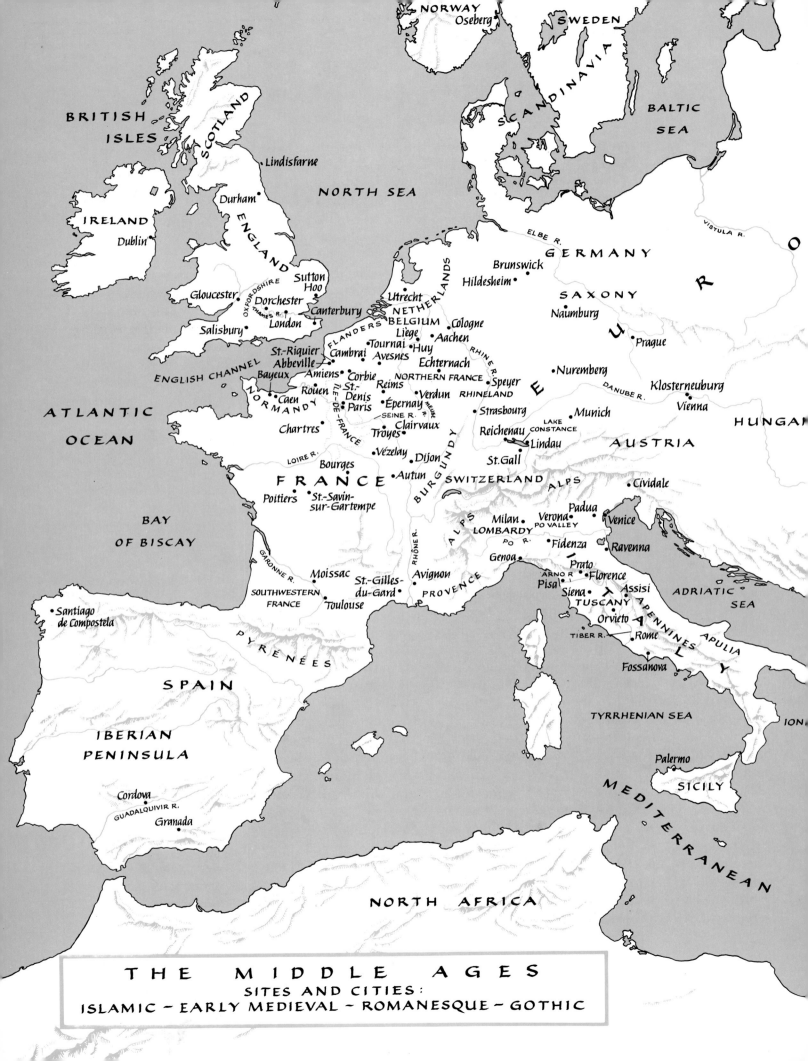

NORWAY
Oseberg

SWEDEN

BALTIC
SEA

BRITISH
ISLES

SCOTLAND

SCANDINAVIA

• Lindisfarne

NORTH SEA

ELBE R.

VISTULA R.

IRELAND

• Durham

ENGLAND

GERMANY

• Dublin

• Brunswick
• Hildesheim

SAXONY
• Naumburg

EUR O

Utrecht
Sutton
Hoo
OXFORDSHIRE
• Gloucester
• Dorchester
THAMES R.
London
Canterbury
• Salisbury

NETHERLANDS

BELGIUM
Liège
Tournai
Avesnes
Huy

• Cologne
• Aachen
Echternach

RHINE R.
NORTHERN FRANCE
RHINELAND

• Prague

• Nuremberg

DANUBE R.

• Klosterneuburg
• Vienna

HUNGAR

FLANDERS
St.-Riquier
Abbeville
Bayeux
Amiens
Cambrai

Corbie
St.-
Denis

Reims
Paris

Speyer

• Strasbourg

Verdun
Épernay

MEUSE R.
SEINE R.

• Munich

• Reichenau
LAKE
CONSTANCE
Lindau

ATLANTIC

OCEAN

ENGLISH CHANNEL

NORMANDY
Rouen
Caen

ÎLE-
DE-
FRANCE

Chartres

Troyes
Clairvaux

Vézelay
Dijon

LOIRE R.
Bourges

FRANCE
• Autun

BURGUNDY

St.Gall

AUSTRIA

ALPS

• Cividale

BAY

OF BISCAY

Poitiers

St.-Savin-
sur-Gartempe

RHÔNE R.

ALPS

Milan
LOMBARDY
PO VALLEY
PO R.
Genoa

Padua
Verona
Venice
• Fidenza
Ravenna

ADRIATIC

SEA

GARONNE R.

Moissac

Avignon

St.-Gilles-
du-Gard

SOUTHWESTERN
FRANCE

Toulouse

PROVENCE

ARNO R.
Pisa

Prato
Siena

Florence
Assisi
TUSCANY
Orvieto

APENNINES

TIBER R.

Rome

APULIA

Santiago
de Compostela

PYRENEES

SPAIN

Fossanova

IBERIAN
PENINSULA

TYRRHENIAN SEA

ION

Palermo

SICILY

Cordova

GUADALQUIVIR R.

Granada

MEDITERRANEAN

NORTH AFRICA

# THE MIDDLE AGES
## SITES AND CITIES:
### ISLAMIC – EARLY MEDIEVAL – ROMANESQUE – GOTHIC

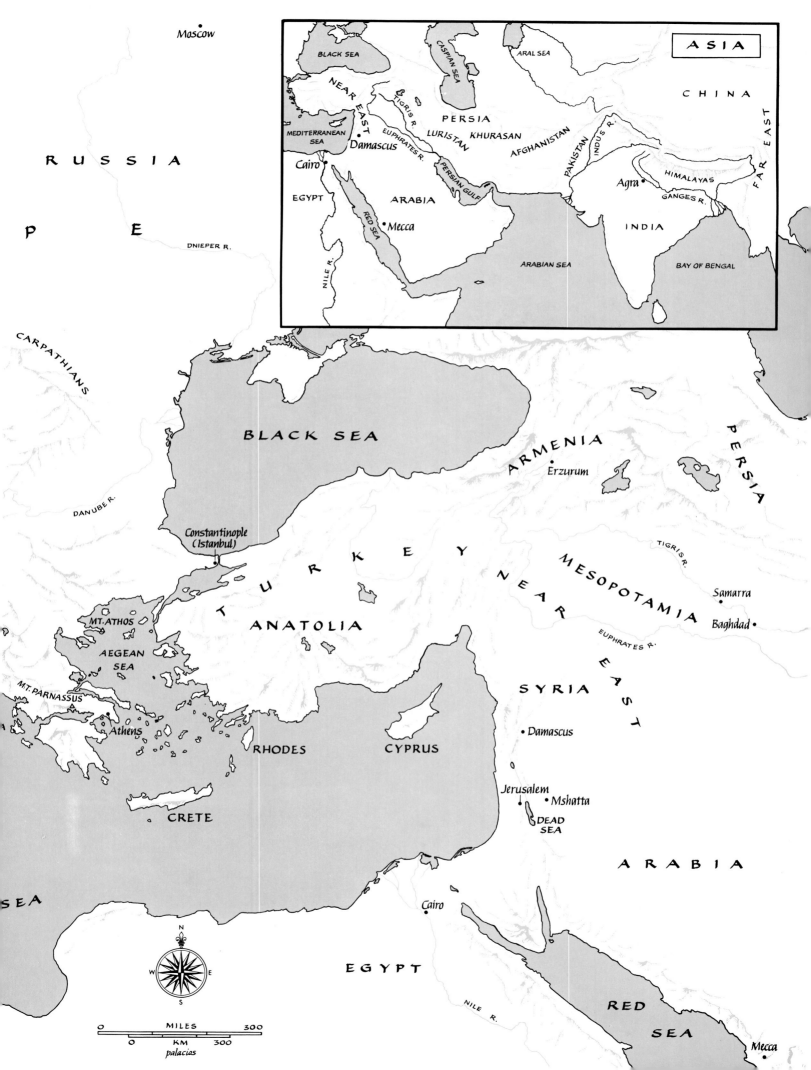

ASIA

BLACK SEA
CASPIAN SEA
ARAL SEA
NEAR EAST
CHINA
TIGRIS R.
PERSIA
KHURASAN
AFGHANISTAN
MEDITERRANEAN SEA
LURISTAN
EUPHRATES R.
PAKISTAN
INDUS R.
FAR EAST
Damascus
Cairo
PERSIAN GULF
HIMALAYAS
Agra
EGYPT
ARABIA
RED SEA
GANGES R.
Mecca
INDIA
ARABIAN SEA
BAY OF BENGAL

RUSSIA
Moscow
E P
DNIEPER R.

CARPATHIANS

DANUBE R.

BLACK SEA

ARMENIA
Erzurum

PERSIA

TIGRIS R.

MESOPOTAMIA
Samarra
Baghdad

Constantinople
(Istanbul)

T U R K E Y
NEAR EAST

MT. ATHOS

ANATOLIA

EUPHRATES R.

AEGEAN SEA

SYRIA

MT. PARNASSUS

Damascus

Athens

RHODES
CYPRUS

Jerusalem
Mshatta
DEAD SEA

CRETE

ARABIA

SEA

Cairo

N
W      E
S

EGYPT

MILES
0                    300
0          KM          300
palacios

NILE R.

RED SEA

Mecca

# CHAPTER ONE
# ISLAMIC ART

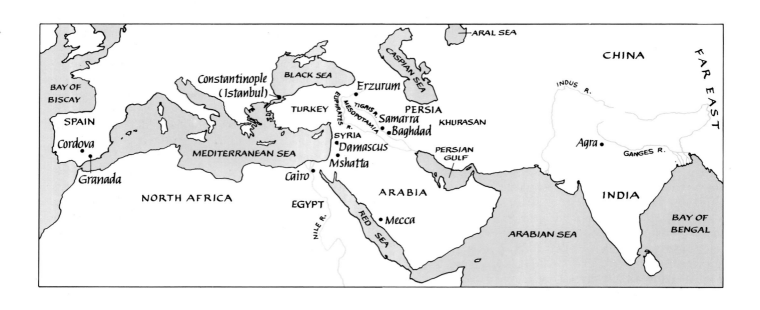

The incredible speed with which Islam spread throughout the Near East and North Africa remains one of the most astonishing phenomena in world history. In two generations, the new faith conquered a larger territory and greater numbers of believers than Christianity had in three centuries. How was it possible for a group of semicivilized desert tribes suddenly to burst forth from the Arab peninsula and to impose their political and religious dominance on populations far superior to them in numbers, wealth, and cultural heritage? That they had the advantage of surprise, great fighting skill, and a fanatical will to win, that both Byzantine and Persian military power was at a low ebb, has been pointed out often enough; these favorable circumstances may help to account for the initial Arab successes but not for the enduring nature of their conquests. What had begun as a triumph of force soon turned into a spiritual triumph as Islam gained the allegiance of millions of converts. Clearly, the new faith must have satisfied the needs of vast multitudes of people more fully than any of the older religions of the Hellenized Orient.

Islam owes many of its essential elements to the Judaeo-Christian tradition. The word Islam means "submission"; Moslems are those who submit to the will of Allah, the one and all-powerful God, as revealed to Mohammed in the Koran, the sacred scriptures of Islam. The Koran often draws upon the contents of the Bible and counts the Old Testament prophets as well as Jesus among the predecessors of Mohammed. Its teachings include the concepts of the Last Judgment, of Heaven and Hell, of angels and devils.

The ethical commands of Islam, too, are basically similar to those of Judaism and Christianity. As to dissimilarities, there is no ritual demanding a priesthood; all Moslems have equal access to Allah, and the observances required of them are simple: prayer at stated times of day (alone or in a mosque), almsgiving, fasting, and a pilgrimage to Mecca. All true believers, according to Mohammed, are members of one great community. During his lifetime, he was their leader not only in the religious sense but in all temporal affairs as well, so that he bequeathed to posterity a faith which was also a new pattern of society. The tradition of placing both religious and political leadership in the hands of a single ruler persisted after the Prophet's death; his successors were the caliphs, the deputies of Mohammed, whose claim to authority rested on their descent from the families of the Prophet or his early associates.

The unique quality of Islam—and the core of its tremendous appeal—is the blending of ethnic and universal elements. Like Christianity, it opened its ranks to everyone, stressing the kinship of the faithful before God, regardless of race or culture. Yet, like Judaism, it was also a national religion, firmly centered in Arabia. The Arab warriors under the early caliphs who set out to conquer the earth for Allah did not expect to convert the unbelievers to Islam; their aim was simply to rule, to enforce obedience to themselves as the servants of the One True God. Those who wanted to share this privileged status by joining Islam had to become Arabs-by-adoption: they not only had to learn Arabic in order to read the Koran (since Allah had chosen to speak in that language, his words must not be translated into lesser tongues), but also had to adopt the social, legal, and political framework of the Moslem community. As a result, the Arabs, though few in numbers, were never in danger of being absorbed by the inhabitants of the regions they ruled. Instead, they absorbed the conquered populations, along with their cultural heritage, which they skillfully adapted to the requirements of Islam.

# ARCHITECTURE

In art, this heritage encompassed the Early Christian and Byzantine style, with its echoes of Hellenistic and Roman forms, as well as the artistic traditions of Persia (see pages 131–35). Pre-Islamic Arabia contributed nothing except the beautifully ornamental Arabic script; populated largely by nomadic tribes, it had no monumental architecture, and its sculptured images of local deities fell under Mohammed's ban against idolatry. Originally, Islam, like early Christianity, made no demands at all upon the visual arts. During the first fifty years after the death of the Prophet, the Moslem place of prayer could be a church taken over for the purpose, a Persian columned hall, or even a rectangular field surrounded by a fence or a ditch. The one element these improvised mosques had in common was the marking of the *qibla* (the direction to which Moslems turn in praying): the side facing toward Mecca had to be emphasized by a colonnade, or merely by placing the entrance on the opposite side.

At the end of the seventh century, however, the Moslem rulers, now firmly established in their conquered domains, began to erect mosques and palaces on a large scale as visible symbols of their power, intended to outdo all pre-Islamic structures in size and splendor. These early monuments of Moslem architecture do not, for the most part, survive in their original form. What we know of their design and decoration shows that they were produced by craftsmen gathered from Egypt, Syria, Persia, and even Byzantium, who continued to practice the styles in which they had been trained. A distinctive Islamic tradition crystallized only in the course of the eighth century.

## Eastern Islam

GREAT MOSQUE, DAMASCUS. Thus the Great Mosque at Damascus, built 706–15 within the enclosure of a Roman sanctuary, had its walls covered with wonderful glass mosaics of Byzantine origin. The surviving remnants, such as the section reproduced in figure 362, consist entirely of views of landscape and architecture framed by richly ornamented borders against a gold background. Nothing quite like them is known in Byzantine art, but their style obviously reflects an illusionism familiar to us from Pompeian painting. Apparently, ancient traditions persisted more strongly in the Near Eastern provinces of Byzantium than in Europe. Caliph al-Walid, who built the mosque, must have welcomed these Hellenistic-Roman motifs, so different from the symbolic and narrative content of Christian mosaics. A somewhat later Arabic author records that the country contained many

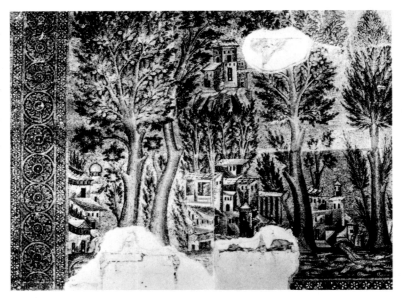

362. Landscape mosaic. 715 A.D. The Great Mosque, Damascus, Syria

churches "enchantingly fair and renowned for their splendor," and that the Great Mosque at Damascus was meant to keep the Moslems from being dazzled by them.

PALACE AT MSHATTA. The date of the huge desert palace at Mshatta (in the present-day kingdom of Jordan) has been much disputed; we can well understand why, for the style of the façade decoration (fig. 363) harks back to various pre-Islamic sources. According to the best available evidence, the palace was erected by one of al-Walid's successors, probably about 743. The lace-like carving and the character of the plant motifs are strongly reminiscent of Byzantine architectural ornament (compare fig. 343), and variations within the reliefs indicate that they were done by craftsmen conscripted from several provinces of the former Byzantine domain in the Near East. There is also, however, a notable Persian element, evidenced by winged lions and similar mythical animals familiar from Sassanian textiles or metalwork (see fig. 136). On the other hand, the geometric framework of zigzags and rosettes, uniformly repeated over the entire width of the façade, suggests a taste for symmetrical abstract patterns characteristic of Moslem art.

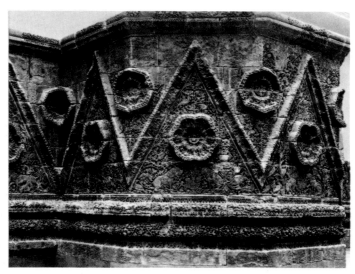

363. Portion of the façade of the Palace at Mshatta, Jordan.
c. 743 A.D. Height of triangles 9½″ (24 cm).
Staatliche Museen, Berlin

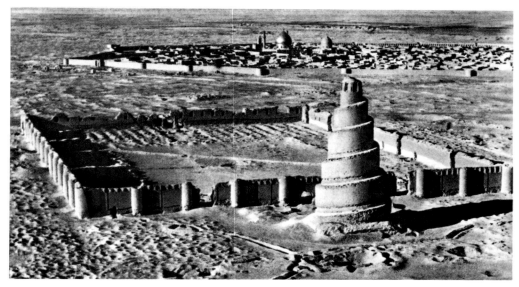

364. Mosque of al-Mutawakkil (view from the north), Samarra, Iraq. 848–52 A.D.

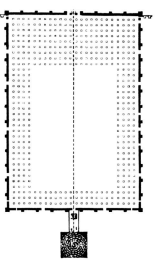

365. Plan of the
Mosque of al-Mutawakkil
(after Creswell)

GREAT MOSQUE, SAMARRA. A striking example of the early caliphs' architectural enterprises, all of which were built on an immense scale at incredible speed, is the Great Mosque at Samarra (on the Tigris, northwest of Baghdad), built under al-Mutawakkil, 848–52. Only an aerial view (fig. 364) can convey its vast dimensions, which make it the largest mosque in the world. The basic features of the plan (fig. 365) are typical of the mosques of this period: a rectangle, its main axis pointing south (up) to Mecca, encloses a court surrounded by aisles that run toward the *qibla* side, the center of which is marked by a small niche, the *mihrab*; on the northern side rises the minaret, a tower from which the faithful were summoned to prayer by the cry of the muezzin. (This feature was derived from the towers of Early Christian churches in Syria, which may also have influenced the church towers of medieval Europe.) The floor area of the Great Mosque at Samarra is more than 45,000 square yards—almost ten acres, of which five and a half were covered by a wooden roof resting on 464 supports. These have all disappeared now, along with the mosaics that once covered the walls. The most spectacular aspect of the building is the minaret, linked with the mosque by a ramp. Its bold and unusual design, with a spiral staircase leading to the platform at the top, reflects the ziggurats of ancient Mesopotamia, such as the famed Tower of Babel (see page 119), at that time still in a fair state of repair. Did al-Mutawakkil wish to announce to the world that the realm of the caliphs was heir to the empires of the ancient Near East?

## Western Islam

MOSQUE, CORDOVA. In order to gain some notion of the interior effect of the Great Mosque at Samarra, we must turn to the mosque at Cordova in Spain, begun in 786. Although converted to Christian use after the reconquest of the city in 1236, the structure retains its Islamic character. The plan (fig. 366) was originally designed as a simpler version of the type we came to know at Samarra, the aisles being confined to the *qibla* side. Half a century later, the mosque was enlarged by extending the length of these aisles; in 961–65 they were lengthened again, and twenty years later eight more aisles were added on the east side, since a river bank barred any further extension to the south. These successive stages illustrate the flexible nature of early mosque plans, which made it possible to quadruple the size of the sanctuary without departing from the original pattern. As we enter, a seemingly endless forest of columns confronts us, with nothing but the direction of the aisles to guide us toward the *qibla* side.

366. Plan of the Mosque at Cordova, Spain
enlarged in 987 A.D. (from Gomez-Moreno)

*Qibla* wall
Mihrab niche
Hypostyle hall

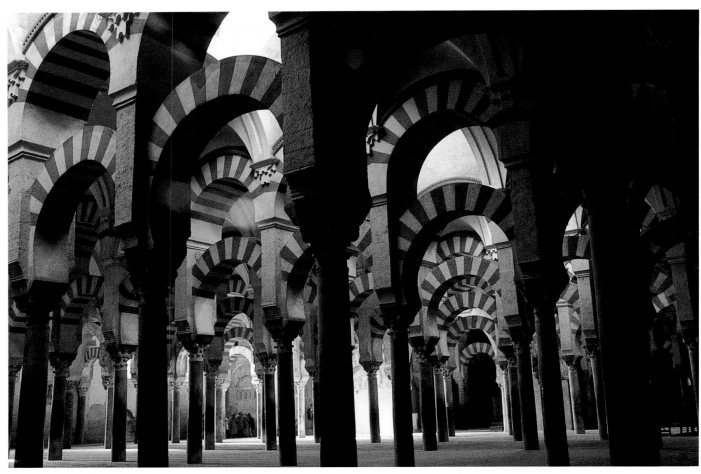

367. Interior of the sanctuary (view from the east), Mosque, Cordova

The sanctuary was covered by a wooden roof (now replaced by vaults) resting on double arcades of remarkable and picturesque design (fig. 367). The lower arches are horseshoe-shaped, a form that sometimes occurs in Near Eastern buildings of pre-Islamic date but which Moslem architecture made peculiarly its own. They rise from short, slender columns of a kind familiar to us from Roman and Early Christian times. These columns, however, also support stone piers that carry a second tier of arches. Was this piggy-back arrangement a practical necessity because the architect who began the building of the mosque—apparently at maximum speed—had to utilize a set of too-short columns from some earlier structure? If so, he certainly has used the device to excellent advantage, for it produces an effect far lighter and airier than a system of single arches and supports could have achieved.

A further elaboration of the same principle is found in the Capilla de Villaviciosa (fig. 368), a vaulted chamber to the north of the *mihrab,* which dates from the building campaign of 961–65. Here we meet lobed arches in three tiers, interlaced in such a way as to form a complex, ornamental screen. The vault is even more imaginative; eight slender arches, or ribs, cross each other above the square compartment, subdividing it into a network of cells. It is instructive to compare the spatial effects of the Mosque at Cordova and

of a Byzantine church (fig. 344): in the latter, space always is treated as volume and has a clearly defined shape, while at Cordova its limits are purposely obscured, so that we experience it as something fluid, limitless, and mysterious. Even in the Capilla de Villaviciosa, the surfaces and cavities prevent us from perceiving walls or vaults as continuous surfaces; the space is like that of an openwork cage, screened off yet continuous with its surroundings.

This distinctively Moorish (North African and Spanish) style reaches its ultimate stage of refinement in the Alhambra Palace in Granada, the last Islamic stronghold on the Iberian peninsula during the late Middle Ages. Its richest portion, the Court of the Lions and the rooms around it, was built between 1354 and 1391 (fig. 369). The columns now have become slender as flower stalks; they support stilted arches of extravagantly complex shape, cut into walls that seem to consist of nothing more than gossamerlike webs of ornament.

On the interior surfaces (fig. 370) we find the same lacework of arabesque decoration, carried out in delicately colored stucco or tile—a limitless variety of designs, including bands of inscriptions, yet disciplined by symmetry and rhythmic order. The effect is infinitely richer than that of the Mshatta façade, but in retrospect the two monuments, separated by six centuries and the entire expanse of the

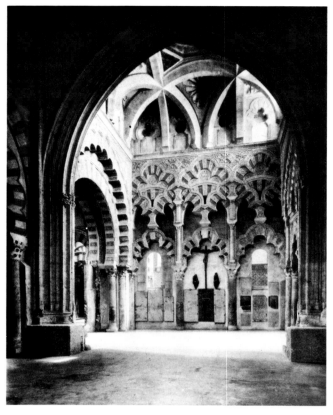

368. Capilla de Villaviciosa, Mosque,
Cordova. 961–65 A.D.

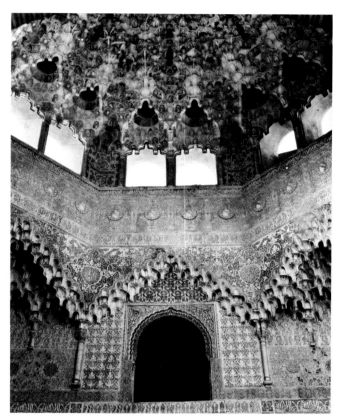

370. Stucco decoration, Hall of the Two Sisters, the Alhambra

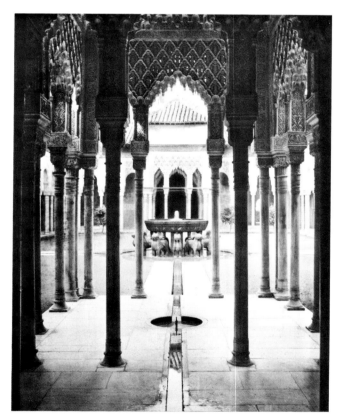

369. Court of the Lions, the Alhambra, Granada, Spain. 1354–91

Mediterranean, appear clearly linked by the same basic process of evolution: the ribs of the Capilla de Villaviciosa have disappeared behind a honeycomb of ever-multiplying cells framed by tiny arches that hang like stalactites from the ceilings. Little wonder that the Alhambra is enshrined in the romantic imagination of the West as the visible counterpart of all the wonders of *The Thousand and One Nights*.

## The Turks

From the tenth century onward, the Seljuk Turks gradually advanced into the Near East, where they adopted Islam, seized control of most of Persia, Mesopotamia, Syria, and the Holy Land, and advanced against the Byzantine Empire in Asia Minor. They were followed in the thirteenth century by the Mongols of Genghis Khan—whose armies included the Mamelukes (a people related to the Turks)—and by the Ottoman Turks. The latter not only put an end to the Byzantine Empire by their capture of Constantinople in 1453, but occupied the entire Near East and Egypt as well, thus becoming the most important power in the Moslem world. The growing weight of the Turkish element in Islamic civilization is reflected by the westward spread of a new type of mosque, the madrasah, which had been created in Persia under Seljuk domination in the eleventh century.

MADRASAH OF SULTAN HASAN, CAIRO. One of the most imposing examples is the Madrasah of Sultan Hasan in

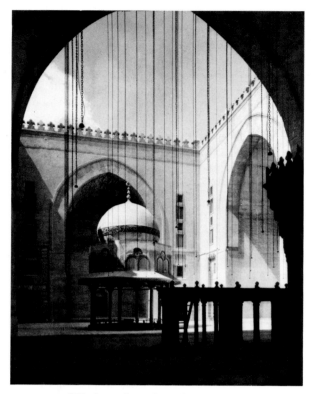

371. Court (view from the *qibla* side),
Madrasah of Sultan Hasan, Cairo, Egypt. 1356–63

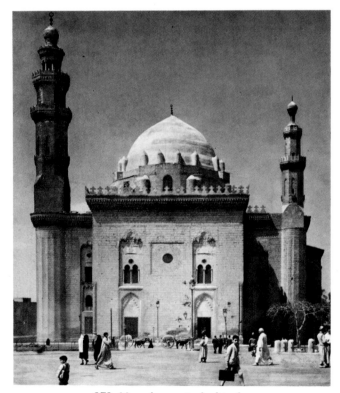

372. Mausoleum attached to the
Madrasah of Sultan Hasan

373. (*opposite*) Taj Mahal, Agra, India. 1630–48

Cairo, contemporary with the Alhambra but very different in spirit. Its main feature is a square court (fig. 371), with a fountain in the center. Opening onto each side of this court is a rectangular vaulted hall; that on the *qibla* side, larger than the other three, serves as the sanctuary. The monumental scale of these halls seems to echo palace architecture of Sassanian Persia (see fig. 135), while the geometric clarity of the whole design, emphasized by the severe wall surfaces, is a Turkish contribution that we shall meet again. It represents an attitude toward architectural space completely opposed to that of many-aisled Arabic mosques.

Attached to the *qibla* side of the Madrasah of Sultan Hasan is the sultan's mausoleum, a large cubic structure surmounted by a dome (fig. 372). Such funerary monuments had been unknown to early Islam; they were borrowed from the West (see page 257) in the ninth century and became especially popular among the Mameluke sultans of Egypt. The dome in our example betrays its descent from Byzantine domes.

TAJ MAHAL, AGRA. The most famous mausoleum of Islamic architecture is the Taj Mahal at Agra (fig. 373), built three centuries later by one of the Moslem rulers of India, Shah Jahan, as a memorial to his wife. He belonged to the Mogul dynasty, which had come from Persia, so that the basic similarity of the Taj Mahal and the mausoleum of Sultan Hasan is less surprising than it might seem at first glance. At the same time, such a comparison emphasizes the special qualities that make the Taj Mahal a masterpiece of its kind. The massiveness of the Cairo mausoleum, with its projecting cornice and firmly anchored dome, has given way to a weightless elegance not unlike that of the Alhambra. The white marble walls, broken by deep shadowy recesses, seem paper-thin, almost translucent, and the entire building gives the impression of barely touching the ground, as if it were suspended from the balloonlike dome. Its mood of poetic reverie is greatly enhanced by the setting; the long reflecting pool lined with dark green shrubs sets off the cool whiteness of the great pavilion in truly magnificent fashion.

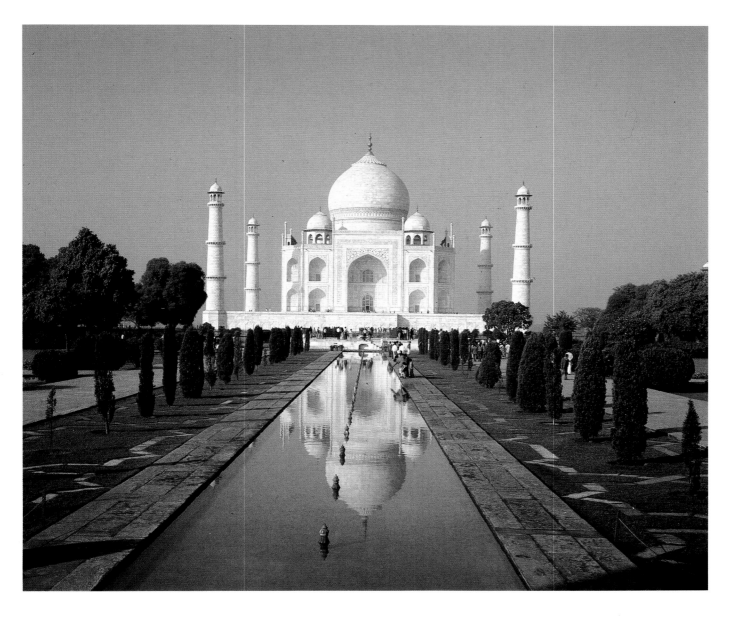

MOSQUES AT ERZURUM AND ISTANBUL. The Turks, once they settled in Asia Minor, developed a third variety of mosque by interbreeding the Seljuk madrasah with the domed Byzantine church. Among the earliest and most astonishing results of this process is the wooden dome of the Ulu Mosque at Erzurum (see fig. 764), which has successfully withstood the earthquakes common in that region. The Turks, therefore, were well prepared to appreciate the beauty of Hagia Sophia when they entered Constantinople. It impressed them so strongly that echoes of it appear in numerous mosques built in that city and elsewhere after 1453. One of the most impressive is that of Sultan Ahmed I, erected 1609–16 (figs. 374–76). Its plan elaborates and regularizes the design of Hagia Sophia into a square, with the main dome abutted by four half domes instead of two, and four smaller domes next to the minarets at the corners. The mounting sequence of these domes has been handled with marvelous logic and geometric precision, so that the exterior is far more harmonious than that of Hagia Sophia. Thus, the first half of the seventeenth century, which produced both the Taj Mahal and the Mosque of Ahmed I, marks the final flowering of Moslem architectural genius.

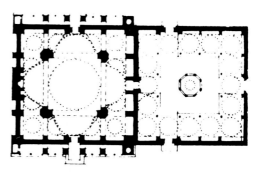

374. Plan of the Mosque
of Ahmed I (after Unsal)

375. (*below*) Mosque of Ahmed I
(view from the west), Istanbul, 1609–16

376. (*opposite*) Detail, Mosque of Ahmed I

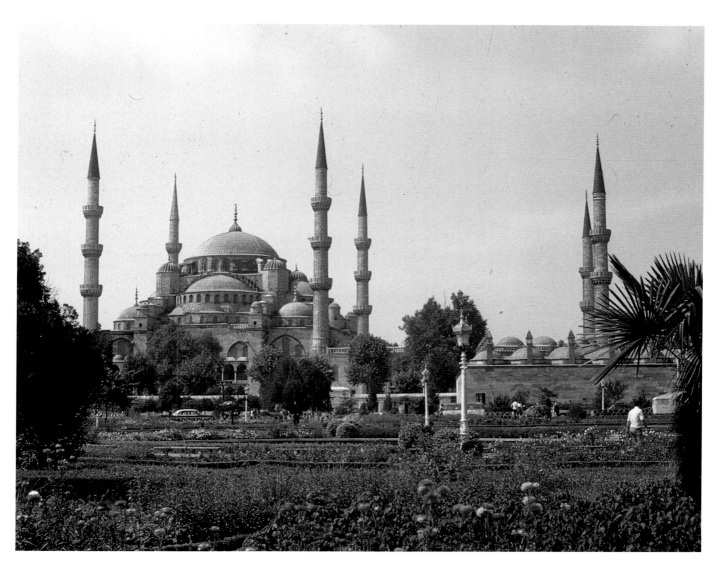

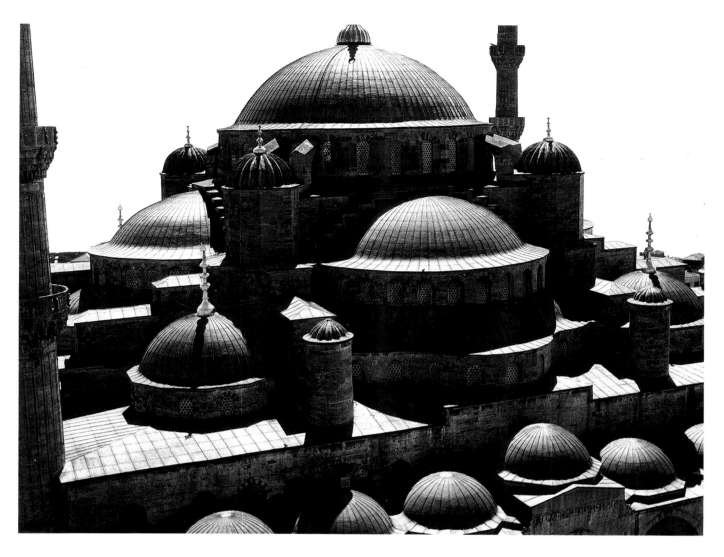

# REPRESENTATION

Before we can enter into a discussion of Islamic painting and sculpture, we must understand the Moslem attitude toward representation. It has often been likened to that of the Byzantine Iconoclasts (see pages 279–81), but there are significant differences. The Iconoclasts, we will recall, were opposed to sacred images (that is, images of religious personages) rather than to representation as such. Mohammed, too, condemned idolatry; one of his first acts after his triumphant return to Mecca in 630 was to take over the Kaaba, an age-old Arabic sanctuary, and to remove all the idols he found there. These were always understood to have been statues, and the Koran expressly places statues among the handiwork of Satan, while painting and representation in general are not mentioned.

Mohammed's attitude toward painting seems to have been ambiguous. An early Arabic source informs us that in 630 the Kaaba also contained murals of religious (apparently biblical) subjects; the Prophet ordered them all to be destroyed, except for a picture of Mary with the Infant Jesus, which he protected with his own hands. This incident, as well as the lack of any discussion of the subject in early Moslem theology, suggests that *painted* sacred images never posed a serious problem to Mohammed and his immediate successors; since there was no pictorial tradition among the Arabs, Islamic religious painting could have been created only by borrowing from outside sources, and such a development was most unlikely as long as the authorities did not encourage it. They could afford to display indifference or even at times a certain tolerance toward the sacred pictures of other faiths. (Mohammed may have saved the Virgin and Child from destruction in order not to hurt the feelings of former Christians among his followers.)

This passive iconoclasm did not prevent the Arabs from accepting the nonreligious representational art they found in the newly conquered territories. Statues of any sort they surely abominated, but Hellenistic landscapes could be introduced into mosques (see fig. 362) and Sassanian animals scattered among the relief decoration of the Mshatta façade (see fig. 363). The ruins of another palace, contemporary with Mshatta, have even yielded fresco fragments with human figures. Only from about 800 on do we find strictures against representation as such in Moslem religious literature, perhaps under the influence of prominent Jewish converts. The chief argument became not the danger of idolatry but of human presumption: in making images of living things, the artist usurps a creative act that is reserved to God alone, since only He can breathe a soul into living creatures.

DECORATED OBJECTS. Theoretically, therefore, human or animal figures of any kind were forbidden by Islamic law. Yet in actual practice the ban was effective only against large-scale representational art for public display. There seems to have been a widespread conviction, especially at the luxury-loving courts of the caliphs and other Moslem princes, that images of living things were harmless if they did not cast a shadow, if they were on a small scale, or applied to objects of daily use, such as rugs, fabrics, and pottery. As a result, human and animal figures did survive in Islamic art, but they tended to become reduced to decorative motifs, intrinsically no more important than geometric or plant ornament.

We must remember, too, that this tendency was an age-old tradition; among the peoples who shaped Moslem civilization, Arabs, Persians, Turks, and Mongols all shared a love of portable, richly decorated objects as the common heritage of their nomadic past (see pages 131–32). Islam, then, merely reinforced a taste that was natural to these cultures. When the techniques of the nomads' arts—rugmaking, metalwork, and leathercraft—merged with the vast repertory of forms and materials accumulated by the craftsmen of Egypt, the Near East, and the Graeco-Roman world, the decorative arts of Islam reached a level of sumptuousness never equaled before or since. The few samples illustrated here can convey only the faintest suggestion of their endless variety.

Characteristically enough, a good number of the finest specimens are to be found in the churches and palaces of western Europe; whether acquired by trade, by gift, or as crusaders' booty, they were treasured throughout the Middle Ages as marvels of imaginative craftsmanship and often imitated. Such a piece is the embroidered coronation cloak of the German emperors (fig. 377), made by Islamic artisans in Palermo for Roger II of Sicily in 1133–34, fifty years after the Normans had captured that city from the Moslems (who had held it for 241 years). The symmetrical grouping of two lions attacking camels on either side of a symbolic tree of life is a motif whose ancestry goes back thousands of years in the ancient Near East (compare fig. 127); here, inscribed within quarter-circles and filled with various kinds of ornament, the animals have yielded their original fierceness to a splendid sense of pattern.

It is the element of pattern that links them with the bronze creature made fifty years later in a very different part of the Moslem world, northeast Persia (fig. 378). This one certainly casts a shadow, and a sizable one at that, since it is almost three feet tall; it is, in fact, one of the largest pieces of free-standing sculpture in all of Islamic art. Yet to call it the statue of an animal hardly does justice to its peculiar character. It is primarily a vessel, a perforated incense burner whose shape approaches that of an animal; the representational aspect of the forms seems secondary and casual. We cannot tell what kind of beast this is meant to be; if only a part of it had survived, we might even be doubtful whether it represented anything at all, so abstract and ornamental is the handling of the body. The object becomes a "living crea-

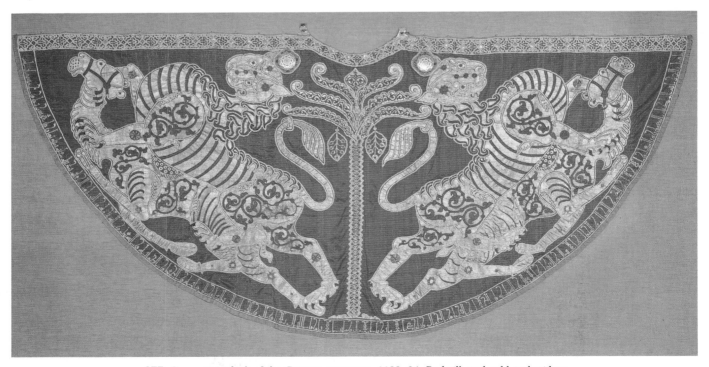

377. Coronation cloak of the German emperors. 1133–34. Red silk and gold embroidery, width 11′2″ (3.4 m). Kunsthistorisches Museum, Vienna

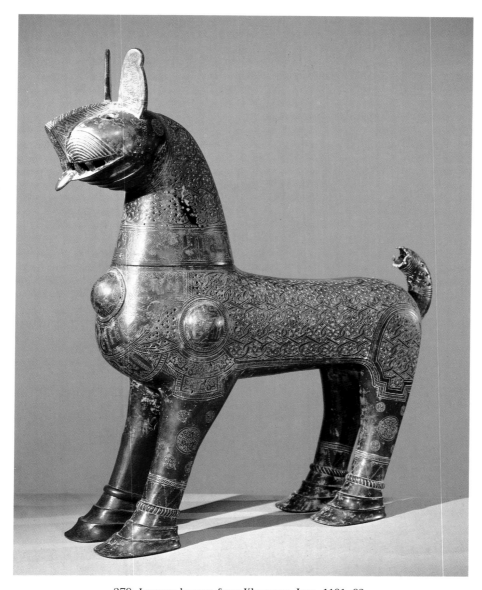

378. Incense burner, from Khurasan, Iran. 1181–82.
Bronze, height 33½″ (85 cm). The Metropolitan Museum of Art,
New York. Rogers Fund, 1951

ture" only while it is serving its proper function; filled with burning incense, breathing fire and smoke, our animal might well have seemed terrifyingly real to a naïve beholder. The Seljuk prince who owned it undoubtedly enjoyed the performance of this half-comic, half-demoniacal guardian monster, which he himself could "bring to life" whenever he wished.

PAINTING. The fate of painting in the Moslem world between the eighth and thirteenth centuries remains almost entirely unknown to us. So little has survived from the five hundred years following the Damascus mosaics that we should be tempted to assume the complete disappearance of pictorial expression under Islam if literary sources did not contain evidence to the contrary. Even so, it seems clear that the tradition of painting was kept alive, not by Moslems but by artists of other faiths. Byzantine masters were imported occasionally to work for Arab rulers, and the Oriental Christian churches that survived within the Islamic empire must have included many painters who were available to Moslem art patrons. But what kind of pictures could the Moslems have wanted?

We may assume that there was a more or less continuous demand for the illustration of scientific texts. The Arabs had inherited such manuscripts from the Byzantines in the Near East, and, being keenly interested in Greek science, they reproduced them in their own language. This meant that the illustrations had to be copied as well, since they formed an essential part of the content, whether they were abstract diagrams or representational images (as in zoological, medical, or botanical treatises). Works of this sort are among the earliest Islamic illuminated manuscripts known so far, al-

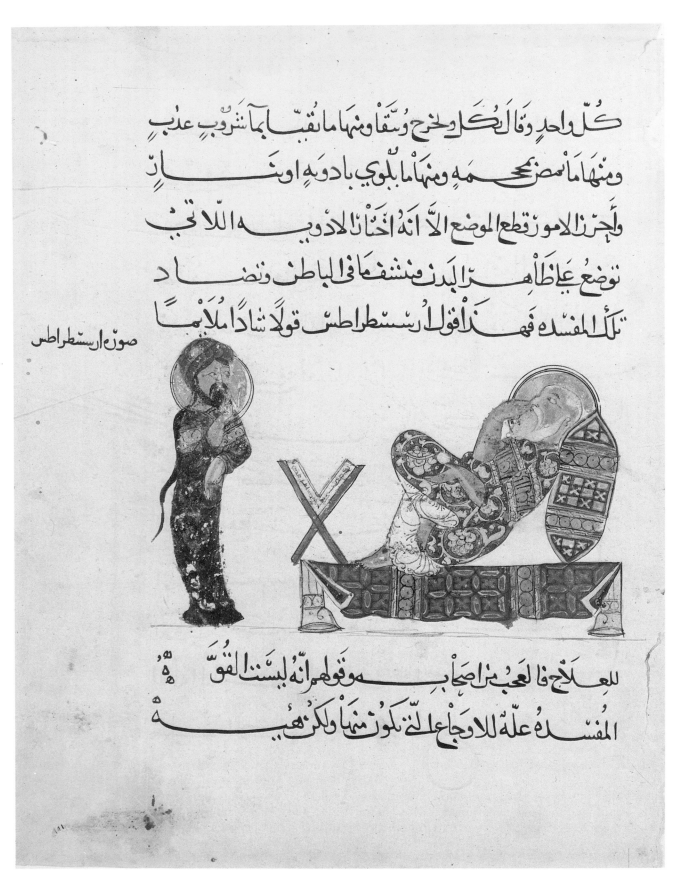

كُلّ وَاحِدٍ رَقَالَ أَكُلَّ وَاخْرَجَ رَسَقَا مَا نَقِيَّا بِمَا شَرُوبٍ عَذَبٍ
وَمِنْهَا مَا نَصَرَ يَحْمَدُ وَمِنْهَا مَا يَقَوِي بَادِوَيْهِ اوِنَازٍ
وَأَجَزَّ الْأَمُورَ قِطَعَ الْمَوْضِعَ إِلَّا أَنَّهُ أَخَاَ الْأَدُويِهَ اللَّاتِب
تُوضَعُ عَلَى ظَاهِرِ الْبَدَنِ مُنْشَفَا فِى الْبَاطِنِ وَنَضَادُ
تِلْكَ الْمُفْسِدُ فَهَذَا أَقَوْلَ أَرَسَطَرَاطِسَ قَوْلًا شَاذًا مُلَائِمًا

صُورَةُ أَرَسَطَرَاطِسَ

لِلْعِلَاجِ فَالْعَجَبُ مِنْ أَصْحَابِهِ وَقَوْلِهُمْ إِنَّهُ لَيْسَ الْقَوَّ
الْمُفْسِدُ عِلَّةٌ لِلْأَوْجَاعِ عَلَّةً تَكُونُ مِنْهَا وَلَكِنَّ هِيَ

379. *ERASISTRATUS AND AN ASSISTANT,* from an Arabic translation of Dioscorides' *De Materia Medica.*
Baghdad School. 1224. 12⅞ × 9¾″ (32.5 × 24.8 cm). Courtesy of the Freer Gallery of Art, Smithsonian Institution, Washington, D.C.

306 • ISLAMIC ART

though none of them can be dated before about 1200. This example (fig. 379) is from an Arabic translation, signed and dated 1224, of Dioscorides' *De Materia Medica*; it shows the Greek physician Erasistratus reclining on a couch and discoursing with an assistant. (Both are equipped with halos to indicate their venerability.) Interestingly enough, the scribe in this instance also did the illustration; or, rather, he copied it along with the text. The ultimate source of the picture must have been a late Antique miniature with three-dimensional figures in a spatial setting, but it takes a real effort of the imagination to see remnants of these qualities in the present version, in which everything is flattened out and ornamentalized. The forms remain strictly on the surface of the page, like the script itself, and our artist's pen lines have a rhythmic assurance akin to that of the lettering.

It is tempting to think that manuscript illumination found its way into Islamic art through scribes who doubled as draftsmen, for to a Moslem the calling of scribe was an ancient and honorable one; a skilled calligrapher might do pictures if the text demanded them, without having to feel that this incidental activity stamped him as a painter (and an abomination in the sight of Allah). Be that as it may, the calligrapher's style of pen-drawn illustrations, with or without the addition of color, soon made its appearance in secular Arabic literature such as the *Maqamat* of Hariri. These delightful stories, composed about 1100, were probably illustrated within a hundred years after they were written, since we have illuminated Hariri manuscripts from the thirteenth century on. The drawing in figure 380, from a copy dated 1323, is clearly a descendant of the style we saw in the Dios-

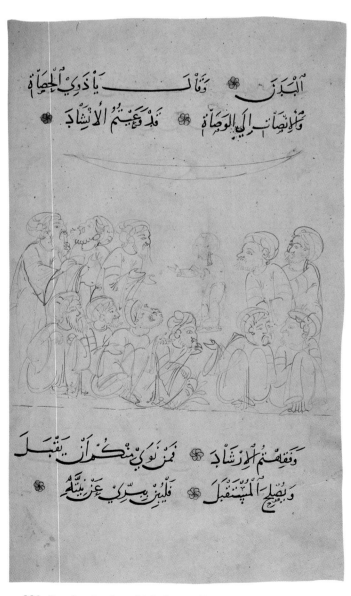

380. Pen drawing in red ink, from a Hariri manuscript.
Mesopotamian (?). 1323. British Museum, London

corides illustration of a century before. The lines have the same quick, rhythmic quality, but they are handled very much more freely now, and with an extraordinary expressive power. Our artist's grasp of human character, showing the response of the eleven men to the plea of the clever rascal in the center, is so precise and witty that we must regard him as far more important than a mere copyist.

## Persia

Arab merchants had been in touch with the Far East even before the advent of Islam, and occasional references to Chinese painters by early Moslem authors indicate that these contacts had brought about some acquaintance with the art of China. It was only after the Mongol invasion of the thirteenth century, however, that Chinese influence became an important factor in Islamic art. It can be felt most strongly in Persian illuminated manuscripts done under Mongol rule, from about 1300 on, such as the *Summer Landscape* in figure 381. More than three centuries earlier, under the Song Dynasty, the painters of China had created a landscape art of great atmospheric depth, mist-shrouded mountains and rushing streams embodying a poetic vision of untamed nature. Our Mongol painter must have known this tradition well; most of the essential elements recur in his own work, enhanced by a lively sense of color that made him stress the red and yellow of leaves turning in early fall. Did such landscapes reach medieval Europe? We do not know, but it may be more than coincidence that landscape painting in the West, which had been dormant since the end of antiquity, began to revive about this time (see figs. 534 and 539).

The extent to which Chinese influence transformed the tradition of Islamic miniature painting is well demonstrated by the combat scene of prince and princess in a landscape (fig. 382): this is no colored drawing but an ambitious pictorial composition that fills the entire page. The narrative to be illustrated has served merely as a point of departure for our artist; most of his effort is devoted to the setting, rather than to the action described in the text. He must have been a great admirer of Chinese landscapes, for the graceful and delicately shaded rocks, trees, and flowers of our picture clearly reflect their Far Eastern source. At the same time, the design has a decorative quality that is characteristically Islamic; in this respect, it seems more akin to the pattern of a Persian carpet than to the airy spaciousness of Chinese landscape painting.

Another important result of Far Eastern influence, it would seem, was the emergence of religious themes in Persian miniatures. The Mongol rulers, familiar with the rich tradition of Buddhist religious art in India and China, did not share their predecessors' horror at the very idea of pictures of Mohammed. In any event, scenes from the life of the Prophet do occur in Persian illuminated manuscripts from the early fourteenth century on. Since they had never been represented before, the artists who created them had to rely on both Christian and Buddhist art as their source of inspiration. The result was a curious mixture of elements, often far from well integrated.

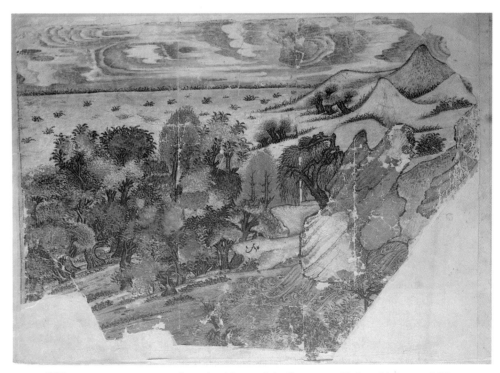

381. *SUMMER LANDSCAPE,* from the *Album of the Conqueror (Sultan Mohammed II).*
Mongol. Mid-14th century. Topkapu Palace Museum, Istanbul

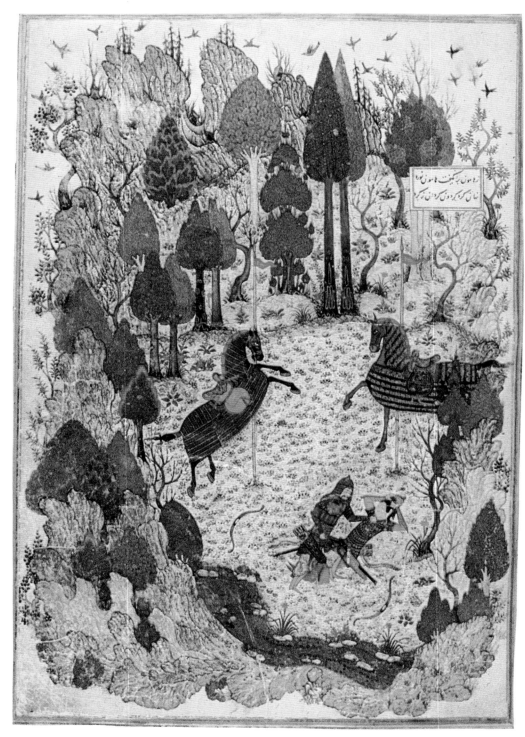

382. JUNYAD. *SOLITARY COMBAT OF PRINCE HUMAY AND PRINCESS HUMAYUN*,
from a Persian manuscript. 1396. British Museum, London

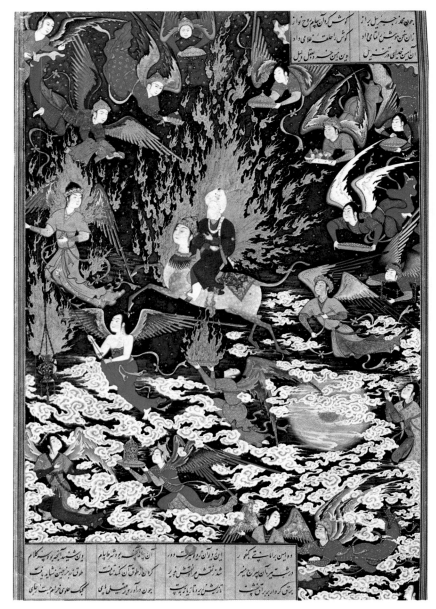

383. *THE ASCENSION OF MOHAMMED,* from a Persian manuscript.
1539–43. British Library, London

Only on rare occasions does Islamic religious painting rise to a level that bears comparison with the art of older faiths. Such a picture is the wonderful miniature in figure 383, showing Mohammed's ascension to Paradise. In the Koran, we read that the Lord "caused His servant to make a journey by night...to the remote place of worship which We have encircled with blessings, that We might show him of Our signs." Later Moslem authors added elaborate details to this brief account: the ascent was made from Jerusalem, under the guidance of the angel Gabriel; Mohammed rose through the seven heavens, where he met his predecessors, including Adam, Abraham, Moses, and Jesus, before he was brought into the presence of Allah. The entire journey apparently was thought of as analogous to that of Elijah, who ascended to heaven in a fiery chariot. Mohammed, however,

was said to have ridden a miraculous mount named *buraq,* "white, smaller than a mule and larger than an ass," and having a cheek—or a face—like that of a human being; some authors also gave it wings. We will recognize the ancestry of this beast: it derives from the winged, human-headed guardian monsters of ancient Mesopotamia (see fig. 121) and their kin, the sphinxes and centaurs, all of which had survived as ornamental motifs in the great melting pot of Islamic decorative art, where they lay dormant, as it were, until Moslem writers identified them with *buraq.* In our miniature, the wings are reduced to a ring of feathers around *buraq's* neck, so as not to interfere with the saddle. The animal follows Gabriel across a deep-blue, star-studded sky; below, among scattered clouds, there is a luminous celestial body, probably the moon. The Far Eastern elements

384. Calligraphic page from the *Album of the Conqueror (Sultan Mohammed II).*
Turkish (?). Topkapu Palace Museum, Istanbul

in this poetic vision are striking. We find them in the flame-like golden halos behind Gabriel and Mohammed, a familiar feature of Buddhist art; in the curly, "intestinal" stylization of the clouds; in the costumes and facial types of the angels. Yet the composition as a whole—the agitated movement of the angelic servitors converging from all sides upon the Prophet—strongly recalls Christian art. Our miniature thus represents a true, and singularly felicitous, meeting of East and West. There is only one small concession to Islamic iconoclasm: the Prophet's face has been left blank, evidently because it was thought too holy to be depicted.

Scenes such as this one occur in manuscripts of historical or literary works, but not of the Koran. Even the Persians apparently did not dare to illustrate the Sacred Book directly, although—or perhaps because—illustrated copies of the Bi-

ble were not altogether unknown in the Moslem world. The Koran remained the calligraphers' domain, as it had been from the very beginning of Islam. In their hands, Arabic lettering became an amazingly flexible set of shapes, capable of an infinite variety of decorative elaborations, both geometric and curvilinear. At their best, these designs are masterpieces of the disciplined imagination that seem to anticipate, in a strange way, the abstract art of our own time. The page shown in figure 384, probably done by a Turkish calligrapher of the fifteenth century, renders the single word Allah. It is indeed a marvel of intricacy within a rigorous set of formal rules, sharing the qualities of a maze, of a rug pattern, and even of certain non-objective paintings. More than any other single object, it sums up the essence of Islamic art.

# CHAPTER TWO

# EARLY MEDIEVAL ART

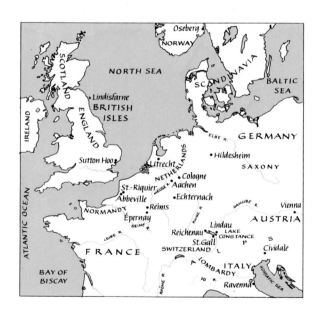

# THE DARK AGES

The labels we use for historical periods tend to be like the nicknames of people: once established, they are almost impossible to change, even though they may no longer be suitable. Those who coined the term "Middle Ages" thought of the entire thousand years from the fifth to the fifteenth century as an age of darkness, an empty interval between classical antiquity and its rebirth, the Renaissance in Italy. Since then, our view of the Middle Ages has changed completely; we no longer think of the period as "benighted" but as the "Age of Faith."

With the spread of this new, positive conception, the idea of darkness has become confined more and more to the early part of the Middle Ages. A hundred years ago, the "Dark Ages" were generally thought to extend as far as the twelfth century: they have been shrinking steadily ever since, so that today the term covers no more than the two hundred-year interval between the death of Justinian and the reign of Charlemagne. Perhaps we ought to pare down the Dark Ages even further; for in the course of the century 650–750 A.D., as we have pointed out earlier, the center of gravity of European civilization shifted northward from the Mediterranean, and the economic, political, and spiritual framework of the Middle Ages began to take shape. We shall now see that the same century also gave rise to some important artistic achievements.

## Celtic-Germanic Style

ANIMAL STYLE. The Germanic tribes that had entered western Europe from the east during the declining years of the Roman Empire carried with them, in the form of nomads' gear, an ancient and widespread artistic tradition, the so-called animal style. We have encountered early examples of it in the Luristan bronzes of Iran and the Scythian gold ornaments from southern Russia (see page 132 and figs. 127 and 128). This style, with its combination of abstract and organic shapes, of formal discipline and imaginative freedom, became an important element in the Celtic-Germanic art of the Dark Ages, such as the gold-and-enamel purse cover (fig. 385) from the grave, at Sutton Hoo, of an East Anglian king who died between 625 and 633.

On it are four pairs of symmetrical motifs: each has its own distinctive character, an indication that the motifs have been assembled from four different sources. One motif, the standing man between confronted animals, has a very long history indeed—we first saw it in Sumerian art more than 3,000 years before (see fig. 113). The eagles pouncing on ducks bring to mind similar pairings of carnivore-and-victim in Luristan bronzes. The design above them, on the other hand, is of more recent origin. It consists of fighting animals whose tails, legs, and jaws are elongated into bands forming a complex interlacing pattern. Interlacing bands as an ornamental device occur in Roman and Early Christian art, especially along the southern shore of the Mediterranean, but their combination with the animal style, as shown here, seems to be an invention of the Dark Ages, not much before the date of our purse cover.

Metalwork, in a variety of materials and techniques and often of exquisitely refined craftsmanship, had been the principal medium of the animal style. Such objects, small, durable, and eagerly sought after, account for the rapid dif-

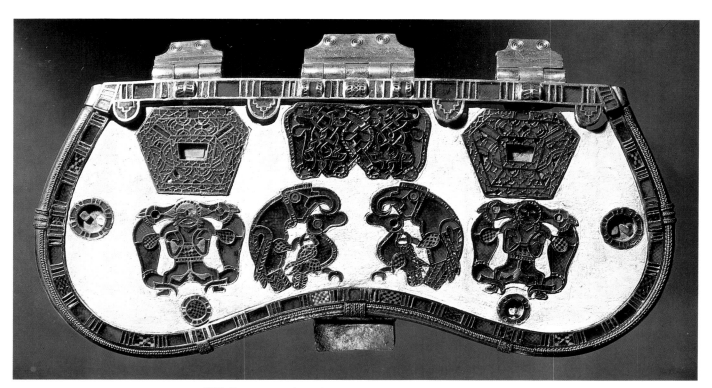

385. Purse cover, from the Sutton Hoo Ship-Burial. 625–33 A.D.
Gold with garnets and enamels, length 8″ (20.3 cm). British Museum, London

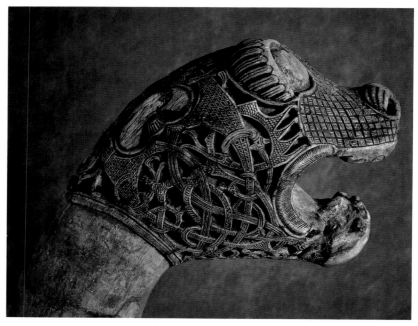

386. *ANIMAL HEAD,* from the Oseberg Ship-Burial. c. 825 A.D.
Wood, height c. 5″ (12.7 cm). University Museum of National Antiquities, Oslo

fusion of its repertory of forms. During the Dark Ages, however, these forms migrated not only in the geographic sense but also technically and artistically, into wood, stone, and even manuscript illumination.

Wooden specimens, as we might expect, have not survived in large numbers; most of them come from Scandinavia, where the animal style flourished longer than anywhere else. The splendid animal head in figure 386, of the early ninth century, is the terminal of a post that was found, along with much other equipment, in a buried Viking ship at Oseberg in southern Norway. Like the motifs on the Sutton Hoo purse cover, it shows a peculiarly composite quality: the basic shape of the head is surprisingly realistic, as are certain details (teeth, gums, nostrils), but the surface has been spun over with interlacing and geometric patterns that betray their derivation from metalwork. Snarling monsters such as this used to rise from the prows of Viking ships, endowing them with the character of mythical sea dragons.

## Hiberno-Saxon Style

The earliest Christian works of art that were made north of the Alps also reflected the pagan Germanic version of the animal style. In order to understand how they came to be produced, however, we must first acquaint ourselves with the important role played by the Irish (Hibernians), who, during the Dark Ages, assumed the spiritual and cultural leadership of western Europe. The period 600–800 A.D. deserves, in fact, to be called the Golden Age of Ireland. Unlike their English neighbors, the Irish had never been part of the Roman Empire; thus the missionaries who carried the Gospel to them from England in the fifth century found a Celtic society entirely barbarian by Roman standards. The Irish readily accepted Christianity, which brought them into contact with Mediterranean civilization, but they did not become Rome-oriented. Rather, they adapted what they had received in a spirit of vigorous local independence.

The institutional framework of the Roman Church, being essentially urban, was ill-suited to the rural character of Irish life. Irish Christians preferred to follow the example of the desert saints of Egypt and the Near East who had left the temptations of the city to seek spiritual perfection in the solitude of the wilderness. Groups of such hermits, sharing a common ideal of ascetic discipline, had founded the earliest monasteries. By the fifth century, monasteries had spread as far north as western Britain, but only in Ireland did monasticism take over the leadership of the Church from the bishops. Irish monasteries, unlike their Egyptian prototypes, soon became seats of learning and the arts; they also developed a missionary fervor that sent Irish monks to preach to the heathen and to found monasteries in northern Britain as well as on the European mainland, from Poitiers to Vienna. These Irishmen not only speeded the conversion to Christianity of Scotland, northern France, the Netherlands, and Germany, they also established the monastery as a cultural center throughout the European countryside. Although their Continental foundations were taken over before long by the monks of the Benedictine order, who were advancing north from Italy during the seventh and eighth centuries, Irish influence was to be felt within medieval civilization for several hundred years to come.

MANUSCRIPTS. In order to spread the Gospel, the Irish monasteries had to produce copies of the Bible and other Christian books in large numbers. Their writing workshops (scriptoria) also became centers of artistic endeavor, for a manuscript containing the Word of God was looked upon as a sacred object whose visual beauty should reflect the importance of its contents. Irish monks must have known Ear-

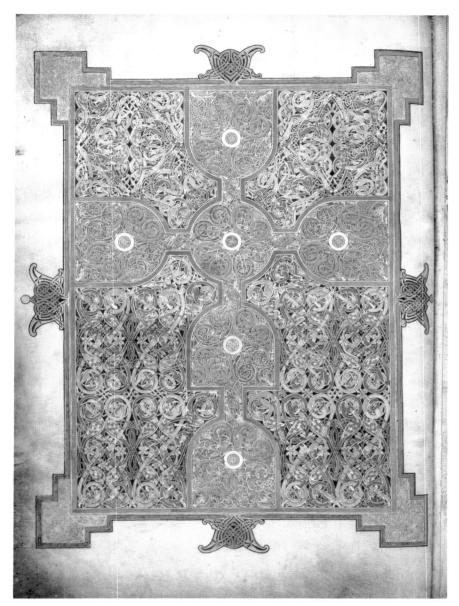

387. Cross Page from the *Lindisfarne Gospels*.
c. 700 A.D. 13½ × 9¼" (34.3 × 23.5 cm). British Library, London

ly Christian illuminated manuscripts, but here again, as in so many other respects, they developed an independent tradition instead of simply copying their models. While pictures illustrating biblical events held little interest for them, they devoted great effort to decorative embellishment. The finest of these manuscripts belong to the Hiberno-Saxon style, combining Celtic and Germanic elements, which flourished in the monasteries founded by Irishmen in Saxon England.

The Cross Page in the *Lindisfarne Gospels* (fig. 387) is an imaginative creation of breathtaking complexity; the miniaturist, working with a jeweler's precision, has poured into the compartments of his geometric frame an animal interlace so dense and yet so full of controlled movement that the fighting beasts on the Sutton Hoo purse cover seem childishly simple in comparison. It is as if the world of paganism, embodied in these biting and clawing monsters, had sud-

denly been subdued by the superior authority of the Cross. In order to achieve this effect, our artist has had to impose an extremely severe discipline upon himself. His "rules of the game" demand, for instance, that organic and geometric shapes must be kept separate; that within the animal compartments every line must turn out to be part of an animal's body, if we take the trouble to trace it back to its point of origin. There are also rules, too complex to go into here, concerning symmetry, mirror-image effects, and repetitions of shapes and colors. Only by working these out for ourselves by intense observation can we hope to enter into the spirit of this strange, mazelike world.

Of the representational images they found in Early Christian manuscripts, the Hiberno-Saxon illuminators generally retained only the symbols of the four evangelists, since these could be translated into their ornamental idiom without

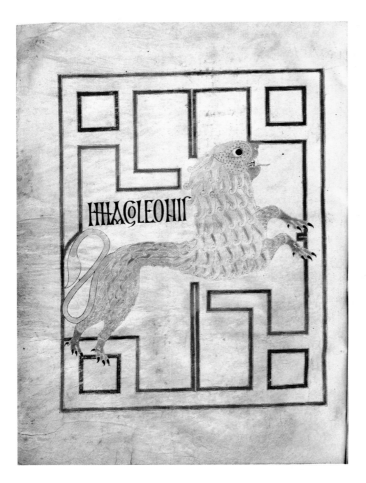

much difficulty. The lion of St. Mark in the *Echternach Gospels* (fig. 388), sectioned and patterned like the enamel inlays of the Sutton Hoo purse cover, is animated by the same curvilinear sense of movement we saw in the animal interlaces of the previous illustration. Here again we marvel at the masterly balance between the shape of the animal and the geometric framework on which it has been superimposed (and which, in this instance, includes the inscription, *imago leonis*).

The human figure, on the other hand, remained beyond the Celtic or Germanic artist's reach for a long time. The bronze plaque of the *Crucifixion* (fig. 389), probably made for a book cover, shows how helpless he was when faced with the image of a man. In his attempt to reproduce an Early Christian composition, he suffers from an utter inability to conceive of the human frame as an organic unit, so that the figure of Christ becomes disembodied in the most literal sense: the head, arms, and feet are all separate elements joined to a central pattern of whorls, zigzags, and interlacing bands. Clearly, there is a wide gulf between the Celtic-Germanic and the Mediterranean traditions, a gulf that the Irish artist who modeled the *Crucifixion* did not know how to bridge.

388. *SYMBOL OF ST. MARK,* from the *Echternach Gospels.* c. 690 A.D. 12¾ × 10⅜″ (32.4 × 26.4 cm). Bibliothèque Nationale, Paris

389. *CRUCIFIXION,* plaque from a book cover (?). 8th century A.D. Bronze. National Museum of Ireland, Dublin

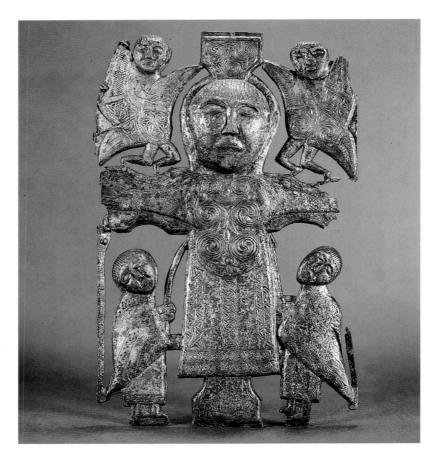

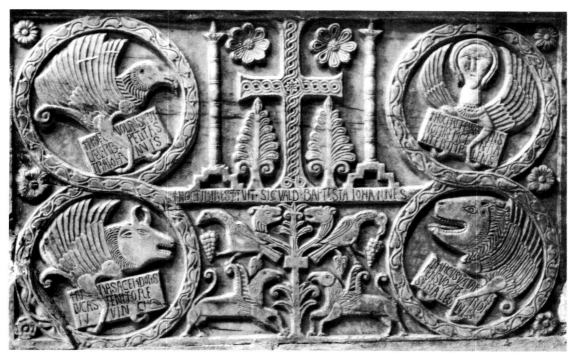

390. Balustrade relief inscribed by the Patriarch Sigvald (762–76 A.D.), probably carved c. 725–50 A.D. Marble, c. 3×5′ (91.3×152.3 cm). Cathedral Baptistery, Cividale, Italy

## Lombard Style

The situation was much the same in Continental Europe: we even find it among the Lombards in northern Italy. The Germanic stone carver who did the marble balustrade relief in the Cathedral Baptistery at Cividale (fig. 390) was just as perplexed as his Irish contemporaries by the problem of representation. His evangelists' symbols are strange creatures indeed; all four of them have the same spidery front legs, and their bodies consist of nothing but head, wings, and (except for the angel) a little spiral tail. Apparently he did not feel he was violating their integrity by forcing them into their circular frames in this Procrustean fashion. On the other hand, he had a well-developed sense of ornament; the panel as a whole, with its flat, symmetrical pattern, is an effective piece of decoration, rather like an embroidered cloth. He may, in fact, have derived his design in part from Oriental textiles (compare fig. 136).

# CAROLINGIAN ART

The empire built by Charlemagne (see page 291) did not endure for long. His grandsons divided it into three parts, and proved incapable of effective rule even in these, so that political power reverted to the local nobility. The cultural achievements of his reign, in contrast, have proved far more lasting; this very page would look different without them, for it is printed in letters whose shapes derive from the script in Carolingian manuscripts. The fact that these letters are known today as "roman" rather than Carolingian recalls another aspect of the cultural reforms sponsored by Charle-

magne: the collecting and copying of ancient Roman literature. The oldest surviving texts of a great many classical Latin authors are to be found in Carolingian manuscripts, which, until not very long ago, were mistakenly regarded as Roman, hence their lettering, too, was called roman.

This interest in preserving the classics was part of an ambitious attempt to restore ancient Roman civilization, along with the imperial title. Charlemagne himself took an active hand in this revival, through which he expected to implant the cultural traditions of a glorious past in the minds of the semibarbaric people of his realm. To an astonishing extent, he succeeded. Thus the "Carolingian revival" may be termed the first—and in some ways the most important—phase of a genuine fusion of the Celtic-Germanic spirit with that of the Mediterranean world.

## Architecture

PALACE CHAPEL, AACHEN. The fine arts played an important role in Charlemagne's cultural program from the very start. On his visits to Italy, he had become familiar with the architectural monuments of the Constantinian era in Rome and with those of the reign of Justinian in Ravenna; his own capital at Aachen, he felt, must convey the majesty of Empire through buildings of an equally impressive kind. His famous Palace Chapel (figs. 391 and 392) is, in fact, directly inspired by S. Vitale (compare figs. 334–37). To erect such a structure on Northern soil was a difficult undertaking; columns and bronze gratings had to be imported from Italy, and expert stonemasons must have been hard to find. The design, by Odo of Metz (probably the earliest architect

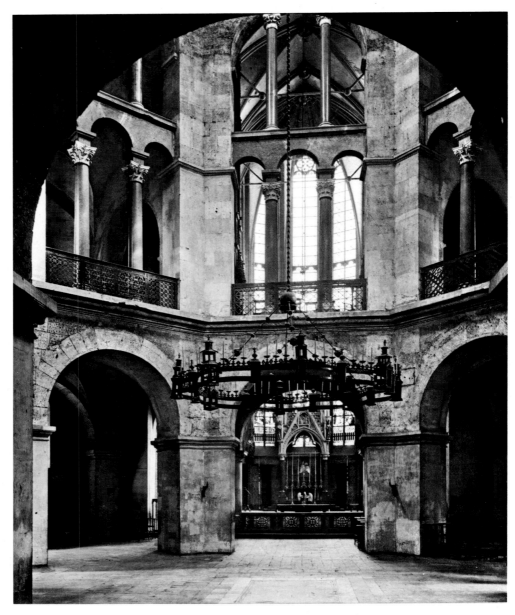

391. Interior of the Palace Chapel of Charlemagne, Aachen. 792–805 A.D.

north of the Alps known to us by name), is by no means a mere echo of S. Vitale but a vigorous reinterpretation, with piers and vaults of Roman massiveness and a geometric clarity of the spatial units very different from the fluid space of the earlier structure.

Equally significant is Odo's scheme for the western entrance (now largely obscured by later additions and rebuilding); at S. Vitale, the entrance consists of a broad, semidetached narthex with twin stair turrets, at an odd angle to the main axis of the church, while at Aachen these elements have been molded into a tall, compact unit, in line with the main axis and closely attached to the chapel proper. This monumental entrance structure, or westwork (from the German *Westwerk*), which makes one of its first known appearances here, holds the germ of the two-tower façade familiar from so many later medieval churches.

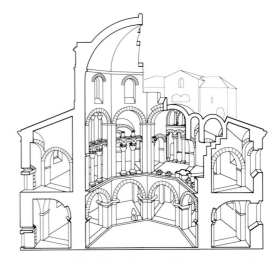

392. Cross section of the Palace Chapel of Charlemagne (after Kubach)

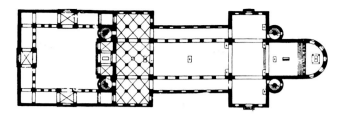

393. Plan of the Abbey Church of St.-Riquier, France.
Consecrated 799 A.D. (after Effmann, 1912)

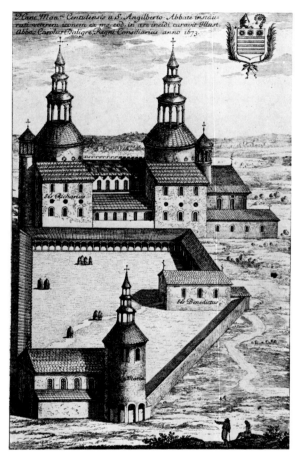

394. Abbey Church of St.-Riquier (engraved view by Petau, 1612, after an 11th-century manuscript illumination)

ST.-RIQUIER, ABBEVILLE. An even more elaborate westwork formed part of the greatest basilican church of Carolingian times, that of the monastery of St.-Riquier (also called Centula), near Abbeville in northeastern France. It has been completely destroyed, but its design is known in detail from drawings and descriptions (figs. 393 and 394). Several innovations in the church were to become of basic importance for the future: the westwork leads into a vaulted narthex which is in effect a western transept; the crossing (the area where the transept intersects the nave) was crowned by a tower, and the same feature recurred above the crossing of the eastern transept, again with two round

stair towers. The apse, unlike that of Early Christian basilicas (compare fig. 317), is separated from the eastern transept by a square compartment, called the choir. St.-Riquier was widely imitated in other Carolingian monastery churches, but these, too, have been destroyed or rebuilt in later times (a fine westwork of the tenth century is shown in figure 403).

PLAN OF A MONASTERY, ST. GALL. The importance of monasteries, and their close link with the imperial court, are vividly suggested by a unique document of the period, the large drawing of a plan for a monastery preserved in the Chapter Library at St. Gall in Switzerland (fig. 395). Its basic features seem to have been determined at a council held near Aachen in 816–17; this copy was then sent to the abbot of St. Gall for his guidance in rebuilding the monastery. We may regard it, therefore, as a standard plan, to be modified according to local needs.

The monastery is a complex, self-contained unit, filling a rectangle about 500 by 700 feet (fig. 396). The main entrance-way, from the west, passes between stables and a hostelry toward a gate which admits the visitor to a colonnaded semicircular portico flanked by two round towers, a sort of strung-out westwork that looms impressively above the low outer buildings. It emphasizes the church as the center of the monastic community. The church is a basilica, with a transept and choir in the east but an apse and altar at either end; the nave and aisles, containing numerous other altars, do not form a single continuous space but are subdivided into compartments by screens. There are numerous entrances: two beside the western apse, others on the north and south flanks.

This entire arrangement reflects the functions of a monastery church, designed for the liturgical needs of the monks rather than for a lay congregation. Adjoining the church to the south is an arcaded cloister, around which are grouped the monks' dormitory (on the east side), a refectory and kitchen (on the south side), and a cellar. The three large buildings north of the church are a guest house, a school, and the abbot's house. To the east are the infirmary, a chapel and quarters for novices, the cemetery (marked by a large cross), a garden, and coops for chickens and geese. The south side is occupied by workshops, barns, and other service buildings. There is, needless to say, no monastery exactly like this anywhere—even in St. Gall the plan was not carried out as drawn—yet its layout conveys an excellent notion of such establishments throughout the Middle Ages.

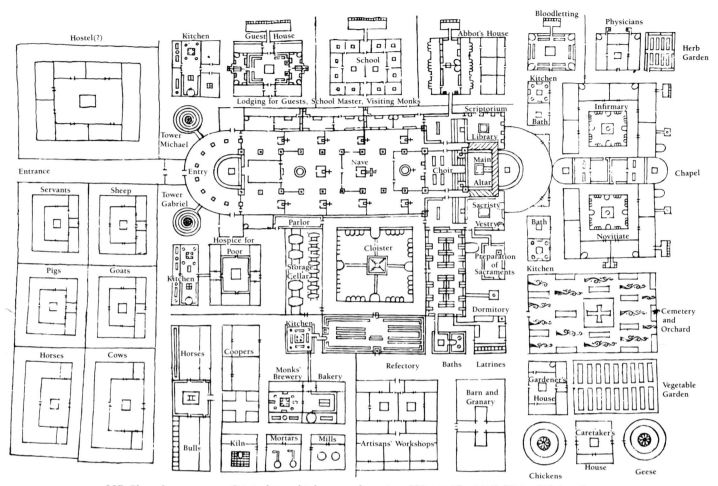

Hostel(?)

Kitchen

Guest House

School

Abbot's House

Bloodletting

Physicians

Herb Garden

Lodging for Guests, School Master, Visiting Monks

Scriptorium

Kitchen

Bath

Infirmary

Tower Michael

Library

Entry

Nave

Choir

Main Altar

Chapel

Entrance

Tower Gabriel

Sacristy

Vestry

Bath

Novitiate

Servants

Sheep

Hospice for Poor

Parlor

Cloister

Preparation of Sacraments

Kitchen

Pigs

Goats

Kitchen

Storage Cellar

Horses

Cows

Horses

Coopers

Dormitory

Cemetery and Orchard

Monks' Brewery

Bakery

Refectory

Baths

Latrines

Barn and Granary

Gardener's House

Vegetable Garden

Bulls

Kiln

Mortars

Mills

Artisans' Workshops

Chickens

Caretaker's House

Geese

395. Plan of a monastery. Original in red ink on parchment, c. 820 A.D. 28 × 44⅛″ (71.1 × 112.1 cm). Stiftsbibliothek, St. Gall, Switzerland (inscriptions translated into English from Latin)

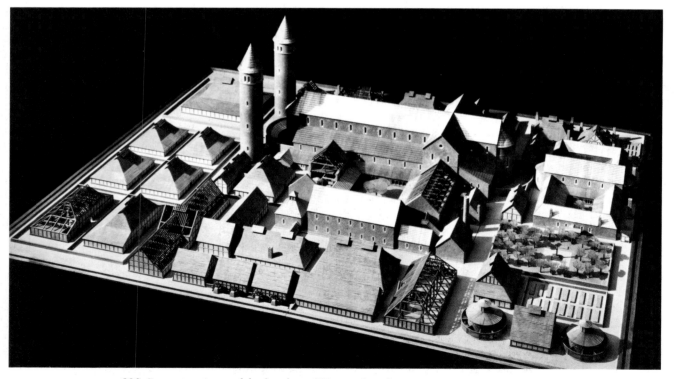

396. Reconstruction model, after the c. 820 A.D. plan of a monastery (Walter Horn, 1965)

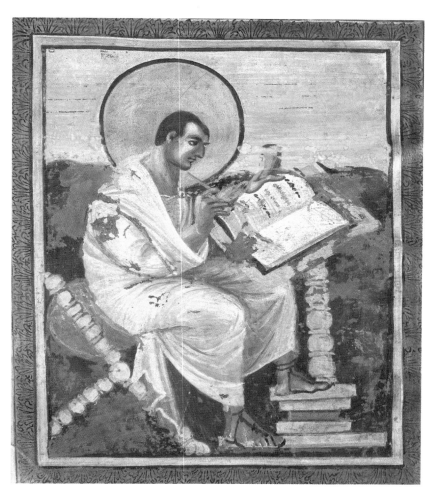

397. *ST. MATTHEW,*
from the *Gospel Book of Charlemagne.*
c. 800–10 A.D. 13 × 10″ (33 × 25.4 cm).
Kunsthistorisches Museum, Vienna

398. *PORTRAIT OF MENANDER.*
Wall painting. c. 70 A.D.
House of Menander, Pompeii

## Manuscripts and Book Covers

GOSPEL BOOK OF CHARLEMAGNE. We know from literary sources that Carolingian churches contained murals, mosaics, and relief sculpture, but these have disappeared almost entirely. Illuminated manuscripts, ivories, and goldsmiths' work, on the other hand, have survived in considerable numbers. They demonstrate the impact of the Carolingian revival even more strikingly than the architectural remains of the period. The former Imperial Treasury in Vienna contains a Gospel Book said to have been found in the tomb of Charlemagne and, in any event, closely linked with his court at Aachen. As we look at the picture of St. Matthew from that manuscript (fig. 397), we find it hard to believe that such a work could have been executed in northern Europe about the year 800; if it were not for the large golden halo, the Evangelist Matthew might almost be mistaken for a classical author's portrait like the one of Menander (fig. 398), painted at Pompeii almost eight centuries earlier. Whoever the artist was—Byzantine, Italian, or Frankish—he plainly was fully conversant with the Roman tradition of painting, down to the acanthus ornament on the wide frame, which emphasizes the "window" aspect of the picture. The *St. Matthew* represents the most orthodox phase of the Carolingian revival; it is the visual counterpart of copying the text of a classical work of literature.

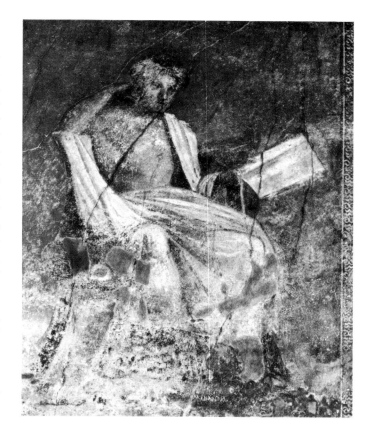

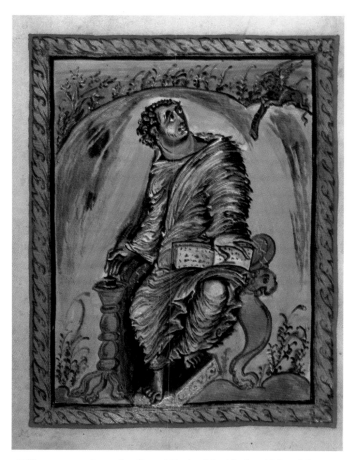

**GOSPEL BOOK OF ARCHBISHOP EBBO.** A miniature of some three decades later for the *Gospel Book of Archbishop Ebbo of Reims* (fig. 399) shows the classical model translated into a Carolingian idiom. It must have been based on an evangelist's portrait of the same style as the *St. Matthew*, but now the entire picture is filled with a vibrant energy that sets everything into motion: the drapery swirls about the figure, the hills heave upward, the vegetation seems to be tossed about by a whirlwind, and even the acanthus pattern on the frame assumes a strange, flamelike character. The Evangelist himself has been transformed from a Roman author setting down his own thoughts into a man seized with the frenzy of divine inspiration, an instrument for recording the Word of God. His gaze is fixed not upon his book but upon his symbol (the winged lion with a scroll), which acts as the transmitter of the Sacred Text. This dependence upon the Will of the Lord, so powerfully expressed here, marks the contrast between classical and medieval images of men. But the *means* of expression—the dynamism of line that distinguishes our miniature from its predecessor—recalls the passionate movement in the ornamentation of Irish manuscripts of the Dark Ages (figs. 387 and 388).

399. *ST. MARK,* from the *Gospel Book of Archbishop Ebbo of Reims.* 816–35 A.D. Bibliothèque Municipale, Epernay, France

**UTRECHT PSALTER.** The Reims School also produced the most extraordinary of all Carolingian manuscripts, the *Utrecht Psalter* (fig. 400). It displays the style of the *Ebbo Gospels* in an even more energetic form, since the entire book is illustrated with pen drawings. Here again the artist has followed a much older model, as indicated by the architectural and landscape settings of the scenes and by the use of Roman capital lettering, which had gone out of general use several centuries before. The wonderfully rhythmic

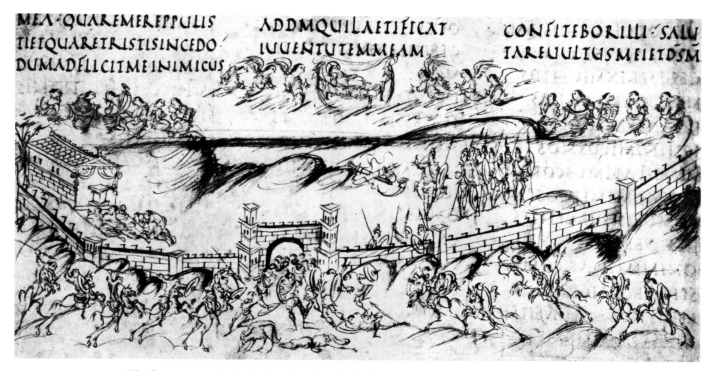

400. Illustration to Psalm 44, from the *Utrecht Psalter.* c. 820–32 A.D. University Library, Utrecht

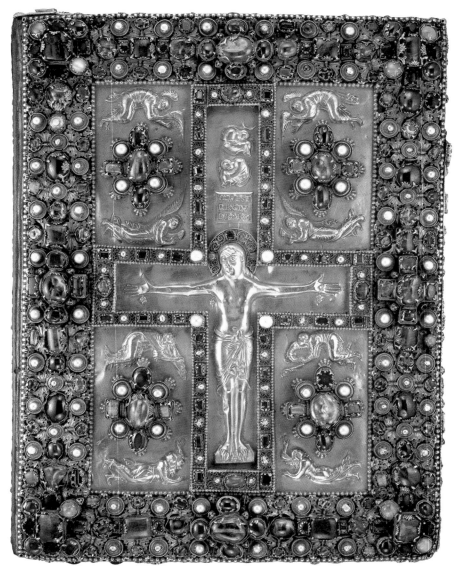

401. Upper cover of binding, the *Lindau Gospels*. c. 870 A.D.
Gold and jewels, 13¾ × 10½″ (35 × 26.7 cm). The Pierpont Morgan Library, New York

quality of his draftsmanship, however, gives to these sketches a kind of emotional coherence that could not have been present in the earlier pictures. Without it, the drawings of the *Utrecht Psalter* would carry little conviction, for the poetic language of the Psalms does not lend itself to illustration in the same sense as the narrative portions of the Bible.

The Psalms can be illustrated only by taking each phrase literally and then by visualizing it in some manner. Thus, at the top of our picture, we see the Lord reclining on a bed, flanked by pleading angels, an image based on the words, "Awake, why sleepest thou, O Lord?" On the left, the faithful crouch before the Temple, "for . . . our belly cleaveth unto the earth," and at the city gate in the foreground they are killed "as sheep for the slaughter." In the hands of a pedestrian artist, this procedure could well turn into a wearisome charade; here, it has the force of a great drama.

LINDAU GOSPELS COVER. The style of the Reims School can still be felt in the reliefs of the jeweled front cover of the *Lindau Gospels* (fig. 401), a work of the third quarter of the ninth century. This masterpiece of the goldsmith's art shows how splendidly the Celtic-Germanic metalwork tradition of the Dark Ages adapted itself to the Carolingian revival. The clusters of semiprecious stones are not mounted directly on the gold ground but raised on claw feet or arcaded turrets, so that the light can penetrate beneath them, to bring out their full brilliance. Interestingly enough, the crucified Christ betrays no hint of pain or death; He seems to stand rather than to hang, His arms spread out in a solemn gesture. To endow Him with the signs of human suffering was not yet conceivable, even though the means were at hand, as we can see from the eloquent expressions of grief among the small figures in the adjoining compartments.

# OTTONIAN ART

In 870, about the time when the *Lindau Gospels* cover was made, the remains of Charlemagne's empire were ruled by his two surviving grandsons: Charles the Bald, the West Frankish king, and Louis the German, the East Frankish king, whose domains corresponded roughly to the France and Germany of today. Their power was so weak, however, that Continental Europe once again lay exposed to attack. In the south, the Moslems resumed their depredations, Slavs and Magyars advanced from the east, and Vikings from Scandinavia ravaged the north and west.

These Norsemen (the ancestors of today's Danes and Norwegians) had been raiding Ireland and Britain by sea from the late eighth century on; now they invaded northwestern France as well, occupying the area that ever since has been called Normandy. Once established there, they soon adopted Christianity and Carolingian civilization, and, from 911 on, their leaders were recognized as dukes nominally subject to the authority of the king of France. During the eleventh century, the Normans assumed a role of major importance in shaping the political and cultural destiny of Europe, with William the Conqueror becoming king of England while other Norman nobles expelled the Arabs from Sicily and the Byzantines from South Italy.

In Germany, meanwhile, after the death of the last Carolingian monarch in 911, the center of political power had shifted north to Saxony. The Saxon kings (919–1024) reestablished an effective central government, and the greatest of them, Otto I, also revived the imperial ambitions of Charlemagne. After marrying the widow of a Lombard king, he extended his rule over most of Italy and had himself crowned emperor by the pope in 962. From then on the Holy Roman Empire was to be a German institution—or perhaps we ought to call it a German dream, for Otto's successors never managed to consolidate their claim to sovereignty south of the Alps. Yet this claim had momentous consequences, since it led the German emperors into centuries of conflict with the papacy and local Italian rulers, linking North and South in a love-hate relationship whose echoes can be felt to the present day.

## Sculpture

During the Ottonian period, from the mid-tenth century to the beginning of the eleventh, Germany was the leading nation of Europe, politically as well as artistically. German

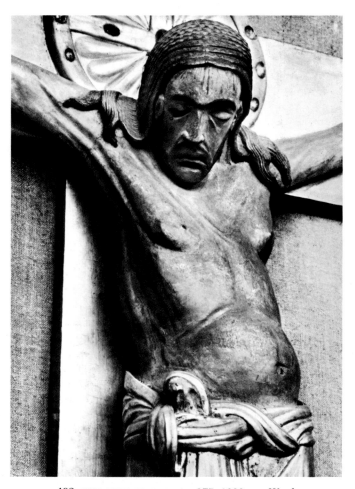

402. *THE GERO CRUCIFIX.* c. 975–1000 A.D. Wood,
height 6'2" (2 m). Cathedral, Cologne

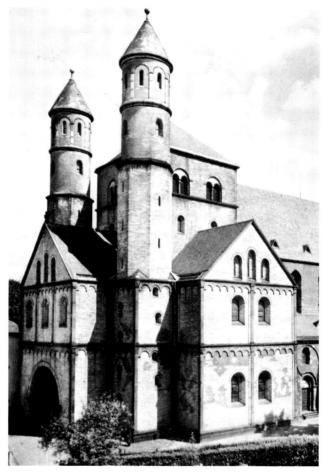

403. Westwork, St. Pantaleon, Cologne. Consecrated 980 A.D.

achievements in both areas began as revivals of Carolingian traditions but soon developed new and original traits.

GERO CRUCIFIX. These changes of outlook are impressively brought home to us if we compare the Christ on the cover of the *Lindau Gospels* with *The Gero Crucifix* (fig. 402) in the Cathedral at Cologne. The two works are separated by little more than a hundred years' interval, but the contrast between them suggests a far greater span. In *The Gero Crucifix* we meet an image of the crucified Saviour new to Western art: monumental in scale, carved in powerfully rounded forms, and filled with a deep concern for the sufferings of the Lord. Particularly striking is the forward bulge of the heavy body, which makes the physical strain on arms and shoulders seem almost unbearably real. The face, with its deeply incised, angular features, has turned into a mask of agony, from which all life has fled.

How did the Ottonian sculptor arrive at this startlingly bold conception? We do not belittle his greatness by recalling that the compassionate view of Christ on the Cross had been created in Byzantine art of the Second Golden Age (see fig. 355) and that *The Gero Crucifix* clearly derives from that source. Nor need we be surprised that Byzantine influence should have been strong in Germany at that time, for Otto II

had married a Byzantine princess, establishing a direct link between the two imperial courts. It remained for the Ottonian artist to translate the Byzantine image into large-scale sculptural terms and to replace its gentle pathos with an expressive realism that has been the main strength of German art ever since.

## Architecture

Cologne was closely connected with the imperial house through its archbishop, Bruno, the brother of Otto I, who left a strong mark on the city through the numerous churches he built or rebuilt. His favorite among these, the Benedictine Abbey of St. Pantaleon, became his burial place as well as that of the wife of Otto II. Only the monumental westwork (fig. 403) has retained its original shape essentially unchanged until modern times: we recognize it as a massive and well-proportioned successor to Carolingian westworks, with the characteristic tower over the crossing of the western transept and a deep porch flanked by tall stair turrets.

ST. MICHAEL'S, HILDESHEIM. The most ambitious patron of architecture and art in the Ottonian age, however, judged in terms of surviving works, was Bernward, who,

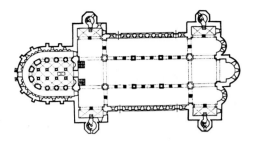

404. Reconstructed plan, Hildesheim Cathedral
(St. Michael's). 1001–33

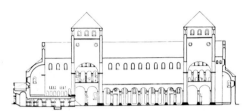

405. Reconstructed longitudinal section,
Hildesheim Cathedral (after Beseler)

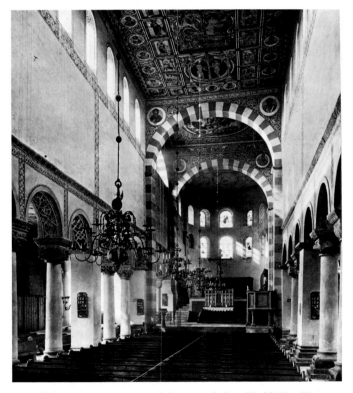

406. Interior (view toward the west, before World War II),
Hildesheim Cathedral

after having been one of the tutors of Otto III, became Bishop of Hildesheim. His chief monument is another Benedictine abbey church, St. Michael's (figs. 404–6). The plan, with its two choirs and lateral entrances, recalls the monastery church of the St. Gall plan (fig. 395). But in St. Michael's the symmetry is carried much further: not only are there two identical transepts, with crossing towers and stair turrets (see St.-Riquier, figs. 393 and 394), but the supports of the nave arcade, instead of being uniform, consist of pairs of columns separated by square piers. This alternate system divides the arcade into three equal units of three openings each; the first and third units are correlated with the entrances, thus echoing the axis of the transepts. Since, moreover, the aisles and nave are unusually wide in relation to their length, Bernward's intention must have been to achieve a harmonious balance between the longitudinal and transverse axes throughout the structure.

The exterior, as well as the choirs, of Bernward's church have been disfigured by rebuilding, but the interior of the nave (figs. 405 and 406), with its great expanse of wall space between arcade and clerestory, retained the majestic spatial feeling of the original design until World War II reduced it to ruins. (The capitals of the columns date from the twelfth century, the painted wooden ceiling from the thirteenth.) The Bernwardian western choir, as reconstructed in our plan on the basis of recent studies, is particularly interesting: its floor was raised above the level of the rest of the church, so as to accommodate a half-subterranean basement chapel, or crypt, apparently a special sanctuary of St. Michael, which could be entered both from the transept and from the west. The crypt was roofed by groined vaults resting on two rows of columns, and its walls were pierced by arched openings that linked it with the U-shaped corridor, or ambulatory, wrapped around it. This ambulatory must have been visible above ground, enriching the exterior of the western choir, since there were windows in its outer wall. Such crypts with ambulatories, usually housing the venerated tomb of a saint, had been introduced into the repertory of Western church architecture during Carolingian times; the Bernwardian design stands out for its large scale and its carefully planned integration with the rest of the building.

## Metalwork

BRONZE DOORS OF BISHOP BERNWARD. How much importance Bernward himself attached to the crypt at St. Michael's can be gathered from the fact that he commissioned a pair of richly sculptured bronze doors which were probably meant for the two entrances leading from the transept to the ambulatory (they were finished in 1015, the year the crypt was consecrated). The idea may have come to him as a result of his visit to Rome, where he could see ancient Roman—and perhaps Byzantine—bronze doors. The Bernwardian doors, however, differ from their predecessors; they are divided into broad horizontal fields rather than vertical panels, and each field contains a biblical scene in high relief.

Our detail (fig. 407) shows Adam and Eve after the Fall. Below it, in inlaid letters remarkable for their classical Roman character, is part of the dedicatory inscription, with the date and Bernward's name. In these figures we find nothing

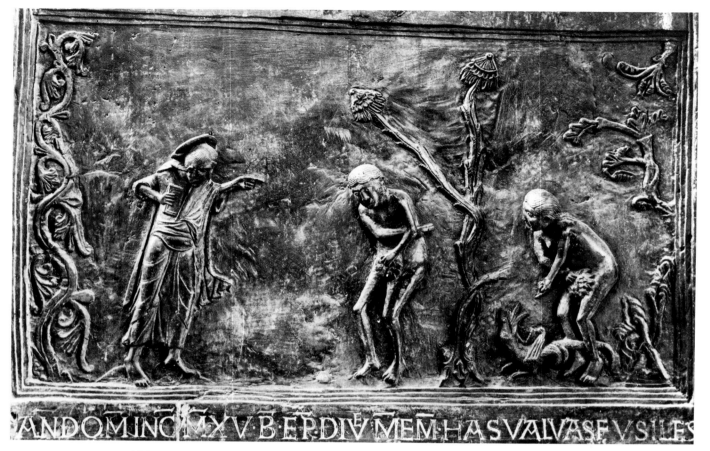

407. *ADAM AND EVE REPROACHED BY THE LORD*, from the Bronze Doors of Bishop Bernward.
1015. c. 23 × 43″ (58.3 × 109.3 cm). Hildesheim Cathedral

of the monumental spirit of *The Gero Crucifix:* they seem far smaller than they actually are, so that one might easily mistake them for a piece of goldsmith's work such as the *Lindau Gospels* cover (compare fig. 401). The entire composition must have been derived from an illuminated manuscript; the oddly stylized bits of vegetation have a good deal of the twisting, turning movement we recall from Irish miniatures. Yet the story is conveyed with splendid directness and expressive force. The accusing finger of the Lord, seen against a great void of blank surface, is the focal point of the drama; it points to a cringing Adam, who passes the blame to his mate, while Eve, in turn, passes it to the serpent at her feet.

## Manuscripts

GOSPEL BOOK OF OTTO III. The same intensity of glance and of gesture characterizes Ottonian manuscript painting, which blends Carolingian and Byzantine elements into a new style of extraordinary scope and power. The most important center of Manuscript illumination at that time was the Reichenau Monastery, on an island in the Lake of Constance. Perhaps its finest achievement—and one of the great masterpieces of medieval art—is the *Gospel Book of Otto III*, from which we reproduce two full-page miniatures (figs. 408 and 409).

The scene of Christ washing the feet of St. Peter contains notable echoes of ancient painting, transmitted through Byzantine art; the soft pastel hues of the background recall the illusionism of Graeco-Roman landscapes, and the architectural frame around Christ is a late descendant of such architectural perspectives as the mural from Boscoreale (see fig. 305). That these elements have been misunderstood by the Ottonian artist is obvious enough; but he has also put them to a new use, so that what was once an architectural vista now becomes the Heavenly City, the House of the Lord filled with golden celestial space as against the atmospheric earthly space without. The figures have undergone a similar transformation: in ancient art, this composition had been used to represent a doctor treating a patient. Now St. Peter takes the place of the sufferer, and Christ that of the physician (note that He is still the beardless young philosopher type here). As a consequence, the emphasis has shifted from physical to spiritual action, and this new kind of action is not only conveyed through glances and gestures, it also governs the scale of things: Christ and St. Peter, the most active figures, are larger than the rest; Christ's "active" arm is longer than His "passive" one; and the eight disciples who merely watch have been compressed into a tiny space, so that we see little more than their eyes and hands.

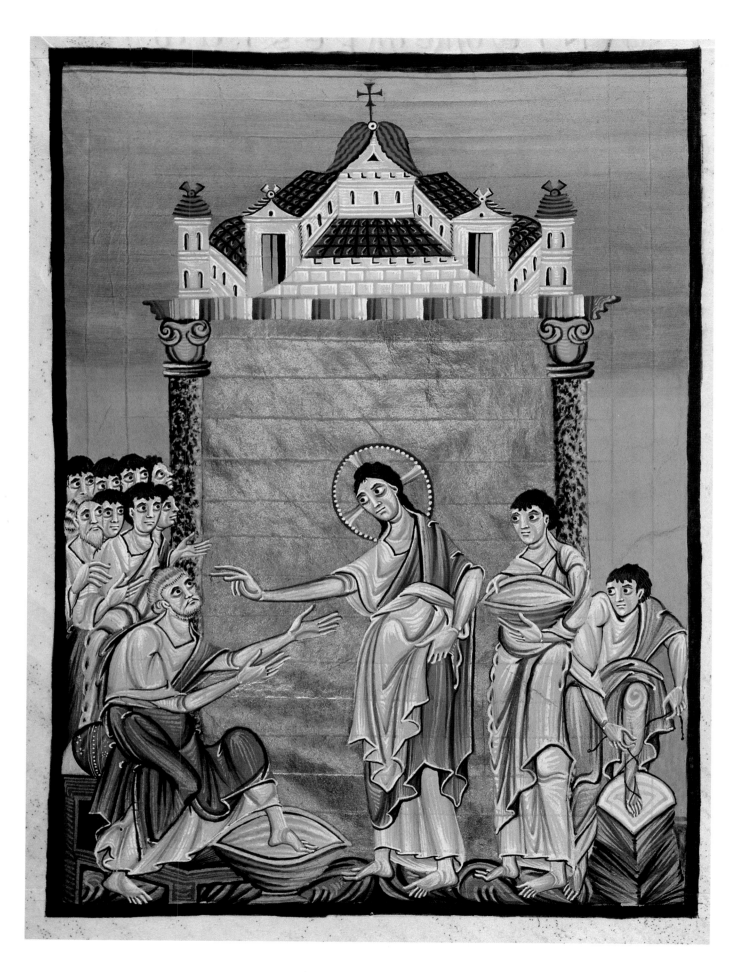

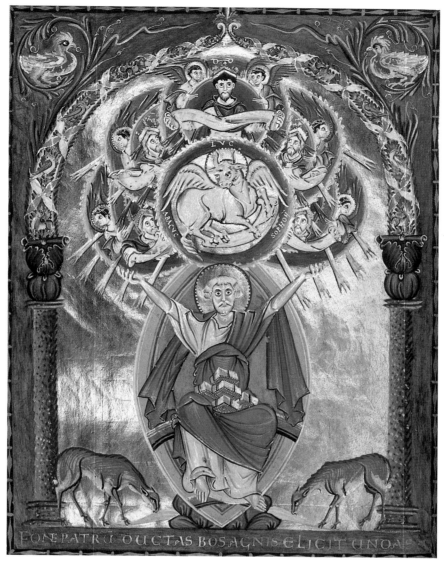

409. *ST. LUKE*, from the *Gospel Book of Otto III*.
c. 1000. 13×9⅜" (33×23.8 cm). Staatsbibliothek, Munich

The other miniature, the painting of St. Luke, is a symbolic image of overwhelming grandeur. Unlike his Carolingian predecessors, the Evangelist is no longer shown writing; his Gospel lies completed on his lap. Enthroned on two rainbows, he holds aloft a huge cluster of clouds from which tongues of light radiate in every direction. Within it we see

408. *(opposite) CHRIST WASHING THE FEET OF PETER,*
from the *Gospel Book of Otto III*. c. 1000. 13×9⅜" (33×23.8 cm).
Staatsbibliothek, Munich

his symbol, the ox, surrounded by five Old Testament prophets and an outer circle of angels. At the bottom, two lambs drink the life-giving waters that spring from beneath the Evangelist's feet. The key to the entire design is in the inscription: *Fonte patrum ductas bos agnis elicit undas*— "From the source of the fathers the ox brings forth a flow of water for the lambs"—that is, St. Luke makes the prophets' message of salvation explicit for the faithful. The Ottonian artist has truly "illuminated" the meaning of this terse and enigmatic phrase by translating it into such compelling visual terms.

# CHAPTER THREE
# ROMANESQUE ART

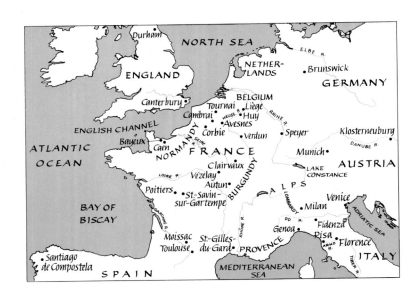

Looking back over the ground we have covered in this book so far, a thoughtful reader will be struck by the fact that almost all of our chapter headings and subheadings might serve equally well for a general history of civilization. Some are based on technology (for example, the Old Stone Age), others on geography, ethnology, religion; whatever the source, they have been borrowed from other fields, even though in our context they also designate artistic styles. There are only two important exceptions to this rule: Archaic and Classical are primarily terms of style; they refer to qualities of form rather than to the setting in which these forms were created. Why don't we have more terms of this sort? We do, as we shall see—but only for the art of the past nine hundred years.

Those who first conceived the idea of viewing the history of art as an evolution of styles started out with the conviction that art in the ancient world developed toward a single climax: Greek art from the age of Pericles to that of Alexander the Great. This style they called Classical (that is, perfect). Everything that came before was labeled Archaic, to indicate that it was still old-fashioned and tradition-bound, not-yet-Classical but striving in the right direction, while the style of post-Classical times did not deserve a special term since it had no positive qualities of its own, being merely an echo or a decadence of Classical art.

The early historians of medieval art followed a similar pattern; to them, the great climax was the Gothic style, from the thirteenth century to the fifteenth. For whatever was not-yet-Gothic they adopted the label Romanesque. In doing so, they were thinking mainly of architecture; pre-Gothic churches, they noted, were round-arched, solid, and heavy (as against the pointed arches and the soaring lightness of Gothic structures), rather like the ancient Roman style of building, and the term "Romanesque" was meant to convey just that. In this sense, all of medieval art before 1200, insofar as it shows any link with the Mediterranean tradition, could be called Romanesque. Some scholars speak of medieval art before Charlemagne as pre-Romanesque, and of Carolingian and Ottonian as proto- or early Romanesque, and they are right to the extent that Romanesque art proper (that is, medieval art from about 1050 to 1200) would be unthinkable without the contributions of these earlier styles. On the other hand, if we follow this practice we are likely to do less than justice to those qualities that make the art of the Dark Ages and of Carolingian and Ottonian times different from the Romanesque.

Carolingian art, we will recall, was brought into being by Charlemagne and his circle, as part of a conscious revival policy; even after his death, it remained strongly linked with his imperial court. Ottonian art, too, had this sponsorship, and a correspondingly narrow base. The Romanesque, in contrast, sprang up all over western Europe at about the same time; it consists of a large variety of regional styles, distinct yet closely related in many ways, and without a central source. In this respect, it resembles the art of the Dark Ages rather than the court styles that had preceded it, although it includes the Carolingian-Ottonian tradition along with a good many other, less clearly traceable ones, such as Late Classical, Early Christian, and Byzantine elements, some Is-lamic influence, and the Celtic-Germanic heritage.

What welded all these different components into a coherent style during the second half of the eleventh century was not any single force but a variety of factors that made for a new burgeoning of vitality throughout the West. Christianity had at last triumphed everywhere in Europe; the Vikings, still largely pagan in the ninth and tenth centuries when their raids terrorized the British Isles and the Continent, had entered the Catholic fold, not only in Normandy but in Scandinavia as well; the Caliphate of Cordova had disintegrated in 1031 into many small Moslem states, opening the way for the reconquest of the Iberian peninsula; and the Magyars had settled down in Hungary.

There was a growing spirit of religious enthusiasm, reflected in the greatly increased pilgrimage traffic to sacred sites and culminating, from 1095 on, in the crusades to liberate the Holy Land from Moslem rule. Equally important was the reopening of Mediterranean trade routes by the navies of Venice, Genoa, and Pisa; the revival of commerce and manufacturing; and the consequent growth of city life. During the turmoil of the early Middle Ages, the towns of the West Roman Empire had shrunk greatly in size (the population of Rome, about one million in 300 A.D., fell to less than 50,000 at one point); some were deserted altogether. From the eleventh century on, they began to regain their former importance. New towns sprang up everywhere, and an urban middle class of craftsmen and merchants established itself between the peasantry and the landed nobility as an important factor in medieval society.

In many respects, then, western Europe between 1050 and 1200 became a great deal more "Roman-esque" than it had been since the sixth century, recapturing some of the international trade patterns, the urban quality, and the military strength of ancient imperial times. The central political authority was lacking, to be sure, (even the empire of Otto I did not extend much farther west than modern Germany does), but the central spiritual authority of the pope took its place to some extent as a unifying force. The international army that responded to Urban II's call for the First Crusade was more powerful than anything a secular ruler could have raised for the purpose.

# ARCHITECTURE

The most conspicuous difference between Romanesque architecture and that of the preceding centuries is the amazing increase in building activity. An eleventh-century monk, Raoul Glaber, summed it up well when he triumphantly exclaimed that the world was putting on a "white mantle of churches." These churches were not only more numerous than those of the early Middle Ages, they were also generally larger, more richly articulated, and more "Roman-looking," for their naves now had vaults instead of wooden roofs, and their exteriors, unlike those of Early Christian, Byzantine, Carolingian, and Ottonian churches, were decorated with both architectural ornament and sculpture. Geographically, Romanesque monuments of the first importance are distributed over an area that might well have represented the

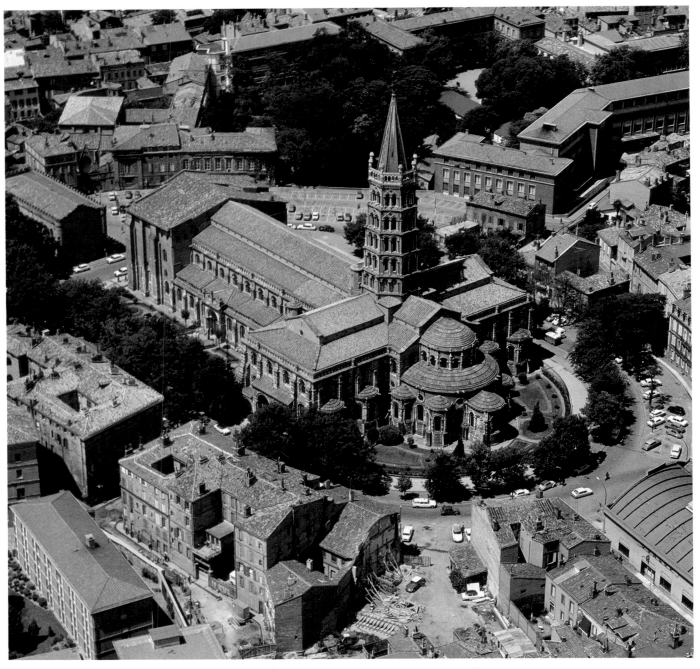

410. St.-Sernin, Toulouse (aerial view). c. 1080–1120

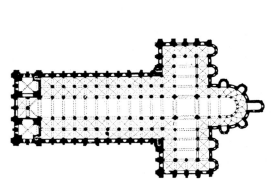

411. Plan of St.-Sernin (after Conant)

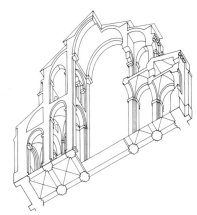

412. Axonometric projection of nave, St.-Sernin (after Choisy)

world—the Catholic world, that is—to Raoul Glaber: from northern Spain to the Rhineland, from the Scottish-English border to central Italy. The richest crop, the greatest variety of regional types, and the most adventurous ideas are to be found in France. If we add to this group those destroyed or disfigured buildings whose original designs are known to us through archaeological research, we have a wealth of architectural invention unparalleled by any previous era.

## Southwestern France

ST.-SERNIN, TOULOUSE. We begin our sampling of Romanesque churches—it cannot be more than that—with St.-Sernin, in the southern French town of Toulouse (figs. 410–13), one of a group of great churches of the "pilgrimage type," so called because they were built along the roads leading to the pilgrimage center of Santiago de Compostela in northwestern Spain. The plan immediately strikes us as very much more complex and more fully integrated than those of earlier structures such as St.-Riquier, or St. Michael's at Hildesheim (see figs. 393 and 404). It is an emphatic Latin cross, with the center of gravity at the eastern end. Clearly, this church was not designed to serve a monastic community only but (like Old St. Peter's in Rome, fig. 316) to accommodate large crowds of lay worshipers in its long nave and transept.

The nave is flanked by two aisles on either side, the inner aisle continuing around the arms of the transept and the apse and thus forming a complete ambulatory circuit anchored to the two towers of the west façade. The ambulatory, we will recall, had developed as a feature of the crypts of earlier churches (as at St. Michael's); now it has emerged above ground and it is linked with the aisles of nave and transept, and enriched with apsidal chapels that seem to radiate from the apse and continue along the eastern face of the transept. (Apse, ambulatory, and radiating chapels form a unit known as the pilgrimage choir.) The plan also shows that the aisles of St.-Sernin are groin-vaulted throughout. This, in conjunction with the features already noted, imposes a high degree of regularity upon the entire design: the aisles are made up of square bays, which serve as a basic unit, or module, for the other dimensions, so that the nave and transept bays equal two such units, the crossing and the façade towers four units.

On the exterior, this rich articulation is further enhanced by the different roof levels that set off the nave and transept against the inner and outer aisles, the apse, the ambulatory, and the radiating chapels; by the buttresses reinforcing the walls between the windows, so as to contain the outward thrust of the vaults; by the decorative framing of windows and portals; and by the great crossing tower (completed in Gothic times and taller than originally intended). The two façade towers, unfortunately, have remained stumps.

As we enter the nave, we are impressed with its tall proportions, the architectural elaboration of the nave walls, and the dim, indirect lighting, all of which create a sensation very different from the ample and serene interior of St. Michael's, with its simple and clearly separated "blocks" of space (see figs. 405 and 406). The contrast between these structures is such as to make the nave walls of St. Michael's

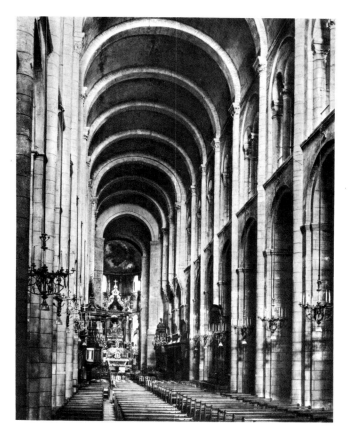

413. Nave and choir, St.-Sernin

look Early Christian (see fig. 318), while those of St.-Sernin seem more akin to structures such as the Colosseum (see fig. 263). The syntax of ancient Roman architecture—vaults, arches, engaged columns, and pilasters firmly knit together into a coherent order—has indeed been recaptured here to a remarkable degree; yet the forces whose interaction is expressed in the nave of St.-Sernin are no longer the physical, "muscular" forces of Graeco-Roman architecture but spiritual forces—spiritual forces of the kind we have seen governing the human body in Carolingian and Ottonian miniatures. The half-columns running the entire height of the nave wall would appear just as unnaturally drawn-out to an ancient Roman beholder as the arm of Christ in figure 409. They seem to be driven upward by some tremendous, unseen pressure, hastening to meet the transverse arches that subdivide the barrel vault of the nave. Their insistently repeated rhythm propels us toward the eastern end of the church, with its light-filled apse and ambulatory (now obscured by a huge altar of later date).

In thus describing our experience we do not, of course, mean to suggest that the architect consciously set out to achieve this effect. For him, beauty and engineering were inseparable. Vaulting the nave so as to eliminate the fire hazard of a wooden roof was not only a practical aim; it also challenged him to make the House of the Lord grander and more impressive. And since a vault becomes the more difficult to sustain the farther it is from the ground, he strained every resource to make the nave as tall as he dared. He had, however, to sacrifice the clerestory for safety's sake. Instead, he built galleries over the inner aisles, to abut the lateral pressure of the nave vault, hoping that enough light would filter through them into the central space. St.-Sernin serves to remind us that architecture, like politics, is "the art of the possible," and that its success, here as elsewhere, is measured by the degree to which the architect has explored the limits of what was possible to him under those particular circumstances, structurally and aesthetically.

## Burgundy and Western France

The builders of St.-Sernin would have been the first to admit that their answer to the problem of the nave vault was not a final one, impressive though it is in its own terms.

AUTUN CATHEDRAL. The architects of Burgundy arrived at a more elegant solution, as evidenced by the Cathedral of Autun (fig. 414), where the galleries are replaced by a blind arcade (called a triforium, since it often has three openings per bay) and a clerestory. What made this three-story elevation possible was the use of the pointed arch for the nave vault, which produced a thrust more nearly downward than outward. For reasons of harmony, the pointed arch also appears in the nave arcade (it had probably reached France from Islamic architecture, where it had been employed for some time). Autun, too, comes close to straining the limits of the possible, for the upper part of the

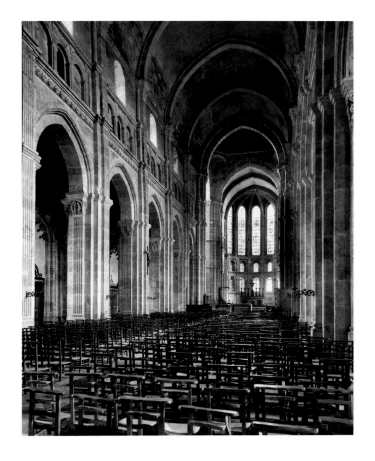

414. (*above*) Nave wall, Autun Cathedral c. 1120–32

415. (*left*) Choir (c. 1060–75) and nave (1095–1115), St.-Savin-sur-Gartempe

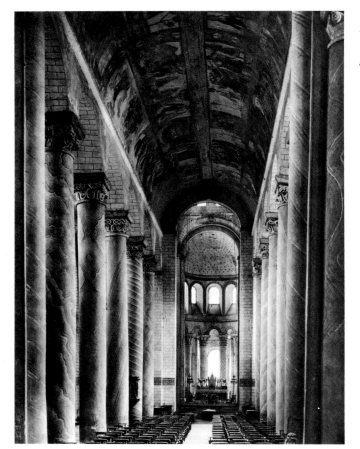

nave wall shows a slight but perceptible outward lean under the pressure of the vault, a warning against any further attempts to increase the height of the clerestory or to enlarge the windows.

HALL CHURCHES. A third alternative, with virtues of its own, appears in the west of France, in such churches as that of St.-Savin-sur-Gartempe (fig. 415). The nave vault here lacks the reinforcing arches, since it was meant to offer a continuous surface for murals (see fig. 446 for this cycle, the finest of its kind). Its great weight rests directly on the nave arcade, which is supported by a majestic set of columns. Yet the nave is fairly well lit, for the two aisles are carried almost to the same height, making it a "hall church," and their outer walls have generously sized windows. At the eastern end of the nave, there is a pilgrimage choir—happily unobstructed in this case—beyond the crossing tower.

The nave and aisles of hall churches are covered by a single roof, as at St.-Savin. The west façade, too, tends to be low and wide, and may become a richly sculptured screen. That of Notre-Dame-la-Grande at Poitiers (fig. 416), due west from St.-Savin, is particularly noteworthy in this respect, with its elaborately bordered arcades housing large seated or standing figures. A wide band of relief stretches across the façade on either side of the doorway, which is deeply recessed and framed by a series of arches resting on stumpy columns. Taller bundles of columns enhance the turrets, whose conical helmets match the height of the gable in the center (which rises above the actual height of the roof behind it). The sculptural program spread out over this entire

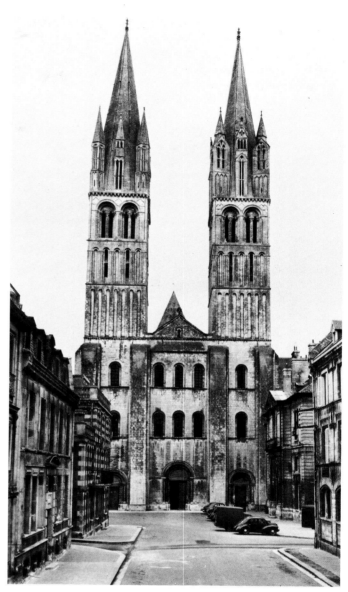

417. West façade, St.-Etienne, Caen. Begun 1068

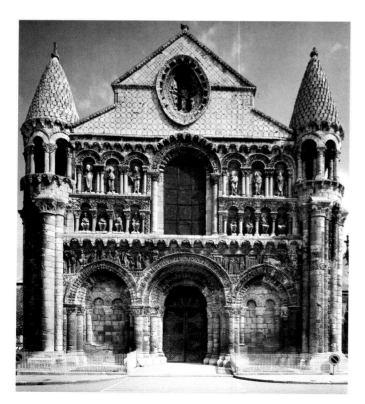

416. West façade, Notre-Dame-la-Grande, Poitiers.
Early 12th century

area is a visual exposition of Christian doctrine that is a feast for the eyes as well as the mind.

## England and Normandy

Farther north, in Normandy, the west façade evolved in an entirely different direction. That of the abbey church of St.-Etienne at Caen (fig. 417), founded by William the Conqueror a year or two after his invasion of England, offers a striking contrast with Notre-Dame-la-Grande. Decoration is at a minimum, four huge buttresses divide the front of the church into three vertical sections, and the vertical impetus continues triumphantly in the two splendid towers, whose height would be impressive enough even without the tall Early Gothic helmets. The interior is equally remarkable, but in order to understand its importance we must first turn to the extraordinary development of Anglo-Norman architecture in Britain during the last quarter of the eleventh century.

DURHAM CATHEDRAL.  Its most ambitious product is the Cathedral of Durham (figs. 418–20), just south of the Scottish border, begun in 1093. Though somewhat more austere in plan, it has a nave one-third wider than St.-Sernin's, and a greater overall length (400 feet), which places it among the largest churches of medieval Europe. The nave may have been designed to be vaulted from the start; and the vault over its eastern end had been completed by 1107; the rest of the nave, following the same pattern, by 1130. This vault is of great interest, for it represents the earliest systematic use of a ribbed groined vault over a three-story nave, and thus marks a basic advance beyond the solution we saw at Autun. Looking at the plan, we see that the aisles consist of the usual groin-vaulted compartments closely approaching a square, while the bays of the nave, separated by strong transverse arches, are decidedly oblong and groin-vaulted in such a way that the ribs form a double-X design, dividing the vault into seven sections rather than the conventional four. Since the nave bays are twice as long as the aisle bays, the transverse arches occur only at the odd-numbered piers of the nave arcade, and the piers therefore alternate in size, the larger ones being of compound shape (that is, bundles of column and pilaster shafts attached to a square or oblong core), the others cylindrical.

Perhaps the easiest way to visualize the origin of this peculiar system is to imagine that the architect started out by designing a barrel-vaulted nave, with galleries over the aisles, and without a clerestory, as at St.-Sernin, but with

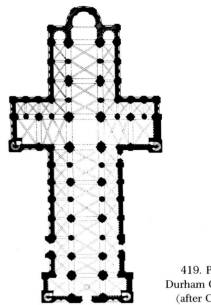

419. Plan of
Durham Cathedral
(after Conant)

420. Transverse section of
Durham Cathedral
(after Acland)

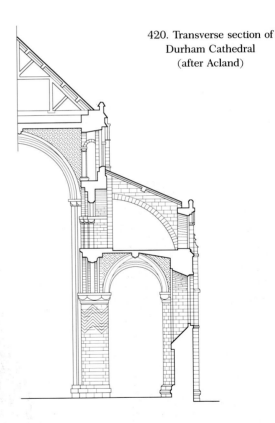

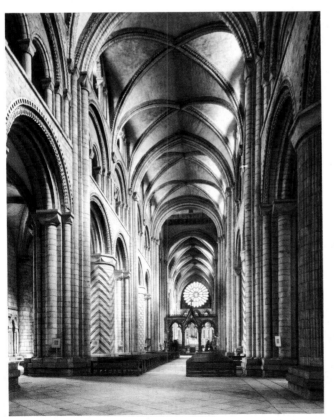

418. Nave (looking east), Durham Cathedral. 1093–1130

the transverse reinforcing arches spaced more widely. As he was doing so, he realized that he could have a clerestory after all if the barrel vault of each nave bay was intersected by two transverse barrel vaults of *oval* shape (see fig. 421); the result would be a pair of Siamese-twin groined vaults, and the ends of the transverse barrel vaults could become the clerestory, since the outward thrust and the weight of the whole vault would be concentrated at six securely anchored points on the gallery level. The ribs, of course, were necessary to provide a stable skeleton for the groined vault,

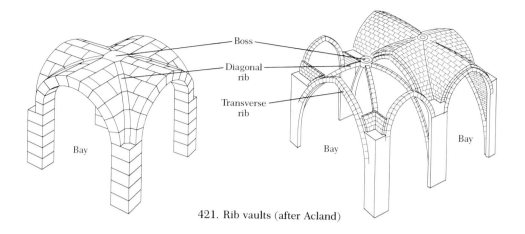

421. Rib vaults (after Acland)

so that the curved surfaces between them could be filled in with masonry of minimum thickness, thus reducing both weight and thrust. We do not know whether this ingenious scheme was actually invented at Durham, but it could not have been created much earlier, for it is still in an experimental stage. While the transverse arches at the crossing are round, those to the west of it are slightly pointed, indicating a continuous search for improvements in detail. Aesthetically, the nave at Durham is among the finest in all Romanesque architecture: the wonderful sturdiness of the alternating piers makes a splendid contrast with the dramatically lighted, saillike surfaces of the vault.

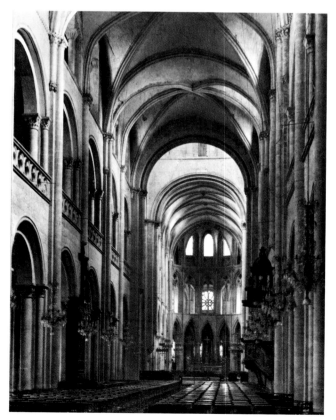

422. Nave (vaulted c. 1115–20), St.-Etienne, Caen

ST.-ETIENNE, CAEN. Let us now return to the interior of St.-Etienne at Caen (fig. 422). The nave, it seems, had originally been planned with galleries and clerestory, and a wooden ceiling. After the experience of Durham, it became possible, in the early twelfth century, to build a groined nave vault instead, with only slight modifications of the wall design. But the bays of the nave here are approximately square, so that the double-X rib pattern could be replaced by a single X with an additional transverse rib (see fig. 421), producing a groined vault of six sections instead of seven. These sexpartite vaults are no longer separated by heavy transverse arches but by simple ribs—another saving in weight that, besides, gives a stronger sense of continuity to the nave vault as a whole and makes for a less emphatic alternating system of piers. Compared to Durham, the nave of St.-Etienne creates an impression of graceful, airy lightness closely akin to the quality of the Gothic choir that was added in the thirteenth century. And structurally, too, we have here reached the point where Romanesque merges into Early Gothic.

## Lombardy

At the time when the Normans and Anglo-Normans constructed their earliest ribbed groined nave vaults, the same problem was being explored in Lombardy, where ancient cities had once again grown large and prosperous. Lombard Romanesque architecture was both nourished and impeded by a continuous building tradition reaching back to Roman and Early Christian times and including the monuments of Ravenna.

S. AMBROGIO, MILAN. We sense this background as we approach one of its most venerable and important structures, S. Ambrogio in Milan (figs. 423–25), on a site that had been occupied by a church since the fourth century. The present building was begun in the late eleventh century, except for the apse and southern tower, which date from the tenth. The brick exterior, though more ornate and far more monumental, recalls the proportions and the geometric simplicity of the Ravennate churches (compare figs. 319 and 334). Upon entering the atrium, we are confronted by the severely handsome façade, with its deeply recessed arcades; just beyond it are two bell towers, separate structures just touching the outer walls of the church. We had seen a round tower of this kind—probably the earliest surviving example, of the ninth or tenth century—on the north side of S. Apollinare in Classe (fig. 319); most of its successors are square, but the tradition of the free-standing bell tower, or campanile, remained so strong in Italy that they hardly ever became an integral part of the church proper.

The nave of S. Ambrogio, low and broad (it is some ten feet wider than that at Durham), consists of four square

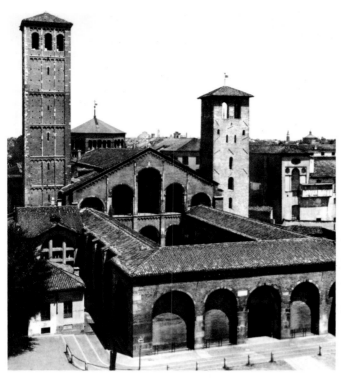

423. S. Ambrogio, Milan. Late 11th and 12th centuries

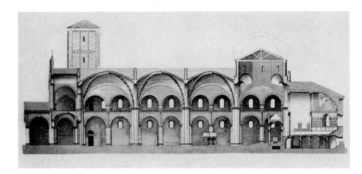

425. Longitudinal section of S. Ambrogio

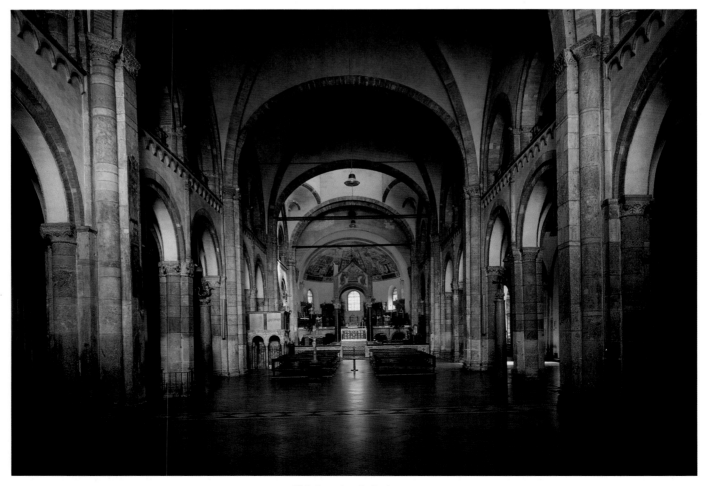

424. Interior, S. Ambrogio

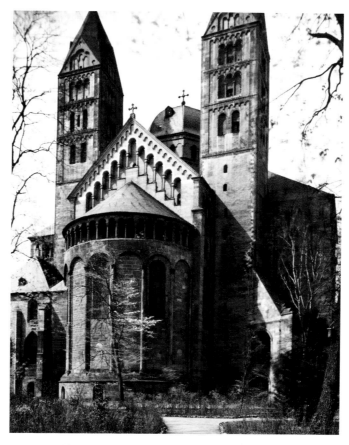

426. Speyer Cathedral, from the east. Begun 1030

bays separated by strong transverse arches. There is no transept, but the easternmost nave bay carries an octagonal, domed crossing tower or lantern. This was an afterthought, and we can easily see why, for the nave has no clerestory and the windows of the lantern provide badly needed illumination. As at Durham, or Caen, there is an alternate system of nave piers, since the length of each nave bay equals that of two aisle bays; the latter are groin-vaulted, like the first three of the nave bays, and support galleries. The nave vaults, however, differ significantly from their northern counterparts. Constructed of brick and rubble, in a technique reminiscent of Roman groined vaults such as those in the Basilica of Constantine, they are a good deal heavier; the diagonal ribs, moreover, form true half circles (at Durham and Caen, they are flattened), so that the vaults rise to a point considerably above the transverse arches. This produces a domed effect and gives each bay the appearance of a separate entity, apart from further increasing the weight of the vault.

On a smaller scale, the Milanese architect might have attempted a clerestory instead of galleries; but the span of the nave was determined by the width of the tenth-century apse, and he shared with his patrons a taste for ample interior proportions like those of Early Christian basilicas (compare fig. 321) instead of striving for height and light as his Norman contemporaries did. Under these circumstances,

he saw no reason to take risks by experimenting with more economical shapes and lighter construction, so that the ribbed groined vault in Lombardy remained conservative and never approached the proto-Gothic stage.

## Germany and the Low Countries

SPEYER CATHEDRAL. German Romanesque architecture, centered in the Rhineland, was equally conservative, although its conservatism reflects the persistence of Carolingian-Ottonian rather than earlier traditions. Its finest achievement, the Imperial Cathedral of Speyer, begun about 1030 but not completed until more than a century later, has a westwork (now sheathed by a modern reconstruction) and an equally monumental eastern grouping of crossing tower and paired stair towers (fig. 426). The architectural detail derives from Lombardy, long a focus of German imperial ambitions (compare S. Ambrogio), but the tall proportions are northern, and the scale is so vast as to dwarf every other church of the period. The nave, one-third taller and wider than that of Durham, has a generous clerestory, since it was planned for a wooden roof; in the early twelfth century, it was divided into square bays and covered with heavy, unribbed groined vaults akin to the Lombard rather than the Norman type.

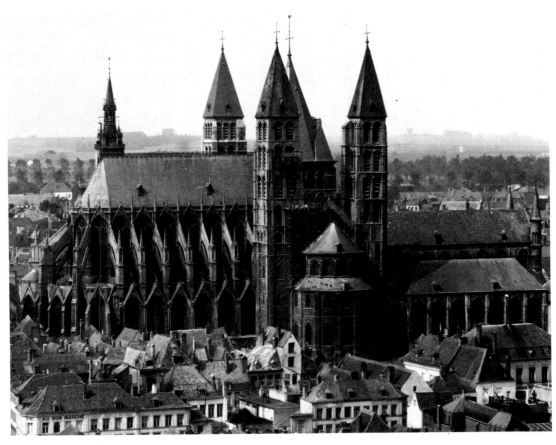

427. Tournai Cathedral. Nave 1110–71; transept and crossing c. 1165–1213

TOURNAI CATHEDRAL. The impressive eastern end of Speyer Cathedral is echoed in a number of churches of the Rhine Valley and the Low Countries. In the Cathedral of Tournai (fig. 427), it occurs twice, at either end of the transept—the most memorable massing of towers anywhere in Romanesque architecture. Originally, there were to have been four more: two at the west façade (later reduced to turrets) and two flanking the eastern apse (replaced by a huge Gothic choir). Such multiple towers had been firmly established in medieval church design north of the Alps since the time of Charlemagne (see St.-Riquier, fig. 394), although few complete sets were ever finished and even fewer have survived. Whatever their practical functions (as stair towers, bell towers, or watchtowers), their popularity can hardly be accounted for on this basis. In a way not easily fathomed today, they expressed medieval man's relation to the supernatural, as the ziggurats had done for the ancient Mesopotamians (the story of the Tower of Babel always fascinated the people of the Middle Ages). Perhaps their symbolic meaning is best illustrated by a "case history." A certain count had a quarrel with the people of a nearby town, led by their bishop. He finally laid siege to the town, captured it, and, to express his triumph and humiliate his enemies, he lopped the top off their cathedral tower. Evidently, loss of tower meant loss of face, towers being architectural symbols of strength, power, and authority.

## Tuscany

CAMPANILE, BAPTISTERY, AND CATHEDRAL, PISA. The most famous tower of all, however, owes its renown to an accident. It is the Leaning Tower of Pisa (or, more precisely, the Campanile of Pisa Cathedral), which began to assume its present angle, because of poor foundations, even before completion (figs. 428 and 429; note that its axis is slightly bent). The tower forms part of a magnificent ensemble on an open site north of the city that includes the Cathedral and the circular, domed Baptistery to the west of it. They represent the most ambitious monument of the Tuscan Romanesque, reflecting the wealth and pride of the city republic of Pisa.

Far more than Lombardy, with its strong northward connections, Tuscany retained an awareness of its classical heritage throughout the Middle Ages. The plan of Pisa Cathedral is essentially that of an Early Christian basilica, elaborated into a Latin cross by the addition of two transept arms that resemble smaller basilicas in themselves, with apses of their own; the crossing is marked by a dome, but the rest of the church is wooden-roofed except for the aisles (four in the nave, two in the transept arms), which have groined vaults. The interior (fig. 430) has somewhat taller proportions than an Early Christian basilica, because there are galleries over the aisles, as well as a clerestory, yet the

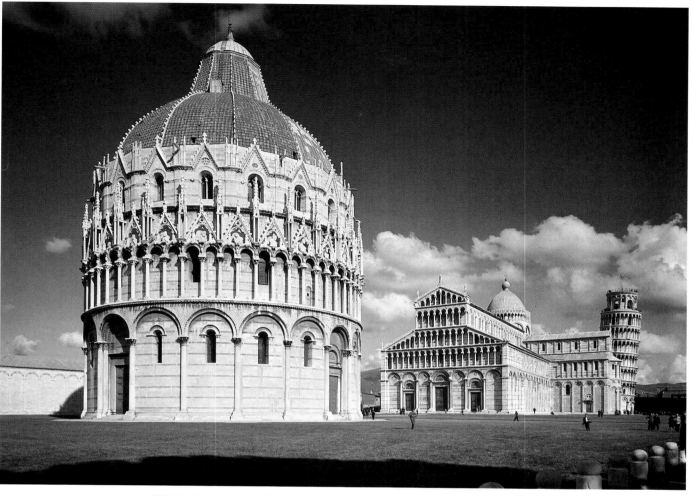

428. Pisa Baptistery, Cathedral, and Campanile (view from the west). 1053–1272

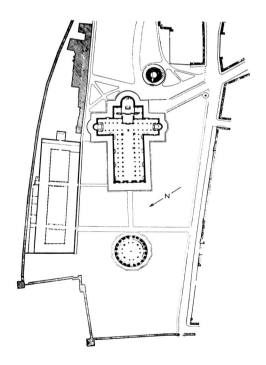

429. Plan of Pisa Cathedral,
Baptistery, and Campanile

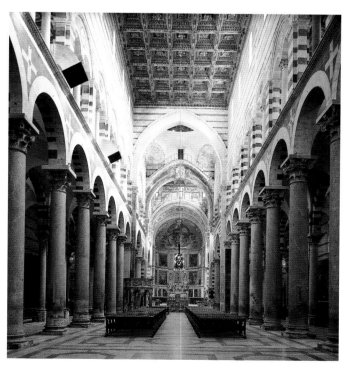

430. Interior, Pisa Cathedral

splendid files of classical columns supporting the nave and aisle arcades inevitably recall such Roman structures as St. Paul Outside the Walls (see fig. 318).

Pisa Cathedral and its companions are sheathed entirely in white marble inlaid with horizontal stripes and ornamental patterns in dark-green marble. This practice, familiar from Imperial Roman times, survived (or was revived) only in central Italy during the Middle Ages. On the exteriors, it is combined with blind arcades and galleries, producing a lacelike richness of texture and color very different from the austerely simple Early Christian exteriors. But then the time had long passed when it might be thought undesirable for a church to compete with the outward splendor of classical temples.

BAPTISTERY OF S. GIOVANNI, FLORENCE. In Florence, which was to outstrip Pisa commercially and artistically, the greatest achievement of the Tuscan Romanesque is the Baptistery (fig. 431), opposite the Cathedral, a domed octagonal structure of impressive size. Here the marble paneling follows severe geometric lines, and the blind arcades are extraordinarily classical in proportion and detail. The entire building, in fact, exudes so classical an air that the Florentines themselves came to believe, a few hundred years later, that it had originally been a temple of Mars. And even today the controversy over its date has not yet been settled to everyone's satisfaction. We shall have to return to this baptistery a number of times, since it was destined to play an important role in the Renaissance.

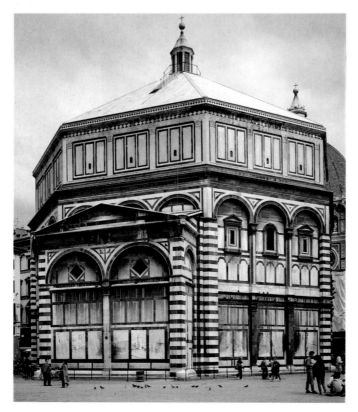

431. Baptistery of S. Giovanni, Florence. c. 1060–1150

# SCULPTURE

The revival of monumental stone sculpture is even more astonishing than the architectural achievements of the Romanesque era, since neither Carolingian nor Ottonian art had shown any tendencies in this direction. Free-standing statues, we will recall, all but disappeared from Western art after the fifth century; stone relief survived only in the form of architectural ornament or surface decoration, with the depth of the carving reduced to a minimum. Thus the only continuous sculptural tradition in early medieval art was that of sculpture-in-miniature: small reliefs, and occasional statuettes, in metal or ivory. Ottonian art, in works such as the bronze doors of Bishop Bernward (see fig. 407), had enlarged the scale of this tradition but not its spirit; and its truly large-scale sculptural efforts, represented by the impressive *Gero Crucifix* (fig. 402), were limited almost entirely to wood. What little stone carving there was in western Europe before the mid-eleventh century hardly went beyond the artistic and technical level of the Sigvald relief (fig. 390).

## Southwestern France

Fifty years later, the situation had changed dramatically. Just when and where the revival of stone sculpture began we cannot say with assurance, but if any one area has a claim to priority it is southwestern France and northern Spain, along the pilgrimage roads leading to Santiago de Compostela. The link with the pilgrimage traffic seems logical enough, for architectural sculpture, especially when applied to the exterior of a church, is meant to appeal to the lay worshiper rather than to the members of a closed monastic community.

ST.-SERNIN, TOULOUSE. Like Romanesque architecture, the rapid development of stone sculpture between 1050 and 1100 reflects the growth of religious fervor among the lay population in the decades before the First Crusade. St.-Sernin at Toulouse contains several important examples probably carved about 1090, including the *Apostle* in figure 432. This panel is now in the ambulatory; its original location remains uncertain—perhaps it decorated the front of an altar. Be that as it may, the figure (which is somewhat more than half lifesize) was not intended for viewing at close range only. Its impressive bulk and weight "carry" over a considerable distance. This emphasis on massive volume hints at what may well have been the main impulse behind the revival of large-scale sculpture: a stone-carved image, being tangible and three-dimensional, is far more "real" than a painted one. To the mind of a cleric steeped in the abstractions of theology, this might seem irrelevant, or even dangerous. St. Bernard of Clairvaux, writing in 1127, denounced the sculptured decoration of churches as a vain folly and diversion that tempts us "to read in the marble rather than in our books." His was a voice not very much heeded, however; for the unsophisticated layman, any large piece of sculpture inevitably had something of the quality of an idol, and it was this very fact that gave it such great appeal.

close-fitting cap, the body severe and blocklike. Our *Apostle* has, in fact, much the same dignity and directness as the sculpture of Archaic Greece.

ST.-PIERRE, MOISSAC. Another important early center of Romanesque sculpture was the abbey at Moissac, some distance north of Toulouse. The south portal of its church, carved a generation later than the *Apostle* from St.-Sernin, displays a richness of invention that would have made St. Bernard wince. (The parts of the medieval portal are shown in figure 435.) In figure 433 we see the magnificent *trumeau* (the center post supporting the lintel) and the western jamb. Both have a scalloped profile—apparently a bit of Moorish influence (see fig. 368)—and the shafts of the half-columns applied to jambs and *trumeau* follow this scalloped pattern as if they had been squeezed from a giant pastry tube. Human and animal forms are treated with the same

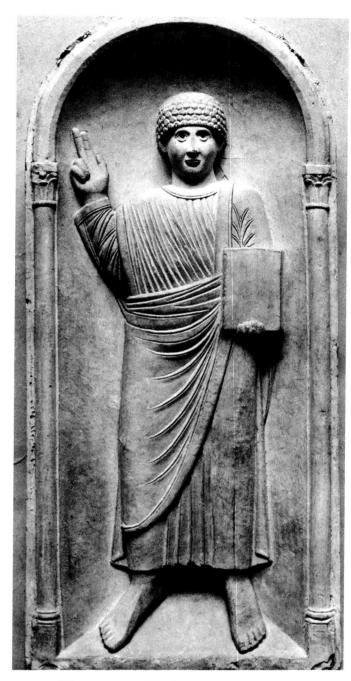

432. *APOSTLE*. c. 1090. Stone. St.-Sernin, Toulouse

But let us return to the *Apostle* from St.-Sernin. Where have we seen its like before? The solidity of the forms has a strongly classical air, indicating that our artist must have had a close look at late Roman sculpture (of which there are considerable remains in southern France). The design as a whole, on the other hand—the solemn frontality of the figure, its placement in the architectural frame—derives from a Byzantine source, in all likelihood an ivory panel descended from the *Archangel Michael* in figure 332. Yet in enlarging such a miniature, the carver of our relief has also reinflated it: the niche is a real cavity, the hair a round,

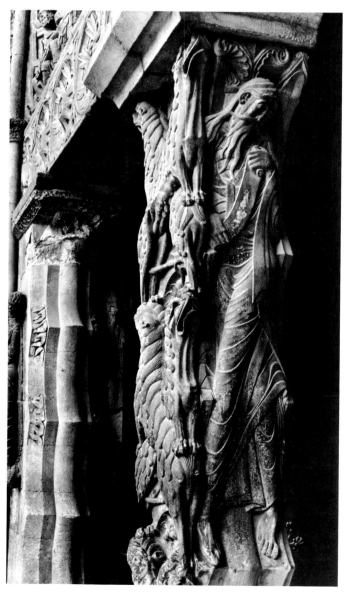

433. South portal (portion), St.-Pierre, Moissac. Early 12th century

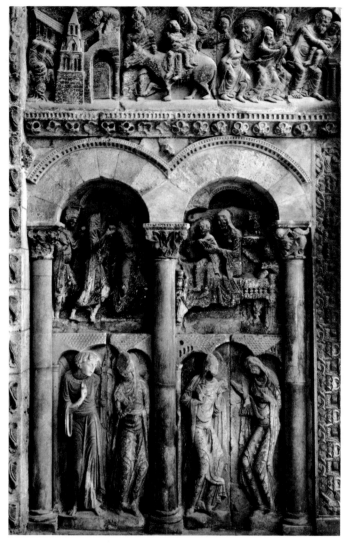

434. East flank, south portal, St.-Pierre, Moissac
(the angel of the *Annunciation,* bottom left, is modern)

cannot fully account for their presence at Moissac in terms of their effectiveness as ornament. They belong to a vast family of savage or monstrous creatures in Romanesque art that retain their demoniacal vitality even though they are compelled—like our lions—to perform a supporting function. (Similar examples may be seen in figs. 433 and 439). Their purpose is thus not merely decorative but expressive; they embody dark forces that have been domesticated into guardian figures or banished to a position that holds them fixed for all eternity, however much they may snarl in protest.

The portal proper at Moissac is preceded by a deep porch, with lavishly sculptured sides. On the east flank (fig. 434) we see, within the arcade, the *Annunciation* and *Visitation,* as well as the *Adoration of the Magi.* Other events from the early life of Christ are shown on the frieze above. Here we find the same thin limbs, the same eloquent gestures we saw in the prophet on the *trumeau* (note especially the wonderful play of hands in the *Visitation* and *Annunciation*); only the proportions of the bodies and the size of the figures vary with the architectural context. What matters is the vividness of the narrative, rather than consistency of treatment.

## Burgundy

AUTUN CATHEDRAL. The tympanum (the lunette above the lintel) of the main portal of Romanesque churches (see fig. 435) is usually given over to a composition centered on the Enthroned Christ, most often the Apocalyptic Vision or the Last Judgment, the most awesome scene of Christian art. At Autun Cathedral, the latter subject has been visualized with singularly expressive force. Our detail (fig. 436) shows part of the right half of the tympanum, with the weighing of the souls. At the bottom, the dead rise from their graves in fear and trembling; some are already beset by snakes or gripped by huge, clawlike hands. Above, their fate quite literally hangs in the balance, with devils yanking at one end of the scales and angels at the other. The saved souls cling like children to the hem of the angel's garment for protection, while the condemned are seized by grinning devils and cast into the mouth of Hell. These devils betray the same nightmarish imagination we observed in the Romanesque animal world; they are composite creatures, human in general outline but with spidery, birdlike legs, furry thighs, tails, pointed ears, and enormous, savage mouths. But their violence, unlike that of the animal monsters, is unchecked; they enjoy themselves to the full in their grim occupation. No visitor, having "read in the marble" here (to speak with St. Bernard), could fail to enter the church in a chastened spirit.

STE.-MADELEINE, VÉZELAY. Perhaps the most beautiful of all Romanesque tympanums is that of Ste.-Madeleine in Vézelay, not far from Autun in Burgundy (fig. 437). Its subject, the Mission of the Apostles, had a special meaning for this age of crusades, since it proclaims the duty of every Christian to spread the Gospel to the ends of the earth. From the hands of the majestic ascending Christ we see the rays of the Holy Spirit pouring down upon the apostles, all of

incredible flexibility, so that the spidery prophet on the side of the *trumeau* seems perfectly adapted to his precarious perch (notice how he, too, has been fitted into the scalloped outline). He even remains free to cross his legs in a dancelike movement and to turn his head toward the interior of the church as he unfurls his scroll.

But what of the crossed lions that form a symmetrical zigzag on the face of the *trumeau*—do they have a meaning? So far as we know, they simply "animate" the shaft as the interlacing beasts of Irish miniatures (whose descendants they are) animate the compartments assigned to them. In manuscript illumination, this tradition had never died out; our sculpture has undoubtedly been influenced by it, just as the agitated movement of the prophet has its ultimate origin in miniature painting (see fig. 444). The crossed lions, however, reflect another source as well; we find them in Persian metalwork (although not in this towerlike formation), whence they can be traced back to the confronted animals of ancient Near Eastern art (see figs. 113 and 152). Yet we

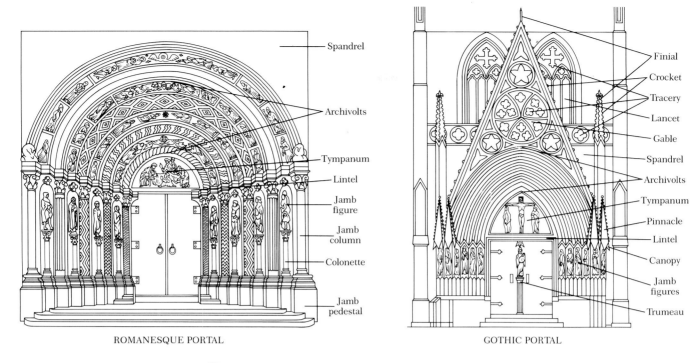

Spandrel

Archivolts

Tympanum

Lintel

Jamb figure

Jamb column

Colonette

Jamb pedestal

ROMANESQUE PORTAL

Finial

Crocket

Tracery

Lancet

Gable

Spandrel

Archivolts

Tympanum

Pinnacle

Lintel

Canopy

Jamb figures

Trumeau

GOTHIC PORTAL

435. Romanesque and High Gothic portal ensembles

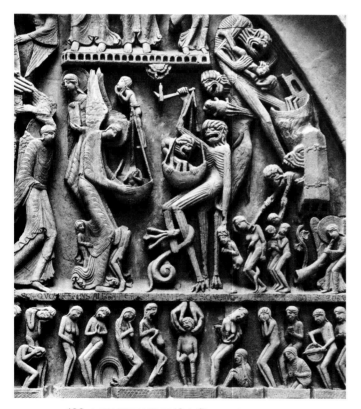

436. *LAST JUDGMENT* (detail), west tympanum, Autun Cathedral. c. 1130–35

them equipped with copies of the Scriptures in token of their mission. The lintel and the compartments around the central group are filled with representatives of the heathen world, a veritable encyclopedia of medieval anthropology which includes all sorts of legendary races (fig. 438). On the archivolt (the arch framing the tympanum) we recognize the signs of the zodiac and the labors appropriate to every month of the year, to indicate that the preaching of the Faith is as unlimited in time as it is in space.

## Romanesque Classicism

PROVENCE. The portal sculpture at Moissac, Autun, and Vézelay, although varied in style, has many qualities in common: intense expression, unbridled fantasy, and a nervous agility of form that owes more to manuscript illumination and metalwork than to the sculptural tradition of antiquity. The *Apostle* from St.-Sernin, in contrast, had impressed us with its stoutly "Roman" flavor. The influence of classical monuments is particularly strong in Provence, the coastal region of southeastern France (which had been part of the Graeco-Roman world far longer than the rest of the country and is full of splendid Roman remains), as well as in Italy. Perhaps for this reason, the Romanesque style persisted longer in these areas than elsewhere. Looking at the center portal of the church at St.-Gilles-du-Gard (fig. 439), one of the great masterpieces of Romanesque art, we are struck immediately by the classical flavor of the architectural framework, with its free-standing columns, meander patterns, and fleshy acanthus ornament. The two large statues, carved almost in the round, have a sense of weight and volume akin to that of the *Apostle* from St.-Sernin, although, being half a century later in date, they also display the richness of detail we have observed in the intervening monu-

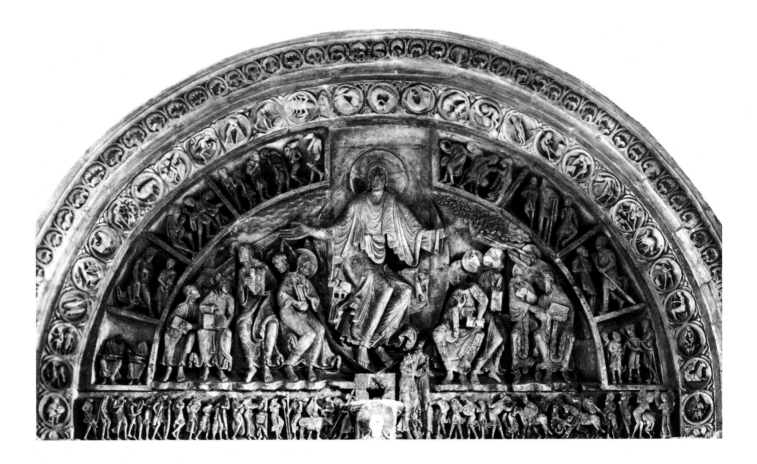

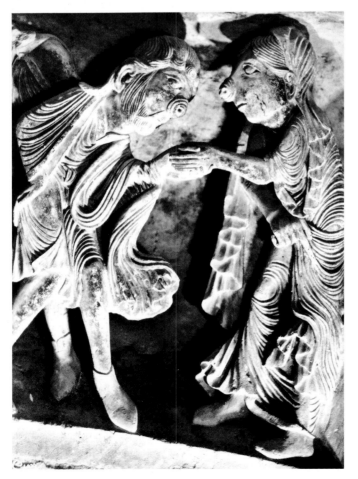

437. *THE MISSION OF THE APOSTLES,* tympanum of center portal of narthex, Ste.-Madeleine, Vézelay. 1120–32

438. *PIG-SNOUTED ETHIOPIANS,* portion of tympanum, Ste.-Madeleine, Vézelay

ments. They stand on brackets supported by crouching beasts of prey, and these, too, show a Roman massiveness, while the small figures on the base (Cain and Abel) recall the style of Moissac.

FIDENZA CATHEDRAL. The two statues at St.-Gilles are akin to the splendid figure of King David from the façade of Fidenza Cathedral in Lombardy (fig. 440), by Benedetto Antelami, the greatest sculptor of Italian Romanesque art. That we should know his name is not surprising in itself—artists' signatures are far from rare in Romanesque times; what makes Antelami exceptional is the fact that his work shows a considerable degree of individuality, so that, for the first time since the ancient Greeks, we can begin to speak (though with some hesitation) of a personal style. And his *David,* too, approaches the ideal of the self-sufficient statue more closely than any medieval work we have seen so far. The *Apostle* from St.-Sernin is one of a series of figures, all of them immutably fixed to their niches, while Antelami's *David* stands physically free and even shows an attempt to recapture the Classical *contrapposto.* To be sure, he would look awkward if placed on a pedestal in isolation; he *demands* the architectural framework for which he was made,

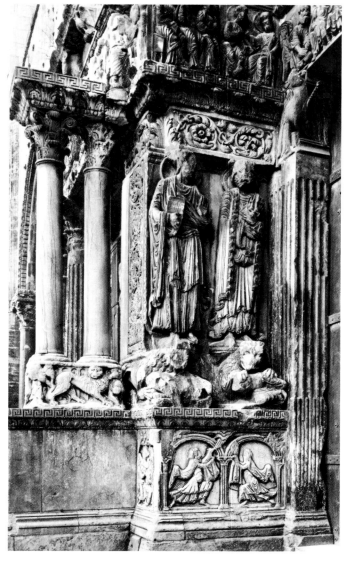

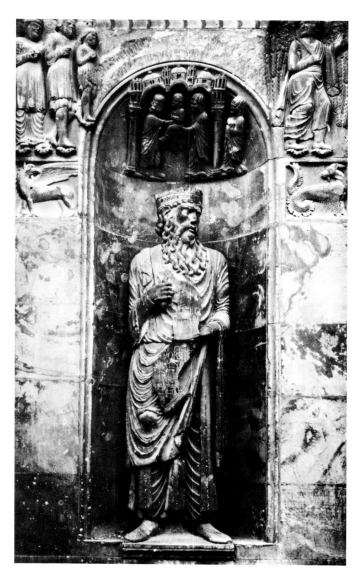

439. North jamb, center portal, St.-Gilles-du-Gard.
Second quarter of the 12th century

440. BENEDETTO ANTELAMI. *KING DAVID.* c. 1180–90.
West façade, Fidenza Cathedral

but certainly to a far lesser extent than do the two statues at St.-Gilles. Nor is he subject to the group discipline of a series; his only companion is a second niche statue on the other side of the portal. An extraordinary achievement indeed, especially if we consider that not much more than a hundred years separate it from the beginnings of the sculptural revival.

## The Meuse Valley

The emergence of distinct artistic personalities in the twelfth century is a phenomenon that is rarely acknowledged, perhaps because it contravenes the widespread assumption that all medieval art is anonymous. It does not happen very often, of course, but it is no less significant for all that. Antelami is not an isolated case; he cannot even claim to be the earliest. Nor is the revival of individuality confined to Italy. We also find it in one particular region of

the north, in the valley of the Meuse River, which runs from northeastern France into Belgium and Holland. This region had been the home of the "Reims style" in Carolingian times (see figs. 399 and 400), and that awareness of classical sources pervades its art during the Romanesque period. Here again, then, interestingly enough, the revival of individuality is linked with the influence of ancient art, although this influence did not produce works on a monumental scale. "Mosan" Romanesque sculpture excelled in metalwork, such as the splendid baptismal font of 1107–18 in Liège (fig. 441), which is also the masterpiece of the earliest among the individually known artists of the region, Renier of Huy. The vessel rests on twelve oxen (symbols of the twelve apostles), like Solomon's basin in the Temple at Jerusalem as described in the Bible. The reliefs make an instructive contrast with those of Bernward's doors (see fig. 407), since they are about the same height. Instead of the rough expressive power of the Ottonian panel, we find here a harmonious balance of design, a subtle control of the sculptured surfaces, and an understanding of organic structure that, in medieval terms, are amazingly classical. The figure seen from the back (beyond the tree on the left in our picture), with its graceful turning movement and Greek-looking drapery, might almost be taken for an ancient work.

## Germany

The one monumental free-standing statue of Romanesque art—perhaps not the only one made, but the only one that has survived—is that of an animal, and in a secular rather than a religious context: the lifesized bronze lion on top of a tall shaft that Duke Henry the Lion of Saxony had placed in front of his palace at Brunswick in 1166 (fig. 442). The wonderfully ferocious beast (which, of course, personifies the duke, or at least that aspect of his personality that earned him his nickname) reminds us in a curious way of the archaic bronze she-wolf of Rome (see fig. 248). Perhaps the resemblance is not entirely coincidental, since the she-wolf was on public view in Rome at that time and must have had a strong appeal for Romanesque artists.

The more immediate relatives of the Brunswick lion, however, are the countless bronze water ewers in the shape of lions, dragons, griffins, and such, that came into use in the twelfth century for the ritual washing of the priest's hands during Mass. These vessels—another instance of monsters doing menial service for the Lord—were of Near Eastern inspiration. The beguiling specimen reproduced in figure 443 still betrays its descent from the winged beasts of Persian art, transmitted to the West through trade with the Islamic world.

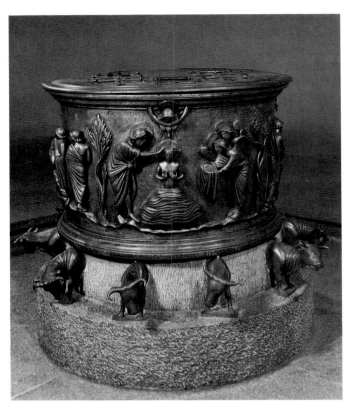

441. RENIER OF HUY. Baptismal Font. 1107–18. Bronze, height 25″ (63.5 cm). St.-Barthélemy, Liège

442. Lion Monument. 1166. Bronze, length c. 6′ (1.8 m). Cathedral Square, Brunswick, Germany

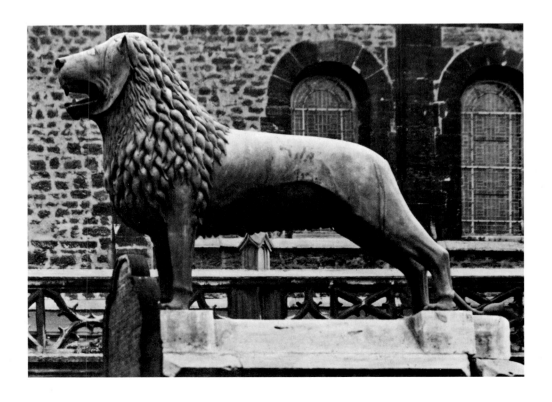

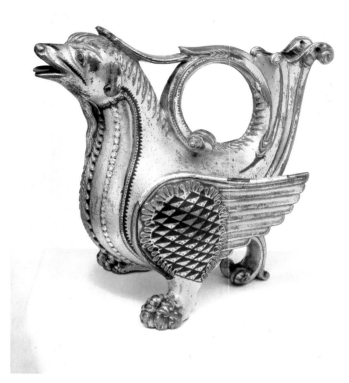

443. Ewer. Mosan. c. 1130. Gilt bronze, height 7¼" (18.5 cm). Victoria & Albert Museum, London (Crown copyright reserved)

dimensional aspects of the picture are reduced to overlapped planes. Even Ottonian painting (see figs. 408 and 409) seems illusionistic in comparison. Yet by sacrificing the last remnants of modeling in terms of light and shade, the Romanesque artist has endowed his work with an abstract clarity and precision that had not been possible in Carolingian or Ottonian times; only now can we truly say that the representational, the symbolic, and the decorative elements of the design are knit together into a single, unified structure.

This style of rhythmic lines and planes eschews all effects that might be termed specifically pictorial—not only tonal values but the rendering of textures and highlights such as we still find in Ottonian painting—and because of this it gains a new universality of scale. The evangelists of the *Ebbo Gospels,* the drawings of the *Utrecht Psalter,* and the miniatures in the *Gospel Book of Otto III* are made up of open, spontaneous flicks and dashes of brush or pen that

## PAINTING AND METALWORK

Unlike architecture and sculpture, Romanesque painting shows no sudden revolutionary developments that set it apart immediately from Carolingian or Ottonian. Nor does it look more "Roman" than Carolingian or Ottonian painting. This does not mean, however, that in the eleventh and twelfth centuries painting was any less important than it had been during the earlier Middle Ages; it merely emphasizes the greater continuity of the pictorial tradition, especially in manuscript illumination.

### France

GOSPEL BOOK, CORBIE. Nevertheless, soon after the year 1000 we find the beginnings of a painting style that corresponds to—and often anticipates—the monumental qualities of Romanesque sculpture. The new attitude is clearly evident in the *St. Mark* (fig. 444), from a Gospel Book probably done toward 1050 at the monastery of Corbie in northern France. The twisting and turning movement of the lines, which pervades not only the figure of the Evangelist but the winged lion, the scroll, and the curtain, recalls Carolingian miniatures of the Reims School such as the *Ebbo Gospels* (see fig. 399). This very resemblance helps us see the differences between the two works: in the Corbie manuscript, every trace of classical illusionism has disappeared; the fluid modeling of the Reims School, with its suggestion of light and space, has been replaced by firmly drawn contours filled in with bright, solid colors, so that the three-

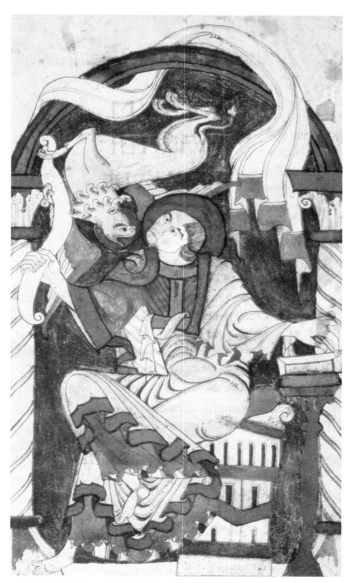

444. *ST. MARK,* from a Gospel Book produced at Corbie. c. 1050. Bibliothèque Municipale, Amiens

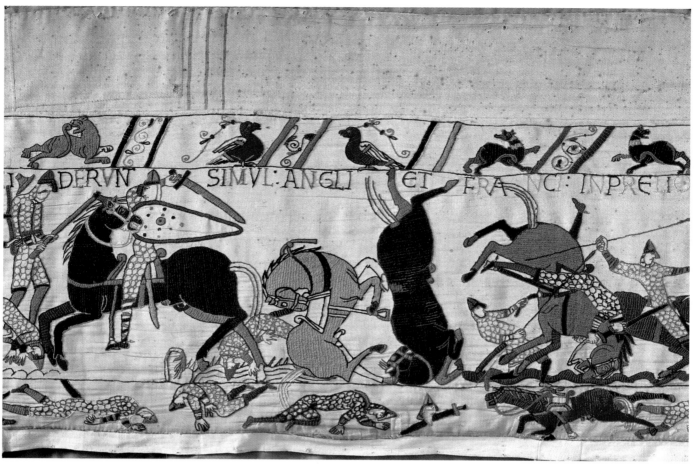

445. THE BATTLE OF HASTINGS. Detail of the *BAYEUX TAPESTRY.* c. 1073–83. Wool embroidery on linen, height 20″ (50.7 cm). Centre Guillaume le Conquerant, Bayeux, France

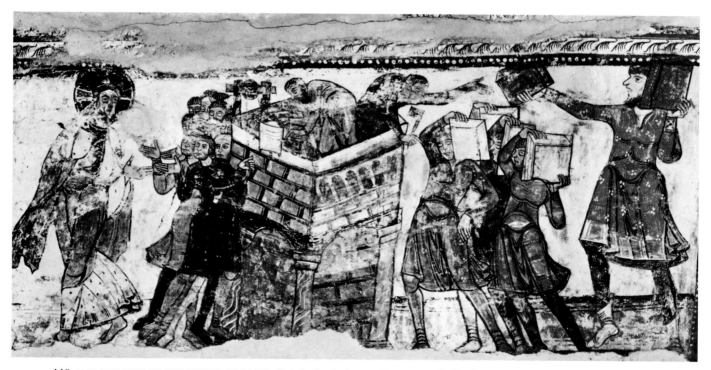

446. *THE BUILDING OF THE TOWER OF BABEL.* Detail of painting on the nave vault, St.-Savin-sur-Gartempe Early 12th century

have an intimate, hand-written flavor; they would look strange if copied on a larger scale or in another medium. The Corbie miniature, on the contrary, might be translated into a mural, a stained-glass window, a tapestry, or a relief panel without losing any of its essential qualities.

BAYEUX TAPESTRY. This monumentality is the same as in the Vézelay tympanum (fig. 437), where much the same pleated drapery patterns are rendered in sculptural terms; or in the so-called Bayeux Tapestry, an embroidered frieze 230 feet long illustrating William the Conqueror's invasion of England. Our detail (fig. 445), portraying the Battle of Hastings, has stylistic kinship with the Corbie manuscript even in the lively somersaults of the falling horses, so strikingly like the pose of the lion in the miniature. Again we marvel at the ease with which the designer has integrated narrative and ornament: the main scene is enclosed by two border strips that perform their framing function equally well, although the upper one is purely decorative while the other consists of dead warriors and horses and thus forms part of the story.

ST.-SAVIN-SUR-GARTEMPE. Firm outlines and a strong sense of pattern are equally characteristic of Romanesque wall painting. *The Building of the Tower of Babel* (fig. 446) is taken from the most impressive surviving cycle, on the nave vault of the church at St.-Savin-sur-Gartempe (compare fig. 415). It is an intensely dramatic design, crowded with strenuous action; the Lord Himself, on the far left, participates directly in the narrative as He addresses the builders of the colossal structure. He is counterbalanced, on the right, by the giant Nimrod, the leader of the enterprise, who frantically hands blocks of stone to the masons atop the tower, so that the entire scene becomes a great test of strength between God and man. The heavy dark contours and the emphatic play of gestures make the composition eminently readable from a distance, yet these same qualities occur in the illuminated manuscripts of the region, which can be equally monumental despite their small scale.

## The Channel Region

While Romanesque painting, like architecture and sculpture, developed a wide variety of regional styles throughout western Europe, its greatest achievements emerged from the monastic scriptoria of northern France, Belgium, and southern England. The works produced in this area are so closely related in style that it is at times impossible to be sure on which side of the English Channel a given manuscript belongs.

GOSPEL BOOK OF ABBOT WEDRICUS. Thus the style of the wonderful miniature of St. John (fig. 447) has been linked with both Cambrai and Canterbury. The abstract linear draftsmanship of the Corbie manuscript (fig. 444) has been influenced by Byzantine style (note the ropelike loops of drapery, whose origin can be traced back to such works as fig. 332) but without losing its energetic rhythm. It is the precisely controlled dynamics of every contour, both in the main figure and in the frame, that unite the varied elements

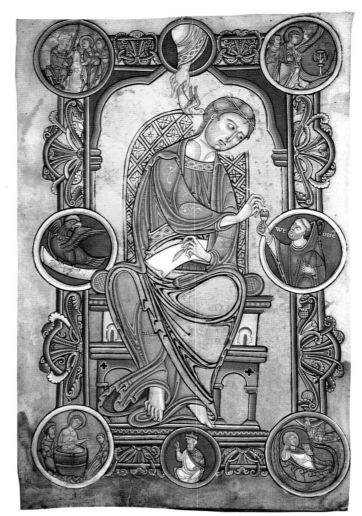

447. *ST. JOHN THE EVANGELIST*, from the *Gospel Book of Abbot Wedricus*. Shortly before 1147. Société Archéologique et Historique, Avesnes-sur-Helpe, France

of the composition into a coherent whole. This quality of line still betrays its ultimate source, the Celtic-Germanic heritage; if we compare our miniature with the *Lindisfarne Gospels* (fig. 387), we see how much the interlacing patterns of the Dark Ages have contributed to the design of the St. John page. The drapery folds and the clusters of floral ornament have an impulsive yet disciplined aliveness that echoes the intertwined snakelike monsters of the animal style, even though the foliage is derived from the classical acanthus and the human figures are based on Carolingian and Byzantine models. The unity of the entire page, however, is conveyed not only by the forms but by the content as well. The Evangelist "inhabits" the frame in such a way that we could not remove him from it without cutting off his ink supply (proffered by the donor of the manuscript, Abbot Wedricus), his source of inspiration (the dove of the Holy Spirit in the hand of God), or his identifying symbol, the eagle. The other medallions, less directly linked with the main figure, show scenes from the life of St. John.

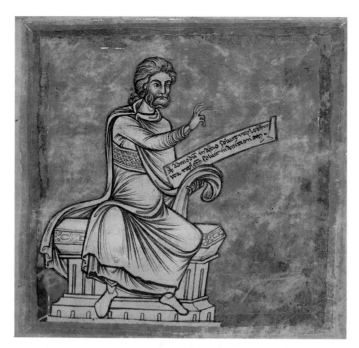

448. *PORTRAIT OF A PHYSICIAN*, from a medical treatise.
c. 1160. British Museum, London

clothed in rippling, "wet" draperies familiar to us from countless classical statues, have achieved so high a degree of organic body structure and freedom of movement that we tend to think of them as harbingers of Gothic art rather than as the final phase of the Romanesque. Whatever we choose to call it, the style of the Klosterneuburg Altar was to have a profound impact upon both painting and sculpture during the next fifty years (see figs. 496 and 497).

The astonishing humanity of Nicholas of Verdun's art must be understood against the background of a general reawakening of interest in man and the natural world throughout northwestern Europe. This attitude could express itself in various ways: as a new regard for classical literature and mythology, an appreciation of the beauty of ancient works of art, or simply as a greater readiness to acknowledge the enjoyment of sensuous experience.

CARMINA BURANA. The latter aspect is reflected particularly in such lighthearted poetry as the well-known *Carmina Burana*, composed during the later twelfth century and preserved in an illuminated manuscript of the early thirteenth. That a collection of verse devoted largely—and at times all too frankly—to the delights of nature, love, and drinking should have been embellished with illustrations is signif-

PORTRAIT OF A PHYSICIAN. Soon after the middle of the twelfth century, an important change of style began to make itself felt in Romanesque painting on either side of the English Channel. The *Portrait of a Physician* (fig. 448), from a medical manuscript of about 1160, is surprisingly different from the St. John miniature, although it was produced in the same region. Instead of abstract patterns, we suddenly find lines that have regained the ability to describe three-dimensional shapes; the drapery folds no longer lead an ornamental life of their own but suggest the rounded volume of the body underneath; there is even a renewed interest in foreshortening. Here at last, then, we meet the pictorial counterpart of that classicism which we saw earlier in the baptismal font of Renier of Huy at Liège (see fig. 441). In fact, our miniature was probably done at Liège, too, and its sharp, deliberate lines look as if they had been engraved in metal, rather than drawn with pen or brush.

NICHOLAS OF VERDUN. That a new painting style should have originated in metalwork is perhaps less strange than it might seem at first, for the style's essential qualities are sculptural rather than pictorial; moreover, metalwork (which includes not only cast or embossed sculpture but also engraving, enameling, and goldsmithing) had been a highly developed art in the Meuse valley area since Carolingian times. Its greatest practitioner after Renier of Huy was Nicholas of Verdun, in whose work the classicizing, three-dimensional style of draftsmanship reaches full maturity. The engraved and enameled plaques of the Klosterneuburg Altar, which he completed in 1181 (fig. 449 shows one of them, *The Crossing of the Red Sea*), clearly belong to the same tradition as the Liège miniature, but the figures,

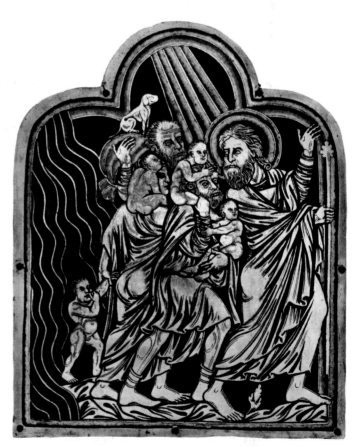

449. NICHOLAS OF VERDUN. *THE CROSSING OF THE RED SEA.*
1181. Enamel on gold plaque, from the
*KLOSTERNEUBURG ALTAR*, height 5½" (14 cm).
Klosterneuburg Abbey, Austria

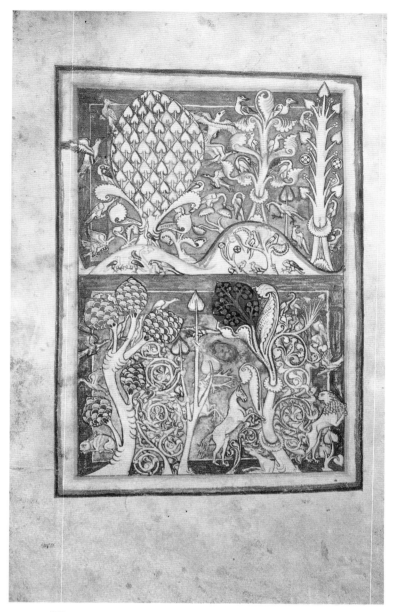

450. Page with *SUMMER LANDSCAPE*, from a manuscript of
*Carmina Burana*. Early 13th century. 7 × 4⅞″ (17.8 × 12.5 cm).
Bayerische Staatsbibliothek, Munich

icant in itself. We are even more surprised, however, to find that one of the miniatures (fig. 450), coupled with a poem praising spring, represents a landscape—the first, so far as we know, in Western art since late classical times.

Echoes of ancient landscape painting, derived from Early Christian and Byzantine sources, can be found in Carolingian art (see figs. 399 and 400), but only as background for the human figure. Later on, these remnants had been reduced still further, even when the subject required a landscape setting; the Garden of Eden on Bernward's doors (see fig. 407) is no more than a few strangely twisted stems and bits of foliage. Thus the *Carmina Burana* illustrator, called upon to depict the life of nature in summertime, must have found his task a rather perplexing one. He has solved it in the only way possible for him—by filling his page with a sort of anthology of Romanesque plant ornament interspersed with birds and animals.

The trees, vines, and flowers remain so abstract that we cannot identify a single species (the birds and animals, probably copied from a zoological treatise, are far more realistic), yet they have an uncanny vitality of their own that makes them seem to sprout and unfold as if the growth of an entire season were compressed into a few frantic moments. These giant seedlings convey the exuberance of early summer, of stored energy suddenly released, far more intensely than any normal vegetation could. Our artist has created a fairytale landscape, but his enchanted world nevertheless evokes essential aspects of reality.

# CHAPTER FOUR
# GOTHIC
# ART

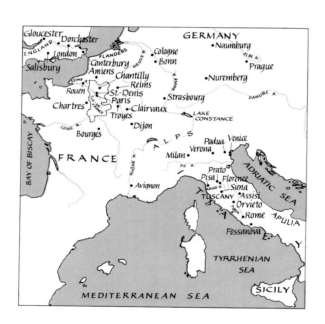

Time and space, we have been taught, are interdependent. Yet we tend to think of history as the unfolding of events in time without sufficient awareness of their unfolding in space—we visualize it as a stack of chronological layers, or periods, each layer having a specific depth that corresponds to its duration. For the more remote past, where our sources of information are scanty, this simple image works reasonably well. It becomes less and less adequate as we draw closer to the present and our knowledge grows more precise. Thus we cannot define the Gothic era in terms of time alone; we must consider the changing surface area of the layer as well as its depth.

At the start, about 1140, this area was small indeed. It embraced only the province known as the Île-de-France (that is, Paris and vicinity), the royal domain of the French kings. A hundred years later, most of Europe had "gone Gothic," from Sicily to Iceland, with only a few Romanesque pockets left here and there; through the crusaders, the new style had even been introduced to the Near East. About 1450, the Gothic area had begun to shrink—no longer including Italy—and by about 1550 it had disappeared almost entirely. The Gothic layer, then, has a rather complicated shape, its depth varying from close to 400 years in some places to a minimum of 150 in others. This shape, moreover, does not emerge with equal clarity in all the visual arts.

The term "Gothic" was first coined for architecture, and it is in architecture that the characteristics of the style are most easily recognized. And although we speak of Gothic sculpture and painting, there is, as we shall see, some uncertainty about the exact limits of the Gothic style in these fields. This evolution of our concept of Gothic art suggests the way the new style actually grew: it began with architecture, and for a century—from about 1150 to 1250, during the Age of the Great Cathedrals—architecture retained its dominant role. Gothic sculpture, at first severely architectural in spirit, tended to become less and less so after 1200; its greatest achievements are between the years 1220 and 1420. Painting, in turn, reached a climax of creative endeavor between 1300 and 1350 in central Italy. North of the Alps, it became the leading art from about 1400 on. We thus find, in surveying the Gothic era as a whole, a gradual shift of emphasis from architecture to painting or, better perhaps, from architectural to pictorial qualities. (Characteristically enough, Early Gothic sculpture and painting both reflect the discipline of their monumental setting, while Late Gothic architecture and sculpture strive for "picturesque" effects rather than clarity or firmness).

Overlying this broad pattern is another one: international diffusion as against regional independence. Starting as a local development in the Île-de-France, Gothic art radiates from there to the rest of France and to all Europe, where it comes to be known as *opus modernum* or *francigenum* (modern or French work). In the course of the thirteenth century, the new style gradually loses its "imported" flavor; regional variety begins to reassert itself. Toward the middle of the fourteenth century, we notice a growing tendency for these regional achievements to influence each other until, about 1400, a surprisingly homogeneous "International Gothic" style prevails almost everywhere. Shortly thereafter,

this unity breaks apart: Italy, with Florence in the lead, creates a radically new art, that of the Early Renaissance, while north of the Alps, Flanders assumes an equally commanding position in the development of Late Gothic painting and sculpture. A century later, finally, the Italian Renaissance becomes the basis of another international style. With this skeleton outline to guide us, we can now explore the unfolding of Gothic art in greater detail.

# ARCHITECTURE

## France

ST.-DENIS AND ABBOT SUGER.   We can pinpoint the origin of no previous style as exactly as that of Gothic. It was born between 1137 and 1144 in the rebuilding, by Abbot Suger, of the royal Abbey Church of St.-Denis just outside the city of Paris. If we are to understand how Gothic architecture happened to come into being at this particular spot, we must first acquaint ourselves with the special relationship between St.-Denis, Suger, and the French monarchy. The kings of France derived their claim to authority from the Carolingian tradition, although they belonged to the Capetian line (founded by Hugh Capet after the death of the last Carolingian in 987). But their power was eclipsed by that of the nobles who, in theory, were their vassals; the only area they ruled directly was the Île-de-France, and they often found their authority challenged even there. Not until the early twelfth century did the royal power begin to expand; and Suger, as chief adviser to Louis VI, played a key role in this process. It was he who forged the alliance between the monarchy and the Church, which brought the bishops of France (and the cities under their authority) to the king's side, while the king, in turn, supported the papacy in its struggle against the German emperors.

Suger, however, championed the monarchy not only on the plane of practical politics but on that of "spiritual politics"; by investing the royal office with religious significance, by glorifying it as the strong right arm of justice, he sought to rally the nation behind the king. His architectural plans for the Abbey of St.-Denis must be understood in this context, for the church, founded in the late eighth century, enjoyed a dual prestige that made it ideally suitable for Suger's purpose: it was the shrine of the Apostle of France, the sacred protector of the realm, as well as the chief memorial of the Carolingian dynasty (both Charlemagne and his father, Pepin, had been consecrated kings there, and it was also the burial place of Charles Martel, Pepin, and Charles the Bald). Suger wanted to make the abbey the spiritual center of France, a pilgrimage church to outshine the splendor of all the others, the focal point of religious as well as patriotic emotion. But in order to become the visible embodiment of such a goal, the old edifice had to be enlarged and rebuilt. The great abbot himself has described the entire campaign in such eloquent detail that we know more about what he desired to achieve than we do about the final result, for the west façade and its sculpture are sadly mutilated today, and the choir, which Suger regarded as the most important part

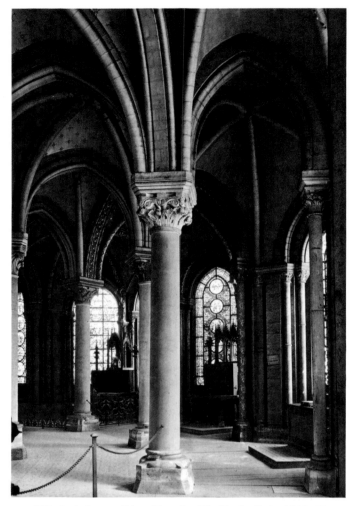

451. Ambulatory, Abbey Church of St.-Denis, Paris. 1140–44

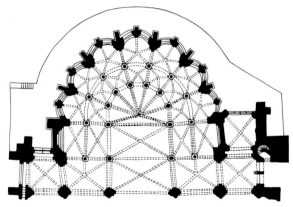

452. Plan of the choir and ambulatory of St.-Denis
(after Sumner Crosby)

of the enterprise, retains its original appearance only in the ambulatory (figs. 451 and 452).

Looking at the plan, we recognize familiar elements of the **Romanesque pilgrimage choir (compare fig. 412)**, with an arcaded apse surrounded by an ambulatory and radiating chapels. Yet these elements have been integrated in strikingly novel fashion; the chapels, instead of remaining separate entities, are merged so as to form, in effect, a second

ambulatory, and ribbed groined vaulting based on the pointed arch is employed throughout (in the Romanesque pilgrimage choir, only the ambulatory had been groin-vaulted). As a result, the entire plan is held together by a new kind of geometric order: it consists of seven identical wedge-shaped units fanning out from the center of the apse. We experience this double ambulatory not as a series of separate compartments but as a continuous (though articulated) space, whose shape is outlined for us by the network of slender arches, ribs, and columns that sustains the vaults.

What distinguishes this interior immediately from its predecessors is its lightness, in both senses; the architectural forms seem graceful, almost weightless as against the massive solidity of the Romanesque, and the windows have been enlarged to the point that they are no longer openings cut into a wall—they fill the entire wall area, so that they themselves become translucent walls. If we now examine the plan once more, we realize what makes this abundance of light possible. The outward pressure of the vaults is contained by heavy buttresses jutting out between the chapels (in the plan, they look like stubby black arrows pointing toward the center of the apse). The main weight of the masonry construction is concentrated there, visible only from the outside. No wonder, then, that the interior appears so amazingly airy and weightless, since the heaviest members of the structural skeleton are beyond our view. The same impression would be even more striking if we could see all of Suger's choir, for the upper part of the apse, rising above the double ambulatory, had very large, tall windows (the effect, from the nave, must have been similar to that of the somewhat later choir of Notre-Dame in Paris; see fig. 454).

SUGER AND GOTHIC ARCHITECTURE. In describing Suger's choir, we have also described the essentials of Gothic architecture. Yet none of the individual elements that entered into its design is really new; the pilgrimage choir plan, the pointed arch, and the ribbed groined vault are familiar to us from the various regional schools of the French (and Anglo-Norman) Romanesque, even though we never encounter them all combined in the same building until St.-Denis. The Île-de-France had failed to develop a Romanesque tradition of its own, so that Suger—as he himself tells us—had to bring together artisans from many different regions for his project. We must not conclude from this, however, that Gothic architecture originated as a mere synthesis of Romanesque traits. If it were no more than that, we would be hard pressed to explain the new spirit that strikes us so forcibly at St.-Denis: the emphasis on strict geometric planning and the quest for luminosity. Suger's account of the rebuilding of his church insistently stresses both of these as the highest values achieved in the new structure. "Harmony" (that is, the perfect relationship among parts in terms of mathematical proportions or ratios) is the source of all beauty, since it exemplifies the laws according to which divine reason has constructed the universe; the "miraculous" light that floods the choir through the "most sacred" windows becomes the Light Divine, a mystic revelation of the spirit of God.

This symbolic interpretation of light and of numerical harmony had been established over the centuries in Christian thought. It derived from the writings of a fifth-century Greek theologian who, in the Middle Ages, was believed to have been Dionysius the Areopagite, an Athenian disciple of St. Paul. Through this identification, the works of the fifth-century writer, known as the Pseudo-Dionysius, came to be vested with great authority. In Carolingian France, however, Dionysius the disciple of St. Paul was identified both with the author of the Pseudo-Dionysian writings and with St. Denis, the Apostle of France and the special protector of the realm.

The revival of monarchic power during the early twelfth century gave new importance to the theology of the Pseudo-Dionysius, attributed to St. Denis and therefore regarded as France's very own. For Suger, the light-and-number symbolism of Dionysian thought must have had a particularly strong appeal. We can well understand why his own mind was steeped in it, and why he wanted to give it visible expression when he rebuilt the church of the royal patron saint. That he succeeded is proved not only by the inherent qualities of his choir design but also by its extraordinary impact; every visitor to St.-Denis, it seems, was overwhelmed by Suger's achievement, and within a few decades the new style had spread far beyond the confines of the Île-de-France.

SUGER AND THE MEDIEVAL ARCHITECT. The how and why of Suger's success are a good deal more difficult to explain. Here we encounter a controversy we have met several times before—that of form versus function. To the advocates of the functionalist approach, Gothic architecture has seemed the result of advances in architectural engineering, which made it possible to build more efficient vaults, to concentrate their thrust at a few critical points, and thus eliminate the solid walls of the Romanesque. Suger, they would argue, was fortunate in securing the services of an architect who evidently understood the principles of ribbed groined vaulting better than anybody else at that time. If the abbot chose to interpret the resulting structure as symbolic of Dionysian theology, he was simply expressing his enthusiasm over it in the abstract language of the churchman; his account does not help us to understand the origin of the new style.

It is perfectly true, of course, that the choir of St.-Denis is more rationally planned and constructed than any Romanesque church. The pointed arch (which can be "stretched" to reach any desired height regardless of the width of its base) has now become an integral part of the ribbed groined vault. As a result, these vaults are no longer restricted to square or near-square compartments; they have gained a flexibility that permits them to cover areas of almost any shape (such as the trapezoids and pentagons of the ambulatory). The buttressing of the vaults, too, is more fully understood than before. How could the theological ideas of Suger have led to these technical advances, unless we are willing to assume that he was a professionally trained architect? If we grant that he was not, can he claim any credit at all for the style of what he so proudly calls "his" new church? Perhaps the question poses a false alternative, somewhat like

the conundrum of the chicken and the egg. The function of a church, after all, is not merely to enclose a maximum of space with a minimum of material; for the master who built the choir of St.-Denis under Suger's supervision, the technical problems of vaulting must have been inextricably bound up with considerations of form (that is, of beauty, harmony, fitness, and so forth). As a matter of fact, his design includes various elements that *express* function without actually performing it, such as the slender shafts (called responds) that seem to carry the weight of the vaults to the church floor.

But in order to know what constituted beauty, harmony, and fitness, the medieval architect needed the guidance of ecclesiastical authority. Such guidance might be a simple directive to follow some established model or, in the case of a patron as actively concerned with architectural aesthetics as Suger, it might amount to full participation in the designing process. Thus Suger's desire to "build Dionysian theology" is likely to have been a decisive factor from the very beginning: it shaped his mental image of the kind of structure he wanted, we may assume, and determined his choice of a master of Norman background as the chief architect. This man, a great artist, must have been singularly responsive to the abbot's ideas and instructions. Between them, the two together created the Gothic style.

NOTRE-DAME, PARIS. Although St.-Denis was an abbey, the future of Gothic architecture lay in the towns rather than in rural monastic communities. There had been a vigorous revival of urban life, we will recall, since the early eleventh century; this movement continued at an accelerated pace, and the growing weight of the cities made itself felt not only economically and politically but in countless other ways as well: bishops and the city clergy rose to new importance; cathedral schools and universities took the place of monasteries as centers of learning, while the artistic efforts of the age culminated in the great cathedrals. That of Notre-Dame ("Our Lady," the Virgin Mary) at Paris, begun in 1163, reflects the salient features of Suger's St.-Denis more directly than any other (figs. 453–57).

The plan (fig. 453), with its emphasis on the longitudinal axis, is extraordinarily compact and unified as against that of major Romanesque churches; the double ambulatory of the choir continues directly into the aisles, and the stubby transept barely exceeds the width of the façade. In the interior (fig. 454) we still find echoes of the Norman Romanesque: sexpartite nave vaults over squarish bays, and galleries above the inner aisles. The columns of the nave arcade are another conservative feature. Yet the large clerestory windows and the lightness and slenderness of the forms create an unmistakably Gothic effect (note how thin the nave walls are made to seem). Gothic, too, is the "verticalism" of the interior space. This depends less on the actual proportions of the nave—for some Romanesque naves are equally tall, relative to their width—than on the constant accenting of the verticals and on the soaring ease with which the sense of height is attained. Romanesque interiors (such as fig. 413), by contrast, emphasize the great effort required in supporting the weight of the vaults.

In Notre-Dame, as in Suger's choir, the buttresses (the

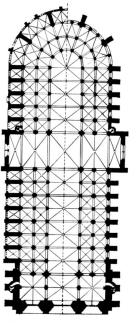

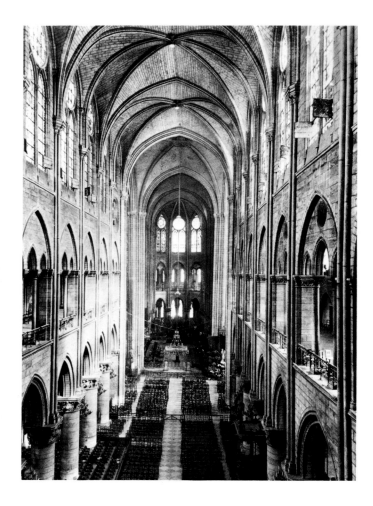

453. Plan of Notre-Dame, Paris. 1163–c. 1250

454. (*right*) Nave and choir, Notre-Dame, Paris

455. (*below*) Notre-Dame (view from the southeast), Paris

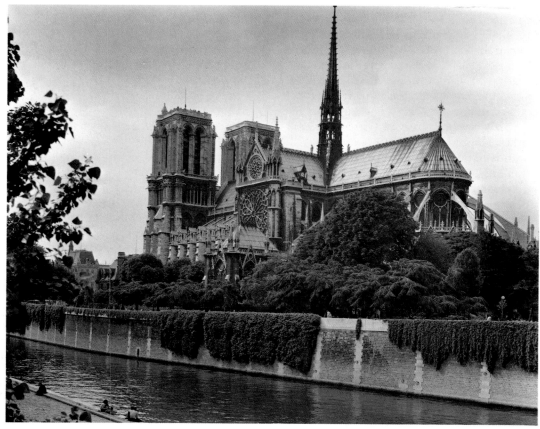

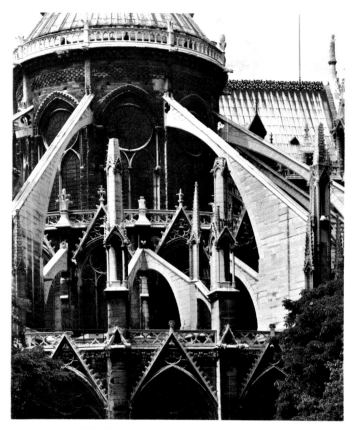

456. Flying buttresses, Notre-Dame, Paris

Much more important than these resemblances are the qualities that distinguish the façade of Notre-Dame from its Romanesque ancestors. Foremost among these is the way all the details have been integrated into a wonderfully balanced and coherent whole; the meaning of Suger's emphasis on harmony, geometric order, and proportion becomes evident here even more strikingly than in St.-Denis itself. This formal discipline also embraces the sculpture, which is no longer permitted the spontaneous (and often uncontrolled) growth so characteristic of the Romanesque but has been assigned a precisely defined role within the architectural framework. At the same time, the cubic solidity of the façade of St.-Etienne at Caen has been transformed into its very opposite; lacelike arcades, huge portals and windows dissolve the continuity of the wall surfaces, so that the total effect approximates that of a weightless openwork screen. How rapidly this tendency advanced during the first half of the thirteenth century can be seen by comparing the west façade of Notre-Dame with the somewhat later façade of the south transept, visible in figure 455. In the former the rose window in the center is still deeply recessed and, as a result, the stone tracery that subdivides the opening is clearly set

"heavy bones" of the structural skeleton) are not visible from the inside. The plan shows them as massive blocks of masonry that stick out from the building like a row of teeth. Above the aisles, these piers turn into flying buttresses—arched bridges that reach upward to the critical spots between the clerestory windows where the outward thrust of the nave vault is concentrated (fig. 455). This method of anchoring vaults, a characteristic feature of Gothic architecture, certainly owed its origin to functional considerations. Even the flying buttress, however, soon became aesthetically important as well, and its shape could express support (apart from actually providing it) in a variety of ways, according to the designer's sense of style (fig. 456).

The most monumental aspect of the exterior of Notre-Dame is the west façade (fig. 457). Except for its sculpture, which suffered heavily during the French Revolution and is for the most part restored, it retains its original appearance. The design reflects the general disposition of the façade of St.-Denis, which in turn had been derived from Norman Romanesque façades such as that of St.-Etienne at Caen (see fig. 417). Comparing the latter with Notre-Dame, we note the persistence of some basic features: the pier buttresses that reinforce the corners of the towers and divide the façade into three main parts; the placing of the portals; the three-story arrangement. The rich sculptural decoration, however, recalls the façades of the west of France (see fig. 416) and the elaborately carved portals of Burgundy.

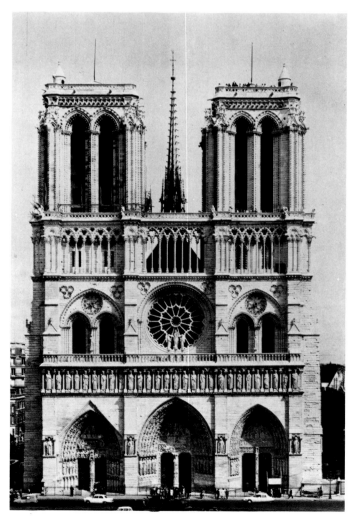

457. West façade, Notre-Dame, Paris

off against the surrounding wall surface; on the transept façade, in contrast, we can no longer distinguish the rose window from its frame—a single network of tracery covers the entire area.

CHARTRES CATHEDRAL. Toward 1145 the bishop of Chartres, who befriended Abbot Suger and shared his ideas, began to rebuild his cathedral in the new style. Fifty years later, all but the west façade, which provided the main entrance to the church, and the east crypt were destroyed by a disastrous fire (for sculpture of the west portals, see figs. 493 and 494); a second rebuilding was begun in 1194 (fig. 458), and as the result of a huge campaign was largely accomplished within the astonishingly brief span of twenty-six years. The basic design is so unified that it must have been planned by a single master builder. However, because the construction proceeded in several stages and was never entirely finished, the church incorporates an evolutionary, rather than a systematic, harmony. For example, the two west towers, though similar, are by no means identical. Moreover, their spires are radically different: the north spire on the left dates from the early sixteenth century, nearly three hundred years later than the other.

The church was erected on the highest point in town and the spires can be seen for miles in the surrounding farmland (fig. 459). Had the seven other spires been completed as originally planned, Chartres would convey a less insistent directionality. Both arms of the transept have three deeply recessed portals lavishly embellished with sculpture and surmounted by an immense rose window over five smaller lancets (fig. 460). Perhaps the most striking feature of the

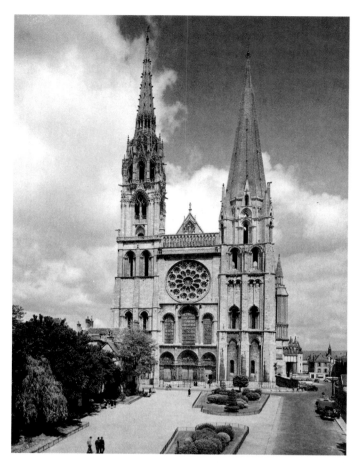

458. West façade, Chartres Cathedral
(north spire is 16th century). 1145–1220

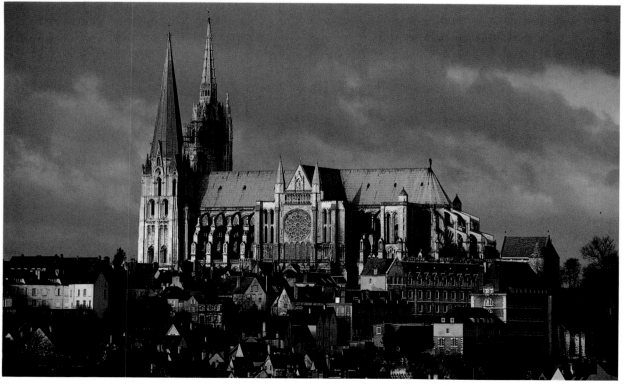

459. Chartres Cathedral (aerial view)

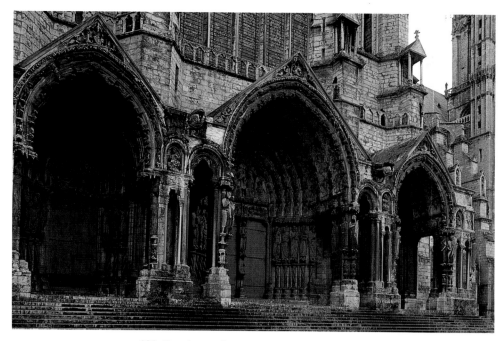

460. Portals, north transept, Chartres Cathedral

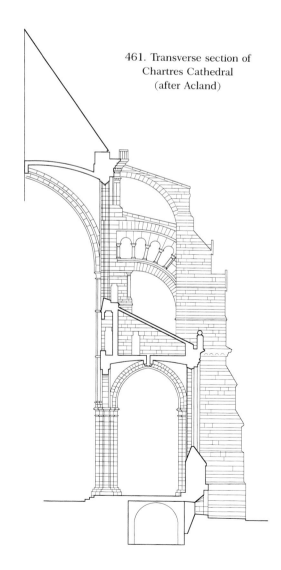

461. Transverse section of
Chartres Cathedral
(after Acland)

flanks is the flying buttresses, whose massing lends a powerfully organic presence to the semicircular apse at the east end, with its seven subsidiary chapels (figs. 459 and 461).

The impressive west façade, divided into units of two and three, is a model of lucidity. Its soaring verticality and punctuated surface are important in shaping our expectations about the interior. The shape of the doors tells us, too, that we will first be ushered into a low chamber. As soon as we enter the narthex, as the covered anteroom is called, we have left the temporal world completely behind. It takes some time for our eyes to adjust to the darkness of the interior. The noise of daily life has been shut out as well; at first, sounds are eerily muffled, as if swallowed up with light by the void. Once we recover from the disorienting effect of this strangely cavernous realm, we become aware of a glimmering light, which guides us into the full height of the church.

Conceived one generation after the nave of Notre-Dame in Paris, the rebuilt nave (fig. 462) represents the first masterpiece of the mature, or High Gothic, style. The openings of the pointed nave arcade are taller and narrower (see fig. 454). They are joined to a clerestory of the same height by a short triforium screening the galleries, which have now been reduced to a narrow wall. Responds have been added to the columnar supports, so as to stress the continuity of the vertical lines and guide our eye upward to the quadripartite vaults, which seem like diaphanous webs stretched across the slender ribs. Because there are so few walls, the vast interior space of Chartres Cathedral initially seems indeterminate. It is made to seem even larger by the sense of disembodied sound. The effect is so striking that it would seem to have been thought of from the beginning with music in mind, both antiphonal choirs and large pipe organs, which had already been in use for over two centuries in some parts of Europe.

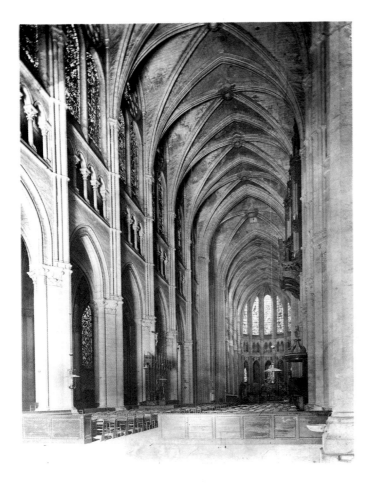

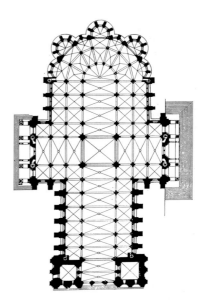

The alternating sequence of round and octagonal piers that demark each bay marches down the nave toward the apse—the east end of the church—where the liturgy is performed. Beneath the apse is the crypt, which houses Chartres' most important possession: remnants of the robe said to have been worn by the Virgin Mary, to whom the cathedral is dedicated. The venerable relic, which miraculously survived the great fire of 1194, drew pilgrims from all over

462. Nave and choir, Chartres Cathedral

463. (*above right*) Plan, Chartres Cathedral

464. (*below right*) Clerestory wall of the nave, Chartres Cathedral.

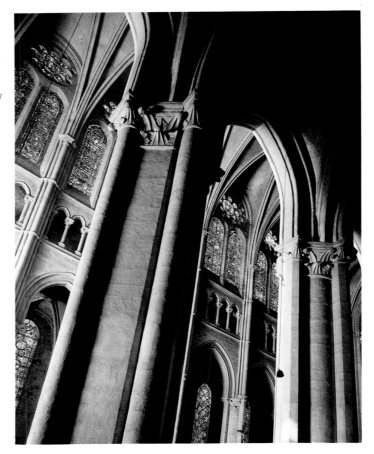

Europe. In order to accommodate large numbers of visitors without disturbing worshipers, the church incorporates a wide aisle running the length of the nave and around the transept; it is joined at the choir by a second aisle, forming an ambulatory that connects the apsidal chapels (see plan, fig. 463).

Alone among all major Gothic cathedrals, Chartres still retains most of its more than 180 original stained-glass windows. The magic of the colored light streaming down from the clerestory through the large windows is unforgettable to anyone who has experienced their intense, jewellike hues on the spot (fig. 464). The windows admit far less light than one might expect; they act mainly as multicolored diffusing filters that change the *quality* of ordinary daylight, endow- ing it with the poetic and symbolic values—the "miraculous light"—so highly praised by Abbot Suger. The sensation of ethereal light, which dissolves the physical solidity of the church and, hence, the distinction between the temporal and the divine realms, creates the intensely mystical experi- ence that lies at the heart of Gothic spirituality. The aisles, however, are considerably darker because the stained-glass windows on the outer walls, though relatively large, are at ground level, where they admit much less light than at the clerestory level.

AMIENS CATHEDRAL. The High Gothic style defined at Chartres reaches its climax a generation later in the interior of Amiens Cathedral (figs. 465 and 466). Breathtaking

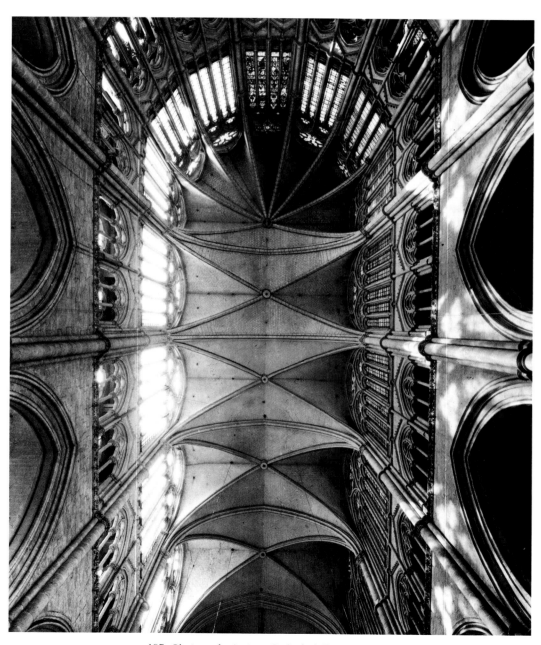

465. Choir vault, Amiens Cathedral. Begun 1220

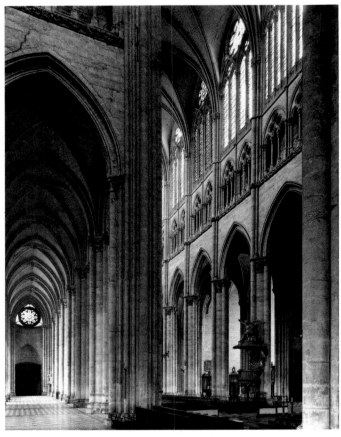

466. Nave and side aisle, Amiens Cathedral

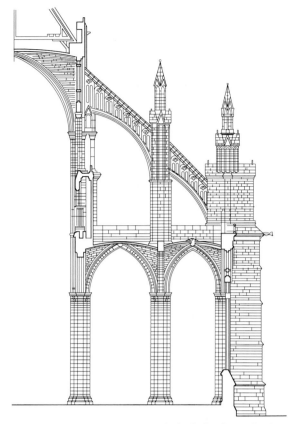

467. Transverse section, Amiens Cathedral (after Acland)

height has become the dominant aim, both technically and aesthetically (see fig. 467); skeletal construction is carried to its most precarious limits. The inner logic of the system forcefully asserts itself in the shape of the vaults, taut and thin as membranes, and in the expanded window area, which now includes the triforium so that the entire wall above the nave arcade becomes a clerestory (fig. 466).

REIMS CATHEDRAL. The same emphasis on verticality and translucency can be traced in the development of the High Gothic façade. The most famous of these, at Reims Cathedral (fig. 468), makes an instructive contrast with the west façade of Notre-Dame in Paris, even though its basic design was conceived only about thirty years later. Many of the same elements are common to both (as the Coronation Cathedral of the kings of France, Reims was closely linked to Paris), but in the younger structure they have been reshaped into a very different ensemble. The portals, instead of being recessed, are projected forward as gabled porches, with windows in place of tympanums above the doorways; the gallery of royal statues, which in Paris forms an incisive horizontal between the first and second stories, has been raised until it merges with the third-story arcade; every detail except the rose window has become taller and narrower than before; and a multitude of pinnacles further accentuates the restless upward-pointing movement. The sculptural decoration, by far the most lavish of its kind (see figs. 497

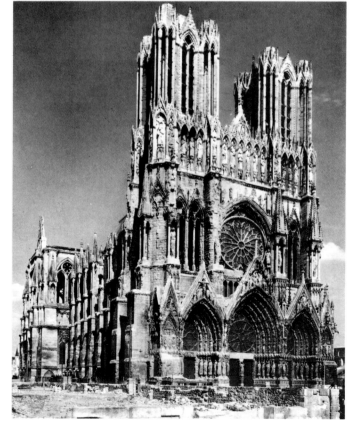

468. West façade, Reims Cathedral. c. 1225–99

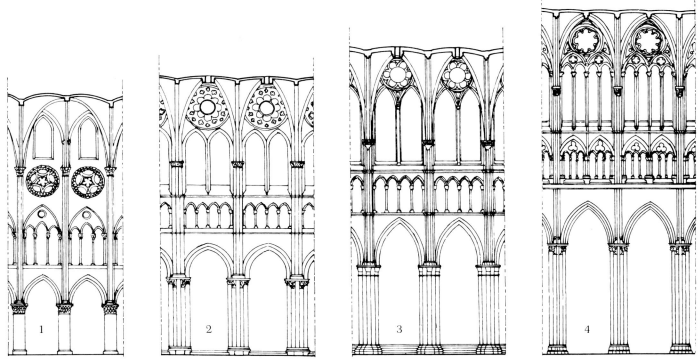

469. Comparison of nave elevations in same scale. 1) Nôtre-Dame, Paris; 2) Chartres Cathedral;
3) Reims Cathedral; 4) Amiens Cathedral (after Grodecki)

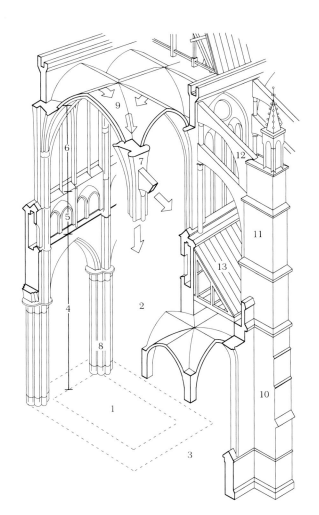

470. Axonometric projection of a High Gothic cathedral
(after Acland). 1) Bay; 2) Nave; 3) Side aisle;
4) Nave arcade; 5) Triforium; 6) Clerestory; 7) Pier;
8) Compound pier; 9) Sexpartite vault; 10) Buttress;
11) Flying buttress; 12) Flying arch; 13) Roof (after Acland)

and 498), no longer remains in clearly marked-off zones; it has now spread to so many hitherto unaccustomed perches, not only on the façade but on the flanks as well, that the exterior of the cathedral begins to look like a dovecote for statues. The relatively swift progression toward verticality in French Gothic cathedral architecture is clearly seen in figure 469, while figure 470 shows how both height and large expanses of window were achieved toward the end of this development.

LATER THIRTEENTH-CENTURY GOTHIC. The High Gothic cathedrals of France represent a concentrated expenditure of effort such as the world has rarely seen before or since. They are truly national monuments, whose immense cost was borne by donations collected all over the country and from all classes of society—the tangible expression of that merging of religious and patriotic fervor that had been the goal of Abbot Suger. As we approach the second half of the thirteenth century, we sense that this wave of enthusiasm has passed its crest: work on the vast structures begun during the first half now proceeds at a slower pace; new projects are fewer and generally on a far less ambitious scale; and the highly organized teams of masons and sculptors that had developed at the sites of the

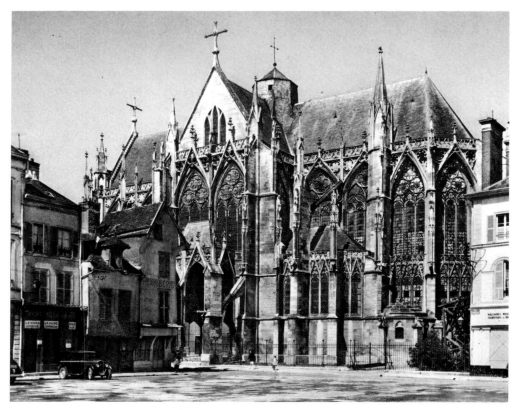

471. St.-Urbain, Troyes. 1261–75

great cathedrals during the preceding decades gradually break up into smaller units.

A characteristic church of the later years of the century, St.-Urbain in Troyes (figs. 471 and 472), leaves no doubt that the "heroic age" of the Gothic style is past. Refinement of detail, rather than towering monumentality, has been the designer's chief concern; by eliminating the triforium and simplifying the plan, he has created a delicate cage of glass (in the choir the windows begin ten feet above the floor), sustained by flying buttresses so thin as to be hardly noticeable. The same spiny, attenuated elegance can be felt in the architectural ornament.

FLAMBOYANT GOTHIC. In some respects, St.-Urbain is prophetic of the Late, or Flamboyant, phase of Gothic architecture. The beginnings of Flamboyant Gothic do indeed seem to go back to the late thirteenth century, but its growth was delayed by the Hundred Years' War with England, so that we do not meet any full-fledged examples of it until the early fifteenth. Its name, which means flamelike, refers to the undulating patterns of curve and countercurve that are a prevalent feature of Late Gothic tracery, as at St.-Maclou in Rouen (fig. 473). Structurally, Flamboyant Gothic shows no significant developments of its own; what distinguishes St.-Maclou from such churches as St.-Urbain in Troyes is the luxuriant profusion of ornament. The architect has turned into a virtuoso who overlays the structural skeleton with a web of decoration so dense and fanciful as to obscure it al-

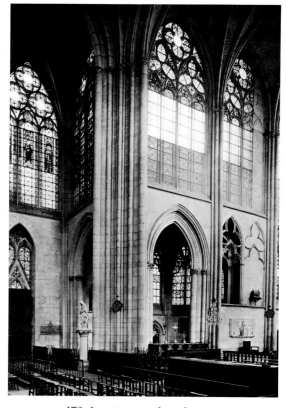

472. Interior toward northeast, St.-Urbain

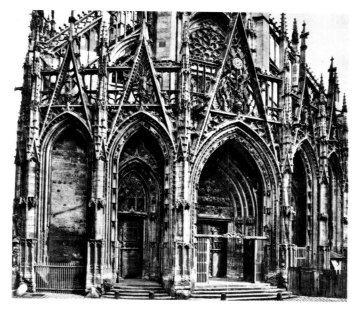

473. St.-Maclou, Rouen. Begun 1434

most completely. It becomes a fascinating game of hide-and-seek to locate the "bones" of the building within this picturesque tangle of lines.

SECULAR ARCHITECTURE. Since our account of medieval architecture is mainly concerned with the development of style, we have until now confined our attention to religious structures, the most ambitious as well as the most representative efforts of the age. Secular building, indeed, reflects the same general trends, but these are often obscured by the diversity of types, ranging from bridges and fortifications to royal palaces, from barns to town halls. Moreover, social, economic, and practical factors play a more important part here than in church design, so that the useful life of the buildings is apt to be much briefer and their chance of preservation correspondingly less. (Fortifications, indeed, are often made obsolete by even minor advances in the technology of warfare.) As a consequence, our knowledge of secular structures of the pre-Gothic Middle Ages remains extremely fragmentary, and most of the surviving examples from Gothic times belong to the latter half of the period. This fact, however, is not without significance; nonreligious architecture, both private and public, became far more elaborate during the fourteenth and fifteenth centuries than it had been before.

The history of the Louvre in Paris provides a telling example: the original building, erected about 1200, followed the severely functional plan of the castles of that time—it consisted mainly of a stout tower, the donjon or keep, surrounded by a heavy wall. In the 1360s, King Charles V had it built as a sumptuous royal residence. Although this second Louvre, too, has now disappeared, we know what it looked like from a fine miniature painted in the early fifteenth century (see fig. 543). There is still a defensive outer wall, but

the great structure behind it has far more the character of a palace than of a fortress. Symmetrically laid out around a square court, it provided comfortable quarters for the royal family and household (note the countless chimneys) as well as lavishly decorated halls for state occasions. (Figure 544, another miniature from the same manuscript, conveys a good impression of such a hall.)

If the exterior of the second Louvre still has some of the forbidding qualities of a stronghold, the sides toward the court displayed a wealth of architectural ornament and sculpture. The same contrast also appears in the house of Jacques Coeur in Bourges, built in the 1440s. We speak of it as a house, not a palace, only because Jacques Coeur was a silversmith and merchant, rather than a nobleman. Since, however, he also was one of the richest men of his day, he could well afford an establishment obviously modeled on the mansions of the aristocracy. The courtyard (fig. 474), with its high-pitched roofs, its pinnacles and decorative carvings, suggests the picturesque qualities familiar to us from Flamboyant church architecture (fig. 473). That we should find an echo of the Louvre court in a merchant's residence is striking proof of the importance attained by the urban middle class during the later Middle Ages.

## England

Among the astonishing things about Gothic art is the enthusiastic response this "royal French style of the Paris region" evoked abroad. Even more remarkable was its ability to ac-

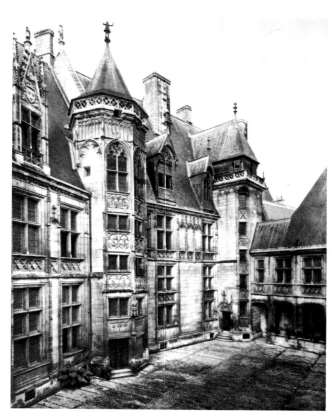

474. Court, House of Jacques Coeur, Bourges. 1443–51

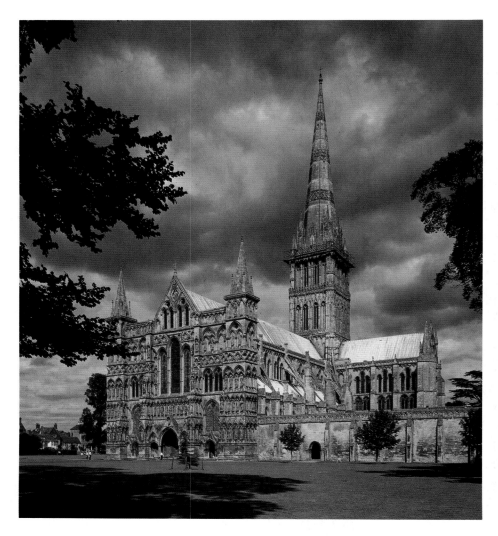

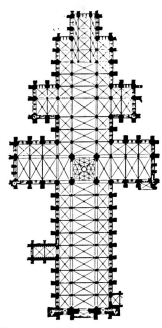

476. Plan of Salisbury Cathedral

477. (below) Nave and choir, Salisbury Cathedral

climate itself to a variety of local conditions—so much so, in fact, that the Gothic monuments of England and Germany have become objects of intense national pride in modern times, and critics in both countries have acclaimed Gothic as a peculiarly "native" style. How are we to account for the rapid spread of Gothic art? A number of factors might be cited, singly or in combination: the superior skill of French architects and stone carvers; the vast intellectual prestige of French centers of learning, such as the Cathedral School of Chartres and the University of Paris; and the influence of the Cistercians, the reformed monastic order founded by St. Bernard of Clairvaux. He, we will recall, had violently denounced the flights of fancy of Romanesque sculpture (see page 333). In conformity with his ascetic ideals, Cistercian abbey churches were a distinctive, severe type—decoration of any sort was held to a minimum, and a square choir took the place of apse, ambulatory, and radiating chapels. For that very reason, however, Cistercian architects put special emphasis on harmonious proportions and exact craftsmanship; and their "anti-Romanesque" outlook prompted them to adopt certain basic features of the Gothic style. During the latter half of the twelfth century, as the reform movement gathered momentum, this austere Cistercian Gothic came to be known throughout western Europe.

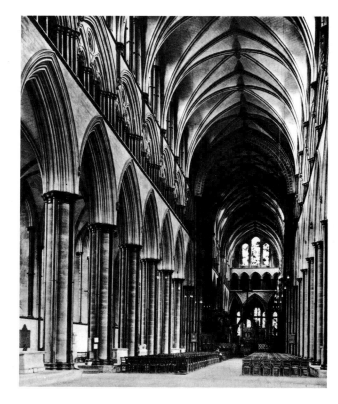

Still, one wonders whether any of the explanations we have mentioned really go to the heart of the matter. The ultimate reason for the international victory of Gothic art seems to have been the extraordinary persuasive power of the style itself, its ability to kindle the imagination and to arouse religious feeling even among people far removed from the cultural climate of the Île-de-France.

That England should have proved particularly receptive to the new style is hardly surprising. Yet English Gothic did not grow directly from Anglo-Norman Romanesque but from the Gothic of the Île-de-France (introduced in 1175 by the French architect who rebuilt the choir of Canterbury Cathedral) and from that of the Cistercians. Within less than fifty years, it developed a well-defined character of its own, known as the Early English style, which dominated the second quarter of the thirteenth century. Although there was a great deal of building activity during those decades, it consisted mostly of additions to Anglo-Norman structures. A great many English cathedrals had been begun about the same time as Durham (see figs. 418–20) but remained unfinished; they were now completed or enlarged. As a consequence, we find few churches that are designed in the Early English style throughout.

SALISBURY CATHEDRAL. Among cathedrals, only Salisbury meets this requirement (figs. 475–77). Viewing the exterior, we realize immediately how different it is from its counterparts in France—and how futile it would be to judge it by French Gothic standards. Compactness and verticality have given way to a long, low, sprawling look (the great crossing tower, which provides a dramatic unifying accent, was built a century later than the rest and is much taller than originally planned). Since there is no straining after height, flying buttresses have been introduced only as an afterthought. Characteristically enough, the west façade has become a screen wall, wider than the church itself and stratified by emphatic horizontal bands of ornament and statuary, while the towers have shrunk to stubby turrets. The plan, with its strongly projecting double transept, retains the segmented quality of Romanesque structures; the square east end derives from Cistercian architecture.

As we enter the nave, we recognize the same elements familiar to us from French interiors of the time, such as Chartres (see fig. 462), but the English interpretation of these elements produces a very different total effect. As on the façade, the horizontal divisions are stressed at the expense of the vertical, so that we see the nave wall not as a succession of bays but as a continuous series of arches and supports. These supports, carved of dark marble, stand out against the rest of the interior—a method of stressing their special function that is one of the hallmarks of the Early English style. Another insular feature is the steep curve of the nave vault. The ribs ascend all the way from the triforium level, and the clerestory, as a result, gives the impression of being "tucked away" among the vaults. At Durham, more than a century earlier, the same treatment had been a technical necessity (compare fig. 420); now it has become a matter of style, thoroughly in keeping with the character of Early English Gothic as a whole. This character might be

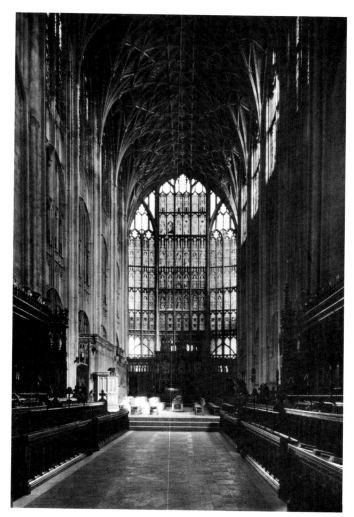

478. Choir, Gloucester Cathedral. 1332–57

described as conservative in the positive sense: it accepts the French system but tones down its revolutionary aspects so as to maintain a strong sense of continuity with the Anglo-Norman past.

PERPENDICULAR STYLE. The contrast between the bold upward thrust of the crossing tower and the leisurely horizontal progression throughout the rest of Salisbury Cathedral suggests that English Gothic had developed in a new direction during the intervening hundred years. The change becomes very evident if we compare the interior of Salisbury with the choir of Gloucester Cathedral, built in the second quarter of the next century (fig. 478). This is a striking example of English Late Gothic, also called "Perpendicular." The name certainly fits, since we now find the dominant vertical accent that is so conspicuously absent in the Early English style (note the responds running in an unbroken line from the vault to the floor). In this respect Perpendicular Gothic is much more akin to French sources, yet it includes so many features we have come to know as English that it would look very much out of place on the Continent. The repetition of small uniform tracery panels recalls the

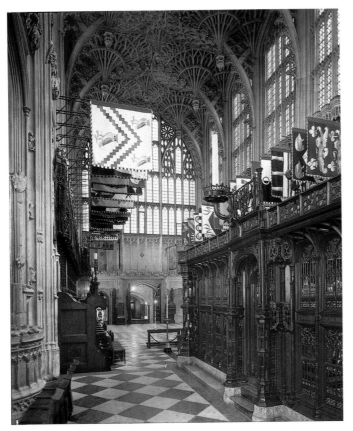

479. Chapel of Henry VII, Westminster Abbey, London
(view toward west). 1503–19

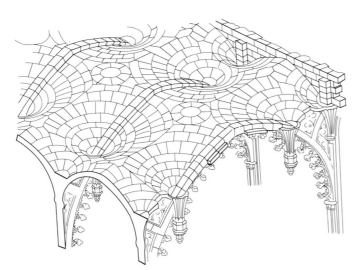

480. Diagram of vault construction, Chapel of Henry VII,
Westminster Abbey (after Swaan)

form an ornamental network that screens the boundaries between the bays and thus makes the entire vault look like one continuous surface. This, in turn, has the effect of emphasizing the unity of the interior space. Such decorative elaboration of the "classic" quadripartite vault is characteristic of the Flamboyant style on the Continent as well, but the English started it earlier and carried it to greater lengths. The ultimate is reached in the amazing pendant vault of Henry VII's Chapel at Westminster Abbey, built in the early years of the sixteenth century (figs. 479 and 480), with its lanternlike knobs hanging from conical "fans." This fantastic scheme merges ribs and tracery patterns in a dazzling display of architectural pageantry.

## Germany

In Germany, Gothic architecture took root a good deal more slowly than in England. Until the mid-thirteenth century, the Romanesque tradition, with its persistent Ottonian reminiscences, remained dominant, despite the growing acceptance of Early Gothic features. From about 1250 on, the High Gothic of the Île-de-France had a strong impact on the Rhineland; Cologne Cathedral (begun in 1248) represents an ambitious attempt to carry the full-fledged French system beyond the stage of Amiens. Significantly enough, however, the building remained a fragment until it was finally completed in modern times; nor did it have any successors.

bands of statuary on the west façade at Salisbury; the plan simulates the square east end of earlier English churches; and the upward curve of the vault is as steep as in the nave of Salisbury.

The ribs of the vaults, on the other hand, have assumed an altogether new role—they have been multiplied until they

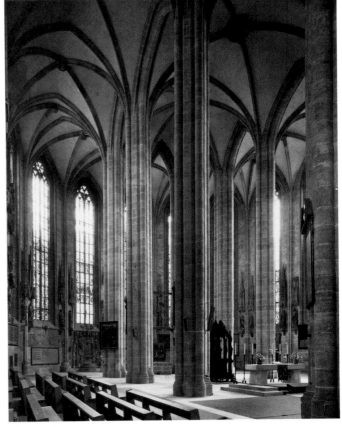

481. Choir, St. Sebald, Nuremberg. 1361–72

HALL CHURCHES. Far more characteristic of German Gothic is the development of the hall church, or *Hallenkirche*. Such churches—with aisles and nave of the same height—are familiar to us from Romanesque architecture (see fig. 415). For reasons not yet well understood, the type found particular favor on German soil, where its artistic possibilities were very fully explored. The large hall choir added in 1361–72 to the church of St. Sebald in Nuremberg (fig. 481) is one of many fine examples from central Germany. The space here has a fluidity and expansiveness that enfold us as if we were standing under a huge canopy; there is no pressure, no directional command to prescribe our path. And the unbroken lines of the pillars, formed by bundles of shafts which gradually diverge as they turn into ribs, seem to echo the continuous movement that we feel in the space itself.

## Italy

Italian Gothic architecture stands apart from that of the rest of Europe. Judged by the formal criteria of the Île-de-France, most of it hardly deserves to be called Gothic at all. Yet it produced structures of singular beauty and impressiveness that cannot be understood as mere continuations of the local Romanesque. We must be careful, therefore, to avoid too rigid or technical a standard in approaching these monuments, lest we fail to do justice to their unique blend of Gothic qualities and Mediterranean tradition. It was the Cistercians, rather than the cathedral builders of the Île-de-France, who provided the chief exemplars on which Italian architects based their conception of the Gothic style. As early as the end of the twelfth century, Cistercian abbeys sprang up in both north and central Italy, their designs patterned directly after those of the French abbeys of the order.

ABBEY CHURCH, FOSSANOVA. One of the finest buildings, at Fossanova, some sixty miles south of Rome, was consecrated in 1208 (figs. 482 and 483). Without knowing its location, we would be hard put to decide where to place it on a map—it might as well be Burgundian or English; the plan looks like a simplified version of Salisbury, and the finely proportioned interior bears a strong family resemblance to all Cistercian abbeys of the time. There are no façade towers, only a lantern over the crossing, as befits the Cistercian ideal of austerity. The groined vaults, although based on the pointed arch, have no diagonal ribs, the windows are small, and the architectural detail retains a good deal of Romanesque solidity, but the flavor of the whole is unmistakably Gothic.

Churches such as the one at Fossanova made a deep impression upon the Franciscans, the monastic order founded by St. Francis of Assisi in the early thirteenth century. As mendicant friars dedicated to poverty, simplicity, and humility, they were the spiritual kin of St. Bernard, and the severe beauty of Cistercian Gothic must have seemed to them to express an ideal closely related to theirs. Be that as it may, their churches from the first reflected Cistercian influence and thus played a leading role in establishing Gothic architecture in Italy.

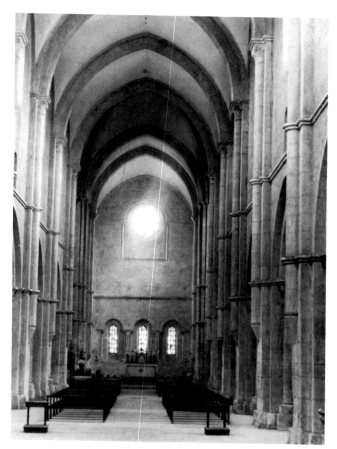

482. Nave and choir, Abbey Church of Fossanova.
Consecrated 1208

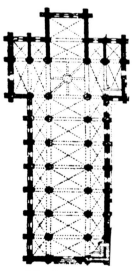

483. Plan of the
Abbey Church of Fossanova

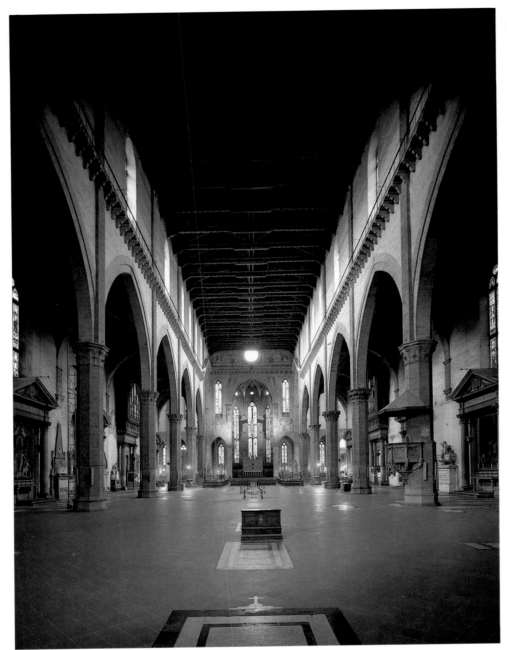

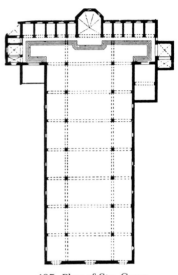

484. Nave and choir,
Sta. Croce, Florence. Begun c. 1295

485. Plan of Sta. Croce

STA. CROCE, FLORENCE. Sta. Croce in Florence, begun about a century after Fossanova, may well claim to be the greatest of all Franciscan structures (figs. 484 and 485); it is also a masterpiece of Gothic architecture, even though it has wooden ceilings instead of groined vaults. There can be no doubt that this was a matter of deliberate choice, rather than of technical or economic necessity—a choice made not only on the basis of local practice (we recall the wooden ceilings of the Tuscan Romanesque) but also perhaps from a desire to evoke the simplicity of Early Christian basilicas and, in doing so, to link Franciscan poverty with the traditions of the early Church. The plan, too, combines Cistercian and Early Christian features. We note, however, that it shows no trace of the Gothic structural system, except for the groin-

vaulted choir; the walls remain intact as continuous surfaces (indeed, Sta. Croce owes part of its fame to its wonderful murals) and, in contrast to Fossanova, there are no longer any buttresses, since the wooden ceilings do not require them.

Why, then, do we speak of Sta. Croce as Gothic? Surely the use of the pointed arch is not sufficient to justify the term? A glance at the interior will dispel our misgivings. For we sense immediately that this space creates an effect fundamentally different from that of either Early Christian or Romanesque architecture. The nave walls have the weightless, "transparent" quality we saw in northern Gothic churches, and the dramatic massing of windows at the eastern end conveys the dominant role of light as forcefully as

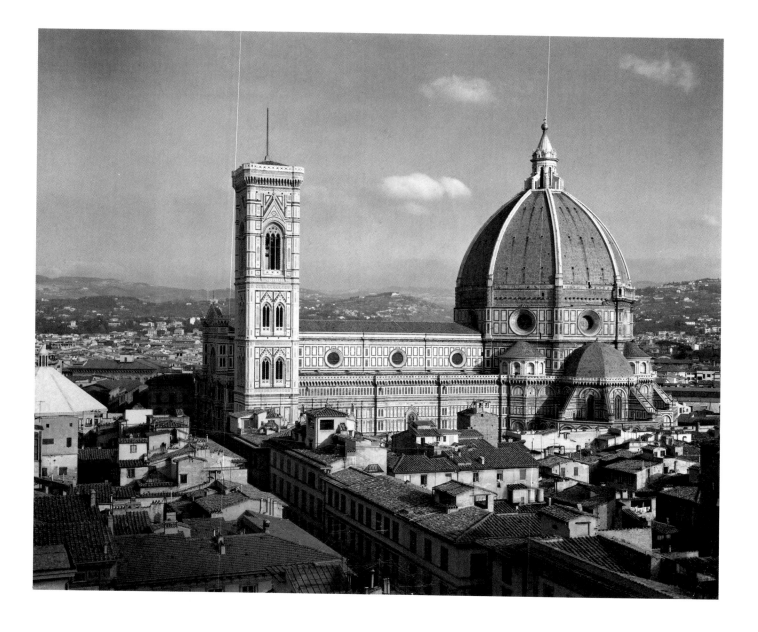

486. Florence Cathedral (S. Maria del Fiore).
Begun by ARNOLFO DE CAMBIO, 1296;
dome by FILIPPO BRUNELLESCHI, 1420–36

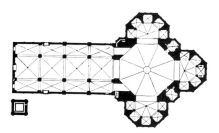

487. Plan of Florence Cathedral

Abbot Suger's choir at St.-Denis. Judged in terms of its emotional impact, Sta. Croce is Gothic beyond doubt; it is also profoundly Franciscan—and Florentine—in the monumental simplicity of the means by which this impact has been achieved.

FLORENCE CATHEDRAL. If in Sta. Croce the architect's main concern was an impressive interior, Florence Cathedral was planned as a monumental landmark to civic pride towering above the entire city (figs. 486 and 487). The original design, by the sculptor Arnolfo di Cambio, which dates from 1296—about the same time construction was begun at Sta. Croce—is not known in detail; although somewhat smaller than the present building, it probably showed the same basic plan. The building as we know it, however, is based largely on a design by Francesco Talenti, who took over around 1343. The most striking feature is the great octagonal dome with its subsidiary half-domes, a motif ultimately of late Roman origin (see figs. 266, 267, and 322–

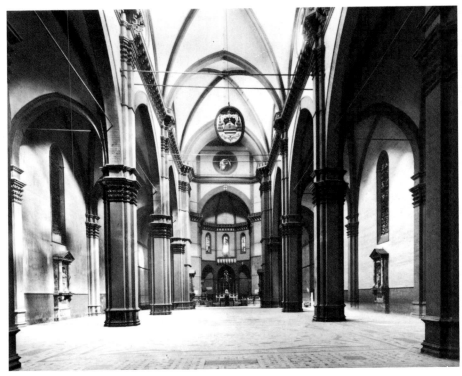

488. Nave and choir, Florence Cathedral

24). It may have been thought of at first as an oversize dome above the crossing of nave and transept, but it soon grew into a huge central pool of space that makes the nave look like an afterthought. The basic characteristics of the dome were set by a committee of leading painters and sculptors in 1367; the actual construction, however, belongs to the early fifteenth century (see page 455).

Apart from the windows and the doorways, there is nothing Gothic about the exterior of Florence Cathedral (flying buttresses to sustain the nave vault may have been planned but proved unnecessary). The solid walls, encrusted with geometric marble inlays, are a perfect match for the Romanesque Baptistery (see fig. 431). The interior, on the other hand, recalls Sta. Croce, even though the dominant impression is one of chill solemnity rather than lightness and grace. The ribbed groined vault of the nave rests directly on the huge nave arcade, producing an emphasis on width instead of height, and the architectural detail throughout has a massive solidity that seems more Romanesque than Gothic (fig. 488). Thus, the unvaulted interior of Sta. Croce reflects the spirit of the new style more faithfully than does the Cathedral, which, on the basis of its structural system, ought to be the more Gothic of the two.

Typically enough, a separate campanile takes the place of the façade towers familiar to us in northern Gothic churches. It was begun by the great painter Giotto, who managed to finish only the first story, and continued by the sculptor Andrea Pisano, son of Nicola Pisano (see page 386), who was responsible for the niche zone. The rest represents the work of Talenti, who completed it by about 1360.

The west façade, so dramatic a feature in French cathedrals, never achieved the same importance in Italy. It is re-

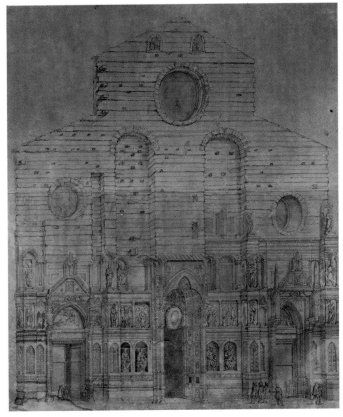

489. BERNARDINO POCCETTI
Drawing of ARNOLFO DI CAMBIO'S
design for the façade of Florence Cathedral. c. 1587.
Museo dell'Opera di S. Maria del Fiore, Florence

markable how few Italian Gothic façades were ever carried to completion before the onset of the Renaissance. Those of Sta. Croce and Florence Cathedral both date from the nineteenth century. Fortunately, Arnolfo's design for the latter is preserved in a drawing made by Bernardino Poccetti just before being demolished in 1587 (fig. 489). Only the bottom half of the decorations is shown in detail, but it provides us with a clear idea of what an Italian Gothic façade would have looked like, though it is not without later alterations. Arnolfo devised an ornate scheme of pilasters and niches with sculptures to articulate the surface, which was further embellished by mosaics. The over-all effect must have been a dazzling fusion of sculpture and architecture, classical severity and Gothic splendor.

MILAN CATHEDRAL. Work on Italian Gothic churches often continued for hundreds of years. Such was the case with Milan Cathedral, by far the largest Gothic church on Italian soil as well as the one most nearly comparable to Northern structures. Begun in 1386, it was completed only in 1910. Its structural design was the subject of a famous dispute between the local architects and consulting experts from France and Germany. Only the apse, begun first, retains the original flavor of the building, which belongs to the late, Flamboyant phase of Gothic architecture (fig. 490). Otherwise the decoration strikes us as an overly elaborate piling up of detail applied in mechanical fashion over the centuries without any unity of feeling.

SECULAR ARCHITECTURE. The secular buildings of Gothic Italy convey as distinct a local flavor as the churches. There is nothing in the cities of northern Europe to match the impressive grimness of the Palazzo Vecchio (fig. 491), the town hall of Florence. Fortresslike structures such as this reflect the factional strife—among political parties, social classes, and prominent families—so characteristic of life within the Italian city-states. The wealthy man's home (or *palazzo*, a term denoting any large urban house) was quite literally his castle, designed both to withstand armed assault and to proclaim the owner's importance. The Palazzo Vecchio, while larger and more elaborate, follows the same pattern. Behind its battlemented walls, the city government

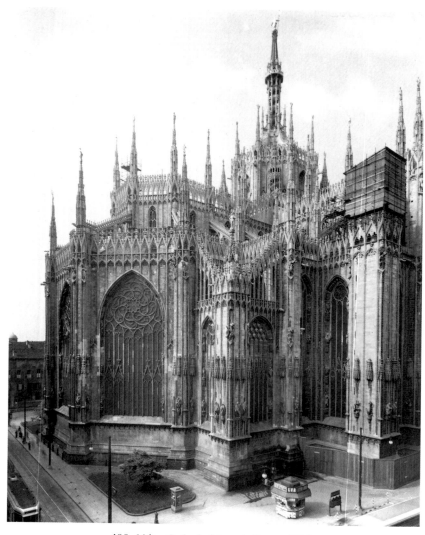

490. Milan Cathedral (apse). Begun 1386

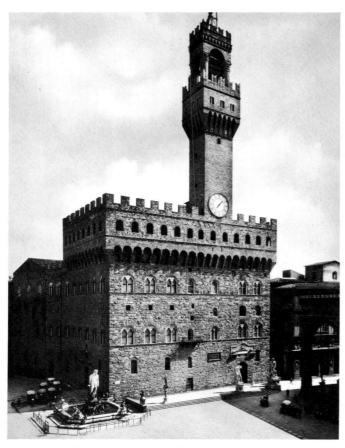

491. Palazzo Vecchio, Florence. Begun 1298

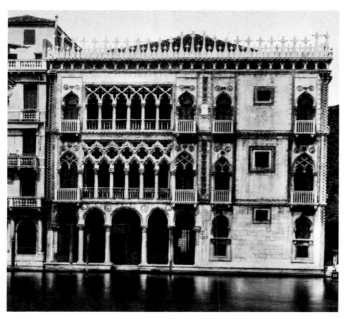

492. Ca' d'Oro, Venice. 1422–c. 1440

could feel well protected from the wrath of angry crowds. The tall tower not only symbolizes civic pride but has an eminently practical purpose; dominating the city as well as the surrounding countryside, it served as a lookout against enemies from without or within.

Among Italian cities Venice alone was ruled by a merchant aristocracy so firmly established that internal disturbances were the exception rather than the rule. As a consequence, Venetian *palazzi*, unhampered by defensive requirements, developed into graceful, ornate structures such as the Ca' d'Oro (fig. 492). There is more than a touch of the Orient in the delicate latticework effect of this façade, even though most of the decorative vocabulary derives from the Late Gothic of northern Europe. Its rippling patterns, ideally designed to be seen against their own reflection in the water of the Grand Canal, have the same fairy-tale quality we recall from the exterior of St. Mark's (see fig. 350).

# SCULPTURE

## France

Although Abbot Suger's story of the rebuilding of St.-Denis does not deal at length with the sculptural decoration of the church, he must have attached considerable importance to this aspect of the enterprise. The three portals of his west façade were far larger and more richly carved than those of Norman Romanesque churches. Unhappily, their condition today is so poor that they do not tell us a great deal about Suger's ideas of the role of sculpture within the total context of the structure he had envisioned.

CHARTRES CATHEDRAL, WEST PORTALS. We may assume, however, that Suger's ideas had prepared the way for the admirable west portals of Chartres Cathedral (fig. 493), begun about 1145 under the influence of St.-Denis, but even more ambitious. They probably represent the oldest full-fledged example of Early Gothic sculpture. Comparing them with Romanesque portals, we are impressed first of all with a new sense of order, as if all the figures had suddenly come to attention, conscious of their responsibility to the architectural framework. The dense crowding and the frantic movement of Romanesque sculpture have given way to an emphasis on symmetry and clarity; the figures on the lintels, archivolts, and tympanums are no longer entangled with each other but stand out as separate entities, so that the entire design carries much farther than that of previous portals.

Particularly striking in this respect is the novel treatment of the jambs (fig. 494), which are lined with tall figures attached to columns. Similarly elongated figures, we recall, had occurred on the jambs or *trumeaux* of Romanesque portals (see figs. 433 and 439), but they had been conceived as reliefs carved into—or protruding from—the masonry of the doorway. The Chartres jamb figures, in contrast, are essentially statues, each with its own axis; they could, in theory at least, be detached from their supports. Here, then, we wit-

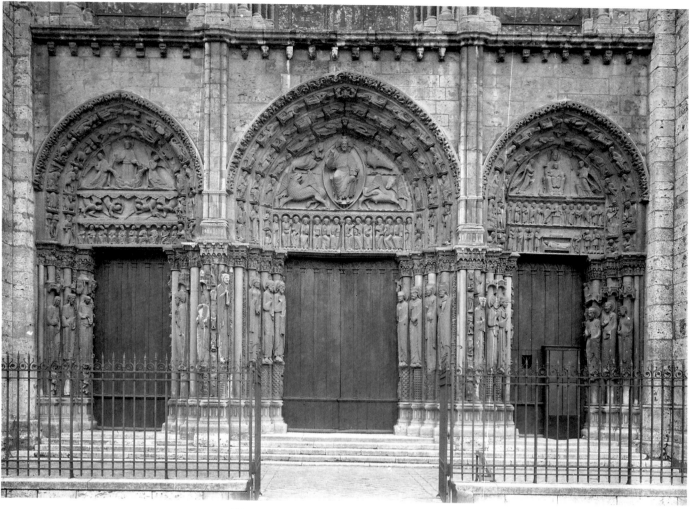

493. West portal, Chartres Cathedral. c. 1145–70

ness a development of truly revolutionary importance; the first basic step toward the reconquest of monumental sculpture in the round since the end of classical antiquity. Apparently, this step could be taken only by "borrowing" the rigid cylindrical shape of the column for the human figure, with the result that these statues seem more abstract than their Romanesque predecessors. Yet they will not regain their immobility and unnatural proportions for long; the very fact that they are round endows them with a more emphatic presence than anything in Romanesque sculpture, and their heads show a gentle, human quality that betokens the fundamentally realistic trend of Gothic sculpture.

Realism is, of course, a relative term whose meaning varies greatly according to circumstances. On the Chartres west portals, it appears to spring from a reaction against the fantasic and demoniacal aspects of Romanesque art, a reaction that may be seen not only in the calm, solemn spirit of the figures and their increased physical bulk (compare the Christ of the center tympanum with that at Vézelay, fig. 437) but in the rational discipline of the symbolic program underlying the entire scheme. While the subtler aspects of this program are accessible only to a mind fully conversant

with the theology of the Chartres Cathedral School, its main elements can be readily understood.

The jamb statues, a continuous sequence linking all three portals, represent the prophets, kings, and queens of the Bible; their purpose is both to acclaim the rulers of France as the spiritual descendants of Old Testament royalty and to stress the harmony of secular and spiritual rule, of priests (or bishops) and kings—an ideal insistently put forward by Abbot Suger. Christ Himself appears enthroned above the main doorway as Judge and Ruler of the Universe, flanked by the symbols of the four evangelists, with the apostles assembled below and the twenty-four elders of the Apocalypse in the archivolts. The right-hand tympanum shows His incarnation—the Birth, the Presentation in the Temple, and the Infant Christ on the lap of the Virgin (who also stands for the Church)—while in the archivolts we see the personifications and representatives of the liberal arts: human wisdom paying homage to the divine wisdom of Christ. In the left-hand tympanum, finally, we see the timeless Heavenly Christ, the Christ of the Ascension, framed by the signs of the zodiac and their earthly counterparts, the labors of the twelve months—the ever-repeating cycle of the year.

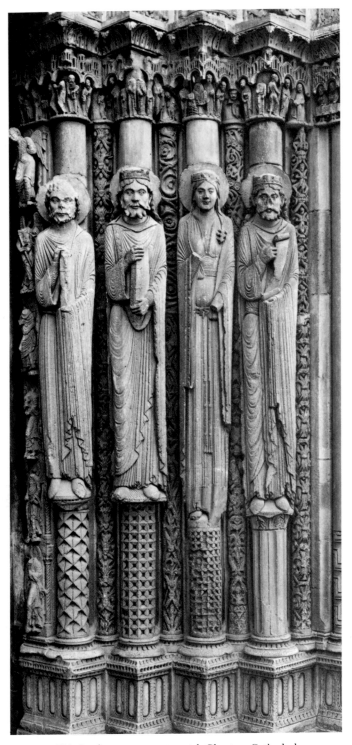

494. Jamb statues, west portal, Chartres Cathedral

ture. By now, the symbiosis of statue and column has begun to dissolve: the columns are quite literally put in the shade by the greater width of the figures, by the strongly projecting canopies above, and by the elaborately carved bases of the statues.

In the three saints on the right, we still find echoes of the rigid cylindrical shape of Early Gothic jamb statues, but even here the heads are no longer strictly in line with the central axis of the body; and St. Theodore, the knight on the left, already stands at ease, in a semblance of classical *contrapposto*. His feet rest on a horizontal platform, rather than on a sloping shelf as before, and the axis of his body, instead of being straight, describes a slight but perceptible S-curve. Even more astonishing is the abundance of precisely observed detail—the weapons, the texture of the tunic and chain mail—and, above all, the organic structure of the body. Not since imperial Roman times have we seen a figure as thoroughly alive as this. Yet the most impressive quality of the statue is not its realism; it is, rather, the serene, balanced image of man which this realism conveys. In this ideal portrait of the Christian Soldier, the spirit of the crusades has been cast into its most elevated form.

The style of the *St. Theodore* could not have evolved directly from the elongated columnar statues of Chartres' west façade. It incorporates another, equally important tradition:

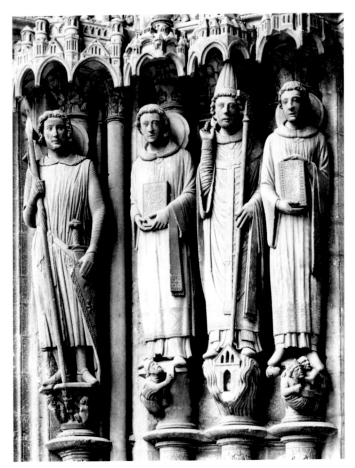

495. Jamb statues, south transept portal,
Chartres Cathedral. c. 1215–20

GOTHIC CLASSICISM. When Chartres Cathedral was rebuilt after the fire of 1195, the so-called Royal Portals of the west façade must have seemed rather small and old-fashioned in relation to the rest of the new edifice. Perhaps for that reason, the two transept façades each received three large and lavishly carved portals preceded by deep porches. The jamb statues of these portals, such as the group shown in figure 495, represent an early phase of High Gothic sculp-

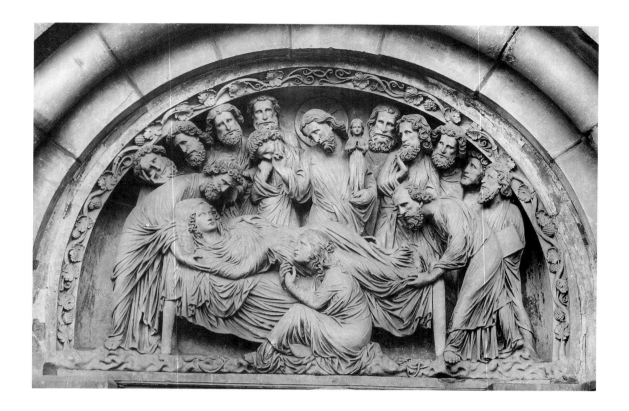

the classicism of the Meuse valley, which we traced in the previous chapter from Renier of Huy to Nicholas of Verdun (compare figs. 441, 448, and 449). At the end of the twelfth century this trend, hitherto confined to metalwork and miniatures, began to appear in monumental stone sculpture as well, transforming it from Early Gothic to Classic High Gothic. The link with Nicholas of Verdun is striking in the *Death of the Virgin* (fig. 496), a tympanum from Strasbourg Cathedral contemporary with the Chartres transept portals; here the draperies, the facial types, and the movements and gestures have a classical flavor that immediately recalls the Klosterneuburg Altar (fig. 449).

What marks it as Gothic rather than Romanesque, on the other hand, is the deeply felt tenderness pervading the entire scene. We sense a bond of shared emotion among the figures, an ability to communicate by glance and gesture such as we have never met before. This quality of pathos, too, has classical roots—we recall its entering into Christian art during the Second Golden Age in Byzantium (see fig. 355). But how much warmer and more eloquent it is at Strasbourg than at Daphnē!

The climax of Gothic classicism is reached in some of the statues at Reims Cathedral, the most famous among them being the Visitation group (fig. 497, right). To have a pair of jamb figures enact a narrative scene such as this would have been unthinkable in Early Gothic sculpture; the fact that they can do so now shows how far the sustaining column has receded into the background. Characteristically enough, the S-curve, much more conspicuous than in the *St. Theodore*, dominates the side view as well as the front view, and the physical bulk of the body is further emphasized by horizontal folds pulled across the abdomen. The re-

496. *DEATH OF THE VIRGIN*, tympanum of the south transept portal, Strasbourg Cathedral. c. 1220

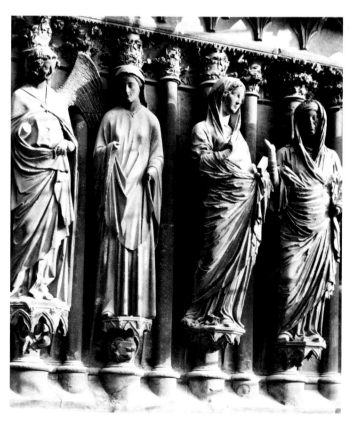

497. *ANNUNCIATION* and *VISITATION*, west portal, Reims Cathedral. c. 1225–45

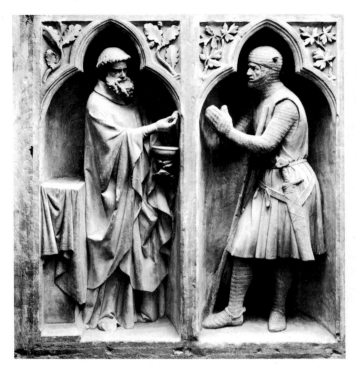

498. *MELCHIZEDEK AND ABRAHAM*, interior west wall,
Reims Cathedral. After 1251

lationship of the two women shows the same human
warmth and sympathy we found in the Strasbourg tympanum, but their classicism is of a far more monumental
kind; they remind us so forcibly of ancient Roman matrons
(compare fig. 286) that we wonder if the artist could have
been inspired directly by large-scale Roman sculpture. The
influence of Nicholas of Verdun alone could hardly have
produced such firmly rounded, solid volumes.

The vast scale of the sculptural program for Reims Cathedral had made it necessary to call upon the services of masters and workshops from various other building sites, and so
we encounter several distinct styles among the Reims sculpture. Two of these styles, both clearly different from the classicism of the *Visitation*, appear in the Annunciation group
(fig. 497, left). The Virgin exhibits a severe manner, with a
rigidly vertical body axis and straight, tubular folds meeting
at sharp angles, a style probably invented about 1220 by the
sculptors of the west portals of Notre-Dame in Paris; from
there it traveled to Reims as well as Amiens (see fig. 500,
above). The angel, in contrast, is conspicuously graceful: we
note the tiny, round face framed by curly locks, the emphatic smile, the strong S-curve of the slender body, the ample,
richly accented drapery. This "elegant style," created
around 1240 by Parisian masters working for the royal court,
was to spread far and wide during the following decades; it
soon became, in fact, the standard formula for High Gothic
sculpture. We shall feel its effect for many years to come, not
only in France but abroad.

A characteristic instance of the "elegant style" is the fine
group of *Melchizedek and Abraham*, carved shortly after the
middle of the century for the interior west wall of Reims Ca-

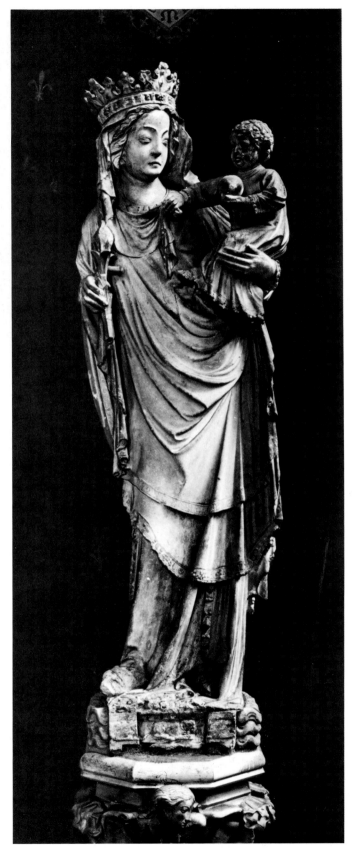

499. *THE VIRGIN OF PARIS*. Early 14th century. Stone.
Notre-Dame, Paris

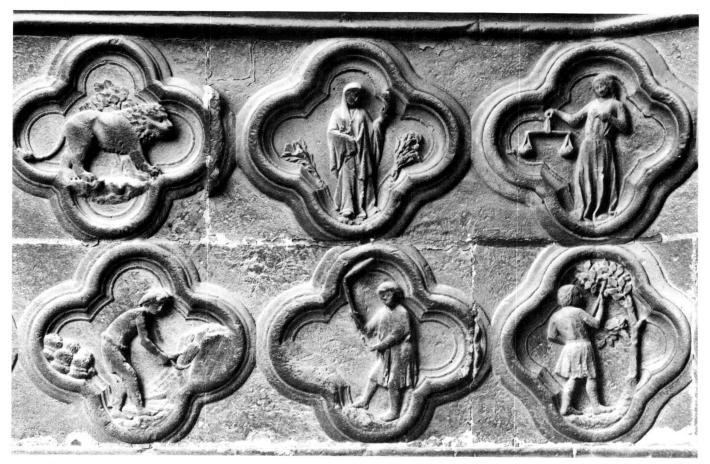

500. *SIGNS OF THE ZODIAC* and *LABORS OF THE MONTHS (JULY, AUGUST, SEPTEMBER),* west façade, Amiens Cathedral. c. 1220–30

thedral (fig. 498). Abraham, in the costume of a medieval knight, still recalls the vigorous realism of the *St. Theodore* at Chartres; Melchizedek, however, shows clearly his descent from the angel of the Reims *Annunciation*—his hair and beard are even more elaborately curled, the draperies more lavishly ample, so that the body almost disappears among the rich play of folds. The deep recesses and sharply projecting ridges betray a new awareness of effects of light and shadow that seem more pictorial than sculptural; the same may be said of the way the figures are placed in their cavernous niches.

A half century later every trace of classicism has disappeared from Gothic sculpture. The human figure itself now becomes strangely abstract. Thus the famous *Virgin of Paris* (fig. 499) in Notre-Dame Cathedral consists largely of hollows, the projections having been reduced to the point where they are seen as lines rather than volumes. The statue is quite literally disembodied—its swaying stance no longer bears any relationship to the classical *contrapposto.* Compared to such unearthly grace, the angel of the Reims *Annunciation* seems solid and tangible indeed, yet it contains the seed of the very qualities so strikingly expressed in *The Virgin of Paris.*

When we look back over the century and a half that separates *The Virgin of Paris* from the Chartres west portals, we cannot help wondering what brought about this retreat from

the realism of Early and classic High Gothic sculptures. Despite the fact that the new style was backed by the royal court and thus had special authority, we find it hard to explain why attenuated elegance and calligraphic, smoothly flowing lines came to dominate Gothic art throughout northern Europe from about 1250 to 1400. It is clear, nevertheless, that *The Virgin of Paris* represents neither a return to the Romanesque nor a complete repudiation of the earlier realistic trend.

Gothic realism had never been of the all-embracing, systematic sort; it had been a "realism of particulars," focused on specific details rather than on the over-all structure of the visible world. Its most characteristic products are not the classically oriented jamb statues and tympanum compositions of the early thirteenth century, but small-scale carvings such as the *Labors of the Months* in quatrefoil frames on the façade of Amiens Cathedral (fig. 500), with their delightful observation of everyday life. This intimate kind of realism survives even within the abstract formal framework of *The Virgin of Paris*; we see it in the Infant Christ, who appears here not as the Saviour-in-miniature austerely facing the beholder, but as a thoroughly human child playing with his mother's veil. Our statue thus retains an emotional appeal that links it to the Strasbourg *Death of the Virgin* and to the Reims *Visitation.* It is this appeal, not realism or classicism as such, that is the essence of Gothic art.

## England

The spread of Gothic sculpture beyond the borders of France began only toward 1200—the style of the Chartres west portals had hardly any echoes abroad—but, once under way, it proceeded at an astonishingly rapid pace. England may well have led the way, as it did in evolving its own version of Gothic architecture. Unfortunately, so much English Gothic sculpture was destroyed during the Reformation that we can study its development only with difficulty. Our richest materials are the tombs, which did not arouse the iconoclastic zeal of anti-Catholics. They include a type, illustrated by the splendid example in figure 501, that has no counterpart on the other side of the Channel: it shows the deceased, not in quiet repose as does the vast majority of medieval tombs, but in violent action, a fallen hero, fighting to the last breath. According to an old tradition, these dramatic figures, whose agony so oddly recalls the *Dying Gaul* (see fig. 224), honor the memory of crusaders who died in the struggle for the Holy Land. If so, they would, as the tombs of Christian Soldiers, carry a religious meaning that might help to account for their compelling expressive power. In any event, they are among the finest achievements of English Gothic sculpture.

## Germany

In Germany, the growth of Gothic sculpture can be traced more easily. From the 1220s on, German masters trained in the sculptural workshops of the great French cathedrals transplanted the new style to their homeland, although German architecture at that time was still predominantly Romanesque. However, even after the middle of the century, Germany failed to emulate the vast statuary cycles of France. As a consequence, German Gothic sculpture tended to be less closely linked with its architectural setting (the finest work was often done for the interiors rather than the exteriors of churches) and this, in turn, permitted it to develop an individuality and expressive freedom greater than that of its French models.

THE NAUMBURG MASTER. All these qualities are strikingly evident in the style of the Naumburg Master, an artist of real genius whose best-known work is the magnificent se-

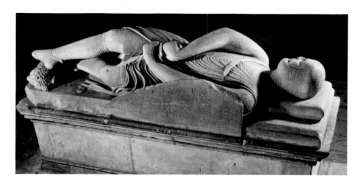

501. Tomb of a Knight. c. 1260. Stone.
Dorchester Abbey, Oxfordshire

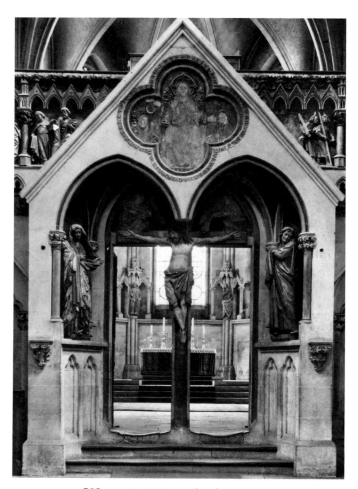

502. *CRUCIFIXION,* on the choir screen,
Naumburg Cathedral. c. 1240–50. Stone

ries of statues and reliefs he carved, about 1240–1250, for Naumburg Cathedral. The *Crucifixion* (fig. 502) forms the central feature of the choir screen; enclosed by a deep, gabled porch, the three figures frame the opening that links the nave with the sanctuary. Placing the group as he did (rather than above the screen, in accordance with the usual practice), our sculptor has brought the sacred subject down to earth both physically and emotionally: the suffering of Christ becomes a human reality because of the emphasis on the weight and volume of the Saviour's body, and Mary and John, pleading with the beholder, convey their grief more eloquently than ever before.

The pathos of these figures is heroic and dramatic, as against the lyricism of the Strasbourg tympanum or the Reims *Visitation.* If the Classic High Gothic sculpture of France evokes comparison with Phidias, the Naumburg Master might be termed the temperamental kin of Scopas (see pages 191–92). The same intensity of feeling dominates the Passion scenes, such as *The Kiss of Judas* (fig. 503), with its unforgettable contrast between the meekness of Christ and the violent, sword-wielding St. Peter. Finally there are, attached to the responds inside the choir, the statues of nobles associated with the founding of the cathedral, among them the famous pair *Ekkehard and Uta* (fig. 504).

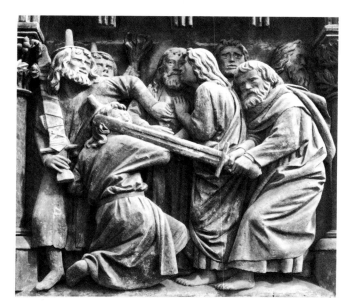

503. *THE KISS OF JUDAS*, on the choir screen,
Naumburg Cathedral. c. 1240–50. Stone

Although these men and women were not of the artist's own time, so that he knew them only as names in a chronicle, he has given each of them a personality as distinctive and forceful as if he had portrayed them from life. They make an instructive contrast with the *St. Theodore* at Chartres (see fig. 495).

THE PIETÀ. Gothic sculpture, as we have come to know it so far, reflects a desire to endow the traditional themes of Christian art with an ever greater emotional appeal. Toward the end of the thirteenth century, this tendency gave rise to a new kind of religious imagery, designed to serve private devotion; it is often referred to by the German term *Andachtsbild*, since Germany played a leading part in its development. The most characteristic and widespread type of *Andachtsbild* was the *Pietà* (an Italian word derived from the Latin *pietas*, the root word for both "pity" and "piety"), a representation of the Virgin grieving over the dead Christ. No such scene occurs in the scriptural account of the Pas-

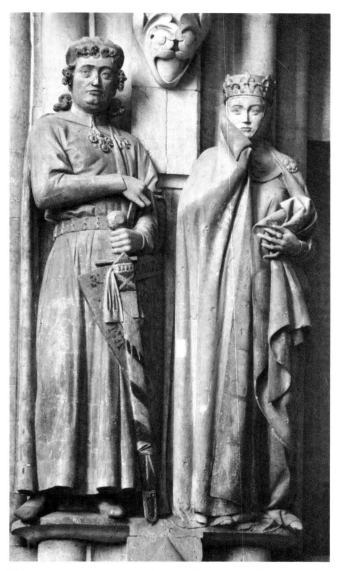

504. *EKKEHARD AND UTA*, c. 1240–50. Stone. Naumburg Cathedral

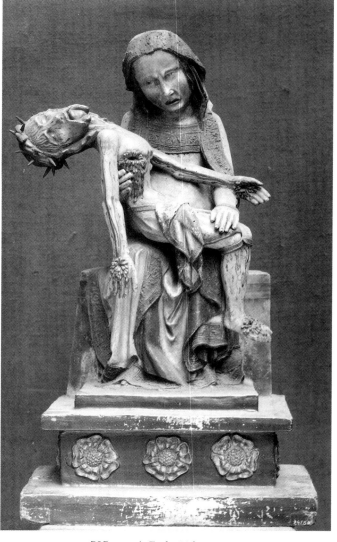

505. *PIETÀ*. Early 14th century.
Wood, height 34½″ (87.5 cm). Provinzialmuseum, Bonn

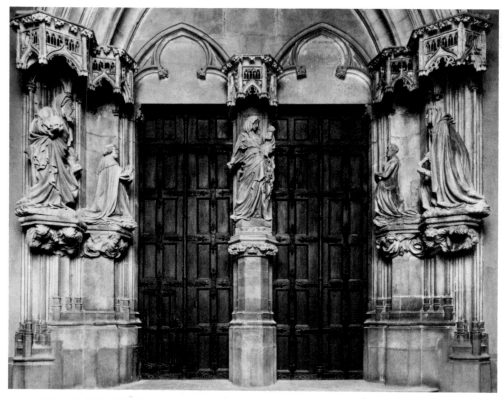

506. CLAUS SLUTER. Portal of the Chartreuse de Champmol, Dijon. 1385–93. Stone

sion; it was invented, rather—we do not know exactly where or when—as a tragic counterpart to the familiar motif of the Madonna and Child.

The *Pietà* reproduced in figure 505 dates from the same period as *The Virgin of Paris*; like most such groups, it is carved of wood, with a vividly painted surface to enhance its impact. Realism here has become purely a vehicle of expression—the agonized faces; the blood-encrusted wounds of Christ that are enlarged and elaborated to an almost grotesque degree; and the bodies and limbs, puppetlike in their thinness and rigidity. The purpose of the work, clearly, is to arouse so overwhelming a sense of horror and pity that the beholder will identify his own feelings completely with those of the grief-stricken Mother of God.

At a glance, our *Pietà* would seem to have little in common with *The Virgin of Paris*. Yet they both share a lean, "deflated" quality of form that is the characteristic period flavor of Northern European art from the late thirteenth century to the mid-fourteenth. Only after 1350 do we again find an interest in weight and volume, coupled with a renewed impulse to explore tangible reality.

## The International Style in the North

SLUTER. The climax of this new trend came around 1400, during the period of the so-called International Style (see pages 338–39 and 404–11), and its greatest exponent was Claus Sluter, a sculptor of Netherlandish origin working for the duke of Burgundy at Dijon. The portal of the Chartreuse de Champmol (fig. 506), which he did in 1385–93, recalls the monumental statuary on thirteenth-century cathedral portals, but the figures have grown so large and expansive that they almost overpower their architectural framework. This effect is due not only to their size and the bold three-dimensionality of the carving, but also to the fact that the jamb statues (Duke Philip the Bold and his wife, accompanied by their patron saints) are turned toward the Madonna on the *trumeau*, so that the five figures form a single, coherent unit, like the *Crucifixion* group at Naumburg. In both instances, the sculptural composition has simply been superimposed—however skillfully—on the shape of the doorway, not developed from it as at Chartres, Notre-Dame, or Reims. Significantly enough, the Champmol portal did not pave the way for a revival of architectural sculpture; it remained an isolated effort.

Sluter's other works belong to a different category, which for lack of a better term we must label church furniture (tombs, pulpits, and the like), combining large-scale sculpture with a small-scale architectural setting. The most impressive of these is *The Moses Well* at the Chartreuse de Champmol (fig. 507), a symbolic well surrounded by statues of Moses and other Old Testament prophets and once surmounted by a crucifix. The majestic Moses epitomizes the same qualities we find in Sluter's portal statues; soft, lavishly draped garments envelop the heavy-set body like an am-

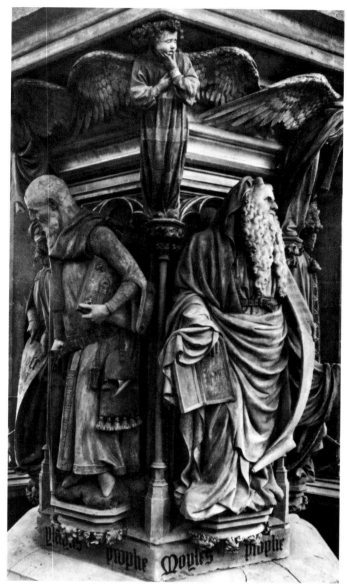

507. CLAUS SLUTER. *THE MOSES WELL*. 1395–1406. Stone,
height of figures c. 6′ (1.8 m). Chartreuse de Champmol, Dijon

ple shell, the swelling forms seem to reach out into the surrounding space, determined to capture as much of it as possible (note the outward curve of the scroll).

In the Isaiah, facing left in our illustration, these aspects of our artist's style are less pronounced; what strikes us, rather, is the precise and masterful realism of every detail, from the minutiae of the costume to the texture of the wrinkled skin. The head, unlike that of Moses, has all the individuality of a portrait. Nor is this impression deceiving, for the sculptural development that culminated in Claus Sluter had produced, from about 1350 on, the first genuine portraits since late Antiquity. And Sluter himself has left us two splendid examples in the heads of the duke and duchess on the Chartreuse portal. It is this attachment to the tangible and specific that distinguishes his realism from that of the thirteenth century.

## Italy

We have left a discussion of Italian Gothic sculpture to the last, for here, too, as in Gothic architecture, Italy stands apart from the rest of Europe. The earliest Gothic sculpture on Italian soil was probably produced in the extreme south, in Apulia and Sicily, the domain of the German Emperor Frederick II, who employed Frenchmen and Germans along with native artists at his court. Of the works he sponsored little has survived, but there is evidence that his taste favored a strongly classic style derived from the sculpture of the Chartres transept portals and the *Visitation* group at Reims. This style not only provided a fitting visual language for a ruler who saw himself as the heir of the Caesars of old; it also blended easily with the classical tendencies in Italian Romanesque sculpture (see above, page 345).

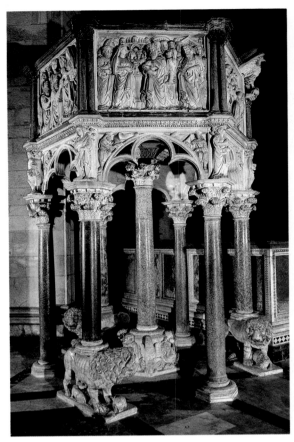

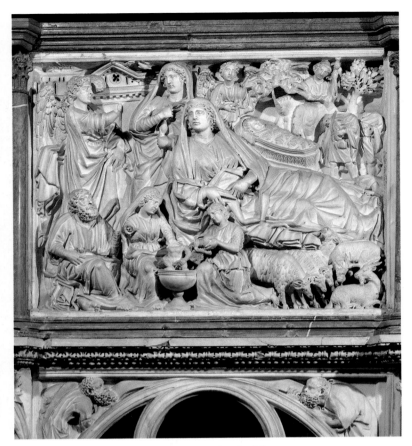

508. NICOLA PISANO. Pulpit. 1259–60. Marble, height 15' (4.6 m). Baptistery, Pisa

509. *NATIVITY*, detail of the Pulpit by NICOLA PISANO, Baptistery, Pisa

NICOLA PISANO. Such was the background of Nicola Pisano, who came to Tuscany from southern Italy about 1250 (the year of Frederick II's death). In 1260 he completed the marble pulpit in the Baptistery of Pisa Cathedral (fig. 508). His work has been well defined as that of "the greatest—and in a sense the last—of medieval classicists." In the Pisa Baptistery pulpit the classical flavor is indeed so strong, whether we look at the architectural framework or at the sculptured parts, that the Gothic elements are hard to detect at first glance. But we do find such elements in the design of the arches, in the shape of the capitals, and in the standing figures at the corners (which look like small-scale descendants of the jamb statues on French Gothic cathedrals).

More striking, perhaps, is the Gothic quality of human feeling in the reliefs of narrative scenes such as the *Nativity* (fig. 509). The dense crowding of figures, on the other hand, has no counterpart in northern Gothic sculpture (aside from the Nativity, the panel also shows the Annunciation and the shepherds in the fields receiving the glad tidings of the birth of Christ). This treatment of the relief as a shallow box filled almost to the bursting point with solid, convex shapes tells us that Nicola Pisano must have been thoroughly familiar with Roman sarcophagi (compare fig. 329).

GIOVANNI PISANO. Half a century later Nicola's son Giovanni (1245/50–after 1314), who was an equally gifted sculptor, did a marble pulpit for Pisa Cathedral. It, too, includes a *Nativity* (fig. 510). Both panels have a good many things in common, as we might well expect, yet they also offer a sharp—and instructive—contrast. Giovanni's slender, swaying figures, with their smoothly flowing draperies, recall neither classical Antiquity nor the Visitation group at Reims; instead, they reflect the elegant style of the royal court at Paris that had become the standard Gothic formula during the later thirteenth century. And with this change there has come about a new treatment of relief: to Giovanni Pisano, space is as important as plastic form. The figures are no longer tightly packed together; they are now spaced far enough apart to let us see the landscape setting that contains them, and each figure has been allotted its own pocket of space. If Nicola's *Nativity* strikes us as essentially a sequence of bulging, rounded masses, Giovanni's appears to be made up mainly of cavities and shadows.

Giovanni Pisano, then, seems to follow the same trend toward "disembodiment" that we encountered north of the Alps around 1300. He does so, however, only within limits. Compared to *The Virgin of Paris*, his *Madonna* at Prato Cathedral (figs. 511 and 512) immediately evokes memories of Nicola's style. The three-dimensional firmness of the modeling is further emphasized by the strong turn of the head and the thrust-out left hip; we also note the heavy, buttresslike folds that anchor the figure to its base. Yet there can be no

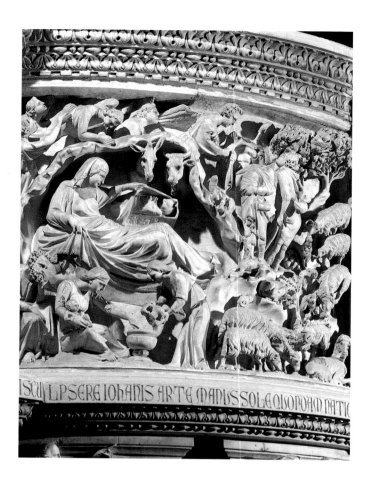

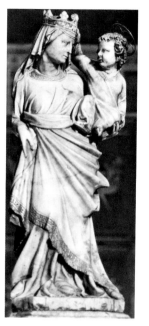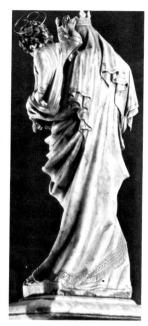

510. *(left)* GIOVANNI PISANO. *THE NATIVITY*,
detail of pulpit. 1302–10. Marble.
Pisa Cathedral

511, 512. GIOVANNI PISANO. *MADONNA*. c. 1315.
Marble, height 27″ (68.7 cm). Prato Cathedral

doubt that the Prato statue derives from a French prototype which must have been rather like *The Virgin of Paris*. (The back view, with its suggestion of "Gothic sway," reveals the connection more clearly than the front view.)

CHURCH FAÇADES. The façades of Italian Gothic churches, we will recall, do not rival those of the French cathedrals as focal points of architectural and sculptural endeavor. The French Gothic portal, with its jamb statues and richly carved tympanum, never found favor in the south. Instead, we often find a survival of Romanesque traditions of architectural sculpture, such as statues in niches or small-scale reliefs overlaying the wall surfaces (compare fig. 440).

At Orvieto Cathedral, Lorenzo Maitani (before 1270–1330) covered the wide pilasters between the portals with relief carvings of such lacelike delicacy that we become aware of them only if we see them at close range. The tortures of the damned from *The Last Judgment* on the southernmost pilaster (fig. 513) make an instructive comparison with similar scenes in Romanesque art (such as fig. 436): the hellish monsters are as vicious as ever, but the sinners now evoke compassion rather than sheer horror. Even here, then, we feel the spirit of human sympathy that distinguishes the Gothic from the Romanesque.

TOMBS. If Italian Gothic sculpture failed to emulate the vast sculptural programs of northern Europe, it excelled in the field which we have called church furniture, such as

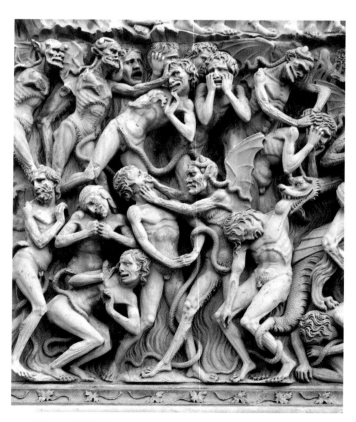

513. LORENZO MAITANI. *THE LAST JUDGMENT* (detail),
from the façade of Orvieto Cathedral. c. 1320

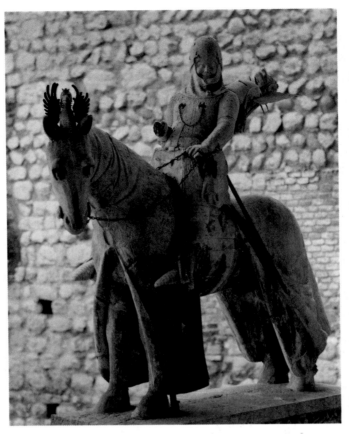

514. *EQUESTRIAN STATUE OF CAN GRANDE DELLA SCALA,*
from his tomb. 1330. Stone. Museo di Castelvecchio, Verona

pulpits, screens, shrines, and tombs. Among the latter, the most remarkable perhaps is the monument of Can Grande della Scala, the lord of Verona. A tall structure built out-of-doors next to the church of Sta. Maria Antica (and now in the courtyard of the Castelvecchio), it consists of a vaulted canopy housing the sarcophagus and surmounted by a truncated pyramid which in turn supports an equestrian statue of the deceased (fig. 514). The ruler, astride his richly caparisoned mount, is shown in full armor, sword in hand, as if he were standing on a windswept hill at the head of his troops; and, in a supreme display of self-confidence, he wears a broad grin. Clearly, this is no Christian Soldier, no crusading knight, no embodiment of the ideals of chivalry, but a frank glorification of power.

Can Grande, remembered today mainly as the friend and protector of Dante, was indeed an extraordinary figure; although he held Verona as a fief from the German emperor, he styled himself "the Great Khan," thus asserting his claim to the absolute sovereignty of an Asiatic potentate. His free-standing equestrian statue—a form of monument traditionally reserved for emperors—conveys the same ambition in visual terms.

## The International Style in the South

During the later fourteenth century, northern Italy proved particularly hospitable to artistic influences from across the Alps, not only in architecture (see Milan Cathedral, fig. 490), but in sculpture as well. The *Apostles* atop the choir screen of St. Mark's in Venice (fig. 515), carved by Jacobello and Pierpaolo dalle Masegne about 1394, reflect the trend toward greater realism and the renewed interest in weight and volume that culminated in the work of Claus Sluter, even though these qualities are not yet fully developed here. With the *Apostles* from St. Mark's, we are on the threshold of the "International Style," which flourished throughout western Europe about 1400 to 1420.

GHIBERTI. The style's outstanding representative in Italian sculpture was a Florentine, Lorenzo Ghiberti (c. 1381–1455), who as a youth must have had close contact with French art. We first encounter him in 1401–02, when he won a competition for a pair of richly decorated bronze doors for the Baptistery of S. Giovanni in Florence. (It took him more than two decades to complete these doors, which fill the north portal of the building.) Each of the competing artists had to submit a trial relief, in a Gothic quatrefoil frame, representing the Sacrifice of Isaac. Ghiberti's panel (fig. 516) strikes us first of all with the perfection of its craftsmanship, which reflects his training as a goldsmith. The silky shimmer of the surfaces, the wealth of beautifully articulated detail, make it easy to understand why this entry was awarded the prize. If the composition seems somewhat

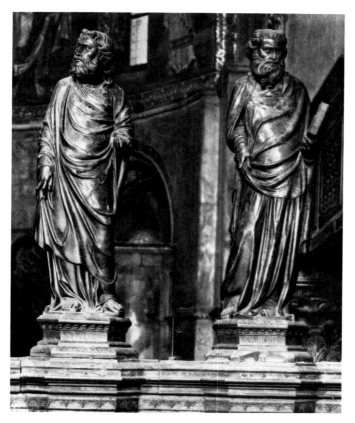

515. JACOBELLO and PIERPAOLO DALLE MASEGNE
*APOSTLES,* on the choir screen. 1394.
Marble, height c. 53″ (134.6 cm). St. Mark's, Venice

lacking in dramatic force, that is as characteristic of Ghiberti's calm, lyrical temper as of the taste of the period, for the realism of the International Style did not extend to the realm of the emotions. The figures, in their softly draped, ample garments, retain an air of courtly elegance even when they enact scenes of violence.

However much his work may owe to French influence, Ghiberti proves himself thoroughly Italian in one respect: his admiration for ancient sculpture, as evidenced by the beautiful nude torso of Isaac. Here our artist revives a tradition of classicism that had reached its highest point in Nicola Pisano but had gradually died out during the fourteenth century.

But Ghiberti is also the heir of Giovanni Pisano. In the latter's *Nativity* panel (fig. 510) we noted a bold new emphasis on the spatial setting; the trial relief carries this same tendency a good deal further, achieving a far more natural sense of recession. For the first time since classical antiquity, we are made to experience the background of the panel not as a flat surface but as empty space from which the sculptured forms emerge toward the beholder (note particularly the angel in the upper right-hand corner). This "pictorial" quality relates Ghiberti's work to the painting of the International Style, where we find a similar concern with spatial depth and atmosphere (see below, pages 407–11). While not a revolutionary himself, he prepares the ground for the great revolution that will mark the second decade of the fifteenth century in Florentine art and that we call the Early Renaissance.

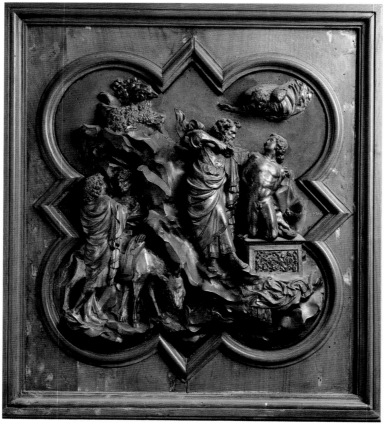

516. LORENZO GHIBERTI
*THE SACRIFICE OF ISAAC.*
1401–02.
Gilt bronze,
21 × 17″ (53.3 × 43.4 cm).
Museo Nazionale del Bargello,
Florence

# PAINTING

## France

STAINED GLASS. Although Gothic architecture and sculpture began so dramatically at St.-Denis and Chartres, Gothic painting developed at a rather slow pace in its early stages. The new architectural style sponsored by Abbot Suger gave birth to a new conception of monumental sculpture almost at once but did not demand any radical change of style in painting. Suger's account of the rebuilding of his church, to be sure, places a great deal of emphasis on the miraculous effect of stained-glass windows, whose "continuous light" flooded the interior. Stained glass was thus an integral element of Gothic architecture from the very beginning. Yet the technique of stained-glass painting had already been perfected in Romanesque times; the "many masters from different regions" whom Suger assembled to do the choir windows at St.-Denis may have faced a larger task and a more complex pictorial program than before, but the style of their designs remained Romanesque.

During the next half century, as Gothic structures became ever more skeletal and clerestory windows grew to vast size, stained glass displaced manuscript illumination as the leading form of painting. Since the production of stained glass was so intimately linked with the great cathedral workshops, the designers came to be influenced more and more by architectural sculpture, and in this way, about the year 1200, arrived at a distinctively Gothic style of their own.

The majestic *Iohel* (Joel) of Bourges Cathedral (fig. 517), one of a series of windows representing Old Testament prophets, is the direct kin of the jamb statues on the Chartres transept portals and of the *Visitation* at Reims. All these works share a common ancestor, the classicizing style of Nicholas of Verdun (compare fig. 449), yet the Joel figure resembles a statue projected onto a translucent screen rather than an enlarged figure from the enamel plaques of the Klosterneuburg Altar.

The window consists not of large panes but of hundreds of small pieces of tinted glass bound together by strips of lead. The maximum size of these pieces was severely limited by the primitive methods of medieval glass manufacture, so that the artist who created this window could not simply "paint on glass"; rather, he painted *with* glass, assembling his design, somewhat the way one would a mosaic or a jigsaw puzzle, out of odd-shaped fragments which he cut to fit the contours of the forms. Only the finer details, such as eyes, hair, and drapery folds, were added by actually painting—or, better perhaps, drawing—in black or gray on the glass surfaces. While this process encourages an abstract, ornamental style, it tends to resist any attempt to render three-dimensional effects. Yet in the hands of a great master the maze of lead strips could resolve itself into figures having the looming monumentality of our *Iohel*.

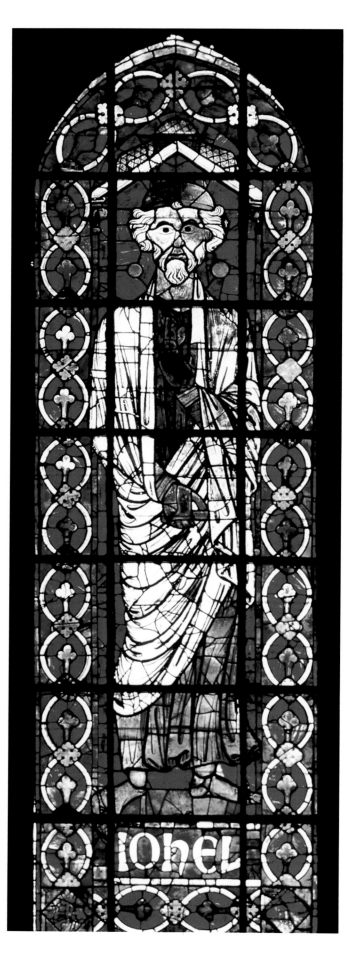

517. *IOHEL.* c. 1220. Stained-glass window, height c. 14' (4.3 m). Bourges Cathedral

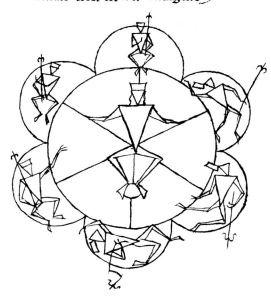

**518. VILLARD DE HONNECOURT.** *WHEEL OF FORTUNE.*
c. 1240. Bibliothèque Nationale, Paris

Apart from the peculiar demands of their medium, the stained-glass workers who filled the windows of the great Gothic cathedrals also had to face the difficulties arising from the enormous scale of their work. No Romanesque painter had ever been called upon to cover areas so vast—the *Iohel* window is more than 14 feet tall—or so firmly bound into an architectural framework. The task required a technique of orderly planning for which the medieval painting tradition could offer no precedent.

VILLARD DE HONNECOURT. Only architects and stone masons knew how to deal with this problem, and it was their methods that the stained-glass workers borrowed in mapping out their own compositions. Gothic architectural design, as we recall from our discussion of the choir of St.-Denis (see figs. 451 and 452), uses a system of geometric relationships; the same rules could be used to control the design of a stained-glass window, or even of an individual figure.

We gain some insight into this procedure from the drawings in a notebook compiled about 1240 by the architect Villard de Honnecourt, such as the *Wheel of Fortune* (fig. 518). What we see here is not the final version of the design but the scaffolding of circles and triangles on which the image is to be constructed. The pervasiveness of these geometric schemes is well illustrated by another drawing from the same notebook, the *Front View of a Lion* (fig. 519). According to the inscription, Villard has portrayed the animal from life, but a closer look at the figure will convince us that he was able to do so only after he had laid down a geometric pattern: a circle for the face (the dot between the eyes is its center) and a second, larger circle for the body. To Villard, then, drawing from life meant something far different from

what it does to us—it meant filling in an abstract framework with details based on direct observation. If we now turn back once more to the firmly drawn, simplified outlines of the *Iohel*, we cannot help wondering to what extent they, too, reflect a geometric scaffolding of some sort.

The period 1200–1250 might be termed the golden age of stained glass. After that, as architectural activity declined and the demand for stained glass began to slacken, manuscript illumination gradually recaptured its former position of leadership. By then, however, miniature painting had been thoroughly affected by the influence of both stained glass and stone sculpture, the artistic pacemakers of the first half of the century.

ILLUMINATED MANUSCRIPTS. The resulting change of style is fully evident in figure 520, from a psalter done about 1260 for King Louis IX (St. Louis) of France. The scene illustrates I Samuel 11:2, in which Nahash the Ammonite threatens the Jews at Jabesh. We notice first of all the careful symmetry of the framework, which consists of flat, ornamented panels very much like those in the *Iohel* window, and of an architectural setting. The latter recalls the canopies above the heads of jamb statues (see fig. 495) and the arched twin niches enclosing the relief of *Melchizedek and Abraham* at Reims (fig. 498).

Against this emphatically two-dimensional background, the figures are "relieved" by smooth and skillful modeling. But their sculptural quality stops short at the outer contours, which are defined by heavy dark lines rather like the lead strips in stained-glass windows. The figures themselves show all the characteristics of the elegant style originated about twenty years before by the sculptors of the royal court

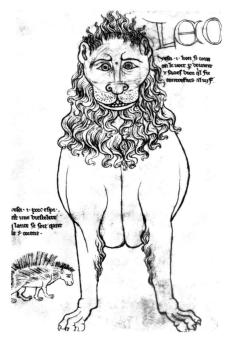

**519. VILLARD DE HONNECOURT**
*FRONT VIEW OF A LION.* c. 1240.
Bibliothèque Nationale, Paris

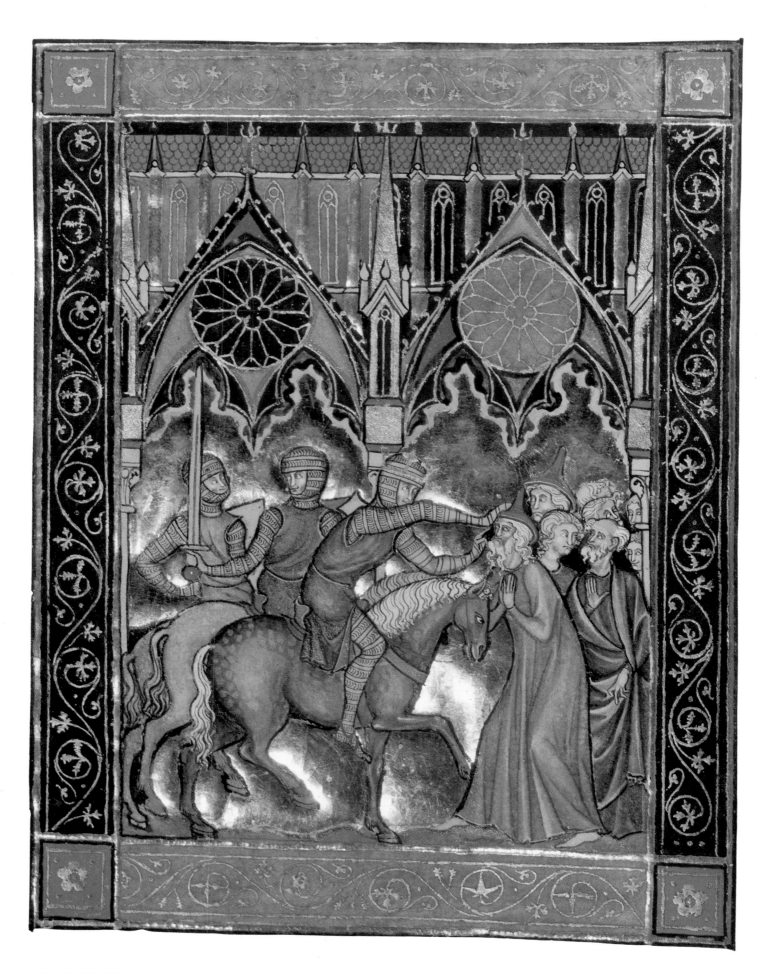

(compare the Annunciation angel in figure 497 and Melchizedek in figure 498): graceful gestures, swaying poses, smiling faces, neatly waved strands of hair. Of the expressive energy of Romanesque painting we find no trace (figs. 408 and 409); our miniature exemplifies the subtle and refined taste that made the court art of Paris the standard for all Europe.

Until the thirteenth century, the production of illuminated manuscripts had been centered in the scriptoria of monasteries. Now, along with a great many other activities once the special preserve of monasteries, it shifted ever more to urban workshops organized by laymen, the ancestors of the publishing houses of today. Here again the workshops of sculptors and stained-glass painters may have set the pattern.

Some members of this new, secular breed of illuminator are known to us by name, such as Master Honoré of Paris, who in 1295 did the miniatures in the *Prayer Book of Philip the Fair.* Our sample (fig. 521) shows him working in a style derived from the *Psalter of St. Louis.* Significantly enough, however, the framework no longer dominates the composition; the figures have become larger, and their relieflike modeling is more emphatic; they are even permitted to overlap the frame, a device that helps to detach them from the flat pattern of the background and thus introduces a certain—though very limited—spatial range into the picture.

## Italy

We must now turn our attention to Italian painting, which at the end of the thirteenth century produced an explosion of creative energy as spectacular, and as far-reaching in its impact upon the future, as the rise of the Gothic cathedral in France. A single glance at Giotto's *Lamentation* (fig. 528) will convince us that we are faced with a truly revolutionary development here. How, we wonder, could a work of such intense dramatic power be conceived by a contemporary of Master Honoré? What were the conditions that made it possible? Oddly enough, as we inquire into the background of Giotto's art, we find that it arose from the same "old-fashioned" attitudes we met in Italian Gothic architecture and sculpture.

Medieval Italy, although strongly influenced by Northern art from Carolingian times on, nevertheless had always maintained close contact with Byzantine civilization. As a result, panel painting, mosaics, and murals—techniques that had never taken firm root north of the Alps—were kept alive on Italian soil; and at the very time when stained glass became the dominant pictorial art in France, a new wave of Byzantine influence overwhelmed the lingering Romanesque elements in Italian painting.

There is a certain irony in the fact that this neo-Byzantine style (or "Greek manner," as the Italians called it) made its

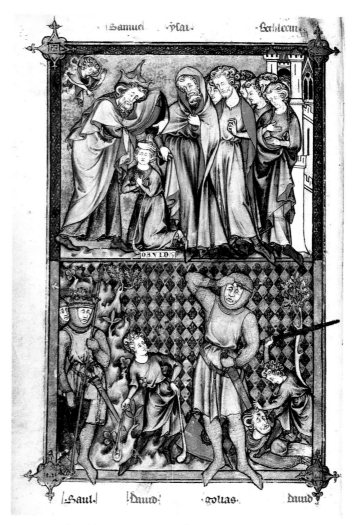

**521. MASTER HONORÉ.** *DAVID AND GOLIATH,* from the *Prayer Book of Philip the Fair,* 1295. Bibliothèque Nationale, Paris

520. (*opposite*) *NAHASH THE AMMONITE THREATENING THE JEWS AT JABESH,* from the *Psalter of St. Louis.* c. 1260. Bibliothèque Nationale, Paris

appearance soon after the conquest of Constantinople by the armies of the Fourth Crusade in 1204—one thinks of the way Greek art had once captured the taste of the victorious Romans of old. Be that as it may, the Greek manner prevailed almost until the end of the thirteenth century, so that Italian painters were able to absorb the Byzantine tradition far more thoroughly than ever before. During this same period, we recall, Italian architects and sculptors followed a very different course; untouched by the Greek manner, they were assimilating the Gothic style. Eventually, toward 1300, Gothic influence spilled over into painting as well, and it was the interaction of this element with the neo-Byzantine that produced the revolutionary new style of which Giotto is the greatest exponent.

TEMPERA. Altarpieces of the Gothic era were painted on wood panel in tempera, an egg-based medium that dries quickly to form an extremely tough surface. The preparation of the panel was a complex, time-consuming process. First it was planed and coated with a mixture of plaster and glue

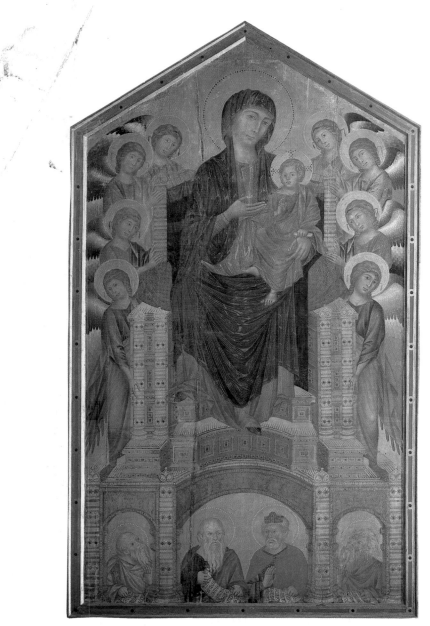

522. CIMABUE. *MADONNA ENTHRONED*. c. 1280–90. Tempera on panel,
12'7½" × 7'4" (3.9 × 2.2 m). Galleria degli Uffizi, Florence

known as gesso, which was sometimes reinforced with linen. Once the design had been drawn, the background was almost invariably filled in with gold leaf over red sizing; then the underpainting, generally a green earth (*terra verde*) pigment, was added. The image itself was executed in multiple layers of thin tempera with very fine brushes, a painstaking process that placed a premium on neatness, since few corrections were possible.

CIMABUE. Among the painters of the Greek manner, the Florentine master Cimabue (c. 1250–after 1300), who may have been Giotto's teacher, enjoyed special fame. His huge altar panel, *Madonna Enthroned* (fig. 522), rivals the finest Byzantine icons or mosaics (compare figs. 345 and 358); what distinguishes it from them is mainly a greater severity of design and expression, which befits its huge size. Panels

on such a monumental scale had never been attempted in the East. Likewise un-Byzantine is the picture's gabled shape, and the way the throne of inlaid wood seems to echo this shape. The geometric inlays—indeed, the throne's architectural style—remind us of the Florence Baptistery (see fig. 431).

DUCCIO. The *Madonna Enthroned* (fig. 523), of a quarter century later by Duccio of Siena (c. 1255–before 1319) for the main altar of Siena Cathedral, makes an instructive comparison with Cimabue's. The Sienese honored this panel by calling it the *Maestà*—"majesty"—to identify the Virgin's role here as the Queen of Heaven surrounded by her celestial court of saints and angels. At first glance, the two pictures may seem much alike, since both follow the same basic scheme; yet the differences are important. They

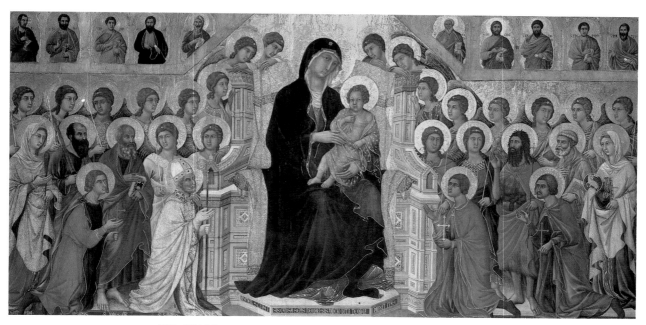

523. DUCCIO. *MADONNA ENTHRONED*, center of the *Maestà Altar*.
1308–11. Tempera on panel, height 6'10½" (2.1 m). Museo dell'Opera del Duomo, Siena

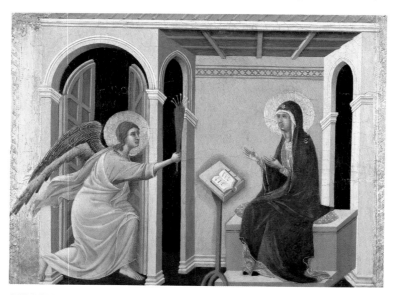

524. DUCCIO. *ANNUNCIATION OF THE DEATH OF THE VIRGIN*, from the *Maestà Altar*

reflect not only two contrasting personalities and contrasting local tastes—the gentleness of Duccio is characteristic of Siena—but also the rapid evolution of style.

In Duccio's hands, the Greek manner has become unfrozen, as it were: the rigid, angular draperies have given way to an undulating softness, the abstract shading-in-reverse with lines of gold is reduced to a minimum, and the bodies, faces, and hands are beginning to swell with a subtle three-dimensional life. Clearly, the heritage of Hellenistic-Roman illusionism that had always been part of the Byzantine tradition, however dormant or submerged, is asserting itself once more. But there is also a half-hidden Gothic element here; we sense it in the fluency of the drapery folds, the appealing naturalness of the Infant Christ, and the tender glances by

which the figures communicate with each other. The chief source of this Gothic influence must have been Giovanni Pisano (see page 386), who was in Siena from 1285 to 1295 as the sculptor-architect in charge of the cathedral façade.

Apart from the *Madonna*, the *Maestà* includes many small compartments with scenes from the lives of Christ and the Virgin. In these panels, the most mature works of Duccio's career, the cross-fertilization of Gothic and Byzantine elements has given rise to a development of fundamental importance—a new kind of picture space. The *Annunciation of the Death of the Virgin* (fig. 524) shows us something we have never seen before in the history of painting: two figures enclosed by an architectural interior.

Ancient painters (and their Byzantine successors) were

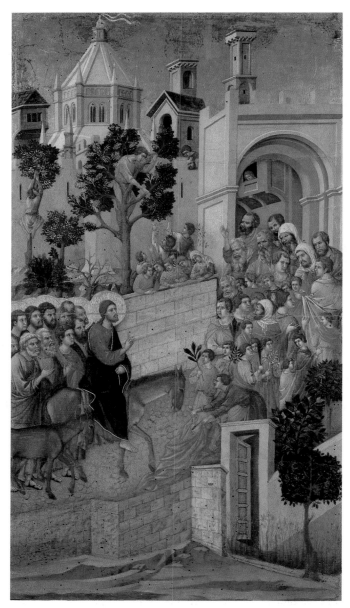

525. DUCCIO. *CHRIST ENTERING JERUSALEM,*
from the back of the *Maestà Altar.* 1308–11.
Tempera on panel, 40½ × 21⅛″ (103 × 53.7 cm).
Museo dell'Opera del Duomo, Siena

quite unable to achieve this space; their architectural settings always stay *behind* the figures, so that their indoor scenes tend to look as if they were taking place in an open-air theater, on a stage without a roof. Duccio's figures, in contrast, inhabit a space that is created and defined by the architecture, as if the artist had carved a niche into his panel. Perhaps we will recognize the origin of this spatial framework: it derives from the architectural "housing" of Gothic sculpture (compare especially figs. 498 and 502). Northern Gothic painters, too, had tried to reproduce these architectural settings, but they could do so only by flattening them out completely (as in the *Psalter of St. Louis,* fig. 520). The Italian painters of Duccio's generation, on the other hand, trained as they were in the Greek manner, had acquired

enough of the devices of Hellenistic-Roman illusionism to let them render such a framework without draining it of its three-dimensional qualities. Even in the outdoor scenes on the back of the *Maestà,* such as *Christ Entering Jerusalem* (fig. 525), the architecture keeps its space-creating function: the diagonal movement into depth is conveyed not by the figures—which have the same scale throughout—but by the walls on either side of the road leading to the city, by the gate that frames the welcoming crowd, and by the structures beyond. Whatever the shortcomings of Duccio's perspective, his architecture again demonstrates its capacity to contain and enclose, and for that very reason strikes us as more intelligible than similar vistas in ancient art (compare fig. 305).

GIOTTO. Turning from Duccio to Giotto (1267?–1336/7), we meet an artist of far bolder and more dramatic temper. Ten to fifteen years younger, Giotto was less close to the Greek manner from the start, despite his probable apprenticeship under Cimabue. As a Florentine, he fell heir to Cimabue's sense of monumental scale, which made him a wall painter by instinct, rather than a panel painter. Of his surviving murals, those in the Arena Chapel in Padua, done in 1305–6, are the best preserved as well as the most characteristic. The decorations are devoted principally to scenes from the life of Christ, laid in a carefully arranged program consisting of three tiers of narrative scenes and culminating in the Last Judgment at the east end of the chapel (fig. 526).

Giotto includes many of the same subjects that we find on the reverse of Duccio's *Maestà,* such as *Christ Entering Jerusalem* (fig.527). The two versions have many elements in common, since they both ultimately derive from the same Byzantine source; but where Duccio has enriched the traditional scheme, spatially as well as in narrative detail, Giotto subjects it to a radical simplification. The action proceeds parallel to the picture plane; landscape, architecture, and figures have been reduced to the essential minimum. And the sober technique of fresco painting (water-based paint applied to the freshly plastered wall), with its limited range and intensity of tones, further emphasizes the austerity of Giotto's art as against the jewellike brilliance of Duccio's picture, which is executed in egg tempera on gold ground. (Note the sparkling colors of the *Maestà* panel in figure 525.) Yet Giotto's work has far the more powerful impact of the two; it makes us feel so close to the event that we have a sense of being participants rather than distant observers.

How does the artist achieve this extraordinary effect? He does so, first of all, by having the entire scene take place in the foreground and—even more important—by presenting it in such a way that the beholder's eye-level falls within the lower half of the picture. Thus we can imagine ourselves standing on the same ground plane as these painted figures, even though we see them from well below, while Duccio makes us survey the scene from above in bird's-eye perspective. The consequences of this choice of viewpoint are truly epoch-making; choice implies conscious awareness—in this case, awareness of a relationship in space between the beholder and the picture—and Giotto may well claim to be the first to have established such a relationship. Duccio, cer-

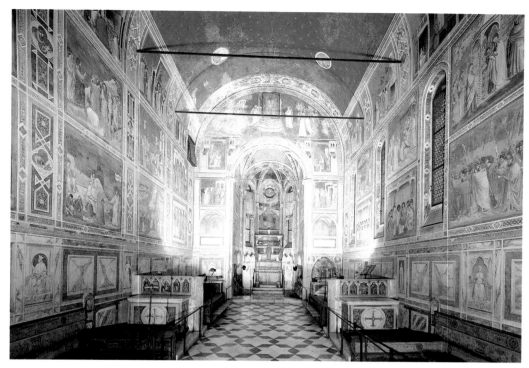

526. Interior, Arena (Scrovegni) Chapel, Padua

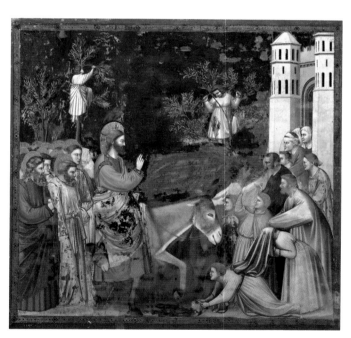

527. GIOTTO. *CHRIST ENTERING JERUSALEM.* 1305–6.
Fresco. Arena (Scrovegni) Chapel, Padua

tainly, does not yet conceive his picture space as continuous with the beholder's space (hence we have the sensation of vaguely floating above the scene, rather than of knowing where we stand), and even ancient painting at its most illusionistic provides no more than a pseudo-continuity in this respect (see page 235, discussion of figures 268, 288, and 289). Giotto, on the other hand, tells us where we stand, and he also endows his forms with a three-dimensional reality so forceful that they seem as solid and tangible as sculpture in the round.

With Giotto it is the figures, rather than the architectural framework, that create the picture space. As a result, this space is more limited than Duccio's—its depth extends no further than the combined volumes of the overlapping bodies in the picture—but within its limits it is very much more persuasive. To his contemporaries, the tactile quality of Giotto's art must have seemed a near-miracle; it was this that made them praise him as equal, or even superior, to the greatest of the ancient painters, because his forms looked so lifelike that they could be mistaken for reality itself. Equally significant are the stories linking Giotto with the claim that painting is superior to sculpture—not an idle boast, as it turned out, for Giotto does indeed mark the start of what might be called "the era of painting" in Western art. The symbolic turning point is the year 1334, when he was appointed the head of the Florence Cathedral workshop, an honor and responsibility hitherto reserved for architects or sculptors.

Yet Giotto's aim was not simply to transplant Gothic statuary into painting. By creating a radically new kind of picture space, he had also sharpened his awareness of the picture surface. When we look at a work by Duccio (or his ancient and medieval predecessors), we tend to do so in installments, as it were; our glance travels from detail to detail at a leisurely pace until we have surveyed the entire area. Giotto, on the contrary, invites us to see the whole at one glance. His large, simple forms, the strong grouping of his figures, the limited depth of his "stage," all these factors help to endow his scenes with an inner coherence such as we have never found before. Notice how dramatically the massed verticals of the "block" of apostles on the left are contrasted with the upward slope formed by the welcoming crowd on the right; how Christ, alone in the center, bridges the gulf between the two groups. The more we study the composition, the more we come to realize its majestic firmness and clarity.

Giotto's achievement as a master of design does not fully emerge from any single work. Only if we compare a number of scenes from the Padua fresco cycle do we understand how perfectly the composition in each instance is attuned to the emotional content of the subject. Thus the artist has "rephrased" the traditional pattern of Christ's Entry into Jerusalem to stress the solemnity of the event as a triumphal procession of the Prince of Peace, while the tragic mood of *The Lamentation* (fig. 528) is brought home to us by the formal rhythm of the design as much as by the gestures and expressions of the participants. The very low center of gravity, and the hunched, bending figures communicate the somber quality of the scene and arouse our compassion even before we have grasped the specific meaning of the event depicted. With extraordinary boldness, Giotto sets off the frozen grief of the human mourners against the frantic movement of the weeping angels among the clouds, as if the figures on the ground were restrained by their collective duty to maintain the stability of the composition while the angels, small and weightless as birds, do not share this burden.

Let us note, too, how the impact of the drama is heightened by the severely simple setting; the descending slope of the hill acts as a unifying element and at the same time directs our glance toward the heads of Christ and the Virgin, which are the focal point of the scene. Even the tree has a twin function. Its barrenness and isolation suggest that all of nature somehow shares in the Saviour's death, yet it also invites us to ponder a more precise symbolic message. For it alludes—as does Dante in a passage in the *Divine Comedy*—to the Tree of Knowledge, which the sin of Adam and Eve had caused to wither and which was to be restored to life through the sacrificial death of Christ.

The art of Giotto is so daringly original that its sources are far more difficult to trace than those of Duccio's style. Apart from his Florentine background as represented by the Greek manner of Cimabue, the young Giotto seems to have been familiar with the neo-Byzantine painters of Rome; in that city, he probably also became acquainted with older monuments—Early Christian and ancient Roman mural decora-

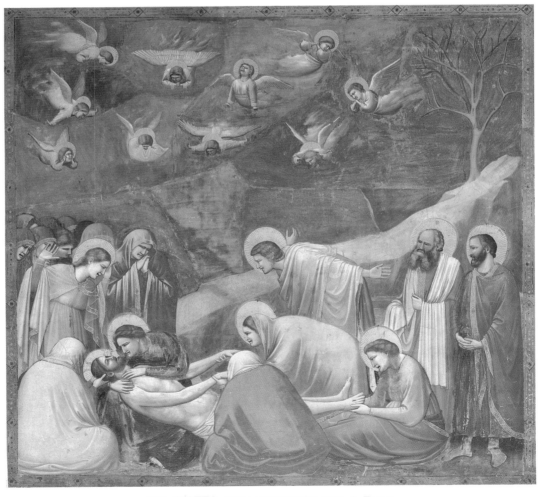

528. GIOTTO. *THE LAMENTATION.* 1305–6. Fresco.
Arena (Scrovegni) Chapel, Padua

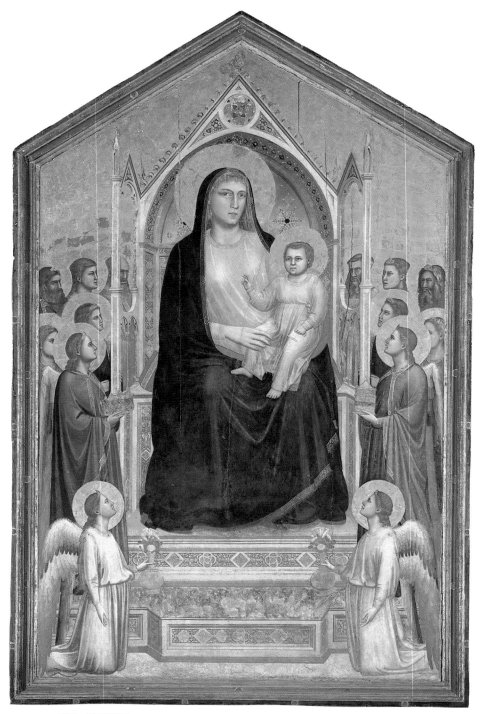

529. GIOTTO. *MADONNA ENTHRONED.* c. 1310. Tempera on panel,
10'8″×6'8″ (3.3×2 m). Galleria degli Uffizi, Florence

tion. Classical sculpture, too, left an impression on him.
More fundamental than any of these, however, was the influence of the Pisanos—Nicola, and especially Giovanni—
the founders of Italian Gothic sculpture. They were the
chief intermediaries through whom Giotto first came in contact with the world of Northern Gothic art. And the latter
remains the most important of all the elements that entered
into Giotto's style. Without the knowledge, direct or indirect,
of Northern works such as those illustrated in figure 496 or

figure 503, he could never have achieved the emotional impact of his *Lamentation.*

What we have said of the Padua frescoes applies equally to
the *Madonna Enthroned* (fig. 529), the most important
among the small number of panel paintings by our master.
Done about the same time as Duccio's *Maestà*, it illustrates
once again the difference between Florence and Siena; its
architectural severity clearly derives from Cimabue (see fig.
522). The figures, however, have the same overpowering

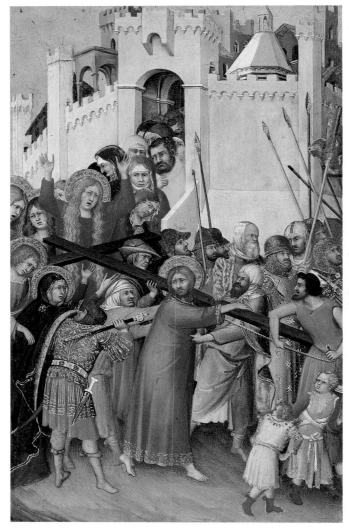

530. **SIMONE MARTINI.** *THE ROAD TO CALVARY.* c. 1340.
Panel, 9⅞ × 6⅛″ (25 × 15.5 cm). Musée du Louvre, Paris

greatness, however, tended to dwarf the next generation of Florentine painters, which produced only followers rather than new leaders. Their contemporaries in Siena were more fortunate in this respect, since Duccio never had the same overpowering impact. As a consequence, it was they, not the Florentines, who took the next decisive step in the development of Italian Gothic painting. Simone Martini (c. 1284–1344), who painted the tiny but intense *The Road to Calvary* (fig. 530) about 1340, may well claim to be the most distinguished of Duccio's disciples. He spent the last years of his life in Avignon, the town in southern France that served as the residence-in-exile of the popes during most of the fourteenth century. Our panel, originally part of a small altar, was probably done there.

In its sparkling colors, and especially in the architectural background, it still echoes the art of Duccio (see fig. 525). The vigorous modeling of the figures, on the other hand, as well as their dramatic gestures and expressions, betray the influence of Giotto. While Simone Martini is not much concerned with spatial clarity, he proves to be an extraordinarily acute observer; the sheer variety of costumes and physical types and the wealth of human incident create a sense of down-to-earth reality very different from both the lyricism of Duccio and the grandeur of Giotto.

THE LORENZETTI BROTHERS. This closeness to everyday life also appears in the work of the brothers Pietro and Ambrogio Lorenzetti (both died 1348?), but on a more monumental scale and coupled with a keen interest in problems of space. The boldest spatial experiment is Pietro's triptych of 1342, *The Birth of the Virgin* (fig. 531), where the painted architecture has been correlated with the real architecture of the frame in such a way that the two are seen as a single system. Moreover, the vaulted chamber where the birth takes place occupies two panels—it continues unbroken behind the column that divides the center from the right wing. The left wing represents an anteroom which leads to a vast and only partially glimpsed architectural space suggesting the interior of a Gothic church. What Pietro Lorenzetti achieved here is the outcome of a development that began three decades earlier in the work of Duccio (compare fig. 525), but only now does the picture surface assume the quality of a transparent window through which—not *on* which—we perceive the same kind of space we know from daily experience.

Yet Duccio's work alone is not sufficient to explain Pietro's astonishing breakthrough; it became possible, rather, through a combination of the *architectural* picture space of Duccio and the *sculptural* picture space of Giotto. The same procedure enabled Ambrogio Lorenzetti, in his frescoes of 1338–40 in the Siena city hall, to unfold a comprehensive view of the entire town before our eyes (fig. 532). Again we marvel at the distance that separates this precisely articulated "portrait" of Siena from Duccio's Jerusalem (fig. 525). Ambrogio's mural forms part of an elaborate allegorical program depicting the contrast of good and bad government; hence the artist, in order to show the life of a well-ordered city-state, had to fill the streets and houses with teeming activity.

sense of weight and volume we saw in the frescoes in the Arena Chapel, and the picture space is just as persuasive—so much so, in fact, that the golden halos look like foreign bodies in it.

Characteristically enough, the throne, of a design based on Italian Gothic architecture, has now become a nichelike structure that encloses the Madonna on three sides and thus "insulates" her from the gold background. Its lavish ornamentation includes one feature of special interest: the colored marble surfaces of the base and of the quatrefoil within the gable. Such make-believe stone textures had been highly developed by ancient painters (see figs. 304 and 305), but the tradition had died out in Early Christian times. Its sudden reappearance here offers concrete evidence of Giotto's familiarity with whatever ancient murals could still be seen in medieval Rome.

MARTINI. There are few artists in the entire history of art to equal the stature of Giotto as a radical innovator. His very

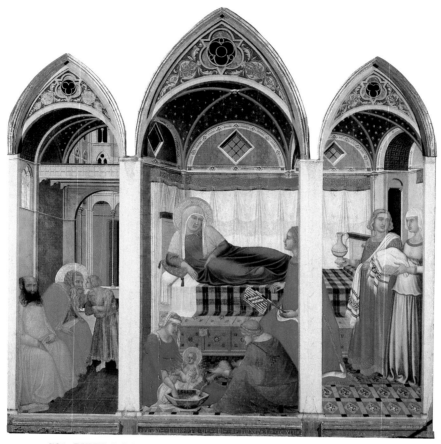

531. PIETRO LORENZETTI. *THE BIRTH OF THE VIRGIN*. 1342.
Tempera on panel, 6'1½" × 5'11½" (1.9 × 1.8 m). Museo dell'Opera del Duomo, Siena

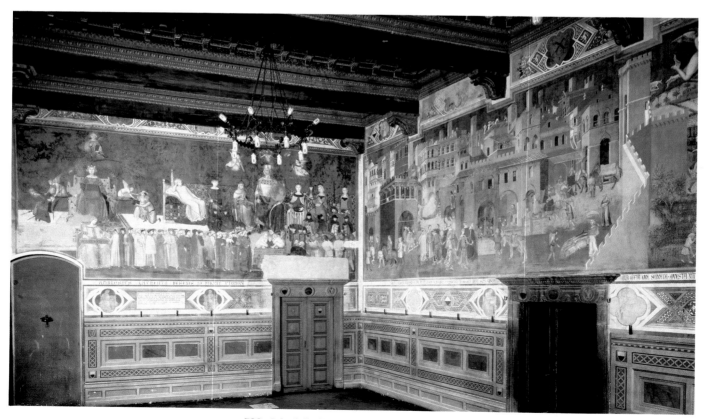

532. Sala della Pace, Palazzo Pubblico, Siena

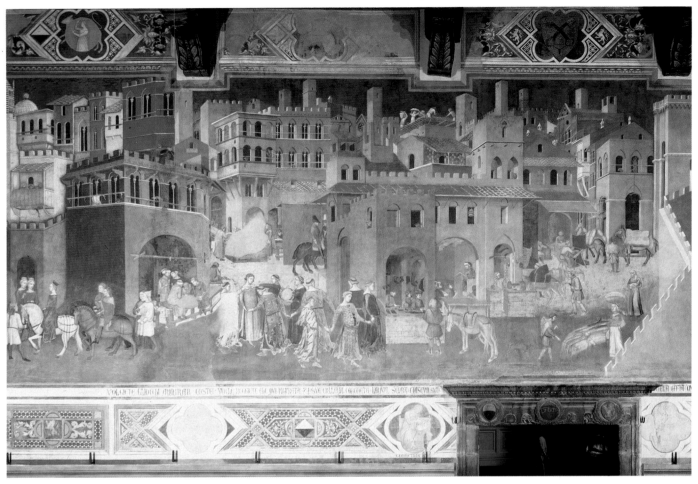

533. AMBROGIO LORENZETTI. *GOOD GOVERNMENT IN THE CITY.*
1338–40. Fresco, width of entire wall 46′ (14 m). Palazzo Pubblico, Siena

The gay and busy crowd gives the architectural vista its striking reality by introducing the human scale. On the right, beyond the margin of figure 533, the *Good Government* fresco provides a view of the Sienese countryside, fringed by distant mountains. It is a true landscape—the first since ancient Roman times—full of sweeping depth yet distinguished from its classical predecessors (such as figure 306) by an ingrained orderliness, a domesticated air. Here the presence of man is not accidental; he has taken full possession of nature, terracing the hillsides with vineyards, patterning the valleys with the geometry of fields and pastures. In such a setting, Ambrogio observes the peasants at their seasonal labors (fig. 534), recording a rural Tuscan scene so characteristic that it has hardly changed during the past six hundred years.

THE BLACK DEATH. The first four decades of the fourteenth century in Florence and Siena had been a period of political stability and economic expansion as well as of great artistic achievement. In the 1340s both cities suffered a series of catastrophes whose echoes were to be felt for many years: banks and merchants went bankrupt by the score, internal upheavals shook the government, there were repeat-ed crop failures, and in 1348 the epidemic of bubonic plague throughout Europe, the Black Death, wiped out more than half their urban population. The popular reaction to these calamitous events was mixed. Many people regarded them as signs of divine wrath, warnings to a sinful humanity to forsake the pleasures of this earth; in such people the Black Death engendered a mood of otherworldly exaltation. To others, such as the gay company in Boccaccio's *Decameron*, the fear of sudden death merely intensified the desire to enjoy life while there was yet time. These conflicting attitudes are reflected in the pictorial theme of the Triumph of Death.

TRAINI. The most impressive version of this subject is an enormous fresco in the Camposanto, the cemetery building next to Pisa Cathedral. From this work, attributed to the Pisan master Francesco Traini (documented c. 1321–1363), we reproduce a particularly dramatic detail (fig. 535). The elegantly costumed men and women on horseback have suddenly come upon three decaying corpses in open coffins; even the animals are terrified by the sight and smell of rotting flesh. Only the hermit, having renounced all earthly pleasures, calmly points out the lesson of the scene. But will the living accept the lesson, or will they, like the characters

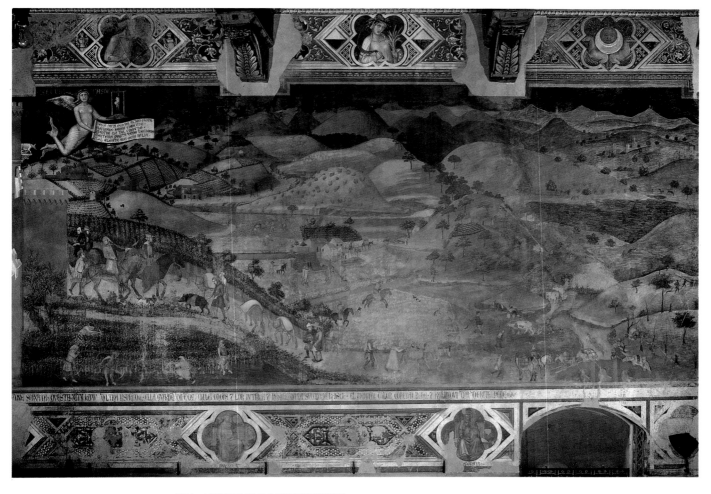

**534. AMBROGIO LORENZETTI.** *GOOD GOVERNMENT IN THE COUNTRY.*
Palazzo Pubblico, Siena

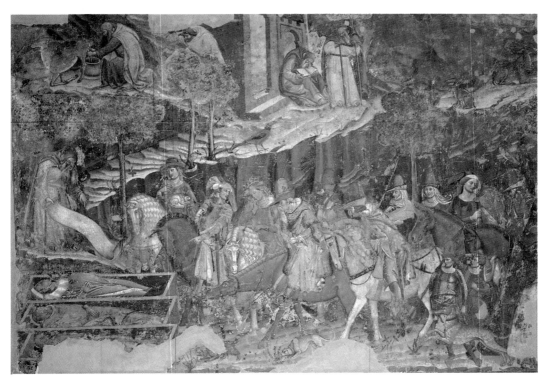

**535. FRANCESCO TRAINI.** *THE TRIUMPH OF DEATH* (portion). c. 1325–50. Fresco. Camposanto, Pisa

of Boccaccio, turn away from the shocking spectacle more determined than ever to pursue their own hedonistic ways? The artist's own sympathies seem curiously divided; his style, far from being otherworldly, recalls the realism of Ambrogio Lorenzetti, although the forms are harsher and more expressive.

In a fire that occurred in 1944, Traini's fresco was badly damaged and had to be detached from the wall in order to save what was left of it. This procedure exposed the first, rough coat of plaster underneath, on which the artist had sketched out his composition (fig. 536). These drawings, of the same size as the fresco itself, are done in red, hence they are called *sinopie* (an Italian word derived from ancient Sinope, in Asia Minor, which was famous as a source of brick-red earth pigment); amazingly free and sweeping, they reveal Traini's personal style more directly than the painted version, which was carried out with the aid of assistants. *Sinopie* also serve to acquaint us with the standard technique of preparing frescoes in the fourteenth century.

Traini still retains a strong link with the great masters of the second quarter of the century. More characteristic of Tuscan painting after the Black Death are the artists who reached maturity around the 1350s. None of them can compare with the men whose work we have discussed; their style, in comparison, seems dry and formula-ridden. Yet they were capable, at their best, of expressing the somber mood of the time with memorable intensity. Giovanni da Milano's (documented 1346–1369) *Pietà* panel of 1365 (fig.

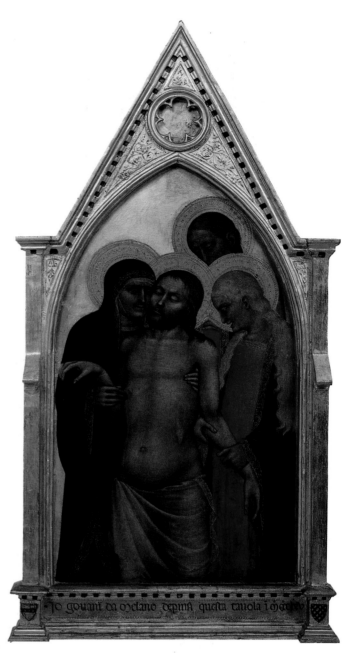

537. GIOVANNI DA MILANO. *PIETÀ*. 1365. Oil on panel, 48 × 22¾″ (122 × 57.5 cm). Galleria dell'Accademia, Florence

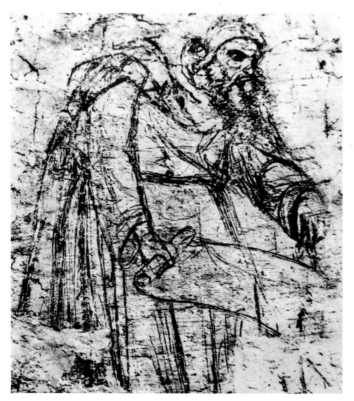

536. FRANCESCO TRAINI. *Sinopia* drawing for the *TRIUMPH OF DEATH* (detail). Camposanto, Pisa

537) has all the emotional appeal of a German *Andachtsbild* (compare fig. 505), although the heritage of Giotto can be clearly felt even here.

## North of the Alps

ILLUMINATED MANUSCRIPTS. We are now in a position to turn once more to Gothic painting north of the Alps. What happened there during the latter half of the fourteenth century was determined in large measure by the influence

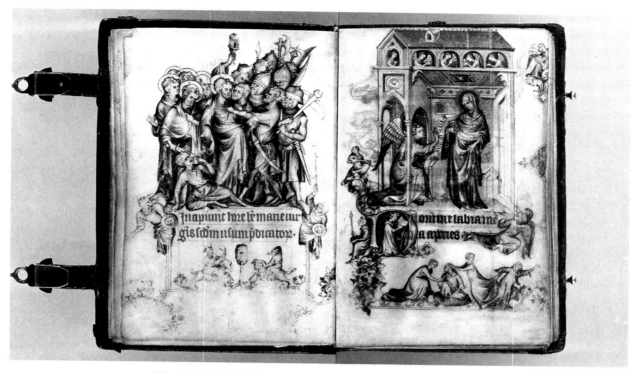

538. JEAN PUCELLE. *BETRAYAL OF CHRIST* and *ANNUNCIATION*, from the
*Hours of Jeanne d'Evreux*. 1325–28. Tempera and gold leaf on parchment (shown actual size)
3½ × 2⁷⁄₁₆″ (8.9 × 6.2 cm). The Metropolitan Museum of Art, New York.
The Cloisters Collection, Purchase, 1954

of the great Italians. Some examples of this influence can be found even earlier, such as *The Annunciation* (fig. 538) from the private prayer book—called "book of hours"—illuminated by Jean Pucelle in Paris about 1325–28 for Jeanne d'Evreux, Queen of France. The style of the figures still recalls Master Honoré (see fig. 521) but the architectural interior clearly derives from Duccio (fig. 524). It had taken less than twenty years for the fame of the *Maestà* to spread from Tuscany to the Île-de-France.

In taking over the new picture space, however, Jean Pucelle had to adapt it to the special character of a manuscript page, which lends itself far less readily than a panel to being treated as a "window." The Virgin's chamber no longer fills the entire picture surface; it has become an ethereal cage that floats on the blank parchment background (note the supporting angel on the right) like the rest of the ornamental framework, so that the entire page forms a harmonious unit. As we explore the details of this framework, we realize that most of them have nothing to do with the religious purpose of the manuscript: the kneeling queen inside the initial D is surely meant to be Jeanne d'Evreux at her devotions, but who could be the man with the staff next to her? He seems to be listening to the lute player perched on the tendril above him. The four figures at the bottom of the page are playing a game of tag outdoors; a rabbit peers from its burrow beneath the girl on the left; and among the foliage leading up to the initial we find a monkey and a squirrel.

DRÔLERIE. These fanciful marginal designs (see fig. 538)—or *drôleries*—are a characteristic feature of Northern Gothic manuscripts. They had originated more than a century before Jean Pucelle in the regions along the English Channel, whence they spread to Paris and all the other centers of Gothic art. Their subject matter encompasses a vast range of motifs: fantasy, fable, and grotesque humor, as well as acutely observed scenes of everyday life, appear side by side with religious themes. The essence of *drôlerie* is its playfulness, which marks it as a special domain where the artist enjoys almost unlimited freedom. It is this freedom, comparable to the license traditionally claimed by the court jester, that accounts for the wide appeal of *drôlerie* during the later Middle Ages.

FRESCOES AND PANEL PAINTINGS. As we approach the middle years of the fourteenth century, Italian influence becomes ever more important in Northern Gothic painting. Sometimes this influence was transmitted by Italian artists working on northern soil; an example is Simone Martini (see page 400). The delightful frescoes with scenes of country life in the Palace of the Popes at Avignon (fig. 539) were done by one of his Italian followers, who must have been thoroughly familiar with the pioneer explorers of landscape and deep space in Sienese painting. His work shows many of the qualities we recall from the *Good Government* fresco by Ambrogio Lorenzetti (see fig. 534). Another gateway of

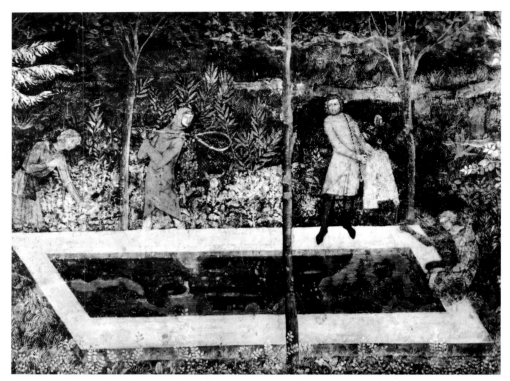

539. Italian follower of SIMONE MARTINI (MATTEO GIOVANNETTI?).
*SCENES OF COUNTRY LIFE* (detail). c. 1345. Fresco. Palace of the Popes, Avignon

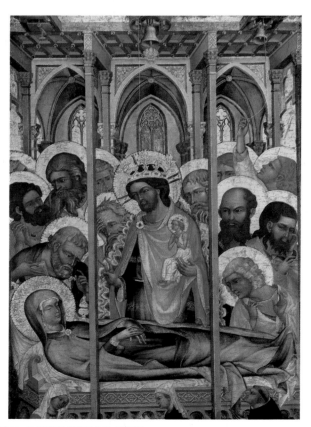

540. BOHEMIAN MASTER. *DEATH OF THE VIRGIN.* 1350–60.
Tempera on panel, 39⅜ × 28″ (100 × 71 cm). Museum of Fine Arts, Boston.
William Francis Warden Fund: Seth K. Sweetser Fund, The Henry C. and Martha B. Angell Coll.,
Juliana Cheney Edwards Collection, Gift of Martin Brimmer, and
Mrs. Frederick Frothingham: by exchange

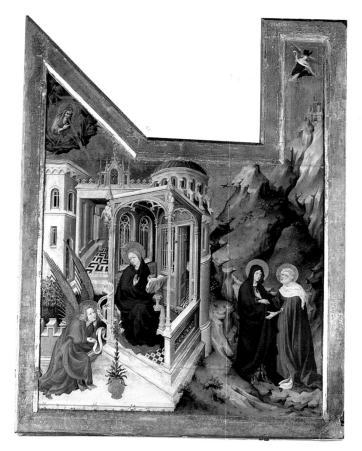
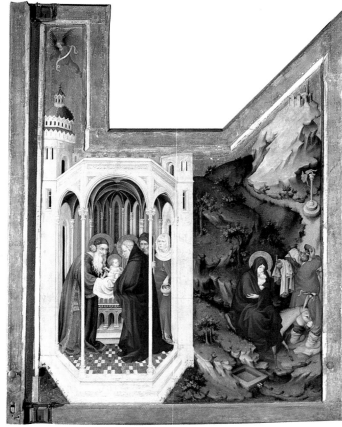

541. MELCHIOR BROEDERLAM. *ANNUNCIATION* and *VISITATION*; *PRESENTATION IN THE TEMPLE*; and *FLIGHT INTO EGYPT.* 1394–99. Oil on panel, 53¾ × 49¼″ (136.5 × 125 cm). Musée de la Ville, Dijon

Italian influence was the city of Prague, which in 1347 became the residence of Emperor Charles IV and rapidly developed into an international cultural center second only to Paris. The *Death of the Virgin* (fig. 540), by an unknown Bohemian painter of about 1360, again brings to mind the achievements of the great Sienese masters, although these were known to our artist only at second or third hand. Its glowing richness of color recalls Simone Martini (compare figure 530), and the carefully articulated architectural interior betrays its descent from such works as Pietro Lorenzetti's *Birth of the Virgin* (fig. 531), although it lacks the spaciousness of its Italian models. Italian, too, is the vigorous modeling of the heads and the overlapping of the figures, which reinforces the three-dimensional quality of the design but raises the awkward question of what to do with the halos. (Giotto, we will remember, had faced the same problem in his *Madonna Enthroned*; compare fig. 529). Still, the Bohemian master's picture is not a mere echo of Italian painting. The gestures and facial expressions convey an intensity of emotion that represents the finest heritage of Northern Gothic art. In this respect, our panel is far more akin to the *Death of the Virgin* at Strasbourg Cathedral (fig. 496) than to any Italian work.

## The International Style

Toward the year 1400, the merging of Northern and Italian traditions had given rise to a single dominant style throughout western Europe. This International Style was not confined to painting—we have used the same term for the sculpture of the period—but painters clearly played the main role in its development.

BROEDERLAM. Among the most important was Melchior Broederlam (flourished c. 1387–1409), a Fleming who worked for the court of the duke of Burgundy in Dijon. Figure 541, showing the panels of a pair of shutters for an altar shrine that he did in 1394–99, is really two pictures within each frame; the temple of the *Presentation* and the landscape of the *Flight into Egypt* stand abruptly side by side, even though the artist has made a halfhearted effort to persuade us that the landscape extends around the building. Compared to Pietro and Ambrogio Lorenzetti, Broederlam's picture space still strikes us as naïve in many ways—the architecture looks like a doll's house, and the details of the landscape are quite out of scale with the figures. Yet the panels convey a far stronger feeling of depth than we have found in any previous Northern work. The reason for this is the subtlety of the modeling; the softly rounded shapes and the dark, velvety shadows create a sense of light and air that more than makes up for any shortcomings of scale or perspective. The same soft, pictorial quality—a hallmark of the International Style—appears in the ample, loosely draped garments with their fluid curvilinear patterns of folds, which remind us of Sluter and Ghiberti (see figs. 507 and 509).

Our panels also exemplify another characteristic of the International Style: its "realism of particulars," the same kind of realism we encountered first in Gothic sculpture (see fig. 500) and somewhat later among the marginal *drôleries* of manuscripts. We find it in the carefully rendered foliage and flowers, in the delightful donkey (obviously drawn from life), and in the rustic figure of St. Joseph, who looks and behaves like a simple peasant and thus helps to emphasize the delicate, aristocratic beauty of the Virgin. It is this painstaking concentration on detail that gives Broederlam's work the flavor of an enlarged miniature rather than of a large-scale painting, even though the panels are more than five feet tall.

THE LIMBOURG BROTHERS. That book illumination remained the leading form of painting in northern Europe at the time of the International Style, despite the growing importance of panel painting, is well attested by the miniatures of *Les Très Riches Heures du Duc de Berry*. Produced for the brother of the king of France, a man of far from admirable character but the most lavish art patron of his day, this luxurious book of hours represents the most advanced phase of the International Style. The artists were Pol de Limbourg and his two brothers, a group of Flemings who, like Sluter and Broederlam, had settled in France early in the fifteenth century. They must have visited Italy as well, for their work includes a great number of motifs and whole compositions borrowed from the great masters of Tuscany.

The most remarkable pages of *Les Très Riches Heures* are those of the calendar, with their elaborate depiction of the life of man and nature throughout the months of the year. Such cycles, originally consisting of twelve single figures each performing an appropriate seasonal activity, had long been an established tradition in medieval art (compare fig. 500). Jean Pucelle had enriched the margins of the calendar pages of his books of hours by emphasizing the changing aspects of nature in addition to the labors of the months. The Limbourg brothers, however, integrated all these elements into a series of panoramas of human life *in* nature. Thus the February miniature (fig. 542), the earliest snow landscape in the history of Western art, gives an enchantingly lyrical account of village life in the dead of winter, with the sheep huddled together in their fold, birds hungrily scratching in the barnyard, and a maid blowing on her frostbitten hands as she hurries to join her companions in the warm cottage (the front wall has been omitted for our benefit), while in the middle distance we see a villager cutting trees for firewood and another driving his laden donkey toward the houses among the hills. Here the promise of the Broederlam panels has been fulfilled, as it were: landscape, architectural interiors, and exteriors are harmoniously united in deep, atmo-

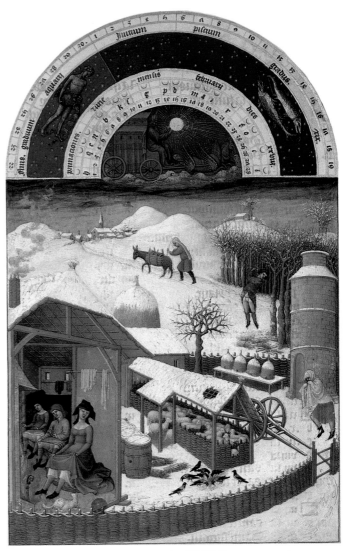

542. THE LIMBOURG BROTHERS. *FEBRUARY*, from
*Les Très Riches Heures du Duc de Berry*. 1413–16.
Musée Condé, Chantilly, France

spheric space. Even such intangible, evanescent things as the frozen breath of the maid, the smoke curling from the chimney, and the clouds in the sky have become "paintable."

Our figure 543 shows the sowing of winter grain during the month of October. It is a bright, sunny day, and the foreground figures—for the first time since classical Antiquity—cast visible shadows on the ground. Once more we marvel at the wealth of realistic detail such as the scarecrow in the middle distance or the footprints of the sower in the soil of the freshly plowed field. That sower is memorable in other ways as well; his tattered clothing, his unhappy mien, go beyond mere description. He is meant to be a pathetic figure, to arouse our awareness of the miserable lot of the peasantry in contrast to the life of the aristocracy, as symbolized by the splendid castle on the far bank of the river. (The castle, we will recall, is a "portrait" of the Gothic Louvre, the most lavish structure of its kind at that time; see page 367.)

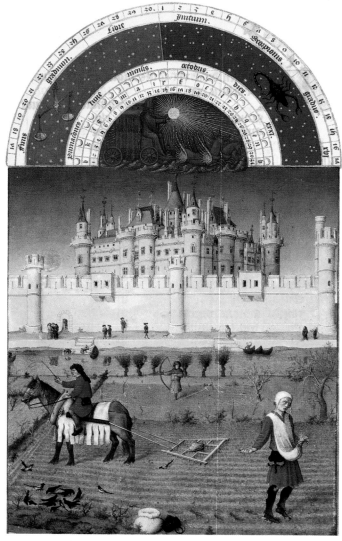

543. THE LIMBOURG BROTHERS. *OCTOBER,* from
*Les Très Riches Heures du Duc de Berry*

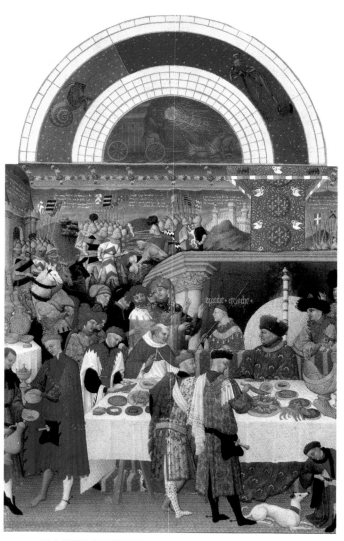

544. THE LIMBOURG BROTHERS. *JANUARY,* from
*Les Très Riches Heures du Duc de Berry*

Several of the calendar pages are devoted to the life of the nobility. The most interesting perhaps is the January picture, the only interior scene of the group, which shows the duke of Berry at a banquet (fig. 544). He is seated next to a huge fireplace, with a screen to protect him and, incidentally, to act as a kind of secular halo that sets him off against the multitude of courtiers and attendants. His features, known to us also from other works of the period, have all the distinctive qualities of a fine portrait, but the rest of the crowd—except for the youth and the cleric on the duke's right—displays an odd lack of individuality. They are all of the same type, in face as well as stature: aristocratic mannequins whose superhuman slenderness brings to mind their feminine counterparts in the fashion magazines of our own day. They are differentiated only by the luxuriance and variety of their clothing. Surely the gulf between them and the melancholy peasant of the October miniature could not have been greater in real life than it appears in these pictures!

GENTILE DA FABRIANO. From the courtly throng of the January page it is but a step to the three Magi and their train in the altarpiece by Gentile da Fabriano (c. 1370–1427), the greatest Italian painter of the International Style (fig. 545). The costumes here are as colorful, the draperies as ample and softly rounded, as in the North. The Holy Family on the left almost seems in danger of being overwhelmed by the gay and festive pageant pouring down upon it from the hills in the distance. Again we admire the marvelously well-observed animals, which now include not only the familiar ones but hunting leopards, camels, and monkeys. (Such creatures were eagerly collected by the princes of the period, many of whom kept private zoos.) The Oriental background of the Magi is further emphasized by the Mongolian facial cast of some of their companions. It is not these exotic touches, however, that mark our picture as the work of an Italian master but something else, a greater sense of weight, of physical substance, than we could hope to find among the

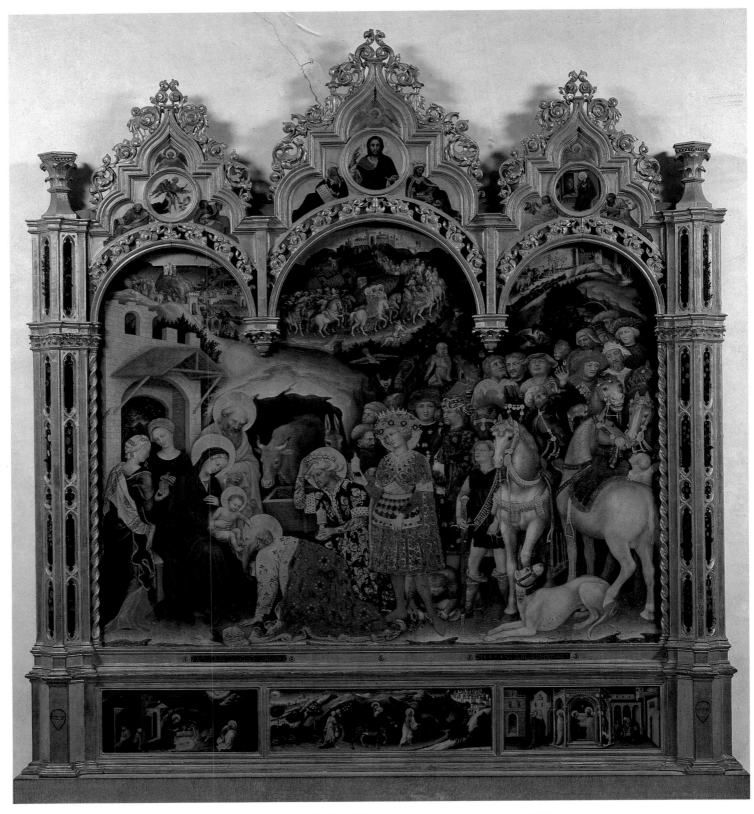

545. GENTILE DA FABRIANO. *THE ADORATION OF THE MAGI.* 1423.
Oil on panel, 9'10⅛" × 9'3" (3 × 2.8 m). Galleria degli Uffizi, Florence

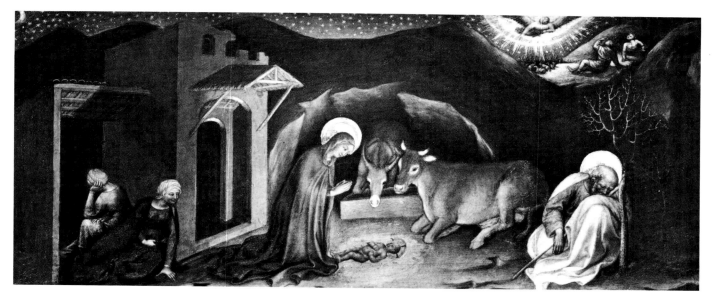

546. GENTILE DA FABRIANO. *THE NATIVITY*, from the predella of the *ADORATION OF THE MAGI*. 1423. 12¼ × 29½″ (31 × 75 cm). Galleria degli Uffizi, Florence

Northern representatives of the International Style.

Gentile, despite his love of fine detail, is obviously a painter used to working on a monumental scale, rather than a manuscript illuminator at heart. Yet he, too, had command of the delicate pictorial effects of a miniaturist, as we see on turning to the small panels decorating the base, or predella, of his altarpiece. In *The Nativity* (fig. 546) the new awareness of light that we first observed in the October page of *Les Très Riches Heures*—light as an independent factor, separate from form and color—dominates the entire picture. Even though the main sources of illumination are the divine radiance of the newborn Child ("the light of the world") and of the angel bringing the glad tidings to the shepherds in the fields, their effect is as natural—note the strong cast shadows—as if the Virgin were kneeling by a campfire. The poetic intimacy of this night scene opens up a whole new world of artistic possibilities, possibilities that were not to be fully explored until two centuries later.

# ILLUSTRATED TIME CHART II

**600**

Golden Age of Ireland, 600–800
Mohammed (570–632)
Omayyad caliphs (Damascus) 661–750
Moslems invade Spain 711–718; defeated
  by Franks, battle of Tours 732
Abbasid caliphate (Baghdad) begins 750
St. Boniface (died 755) converts Germans
Pepin the Short crowned king of Franks
  by St. Boniface 751; conquers Ravenna
  and donates it to papacy 756
Moslem state established in Spain 756
Viking invasions begin 794

Stirrup introduced into Western Europe c. 600
Earliest cast iron in China
Porcelain invented in China c. 700
Paper-making introduced into Near East
  from China
Isidore of Seville, encyclopedist (died 636)
The Venerable Bede, English historian
  (673–735)
*Beowulf* epic, England, early 8th cent.

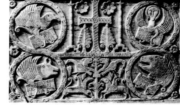
Sigvald relief, Cividale Cathedral

**800**

Charlemagne (r. 768–814) crowned Holy
  Roman Emperor by Pope 800; empire
  extends from northern Spain to western
  Germany and northern Italy
Treaty of Verdun 843, split of Carolingian
  empire: France, Germany, Lorraine
Rhabanus Maurus, German encyclopedist
  (784–856)
Alfred the Great (r. 871–899?), Anglo-
  Saxon king of England, defeats Danish
  invaders

Earliest version of *1001 Nights*, Arabian stories
Earliest documented church organ, Aachen 822
Carolingian revival of Latin classics
Earliest printed book, China, 868
Horse collar adopted in Western Europe
  makes horses efficient draft animals
Vikings discover Iceland 860

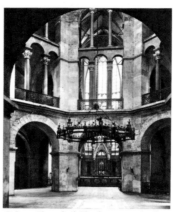
Palace Chapel of Charlemagne, Aachen

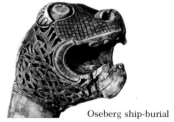
Oseberg ship-burial

**900**

Monastic order of Cluny founded 910
Normandy awarded to Vikings by king of
  France 911
Otto I (the Great) crowned Holy Roman
  Emperor by Pope 962
Otto II (r. 973–983) defeated by Moslems
  in southern Italy
Ethelred the Unready (r. 978–1016) buys
  off Danish invaders of England
Hugh Capet (r. 987–996) founds Cape-
  tian dynasty in France

Earliest documented use of windmills, in
  Near East
Earliest application of water power to in-
  dustry
Vikings discover Greenland c. 980

**1000**

Bishop Bernward of Hildesheim (r. 993–
  1022)
Normans arrive in Italy 1016; conquer
  Bari, last Byzantine stronghold, 1071;
  Sicily 1072–92
Reconquest of Spain from Moslems be-
  gins 1085
William the Conqueror (Norman) defeats
  English king Harold at Battle of Has-
  tings 1066
First Crusade 1095–99 takes Jerusalem
Cistercian order founded 1098; St. Ber-
  nard of Clairvaux (1090–1153) becomes
  principal abbot

Leif Ericson sails to North America 1002
Avicenna (980–1037), chief medical au-
  thority in Middle Ages
Hariri, Arabic writer (1054–1121)
Omar Khayyam, Persian poet (fl. c. 1100)
*Chanson de Roland*, French epic c. 1098

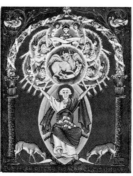
*Gospel Book of Otto III*

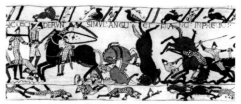
*Bayeux Tapestry*

**1100**

— 600

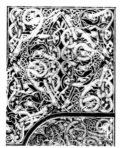

Sutton Hoo ship-burial treasure
*Lindisfarne Gospels*
*Echternach Gospels*
Sigvald relief, Cividale Cathedral
Palace at Mshatta, Jordan
Mosaic, Great Mosque, Damascus
Mosque at Cordova
Abbey Church of St.-Riquier

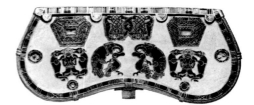

Sutton Hoo ship-burial treasure

*Lindisfarne Gospels*

— 800

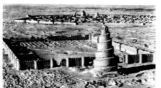

Palace Chapel of Charlemagne, Aachen
*Gospel Book of Charlemagne*
*Gospel Book of Ebbo of Reims*
*Utrecht Psalter*
*Monastery plan*, St. Gall
Oseberg ship-burial
Mosque of Mutawakkil, Samarra, Iraq
Crucifixion relief, cover of *Lindau Gospels*

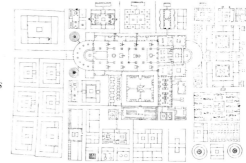

*Monastery plan*, St. Gall

Mosque of Mutawakkil, Samarra, Iraq

— 900

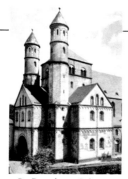

*Gero Crucifix*, Cologne Cathedral
St. Pantaleon, Cologne

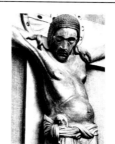

*Gero Crucifix*, Cologne Cathedral

St. Pantaleon, Cologne

— 1000

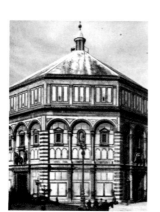

*Gospel Book of Otto III*
St. Michael's, Hildesheim
Bronze doors of Bernward, Hildesheim
*Gospel Book of Corbie*
Speyer Cathedral
Pisa Cathedral, Baptistery, Bell Tower
Baptistery, Florence
St.-Etienne, Caen
*Bayeux Tapestry*
St.-Sernin, Toulouse, and *Apostle*
S. Ambrogio, Milan
Durham Cathedral

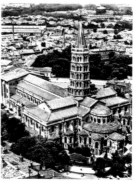

St.-Sernin, Toulouse

Baptistery, Florence

— 1100

Mediterranean made safe for commerce by Italian naval supremacy over Moslems

Knights Hospitalers founded 1113; Templars 1118; Teutonic Knights 1190

Rivalry of Guelfs (Duke Henry the Lion) and Hohenstaufen emperors in Germany

Norman Kingdom of Naples and Sicily 1139–1373

Louis the Fat of France (died 1137) strengthens monarchy

Portugal becomes independent 1143

Frederick I Barbarossa (r. 1155–90) titles himself "Holy Roman Emperor," tries to dominate Italy

King Henry II founds Plantagenet line 1154

Rise of universities (Bologna, Paris, Oxford); faculties of law, medicine, theology

Peter Abelard, French philosopher and teacher (1079–1142)

Geoffrey of Monmouth, English historian (died 1154)

Crossbow gains in use over bow and arrow

St. Bernard denounces sculpture in churches 1127

Flowering of French vernacular literature (epics, fables, chansons); troubadours

Mined coal supplements charcoal as fuel

Earliest use of magnetic compass for navigation

Earliest documented windmill in Europe 1180

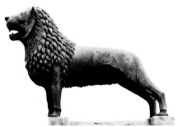

Lion monument, Brunswick

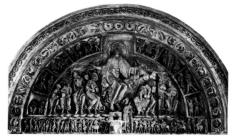

Tympanum, center portal, Vézelay

1200

Fourth Crusade (1202–4) conquers Constantinople

St. Dominic (1170–1221) founds Dominican order; Inquisition established to combat heresy

St. Francis of Assisi (died 1226) founds Franciscan order

Emperor Frederick II (1194–1250) neglects Germany, resides at Palermo

Magna Carta limits power of English kings 1215

King Louis IX (St. Louis, r. 1226–70) leads Seventh and Eighth Crusades

*Nibelung*, German epic c. 1205; minnesingers

*Golden Legend* by Jacobus de Voragine written 1266–83

St. Thomas Aquinas, Italian scholastic philosopher (died 1274)

Albertus Magnus, scholastic philosopher (1193–1280)

Roger Bacon, English philosopher and scientist (Franciscan) (1214–1292)

Dante Alighieri (1265–1321), *Divine Comedy* in Italian vernacular

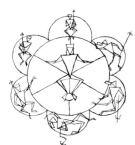

*Sketchbook*, Villard de Honnecourt

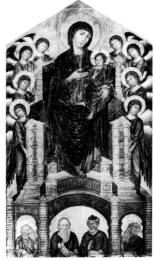

*Madonna Enthroned*, by Cimabue

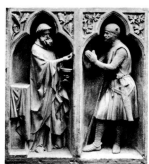

Interior west wall sculpture, Reims Cathedral

Mongol invasion of Russia 1237

Teutonic Knights colonize Prussia

Edward I (r. 1272–1307) conquers Wales

Philip IV (the Fair, r. 1285–1314), king of France, humiliates Pope Boniface VI 1303

Moslems reconquer Acre, last Christian stronghold in Holy Land, 1291

Marco Polo travels to China and India c. 1275–93

Arabic (actually Indian) numerals introduced in Europe

Spectacles invented c. 1286

First documented use of spinning wheel in Europe 1298, replaces distaff and spindle

1300

Nave vault murals, St.-Savin-sur-
  Gartempe
South Portal, Moissac
Notre-Dame-la-Grande, Poitiers
Font, St.-Barthélemy, Liège, by Renier
  of Huy
Tournai Cathedral
Tympanum, center portal, Vézelay
Last Judgment tympanum, Autun
Coronation Cloak of German Emperors
Abbey Church of St.-Denis, Paris
Gospel Book of Wedricus
Portal sculpture, St.-Gilles-du-Gard
West portals, Chartres Cathedral
Notre-Dame, Paris
Lion monument, Brunswick
Klosterneuburg altar, by Nicholas of
  Verdun
Façade sculpture, Fidenza Cathedral, by
  Antelami
Chartres Cathedral (rebuilding after fire)
Abbey Church, Fossanova (Cistercian)

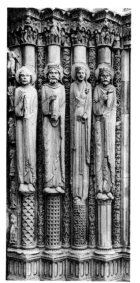

West portals, Chartres Cathedral

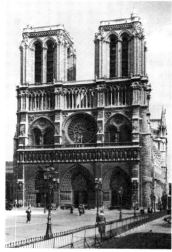

Notre-Dame, Paris

Stained glass, Chartres Cathedral
*Carmina Burana* manuscript, Munich
Transept portals, Chartres Cathedral
Stained glass, Bourges Cathedral
South transept portal, Strasbourg Cathe-
  dral
Amiens Cathedral
Salisbury Cathedral
Illustrated Arabic *Dioscorides*
Reims Cathedral
Tomb of a Knight, Dorchester Abbey
*Sketchbook*, Villard de Honnecourt
Choir screen and "portraits," Naumburg
  Cathedral
Interior west wall sculpture, Reims Cathe-
  dral
Pulpit, Baptistery, Pisa, by Nicola Pisano
*Psalter of St. Louis*
St.-Urbain, Troyes
*Madonna Enthroned*, by Cimabue
*Prayer Book of Philip the Fair*, by Master
  Honoré
Sta. Croce, Florence
Florence Cathedral
Palazzo Vecchio, Florence

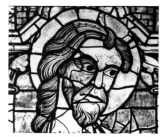

Stained glass, Bourges Cathedral

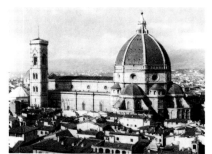

Florence Cathedral

Choir screen and "portraits,"
Naumburg Cathedral

| POLITICAL HISTORY, RELIGION | LITERATURE, SCIENCE, TECHNOLOGY | PAINTING, SCULPTURE, ARCHITECTURE |
|---|---|---|

1300

Exile of papacy in Avignon 1309–76
Hundred Years' War between England and France begins 1337
Black Death throughout Europe 1347–50
Jacquerie (peasant) revolt in France 1358
St. Bridget of Sweden (1303–1373)
Russians defeat Mongols at Kulikovo 1380
Wat Tyler leads peasant uprising in England 1381
John Wycliffe (died 1384) challenges church doctrine; translates Bible into English

First large-scale production of paper in Italy and Germany
Large-scale production of gunpowder; earliest known use of cannon 1326
Earliest cast iron in Europe
Master Eckhart, German mystic (died 1327)
William of Occam, English scholastic philosopher (c. 1300–1349)
Longbow replaces crossbow, Battle of Crécy, 1346
*Canterbury Tales* by Chaucer c. 1387
*Decameron* by Boccaccio 1387

*Virgin of Paris*, Notre Dame
Cathedral pulpit, Pisa, by Giovanni Pisano
Arena Chapel frescoes, Padua, by Giotto
*Maestà* altar, Siena, by Duccio
*Pietà (Andachtsbild)*, Bonn
Façade sculpture, Orvieto Cathedral
*Triumph of Death*, Pisa, by Traini
*Hours of Jeanne d'Evreux*, by Jean Pucelle
Equestrian statue of Can Grande, Verona
Choir, Gloucester Cathedral
*Good and Bad Government* frescoes, Siena, by Ambrogio Lorenzetti
*Country Life* fresco, Avignon
Alhambra Palace, Granada
Madrasah of Sultan Hasan, Cairo
Choir, St. Sebald, Nuremberg
Portal of Chartreuse, Dijon, by Claus Sluter; Moses Well
Altar wings, Dijon, by Broederlam

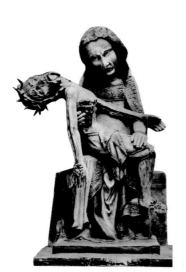

*Pietà (Andachtsbild)*, Bonn

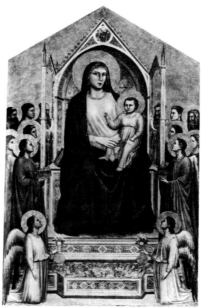

*Madonna Enthroned*, by Giotto

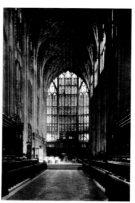

Choir, Gloucester Cathedral

1400

Teutonic Knights beaten by Poles and Lithuanians at Tannenberg 1410
Jan Huss, Czech reformer, burned at stake for heresy 1415
Great Papal Schism (since 1378) settled by election of Martin V at Council of Constance 1417; Pope returns to Rome

Gutenberg invents printing with movable type 1446–50
Earliest account of sea quadrant in navigation 1456

Competition relief for Baptistery doors, Florence
*Très Riches Heures du Duc de Berry*, by Limbourg brothers
Ca' d'Oro, Venice
*Adoration of the Magi* altar, by Gentile da Fabriano
St.-Maclou, Rouen
House of Jacques Coeur, Bourges
Chapel of Henry VII, Westminster Abbey

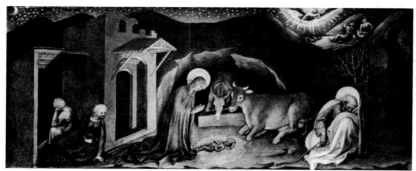

*Adoration of the Magi* altar, by Gentile da Fabriano

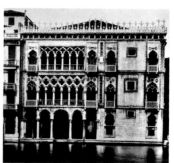

Ca' d'Oro, Venice

# BOOKS FOR FURTHER READING

This list includes standard works and the most recent and comprehensive books in English. Books with material relevant to several chapters are cited only under the first heading. Many authors cited have written other works on their fields. Two useful series, not all volumes of which are cited here, are the *Pelican History of Art* and the *World of Art* series. Two excellent general bibliographies are *Guide to the Literature of Art History* by E. Arntzen and R. Rainwater (American Library Association, 1980) and *Art Books: A Basic Bibliography* by E. L. Lucas (New York Graphic Society, 1968). Many libraries now have access to electronic data bases, such as *Art Bibliographies Modern* and *RLIN*, which can help you find other works. A useful guide to art historical research is *Art Information: Research Methods and Resources* by L. S. Jones (3d ed., Kendall/Hunt Publishing Co., c. 1990). Asterisks (*) indicate titles available in paperback; for publishers, distributors, and the like, see *Paperbound Books in Print* (R.R. Bowker, annual).

## INTRODUCTION

*ARNHEIM, R., *Art and Visual Perception*, 2d ed., Univ. of California Press, Berkeley, 1974
*———, *Visual Thinking*, Univ. of California Press, Berkeley, 1970
BAUMGART, F., *A History of Architectural Styles*, Praeger, N.Y., 1970
BERNHEIMER, R., *The Nature of Representation*, New York Univ. Press, 1961
CAHN, W., *Masterpieces: Chapters on the History of an Idea*, Princeton Univ. Press, 1979
DICKIE, G., *Art and the Aesthetic: An Institutional Analysis*, Cornell Univ. Press, Ithaca, 1974
*DIENHARD, H., *Meaning and Expression: Toward a Sociology of Art*, Beacon Press, Boston, 1970
*ELSEN, A. E., *Purpose of Art*, 3d ed., Holt, Rinehart, Winston, N.Y., 1972
*FEIBELMAN, J. K., *The Quiet Rebellion: The Making and Meaning of the Arts*, Horizon, N.Y., 1972
*FINN, D., *How to Look at Sculpture*, Abrams, N.Y., 1989
*GOMBRICH, E. H., *Art and Illusion*, 4th ed., Pantheon Books, N.Y., 1972
———, *Ideals and Icons: Essays on Value in History and in Art*, Phaidon, Oxford, 1979
*———, *The Sense of Order, a Study in the Psychology of Decorative Art*, Cornell Univ. Press, Ithaca, N.Y., c. 1979, 1984
*HOLT, E. G., *A Documentary History of Art*, 2d ed., 2 vols., Doubleday, Garden City, 1981
KEPES, G., ed., *The Man-Made Object*, Braziller, N.Y., 1966
*KUBLER, G., *The Shape of Time*, Yale Univ. Press, New Haven, 1962
LANG, B., ed., *The Concept of Style*, Univ. of Pennsylvania Press, Philadelphia, 1979
*PANOFSKY, E., *Meaning in the Visual Arts*, Doubleday, Garden City, 1955; reprint, Overlook Press, Woodstock, 1974
PODRO, M., *The Manifold in Perception: Theories of Art from Kant to Hildebrand*, Clarendon Press, Oxford, 1972
READ, H. E., *Art and Alienation: The Role of the Artist in Society*, Horizon, N.Y., 1967
———, *Icon and Idea*, Schocken, N.Y., 1965
*ROSENBERG, H., *The Anxious Object: Art Today and Its Audience*, 2d ed., Horizon, N.Y., 1966
SIRCELLO, G., *Mind and Art*, Princeton Univ. Press, 1972
*TAYLOR, J. C., *Learning to Look: A Handbook for the Visual Arts*, 2d ed., Univ. of Chicago Press, 1981

## PART ONE
## THE ANCIENT WORLD
### 1. PREHISTORIC AND ETHNOGRAPHIC ART

*BASCOM, W. R., *African Art in Cultural Perspective*, Norton, N.Y., 1973
BÜHLER, A., T. BARROW, & C. T. MOUNTFORD, *The Art of the South Sea Islands*, Crown, N.Y., 1962
CHILDE, V. G., *The Dawn of European Civilization*, 6th ed., Knopf, N.Y., 1958
CORNET, J., *Art of Africa*, Phaidon, N.Y., 1971
DAVIES, O., *West Africa Before the Europeans: Archaeology and Prehistory*, Methuen, London, 1967
FEDER, N., *American Indian Art*, Abrams, N.Y., 1971
GIMBUTAS, M. A., *The Gods and Goddesses of Old Europe, 7000–3500 B.C.: Myths, Legends and Cult Images*, Univ. of California Press, Berkeley, 1974
GRAND, P. M., *Prehistoric Art: Paleolithic Painting and Sculpture*, New York Graphic Society, Greenwich, 1967
GRAZIOSI, P., *Paleolithic Art*, McGraw-Hill, N.Y., 1960
*GUIDONI, E., *Primitive Architecture*, Rizzoli, N.Y., 1987
GUNDON, E., *Primitive Architecture*, Abrams, N.Y., 1978
*HEYDEN, D., & P. GENDROP, *Pre-Columbian Architecture of Mesoamerica*, Rizzoli, N.Y., 1988
*LAUDE, J., *The Arts of Black Africa*, Univ. of California Press, Berkeley, 1971
LEROI-GOURHAN, A., *Treasures of Prehistoric Art*, Abrams, N.Y., 1967
*LEUZINGER, E., *The Art of Black Africa*, Rizzoli, N.Y., 1979
LLOYD, S., *Mounds of the Near East*, Edinburgh Univ. Press, 1963
LOMMEL, A., *Shamanism, The Beginnings of Art*, McGraw-Hill, N.Y., 1967
MARSHACK, A., *The Roots of Civilization: The Cognitive Beginnings of Man's First Art, Symbol and Notation*, McGraw-Hill, N.Y., 1971
MEGAW, J. V. S., *Art of the European Iron Age*, Harper & Row, N.Y., 1970
MELLAART, J., *Çatal Hüyük: A Neolithic Town in Anatolia*, McGraw-Hill, N.Y., 1967
———, *The Neolithic of the Near East*, Scribner, N.Y., 1975
PIGGOTT, S., *Ancient Europe*, Aldine, Chicago, 1966
*POWELL, T. G. E., *Prehistoric Art*, Praeger, N.Y., 1966
RENFREW, C., *Before Civilization: The Radiocarbon Revolution and Prehistoric Europe*, Knopf, N.Y., 1973
SANDARS, N. K., *Prehistoric Art in Europe*, Pelican History of Art, Penguin, Baltimore, 1968
SILVERBERG, R., *Mound Builders of Ancient America: The Archaeology of a Myth*, New York Graphic Society, Greenwich, 1968
THOM, A., *Megalithic Sites in Britain*, Clarendon Press, Oxford, 1967
TRACHTENBERG, M., & I. HYMAN, *Architecture: From Prehistory to Post-Modernism*, Abrams, N.Y., 1985
*WILLETT, F., *African Art*, Praeger, N.Y., 1971
WINGERT, P., *Primitive Art: Its Traditions and Styles*, Oxford Univ. Press, N.Y., 1962

### 2. EGYPTIAN ART

ALDRED, C., *Akhenaten and Nefertiti*, Brooklyn Museum/Viking Press, 1973
———, *Art of Ancient Egypt*, 3 vols., Transatlantic, N.Y., 1974
———, *Development of Ancient Egyptian Art from 3200 to 1315 B.C.*, Transatlantic, N.Y., 1975
BADAWY, A., *A History of Egyptian Architecture*, Vol. I, Sh. Studio Misr., Giza, 1954; Vols. II–III, Univ. of California Press, Berkeley, 1966-68
DESROCHES-NOBLECOURT, C., *Tutankhamen*, New York Graphic Society, Greenwich, 1964
*FAKHRY, A., *The Pyramids*, 2d ed., Univ. of Chicago Press, 1962
FLETCHER, B., *A History of Architecture*, 18th ed., rev., R. A. Cordingley, Scribner, N.Y., 1975
GROENEWEGEN-FRANKFORT, H. A., *Arrest and Movement*, Univ. of Chicago Press, 1951; reprint, Hacker Art Books, N.Y., 1972
———, & B. ASHMOLE, *Art of the Ancient World*, Abrams, N.Y., 1975
HAYES, W.C., *The Scepter of Egypt*, 2 vols., Harper, in cooperation with the Metropolitan Museum of Art, N.Y., 1953–59
LANGE, K., & M. HIRMER, *Egypt: Architecture, Sculpture, Painting in Three Thousand Years*, 4th ed., Phaidon, London, 1968
*MEKHITARIAN, A., *Egyptian Painting*, Skira, N.Y., 1954; Rizzoli, N.Y., 1977
MICHALOWSKI, K., *Art of Ancient Egypt*, Abrams, N.Y., 1969; reprint 1985
*PANOFSKY, E., *Tomb Sculpture: Its Aspects from Ancient Egypt to Bernini*, Abrams, N.Y., 1969
PORTER, B., & R. L. B. MOSS, *Topographical Bibliography of Ancient Egyptian Hieroglyphic Texts, Reliefs and Paintings*, 7 vols., Oxford Univ. Press, N.Y., 1927–51; 2d ed., Vol. 1 (2 parts), Vols. 2–3, 1960–74
POULSEN, V., *Egyptian Art*, New York Graphic Society, Greenwich, 1968
SCHÄFER, H., *Principles of Egyptian Art*, Clarendon Press, Oxford, 1974
*SMITH, W. S., & W. K. SIMPSON, *The Art and Architecture of Ancient Egypt*, rev. with additions, Pelican History of Art, Penguin, Baltimore, 1981
WOLF, W., *The Origins of Western Art: Egypt, Mesopotamia, the Aegean*, Universe Books, N.Y., 1971

### 3. ANCIENT NEAR EASTERN ART

AKURGAL, E., *Art of the Hittites*, Abrams, N.Y., 1962
AMIET, P., *Art of the Ancient Near East*, Abrams, N.Y., 1980
*FRANKFORT, H., *The Art and Architecture of the Ancient Orient*, 4th rev. impression with additional bibliography, Pelican History of Art, Penguin, Baltimore, 1969
———, *Cylinder Seals: A Documentary Essay on the Art and Religion of the Ancient Near East*, Gregg, London, 1968
GHIRSHMAN, R., *Iran from the Earliest Times to the Islamic Conquest*, Penguin, Harmondsworth, N.Y., 1978
GOFF, B. L., *Symbols of Prehistoric Mesopotamia*, Yale Univ. Press, New Haven, 1963
KRAMER, S. N., *The Sumerians: Their History, Culture and Characteristics*, Univ. of Chicago Press, 1963
LLOYD, S., *The Archaeology of Mesopotamia: From the Old Stone Age to the Persian Conquest*, Thames & Hudson, London, 1978
LLOYD, S., H. W. MÜLLER, & R. MARTIN, *Ancient Architecture: Mesopotamia, Egypt, Greece*, Abrams, N.Y., 1974
MADHLOOM, T. A., *The Chronology of Neo-Assyrian Art*, Athlone Press, London, 1970
*MELLAART, J., *Earliest Civilizations of the Near East*, McGraw-Hill, N.Y., 1965
MOOREY, P. R. S., *Ancient Iraq: Assyria and Babylonia*, Ashmolean Museum, Oxford, 1976
MOORTGAT, A., *The Art of Ancient Mesopotamia*, Phaidon, N.Y., 1969
PARROT, A., *The Arts of Assyria*, Braziller, N.Y., 1961
PORADA, E., *The Art of Ancient Iran: Pre-Islamic Cultures*, Crown, N.Y., 1965

*SAGGS, H. W. F., *The Greatness That Was Babylon*, Praeger, N.Y., 1968
SMITH, W.S., *Interconnections in the Ancient Near East*, Yale Univ. Press, New Haven, 1965
STROMMENGER, E., & M. HIRMER, *5000 Years of the Art of Mesopotamia*, Abrams, N.Y., 1964
*WOOLLEY, C. L., *Ur of the Chaldees*, Norton, N.Y., 1965

## 4. AEGEAN ART

BLEGEN, C. W., & M. RAWSON, eds., *The Palace of Nestor at Pylos in Western Messenia*, 3 vols., Princeton Univ. Press, 1966–73
BRANIGAN, K., *The Foundations of Palatial Crete: A Survey of Crete in the Early Bronze Age*, Praeger, N.Y., 1970
FOSTER, K. P., *Aegean Faience of the Bronze Age*, Yale Univ. Press, New Haven, 1977
*GRAHAM, J. W., *The Palaces of Crete*, Princeton Univ. Press, 1962
HAMPE, R., & E. SIMON, *The Birth of Greek Art from the Mycenaean to the Archaic Period*, Oxford Univ. Press, N.Y., 1981
HOOD, S., *The Minoans: The Story of Bronze Age Crete*, Praeger, N.Y., 1981
MARINATOS, S. N., & M. HIRMER, *Crete and Mycenae*, Abrams, N.Y., 1960
MYLONAS, G. E., *Mycenae and the Mycenaean Age*, Princeton Univ. Press, 1966
PEROWNE, S., *The Archaeology of Greece and the Aegean*, Viking, N.Y., 1974
RENFREW, C., *The Emergence of Civilization: The Cyclades and the Aegean in the Third Millennium B.C.*, Methuen, London, 1972
*VERMEULE, E., *Greece in the Bronze Age*, Univ. of Chicago Press, 1972

## 5. GREEK ART

ADAM, S., *The Technique of Greek Sculpture in the Archaic and Classical Periods*, Thames & Hudson, London, 1967
ARIAS, P. E., & M. HIRMER, *History of 1000 Years of Greek Vase Painting*, Abrams, N.Y., 1963
ASHMOLE, B., *Architect and Sculptor in Classical Greece*, New York Univ. Press, 1972
ASHMOLE, B., & N. YALOURIS, *Olympia: The Sculptures of the Temple of Zeus*, Phaidon, London, 1967
BEAZLEY, J. D., *Attic Red-Figure Vase-Painters*, 2d ed., 3 vols., Oxford Univ. Press, London, 1963
———, *The Development of Attic Black Figure*, rev. ed., Univ. of California Press, Berkeley, 1986
BEAZLEY, J. D., & B. ASHMOLE, *Sculpture and Painting to the End of the Hellenistic Period*, Cambridge Univ. Press, 1966
BERVÉ, H., G. GRUBEN, & M. HIRMER, *Greek Temples, Theatres, and Shrines*, Abrams, N.Y., 1963
BIEBER, M., *Laocoön: The Influence of the Group Since Its Discovery*, Wayne State Univ. Press, Detroit, 1967
*BOARDMAN, J., *Athenian Black-Figure Vases*, Oxford Univ. Press, N.Y., 1974
———, *Greek Sculpture: The Archaic Period*, Oxford Univ. Press, N.Y., 1978
*———, *Pre-Classical: From Crete to Archaic Greece*, Penguin, Baltimore, 1967
BRILLIANT, R., *Arts of the Ancient Greeks*, McGraw-Hill, N.Y., 1973
*CARPENTER, R., *The Architects of the Parthenon*, Penguin, Baltimore, 1970

CHARBONNEAUX, J., R. MARTIN, & F. VILLARD, *Classical Greek Art*, Braziller, N.Y., 1972
———, *Hellenistic Greek Art*, Braziller, N.Y., 1973
*COOK, R. M., *Greek Art: Its Development, Character and Influence*, Farrar, Straus & Giroux, N.Y., 1973
*DINSMOOR, W. B., *The Architecture of Ancient Greece: An Account of Its Historic Development*, Norton, N.Y.; London, 1975 (reprint of the 1950 ed. [3d rev.] augmented)
HAVELOCK, C. M., *Hellenistic Art*, New York Graphic Society, Greenwich, 1970
HILL, G. F., *Ancient Greek and Roman Coins: A Handbook*, new & enl. ed. (1st Amer. ed.), Argonaut, Chicago, 1964
*HOOD, S., *The Arts in Prehistoric Greece*, Pelican History of Art, Penguin, Harmondsworth, N.Y., 1978
KRAAY, C. M., & M. HIRMER, *Greek Coins*, Abrams, N.Y., 1966
LAWRENCE, A. W., *Greek and Roman Sculpture*, Harper & Row, N.Y., 1972
———, *Greek Architecture*, 4th ed. rev., Pelican History of Art, Penguin, N.Y., 1983
*LULLIES, R., & M. HIRMER, *Greek Sculpture*, Abrams, N.Y., 1960
*MOON, W. G., ed., *Ancient Greek Art and Iconography*, Univ. of Wisconsin Press, Madison, 1983
PAPAIOANNOU, K., *The Art of Greece*, Abrams, N.Y., 1988
PFUHL, E., *Masterpieces of Greek Drawing and Painting*, 2d ed., Macmillan, N.Y., 1955
POLLITT, J. J., *The Ancient View of Greek Art: Criticism, History and Terminology*, Yale Univ. Press, New Haven, 1974
*———, *The Art of Greece: Sources and Documents*, Prentice Hall Englewood Cliffs, 1965
RICHTER, G. M. A., *A Handbook of Greek Art*, 6th ed., redesigned, Phaidon, London, 1969
———, *Kouroi*, 3d ed., Phaidon, N.Y., 1970
———, *The Sculpture and Sculptors of the Greeks*, 4th ed., rev., Yale Univ. Press, New Haven, 1970
ROBERTSON, M., *Greek Painting*, Skira, Geneva, 1959
———, *History of Greek Art*, 2 vols., Cambridge Univ. Press, 1975
SCHWEITZER, B., *Greek Geometric Art*, Phaidon, N.Y., 1971
*SCRANTON, R. L., *Greek Architecture*, Braziller, N.Y., 1962
SCULLY, V. J., *The Earth, the Temple and the Gods: Greek Sacred Architecture*, Yale Univ. Press, New Haven, 1962
*STERLING, C., *Still Life Painting from Antiquity to the Twentieth Century*, 2d rev. ed., Harper & Row, N.Y., 1981
WARD-PERKINS, J. B., *The Cities of Ancient Greece and Italy: Planning in Classical Antiquity*, Braziller, N.Y., 1974,
WEBSTER, T. B. L., *Potter and Painter in Classical Athens*, Methuen, London, 1972

## 6. ETRUSCAN ART

BANTI, L., *Etruscan Cities and Their Culture*, Univ. of California Press, Berkeley, 1973
*BOETHIUS, A., *Etruscan and Early Roman Architecture*, 2d integrated ed., rev., Pelican History of Art, Penguin, Harmondsworth, N.Y., 1978
*BRENDEL, O. J., *Etruscan Art*, Pelican History of Art, Penguin, Harmondsworth, N.Y., 1978
———, *Prolegomena to the Study of Roman Art*, Yale Univ. Press, New Haven, 1979
MORETTI, M., *New Monuments of Etruscan Painting*, Pennsylvania State Univ. Press, University Park, 1970
PALLOTTINO, M., *Etruscan Painting*, Skira, Geneva, 1953
RICHARDSON, E., *The Etruscans: Their Art and Civilization*, Univ. of Chicago Press, 1964
SPRENGER, M., G. BARTOLINI, & M. & A. HIRMER, *The Etruscans, Their History, Art, and Architecture*, Abrams N.Y., 1983

## 7. ROMAN ART

ANDREAE, B., *The Art of Rome*, Abrams, N.Y., 1977
BIANCHI-BANDINELLI, R., *Rome: The Center of Power*, Braziller, N.Y., 1970
———, *Rome: The Late Empire, A.D. 200–400*, Braziller, N.Y., 1971
BRILLIANT, R., *Roman Art from the Republic to Constantine*, Phaidon, N.Y., 1974
*BROWN, F. E., *Roman Architecture*, Braziller, N.Y., 1961
CHARLES-PICARD, G., *Roman Painting*, New York Graphic Society, Greenwich, 1970
HEINTZE, H. VON, *Roman Art*, Universe Books, N.Y., 1971
*HERSEY, G., *The Lost Meaning of Classical Architecture: Speculations on Ornament from Vitruvius to Venturi*, MIT Press, Cambridge, 1988
*L'ORANGE, H. P., *Art Forms and Civic Life in the Late Roman Empire*, Princeton Univ. Press, 1965
MACCORMACK, S., *Art and Ceremony in Late Antiquity*, Univ. of California Press, Berkeley, 1981
*MACDONALD, W. L., *The Architecture of the Roman Empire*, Vol. 1, rev. ed., Yale Univ. Press, New Haven, 1982
———, *The Pantheon: Design, Meaning and Progeny*, Harvard Univ. Press, Cambridge, 1976
MAIURI, A., *Roman Painting*, Geneva, Skira, 1953
NASH, E., *Pictorial Dictionary of Ancient Rome*, 2 vols., 2d ed., rev., Praeger, N.Y., 1968
PERCIVAL, J., *The Roman Villa: An Historical Introduction*, Univ. of California Press, Berkeley, 1976
PERKINS, A., *The Art of Dura-Europas*, Clarendon Press, Oxford, 1963
POBÉ, M., & J. ROUBIER, *The Art of Roman Gaul*, Univ. of Toronto Press, 1961
*POLLITT, J. J., *The Art of Rome and Late Antiquity: Sources and Documents*, Prentice-Hall, Englewood Cliffs, 1966
*STRONG, D. E., *Roman Art*, Pelican History of Art, Penguin, Harmondsworth, 1976
TOYNBEE, J. M. C., *Roman Historical Portraits*, Thames & Hudson, N.Y., 1978
VERMEULE, C. C., III, *Greek Sculpture and Roman Taste*, Univ. of Michigan Press, Ann Arbor, 1977
———, *Roman Imperial Art in Greece and Asia Minor*, Belknap Press, Cambridge, 1968
WARD-PERKINS, J. B., *Roman Architecture*, Abrams, N.Y., 1977
*———, *Roman Imperial Architecture*, Pelican History of Art, Penguin, Harmondsworth, N.Y., 1981

## 8. EARLY CHRISTIAN AND BYZANTINE ART

*ALEXANDER, J. J. G., *The Decorated Letter*, Braziller, N.Y., 1978
BECKWITH, J., *The Art of Constantinople: An Introduction to Byzantine Art (330–1453)*, 2d ed., Phaidon, N.Y., 1968
*———, *Early Christian and Byzantine Art*, 2d integrated ed., Pelican History of Art, Penguin, Harmondsworth, N.Y., 1979
BOVINI, G., & L. VON MATT, *Ravenna*, Abrams, N.Y., 1971
DEMUS, O., *Byzantine Art and the West*, New York Univ. Press, 1970
GALVARIS, G., *The Icon in the Life of the Church: Doctrine, Liturgy, Devotion*, Brill, Leiden, 1981
GRABAR, A., *The Beginnings of Christian Art, 200–395*, Thames & Hudson, London, 1967
———, *Early Christian Art*, Braziller, N.Y., 1971
———, *The Golden Age of Justinian, from the Death of Theodosius to the Rise of Islam*, Braziller, N.Y., 1971
*HAMILTON, G. H., *The Art and Architecture of Russia*, 3d integrated ed., Pelican History of Art, Penguin, N.Y., 1983

KÄHLER, H., & C. MANGO, *Hagia Sophia*, Praeger, N.Y., 1967

*KRAUTHEIMER, R., *Early Christian and Byzantine Architecture*, Pelican History of Art, Penguin, Baltimore, 1965

*——, *Rome: Profile of a City, 312–1308*, Princeton Univ. Press, 1980

*LOWRIE, W., *Art in the Early Church*, Norton, N.Y., 1969

MACDONALD, W. L., *Early Christian and Byzantine Architecture*, Penguin, Baltimore, 1965

MAGUIRE, H., *Art and Eloquence in Byzantium*, Princeton Univ. Press, 1981

*MANGO, C., *The Art of the Byzantine Empire, 312–1453: Sources and Documents*, Prentice-Hall, Englewood Cliffs, 1972

——, *Byzantine Architecture*, Abrams, N.Y., 1976

MATHEWS, T. J., *Byzantine Churches of Istanbul: A Photographic Survey*, Pennsylvania State Univ. Press, University Park, 1976

RICE, D. T., *The Appreciation of Byzantine Art*, Oxford Univ. Press, London, 1972

*RUNCIMAN, S., *Byzantine Style and Civilization*, Penguin, Harmondsworth, Baltimore, 1975

WEITZMANN, K., *Byzantine Book Illumination and Ivories*, Variorum Reprints, London, 1980

*——, *Late Antique and Early Christian Book Illumination*, Braziller, N.Y., 1977

ZARNECKI, G., *Art of the Medieval World*, Abrams, N.Y., 1976

# PART TWO
# THE MIDDLE AGES
## 1. ISLAMIC ART

ATIL, E., ed., *Turkish Art*, Smithsonian Institution Press, Washington, D.C., Abrams; N.Y., 1980

CRESWELL, K. A. C., *Early Muslim Architecture*, 2 vols., 3 parts (reprint, 1932 ed.), Hacker, N.Y., 1976

——, *Muslim Architecture in Egypt*, 2 vols, (reprint, 1952–59 ed.), Hacker, N.Y., 1976

*ETTINGHAUSEN, R., *Arab Painting* (reprint, Skira, Geneva, 1962, ed.), Rizzoli, N.Y., 1977

GOODWIN, G., *A History of Ottoman Architecture*, Johns Hopkins Univ. Press, Baltimore, 1971

GRABAR, O., *The Formation of Islamic Art*, Yale Univ. Press, New Haven, 1973

HILL, D., *Islamic Architecture and Its Decoration: A.D. 800–1500*, Univ. of Chicago Press, 1964

HOAG, J. D., *Islamic Architecture*, Abrams, N. Y., 1977

PAPADOPOULO, A., *Islam and Muslim Art*, Abrams, N. Y., 1979

POPE, A. U., *Persian Architecture: The Triumph of Form and Color*, Braziller, N. Y., 1965

RICE, D. T., *Islamic Painting: A Survey*, Edinburgh Univ. Press, 1971

ROBINSON, B. W., et al., *Islamic Painting and the Arts of the Book*, Faber & Faber, London, 1976

UNSAL, B., *Turkish Islamic Architecture in Seljuk and Ottoman Times*, St. Martin's Press, London, N.Y., 1973

## 2. EARLY MEDIEVAL ART

ALEXANDER, J. J. G., *Insular Manuscripts, 6th to the 9th Century* (A Survey of Manuscript Illumination in the British Isles, I), Miller, London, 1979

BUSCH, H., & B. LOHSE, *Pre-Romanesque Art*, Macmillan, N.Y., 1966

*CONANT, K. J., *Carolingian and Romanesque Architecture, 800–1200*, new ed., Pelican History of Art, Penguin, Norwich, 1974

*DAVIS-WEYER, C., *Early Medieval Art: 300–1150: Sources and Documents*, Prentice-Hall, Englewood Cliffs, 1971

DODWELL, C. R., *Painting in Europe: 800–1200*, Pelican History of Art, Penguin, Harmondsworth, Baltimore, 1971

DUBY, G., *History of Medieval Art, 980–1440*, new 1 vol. ed., Skira/Rizzoli, Geneva/N.Y., 1986

FINLAY, I., *Celtic Art: An Introduction*, Faber & Faber, London, 1973

*GRABAR, A., & C. NORDENFALK, *Early Medieval Painting*, Skira, Geneva, 1957

*GROHSKOPF, B., *The Treasure of Sutton Hoo: Ship Burial for an Anglo-Saxon King*, Atheneum, N.Y., 1970

*HENDERSON, G. D. S., *Early Medieval Style and Civilization*, Penguin, Baltimore, 1972

HENRY, F., ed., *The Book of Kells*, Knopf, N.Y., 1974

——, *Irish Art During the Viking Invasions, 800–1020 A.D.*, Cornell Univ. Press, Ithaca, 1967

*——, *Irish Art in the Early Christian Period, to 800 A.D.*, Cornell Univ. Press, Ithaca, 1965

*HINKS, R. P., *Carolingian Art*, Univ. of Michigan Press, Ann Arbor, 1960

HUBERT, J., *The Carolingian Renaissance*, Braziller, N. Y., 1970

HUBERT, J., J. PORCHER, & W. VOLBACH, *Europe of the Invasions*, Braziller, N. Y., 1969

*KITZINGER, E., *Early Medieval Art in the British Museum*, Indiana Univ. Press, Bloomington, 1964

KLINGENDER, F. D., *Animals in Art and Thought to the End of the Middle Ages*, MIT Press, Cambridge, 1971

*KUBACH, H. E., *Romanesque Architecture*, Rizzoli, N.Y., 1988

LASKO, P., *Ars Sacra, 800–1200*, Pelican History of Art, Penguin, Baltimore, 1972

*MARTINDALE, A., *The Rise of the Artist in the Middle Ages and Early Renaissance*, McGraw-Hill, N.Y., 1972

*MÜTHERICH. F., & J. E. GAEHDE, *Carolingian Painting*, Braziller, N.Y., 1976

*NORDENFALK, C., *Early Medieval Book Illumination*, Skira/Rizzoli, Geneva/N.Y., 1988

PEVSNER, N., *An Outline of European Architecture*, 6th ed., Penguin, Baltimore, 1960

RUSSELL, J. B., *Dissent and Reform in the Early Middle Ages*, Univ. of California Press, Berkeley, 1965

SAALMAN, H., *Medieval Architecture*, Braziller, N.Y., 1962

SNYDER, J., *Medieval Art: Painting, Sculpture, Architecture: 4th–14th Century*, Abrams, N.Y., 1989

*STOKSTAD, M., *Medieval Art*, Icon Ed., Harper & Row, N.Y., 1986

## 3. ROMANESQUE ART

AUBERT, M., *Romanesque Cathedrals and Abbeys of France*, Vane, London, 1966

BOLOGNA, F., *Early Italian Painting: Romanesque and Early Medieval Art*, Van Nostrand, Princeton, 1964

BRAUNFELS, W., *Monasteries of Western Europe: The Architecture of the Orders*, 3d ed., Princeton Univ. Press, 1972

CAHN, W., *Romanesque Bible Illumination*, Cornell Univ. Press, Ithaca, 1982

COLLON-GEVAERT, S., J. LEJEUNE, & J. STIENNON, *A Treasury of Romanesque Art, Metalwork, Illumination and Sculpture from the Valley of the Meuse*, Phaidon, N.Y., 1972

DEMUS, O., *Romanesque Mural Painting*, Abrams, N.Y., 1971

DUBY, G., *The Age of the Cathedrals: Art and Society, 980–1420*, Univ. of Chicago Press, 1981

EVANS, J., *The Romanesque Architecture of the Order of Cluny*, 2d ed., AMS Press, N.Y., 1972

FOCILLON, H., *The Art of the West in the Middle Ages*, ed. by Jean Bony, 2 vols., Phaidon, N.Y., 1963

*GRABAR, A., *Romanesque Painting from the Eleventh to the Thirteenth Century: Mural Painting*, Skira, Geneva, 1958

HAZARD, H., ed., *The Art and Architecture of the Crusader States*. Univ. of Wisconsin Press, Madison, 1977

KAUFMANN, C. M., *Romanesque Manuscripts 1066–1190* (Survey of Manuscripts Illuminated in the British Isles, III), New York Graphic Society, Boston, 1978

KUBACH, H. E., *Romanesque Architecture*, Abrams, N.Y., 1975

*SAALMAN, H., *Medieval Cities*, Braziller, N.Y., 1968

SCHAPIRO, M., *Romanesque Art*, Braziller, N.Y., 1977

STODDARD, W. S., *Art and Architecture in Medieval France*, Harper & Row, N.Y., 1972

*SWARZENSKI, H., *Monuments of Romanesque Art: The Art of Church Treasures in North-Western Europe*, 2d ed., Univ. of Chicago Press, 1967

WEBB, G. F., *Architecture in Britain: The Middle Ages*, 2d ed., Pelican History of Art, Penguin, Baltimore, 1965

ZARNECKI, G., *Romanesque Art*, Universe Books, N.Y., 1971

## 4. GOTHIC ART

*Abbot Suger on the Abbey Church of St. Denis and Its Art Treasures*, tr. by E. Panofsky, Princeton Univ. Press, 1946

ACLAND, J. H., *Medieval Structure: The Gothic Vault*, Univ. of Toronto Press, 1972

*AVRIL, F., *Manuscript Painting at the Court of France: The Fourteenth Century, 1310–1380*, Braziller, N.Y., 1978

BATTISTI, E., *Cimabue*, Pennsylvania State Univ. Press, University Park, 1967

BAXANDALL, M., *Giotto and the Orators: Humanist Observers of Painting in Italy and the Discovery of Pictorial Composition, 1350–1450*, Clarendon Press, Oxford, 1971

BONY, J., *The English Decorated Style: Gothic Architecture Transformed, 1250–1350*, Cornell Univ. Press, Ithaca, 1979

——, *French Gothic Architecture of the 12th and 13th Centuries*, Univ. of California Press, Berkeley, 1983

*BOWIE, T., ed., *The Sketchbook of Villard de Honnecourt*, 3d ed., Indiana Univ. Press, Bloomington, 1968

*BRANNER, R., & S. P. BRANNER, *The Cathedral of Bourges and Its Place in Gothic Architecture*, MIT Press, Cambridge, 1988

——, *Chartres Cathedral*, Norton, N.Y., 1969

*——, *Gothic Architecture*, Braziller, N.Y., 1961

*CENNINI, C., *The Craftsman's Handbook (Il Libro dell'Arte)*, Dover, N.Y., 1954

COLE, B., *Giotto and Florentine Painting, 1280–1375*, Harper & Row, N.Y., 1976

DEUCHLER, F., *Gothic Art*, Universe Books, N.Y., 1973

*DUPONT, J., & C. GNUDI, *Gothic Painting*, Rizzoli, N.Y., 1977

ERLANDE-BRANDENBURG, A., *Gothic Art*, Abrams, N.Y., 1989

FRANKL, P., *Gothic Architecture*, Pelican History of Art, Penguin, Baltimore, 1962

*FRISCH, T. G., *Gothic Art: 1140–1450: Sources and Documents*, Prentice-Hall, Englewood Cliffs 1971

GRODECKI, L., *Gothic Architecture*, Abrams, N.Y., 1977

HARVEY, J. H., *Medieval Craftsmen*, Batsford, London, 1978

*HENDERSON, G. D. S., *Gothic Style and Civilization*, Penguin, Baltimore, 1967

*HOLT, E. G., ed., *A Documentary History of Art: Vol. I, The Middle Ages and the Renaissance*, 2d ed., Doubleday, Garden City, 1957

*JANTZEN, H., *High Gothic: The Classic Cathedrals of Chartres, Rheims, and Amiens*, Pantheon, N.Y., 1962

KRAUTHEIMER, R., & T. KRAUTHEIMER-HESS, *Lorenzo Ghiberti*, 2d ed., Princeton Univ. Press, 1970

LARNER, L., *Culture and Society in Italy, 1290–1420*, Scribner, N.Y., 1971

*MÂLE, E., *The Gothic Image: Religious Art in France of the Thirteenth Century*, Harper, N.Y., 1958

MARLE, R. VAN, *The Development of the Italian Schools of Painting*, 19 vols. (reprint, 1923–38 ed.), Hacker, N.Y., 1971

*MARTINDALE, A., *Gothic Art*, Praeger N.Y., 1967

*MEISS, M., *Giotto and Assisi*, Norton, N.Y., 1967

*——, *Painting in Florence and Siena after the Black Death*, Princeton Univ. Press, 1951

*PETERSEN, K., & J. J. WILSON, *Women Artists: Recognition and Reappraisal from the Early Middle Ages to the Twentieth Century*, Harper & Row, N.Y., 1976

POPE-HENNESSY, J. W., *Italian Gothic Sculpture*, 2d ed., Phaidon, N.Y., 1970

ROWLEY, G., *Ambrogio Lorenzetti*, 2 vols., Princeton Univ. Press, 1958

SAUERLÄNDER, W., *Gothic Sculpture in France, 1140–1270*, Abrams, N.Y., 1973

STUBBLEBINE, J. H., *Duccio di Buoninsegna and His School*, 2 vols., Princeton Univ. Press, 1979

*WATSON, P., *Building the Medieval Cathedrals*, Cambridge Univ. Press, 1976

WHITE, J., *Art and Architecture in Italy, 1250–1400*, Pelican History of Art, Penguin, Baltimore, 1966

——, *Duccio: Tuscan Art and the Medieval Workshop*, Thames & Hudson, N.Y., 1979

# GLOSSARY

ABACUS. A slab of stone at the top of a classical CAPITAL, just beneath the ARCHITRAVE (figs. 159, 161).

ABBEY. 1) A religious community headed by an abbot or abbess. 2) The buildings which house the community. An abbey church often has an especially large CHOIR to provide space for the monks or nuns (fig. 422).

ACADEMY. A place of study, the word coming from the Greek name of a garden near Athens where Plato and, later, Platonic philosophers held philosophical discussions from the 5th century B.C. to the 6th century A.D. The first academy of Fine arts, properly speaking, was the Academy of Drawing founded 1563 in Florence by Giorgio Vasari. Important later academies were the Royal Academy of Painting and Sculpture in Paris, founded 1648, and the Royal Academy of Arts in London, founded 1768. Their purpose was to foster the arts by systematic teaching, exhibitions, discussion, and occasionally by financial assistance.

ACANTHUS. 1) A Mediterranean plant having spiny or toothed leaves. 2) An architectural ornament resembling the leaves of this plant, used on MOLDINGS, FRIEZES, and Corinthian CAPITALS (figs. 151, 164).

AERIAL PERSPECTIVE. See PERSPECTIVE.

AISLE. See SIDE AISLE.

ALLA PRIMA. A painting technique in which PIGMENTS are laid on in one application with little or no UNDERPAINTING.

ALLAH. The unique and personal God of the MOSLEM faith.

ALTAR. 1) A mound or structure on which sacrifices or offerings are made in the worship of a deity. 2) In a Catholic church, a table-like structure used in celebrating the Mass.

ALTARPIECE. A painted or carved work of art placed behind and above the ALTAR of a Christian church. It may be a single panel (colorplate 59) or a TRIPTYCH or a POLYPTYCH having hinged wings painted on both sides (fig. 494). Also called a reredos or retable.

ALTERNATE SYSTEM. A system developed in Romanesque church architecture to provide adequate support for a GROIN-VAULTED NAVE having BAYS twice as long as the SIDE-AISLE bays. The PIERS of the nave ARCADE alternate in size; the heavier COMPOUND piers support the main nave vaults where the THRUST is concentrated, and smaller, usually cylindrical piers support the side-aisle vaults (figs. 391, 396).

AMAZON. One of a tribe of female warriors said in Greek legend to dwell near the Black Sea (fig. 194).

AMBULATORY. A covered walkway. 1) In a BASILICAN church, the semicircular passage around the APSE (fig. 422). 2) In a CENTRAL-PLAN church, the ring-shaped AISLE around the central space (fig. 307). 3) In a CLOISTER, the covered COLONNADED or ARCADED walk around the open courtyard.

AMPHITHEATER. A double THEATER. A building, usually oval in plan, consisting of tiers of seats and access corridors around the central theater area (figs. 235).

AMPHORA (pl. AMPHORAE). A large Greek storage vase with an oval body usually tapering toward the base; two handles extend from just below the lip to the shoulder (figs. 137).

ANDACHTSBILD. German for devotional picture. A picture or sculpture with a type of imagery intended for private devotion, first developed in northern Europe.

ANNULAR. From the Latin word for ring. Signifies a ring-shaped form, especially an annular barrel VAULT.

ANTA (pl. ANTAE). The front end of a wall of a Greek temple, thickened to produce a PILASTER-like member. Temples having COLUMNS between the antae are said to be "in antis" (fig. 160).

APOCALYPSE. The Book of Revelation, the last book of the New Testament. In it St. John the Evangelist describes his visions, experienced on the island of Patmos, of heaven, the future of mankind, and the Last Judgment.

APOSTLE. One of the twelve disciples chosen by Christ to accompany him in his lifetime, and to spread the GOSPEL after his death. The traditional list in Matt. 10:1-4 includes Andrew, Bartholomew, James the Greater (son of Zebedee), James the Less (son of Alphaeus), John, Judas Iscariot, Matthew, Peter, Philip, Simon the Canaanite, Thaddeus (or Jude), and Thomas. In art, however, the same twelve are not always represented since "apostle" was sometimes applied to other early Christians, such as St. Paul.

APSE. 1) A semicircular or polygonal niche terminating one or both ends of the NAVE in a Roman BASILICA (figs. 246). 2) In a Christian church, it is usually placed at the east end of the nave beyond the TRANSEPT or CHOIR (fig. 289); it is also sometimes used at the end of transept arms.

AQUEDUCT. Latin for duct of water. 1) An artificial channel or conduit for transporting water from a distant source. 2) The overground structure which carries the conduit across valleys, rivers, etc. (fig. 234).

ARCADE. A series of ARCHES supported by PIERS or COLUMNS (fig. 290). When attached to a wall, these form a blind arcade (fig. 403).

ARCH. A curved structure used to span an opening. Masonry arches are built of wedge-shaped blocks, called voussoirs, set with their narrow side toward the opening so that they lock together (figs. 226, 234). The topmost voussoir is called the keystone. Arches may take different shapes, as in the pointed Gothic arch (fig. 440), or the STILTED Islamic arch (fig. 341), but all require support from other arches or BUTTRESSES.

ARCHBISHOP. The chief BISHOP of an ecclesiastical district.

ARCHITRAVE. The lowermost member of a classical ENTABLATURE, i.e., a series of stone blocks that rest directly on the COLUMNS (figs. 159, 161).

ARCHIVOLT. A molded band framing an ARCH, or a series of such bands framing a TYMPANUM, often decorated with sculpture (fig. 408).

ARRICCIO. See SINOPIA.

ATRIUM. 1) The central court of a Roman house (fig. 247), or its open entrance court. 2) An open court, sometimes COLONNADED or ARCADED, in front of a church (figs. 289, 395).

ATTIC. A low upper story placed above the main CORNICE or ENTABLATURE of a building, and often decorated with windows and PILASTERS.

AURIGNACIAN. An adjective used for describing artifacts of an Upper PALEOLITHIC culture preceding the MAGDALENIAN; the word comes from Aurignac (Haute-Garonne), a site in southern France where such work was found.

BACCHANT (fem. BACCHANTE). A priest or priestess of the wine god, Bacchus (in Greek mythology, Dionysus), or one of his ecstatic female followers, who were sometimes called maenads (fig. 303).

BALUSTRADE. 1) A railing supported by short pillars called balusters. 2) Occasionally applied to any low parapet (figs. 189, 362).

BAPTISTERY. A building or a part of a church, often round or octagonal, in which the sacrament of baptism is administered (fig. 403). It contains a baptismal font, a receptacle of stone or metal which holds the water for the rite (fig. 412).

BARREL VAULT. See VAULT.

BASE. 1) The lowermost portion of a COLUMN or PIER, beneath the SHAFT (figs. 159, 174). 2) The lowest element of a wall, DOME, or building, or occasionally of a statue or painting (see PREDELLA).

BASILICA. 1) In ancient Roman architecture, a large, oblong building used as a hall of justice and public meeting place, generally having a NAVE, SIDE AISLES, and one or more APSES (fig. 246). 2) In Christian architecture, a longitudinal church derived from the Roman basilica, and having a nave, apse, two or four side aisles or side chapels, and sometimes a

NARTHEX. 3) One of the seven main churches of Rome (St. Peter's, St. Paul Outside the Walls, St. John Lateran, etc.), or another church accorded the same religious privileges.

BATTLEMENT. A parapet consisting of alternating solid parts and open spaces designed originally for defense and later used for decoration (fig. 454).

BAY. A subdivision of the interior space of a building, usually in a series bounded by consecutive architectural supports.

BENEDICTINE ORDER. Founded at Subiaco near Rome in 529 A.D. by St. Benedict of Nursia (c. 480–c. 543). Less austere than other early ORDERS, it spread throughout much of western Europe and England in the next two centuries.

BISHOP. The spiritual overseer of a number of churches or a diocese. His throne, or cathedra, placed in the principal church of the diocese, designates it as a cathedral.

BLIND ARCADE. See ARCADE.

BOOK. A written work of some length on consecutive sheets of PAPER, PARCHMENT, etc., fastened or bound together in a volume. See CODEX.

BOOK COVER. The stiff outer covers protecting the bound pages of a BOOK. In the medieval period, frequently covered with precious metal and elaborately embellished with jewels, embossed decoration, etc. (colorplate 41).

BOOK OF HOURS. A private prayer book containing the devotions for the seven canonical hours of the Roman Catholic church (matins, vespers, etc.), liturgies for local saints, and sometimes a calendar (colorplate 58). They were often elaborately ILLUMINATED for persons of high rank, whose names are attached to certain extant examples (fig. 500).

BRACKET. A stone, wooden, or metal support projecting from a wall and having a flat top to bear the weight of a statue, CORNICE, beam, etc. (fig. 410). The lower part may take the form of a SCROLL: it is then called a scroll bracket.

BROKEN PEDIMENT. See PEDIMENT.

BRONZE. An alloy of copper and tin, used since early times for sculpture. See BRONZE AGE, CIRE-PERDU.

BRONZE AGE. The earliest period in which BRONZE was used for tools and weapons. In the Middle East, the Bronze Age succeeded the NEOLITHIC period in c. 3500 B.C., and preceded the Iron Age, which commenced c. 1900 B.C.

BUTTRESS. 1) A projecting support built against an external wall, usually to counteract the lateral THRUST of a VAULT or ARCH within (fig. 425). 2) FLYING BUTTRESS. An arched bridge above the aisle roof that extends from the upper nave wall, where the lateral thrust of the main vault is greatest, down to a solid pier (fig. 427).

BYZANTIUM. City on the Sea of Marmara, founded by the ancient Greeks and renamed Constantinople in 330 A.D. Today called Istanbul.

CAESAR. The surname of the Roman dictator, Caius Julius Caesar, subsequently used as the title of an emperor; hence the German *Kaiser*, and the Russian *czar* (*tsar*).

CALIPH. A Moslem ruler; the first *caliph* succeeded MOHAMMED and claimed political and religious authority by his descent from the Prophet. Subsequently three caliphates were

recognized: Omayyids, Abbasids, and Fatimids.

CALLIGRAPHY. From the Greek word for beautiful writing. 1) Decorative or formal handwriting executed with a quill or reed pen, or with a brush (colorplates 28, 29; figs. 299, 351). 2) A design derived from or resembling letters, and used to form a pattern (colorplates 37, 38).

CAMPAGNA. Italian word for countryside. When capitalized, it usually refers to the countryside near Rome.

CAMPANILE. From the Italian word *campana*, meaning bell. A bell tower, either round or square in plan, and sometimes freestanding (figs. 291, 395).

CAMPOSANTO. Italian word for holy field. A cemetery near a church, and often enclosed.

CANOPY. In architecture, an ornamental, rooflike projection or cover above a statue or sacred object (fig. 458).

CAPITAL. The uppermost member of a COLUMN or PILLAR supporting the ARCHITRAVE (figs. 159, 173).

CARDINAL. In the Roman Catholic church, a member of the Sacred College, the ecclesiastical body which elects the pope and constitutes his advisory council.

CARMELITE ORDER. Originally a 12th-century hermitage claimed to descend from a community of hermits established by the Prophet Elijah on Mt. Carmel, Palestine. In the early 13th century it spread to Europe and England, where it was reformed by St. Simon Stock and became one of the three great mendicant orders (see FRANCISCAN, DOMINICAN).

CARTHUSIAN ORDER. See CHARTREUSE.

CARVING. 1) The cutting of a figure or design out of a solid material such as stone or wood, as contrasted to the additive technique of MODELING. 2) A work executed in this technique (figs. 55, 206).

CARYATID. A sculptured female figure used as an architectural support (figs. 154, 174). A similar male figure is an atlas (pl. atlantes).

CASTING. A method of duplicating a work of sculpture by pouring a hardening substance such as plaster or molten metal into a mold. See CIRE-PERDU.

CATACOMBS. The underground burial places of the early Christians, consisting of passages with niches for tombs, and small chapels for commemorative services.

CATHEDRA, CATHEDRAL. See BISHOP.

CELLA. 1) The principal enclosed room of a temple, to house an image (fig. 182). Also called the naos. 2) The entire body of a temple as distinct from its external parts.

CENTERING. A wooden framework built to support an ARCH, VAULT, or DOME during its construction.

CENTRAL-PLAN CHURCH. 1) A church having four arms of equal length. The CROSSING is often covered with a DOME. (fig. 322). Also called a Greek-cross church. 2) A church having a circular or polygonal plan. (figs. 306–8).

CHALK. Calcium carbonate, either natural or artificially prepared, finely ground to make a white substance used in GESSO. It may be pressed into sticks and used in its white form, or mixed with colored pigments to make pastels.

CHANCEL. See CHOIR.

CHAPEL. 1) A private or subordinate place of worship. 2) A place of worship that is part of a church, but separately dedicated.

CHARTREUSE. French word for a Carthusian monastery (in Italian, *Certosa*). The Carthusian ORDER was founded by St. Bruno (c. 1030–1101) at Chartreuse near Grenoble in 1084. It is an eremetic order, the life of the

monks being one of silence, prayer, and austerity.

CHASING. 1) A technique of ornamenting a metal surface by the use of various tools. 2) The procedure used to finish a raw bronze cast.

CHEVET. In Gothic architecture, the term for the developed and unified east end of a church, including choir, apse, ambulatory, and radiating chapels (fig. 431).

CHOIR. In church architecture, a square or rectangular area between the APSE and the NAVE or TRANSEPT. It is reserved for the clergy and the singing choir, and is usually marked off by steps, a railing, or a CHOIR SCREEN. Also called the chancel. See PILGRIMAGE CHOIR.

CHOIR SCREEN. A screen, frequently ornamented with sculpture, separating the CHOIR of a church from the NAVE or TRANSEPT (figs. 323, 465). In Orthodox Christian churches it is decorated with ICONS, and thus called an iconostasis (fig. 320).

CIRE-PERDU PROCESS. The lost-wax process of CASTING. A method in which an original is MODELED in wax or coated with wax, then covered with clay. When the wax is melted out, the resulting mold is filled with molten metal (often BRONZE) or liquid plaster.

CISTERCIAN ORDER. Founded at Citeaux in France in 1098 by Robert of Molesme with the objective of reforming the BENEDICTINE ORDER, and reasserting its original ideals of a life of severe simplicity.

CITY-STATE. An autonomous political unit comprising a city and the surrounding countryside.

CLERESTORY. A row of windows in the upper part of a wall that rises above an adjoining roof; built to provide direct lighting, as in a BASILICA or church (colorplate 47).

CLOISTER. 1) A place of religious seclusion such as a monastery or nunnery. 2) An open court attached to a church or monastery and surrounded by a covered ARCADED walk or AMBULATORY, as in Salisbury Cathedral. Used for study, meditation, and exercise.

CODEX (pl. CODICES). A manuscript in BOOK form made possible by the use of PARCHMENT instead of PAPYRUS. During the 1st to 4th centuries A.D., it gradually replaced the ROLL or SCROLL previously used for written documents.

COFFER. 1) A small chest or casket. 2) A recessed, geometrically shaped panel in a ceiling. A ceiling decorated with these panels is said to be coffered (fig. 239).

COLONNADE. A series of regularly spaced COLUMNS supporting a LINTEL or ENTABLATURE (fig. 76).

COLUMN. An approximately cylindrical, upright architectural support, usually consisting of a long, relatively slender SHAFT, a BASE, and a CAPITAL (figs. 159, 161). When imbedded in a wall, it is called an engaged column (fig. 175). Columns decorated with spiral RELIEFS were used occasionally as free-standing commemorative monuments (fig. 265).

COMPOUND PIER. See PIER.

CONCRETE. A mixture of sand or gravel with mortar and rubble, invented in the ancient Near East and further developed by the Romans (figs. 235, 236).

CONTRAPPOSTO. Italian word for set against. A method developed by the Greeks to represent freedom of movement in a figure. The parts of the body are placed asymmetrically in opposition to each other around a central axis, and careful attention is paid to the distribution of the weight (figs. 178, 179).

CORINTHIAN ORDER. See ORDER, ARCHITECTURAL.

CORNICE. 1) The projecting, framing members of a classical PEDIMENT, including the horizontal one beneath and the two sloping or "raking" ones above (figs. 159, 161). 2) Any projecting, horizontal element surmounting a wall or other structure, or dividing it horizontally for decorative purposes.

CRENELATED. See BATTLEMENT.

CROMLECH. From the Welsh for concave stone. A circle of large upright stones, or DOLMENS, probably the setting for religious ceremonies in prehistoric England (figs. 33, 34).

CROSSING. The area in a church where the TRANSEPT crosses the NAVE, frequently emphasized by a DOME (fig. 400), or crossing tower (fig. 383).

CROSS SECTION. See SECTION.

CRYPT. In a church, a VAULTED space beneath the CHOIR, causing the floor of the choir to be raised above the level of that of the NAVE (fig. 379).

CUNEIFORM. Describes the wedge-shaped characters written on clay by the ancient Mesopotamians.

CYCLOPEAN. An adjective describing masonry with large, unhewn stones, thought by the Greeks to have been built by the Cyclopes, a legendary race of one-eyed giants (fig. 131).


DEËSIS. From the Greek word for entreaty. The representation of Christ enthroned between the Virgin Mary and St. John the Baptist, frequent in Byzantine MOSAICS (colorplate 30) and depictions of the Last Judgment refers to the roles of the Virgin Mary and St. John as intercessors for mankind.

DIORITE. An igneous rock, extremely hard and usually black or dark gray in color (fig. 97).

DIPTYCH. 1) Originally a hinged two-leaved tablet used for writing. 2) A pair of ivory CARVINGS or PANEL paintings, usually hinged together (fig. 303).

DIPYLON VASE. A Greek funerary vase with holes in the bottom through which libations were poured to the dead (fig. 135). Named for the cemetery near Athens where the vases were found.

DOLMEN. A structure formed by two or more large, upright stones capped by a horizontal slab; thought to be a prehistoric tomb (fig. 32).

DOME. 1) A true dome is a VAULTED roof of circular, polygonal, or elliptical plan, formed with hemispherical or ovoidal curvature. May be supported by a circular wall or DRUM (fig. 238), and by PENDENTIVES (fig. 309) or related constructions.

DOMINICAN ORDER. Founded as a mendicant ORDER by St. Dominic in Toulouse about 1206–16.

DOMUS. Latin word for house. A Roman detached, one-family house with rooms grouped around one, or frequently two, open courts. The first, the ATRIUM, was used for entertaining and conducting business; the second, usually with a garden and surrounded by a PERISTYLE or COLONNADE, was for the private family (fig. 247).

DONJON. See KEEP.

DONOR. The patron or client at whose order a work of art was executed; the donor may be depicted in the work (fig. 469).

DORIC ORDER. See ORDER, ARCHITECTURAL.

DRÔLERIES. French word for jests. Used to describe the lively animals and small figures in the margins of late medieval manuscripts (fig.

500), and occasionally in wood CARVINGS on furniture.

DRUM. 1) A section of the SHAFT of a COLUMN (figs. 169, 245). 2) A wall supporting a DOME (fig. 322).


ECHINUS. In the Doric or Tuscan ORDER, the round, cushion-like element between the top of the SHAFT and the ABACUS (figs. 159, 162).

ELDERS, TWENTY-FOUR. The twenty-four elders frequently represented on the PORTALS of Romanesque and Gothic churches (fig. 456) are those described by St. John the Evangelist in his vision of heaven, clad in white and seated around the throne of God (Rev. 4:4, 10).

ELEVATION. 1) An architectural drawing presenting a building as if projected on a vertical plane parallel to one of its sides. 2) Term used in describing the vertical plane of a building.

ENAMEL. 1) Colored glassy substances, either opaque or translucent, applied in powder form to a metal surface and fused to it by firing. Two main techniques developed: "champlevé" (from the French for raised field), in which the areas to be treated are dug out of the metal surface; and "cloisonné" (from the French for partitioned), in which compartments or "cloisons" to be filled are made on the surface with thin metal strips. 2) A work executed in either technique (figs. 357, 420).

ENCAUSTIC. A technique of painting with PIGMENTS dissolved in hot wax (colorplate 25).

ENGAGED COLUMN. See COLUMN.

ENTABLATURE. 1) In a classical order, the entire structure above the COLUMNS; this usually includes ARCHITRAVE, FRIEZE, and CORNICE (figs. 159, 161). 2) The same structure in any building of a classical style.

ENTASIS. A swelling of the SHAFT of a COLUMN (figs. 162, 166).

EVANGELISTS. Matthew, Mark, Luke, and John, traditionally thought to be the authors of the GOSPELS, the first four books of the New Testament, which recount the life and death of Christ. They are usually shown with their symbols, which are probably derived from the four beasts surrounding the throne of the Lamb in the Book of Revelation (4:7) or from those in the vision of Ezekiel (1:4-14): a winged man or angel for Matthew (fig. 651), a winged lion for Mark (fig. 372), a winged ox for Luke (colorplate 42), and an eagle for John (colorplate 45). These symbols may also represent the Evangelists (colorplate 27, fig. 362).


FAÇADE. The principal face or the front of a building.

FALISCAN WARE. Pottery made in the Etruscan city of Falerii (the present Città Castellana), its inhabitants known as the Falisci (fig. 192).

FATHERS OF THE CHURCH. Early teachers and defenders of the Christian faith. Those most frequently represented are the four Latin fathers: St. Jerome, St. Ambrose, and St. Augustine, all of the 4th century, and St. Gregory the 6th.

FIBULA. A clasp, buckle, or brooch, often ornamented.

FINIAL. A relatively small, decorative element terminating a GABLE, PINNACLE, or the like (fig. 453).

FLUTING. In architecture, the ornamental grooves channeled vertically into the SHAFT of a COLUMN or PILASTER (fig. 169). They

may meet in a sharp edge as in the Doric ORDER, or be separated by a narrow strip or fillet, as in the Ionic, Corinthian, and Composite orders.

FLYING BUTTRESS. See BUTTRESS.

FONT. See BAPTISTERY.

FORUM (pl. FORA). In an ancient Roman city, the main, public square which was the center of judicial and business activity, and a public gathering place (fig. 233).

FRANCISCAN ORDER. Founded as a mendicant ORDER by St. Francis of Assisi (Giovanni di Bernardone, 1181/82–1226). The monks' aim was to imitate the life of Christ in its poverty and humility, to preach, and to minister to the spiritual needs of the poor.

FRESCO. Italian word for fresh. 1) True fresco is the technique of painting on moist plaster with PIGMENTS ground in water so that the paint is absorbed by the plaster and becomes part of the wall itself (colorplate 53). Fresco secco is the technique of painting with the same colors on dry plaster. 2) A painting done in either of these techniques.

FRIEZE. 1) A continuous band of painted or sculptured decoration (figs. 154, 259). 2) In a classical building, the part of the ENTABLATURE between the ARCHITRAVE and the CORNICE. A Doric frieze consists of alternating TRIGLYPHS and METOPES, the latter often sculptured (fig. 166). An Ionic frieze is usually decorated with continuous RELIEF sculpture (fig. 159).


GABLE. 1) The triangular area framed by the CORNICE or eaves of a building and the sloping sides of a pitched roof (fig. 376). In classical architecture, it is called a PEDIMENT. 2) A decorative element of similar shape, such as the triangular structures above the PORTALS of a Gothic church (fig. 433), and sometimes at the top of a Gothic picture frame.

GALLERY. A second story placed over the SIDE AISLES of a church and below the CLERESTORY (fig. 424), or, in a church with a four-part ELEVATION, below the TRIFORIUM and above the NAVE ARCADE which supports it on its one side.

GESSO. A smooth mixture of ground CHALK or plaster and glue, used as the basis for TEMPERA PAINTING and for OIL PAINTING on PANEL.

GILDING. 1) A coat of gold or of a gold-colored substance that is applied mechanically or chemically to surfaces of a painting, sculpture, or architectural decoration (colorplate 59). 2) The process of applying same.

GLAZE. 1) A thin layer of translucent oil color applied to a painted surface or to parts of it in order to modify the tone. 2) A glassy coating applied to a piece of ceramic work before firing in the kiln; as a protective seal and often as decoration.

GLORIOLE or GLORY. The circle of radiant light around the head or figures of God, Christ, the Virgin Mary, or a saint. When it surrounds the head only, it is called a halo or nimbus (colorplate 56); when it surrounds the entire figure with a large oval (figs. 328, 456), it is called a mandorla (the Italian word for almond). It indicates divinity or holiness, though originally it was placed around the heads of kings and gods as a mark of distinction.

GOLD LEAF, SILVER LEAF. 1) Gold beaten into very thin sheets or "leaves," and applied to ILLUMINATED MANUSCRIPTS and PANEL paintings (colorplates 45, 56, 59), to sculpture, or to the back of the glass TESSERAE used in MOSAICS (colorplates 27, 29). 2) Silver leaf is also used, though ultimately it tarnishes (colorplate 28). Sometimes called gold foil, silver foil.

GORGON. In Greek mythology, one of three hideous, female monsters with large heads, and snakes for hair (fig. 152). Their glance turned men to stone. Medusa, the most famous of the Gorgons, was killed by Perseus only with help from the gods.

GOSPEL. 1) The first four books of the New Testament. They tell the story of Christ's life and death, and are ascribed to the EVANGELISTS Matthew, Mark, Luke, and John. 2) A copy of these, usually called a Gospel Book, often richly ILLUMINATED (figs. 370, 372).

GREEK-CROSS CHURCH. See CENTRAL-PLAN CHURCH.

GROIN VAULT. See VAULT.

GROUND PLAN. An architectural drawing presenting a building as if cut horizontally at the floor level.

GUTTAE. In a Doric ENTABLATURE, small peglike projections above the FRIEZE; possibly derived from pegs originally used in wooden construction (figs. 159, 161).

HALL CHURCH, HALL CHOIR. See HALLENKIRCHE.

HALLENKIRCHE. German word for hall church. A church in which the NAVE and the SIDE AISLES are of the same height. The type was developed in Romanesque architecture, and occurs especially frequently in German Gothic churches (figs. 388, 444).

HALO. See GLORIOLE.

HIEROGLYPH. A picture of a figure, animal, or object, standing for a word, syllable, or sound. These symbols are found on ancient Egyptian monuments as well as in their written records (fig. 73).

HIGH RELIEF. See RELIEF.

ICON. From the Greek word for image. A PANEL painting of one or more sacred personages such as Christ, the Virgin, a saint, etc., particularly venerated in the ORTHODOX Catholic church (colorplate 34).

ICONOSTASIS. See CHOIR SCREEN.

ILLUMINATED MANUSCRIPT. A MANUSCRIPT decorated with drawings (fig. 373) or with paintings in TEMPERA colors (colorplates 42, 45).

ILLUSIONISM. In artistic terms, the technique of manipulating pictorial or other means in order to cause the eye to perceive a particular reality. May be used in architecture and sculpture (fig. 220), as well as in painting (colorplate 23; figs. 277–279).

IN ANTIS. See ANTA.

INSULA (pl. INSULAE). Latin word for island. 1) An ancient Roman city block. 2) A Roman "apartment house": a CONCRETE and brick building or chain of buildings around a central court, up to five stories high. The ground floor contained shops, and above were living quarters (fig. 248).

IONIC ORDER. See ORDER, ARCHITECTURAL.

ISLAM. The religion of the MOSLEMS, based on the submission of the faithful to the will of ALLAH as this was revealed to the Prophet MOHAMMED and recorded in the KORAN. The adjectival form is Islamic.

JAMBS. The vertical sides of an opening. In Romanesque and Gothic churches, the jambs of doors and windows are often cut on a slant outward, or "splayed," thus providing a broader surface for sculptural decoration (figs. 456, 457).

KAABA. An ancient Arabic SANCTUARY in the Great Mosque at Mecca which became the most sacred shrine of the MOSLEMS. The small building in the mosque contains a stone which is said to have been turned black either by the tears of pilgrims, or by the sins of those who have touched it.

KEEP. 1) The innermost and strongest structure or central tower of a medieval castle, sometimes used as living quarters, as well as for defense. Also called a donjon (colorplate 58). 2) A fortified medieval castle.

KEYSTONE. See ARCH.

KORAN. The scriptures of the MOSLEMS, revealed by ALLAH to MOHAMMED at Mecca and Medina, and transcribed by the Prophet himself, or by one of his associates. The text was established 651–52 A.D.

KORE (pl. KORAI). Greek word for maiden. An archaic Greek statue of a clothed, standing female (fig. 150).

KOUROS (pl. KOUROI). Greek word for male youth. An archaic Greek statue of a standing, nude youth (fig. 146).

KYLIX. In Greek and Roman antiquity, a shallow drinking cup with two horizontal handles, often set on a stem terminating in a foot (fig. 140).

LABORS OF THE MONTHS. The various occupations suitable to the months of the year. Scenes or figures illustrating these were frequently represented in ILLUMINATED manuscripts (colorplate 58, fig. 504); sometimes with the symbols of the ZODIAC signs, CARVED around the PORTALS of Romanesque and Gothic churches (figs. 456, 463).

LANTERN. A relatively small structure crowning a DOME, roof, or tower, frequently open to admit light to an enclosed area below (fig. 322).

LAPIS LAZULI. From the Latin for stone of blue. A deep-blue stone used first for ornamental purposes (colorplate 9), or, after the 12th century, for preparing the blue PIGMENT known as ultramarine.

LAPITH. A member of a mythical Greek tribe that defeated the centaurs in a battle, scenes from which are frequently represented in vase painting and sculpture (colorplate 14, fig. 182).

LEKYTHOS (pl. LEKYTHOI). A Greek oil jug with an ellipsoidal body, a narrow neck, a flanged mouth, a curved handle extending from below the lip to the shoulder, and a narrow base terminating in a foot. It was used chiefly for ointments and funerary offerings (colorplate 16).

LIBERAL ARTS. Traditionally thought to go back to Plato, they comprised the intellectual disciplines considered suitable or necessary to a complete education, and included Grammar, Rhetoric, Logic, Arithmetic, Music, Geometry, and Astronomy. During the Middle Ages and the Renaissance, they were often represented allegorically in painting, engravings, and sculpture (fig. 456).

LINTEL. See POST AND LINTEL.

LONGITUDINAL SECTION. See SECTION.

LOW RELIEF. See RELIEF.

MADRASAH. Arabic for place of study. A combination of a Mohammedan mosque and theological school, with living quarters for students (fig. 343).

MAESTÀ. Italian word for majesty, applied in the 14th and 15th centuries to representations of the Madonna and Child enthroned, and surrounded by her celestial court of saints and angels (fig. 487).

MAGDALENIAN. An adjective used for describing artifacts of the latest culture of the Upper PALEOLITHIC; the word comes from La Madeleine (Dordogne), a site in southwestern France where such work was found.

MAGUS (pl. MAGI). 1) A member of the priestly caste of ancient Media and Persia. In Christian literature (Matt. 2:1–12), one of the three Wise Men or Kings who came from the East bearing gifts to the newborn Jesus (fig. 507, colorplate 59).

MANDORLA. See GLORIOLE.

MANUSCRIPT. From the Latin word for handwritten. 1) A document, scroll, or book written by hand, as distinguished from such a work in print (i.e., after c. 1450). 2) A book produced in the Middle Ages, frequently ILLUMINATED.

MASTABA. An ancient Egyptian tomb, rectangular in shape, with sloping sides and a flat roof. It covered a chapel for offerings and a shaft to the burial chamber (fig. 56).

MAUSOLEUM. 1) The huge tomb erected at Halicarnassus in Asia Minor in the 4th century B.C. by King Mausolus and his wife Artemisia (fig. 193). 2) A generic term for any large funerary monument.

MEANDER. From the name Maeander (modern Menderes), a winding river in western Turkey that flows into the Aegean Sea. A decorative motif of intricate, rectilinear character, applied to architecture and sculpture (figs. 261, 410).

MEGALITH. A huge stone such as those used in CROMLECHS and DOLMENS.

MEGARON (pl. MEGARONS, or MEGARA). From the Greek word for large. The central audience hall in a Minoan or Mycenaean palace or home (fig. 118).

MESOLITHIC. Transitional period of the Stone Age, between the PALEOLITHIC and the NEOLITHIC.

METOPE. In a Doric FRIEZE, one of the panels, either decorated or plain, between the TRIGLYPHS. Originally it probably covered the empty spaces between the ends of the wooden ceiling beams (figs. 159–66).

MIHRAB. The small niche which marks the QIBLA wall of a mosque showing the direction of Mecca.

MINARET. A tall, slender tower with balconies from which Moslems are summoned to prayer by the chant of the MUEZZIN (fig. 346).

MINIATURE. 1) A single illustration in an ILLUMINATED manuscript (colorplates 36–39). 2) A very small painting, especially a portrait on ivory, glass, or metal (fig. 285).

MINOTAUR. In Greek mythology, a monster having the head of a bull and the body of a man, who lived in the Labyrinth of the palace of Knossos on Crete.

MODEL. 1) The preliminary form of a sculpture, often finished in itself but preceding the final CASTING or CARVING. 2) Preliminary or reconstructed form of a building, made to scale (figs. 231, 369). 3) A person who poses for an artist (fig. 7).

MODELING. 1) In sculpture, the building up of a figure or design in a soft substance such as clay or wax (colorplate 19). 2) In painting and drawing, producing a three-dimensional effect by changes in color, the use of light and shade, etc.

MOHAMMED (also Muhammad). Arab prophet and the founder of ISLAM (c. 570–632). His first revelations were c. 610 and continued throughout his lifetime; collected and recorded, these form the basis of the KORAN. Mohammed was forced to flee from Mecca, his birthplace, to Medina in 622; the date of this "Hegira" marks the beginning of the Islamic calendar.

MOLDING. In architecture, any of various long, narrow, ornamental bands having a distinctive profile, which project from the surface of the structure and give variety to the surface by means of their patterned contrasts of light and shade (figs. 154, 262).

MOSAIC. Decorative work for walls, VAULTS, ceilings, or floors, composed of small pieces of colored materials (called TESSERAE) set in plaster or CONCRETE. The Romans, whose work was mostly for floors, used regularly shaped pieces of marble in its natural colors (colorplate 21). The early Christians used pieces of glass whose brilliant hues, including gold, and slightly irregular surfaces produced an entirely different, glittering effect (colorplates 27, 29). See also GOLD LEAF.

MOSLEM (also Muslim). 1) One who has embraced ISLAM: a follower of MOHAMMED. 2) An adjective for the religion, law, or civilization of Islam.

MOUNDS. Enormous piles of earth erected by the Indians of the central United States, the so-called Mound Builders, as a grave and/or BASE for a temple or other structure. Sometimes in the form of an animal (fig. 35).

MUEZZIN. In Mohammedan countries, a crier who calls the faithful to prayer from a MINARET or high part of a building.

MURAL. From the Latin word for wall, murus. A large painting or decoration, either executed directly on a wall (FRESCO) or done separately and affixed to it.

MUSES. In Greek mythology, the nine goddesses who presided over various arts and sciences. They are led by Apollo as god of music and poetry, and usually include Calliope, Muse of Epic Poetry; Clio, Muse of History; Erato, Muse of Love Poetry; Euterpe, Muse of Music; Melpomene, Muse of Tragedy; Polyhymnia, Muse of Sacred Music; Terpsichore, Muse of Dancing; Thalia, Muse of Comedy; and Urania, Muse of Astronomy.

NAOS. See CELLA.

NARTHEX. The transverse entrance hall of a church, sometimes enclosed but often open on one side to a preceding ATRIUM (fig. 289).

NAVE. 1) The central aisle of a Roman BASILICA, as distinguished from the SIDE AISLES (fig. 246). 2) The same section of a Christian basilican church extending from the entrance to the APSE or TRANSEPT (fig. 289).

NEOLITHIC. The New Stone Age, thought to have begun c. 9000–8000 B.C. The first society to live in settled communities, to domesticate animals, and to cultivate crops, it saw the beginning of many new skills such as spinning, weaving, and building (fig. 23).

NEW STONE AGE. See NEOLITHIC.

NIKE. The ancient Greek goddess of victory, often identified with Athena, and by the Romans with Victoria. She is usually represented as a winged woman with windblown draperies (figs. 139, 189, 206).

NIMBUS. See GLORIOLE.

OBELISK. A tall, tapering, four-sided stone shaft with a pyramidal top. First constructed as

MEGALITHS in ancient Egypt (fig. 76); certain examples since exported to other countries.

OLD STONE AGE. See PALEOLITHIC.

ORCHESTRA. 1) In an ancient Greek theater, the round space in front of the stage and below the tiers of seats, reserved for the chorus (fig. 176). 2) In a Roman theater, a similar space usually reserved for important guests.

ORDER, ARCHITECTURAL. An architectural system based on the COLUMN and its ENTABLATURE, in which the form of the elements themselves (CAPITAL, SHAFT, BASE, etc.) and their relationships to each other are specifically defined. The five classical orders are the Doric, Ionic, Corinthian, Tuscan, and Composite (fig. 159). See also SUPERIMPOSED ORDER.

ORDER, MONASTIC. A religious society whose members live together under an established set of rules. See BENEDICTINE, CARMELITE, CHARTREUSE, CISTERCIAN, DOMINICAN, FRANCISCAN.

ORTHODOX. From the Greek word for right in opinion. The Eastern Orthodox Church, which split from the Western Catholic Church during the 5th century A.D. and transferred its allegiance from the pope in Rome to the Byzantine emperor in Constantinople and his appointed patriarch. Sometimes called the Byzantine church.

PAINT. See ENCAUSTIC, FRESCO, TEMPERA PAINTING, WATERCOLOR.

PALAZZO (pl. PALAZZI). Italian word for palace (in French, palais). Refers either to large, official buildings (fig. 454), or to important private town houses.

PALEOLITHIC. The Old Stone Age: usually divided into Lower, Middle, and Upper (which began about 35,000 B.C.). A society of nomadic hunters who used stone implements, later developing ones of bone and flint. Some lived in caves, which they decorated during the latter stages of the age (colorplate 2, fig. 15), at which time they also produced small CARVINGS in bone, horn, and stone (figs. 19, 20).

PALETTE. 1) A thin, usually oval or oblong board with a thumb hole at one end, used by painters to hold and mix their colors. 2) The range of colors used by a particular painter. 3) In Egyptian art, a slate slab, usually decorated with sculpture in low RELIEF. The small ones with a recessed circular area on one side are thought to have been used for eye makeup. The larger ones were commemorative objects (figs. 53, 54).

PANEL. 1) A wooden surface used for painting, usually in TEMPERA, and prepared beforehand with a layer of GESSO. Large ALTARPIECES require the joining together of two or more boards

PANTHEON. A temple dedicated to all the gods (figs. 238, 239), or housing tombs of the illustrious dead of a nation, or memorials to them.

PANTOCRATOR. A representation of Christ as ruler of the universe which appears frequently in the DOME or APSE MOSAICS of Byzantine churches (fig. 321).

PAPYRUS. 1) A tall aquatic plant that grows abundantly in the Near East, Egypt, and Abyssinia. 2) A paperlike material made by laying together thin strips of the pith of this plant, and then soaking, pressing, and drying the whole. The resultant sheets were used as writing material by the ancient Egyptians, Greeks, and Romans. 3) An ancient document or SCROLL written on this material.

PARCHMENT. From Pergamum, the name of a Greek city in Asia Minor where parchment was invented in the 2nd century B.C. 1) A paperlike material made from thin bleached animal hides, used extensively in the Middle Ages for MANUSCRIPTS (colorplates 39, 42, 45). Vellum is a superior type of parchment, made from calfskin. 2) A document or miniature on this material.

PASSION. 1) In ecclesiastic terms, the events of Christ's last week on earth. 2) The representation of these events in pictorial, literary, theatrical, or musical form (colorplates 53, 54).

PEDIMENT. 1) In classical architecture, a low GABLE, typically triangular, framed by a horizontal CORNICE below and two raking cornices above; frequently filled with relief sculpture (fig. 156). 2) A similar architectural member, either round or triangular, used over a door, window, or niche. When pieces of the cornice are either turned at an angle or broken, it is called a broken pediment (fig. 249).

PENDENTIVE. One of the spherical triangles which achieve the transition from a square or polygonal opening to the round BASE of a DOME or the supporting DRUM (figs. 316, 320).

PEPLOS. An outer garment worn draped in folds by women in ancient Greece (fig. 150).

PERIPTERAL. An adjective describing a building surrounded by a single row of COLUMNS or COLONNADE (figs. 160, 166).

PERISTYLE. 1) In a Roman house or DOMUS, an open garden court surrounded by a COLONNADE (fig. 252). 2) A colonnade around a building or court (fig. 160).

PICTURE PLANE. The flat surface on which a picture is painted.

PIER. An upright architectural support, usually rectangular, and sometimes with CAPITAL and BASE (fig. 220). When COLUMNS, PILASTERS, or SHAFTS are attached to it, as in many Romanesque and Gothic churches, it is called a compound pier (fig. 391).

PIETÀ. Italian word for both pity and piety. A representation of the Virgin grieving over the dead Christ (fig. 468). When used in a scene recording a specific moment after the Crucifixion, it is usually called a "Lamentation" (fig. 491).

PIGMENT. Colored substances found in organic and inorganic sources. Pigment finely divided and suspended in a liquid medium becomes a paint, ink, etc. See TEMPERA PAINTING, WATERCOLOR, FRESCO.

PILASTER. A flat, vertical element projecting from a wall surface, and normally having a BASE, SHAFT, and CAPITAL. It has generally a decorative rather than structural purpose.

PILGRIMAGE CHOIR. The unit in a Romanesque church composed of the APSE, AMBULATORY, and RADIATING CHAPELS (figs. 384, 423).

PILLAR. A general term for a vertical architectural support which includes COLUMNS, PIERS, and PILASTERS.

PINNACLE. A small, decorative structure capping a tower, PIER, BUTTRESS, or other architectural member, and used especially in Gothic buildings (figs. 434, 436).

PLAN. See GROUND PLAN.

PODIUM. 1) The tall base upon which rests an Etruscan or Roman temple (fig. 227). 2) The ground floor of a building made to resemble such a base.

POLYPTYCH. An ALTARPIECE or devotional work of art made of several panels joined together (colorplate 51), often hinged.

PORCH. General term for an exterior appendage to a building which forms a covered approach to a doorway (fig. 433). See PORTICO for porches consisting of columns.

PORTA. Latin word for door or gate (fig. 226).

PORTAL. A door or gate, usually a monumental one with elaborate sculptural decoration (figs. 456, 469).

PORTICO. A porch supporting a roof or an EN-TABLATURE and PEDIMENT, often approached by a number of steps (fig. 227). It provides a monumental covered entrance to a building, and a link with the space surrounding it.

POST AND LINTEL. A basic system of construction in which two or more uprights, the "posts," support a horizontal member, the "lintel." The lintel may be the topmost element (figs. 33, 34), or support a wall or roof (fig. 131).

PREDELLA. The base of an ALTARPIECE, often decorated with small scenes which are related in subject to that of the main panel or panels (colorplate 59).

PRONAOS. In a Greek or Roman temple, an open vestibule in front of the CELLA (fig. 160).

PROPYLAEUM (pl. PROPYLAEA). 1) The entrance to a temple or other enclosure, especially when it is an elaborate structure. 2) The monumental entry gate at the western end of the Acropolis in Athens (figs. 169).

PSALTER. 1) The book of Psalms in the Old Testament, thought to have been written in part by David, king of ancient Israel. 2) A copy of the Psalms, sometimes arranged for liturgical or devotional use, and often richly ILLUMINATED (colorplate 33).

PULPIT. A raised platform in a church from which the clergyman delivers a sermon or conducts the service. Its railing or enclosing wall may be elaborately decorated (fig. 471).

PYLON. Greek word for gateway. 1) The monumental entrance building to an Egyptian temple or forecourt, consisting of either a massive wall with sloping sides pierced by a doorway, or of two such walls flanking a central gateway (fig. 76). 2) A tall structure at either side of a gate, bridge, or avenue, marking an approach or entrance.

QIBLA. The direction of Mecca, toward which Moslems turn when praying. It is indicated in a mosque by the MIHRAB (niche) in the "qibla wall."

QUARTZITE. An extremely compact, granular rock, consisting essentially of quartz (fig. 72).

QUATREFOIL. An ornamental element composed of four lobes radiating from a common center (figs. 463, 479).

RADIATING CHAPELS. Term for CHAPELS arranged around the AMBULATORY (and sometimes the TRANSEPT) of a medieval church (figs. 383, 423, 434).

REFECTORY. 1) A room for refreshment. 2) The dining hall of a monastery, college, or other large institution.

RELIEF. 1) The projection of a figure or part of a design from the background or plane on which it is CARVED or MODELED. Sculpture done in this manner is described as "high relief" or "low relief" depending on the height of the projection (figs. 55, 265). 2) The apparent projection of forms represented in a painting or drawing.

RESPOND. 1) A half-PIER, PILASTER, or similar element projecting from a wall to support a LINTEL, or an ARCH whose other side is supported by a free-standing COLUMN or pier, as at the end of an ARCADE (colorplate 27). 2) One of several pilasters on a wall behind a COLONNADE (fig. 249) which echo or "respond to" the columns, but are largely decorative. 3) One of the slender shafts of a COMPOUND PIER in a medieval church which seems to carry the weight of the VAULT (figs. 394, 430).

RHYTON. An ancient drinking horn made from pottery or metal, and frequently having a base formed by a human or animal head (fig. 112).

RIB. A slender, projecting archlike member which supports a VAULT either transversely (fig. 386), or at the GROINS, thus dividing the surface into sections (fig. 394). In late Gothic architecture, its purpose is often primarily ornamental (fig. 441).

RIBBED VAULT. See VAULT.

ROLL. A long sheet of PAPYRUS or PARCHMENT with a written text, sometimes illustrated, used as a book before the introduction of the CODEX. Also called a SCROLL, and, in Latin, a *rotulus* (fig. 219).

ROOD SCREEN. See CHOIR SCREEN.

ROSE WINDOW. A large, circular window with stained glass and stone TRACERY, frequently used on FAÇADES and at the ends of TRANSEPTS of Gothic churches (figs. 426, 429).

ROSTRUM. 1) A beak-like projection from the prow of an ancient warship, used for ramming the enemy. 2) In the Roman FORUM, the raised platform decorated with the beaks of captured ships, from which speeches were delivered (fig. 274). 3) A platform, stage, or the like used for public speaking.

SACRISTY. A room near the main altar of a church, or a small building attached to a church, where the vessels and vestments required for the service are kept. Also called a vestry.

SANCTUARY. 1) A sacred or holy place or building. 2) An especially holy place within a building, such as the CELLA of a temple, or the part of a church around the altar.

SANGUINE. A reddish-brown CHALK stick used for drawing.

SARCOPHAGUS (pl. SARCOPHAGI). A large stone coffin usually decorated with sculpture and/or inscriptions (figs. 216, 301). The term is derived from two Greek words meaning flesh and eating, which were applied to a kind of limestone in ancient Greece, since the stone was said to turn flesh to dust.

SATYR. One of a class of woodland gods thought to be the lascivious companions of Dionysus, the Greek god of wine (or of Bacchus, his Roman counterpart). They are represented as having the legs and tail of a goat, the body of a man, and a head with horns and pointed ears. A youthful satyr is also called a faun (colorplate 24, fig. 202).

SCRIPTORIUM (pl. SCRIPTORIA). A workroom in a monastery reserved for copying and illustrating MANUSCRIPTS.

SCROLL. 1) An architectural ornament with the form of a partially unrolled spiral, as on the CAPITALS of the Ionic and Corinthian ORDERS (figs. 159, 174). 2) A form of written text: see ROLL.

SCROLL BRACKET. See BRACKET.

SECTION. An architectural drawing presenting a building as if cut across the vertical plane, at right angles to the horizontal plane. Cross section: a cut along the transverse axis. Longitudinal section: a cut along the longitudinal axis.

SEXPARTITE VAULT. See VAULT.

SHAFT. In architecture, the part of a COLUMN between the BASE and the CAPITAL (fig. 159).

SIDE AISLE. A passageway running parallel to the NAVE of a Roman BASILICA or Christian church, separated from it by an ARCADE or COLONNADE (figs. 246, 289). There may be one on either side of the nave, or two, an inner and outer.

SILENI. A class of minor woodland gods in the entourage of the wine god, Dionysus (or Bacchus). Like Silenus, the wine god's tutor and drinking companion, they are thick-lipped and snub-nosed, and fond of wine. Similar to SATYRS, they are basically human in form except for horse's tails and ears (colorplate 24).

SILVER LEAF. See GOLD LEAF.

SINOPIA (pl. SINOPIE). Italian word taken from Sinope, the ancient city in Asia Minor which was famous for its brick-red PIGMENT. In FRESCO paintings, a full-sized, preliminary sketch done in this color on the first rough coat of plaster or "arriccio" (fig. 498).

SKENE. See THEATER.

SPANDREL. The area between the exterior curves of two adjoining ARCHES, or, in the case of a single arch, the area around its outside curve from its springing to its keystone (figs. 273, 304).

SPHINX. 1) In ancient Egypt, a creature having the head of a man, animal, or bird, and the body of a lion; frequently sculpted in monumental form (fig. 64). 2) In Greek mythology, a creature usually represented as having the head and breasts of a woman, the body of a lion, and the wings of an eagle. It appears in classical, Renaissance, and Neoclassical art.

STEATITE. Soapstone, commonly gray or grayish-green in color (fig. 125).

STELE. From the Greek word for standing block. An upright stone slab or pillar with a CARVED commemorative design or inscription (figs. 95, 190).

STEREOBATE. The substructure of a classical building, especially a Greek temple (fig. 159).

STOA. In Greek architecture, a covered COLONNADE, sometimes detached and of considerable length, used as a meeting place or promenade.

STOIC. A school of philosophy founded by Zeno about 300 B.C., and named after the STOA in Athens where he taught. Its main thesis is that man should be free of all passions.

STUCCO. 1) A CONCRETE or cement used to coat the walls of a building. 2) A kind of plaster used for architectural decorations such as CORNICES, MOLDINGS, etc., (fig. 342) or for sculptured RELIEFS (figs. 220, 262).

STYLOBATE. A platform or masonry floor above the STEREOBATE forming the foundation for the COLUMNS of a classical temple (fig. 159).

STYLUS. From the Latin word *stilus*, a pointed instrument used in ancient times for writing on tablets of a soft material such as clay.

SUPERIMPOSED ORDERS. Two or more rows of COLUMNS, PIERS, or PILASTERS placed above each other on the wall of a building (fig. 236).

TABERNACLE. 1) A place or house of worship. 2) A CANOPIED niche or recess built for an image. 3) The portable shrine used by the Jews to house the Ark of the Covenant (colorplate 26).

TABLINUM. From the Latin word meaning writing tablet, or written record. In a Roman house, a small room at the far end of the ATRIUM, or between it and the second courtyard. It was used for keeping family records.

TEMPERA PAINTING. 1) A painting made with PIGMENTS mixed with egg yolk and water. In the 14th and 15th centuries, it was applied to PANELS which had been prepared with a coating of GESSO; the application of GOLD LEAF and of underpainting in green or brown preceded the actual tempera painting (colorplates 54, 59). 2) The technique of executing such a painting.

TERRACOTTA. Italian word for cooked earth. 1) Earthenware, naturally reddish-brown but often GLAZED in various colors and fired. Used for pottery, sculpture, or as a building material or decoration. 2) An object made of this material. 3) Color of the natural material.

TESSERA (pl. TESSERAE). A small piece of colored stone, marble, glass, or gold-backed glass used in a MOSAIC (colorplate 29, fig. 275).

THEATER. In ancient Greece, an outdoor place for dramatic performances, usually semicircular in plan and provided with tiers of seats, the ORCHESTRA, and the *skene*, or support for scenery (fig. 176). See also AMPHITHEATER.

THERMAE. A public bathing establishment of the ancient Romans which consisted of various types of baths and social and gymnastic facilities.

THOLOS. In classical architecture, a circular building ultimately derived from early tombs (fig. 175).

THRUST. The lateral pressure exerted by an ARCH, VAULT, or DOME, which must be counteracted at its point of greatest concentration either by the thickness of the wall or by some form of BUTTRESS.

TOGA. A garment worn by ancient Roman citizens when appearing in public. It consisted of a single, long piece of material which could be draped in a variety of ways (fig. 255).

TOTEM. Among the Indians of North America, a natural object or animal assumed as the emblem of a tribe or family, or the representation of it, such as those CARVED on the posts or "totem poles" in front of their dwellings.

TRACERY. 1) Ornamental stone work in Gothic windows. In the earlier or "plate tracery," the windows appear to have been cut through the solid stone (colorplate 47). In "bar tracery" the glass predominates, the slender pieces of stone having been added within the windows (figs. 434, 435). 2) Similar ornamentation using various materials and applied to walls, shrines, façades, etc. (figs. 436, 455).

TRANSEPT. A cross arm in a BASILICAN church, placed at right angles to the NAVE, and usually separating it from the CHOIR or APSE (fig. 289).

TREE OF KNOWLEDGE. The tree in the Garden of Eden from which Adam and Eve ate the forbidden fruit which destroyed their innocence (Gen. 2:9, 17).

TREE OF LIFE. A tree in the Garden of Eden whose fruit was reputed to give everlasting life; in medieval art it was frequently used as a symbol of Christ (Gen. 2:9; 3:22).

TRIFORIUM. The section of a NAVE wall above the ARCADE and below the CLERESTORY (colorplate 47). It frequently consists of a BLIND ARCADE with three openings in each bay. When the GALLERY is also present, a four-story ELEVATION results, the triforium being between the gallery and clerestory. It may also occur in the TRANSEPT and the CHOIR walls.

TRIGLYPH. The element of a Doric FRIEZE separating two consecutive METOPES, and being divided by channels (or glyphs) into three sections. Probably an imitation in stone of wooden ceiling beam ends (figs. 159, 166).

TRIPTYCH. An ALTARPIECE or devotional picture, either CARVED or painted, with one central panel and two hinged wings (figs. 332, 494).

TRIUMPHAL ARCH. 1) A monumental ARCH, sometimes a combination of three arches, erected by a Roman emperor in commemoration of his military exploits, and usually decorated with scenes of these deeds in RELIEF sculpture (fig. 273). 2) The great transverse arch at the eastern end of a church which frames ALTAR and APSE and separates them from the main body of the church. It is frequently decorated with MOSAICS or MURAL paintings (colorplate 27, fig. 290).

TROPHY. 1) In ancient Rome, arms or other spoils taken from a defeated enemy and publicly displayed on a tree, PILLAR, etc. 2) A representation of these objects, and others symbolic of victory, as a commemoration or decoration.

TRUMEAU. A central post supporting the LINTEL of a large doorway, as in a Romanesque or Gothic PORTAL, where it was frequently decorated with sculpture (figs. 405, 469).

TRUSS. A triangular wooden or metal support for a roof which may be left exposed in the interior (figs. 290, 447), or be covered by a ceiling (figs. 379, 402).

TUNIC. In classical Greece and Rome, a loose, knee-length garment worn by both sexes. It could have sleeves or not, and was generally worn unbelted.

TURRET. 1) A small tower, part of a larger structure. 2) A small tower at an angle of a building, frequently beginning some distance from the ground.

TYMPANUM. 1) In classical architecture, the recessed, usually triangular area, also called a PEDIMENT, often decorated with sculpture (fig. 161). 2) In medieval architecture, an arched area between an ARCH and the LINTEL of a door or window, frequently carved with RELIEF sculpture (colorplate 49, fig. 408).


UNDERPAINTING. See TEMPERA PAINTING.


VAULT. An arched roof or ceiling usually made of stone, brick, or CONCRETE. Several distinct varieties have been developed; all need BUTTRESSING at the point where the lateral THRUST is concentrated. 1) A barrel vault is a semicylindrical structure made up of successive ARCHES (fig. 388). It may be straight or ANNULAR in plan (fig. 294). 2) A groin vault is the result of the intersection of two barrel vaults of equal size which produces a BAY of four compartments with sharp edges, or "groins," where the two meet (fig. 237). 3) A ribbed groin vault is one in which RIBS are added to the groins, for structural strength and for decoration (fig. 391). When the diagonal ribs are constructed as half circles, the resulting form is a domical ribbed vault (fig. 396). 4) Sexpartite vault: a ribbed groin vault in which each bay is divided into six compartments by the addition of a transverse rib across the center (fig. 394). 5) The normal Gothic vault is quadripartite with all the arches pointed to some degree (fig. 420). 6) A fan vault is an elaboration of a ribbed groin vault, with elements of TRACERY using conelike forms. It was developed by the English in the 15th century, and was employed for decorative purposes (figs. 442, 443).

VELLUM. See PARCHMENT.

VESTRY. See SACRISTY.

VICES. Often represented allegorically in conjunction with the seven VIRTUES, they include Pride, Avarice, Wrath, Gluttony, Unchastity (Luxury), Folly, and Inconstancy, though others such as Injustice are sometimes substituted.

VICTORY, see NIKE.

VILLA. Originally a large country house. See DOMUS.

VIRTUES. The three theological virtues, Faith, Hope, and Charity, and the four cardinal ones, Prudence, Justice, Fortitude, and Temperance, were frequently represented allegorically, particularly in medieval manuscripts and sculpture.

VOLUTE. A spiral architectural element found notably on Ionic and Composite CAPITALS (figs. 174, 227), but also used decoratively on building FAÇADES and interiors.

VOUSSOIR. See ARCH.

WATERCOLOR PAINTING. Painting, usually on paper, in PIGMENTS suspended in water.

WESTWORK. From the German word *Westwerk*. In Carolingian, Ottonian, and German Romanesque architecture, a monumental western front of a church, treated as a tower or combination of towers, and containing an entrance and vestibule below, and a CHAPEL and GALLERIES above. Later examples often added a TRANSEPT and a CROSSING tower (fig. 376).

WING. The side panel of an ALTARPIECE which is frequently decorated on both sides, and also hinged, so that it may be shown either open or closed.

ZIGGURAT. From the Assyrian word *ziqquratu* meaning mountain top or height. In ancient Assyria and Babylonia, a pyramidal tower built of mud brick and forming the BASE of a temple; it was either stepped or had a broad ascent winding around it, which gave it the appearance of being stepped (figs. 86, 89).

ZODIAC. 1) An imaginary belt circling the heavens, including the paths of the sun, moon, and major planets, and containing twelve constellations and thus twelve divisions called signs, which have been associated with the months. The signs are: Aries, the ram; Taurus, the bull; Gemini, the twins; Cancer, the crab; Leo, the lion; Virgo, the virgin; Libra, the balance; Scorpio, the scorpion; Sagittarius, the archer; Capricorn, the goat; Aquarius, the water-bearer; and Pisces, the fish. They are frequently represented around the PORTALS of Romanesque and Gothic churches in conjunction with the LABORS OF THE MONTHS (figs. 408, 463).

# INDEX

Works ascribed to a specific artist are indexed under the artist's name, shown in CAPITAL letters. Insofar as possible, unascribed works, including buildings and archaeological remains, are indexed by site. *See* references (e.g., *Bull's Head, see* Picasso; Colosseum, *see* Rome) are provided to assist in finding the correct name or site. Illustration references, shown in *italic* type, are to *figure numbers* rather than page numbers; but when a figure is also shown on a color plate page, that page number is given with the figure number (e.g., *358* and p. 9).

# LIST OF CREDITS

The author and publisher wish to thank the libraries, museums, and private collectors for permitting the reproduction in black-and-white and in color of paintings, prints, and drawings in their collections. Photographs have been supplied by the following, whose courtesy is gratefully acknowledged. Photographic sources for the Key Monuments section are indicated by page number; all others are figure numbers.

ACL (copyright), Brussels: 427, 441; Alinari, Florence: 242, 244, 251, 286, 290, 291, 296, 300, 423, 490, 491, 492, 515, 546; Altarocca, Terni, Italy: 245; American Museum of Natural History: 70; Archaeological Museum, Teheran, Iran: 133; Artothek, Planegg, West Germany: Page 22; Barsotti, Florence: 511, 512; Mitchell Beazley, *Atlas of World Architecture*, 1984: 279, 412; Beseler (after): 404, 405; Bibliothèque Nationale, Paris: 394, 518, 519; Bildarchiv Foto Marburg/Lahn, West Germany: 195, 402, 434, 468, 472, 498, 499, 503; Bildarchiv Preussischer Kulturbesitz, Berlin, West Germany: Page 3, 100, 101, 125; Erwin Bohm: 109; W. Braunfels, *Mittelalterliche...Toscana*, Pl. III: 429; Brisighelli-Udine, Cividale, Italy: 390; Bulloz, Paris: 436, 437, 439; Bundesamt für Denkmalspflege, Austria: 449; Caisse Nationale des Monuments Historiques et des Sites, Paris: 50, 126, 414, 433, 474, 506, 539; Cameraphoto, Piero Codato, Venice: 526; Ludovico Canali, Rome: Page 6, Page 8, Page 12, Page 20, 21, 136, 183, 184, 202, 207, 238, 247, 248, 253, 255, 270, 275, 283, 289, 294, 296, 301, 302, 303, 304, 306, 307, 308, 309, 310, 311, 322, 326, 334, 337, 338, 424, 430, 431, 484, 508, 509, 510, 523, 531, 532, 533, 534, 535; Canali/Bertoni: Page 14, 281, 516, 537, 545; Canali/Codato: 351, 354; Canali/Rapuzzi: 162; Clarendon Press, Oxford, from K. A. C. Creswell, *Early Muslim Architecture*: 362, 364, 365; Cleveland Museum of Art: 28; Colorphoto Hans Hinz, SWB, Alschwil-Basel, Switzerland: Page 2, 31; Davies, N. de Garis, Chicago: 97; F. De Dartien, *Etude...Lombarde*, pl. 29: 425; Geza De Francovich, Rome: 440; Deutscher Kunstverlag, Munich, West Germany: 37, 198, 277, 391, 406, 426, 502; Pierre Devinoy, Paris: 446; Jean Dieuzaide, Toulouse, France: 410; Walter Dräyer, Zurich: 250; Editions Arthaud, Paris, from S. N. Kramer, *History Begins at Sumer:* 114; Eeva-Inkeri, New York: Page 31; Eliot Elisofon (Copyright Time, Inc., New York): 60; Sir Banister Fletcher, *A History of Architecture*, 19th edition, 1987: 187; Foto Grassi, Siena, Italy: 525; Fotocielo, Rome: 319; Fototeca Unione, Rome: 185, 257, 258, 259, 260, 264, 276, 278, 288, 398; from

H. Frankfort, *The Art and Architecture of the Ancient Orient:* 107; Alison Frantz, Princeton, N.J.: 188, 191, 196, 199, 346; A. Furtwängler (after): 178; Gabinetto Fotografico Nazionale, Rome: 298, 357; German Archaeological Institute, Rome: 6, 285, 273, 282, 293; Edward V. Gorn, New York: 352; Grinnell (after): 182; Gurlitt (after): 341; Haeseler Art Publishers, Lafayette, Calif.: 52; Richard Harrier, New York: 217; Frederick Hartt, *A History of Painting Sculpture Architecture*, 3rd edition, 1989: 452; André Held, Switzerland: 356; Max Hirmer Verlag, Munich, West Germany: 74, 83, 89, 138, 143, 147, 149, 160, 165, 168, 174, 177, 189, 194, 204, 205, 208, 209, 210, 211, 212, 213, 215, 218, 219, 233, 234, 235, 236, 239, 240, 287, 299, 325, 329, 330, 343; Walter Horn (courtesy Schmolz & Urich, Cologne, West Germany): 396; C. Huelsen (after): 271; Hurault, St.-Germain-en-Laye, courtesy Jean M. Porcher: 432; Martin Hürlimann, from *France*: 471; Istituto di Etruscologia e Antichità Italiche, University of Rome: 246; H. W. Janson, New York: 482; S. W. Kenyon, Wellington, England: 40, 41, 42; A. F. Kersting, London: 321, 418, 478, 479; from *Key Monuments in the History of Art*, Abrams, New York: 483; G. E. Kidder-Smith, New York: 22, 24, 263, 292, 340, 342, 369, 372, 374, 376, 457; Nikos Kontos, Athens: Page 5 (right), 1, 139, 141, 144, 146, 150, 151, 152, 154, 158, 167, 171, 172, 192, 193, 201, 203, 206, 221, 231; from R. Krautheimer, *Early Christian and Byzantine Architecture:* 316, 317; F. Krischen (after): 216; Herbert Kuhn, Mainz: 30; Kunsthistorisches Museum, Vienna: 333; Kurt Lange, Obersdorf/Allgäu, West Germany: 72, 73, 94; Jacques Lathion, Oslo, Norway: Page 28; J. P. Lauer (after): 78; from A. W. Lawrence, *Greek Architecture:* 190; Leiris, Galerie Louise, Paris: 2; Tony Linck, Fort Lee, N.J.: 54; Magasins St.-Bernard, Vézelay, France: 438; Barbara Malterm, Rome: 224; Mansell Collection, London: 122; Alexander Marshack, New York, Copyright: 36, 48, 49; Peter Mauss/Esto: Page 32; James Mellaart, London (from *Çatal-Hüyük*): 43, 44, 45, 46, 47; The Metropolitan Museum of Art, New York: 5, 91, 142, 166; Ministry of Works, London, Crown Copyright: 51; Museo Nacional de Antropología, Mexico City: 65; Museum of Fine Arts, Boston: 88; Museum of the American Indian–Heye Foundation, New York: 66; Nippon Television Network Corporation: 10; National Buildings Record, London, Copyright: (F. H. Crossley) 477; The National Gallery of Art, Washington, D.C.: 266; Oriental Institute, University of Chicago: 92, 111, 120, 121, 130, 132; Peabody Museum, Harvard University, Cambridge, Mass.:

68; Penguin Press, Baltimore, Md., from K. J. Conant, *Carolingian and Romanesque Architecture, 850–1200*: 419; from N. Pevsner, *Outline of European Architecture:* 485, 487; Photographie Giraudon, Paris: Pages 18–19, 473, 494, 543; Photo MAS, Barcelona, Spain: 368, 370; Photo Meyer, Vienna: 377; C. Picard, Cambridge, England: 200; Josephine Powell, Rome: 349, 355; Pubbli Aer Photo, Milan: 262, 350; Mario Quattrone, Florence: Page 21, 522, 529; R.M.N., Paris: Page 7, Page 24, Page 26, Page 27, 4, 38, 87, 115, 117, 118, 159, 164, 165, 169, 170, 229, 530; Rheinisches Bildarchiv, Cologne, West Germany: 403, 505; Jean Roubier, Paris: 261, 413, 415, 417, 454, 495, 497, 500; Royal Museum of Central Africa, Terveuren, Belgium: 62; Scala, Florence: 339, 527; J. Schram (after): 227; Edwin Smith, Saffron Walden, England: 124, 127; Soprintendenza ai Monumenti, Pisa, Italy: 536; Soprintendenza all'Antichità, Palermo, Italy: 35; Soprintendenza Archeologica, Ministero per i Beni Culturali Ambientali: 249; Soprintendenza Archeologica all'Etruria Meridionale: 241, 243; Staatliche Antikensammlungen und Glyptothek, Munich, West Germany: 180; Staatliche Museen, Berlin, East Germany: 226, 363; Dr. Franz Stoedtner, Düsseldorf, West Germany: 176; Studio C.N.B. & C., Bologna, Italy: 103; Studio Koppermann, Munich, West Germany: 161, 163, 179, 214; Studio R. Rémy, Dijon, France: 541; Wim Swaan, New York: Page 13, 3, 77, 79, 80, 84, 90, 93, 95, 96, 98, 99, 104, 105, 131, 134, 197, 345, 373, 416, 428, 455, 456, 466, 476, 481, 486, 489, 513, 514, 517; Thames & Hudson, London (from Costa and Lockhart, *Persia*): 135; J. W. Thomas, Oxford, England: 501; Marvin Trachtenberg, New York: 344, 348; UNESCO, from UNESCO World Art Series, *Australia*, Pl. XXII: 39; University Museum, Philadelphia: 113; University of Utrecht, Library: 400; Vatican Archives, Vatican Museum, Rome: 297; Jean Vertut: 32; Leonard von Matt, Buochs, Switzerland: 145; Victoria & Albert Museum, London: 331; Warburg Institute, University of London: 442; Clarence Ward, Oberlin, Ohio: 453, 455, 465; Hildesheim Wehmeyer: 407; David Wilkins, Pittsburgh, Pa.: Page 17; Woodfin Camp & Associates, Inc., New York: 57, 367, 459, 460, 464; Yale Center for British Art, Paul Mellon Collection, New Haven, Conn.: 29; Yan Photo Reportage, Toulouse, France: 34; Yugoslav State Tourist Office: 280.

The text of this book was set in 9½-point Primer,
a typeface designed in 1949 by the American artist and
designer Rudolf Rudzicka (1883–1978) for the Mergenthaler
Linotype Company and made fully available in 1954.
Primer is a refinement of Century Schoolbook, an eminently
legible face designed by Morris Fuller Benton,
which reflects his studies of reading comprehension; it was
released in 1920 by American Type Founders. Display type is
Arrow, condensed 20 percent. The book was printed and
bound in Japan; the paper is 104 GSM (grams per square meter)
Royal coat. Color illustrations are printed in four-color offset;
black-and-white illustrations are printed in duotone offset.